Oscar Wilde: The Complete Interviews

Volume One

ROB MARLAND is the author of *Oscar Wilde: The Season of Sorrow* (2018), a graphic biography that tells the story of Wilde's imprisonment. His research on Wilde has been published in *The Wildean*, the journal of the Oscar Wilde Society, and *Notes and Queries*.

Oscar Wilde
the Complete Interviews

Volume One

Edited by
Rob Marland

Little Eye

First published in 2022 in Jena, Germany by Little Eye

Holland, M., & Hart-Davis, R. (Eds.). (2000). *The Complete Letters of Oscar Wilde.*
London: Fourth Estate. ISBN-10: 0805059156

A CIP catalogue record for this book is available from the British Library.

Hardcover ISBN 978-3-9824134-0-2
Paperback ISBN 978-3-9824134-2-6

Front cover: Oscar Wilde in New York City, plate 14
Photograph by Napoleon Sarony, 1882. Colourisation by Rob Marland, 2021.
Library of Congress, LC-DIG-ppmsca-40827

For errata and updates see https://robmarland.co.uk/wildeints

Contents

Figures

Credits: 1, 3, oscarwildeinamerica.org; 2, Yale Center for British Art, Paul Mellon Collection, B1992.8.13(53); 4, Harvard Theatre Collection TCS 1.3271; 5, Library of Congress, 16-CHIG,43—1; 6, Art Institute of Chicago, 1911.583; 7, 10, 11, 13, editor's collection; 8, Newberry Library, Chicago, Oliver Barrett-Carl Sandburg Papers Photograph Collection, 1860-1950, box 09 072 01; 9, Library of Congress, LC-USZ62-109579; 12, Dayton Metro Library, Lutzenberger Picture Collection, MS 024 0201; 14, Library of Congress, LC-DIG-highsm-30150; 15, Library of Congress, LC-USZ62-77492.

Abbreviations

Listed here are all works cited more than once, and volumes of the OET *Complete Works* cited at least once, in either Volume One or Two. The details of other works cited only once are given in full in the relevant notes.

Archer	Archer. W. (1896). *The Theatrical 'World' of 1895*. Walter Scott.
Bisch	Bisch, M. C. (1996). *Oscar Wilde in Indiana*. [Unpublished master's thesis]. Indiana State University.
Chesson	Chesson, W. H. (1912). A Reminiscence of 1898, *The Bookman, 34*, 389–94.
CL	Holland, M., & Hart-Davis, R. (Eds.). (2000). *The Complete Letters of Oscar Wilde*. Fourth Estate.
Cooper	Cooper, J. *www.oscarwildeinamerica.org*. Accessed October 2019 – December 2021.
CW i	Fong, B., & Beckson, K. (Eds.). (2000). *The Complete Works of Oscar Wilde, Vol. 1: Poems and Poems in Prose*. Oxford University Press.
CW iii	Bristow, J. (Ed.). (2005). *The Complete Works of Oscar Wilde, Vol. 3: The Picture of Dorian Gray: The 1890 and 1891 Texts*. Oxford University Press.
CW iv	Guy, J. M. (Ed.). (2007). *The Complete Works of Oscar Wilde, Vol. 4: Criticism: Historical Criticism, Intentions, The Soul of Man*. Oxford University Press.
CW v	Donohue, J. (Ed.). (2013). *The Complete Works of Oscar Wilde, Vol. 5: Plays, Vol. 1: The Duchess of Padua; Salomé: Drame en Un Acte; Salome: Tragedy in One Act*. Oxford University Press.
CW vi	Stokes, J., & Turner, M. W. (Eds.). (2013). *The Complete Works of Oscar Wilde, Vol. 6: Journalism, Vol. 1*. Oxford University Press.
CW vii	Stokes, J., & Turner, M. W. (Eds.). (2013). *The Complete Works of Oscar Wilde, Vol. 7: Journalism, Vol. 2*. Oxford University Press.
CW x	Donohue, J. (Ed.). (2019). *The Complete Works of Oscar Wilde, Vol. 10: Plays, Vol. 3: The Importance of Being Earnest; 'A Wife's Tragedy' (fragment)*. Oxford University Press.
CW xi	Guy, J. M. (Ed.). (2021). *The Complete Works of Oscar Wilde, Vol. 11: Plays, Vol. 4: Vera; or The Nihilist and Lady Windermere's Fan*. Oxford University Press.
Dearinger	Dearinger, K. L. (2009). *Marie Prescott: A Star of Some Brilliancy*. Fairleigh Dickinson University Press.
Dibb	Dibb, G. (2013). *Oscar Wilde: A Vagabond with a Mission*. The Oscar Wilde Society.
Douglas (1914)	Douglas, A. B. (1914). *Oscar Wilde and Myself*. Duffield & Company.
Douglas	Douglas, A. B. (1929). *The Autobiography of Lord Alfred Douglas*. Martin Secker.
Ellmann	Ellmann, R. (1987). *Oscar Wilde*. Hamish Hamilton. / Ellmann, R. (1988). *Oscar Wilde*. Knopf.
Fitzsimons	Fitzsimons, E. (2015). *Wilde's Women: How Oscar Wilde Was Shaped by the Women He Knew*. Duckworth Overlook.

Friedman	Friedman, D. M. (2014). *Wilde in America*. WW Norton & Co.
Gide	Gide, A. (1905). *Oscar Wilde: A Study*. The Holywell Press.
H & S	Hofer, M., & Scharnhorst, G. (Eds.). (2010). *Oscar Wilde in America: The Interviews*. University of Illinois Press.
Hamilton	Hamilton, W. (1882). *The Aesthetic Movement in England* (3rd ed.). Reeves & Turner.
Harris	Harris, F. (1918). *Oscar Wilde: His Life and Confessions*. Frank Harris.
Holland	Holland, M. (2003). *Irish Peacock & Scarlet Marquess*. Fourth Estate.
Hyde (1963)	Hyde, H. M. (1963). *Oscar Wilde: The Aftermath*. Methuen & Co. Ltd.
Hyde	Hyde, H. M. (1976). *Oscar Wilde*. Eyre Methuen.
Keller–Farmer	Keller-Farmer Co. (1907). *The Writings of Oscar Wilde: His Life, with a Critical Estimate of His Writings*. A. R. Keller & Co.
Langtry	Langtry, L. (1925). *The Days I Knew*. George H. Doran Company.
Mason	Mason, S. (1914). *Bibliography of Oscar Wilde*. T. Werner Laurie Ltd.
Melville	Melville, J. (1994). *Mother of Oscar*. John Murray.
Mendelssohn	Mendelssohn, M. (2018). *Making Oscar Wilde*. Oxford University Press.
Mikhail	Mikhail, E. H. (Ed.). (1979). *Oscar Wilde: Interviews and Recollections*. Macmillan.
Miscellanies	Ross, R. B. (Ed.). (1908). *The Collected Works of Oscar Wilde: Miscellanies*. Methuen and Co.
Moyle	Moyle, F. (2011). *Constance: The Tragic and Scandalous Life of Mrs Oscar Wilde*. John Murray.
Munby	Munby, A. N. L. (Ed.). (1971). *Sale Catalogues of Libraries of Eminent Persons: Poets and Men of Letters*. Mansell.
Nordau	Nordau, M. (1895). *Degeneration*. William Heinemann.
O'Brien	O'Brien, K. (1982). *Oscar Wilde in Canada*. Personal Library.
OED	*Oxford English Dictionary Online*. December 2021. Oxford University Press.
OWDA	Lewis, L., & Smith, H. J. (1936). *Oscar Wilde Discovers America: 1882*. Harcourt, Brace & Co.
Page	Page, N. (1991). *An Oscar Wilde Chronology*. Macmillan.
Pearson	Pearson, H. (1946). *The Life of Oscar Wilde*. Methuen & Co.
Ricketts	Ricketts, C. (1932). *Recollections of Oscar Wilde*. Nonesuch.
Schroeder	Schroeder, H. (2002). *Additions and Corrections to Richard Ellmann's Oscar Wilde*. 2nd ed. Privately printed.
Seaside Library	Wilde, O. (1882). *Poems by Oscar Wilde, and His Lecture on The English Renaissance*. The Seaside Library.
Seeley	Seeley, P. (2019). *Richard D'Oyly Carte*. Routledge.
Sherard	Sherard, R. H. (1902). *Oscar Wilde: The Story of an Unhappy Friendship*. Privately Printed.
Small	Small, I. (1993). *Oscar Wilde Revalued*. ELT Press.
Stratmann	Stratmann, L. (2013). *The Marquess of Queensberry: Wilde's Nemesis*. Yale University Press.
Sturgis	Sturgis, M. (2018). *Oscar: A Life*. Head of Zeus. / Sturgis, M. (2021). *Oscar Wilde: A Life*. Knopf.
Sturgis (2020)	Sturgis, M. (2020). *Wildeana*. Riverrun.
Sutherland	Sutherland, L. (2020). *George Alexander and the Work of the Actor-Manager*. Palgrave Macmillan.
Woman	Ross, R. B. (Ed.). (1908). *The Collected Works of Oscar Wilde: A Woman of No Importance*. Methuen and Co.
Wright	Wright, T. W. (2008). *Oscar's Books*. Chatto & Windus.

Introduction and Acknowledgements

On the morning of 3 January 1882 the SS *Arizona* drew into New York Harbor and anchored at quarantine. A group of men, eager for their first sight of the *Arizona's* most famous passenger, chartered a small steamer and made their way out over the choppy, grey waters. They clambered up an icy ladder onto the deck. There they found a young Oscar Wilde, aesthetically clad in a sealskin cap and a green, fur-lined ulster.

Wilde would later joke that he had thought the men were "literary pirates" who were "coming to seize the first manuscript on board."[1] In fact, they were a contingent of interviewers representing the *Herald*, *Sun*, *Times*, *Tribune*, and *World*. They peppered the poet with questions. Their first—how did he like America?—was greeted with laughter. Wilde had yet to form an opinion on the subject, but pronounced the Atlantic "a disappointment".

Wilde's stated purpose in coming to America was to lecture on the "English Renaissance" of art and to stage his first play, *Vera; or, The Nihilists*, a tragedy of passion and politics set in Russia. But the real reason was that he had been contracted by a canny theatrical impresario, Richard D'Oyly Carte, to act as a walking-talking advertisement for *Patience; or, Bunthorne's Bride*, the latest comic opera by W. S. Gilbert and Arthur Sullivan. *Patience* satirised aestheticism, the movement in favour of "art for art's sake" that had come to prominence in England in the 1870s. D'Oyly Carte felt that American audiences required educating on the craze so that they could properly appreciate Gilbert's gags, and Wilde was just the man to act as tutor. Although by no means a leader of the movement, in the early 1880s Wilde was increasingly being seen as one of its most representative—and eccentric—exponents. His poems in praise of female beauty, as well as his long hair and outrageous aphorisms, had brought him a certain notoriety. He was still a decade from achieving the much-craved immortality that *The Picture of Dorian Gray* and a string of smash hit society comedies would guarantee, but had already been interviewed for a lengthy profile in *The Biograph and Review*.[2] At the outset of his career he was in need of the money that lecturing promised,

1. In his lecture *Personal Impressions of America* (Dibb, 233).
2. "Oscar Wilde," *The Biograph and Review* (London, UK), Aug. 1880, 130–5, pp. 25–31.

and agreed to D'Oyly Carte's proposal of a fifty lecture tour on the proviso that the offer was good. It was.

Throughout 1882, as Wilde rode the rails from New York to San Francisco and San Antonio to New Brunswick, the reporters kept up their pursuit. The candid interview was still a novelty and its practitioners soon learnt that Wilde was a reliable source of copy. By the end of the year at least 176 interviews with the so-called "Apostle of Aestheticism" had hit the American press. Between 1883 and his death in 1900 Wilde gave over 50 further interviews.

Newspapers are, by their nature, ephemeral objects. Wilde's interviews were always more likely to be forgotten than even the most minor of his own works. Nevertheless, over the years, many have been recovered and reprinted. In 1979 E. H. Mikhail included about 30 (the number depends on how one defines an interview) in *Oscar Wilde: Interviews and Recollections*. In 2010 Matthew Hofer and Gary Scharnhorst collected 48 of the more interesting American examples in *Oscar Wilde in America: The Interviews*, and compiled a list of 107 known interviews.[1] In the intervening twelve years more interviews have come to light and been cited in new biographies. And, thanks to the accelerating digitisation of newspaper archives, it is now possible to search through many newspapers that were previously accessible only to those who were willing and able to visit countless local libraries and spool through miles of microfilm. The present collection includes 230 interviews, many new to scholarship. The vast majority have not been reprinted since the nineteenth-century.

Attempting to collect all of Oscar Wilde's interviews is worthwhile for several reasons. The first of many editions of Wilde's complete works was published in 1908; his complete letters appeared in 2000; his plays have rarely been off the stage. Wilde's interviews are less familiar than his writings, and yet they represent perhaps the best record of his opinions on a range of topics from architecture and fashion to the politicians, authors, actors, and artists of his day. What's more, the interviews are a witness to how Wilde talked rather than how he wrote. Many of Wilde's American interviewers, who came expecting to meet a buffoon or huckster, were compelled to admit that his conversational powers and the range of his expertise and interests were impressive. Wilde's friends and acquaintances always maintained that his speech outshone his writings: W. B. Yeats thought that "[o]nly when he spoke, or when his writing was the mirror of his speech [...] had he words exact enough to hold a subtle ear"; André Gide that "[t]he best of his writing is but a pale reflection of his brilliant conversations.

1. In 1916 Guido Bruno began publishing in his New York-based magazine *Bruno's Weekly* what promised to be a collection of 150 interviews, but only a handful appeared before the magazine folded ("The Trail of Oscar Wilde in America," *Bruno's Weekly* (New York, NY), 16 Dec. 1916).

Those who have heard him speak find it disappointing to read him"; and Richard Le Gallienne that, "if the pen is mightier than the sword, in his case the tongue was mightier than the pen".[1] Reading the interviews is the closest any of us will ever come to joining Wilde in conversation. We hear him at his brilliant best and occasionally see the mask slip. He hones rationales for his various philosophies, tests anecdotes, trots out favourite phrases, and airs pet peeves. Differences in Wilde's responses to his questioners are more apparent when reading a complete collection of interviews rather than a selection.

What did Wilde think of the newspaper interview? He told one interviewer that "some of the brightest hours" he had passed in America had been with "the gentlemen of the press," and that he found them "among the most intelligent men" he had encountered in America.[2] The interview was "a capital feature of the paper," and gave an interviewee "an opportunity of saying and explaining things which he could not do as satisfactorily in an ordinary speech." He certainly enjoyed the attention, boasting that, in America, "I used to have them (interviewers) coming to my rooms five or six times a day, and I rather liked it."[3] But, after long train journeys and exhausted by a demanding lecture schedule, he sometimes found the experience tedious, and was annoyed by the repetitive and prying questions. He confided in the magazine proprietor (and his future sister in law) Mrs Frank Leslie that he had "turned his back" on New York's "horrible reporters"; she reminded him that it was their business to interview as it was his to lecture, and that he would be better off giving them something to print, else they would be liable to turn on *him*.[4] Wilde was usually averse to good advice, but he took Leslie's. When, in Chicago, the "gloomy reporters" insisted on asking him to name his favourite colour or for a definition of aestheticism, he steered the conversation to more interesting topics: James Whistler, Henry Labouchère, Henry Irving, and Lillie Langtry.[5] He supplied other reporters with quips and controversial opinions and, after the preacher David Swing attacked him in the press, he even wrote to the Chicago newspapers asking them to send interviewers to his hotel so he could strike back.[6]

Wilde returned to America in 1883 to assist with the rehearsals of *Vera* and there participated in a press junket, speaking with at least ten interviewers in

1. Mikhail, 147, 191; Keller–Farmer Co. (1907). *The Writings of Oscar Wilde: Poems*. A. R. Keller & Co. 12.

2. "Oscar Wilde," *The Cincinnati Enquirer* (Cincinnati, OH), 21 Feb. 1882, 4, p. 195.

3. "Mr. Oscar Wilde Interviewed in Glasgow," *Evening News and Star* (Glasgow, UK), 22 Dec. 1884, 4, p. 575.

4. "An Amazon of Journalism," *The Pall Mall Gazette* (London, UK), 28 Aug. 1886, 1–2, pp. 795–6.

5. CL,154.

6. "Professor Swing and Oscar," *The Daily Inter Ocean* (Chicago, IL), 6 Mar. 1882, 8, p. 251.

sequence in a single day. Back in Europe he was less frequently solicited for interviews simply because there interviewing was not the norm. Although he occasionally agreed to be interviewed by American correspondents, sympathetic English reporters, or friends, by the time he reached the heights of his success in the early nineties he had grown tired of providing columns of conversation for free. In 1894 Robert Sherard was asked by *McClure's Magazine* to obtain an interview "with as many Oscariana as possible"; Wilde declined to oblige unless the editor stumped up £20.[1] Refusals became absolute in 1895, when the Marquess of Queensberry left a card at Wilde's club accusing him of "[?posing as] somdomite [*sic*]". Wilde sued for libel and reporters circled. The case collapsed, Wilde was obliged to swap the witness stand for the dock, and after two trials he was convicted of gross indecency. When the end of his term of two years' hard labour was imminent, Wilde petitioned the Home Secretary to be released four days early because he had heard that English, French, and American journalists intended to meet him at the prison gates. Wilde thought the prospect unseemly and was "anxious to avoid any intrusion of the kind threatened."[2] His petition was denied. He may have agreed to an interview before his release, with the prison governor acting as intermediary, so as to dissuade reporters from ambushing him later.[3]

During the last years of his life, while living in self-imposed exile on the continent, Wilde found himself once more of interest to journalists. He could not resist the attention of young admirers, and in 1897 spoke with two who published their conversations with him in the French press. He must have been happy with at least one of these interviews, as he sent a copy to his friend, Robert Ross.[4] In Naples Wilde complained that he was being chased by Italian journalists: "They write nicely of me, but I don't want to be written about. I want peace—that is all."[5] His servants were under strict instructions not to admit would-be-interviewers, but at least one slipped through the net. Wilde gave his last interview on his deathbed in Paris to the French correspondent of the *Daily Chronicle*,[6] the newspaper a sympathetic guard had regularly smuggled into his prison cell in Reading Gaol.

---

1. CL, 624.
2. CL, 803.
3. Frank Marshall White [and Robert Batho], "Oscar Wilde to Write," *The Chicago Daily Tribune* (Chicago, IL), 17 May 1897, 2, pp. 655–60.
4. CL, 829.
5. CL, 950.
6. [Clifford Millage], "The Late Oscar Wilde," *The Daily Chronicle* (London, UK), 3 Dec. 1900, 5, pp. 679–80.

In assembling this collection I have had to determine which articles qualified as interviews. Many of Wilde's interviews were structured interactions in which a reporter asked questions and Wilde answered. They often took place in Wilde's hotel rooms after he had acceded to a clear request for an interview. These interactions would be recognised as interviews by any definition and most interviews that have been reprinted have been of this type. However, Wilde interacted with reporters in a number of other ways. I have decided to adopt a liberal definition as to what constitutes an interview. In brief, if Wilde conversed with a reporter, or with a group of people that included a reporter (excluding comments made to third parties that were overheard by a reporter), I class this as an interview. Sometimes reporters approached Wilde in public and elicited answers to impromptu questions, conversed with him while visiting his home or accompanying him on a tour of a city, or posed questions via a letter or a transatlantic cable. I class all of these as interviews, no matter how brief the interaction.

Does it matter if Wilde consented to be interviewed? Wilde requested that Lugné-Poe not write up their conversation as an interview, but suspected (correctly) that the temptation might be too great to resist.[1] Other articles relate conversations that Wilde may not have realised were intended for the press. An *Atchison Globe* man approached Wilde after a lecture and represented himself as the accountant for a pottery firm rather than a reporter.[2] Still, he came for an interview and he got one. Similarly, a fellow rail passenger wrote about his conversation with Wilde in a letter to a newspaper editor, and, although Wilde may not have known he was being interviewed, the result was the same.[3] Some reporters moved in the same social circles as Wilde, and Wilde may have spoken to them without knowing that the conversations would be written up as interviews (alternatively, the reporters may have made it clear that he was on the record, but elided the fact in their articles so as to give a sense of informality and spontaneity). I class each of these types of article as interviews.

Not every article that features reported speech, either direct or indirect, necessarily qualifies as an interview. Some are reports of Wilde's social engagements in which it is unclear whether Wilde is speaking to a reporter or to other persons. Some are articles in which the author quotes Wilde, but it is unclear whether the quote was obtained second hand. I have chosen not to class articles as interviews unless it is clear or seems likely that the reporter obtained comments directly from Wilde. An exception is the 1897 prison interview.

1. A.-F. Lugné-Poé, "M. Oscar Wilde en France," *La Presse* (Paris, France), 28 May 1897, 2, pp. 660–3.

2. "A Stranger Within Our Gates," *The Atchison Globe* (Atchison, KS), 24 Apr. 1882, 1, pp. 355–7.

3. John Hague, "Oscar Wilde," *Toronto Evening News* (Toronto, ON), 25 May 1882, 4, pp. 401–3.

Conversations printed after a substantial interval would be better described as reminiscences and are excluded. These are numerous and are well-represented in biographies of Wilde written by his contemporaries and in collections such as E. H. Mikhail's *Oscar Wilde: Interviews and Recollections* and Matthew Sturgis's *Wildeana*. Here the notable exception is William Theodore Peters' profile of Oscar and his wife Constance, which internal evidence indicates was printed two years after Peters visited their home in Tite Street.[1]

As opinions are likely to differ as to what constitutes an interview, I have collected in Appendix C a number of articles that do not meet my criteria but are nevertheless of interest. Appendix D includes interviews others gave about Wilde; Appendix E includes burlesque interviews.

I have transcribed all articles from original sources, silently correcting misspellings and other errors (unless the author's original meaning is unclear) and modernising distracting archaic spellings (e.g. cigaret, trowsers). Words not clearly legible in the original sources are marked [*illeg. wd.*]; if there is a good indication of what the word might be, it is given and preceded by a question mark, for example: "[?word]". Many of the North American interviews include or were printed alongside reports of Wilde's lectures. There is little advantage in including these reports in a collection of interviews, and so they, and any other superfluous content, have been excluded. Where content has been excluded the location is marked "✂". Article headlines and subheads are given in full, regardless of whether they relate to Wilde. Interviews are ordered chronologically according to when they were given, to the extent that this can be ascertained, rather than when they were printed. Ordering strictly by publication date would in some cases give an unclear picture of Wilde's movements, particularly during 1882 when he was interviewed so frequently.

In the footnotes I indicate where the articles collected here have previously been reprinted (in full), excerpted (partially reprinted, either as a standalone excerpt or a block quote set apart from other text), quoted (incorporated in the main text, usually enclosed within quotation marks), or referenced (any use short of quotation, regardless of whether the author explicitly cites the source). I note use at the time of original publication (e.g. reprints in other newspapers) as well as use by biographers. So many biographies of Wilde have been published that the information I give about previous use is necessarily incomplete, but I have recorded all instances of use in four major biographies: Hesketh Pearson's *The Life of Oscar Wilde* (1946), H. Montgomery Hyde's *Oscar Wilde* (1976), Richard Ellmann's *Oscar Wilde* (1987/1888), and Matthew Sturgis's *Oscar: A Life/Oscar Wilde: A Life* (2018/2021). For Ellmann and Sturgis, all use is noted

1. William Theodore Peters, "Oscar Wilde at Home," *The Sunday Inter Ocean* (Chicago, IL), 16 Dec. 1894, 31, pp. 617–21.

for both the United Kingdom and United States editions: page numbers are given in the format "UK/US". I also note, as far as I have been able to ascertain, where the articles were first used, with particular reference to the trailblazing studies of Lloyd Lewis and Henry Justin Smith (*Oscar Wilde Discovers America: 1882*, 1936) and Kevin O'Brien (*Oscar Wilde in Canada*, 1982). When referring to interviews listed by Hofer and Scharnhorst I use their bibliography numbering system, prefixing these numbers with "b" to avoid confusion with page numbers. Christopher Sclater Millard, who published on Wilde under the pseudonym Stuart Mason, is referred to as Mason throughout. Cross-referenced pages are prefixed with "p." to differentiate them from references to page numbers in other sources.

References to Wilde's works are, where possible, to the published volumes in the Oxford English Texts edition of *The Complete Works of Oscar Wilde*. There is no single reliable source for Wilde's lectures. Wilde varied the content of his lectures from city to city and several evolved one from another. This has not made the task of collating authoritative or even representative texts easy for his editors. Where interviews quote or allude to statements Wilde made in a specific lecture on a specific date, my source has been a press report of that lecture. In other cases references to lectures are to the following texts: *The English Renaissance*, the text in *The First Collected Edition of the Works of Oscar Wilde, Miscellanies* edited by Robert Ross (1908); *The Decorative Arts* and the North American version of *The House Beautiful*, O'Brien (1982); and *Modern Art Training* (aka *Lecture to Art Students*), *Personal Impressions of America*, the British version of *The House Beautiful*, and *Dress*, Geoff Dibb's *Oscar Wilde: A Vagabond with a Mission* (2013).

I thank the many people who made this collection possible. Firstly, if Matthew Hofer and Gary Scharnhorst had not compiled and published a bibliography of interviews in their *Oscar Wilde in America: The Interviews*, I could not have begun to contemplate undertaking this project. Merlin Holland allowed me to quote from Wilde's letters and provided useful pointers. John Cooper, whose website is the primary resource for information about Wilde's visits to North America (oscarwildeinamerica.org), identified many interviews and I thank him for sharing his materials and for his invaluable support and encouragement. Cooper's full list of Wilde's North American lectures is my source for all references to those lectures; references to lectures in the United Kingdom are taken from Dibb. I thank Elizabeth Adams of University College Oxford Library for overseeing the archiving of copy text material in the Robert Ross Memorial Collection. I am indebted to John Cooper and Matthew Sturgis for enlightening discussions about Frank Marshall White and Robert Bathos's article, and to Robert Whelan, Joseph Donohue, and Matthew Sturgis for their comments on William

Theodore Peters's article.[1] Horst Schroeder informed me that Peters was present at Wilde's funeral, and his *Additions and Corrections to Richard Ellmann's Oscar Wilde* (2002) has been a crucial resource. Devon Cox shared his research on Constance Wilde's autograph book, a facsimile edition of which will soon be published by the Oscar Wilde Society. Yuki Tsuchiya alerted me to, and shared her research on, Jissen University's copy of Alice B. Woodward's iguanodon drawing annotated by the Marquess of Queensberry. My translations of the French interviews were improved by the astute comments of Doriane Nemes and LibriVox volunteer Sonia (of course, I remain responsible for any errors).

For kindly responding to my queries and for helping me to run to ground elusive articles or opaque references, I express my sincere gratitude to Marilyn Bisch, Scott Burgh, Giuseppe Ciccomascolo, Geoff Dibb, Joseph Donohue, Aaron Eames, Eleanor Fitzsimons, David M. Friedman, Jim Gifford, Fiona Haarer, Richard Haslam, Vanessa Heron, Amy Hitchings, Laura Lee, Dianne Macleod, Wolfgang Maier-Sigrist, Don Mead, Renato Miracco, Brian Nelson, Erin Pauwels, Kate Rhoades, Iain Ross, Geoff Sawers, Michele Stanco, David Stone, John Stratford, Matthew Sturgis, Bobby Tanzio, Georgia Toutziari, and Elisabeth Wittkowski.

Any editor who labels a collection "complete" should be prepared, before long, to find their overconfidence exposed by new discoveries. I am certain that more interviews with Wilde are waiting to be found. Appendix A includes a list of untraced interviews, but, as well as these "known unknowns", there will be other interviews that, as yet, remain "unknown unknowns". I look forward to their rediscovery. In the meantime, I would like to express my heartfelt thanks to Anne Coletta, without whose assistance this collection would be considerably further from the impossible goal of completeness.

Most of the research for this collection was conducted between October 2018 and January 2022, a period that has coincided with the ongoing COVID-19 pandemic. Visits to libraries and archives were impossible for much of this time, and so I have been obliged to rely on the assistance of librarians, historians, and archivists. During the pandemic many institutions have introduced new policies that facilitate remote research, including opening access to online databases and providing scans of materials at reduced or zero cost. I am indebted to the persons responsible for these policies, as I am to those who searched their collections on my behalf. I thank the staff of the Abraham Lincoln Presidential Library and Museum, Biblioteca Nazionale Centrale di Firenze, Biblioteca Universitaria di Napoli, Bibliothèque nationale de France, the British Library, Buffalo and Erie County Public Library, California State Library, Charleston County Public Library, Chicago Public Library, Cincinnati Public Library, Denver Public Library, Des Moines Public Library, Detroit Public Library, Dubuque Carnegie-Stout Library,

1. *Intentions, 120*, Feb. 2022; personal communication.

Falvey Memorial Library (Villanova University), The Filson Historical Society (Louisville), the Free Library of Philadelphia, Halifax Public Libraries, Indianapolis Public Library, Jacksonville Public Library, Jissen Women's University Library, Kansas City Public Library, Library and Archives Canada, the Library of Congress, Liverpool Central Library, Louisiana State University Libraries, Louisville Free Public Library, Milwaukee Public Library, the Minnesota Historical Society, Moncton Public Library, the Newberry Library (Chicago), New York Public Library, New York State Library, Ohio History Connection, Omaha Public Library, Ottawa Public Library, Pikes Peak Library District, Prairie City Public Library, Queen Mary University of London Library, Saint John Free Public Library, San Francisco Public Library, San José Public Library, State Historical Society of Iowa, St. Louis Public Library, Toronto Public Library (particularly the IntelliSearch team), the University College Oxford Library, the University of Illinois Library, the University of Memphis Libraries, Utica Public Library, the William Andrews Clark Memorial Library (University of California, Los Angeles), and the Wisconsin Historical Society.

Several publically accessible digital archives were central to my research: California Digital Newspaper Collection, Chronicling America (the Library of Congress), Colorado Historic Newspapers Collection, Digital Kingston, Fulton History, Gallica (Bibliothèque nationale de France), Georgia Historic Newspapers, Google News, HathiTrust Digital Library, Honma Hisao Collection (Jissen Women's University Library), the Internet Archive, Minnesota Digital Newspaper Hub, Nebraska Public Documents, New York State Historic Newspapers, Numérique (Bibliothèque et Archives nationales du Québec), the Ontario Society of Artists Archives, The Paintings of James McNeill Whistler: A Catalogue Raisonné (University of Glasgow), Papers Past (National Library of New Zealand), Trove (National Library of Australia), and Utah Digital Newspapers. So too were a number of commercial databases: America's Historical Newspapers (Readex), Ancestry, British Newspaper Archive, Gale Primary Sources, GenealogyBank, Newspapers.com, NewspaperArchive, Omaha World Herald Historical Archives, ProQuest American Periodicals, and ProQuest Historical Newspapers.

Rob Marland
Jena, 27 February 2022

The Interviews (1880–1882)

"Oscar Wilde," *The Biograph and Review* (London, UK), Aug. 1880, 130–5[1]

MR. OSCAR WILDE, though he may be considered to have his career still before him, has already attained prominence as one of the elect in a certain modern school of which he is held to be not the least of the apostles. He is a believer in the religion of beauty, a marked figure among the newest group of aesthetics, a dweller in the high places of feeling. To take this position he is specially fitted by reason of a singularly enthusiastic temperament and an exceptional education. He is the offspring of a fervid and emotional race, and the child of two persons of unusual character. In him the strong emotional tendency of the Irish nature which with most of the race feeds personal feeling alone becomes, through intellectual development, an ardour for art and its glories. To such a disposition the intangible delights of the beautiful are the realities of life, and solid comfort is full of the essential unreality of the common-place. Hence arises the craving of aesthetic souls to reach the remote recesses of art, where they believe they will find the swoony sense of a beauty hidden from the common world.

Mr. Wilde was born October 16, 1856 [*sic*];[2] he is the son of Sir William Wilde,[3] a man of great personal influence in Ireland during his life, an eminent ophthalmic and aural surgeon, possessing a European reputation in his profession, and as an archaeologist and man of letters. In 1853 Sir William was made Surgeon-Oculist in Ireland to the Queen, but though his abilities and usefulness in his profession were very great, his love was for the study of archaeology. He possessed a passion for the past, the true antiquarian spirit, which converts a piece of stone into a text for a glowing romance. The world is twice as big for these men—they have the present and they have the past. Sir William wandered about the country looking for archaeological treasures, and took his boy with him; he would linger over a bit of antiquity, filled with the actual delight of build-

1. Referenced in Ellmann, 3/3, 102/106, 122/127, 144/151; and Sturgis, 165–7/160–2. *The Biograph and Review* featured brief biographies or character sketches. Ellmann, 3/3, and Nicholas Frankel (Frankel, N. (1997). "Ave Imperatrix": Oscar Wilde and the poetry of Englishness. *Victorian Poetry*, *35*, 117–37) describe this article as an interview.

2. Wilde was born on 16 October 1854. He habitually shaved one or two years off his age, as can be seen throughout these interviews and in official documents such as the United Kingdom Census records: in 1881 he claimed to be 24 when he was 26; in 1891 that he was 35 when he was 36 (Dibb, G. (2006). Mr & Mrs Wilde! Where are those babies? *The Wildean*, *29*, 40–6). During the Regina vs Queensberry libel trial, after stating under oath that he was 39, Wilde was confronted with his true date of birth by Edward Carson (1854–1935), the QC acting for John Sholto Douglas, the Marquess of Queensberry (1844–1900), and was compelled to admit that he was 40. He maintained that "I have no intention of posing for a younger man at all. I try to be correct in the date." (Holland, 45, 64.)

3. Sir William Wilde (1815–1876).

ing up pictures of the past and its departed glories. Lady Wilde,[1] an author herself, under the signature of "Speranza," had in Dublin the only literary salon which existed there; her passion was for the future, and she surrounded herself with republicans and politicians who put the golden age perpetually into the coming years. Thus the boy lived amid a double enthusiasm, and caught something of the fever of both. Mr. Wilde was constantly with his father and mother, always among grown up persons, and, at eight years old, had heard every subject discussed and every creed defended and demolished at his father's dinner table, where were to be found not only the brilliant genius of Ireland, but also celebrities of Europe and America that visited Dublin. He considers that the best of his education in boyhood was obtained from this association with his father and mother and their remarkable friends. He went to no public school, but had tutors at home, and was given that finest of all educators, the best literature of the day.[2] Although very studious and having a positive antipathy for games, Mr. Wilde was extremely fond of riding. Summer and autumn was generally spent by the Wilde family in the West of Ireland, sometimes at a beautiful place which stood upon the scene of the greatest battle in the Irish legends, and where the very ground was full of memories and crammed with ancient monuments,[3] and sometimes at another place of very different character, on a little island far away in the highlands, in the midst of a heather-covered country.[4] There, the surroundings were natural and savage, and the great amusement, the fishing. As a boy, also, Mr. Wilde travelled a great deal in France and Germany; he cared little for German literature, excepting only Heine and Goethe,[5] but became passionately fond of the French character and writings, which are pervaded by an enthusiasm having some kinship with that peculiar to the Irish nation.

Before going to Oxford, Mr. Wilde went to Trinity College, Dublin, for a year,[6] and there won the gold medal for Greek and a scholarship. He went to Magdalen College, Oxford in 1874, where also he obtained the first scholarship. During the four years he was there, he took two first classes; in 1876, he was first-class in Moderations, and in 1878, he was first-class in "Greats,"[7] and took

1. Jane Francesca, Lady Wilde, née Elgee (1821–1896).

2. Wilde attended Portora Royal School in Enniskillen, County Fermanagh.

3. Wilde's father built Moytura House beside Lough Corrib, County Mayo. He believed it stood on the site of the legendary battle between the Dananns and Firbolgs, two ancient Celtic clans.

4. The family's fishing lodge was built on the peninsula of Illaunroe ("red island"), on Connemara's Loch Fee.

5. Heinrich Heine (1798–1856) was a German poet and literary critic. Johann Wolfgang von Goethe (1749–1832) was a German poet, playwright, and novelist. In prison Wilde requested his *Faust* in the original (Wright, 320).

6. Wilde attended Trinity College Dublin between 1871 and 1874.

7. Oxford's undergraduate classics course is split into Moderations in Classics ("Mods") and *Literae Humaniores* ("Greats").

the Newdigate prize with his poem on Ravenna.[1] Through the first term of Mr. Wilde's residence at Oxford, Ruskin lectured twice a week on Florentine Art, and the other four days devoted himself to teaching the flower and chivalry of English youth how to use its strength in making roads.[2] Mr. Wilde, an avowed Sybarite and a hater of everything uncomfortable or disagreeable, even of an ordinary sort, was yet so ready to do anything which Ruskin thought right, that we hear he actually brought himself to go out upon chilly grey November days, and break stones upon the roadside. But the one consolation to this lover of the beautiful in undertaking so ugly and common-place a task, was that he had the honour of filling Mr. Ruskin's especial wheelbarrow, and that the great teacher of Modern Aestheticism himself taught him how to wheel a barrow.[3] The influence of the master must have been enormous to induce a number of young men, avowed haters of this life and its ugliness, and yearners after something ideal and different, to face the simple un-beautifulness of stone-breaking on a dull morning. But Mr. Ruskin's influence was great enough even for this, and he has left an indelible mark upon his followers. At the end of this term the charmed circle of disciples was suddenly disbanded and cut adrift by the departure of the master; Ruskin went to Venice. But still there were many attractions in Oxford itself for the lover of the aesthetic. Mr. Wilde lived in the most beautiful of the colleges, and he occupied some fine old wainscoted rooms over the river; which he filled with all the treasures of art, from Damascus tiles to Blake drawings, to Burne-Jones and Blue China, and where he held great meetings of High Art, an Academe for the

1. The Newdigate Prize is awarded yearly to a student of the University of Oxford. Wilde recited *Ravenna* in Oxford's Sheldonian Theatre on 26 June 1878 and published the poem the same day (CW i, No. 48).

2. John Ruskin (1819–1900) was the leading art critic of the Victorian era. Wilde drew inspiration from his lectures and writings, and particularly admired his prose style: "Mr Ruskin, whose rhythm and colour and fine rhetoric and marvellous music of words are entirely unattainable." (*The Queen*, 8 Dec. 1888; CW vii, No. 108, lines 160–2.)

3. Wilde would tell this story in an early iteration of his lecture on *The Decorative Arts*, which evolved from his first lecture on *The English Renaissance*. It does not feature in O'Brien's text of *The Decorative Arts*, which is collated from reports of the final North American iteration of this lecture, but there is a lengthy version of the tale in *Art and the Handicraftsmen*, Ross's title for an assemblage of manuscript notes for *The Decorative Arts*: "He [Ruskin] thought, he said, that we should be working at something that would do good to other people [....] So he went out round Oxford and found two villages, Upper and Lower Hinksey, and between them there lay a great swamp, so that the villagers could not pass from one to the other without many miles of a round. And when we came back in winter he asked us to help him to make a road across this morass for these village people to use." (*Miscellanies*, 306–8.) Wilde's audience in Chicago on 13 February 1882 greeted with laughter and applause the story's conclusion: "Our enemies came and mocked us, but we didn't mind it very much then, and don't mind it at all now." ("Oscar Wilde," *The Daily Inter Ocean* (Chicago, IL), 14 Feb. 1882, 2.) Wilde briefly referred to the story in another interview: "The Theories of a Poet," *New York Tribune* (New York, NY), 8 Jan. 1882, 7, p. 54. See also Richards, B. (2012). Oscar Wilde and Ruskin's road. *The Wildean, 40*, 74–88.

elect, and musical parties.[1] During all his stay at Oxford, he found himself surrounded by a number of young men, all of whom were interested in art, in music, in poetry; and all of whom managed, in addition to the ordinary college life, to practise some art. Ruskin had left behind him a nest of enthusiasts, and these dreamers when they enter on the world of every day, find it very disagreeable. Mr. Wilde escaped from England and its too solid comfort. Ruskin's lectures had fired him with the desire to go to Italy, a land which he had not then visited. He went to Florence, and there found a new inspiration and a new passion.[2] Until then, the art which he had chiefly studied was the portrait painting and realistic work of Holland; the solid art which reproduces. Until this visit to Florence, he had been unaware of the spiritual element in art which constitutes its eternal value. In Florence, too, he found a new emotion in a passionate admiration for the Catholic Church. Protestantism cannot attract or interest the aesthetic mind; it is far too ugly and unadorned, and in Ireland even Roman Catholicism forgets to put on its charms. But taught by Fra Angelico and Titian, religion becomes a reality to the soul that craves for beauty. Mr. Wilde came back to Oxford with a mind full of memories of Italy and its gorgeous art, and a soul steeped in the splendour of a religion which is preached through colour and in glow. Then it was that he began to write personal poetry. He produced at this time poems full of the feeling of Roman Catholicism, which appeared in America, and some in the *Month*, the *Catholic Monitor*, and the *Irish Monthly*; the poem in the *Month* on "Rome Unvisited" having attracted considerable attention and high praise from Cardinal Newman.[3] Just after Mr. Wilde's return to Oxford, Cardinal Manning came down to open a church,[4] and delivered a fine sermon on Catholic Oxford; this, and the fact that many of his friends had already gone over to Rome, led Mr. Wilde to contemplate joining the church himself. But a new influence entered his life at this period. In company with Professor Mahaffy, the brilliant author of "Social Life in Greece," once Mr. Wilde's tutor, and always a great friend, he started

1. William Blake (1757–1827) was an English poet and artist. Sir Edward Coley Burne-Jones (1833–1898) was a British painter and designer. According to Ellmann, 66/69, Wilde's rooms were decorated with photographs of Burne-Jones's *The Beguiling of Merlin* (1877), *The Days of the Creation* (1876), and *The Mirror of Venus* (1875).

2. Wilde visited Italy in June 1875 in the company of his former teacher at Dublin, Reverend John Pentland Mahaffy (1839–1919).

3. *Graffiti D'Italia* was published in the *Month and Catholic Review* in September 1876 and in *Poems* (1881) as *Rome Unvisited* (CW i, No. 7). John Henry Newman (1801–1890) had converted to Catholicism and been created Cardinal in 1879. In 1876 Wilde wrote of Newman: "I think that his higher emotions revolted against Rome but that he was swept on by Logic to accept it as the only rational form of Christianity. His life is a terrible tragedy. I fear he is a very unhappy man," (CL, 24).

4. Henry Edward Manning (1808–1892) was an Anglican cleric who converted to Catholicism. Wilde saw him preach at the church opening in Oxford in November 1875 and again in London in July 1876: "He is more fascinating than ever" (CL, 20).

for Greece. Visiting Ravenna by chance on the way, he obtained the material for the prize poem of the following year; in March of 1877, he was at Ravenna, and the subject for the next year's prize was not then given out; in the next March he took the prize. A ride through Greece is a romance, an adventure in its very nature. To a student of Greek literature, such an excursion has a peculiar and absorbing charm; it cuts away the centuries and gives a living reality to that perfect phase of human life which he has learned to know and love. Our travellers went to Corfu, and then took sail in a small boat, landing near Olympia;[1] they rode right across the Peloponnesus, visiting the excavations at Olympia, where they stayed as the guests of the German explorers.[2] They went on through Arcadia—examined the temple at Bassae[3]—to Megalopolis and finally to Argos, where they remained some time examining Schliemann's excavations.[4] Thence they rode to Epidaurus and took a boat to Aegina, to examine the great temple there;[5] from there they sailed to Athens. The effect of this wonderful adventure of riding across Greece upon Mr. Wilde, was that in his mind the Hellenic ideal imperceptibly took the place of the Catholic. Now, as in Italy, art was the medium through

1. Wilde's party took a steamer from Brindisi to Corfu and Zakynthos. They then chartered a small boat and sailed to Katakolo, a port on the Peloponnese mainland about 32 km / 20 miles west of Olympia.

2. German archaeologist Gustav Hirschfeld (1847–1895) led the excavations at Olympia from 1875 to 1877.

3. The Temple of Apollo Epicurius at Bassae.

4. "[R]emained some time" is an exaggeration. Wilde's party arrived at Argos at 00:30 on the night of 10 April 1877, visited the ancient theatre the next morning, in the afternoon drove to Mycenae to inspect the diggings of German archaeologist Heinrich Schliemann (1822–1890), then returned to Argos and departed for Nafplio at 18:30. (George A. Macmillan to Malcolm Macmillan, 14 April 1877, Society for the Promotion of Hellenic Studies; [Macmillan, G. A.], "A Ride Across the Peloponnese," *Blackwood's Edinburgh Magazine*, May 1878, 550–70.)

5. The Temple of Aphaea. There is no evidence that Wilde saw it or even intended to see it. According to his travelling companion, George A. Macmillan (1856–1936), the party chartered a yacht at Epidaurus to sail directly to Athens, but the captain decided to put in at Aegina when a storm came on. Arriving at 19:30 on 12 April they hoped to leave on another boat at 04:00, but had to wait until 14:00 for the wind to change direction. They spent the morning "walking about," and Macmillan, who wrote about the stopover in a letter to his brother, would certainly have mentioned if they had ventured as far as the temple—a five hour round trip by foot (George A. Macmillan to Malcolm Macmillan, 14 April 1877; Society for the Promotion of Hellenic Studies). Neither does Mahaffy, in the second edition of his *Rambles and Studies in Greece* (1878), updated after his travels with Wilde and Macmillan, mention seeing the temple on his "short sojourn" on the island. The author of the *Biograph* article may have assumed that Wilde visited Aegina for the purpose of examining the temple, but it is also possible that Wilde, who often embellished stories of his travels, misled him. It is perhaps worth noting that in April 1880 an article about the marbles of Aegina by Wilde's mentor Water Pater (1839–1894; see p. 653, note 1) had been published in the *Fortnightly Review* (Potolsky, M. (ed.) (2020). *The Collected Works of Walter Pater, Vol. 8: Classical Studies*. Oxford University Press. 145–54). The marbles were—and remain—at the Munich Glyptothek, having been removed from Aegina in 1811.

which the creed was taught. From Greece, Mr. Wilde went back to Rome, and then he recognised "that it was very right for the Greek gods to be in the Vatican."

Mr. Wilde took his degree in 1878. Since leaving Oxford, he has lived in London (with frequent visits to Italy),[1] and devoted himself to poetry, though having some desire to become a painter and find expression through the slightly veiling medium of colour. Some artists feel their passion too intense to be expressed in the simplicity of language, and find in crimson and gold a mode of speech more congenial because not quite so translucent; Mr. Wilde has some of this feeling, and may perhaps some day be so much influenced by it as to become an artist. Mr. Wilde has published a series of sonnets, and a good many translations from Greek tragedies;[2] he wrote "The Conqueror of Time," which was in the first number of Mr. Edmund Yates's new monthly;[3] several of his poems have since then appeared in *Time*, the most remarkable being "The New Helen," a long poem on the worship and the meaning of incarnate beauty.[4] Among his prose writings we may mention an article on Keats, and a critique on the "Grosvenor Gallery of 1877," which appeared in the *Dublin University Magazine*.[5] The following sonnets are examples of Mr. Wilde's style; they show a rhetorical facility, a sense of art, and some youthfulness:—

✂ *Wilde's sonnets* Queen Henrietta Maria, Sonnet Written at Turin, *and* Sara Bernhardt.[6]

1. There is no record of Wilde visiting Italy between leaving Oxford and 1880. He is known to have visited Ireland, France, and Belgium. He was compelled to cut short his first trip to Italy due to lack of funds, and, if this remark is based on a statement of Wilde's rather than the author's conjecture, it may have been motivated by Wilde's desire to appear more a man of means.

2. "[A] good many" is a stretch. *Chorus of Cloud Maidens*, a translation from Aristophanes, was first published in the *Dublin University Magazine* in November 1875 (CW i, No. 2); *ΘΡΗΝΩΙΔΙΑ, a translation from Euripides*, in *Kottabos* in Michaelmas Term 1876 (CW i, No. 20); and *A Fragment from the "Agamemnon" of Aeschylos* in *Kottabos* in Hilary Term 1877 (CW i, No. 25).

3. *The Conqueror of Time*, a poem, was first published in *Time* in April 1879 and in *Poems* as *Athanasia* (CW i, No. 59).

4. *The New Helen* was first published in *Time* in July 1879 (CW i, No. 60).

5. John Keats (1795–1821) was an English Romantic poet. Wilde's article *The Tomb of Keats* was published in the *Irish Monthly* (July 1877; CW vi, No. 2). The Grosvenor Gallery was founded in 1877 and provided a venue for artists sympathetic to the aesthetic movement whose work was less welcome at the Royal Academy. Wilde's review of the first exhibition was published in the *Dublin University Magazine* (July 1877; CW vi, No. 1).

6. *Queen Henrietta Maria* was written in praise of Ellen Terry's performance in W. G. Willis's *Charles I* and was first published in *The World* on 16 July 1879 (CW i, No. 64). *Sonnet Written at Turin* was first published in *The Irish Monthly* in June 1877 as *Salve Saturnia Tellus* and in *Poems* as *Sonnet on Approaching Italy* (CW i, No. 27). *Sara Bernhardt* was written in praise of the French actress (1844–1923) and first published in *The World* on 11 June 1879 as *To Sarah Bernhardt* and in *Poems* as *Phêdre* (CW i, No. 63). All three poems were revised for this article.

At the coming Christmas Mr. Wilde purposes bringing out a blank verse tragedy in four acts, some essays on Greek art, and a collection of poems.[1]

"Oscar Wilde's Arrival," *The New York World, Semi-Weekly Edition* (New York, NY), 3 Jan. 1882, 4[2]

The Apostle of the Intense Coming on a Mission to Frivolous America.

To Lecture and to Produce his Play, Perhaps, If the Public Take Kindly to His Philosophy.

Oscar Wilde, the great English exponent of aestheticism,[3] reached this port last evening on board the Williams & Guion steamship Arizona. Shortly after the vessel came to anchor off the Quarantine Station on Staten Island a WORLD reporter put off in a row-boat managed by two sturdy oarsmen, and although the steamship was not much over a quarter of a mile from the shore it was three-quarters of an hour before he stepped upon the deck of the Arizona. Prior to undertaking the mission he had consulted Worcester, according to whom aesthetics (the good old man gives no such word as aestheticism) is set down as "the science of the sensations, or that which explains the cause of mental pain or pleasure, as derived from a contemplation of the works of art or nature; the science which treats of the beautiful and its various modes of representation in nature and in art; the philosophy of the fine arts."[4] Thus armed the reporter stepped

1. Wilde's prose tragedy *Vera; or, The Nihilists* was privately printed c. September 1880 and premiered in New York as *Vera; or, The Nihilist* in 1883. *The Duchess of Padua*, Wilde's verse tragedy (initially titled *The Duchess of Florence*), was completed in 1883 and premiered as *Guido Ferranti* in 1891 (hereafter, both plays will be referred to by their earlier and more familiar titles). Ellmann, 102/106, suggests that one of the Greek essays was probably *The Rise of Historical Criticism* (CW iv, 3–69), which Wilde wrote for Oxford University's Chancellor's Essay Prize in 1879. Wilde may also have been thinking of his review of the entry for "Greece" in the ninth edition of the *Encyclopaedia Britannica*, published in *The Athenaeum* (4 Sep. 1880; CW vi, No. 6). As a student he had begun, and abandoned, other essays on Greek subjects: *Hellenism* and *The Women of Homer* (Wright, T. (2012). Oscar Wilde: Hellenism. *The Wildean, 41*, 1–50).

2. Printed simultaneously on the front page of the daily edition (which is H & S, b1). Reprinted as "The Apostle of the Intense," *The News and Courier* (Charleston, SC), 5 Jan. 1882, 1; and in H & S, 13–15. Quoted in Ellmann, 151–2/158–9; and Sturgis, 200/194. The reporter was accompanied by the authors of "Ten Minutes with a Poet," *The New York Times* (New York, NY), 3 Jan. 1882, 5, pp. 35–8; "Oscar Wilde in New York," *The Sun* (New York, NY), 3 Jan. 1882, 1, pp. 38–9; [David A. Curtis], "Oscar Wilde," *The New York Herald* (New York, NY), 3 Jan. 1882, 6, pp. 40–2; and "Arrival of Oscar Wilde," *New York Tribune* (New York, NY), 3 Jan. 1882, 5, pp. 43–6.

3. Wilde was Irish but was often described as English in the American press.

4. Joseph Emerson Worcester (1784–1865) was an American lexicographer. The definition of "aesthetics" given here appears on page 27 of his *Dictionary of the English Language* (1860).

upon the broad deck of the Arizona and was soon ushered into the presence of Mr. Wilde in a gangway about amidships.

MR. WILDE'S PERSONAL APPEARANCE.

Mr. Wilde is fully six feet three inches in height, straight as an arrow, and with broad shoulders and long arms, indicating considerable strength. His outer garment was a long ulster trimmed with two kinds of fur, which reached almost to his feet. He wore patent-leather shoes, a smoking cap or turban, and his shirt might be termed ultra-Byronic, or perhaps — décolleté. A sky-blue cravat of the sailor style hung well down upon the chest. His hair flowed over his shoulders in dark-brown waves, curling slightly upwards at the ends. His eyes were of a deep blue, but without that far-away expression that is popularly attributed to poets. In fact they seemed rather every-day and common-place eyes.[1] His teeth were large and regular, disproving a pleasing story which has gone the rounds of the English press that he has three tusks or protuberants far from agreeable to look at. He is beardless, and his complexion is almost colorless. In manner, Mr. Wilde was easy and unconstrained, and his attitude as he conversed with the reporters and others was very graceful. A peculiarity of Mr. Wilde's face is the exaggerated oval of the Italian face carried into the English type of countenance, and tipped with a long sharp chin. It does not, however, impress one as being a strong face. His manner of talking is somewhat affected—judging from an American stand-point—his great peculiarity being a rhythmic chant in which every fourth syllable is accentuated. Thus, when asked what was his mission in America, he replied in a sing-song tone: "I came from *Eng*-land because I *thought* America was the best *place* to see."

AESTHETICISM DEFINED.

"I have come," said the reporter, "to ask you as to your intention in visiting this country. The American public have imbibed an opinion (possibly from *Punch*) that you have visited this country in the interests of aestheticism?[2] And, while we are about it, will you give me your definition of aestheticism?"

1. The allusion is to the comic opera *Patience; or, Bunthorne's Bride* (1881) by dramatist W. S. Gilbert (1836–1911) and composer Arthur Sullivan (1842–1900). When the aesthetic poet Bunthorne threatens his rival, Grosvenor, with a curse, Grosvenor agrees to become "A commonplace young man | A matter-of-fact young man | A steady and stolidy, jolly Bank-holiday | Every-day young man!" He then dances off stage, only to return wearing ordinary clothes and with his long hair cut short.

2. *Punch* was a British satirical magazine edited by F. C. Burnand (1836–1917). It had featured cartoons by George du Maurier (1834–1896) that lampooned the aesthetic movement. Some of the characters in these cartoons were popularly supposed to be based on Wilde.

Figure 1. Oscar Wilde photographed by Napoleon Sarony as he appeared to New York's reporters on the deck of the Arizona *(plate 3).*

"Well," replied Mr. Wilde, "aestheticism is a search after the signs of the beautiful. It is the science through which men look after the correlation which exists in the arts. It is, to speak more exactly, the search after the secret of life."[1]

"It has been said by some of our philosophers that aestheticism, instead of bringing forth principles, develops a certain marked line of individuality."

"It has been noticed in all great movements," replied Mr. Wilde, "that they bring out individuality. A movement that has not sufficient inherent force to develop individual characteristics would be of little or no worth to the world as a general movement of improvement."

THE OBJECT OF HIS VISIT.

"What are your intentions as to your American tour? Will you lecture?"

"That will depend considerably upon the encouragement with which my philosophy meets. I shall lecture in Chickering Hall, in New York, on the 9th of January, but whether I shall continue my labors will depend, as I said, upon the results obtained."

"It is said that you design to introduce a play in this city."

"My play, 'Vera, the Nihilist,' was not produced in London for the reason that I could not get a cast fitted for its representation. It must be produced with able actors. If a satisfactory cast can be obtained here it may be produced."[2]

"You spoke just now of aestheticism as philosophy. Is that your classification of the science?"

"Assuredly. It is a study of what may be found in art and in nature. It is a pursuit of the secret of life. Whatever in art represents eternal truth expresses the great underlying truth of aestheticism."

"Are you here to secure a copyright on your play? Some say that you are."

To this question Mr. Wilde made no reply, then being asked as to the duration of his stay in the United States, replied that he had not decided.

Mr. Wilde is the son of Lady Wilde, who wrote many patriotic poems during the Irish troubles of 1848, under the *nom de plume* of "Speranza." He is, as far as can be judged from his appearance, not over twenty-six years of age.[3]

1. *The English Renaissance* ends: "We spend our days, each one of us, in looking for the secret of life. Well, the secret of life is in art." (*Miscellanies*, 277.)

2. An announcement of the cancellation of a scheduled one-off afternoon performance in London due to "the present state of political feeling in England" was printed in *The World* (London, UK; 30 Nov. 1881, 12). Wilde, on his return to America in 1883, would claim that the play "was not produced in England, because they said it trenched on political subjects" ("Return of Oscar Wilde," *The Cincinnati Commercial Gazette* (Cincinnati, OH), 12 Aug. 1883, 1, p. 541). The more likely reason was lack of funds (Rowell, G. (1993). The truth about Vera. *Nineteenth Century Theatre, 21*, 94–100). *Vera* eventually opened at the Union Square Theatre, New York, on 20 August 1883.

3. Wilde was 27 when he arrived in New York.

DISAPPOINTED WITH THE ATLANTIC.

On the journey over Mr. Wilde did not attain, it appears, to very great popularity among the passengers. Before the ship had been five days out he said to a gentleman with whom he was promenading the deck (and this gentleman kindly retailed the conversation to the writer), "I am not exactly pleased with the Atlantic. It is not so majestic as I expected. I would like to see the ship's bridge carried away!"[1]

"Ten Minutes with a Poet," *The New York Times* (New York, NY), 3 Jan. 1882, 5[2]

A REPORTER GREETS OSCAR WILDE ON HIS ARRIVAL.

WHAT THE YOUNG AUTHOR LOOKS LIKE—HIS DEFINITION OF AESTHETICISM—NOT CERTAIN AS TO HIS FUTURE PLANS—WHAT THE ARIZONA'S PASSENGERS SAY ABOUT HIM.

Oscar Wilde, the young poet whose connection with the aesthetic movement in England has made famous [*sic*], arrived at this port last evening in the Arizona, and spent the night on board that vessel at Quarantine. He sailed from England on the 24th of December. It is understood that he will publish a new volume of poems during his stay in this country,[3] and that he will produce a play

1. This was the most widely circulated remark of Wilde's North American tour. Later a reporter heard it from him directly (see [Robert Batho], "An Interview with Oscar Wilde," *Liverool Daily Post* (Liverpool, UK), 8 Jan. 1883, 7, pp. 521–2). Wilde used the phrase "disappointing Atlantic Ocean" in an article (*Dramatic Review*, 9 May 1885; CW vi, No. 16, line 107).

2. H & S, b2. Excerpted in "Oscar Wilde," *The Chicago Daily Tribune* (Chicago, IL), 3 Jan. 1882, 2. Quoted in Hyde, 51; and Sturgis, 200/194. The reporter was accompanied by the authors of "Oscar Wilde's Arrival," *The New York World, Semi-Weekly Edition* (New York, NY), 3 Jan. 1882, 4, pp. 31–5; "Oscar Wilde in New York," *The Sun* (New York, NY), 3 Jan. 1882, 1, pp. 38–9; [David A. Curtis], "Oscar Wilde," *The New York Herald* (New York, NY), 3 Jan. 1882, 6, pp. 40–2; and "Arrival of Oscar Wilde," *New York Tribune* (New York, NY), 3 Jan. 1882, 5, pp. 43–6.

3. James Rennell Rodd (1858–1941), a friend of Wilde's from Oxford, had published his first book of poems, *Songs in the South*, in the United Kingdom in 1881, dedicating it to his father. Wilde oversaw the publication of the American edition by J. M. Stoddart (1845–1921). It appeared in September 1882 as *Rose Leaf and Apple Leaf* and with a new dedication for which Wilde was responsible: "To Oscar Wilde – 'Heart's Brother' – These Few Songs and Many Songs to Come". Wilde wrote a long self-aggrandising preface (*L'Envoi*; *Miscellanies*, 30–41) that placed Rodd's poetry in the context of the aesthetic movement. Rodd was not pleased and distanced himself from Wilde. Wilde later gave Rodd's *The Unknown Madonna, and other Poems* a mixed review in *The Pall Mall Gazette*: some lines were "excessively tedious" but others had "all the brilliancy of a clever pastel." (6 Apr. 1888; CW vii, No. 97, lines 68–74.) Stoddart later edited *Lippincott's Monthly Magazine*, in which he published Wilde's only novel, *The Picture of Dorian Gray* (1890; revised 1891).

or tragedy in five acts entitled "Vera, the Nihilist."[1] He has made arrangements, also, to lecture in this City on "The English Renaissance." He was born in Dublin, and is 25 years of age. His father was Sir William Wilde, a physician, who was widely known in England and on the Continent. He was President of the Irish Academy, an enthusiastic archaeologist, indefatigable in antiquarian research, and a frequent and brilliant contributor to the press. The poet's mother, Lady Wilde, under the pseudonym of "Speranza," wrote for the Dublin *Nation* and published several volumes of poems.[2] She gathered around her a notable company of artists, litterateurs and politicians. Oscar Wilde was graduated with honor from Magdalen College, Oxford, in 1878. In March of that year he won the Newdigate Prize for English verse, his subject being "Ravenna." The young man traveled extensively through Europe, and paid close attention to what he saw. He has published sonnets and a great many translations from the Greek tragedies. The most remarkable of his later poems was published in Edmund Yates's monthly, *Time*, and is called "The New Helen." Among his prose writings particularly worthy of mention are an article on Keats and a critique on "The Grosvenor Gallery of 1877." A volume of his poems has been printed in this country. He became identified with the aesthetic movement, and has been the subject of much ridicule in the English papers.

Shortly after the arrival of the Arizona at Quarantine last evening several reporters, who braved the raging billows in a small boat from the Health Officer's pier, were rowed to the steamer. After making the perilous ascent of the rope ladder at the ship's side, they were welcomed on deck by several of the passengers, who seemed immensely amused when they learned that the mission of the reporters was to see Mr. Wilde. "Come with us and take a drink," shouted the passengers, laughing heartily, "and we'll tell you all about him." Then one of them said: "Why, he has been groaning all the way over because we didn't have excitement enough. It was too deucedly stupid, you know. He wanted to see a great storm, and have the bridges washed away." As the oarsmen in the small boat had particularly warned the reporters that they would wait for them only 10 minutes, it became necessary to break away from these entertaining passengers, and seek Mr. Wilde. He was found in the Captain's room, and when he learned that someone was looking for him stepped into full view in the companionway. He opened his large mouth as though about to laugh, and displayed white teeth of good size, but he made no noise. He is over six feet in height and has broad shoulders. He is not heavily built, but looks like a not particularly active athletic young man. His face is oval in shape, with a rather massive chin, and nose of more than ordinary size. His complexion is uncertain and would be difficult to describe except per-

1. The 1880 privately printed edition of *Vera* was in four acts.
2. *The Nation* was an Irish nationalist weekly newspaper.

haps in the language of one of the passengers, who said that it is a "pretty complexion." He wears his brown hair so long that it rests in a curling fashion far down upon his shoulders. His face was smooth, no sign of a beard yet having shown itself. He wore a low-necked white shirt, with a turn-down collar of extraordinary size, and a large light-blue silk neck scarf. His hands were in the pockets of his fur-lined ulster, and a turban was perched on his head. He wore pantaloons of light color, and patent leather shoes. His voice was hardy, and by no means musical, and his laugh was a succession of broad "haw, haw, haws." The only jewelry displayed by him was a seal ring on a finger of his left hand. He accented every fourth syllable, as he slowly spoke, and seemed inclined to cross his long legs and rest his back against something. One of the first questions asked of him was how he liked America. At this he gave vent to one of his peculiar laughs, and made no reply. He said that the voyage had been almost without interest, that it had been exceedingly dull. He did not know how many times he would lecture in this country, as that would depend upon how he liked lecturing. He was about to make his début in that line. He desired very much to produce his tragedy here. In England, he said, he could not get it properly cast, and intimated that he expected better luck in America. Of one thing he was certain, that if he accomplished nothing else he will have seen America.

Mr. Wilde was asked to give his definition of aestheticism. By this time a number of the passengers had crowded about. Some of them smiled, but they were bound to hear his reply. He said that aestheticism was the real search of the soul for the true, or, to speak more exactly, the search for the secret of life. In referring to his connection with the aesthetic movement in England, he remarked: "If a movement has not sufficient inherent force to develop individual characteristics it is of little worth to the world as a general movement of improvement." He then proceeded in a somewhat languid manner to explain still further his views, which are by this time rather widely known in both this country and in England, and seemed at a loss what to say of his future plans. He is in the hands of his agent, Mr. D'Oyly Carte,[1] who has much to do with theatrical and operatic management, and this gentleman proposes to make Mr. Wilde a winning card in this country if he can. As the reporters withdrew from the presence of the poet, some of the passengers, who seemed anxious to give vent to their pent-up feelings, made another dash for them, and one of them said: "He told us that when he visited Roumania [*sic*] he saw a gypsy who was one of the most perfect

1. Richard D'Oyly Carte (1844–1901) was a British theatrical impresario. He managed Gilbert and Sullivan. D'Oyly Carte engaged Wilde to lecture in America as a means of educating the public about aestheticism and thereby boosting interest in *Patience*. The link between the two attractions was plain: "The acme of advertising was reached when, as the audience passed out [at the close of Wilde's first lecture], 'Patience' pamphlets, illustrated with pen and ink sketches, were distributed," ("Living up to Beauty," *The New York Herald* (New York, NY), 10 Jan. 1882, 5).

gentlemen he had ever met.[1] He was so delighted with the gypsy that he was much inclined to become a gypsy himself." The oarsmen in the small boat were shouting that they could wait no longer, and the reporters were compelled to cut short the gossip which the passengers were so anxious to deluge them with. Mr. Wilde will be in this City this morning.

"Oscar Wilde in New York," *The Sun* (New York, NY), 3 Jan. 1882, 1[2]

His Definition of Aestheticism—Disappointed in the Atlantic Ocean.

A drenched reporter of THE SUN climbed from a small rowboat to the high deck of the Arizona, while she lay off Quarantine last evening, and sought Mr. Oscar Wilde, the apostle of aestheticism, among the passengers. He was met aft by a tall young man, who was coming out of the Captain's room, saying:

"Ha, ha, ha! Wishes to interview me, does he?"

Mr. Wilde's laugh and accent were remarkable. It was a loud laugh, full of indubitably good nature, yet seeming somewhat forced. He stood at least six feet two inches tall, with broad shoulders and erect carriage. He wore a long ulster, lined with two kinds of fur, patent leather boots, and had a small round fur cap set squarely on his head. He stood at ease with one hand thrust into his ulster pocket and the other, with a large signet ring on its little finger, idly holding a cigarette which he occasionally puffed vigorously. He wore his hair long. It is brown and falls somewhat lankly on his shoulders. He wore a collar that can only be described as low-necked, inasmuch as it opened so very far down on his chest. It was caught at the bottom with a brilliant bit of sky blue plush, which hung down negligently. His face, topped by the round fur cap and flanked by the falling

1. There is no evidence that Wilde visited Romania.

2. H & S, b3. Printed simultaneously as "Awfully Utter," *The Cincinnati Enquirer* (Cincinnati, OH), 3 Jan. 1882, 4; "Oscar Wilde Interviewed," *The Boston Herald* (Boston, MA), 3 Jan. 1882, 1; "Oscar Wilde in New York," *New Haven Evening Register* (New Haven, CT), 3 Jan. 1882, 3; "Wilde is With Us," *Harrisburg Independent* (Harrisburg, PA), 3 Jan. 1882, 1. Reprinted as "Arrival of Oscar Wilde," *The Courier-Journal* (Louisville, KY), 4 Jan. 1882, 4; "Oscar Wilde in New York," *Reading Times* (Reading, PA), 4 Jan. 1882, 2; "Oscar Wilde in New York," *The Chattanooga Daily Times* (Chattanooga, TN), 5 Jan. 1882, 2; and "Oscar Wilde's Reception," *St. Louis Post-Dispatch* (St. Louis, MO), 5 Jan. 1882, 5. Excerpted in "Oscar Wilde," *The Boston Daily Globe* (Boston, MA), 3 Jan. 1882, 1. Quoted in Hyde, 51. Referenced in Sturgis, 200/194. The reporter was accompanied by the authors of "Oscar Wilde's Arrival," *The New York World, Semi-Weekly Edition* (New York, NY), 3 Jan. 1882, 4, pp. 31–35; "Ten Minutes with a Poet," *The New York Times* (New York, NY), 3 Jan. 1882, 5, pp. 35–8; [David A. Curtis], "Oscar Wilde," *The New York Herald* (New York, NY), 3 Jan. 1882, 6, pp. 40–2; and "Arrival of Oscar Wilde," *New York Tribune* (New York, NY), 3 Jan. 1882, 5, pp. 43–6.

hair, was that of a man about twenty-six years of age. He has small blue eyes that are rather expressive, and a straight nose. The face is very long, and terminates in a jaw of unusual size, which is the most prominent and striking feature of his countenance. He threw his head back occasionally when he talked, in a way that made the jaw doubly prominent and gave the face an expression of extraordinary strength. Mr. Wilde accented his words very oddly, with an entire disregard of the customary emphasis, and continually relapsed into his peculiar laugh, without any apparent reason.

"What is aestheticism, Mr. Wilde?"

Laughing again, he replied: "Aestheticism is the science of the beautiful. It is a search for the secret of life. By the way, do you know, I was very much disappointed in the Atlantic Ocean. It was very tame. I expected to have it roar about and be beautiful in its storms. I was disappointed in it."[1]

"Do not the disciples of aestheticism exhibit marked peculiarities in costume in England?"

"Yes; the movement has brought out individualities, but it is because of its force. If a movement has not sufficient force to develop individual characteristics it is of little worth as a movement of improvement. What am I to do? I'm to lecture through the country if I find that I like lecturing, and intend to produce my play."

At the termination of the interview, as the reporter descended over the side of the steamship, a crowd of passengers chanted:

A pallid and lank young man,[2]

and screamed rough jibes about aestheticism.

1. The *World* (p. 35) and *Herald* (p. 42) reporters got this story second hand from another passenger. It is possible that *The Sun* reporter heard it directly from Wilde, but this is unlikely given that the group of reporters appear to have interviewed Wilde together and, as the *Times* reporter points out (p. 36), their time onboard was limited.

2. Lyrics from *Patience* describing Bunthorne, an aesthetic poet.

[David A. Curtis], "Oscar Wilde," *The New York Herald* (New York, NY), 3 Jan. 1882, 6[1]

ARRIVAL OF THE APOSTLE OF AESTHETICISM IN AMERICA—HIS PHILOSOPHY, HIS POETRY AND HIS INTENTIONS.

Oscar Wilde stood on the deck of the Arizona as she steamed up the bay last evening. Men may come, and men may go, but it is not every day that an apostle(thwaite) of aestheticism comes to the shores of America.[2] It was for this reason that the HERALD reporter met Mr. Oscar Wilde at the first available place—namely, Quarantine. Mr. Wilde appeared like a good natured, tall, well dressed, somewhat enthusiastic young man, who was not at all averse to the American process of interviewing. He emerged from the Captain's office when notified that the reporter had arrived, and leaned against the railing of the companionway in a lounging attitude that suggested the negligence of one who had greater things to attend to. Once placed in the proper position Mr. Wilde talked. Indeed, he talked to that extent that the HERALD reporter was unable to follow the full meaning of his words.

"Your mission in America," said the reporter, "is—"

"I am going to lecture soon in Chickering Hall on the Renaissance."

"The Renaissance, meaning—?" suggested the reporter.

1. H & S, b5. Printed simultaneously as "An Apostle of Estheticism," *The Daily Inter Ocean* (Chicago, IL), 3 Jan. 1882, 2. Reprinted as "Mr. Oscar Wilde," *Daily Witness* (Montreal, QC), 4 Jan. 1882, 4; "Oscar Wilde," *The Cincinnati Enquirer* (Cincinnati, OH), 5 Jan. 1882, 5; and "Oscar Wilde," *The Chicago Daily Tribune* (Chicago, IL), 6 Jan. 1882, 5. Excerpted in "An American Interviewer and Mr. Oscar Wilde," *The Pall Mall Gazette* (London, UK), 17 Jan. 1882, 11; and Hamilton, 110–11. Quoted in OWDA, 31; Hyde, 51; and Sturgis, 200/194. David A. Curtis (c. 1846–1923), a Connecticut-born journalist who at this time wrote for the *Herald*, was likely the author. In his lecture *Reporting by the Reporter* he described "his own experience in pushing across the bay on a cold, stormy night, and after twenty minutes had been spent in grasping at the dangling rope ladder swinging from a steamer's side, getting on board only to interview Oscar Wilde" ("Newspaper Reporting," *The New York Herald* (New York, NY), 22 Apr. 1884, 11). Curtis was accompanied by the authors of "Oscar Wilde's Arrival," *The New York World, Semi-Weekly Edition* (New York, NY), 3 Jan. 1882, 4, pp. 31–5; "Ten Minutes with a Poet," *The New York Times* (New York, NY), 3 Jan. 1882, 5, pp. 35–8; "Oscar Wilde in New York," *The Sun* (New York, NY), 3 Jan. 1882, 1, pp. 38–9; and "Arrival of Oscar Wilde," *New York Tribune* (New York, NY), 3 Jan. 1882, 5, pp. 43–6.

2. Postlethwaite, an aesthetic poet, was a character created by the cartoonist, George Du Maurier. A *London World* article of 1881 describes Postlethwaite and his companion Maudle as "effeminate, affected prigs" who are received by society "amid the applause of women and the disgust of men", but judges that the aesthetes may be posing as devotees of art solely to gain entrée to the company of duchesses and the "atmosphere of magnificence, luxury and wealth." Wilde was seen in a similar light by many commentators in the United Kingdom and North America.

"Meaning the revival of the intimate study of the correlation of all arts," replied Mr. Wilde, speaking with the earnest emphasis of a man who had, so to speak, "caught on" to the correlation.

"But," said the reporter, "there is or ought to be a practical side of the study of the correlations. In what manner do you propose to address the American public?"

"I shall lecture," said Mr. Wilde, a little reservedly, "in Chickering Hall on the Renaissance. My future movements will depend entirely upon the results of my lecture in a business sense. I have come here with the intention of producing upon an American stage a play which I have written, and which I have not, for reasons, been able to produce in London. It is exceedingly desirable that it should be produced with a cast of actors who shall be thoroughly able to represent the piece with all the force of its original inception."

"But," said the reporter, "do you not intend to produce a volume of poems while you are in America?"

"No, I shall not, certainly for some time to come, publish another volume; but I hardly care to say what the future may develop."[1]

MR. WILDE'S SCHOOL OF PHILOSOPHY.

"You will certainly lecture, however?" said the reporter.

"I certainly shall, but I do not know whether I shall lecture in other cities besides New York. It will depend entirely upon what encouragement I find in the acceptance of my school of philosophy."

"Do you then call 'aestheticism' a philosophy?" asked the reporter.

"Most certainly it is a philosophy. It is the study of what may be found in art. It is the pursuit of the secret of life. Whatever there is in all art that represents the eternal truth is an expression of the great underlying truth. So far aestheticism may be held to be the study of truth in art."

"Aestheticism," said the reporter, "has been understood in America to be a blind groping after something which is entirely intangible. Can you, as the exponent of aestheticism, give an interpretation which shall serve to give a more respectable standing to the word?"

"I do not know," said Mr. Wilde, "that I can give a much better definition than I have already given. But whatever there has been in poetry since the time of Keats; whatever there has been in art that has served to develop the underlying principles of truth; whatever there has been in science that has served to show to the individual the meaning of truth as expressed to humanity—that has been an exponent of aestheticism."

1. Wilde never published a second volume of poems.

"It has been supposed that you were coming to America to obtain an American copyright?"

Mr. Wilde only laughed.

"Whatever my business may be, whatever I may accomplish in America, whatever I may do in lecturing, whatever the success of my tragedy may be, it is enough to have seen America."

"What, then," said the reporter, "do you propose? Will you stay in America for any extended time?"

"I do not know."

THE AESTHETE'S APPEARANCE.

Mr. Wilde is a man not more than twenty-six years old, apparently. He is three or four inches over six feet in height, and from his patent leather shoes to his round fur cap his dress was unlike that of other men. His fur-lined overcoat was heavier than ordinary men would wear in Arctic winters. He puffed a Russian cigarette the while he talked,[1] with an air of utter unconcern regarding what was written. His tone was affable, his manner entirely polite. His face, devoid of color, did not flush nor blanch at any word he spoke, but all he said was said with an English accent, accentuated with due regard to rhythm. His face is long and oval but exaggerated, his features not unpleasing but accentuated far beyond the face of ordinary men. His eyes are blue, his necktie bluer than his eyes. His shoes are patent leather, and his coat of fashion far surpassing aught that unaesthetic men can reach. There is no beard upon the face of Oscar Wilde, but shorn and shaven he faces criticism. A low-necked shirt displays his throat that stands a column fit to find a place in Songs of Solomon.[2]

The passengers who crossed with Mr. Wilde speak highly of him. "He said," said one, "when we were halfway over, 'The sea seems tame to me. The roaring ocean does not roar. The Atlantic is not what I thought it was. I wish that I could see a storm arise and sweep the bridge from off the ship. I care not for this tame, monotonous trip. I would that I could see a storm arise.' The Captain said," continued the sardonic passenger, "'I would I had that man lashed to the bowsprit on the windward side.' We wished it too." Then the unaesthetic passenger indulged in a most unaesthetic grin.

1. The reporter is presumably speculating here, as in later interviews Wilde claimed to smoke Turkish or Egyptian cigarettes: see "Oscar Wilde," *The Argus* (Albany, NY), 28 Jan. 1882, 8, p. 114); and "Oscar Wilde," *Dayton Daily Journal* (Dayton, OH), 3 May 1882, 4, p. 378.

2. A book of the Old Testament, essentially a collection of love poems in which a man and a woman praise one another.

"Arrival of Oscar Wilde," *New York Tribune* (New York, NY), 3 Jan. 1882, 5[1]

HOW THE POET LOOKS AND TALKS.

THE AESTHETIC ATMOSPHERE WHICH PERVADED THE ARIZONA—A FEW POINTS ON AESTHETICISM—WHAT THE POET WILL DO IN AMERICA.

A large ocean steamer was anchored in the bay last night, its hull looking like a great black shadow above the water. It was the Arizona, which had come over the bar too late to pass quarantine before sundown. The vessel was an object of interest to several persons on shore, because Oscar Wilde, the poet and apostle of English aestheticism, was among the passengers. Finally a small boat was manned and made its way slowly over the waves to the vessel's side. An icy ladder was thrown down, and a TRIBUNE reporter climbing up this tumbled over the rail to the icy deck.

"Where's the poet?" he asked, on going into the companion way. A man in a blue uniform, with gilt letters on his cap, set out to hunt the poet up. He was plainly not in the smoking-room, the door of which was ajar, where several passengers were filling the air with tobacco smoke, and laughing boisterously over jokes of their own making. "That's superlatively aesthetical, ha! ha! ha!"[2] cried a burly voice, whereat the laughing burst out afresh, and was long continued.

"Very true," said another voice, keyed rather high. "If you can tell us something as consummately soulful as that last, we're ready for it." There was more laughter at this, and the person appeared to tell another story.

By this time the man in uniform had found the poet in the captain's room. Presently the door opened from the inside, and a person came out, who was so tall that he had to bend to get through the doorway. This was Oscar Wilde.

The most striking thing about the poet's appearance is his height, which is several inches over six feet, and the next thing to attract attention is his hair,

1. Excerpted in "Aesthetic Oscar," *St. Louis Daily Globe-Democrat* (St. Louis, MO), 3 Jan. 1882, 2; "Of Gangling Gait," *The Atlanta Constitution* (Atlanta, GA), 5 Jan. 1882, 1 (which is H & S, b9); "Oscar Bunthorne Maudle Wilde," *Plain Dealer* (Cleveland, OH), 5 Jan. 1882, 4; and "Oscar Wilde," *The Daily Picayune* (New Orleans, LA), 5 Jan. 1882, 1; "Esthetic Oscar," *The Courier-Journal* (Louisville, KY), 9 Jan. 1882, 6; and "Aesthetic Oscar," *Las Animas Leader* (West Las Animas, CO), 13 Jan. 1882, 1. Quoted in OWDA, 31–2; Hyde, 51; and Ellmann, 151/158, 152/159. The reporter was accompanied by the authors of "Oscar Wilde's Arrival," *The New York World, Semi-Weekly Edition* (New York, NY), 3 Jan. 1882, 4, pp. 31–5; "Ten Minutes with a Poet," *The New York Times* (New York, NY), 3 Jan. 1882, 5, pp. 35–8; "Oscar Wilde in New York," *The Sun* (New York, NY), 3 Jan. 1882, 1, pp. 38–9; and [David A. Curtis], "Oscar Wilde," *The New York Herald* (New York, NY), 3 Jan. 1882, 6, pp. 40–2.

2. "Superlative", as well as "utter", "consummate", "intense", and "too too", were, at least in popular imagination, overused aesthetic slang words.

which is of a dark brown color, and falls far down upon his shoulders. He had broad shoulders, and long legs, which he seemed to be able to use without awkwardness when he walked. His face is oval in shape, and so elongated at the chin as to be almost pointed. His nose in harmony is long and pointed. When he laughs his lips part widely and show a shining row of upper teeth, which are superlatively white. The complexion, instead of being of the rosy hue so common to Englishmen, is so utterly-utterly devoid of color that it can only be said to resemble putty. His eyes are blue, or a light gray, and, instead of being "dreamy," as some of his admirers have imagined them to be, they are bright and quick—not at all like those of one given to perpetual musings on the ineffably beautiful and true. Instead of having a small delicate hand, only fit to caress a lily,[1] his fingers are long, and when doubled up would form a fist that would hit a hard knock, should an occasion arise for the owner to descend to that kind of an argument.

The voice can be said to be anything but aesthetic. It is so far from feminine that it is almost burly, and becomes coarse in a laugh—a form of expression which Mr. Wilde apparently uses immoderately—at least he did so last night. One of the peculiarities of his speech is that he accents almost at regular intervals without regard to the sense, perhaps a result of an effort to be rhythmic in conversation as well as in verse.

Last night the tall form of this modern apostle in poetry was wrapped in a long ulster that reached almost to the heels of his patent-leather boots, and his wilful locks strayed down his back from beneath a turban-shaped dark plush cap. The ulster was lined with fur, and also faced on the flaps and down the edges in front with the same material. This garment was sufficiently open at the throat to bring into view a wide Lord Byron collar worn on a shirt cut very low in the neck; and the cravat, which was broad and neatly looped into a knot, being of sky-blue color, relieved the pale throat and face above it, apparently in accordance with the first principles of aesthetic art. As far as the visitor could take note last night the only jewel that adorned the person of the poet was a seal ring on one of the fingers of his right hand. There might have been a gold watch chain across his waistcoat, but it wasn't visible. The all-enveloping great coat also prevented observation being made as to what sort of trousers one has to wear to be aesthetic.

1. In *Patience* Bunthorne sings: "Though the Philistines may jostle, you will rank as an apostle in the high aesthetic band | If you walk down Piccadilly with a poppy or a lily in your medieval hand." The reporter may also be playing on Wilde's devotion to Lillie Langtry (1853–1929), to whom Wilde was supposed to have carried a lily daily. Wilde denied the story: "Anyone could have done that. The great and difficult thing was what *I* achieved—to make the whole world believe that I had done it." (Maxwell, W. B. (1937). *Time Gathered.* Hutchinson & Co. 96.) See also Jacques Daurelle, "Un Poète Anglais a Paris," *L'Écho de Paris* (Paris, France), 6 Dec. 1891, 2, p. 599.

When the poet thus suddenly confronted his visitors, he was smoking a cigarette, and he bowed gracefully. Being asked how he had enjoyed his voyage, Mr. Wilde replied that he had found it dull. Then someone asked him if he would be kind enough to tell in a few words just what aestheticism is. Thereupon he threw back his chin and gave a British "haw-haw."

"Well," said he, "aesthetics, you know, are the science of the beautiful. In this modern movement there is a searching after the true, you know."

"Oh, yes, the philosophers say that the true and the beautiful are almost synonymous; that what is true is beautiful. That's it, isn't it?"

"Yes."

"What else are you trying to do?"

Hereupon the poet took his cigarette from his lips in a dainty manner and putting his chin into the air gave a second hearty laugh.

"Aestheticism, you know, is a sort of a correlation of all the arts. Its disciples are endeavoring to find out the secret of life." A sense of propriety restrained the questioner from asking if the worshippers of the true and beautiful expected success in this direction.

"Is not it a fact that the aesthetic movement has manifested itself chiefly in developing individual characteristics, rather than a correct taste for the beautiful?" said the reporter.

"Well, you may say that it has. But then, all movements develop characteristics, you know, in the individuals taking part in them. Really a movement that did not do so would be of little worth."

"When do you date the beginning of this new outbreaking?"

"You may say," replied the poet, leaning against a railing and crossing his legs in a fashion that gave him a statuesque pose, "that it began with Keats. Then, you know, others have carried it forward."

"What are your plans respecting your visit to this country?"

"I can hardly say yet. If I do nothing more, I will have an opportunity to see America, and that, you know, will be something."

"Is it true that you are going to publish a volume of poems here?"

"I will bring out a play on the subject of modern Nihilism. It is to be brought out here because I could not get it cast in London to suit me. What success this meets with will determine what I shall do with another play I have brought with me. I don't like, you know, to bring a thing out unless I can get it acted."

"What sort of a play is the second one?"

"It is in blank verse."[1]

1. The reference is surely to Wilde's blank verse tragedy *The Duchess of Padua*. At this stage the play cannot have been much more than an idea. Later in the year the American actress Mary Anderson (1859–1940) would commission Wilde to write the script on the strength of his scenario, but she rejected it in the spring of 1883 (CL, 203).

"Is it your intention to deliver lectures throughout the country?"

Here the poet sent a puff of smoke curling into the air and burst out laughing. At first it appeared that there was something exceedingly ludicrous in the question, and to answer proved that the query was not at fault.

"Now, then," he said when he had got his face straight, "that will depend on how I like lecturing. I may not like it you know."

"You are announced to lecture in Chickering Hall next week. Is that right?"

"It is my purpose to lecture on the evening of January 9." The idea of making an experiment in a new field quite overcame Mr. Wilde, and he fell to laughing again. This ended the conversation.

"A Six-Feet-Four Young Man," *The Evening Telegram* (New York, NY), 3 Jan. 1882, 3rd ed., 5[1]

Arrival of the High Priest of the London Aesthetes.

OSCAR WILDE SPEAKS FOR HIMSELF

He Talks of His Plans for His American Tour.

ALREADY IN LOVE.

A chilled crowd of aesthetic human beings—the men nearly all wearing long hair, *a la* Tilton,[2] and low-necked shirts—beat their hands and stamped their feet on the deck of the Guion Steamship Company this morning while waiting for the Arizona—on which was their apostle, Oscar Wilde—to make her berth. The big ship left Quarantine at ten minutes after seven o'clock, but it was nine before she commenced wearing alongside of her wharf. She came in prow first and stuck fast on a bank of mud twenty feet from the dock. Tugs pushed and pulled, the Arizona's engines worked vigorously, but mud was victor for a time.

1. Excerpted in "Aesthetic Cranks," *The Courier-Journal* (Louisville, KY), 4 Jan. 1882, 2; "Assinine Aesthetics," *The Wheeling Daily Intelligencer* (Wheeling, WV), 4 Jan. 1882, 1; "Morning Dispatches," *Daily Evening Bulletin* (San Francisco, CA), 4 Jan. 1882, 1 (which is H & S, b8); "New York," *The Daily American* (Nashville, TN), 4 Jan. 1882, 1; "Oscar Wilde," *The Chicago Daily Tribune* (Chicago, IL), 4 Jan. 1882, 5 (which is H & S, b7); "Oscar Wilde," *The Detroit Free Press* (Detroit, MI), 4 Jan. 1882, 2; and "Too Utterly Utter," *Milwaukee Daily Sentinel* (Milwaukee, WI), 4 Jan. 1882, 4.

2. Theodore Tilton (1835–1907) was an American newspaper editor and poet. He attended Wilde's lecture in Cincinnati on 23 February, and later that year took Wilde to see the house in New York where American poet Edgar Allan Poe (1809–1849) wrote *The Raven* (Wright, 4).

The battle raged over two hours before the steamship could be reached with a gangplank. While the fight between steam and mud was in progress the shivering mass of humanity on the dock greeted with round after round of applause a towering form on the Arizona's deck.

AN IMPOSING STRANGER.

It was that of a man, youthful in appearance. He stood six feet four inches. He has a smooth face and long flowing locks. An overcoat of bottle-green cloth, fur-lined and fur-collared, a sealskin cap, and yellow kid gloves made the man more conspicuous. It was Mr. Oscar Wilde, the poet and journalist.[1]

"I am here to lecture and see the country," he said with a hearty laugh as he extended his hand to the TELEGRAM reporter. "Will I stay long? Really I can't say. It depends upon circumstances. You see this thing is all new to me. I've made my first trip to America very pleasantly. It has been delightful on deck during the whole passage, with the exception of two days. My fellow-voyagers are splendid people.

IN LOVE WITH THE COUNTRY.

"They have given me such glowing descriptions of the country that I am in love with it already. I want to see what there is in your great metropolis, and the Far West has attractions, unless it is misrepresented, that I must witness. And I am anxious to see something of Mexico."[2] Lighting a fresh cigarette, Mr. Wilde continued: "Already I have experienced something of American courtesy. This gentleman (pointing to Mr. Frank Moseman, a Custom House officer) came on board at Quarantine and relieves [*sic*] me of all trouble concerning my baggage. Then a little steamer met us on the way up the harbor and brought on board an agent of the *International Review*, whose mission was to secure from me an article for that magazine. I had hardly heard the proposition before another steamer hailed us. She had on board Mr. Morse,[3] the business manager of my agent, Mr. R. D'Oyly Carte. I learn from him that our original plans must undergo a change. After lecturing in New York I shall proceed to Baltimore, Boston, Philadelphia and Washington.

1. Although Wilde would later edit the *Woman's World* and publish numerous articles in periodicals such as *The Pall Mall Gazette* and the *Saturday Review*, at this time he had done little work that could justify the title of "journalist". In 1886/1887 he told an unidentified correspondent who had asked for a summary of his journalistic work that he wrote "only on questions of literature and art—am hardly a journalist," (CL, 293).

2. Wilde never visited Mexico, although in *Personal Impressions of America* he would claim that he had: "In the month of June I went south, journeying to the heart of Mexico" (Dibb, 243).

3. Colonel William Francis Morse managed Wilde's American and British lecture tours.

HIS "HONEST" AGE.

"Do tell the people my honest age. I believe the TELEGRAM will report me truthfully. I wish other papers of this city had done so. I was twenty-six last October,[1] and say, too, that I shall remain long enough to see what there is worth seeing in glorious America."

"What is it, steward?" The steward of the Arizona was waiting to speak to Mr. Wilde. "An order for my lecture? Certainly." The lecturer took a card from his card case and writing his name upon the back of it with the words, "Pass bearer," said, "You are the only man in this country that has my autograph. If you can make any money by selling it I'll give you another."

DETERMINED TO GET ACQUAINTED.

Mr. Wilde talked rapidly and laughed merrily several times while making the remarks given above. As he was about passing down the gang plank he turned to the TELEGRAM reporter and said, while a shadow fell over his face:—"I have been misrepresented already, not through malice, I think, but I have come here determined to get acquainted with the big-hearted American people, and (pausing for a moment while his features again lighted up with a good-natured smile) I shan't return to Europe until I do."

"Oscar Wilde," *The Evening Post* (New York, NY), 4 Jan. 1882, 4[2]

A Talk with the Poet of the Aesthetes—The Pursuit of Beauty under Difficulties.

Mr. Oscar Wilde stood on the pier of the Williams & Guion steamship at 11 o'clock this morning when a reporter of the EVENING POST pushed through the crowd of admirers who surrounded him and asked the poet of the aesthetes what he understood by aestheticism.[3]

1. This interview appeared in the 3rd edition (15:00) of the *Evening Telegram*, which explains how Wilde could have already seen other papers published on the same day (perhaps brought by Morse). Wilde claims here that his age is 26 when it was actually 27. On 3 January, the *World, Sun*, and *Herald* reported he was 26, and the *Times* that he was 25.

2. H & S, b4. Printed simultaneously as "The Poet of the Aesthetes," *The Boston Herald* (Boston, MA), 4 Jan. 1882, 6. Reprinted in H & S, 15–17. Excerpted in "The Chief Yearner," *The Boston Daily Globe* (Boston, MA), 4 Jan. 1882, 4; "Running Wilde," *The Topeka Daily Capital* (Topeka, KS), 4 Jan. 1882, 1; "Aestheticism's Expositor," *The Atchison Globe* (Atchison, KS), 5 Jan. 1882, 6; "Arrival of Oscar Wilde," *The Emporia Daily News* (Emporia, KS), 5 Jan. 1882, 1; and "Oscar Wilde," *The Argus* (Albany, NY), 10 Jan. 1882, 5. Quoted in OWDA, 35; Hyde, 52; Ellmann, 151/158, 152/159; and Sturgis, 201/195.

3. Wilde disembarked on the morning of the 3rd and not the 4th as implied here.

"I've defined it about two hundred times since last night," answered Mr. Wilde, with a patient smile, "but I am here to diffuse beauty and I have no objection to saying that—I say, porter, handle that box more carefully, will you?" This was said to a hotel porter, who had seized Mr. Wilde's luggage and was tossing it, box after box, up to the roof of the hotel stage, unmindful that the boxes might contain frail objects, such as lilies and the like.

While Mr. Wilde expostulated with the man the reporter was able to get a good look at him: a tall, well-built, blue-eyed, beardless young man, six feet high at least, with a large, white, flat face, surmounted by a seal-skin cap many sizes too small for him; irregular and protruding teeth; light long hair flowing over the collar of a sort of bottle-green dressing gown extending down to the feet; a manner in which ease and amusement contrasted strangely with an embarrassed laugh used in lieu of punctuation. Such is Mr. Oscar Wilde at the first glance. Further study reveals the ends of a sky-blue neck-tie, a pair of patent-leather boots, and large hands. That Mr. Wilde had with very moderate success attempted something after the style of Raphael's famous portrait of himself would occur to anyone who sees him with his seal-skin cap on.[1]

"Aestheticism," he continued, "is an attempt to color the commonplace, to make beauty stand out wherever it is. There is a subtle relation between beauty and everything—a correlation of one sensible beauty with another—that is not seen or felt, except by—by—well, by persons who have studied the matter."

"For instance," asked the reporter, "where is the beauty in that striking grain elevator which is the chief object in New Jersey's landscape across the river there?"

Mr. Wilde looked across the river, but said that he was too near-sighted to see the object in question; he would examine it some other day and make a note of it.

"Beauty," went on the poet, puffing vigorously at a cigarette and plunging both hands deep into the pockets of his dressing gown, "is nearer to most of us than we are aware; the material is all around us, but we want a systematic way of bringing it out. It may be subjective, don't you know, or objective, but it is there and the science of how to get at it is what I come to lecture about."

"Then you have found a key to pure beauty or to such beauty as there may be in the lily or the Hoboken. Is that it?"

1. Wilde was photographed by Napoleon Sarony (1821–1896) wearing this cap in January 1882 (plate 3 of the series of photographs of Wilde). His appearance is not dissimilar to that of Raffaello Sanzio (1483–1520), or Raphael, the Italian Renaissance artist, in his presumed self-portrait. Another interviewer noticed the resemblance: [Robert Batho], "An Interview with Oscar Wilde," *Liverpool Daily Post* (Liverpool, UK), 8 Jan. 1883, 7, p. 519.

"Something of the kind. It's a wide field which has no limit, and all definitions are unsatisfactory. Some people might search and not find anything. But the search, if carried on according to right laws, would constitute aestheticism. They would find happiness in striving, even in despair of ever finding what they seek. The renaissance of beauty is not to be hoped for without strife internal and external."

"Where is this movement going to end?" asked the reporter.

"There is no end to it: it will go on forever, just as it had no beginning. I have used the word renaissance to show that it is no new thing with me. It has always existed. As time goes on the men and the forms of expression may change, but the principles will remain. Man is hungry for beauty: therefore he must be filled. There is a void; nature will fill it. The ridicule which aesthetes have been subjected to is only the envy of blind, unhappy souls who cannot find the path to beauty."

"What will the last expression of aestheticism be? Has anyone yet succeeded in carrying the science to its highest degree?"

"Now, see here, don't you know I came here to lecture? You come next Monday night to the hall and I'll answer those questions. The last expression of aestheticism is one of the points of my lecture. I must get some breakfast now and see the town. Our voyage over was so monotonous that I am glad to get on land and see some people. Goodbye. You can define aestheticism for your paper as the science of finding the beautiful by looking for it in pursuance of fixed laws. As I said before, there is beauty all around us—even here," looking around upon the horde of hackmen shouting "Carriage, sir!" at the top of their lungs. "Where?" eagerly asked the reporter, following the direction of Mr. Wilde's gaze to an old lady selling apples.

"Everywhere," said the poet, relapsing into the indefinite.

Mr. Wilde's agent hurried him into a carriage, and the party drove off to the Brunswick Hotel.[1] The most noticeable peculiarities about Mr. Wilde's talk were a sing-song division of words into a species of blank verse of his own, and a vacant smile which seemed to be part and parcel of the spoken lines.[2] When talking of aestheticism the smile seemed to suggest that he looked upon the whole business as an absurd farce, and his arrival in New York upon a lecturing tour as its most ridiculous incident.

1. The Brunswick was full and Wilde was turned away. See "Preparing the Poet for Work," *New York Tribune* (New York, NY), 5 Jan. 1882, 3, p. 751.

2. This and the following sentence also appear in "Our New York Letter," *The Philadelphia Inquirer* (Philadelphia, PA), 4 Jan. 1882, 7, p. 875.

"In Honor of Oscar Wilde," *The New York Times* (New York, NY), 6 Jan. 1882, 8[1]

A LARGE NUMBER OF LADIES AND GENTLEMEN CALL TO SEE THE POET.

The parlors of the residence of Mr. Augustus A. Hayes, Jr., at 112 East Twenty-fifth street, were thrown open yesterday afternoon, between the hours of 3 and 6 o'clock, for a reception given in honor of Oscar Wilde, the poet and aesthete.[2] A line of private conveyances with liveried coachmen filled the street, and invited guests were constantly arriving or departing during the hours mentioned. The parlors were arranged in the most attractive manner. Mr. Wilde was in plain black. He wore no flower in the lapel of his coat, but a dark blue handkerchief peeped from a breast pocket. He stood perfectly at ease, and spoke freely with all who were introduced to him by Mr. Hayes. The ladies clustered about him, and seemed greatly interested in what he said. He cordially greeted a reporter of THE TIMES, and spoke of his trip across the Atlantic, saying he had never experienced such loneliness before. "There was such a broad expanse of water," he added with a smile, "a desert, one might say, and I felt at times as though it would have been a great relief could I have seen even a fishing-smack. But I found some splendid people on board the steamer. There was one gentleman in particular who, I think, was one of the most perfect gentlemen I ever met—Gen. Palmer, of Colorado.[3] I was greatly pleased with him." To the question whether he had seen much of New-York since his arrival, he replied that he had not, but from what he had observed he was reminded of Paris. On Wednesday evening, he said, he went to Booth's Theatre, and saw Miss Mary Anderson as Juliet. "She is a very beautiful woman," continued Mr. Wilde, "but there are traditions about dress in Shakespearean performances that detract much from the pleasure, I think, of witnessing those plays. Miss Anderson did excellently well, however, but I should prefer to see her in other plays than those of Shakespeare.[4]

1. Quoted in OWDA, 47; Ellmann, 155/163; and Sturgis, 263/250–1.

2. Augustus Allen Hayes, Jr. (1837–1892) was an American businessman and author of non-fiction works on travel.

3. General William Jackson Palmer (1836–1909) is listed on the relevant passenger manifest of the SS *Arizona*. He served in the Union Army during the Civil War, reaching the rank of Brevet Brigadier General. He was awarded the Medal of Honor. In 1871 he founded the city of Colorado Springs.

4. Wilde saw Anderson again at the same theatre on 14 January in *Pygmalion and Galatea*. Wilde's opinion of her Juliet as given in here contrasts with his less diplomatic appraisal in "Sunflowers and Lilies," *Fort Wayne Daily Gazette* (Fort Wayne, IN), 16 Feb. 1882, 6, p. 177. In 1887 Wilde reviewed her performance in London of *The Winter's Tale* for *The Court and Society Review*: "A certain artificial staginess has, up to this, marred to a certain degree most, if not all, of Miss Anderson's performances. Her manner has been too self conscious, her method too theatrical. In Perdita, however, no trace of these defects could be seen [...]" (14 Sep. 1887; CW vi, No. 77,

Why, Modjeska delighted London until she made her appearance as Juliet. Then she seemed to lose her hold upon her audiences, and they were never satisfied with her after that performance, no matter what she undertook."[1] Mr. Wilde said he had been so extremely busy that he had not yet had time to look at New York as much as he desired. After his lecture in this City next week he goes to Philadelphia, thence to Washington, Boston, and other cities.

✂ *A list of guests at the reception.*

During Mr. Wilde's brief stay in the City he has received a large number of invitations to visit the residences of notable persons, but he has been compelled, through the urgency of preparation for his coming lecture, to decline them all.

"The Theories of a Poet," *New York Tribune* (New York, NY), 8 Jan. 1882, 7[2]

AN INTERVIEW WITH OSCAR WILDE

THE BEGINNING OF THE AESTHETIC MOVEMENT IN ENGLAND—ITS INFLUENCE ON DRESS—DU MAURIER'S CARICATURES

Oscar Wilde, the poet and apostle of aestheticism, is at present living in a private house so that he may secure the quiet and freedom from interruption

lines 37–41). He still took issue with the way she spoke Shakespeare's lines: "Those who act Shakespeare should be perfect in each word and syllable of the text, but on more than one occasion Miss Anderson marred and missed the music of her lines by addition and alteration [...]" (ibid, lines 53–6).

1. Helena Modjeska (1840–1909) was a Polish actress who specialised in Shakespearean and tragic roles. Having previously given her Juliet elsewhere, she first played the part in London at the Court Theatre on 26 March 1881. As she acknowledged in her autobiography, her performance "called forth many notices, some good, some adverse, as might have been expected by a foreigner 'tackling Shakespeare'" (Modjeska, H. (1910). *Memories and Impressions of Helena Modjeska*. Macmillan. 420). She might have responded to Wilde's dismissal in these words: "my chief object was to act Juliet to the best of my ability, and I did so. It seems that the part was a success, for I kept it in my repertoire until the year 1888, just one year after the birth of my first grandchild" (ibid, 380).

2. H & S, b11. Reprinted as "The Aesthete at Home," *The Boston Daily Globe* (Boston, MA), 10 Jan. 1882, 1; and "Oscar Wilde," *The Globe* (Toronto, ON), 12 Jan. 1882, 4; and in Mikhail, 39–42; and H & S, 19–22. Excerpted in OWDA, 46–7. Quoted in Pearson, 33–4. The reporter appears to have been accompanied by the authors of "The Science of the Beautiful," *The New York World, Semi-Weekly Edition* (New York, NY), 10 Jan. 1882, 7, pp. 56–9; and "The Art of Dining," *The Cincinnati Commercial* (Cincinnati, OH), 14 Jan. 1882, 4, pp. 60–2.

which his work demands.[1] He occupies two rooms furnished in a matter-of-fact style, and has his meals sent in from a neighbouring restaurant. The centre table of his parlor yesterday was covered with letters and invitations of all kinds and a few books. The poet himself had on a brown dressing-gown with red cuffs, and brown trousers, with red silk cord along the sides. His shoes were patent leather, with red silk stockings. On the lounge was thrown carelessly a heavy ulster of olive green, with a fur collar and cuffs.

"The groundwork of aestheticism," said Mr. Wilde, in answer to the question of a TRIBUNE reporter, "is that you cannot teach a knowledge of the beautiful; it must be revealed. A boy could become learned in a scientific subject by the study of books; the knowledge of the beautiful is personal, and can only be acquired by one's own eyes and ears. This truth was the origin of the theory of beautiful surroundings. A child should have around him from his infancy beautiful things. Suppose you take up a volume of Keats. If you are in a library furnished as most are you have to take a spiritual jump, so to speak, before you are in the proper frame of mind to appreciate his poetry."

"Where were you first impressed with these ideas?"

"When I went to Oxford, which was the most beautiful city I had ever been in. I was given a wonderful set of old wainscoted rooms in Magdalen overlooking the river, near that graceful bridge which they are now pulling down for the sake of a tramway.[2] Ruskin was then delivering a series of lectures on 'Florentine Art,'

1. Interviewers were able to find their way to Wilde's private house at 46 West 28th Street because the address had been leaked by the editor of New York's *The Daily Star*, Stephen Ryder Fiske (1840–1916). A native of New Jersey, Fiske had previously worked as a foreign correspondent for *The New York Herald.* Settling in London he managed the St. James's Theatre and befriended Charles Dickens. He returned to America in 1874 and managed the Fifth Avenue Theatre for several years before resuming his career in journalism. According to a report in London's *The Referee* (29 Jan. 1882, 3), Fiske "has been treading on the toes of the Apostle of the Lily and the Sunflower, and Oscar has described his method of doing him a turn as 'very curious,' contrasting it with the 'charming' way in which he was treated by a reverend editor of another paper [William Henry Hurlbert (1827–1895), the editor of *The New York World*]. The reverend one gave him a dinner. Fiske gave him notoriety, publicity, popularity, and published his address, so that all the pseudo-fashionables could call upon him and buy tickets for his lectures. 'Our way,' says Stephen, 'will provide him with many good dinners after the reverend one's is digested and forgotten.'" See also "Wilde's Experience," *The Topeka Daily Capital* (Topeka, KS), 23 Jan. 1882, 3, p. 761.

2. In 1881 the Oxford Local Board resolved to widen the bridge on the south-west side (the opposite side to Magdalen College) by twenty feet to accommodate increased traffic; work began the following year. There were unfounded rumours that the bridge would be demolished at the behest of the City of Oxford and District Tramways Company, leading to protests from the Society for the Protection of Ancient Buildings (Walter Pater was on the committee). In fact, the new horse-drawn tramway was not reliant on the widening, and by November 1881 tracks had already been laid over the still unwidened bridge. The trams ran until 1913, when they were replaced by motor-buses. See articles in *Jackson's Oxford Journal* (Oxford, UK), e.g. 16 Apr. 1881, 5; 23 Apr. 1881, 5; 29 Oct. 1881, 5; 7 Jan. 1882, 6; and 4 Mar. 1882, 6.

and I came under his influence. I am rather luxurious in my nature, I think, but I used to assist Mr. Ruskin on dull November mornings in the prosaic occupation of breaking stones and making roads.[1] In 1876 I went to Florence and there the whole splendor of Italian art was revealed to me.[2] When I returned to Oxford I sounded my companions (most of them have since become artists or literary men in London), and finding that their opinions coincided with mine we formed a little coterie for the purpose of carrying out our ideas, and laid out plans for a great revolution in English life and art. In doing this, there is no doubt but that we all purposely went to the wildest extremes in dress and expressions.

"The first time that the absolute stupidity of the English people was ever revealed to me was one Sunday at the University Church, when the preacher opened his sermon in something this way: 'When a young man says, not in polished banter, but in sober earnestness, that he finds it difficult to live up to the level of his blue china, there has crept into these cloistered shades a form of heathenism which it is our bounden duty to fight against and crush out, if possible. I need hardly say that we were delighted and amused at the typical English way in which our ideas were misunderstood. They took our epigrams as earnest, and our paradoxes as prose. In 1877 rumors of the movement began to reach London, and extravagant expressions which we had used were quoted in the public prints. Du Maurier finally began his illustrations, which have been kept up ever since. I had never met him when he did so. I have never felt pained at all by his caricatures or those of anyone else, and I think I have enjoyed them fully as much as anyone."

"Will you tell me something of your life in London?"

"In 1878 I went to London and took a house on the banks of the Thames, near Charing Cross Bridge. It was almost a counterpart of the one in which I lived in Oxford, and embodied our ideas.[3] Since then I have frequently met Du Maurier in society, and have talked with him about his caricatures as if I were not interested in them at all. When I have thought they were clever I have told him so, as I did when I thought them stupid. A party of my friends and myself went to see 'Patience' on the first night,[4] and we laughed, or jeered, at it as it deserved. As to Du Maurier's characters, I suppose that I am the original of *Maudle*, the poet.[5] *Postlethwaite*, the artist, has no original, but is a combination or a conglomeration of the peculiarities of a number of my friends. As an artist, my attitude toward all this is that a true artist who believes in his art and his mission must nec-

1. Ruskin's road: see p. 27, note 3.
2. Wilde visited Florence in 1875.
3. 13 Salisbury Street, off the Strand. Wilde lived there with the artist Frank Miles (1852–1891).
4. At the Opera Comique, 23 April 1881.
5. The poet Algernon Charles Swinburne (1837–1909) is another likely candidate.

essarily be altogether insensible to praise or blame. If he is not a mere sham, he cannot be disturbed by any caricature or exaggeration. He has the truth on his side, and the opinion of the whole world should be of no consequence to him."

"How far has this theory of beautiful surroundings spread?"

"It has had the widest influence among the best classes of society. Its effect is plainly marked in their houses and their furniture. No one in the best society in England would think now of building a house without taking into consideration the ideas which are the basis of aestheticism. The rich middle-class it has not influenced, and nothing can influence them. The real strength of our movement lies in the great spread of beautiful designs among the handicraftsmen of the various cities."

"What influence has aestheticism had in regard to dress?"

"As far as men are concerned it is not so perceptible. But among women there is a distinct tendency toward the most radical change both in the form of the dress and in the introduction of novel and beautiful colors."

"But in America it has been understood that in the matter of color the tendency of the movement was towards neutral tints."

"There can be no beautiful color without tone. If any tone in an orchestra is intensified two or three times it ceases to be music and is mere sound. The people who believe in aestheticism follow out this same theory in regard to color; but this doesn't shut out any ordinary ones [*sic*].[1] This is the only concession they make to neutral tints. So far as the form of the dress is concerned, there has been a tendency among ladies toward a suppression of tight waists and French millinery, and return to more natural drapery. I have seen many lovely dresses on ladies in society not unlike those in 'Patience.' I mean, of course, without that exaggeration in embroidery which you see in the dresses in 'Patience,' particularly that of *Lady Jane*.[2] As far as the men are concerned I have a hope that they

1. Possibly "ones" should be "tones".

2. Alice Barnett (1846–1901) created the role of Lady Jane and wore a gown embroidered with a massive peacock perching in a tree. The review of the first production in *The Times* (London, UK), 25 Apr. 1881, 10, noted that "the dresses and colours of the rapturous maidens (not excepting the peacock embroidered gown of the formidable Lady Jane), would scarcely pass muster in an aesthetic drawing-room. Such at least will probably be the impression of most observers in this country; in America no doubt the new opera will be hailed with welcome as a faithful counterfeit presentment of London society in its latest development." The dress worn by Augusta Roche (1849–1893) in the first authorised New York production was described by one reviewer as "a wonderful aesthetic frenzy of embroidery; on a black background appear, or seem to, a weeping willow in gold, cranes, storks and canvas-back ducks in various metals and colors; a select assortment of pine trees and cactuses, a section of country road, upon which a badger—perhaps it is a seal or guinea pig—meanders along, and there are also suggestions of chain armor, sheet lightning, rail fence, country garden, telegraph wire, moonlit lake, Brussels sprouts, ash heaps and Japanese fans." ("Music and the Drama," *Buffalo Commercial Advertiser* (Buffalo, NY), 1 Oct. 1881, 4.)

will find their dress so utterly incongruous and discordant with that of the ladies that they will be insensibly influenced, so that there will be a complete and radical reform in the matter."

"Have you carried out your ideas in your own dress?"

"Well," said Mr. Wilde, with a laugh, "I don't know. I have conformed it somewhat to my theories, but I intend after a right interval to follow them out entirely. The essence of good dressing is perfect congruity. One must be careful not to be too premature, but I feel that at present velvet is the most beautiful dress for a man. As a rule I wear gray or brown velvet myself."

"I believe myself," said Mr. Wilde, in conclusion, "in the correlation of the arts; that painting, poetry, and sculpture are only different forms of the same truth.[1] I do not believe that poets and artists should live in solitude, but rather that they should associate with each other and mix freely in society. I have always done this myself, and I have preached my theories in every salon in London. I have not the slightest doubt of the complete success of the movement; the desire for beauty is merely a heightened form of the desire for life."

"The Science of the Beautiful," *The New York World, Semi-Weekly Edition* (New York, NY), 10 Jan. 1882, 7[2]

Mr. Oscar Wilde Explains How He Developed the Theory He Imbibed from Mr. Ruskin.

Mr. Oscar Wilde was visited by a WORLD reporter Saturday morning in his new home in Twenty-eighth street.[3] He was seated before a writing-table which was covered with invitations. He was dressed in a simple black velvet jacket, below which he wore a pair of beautiful brown trousers, from the bottoms of which his patent-leather pumps were seen covering a very shapely pair of feet. His cravat was of a light olive green; brown and green being apparently his favorite colors. Being asked to explain his peculiar theory Mr. Wilde said: "My theory is that

1. Wilde maintained this position. In a review of the 10 o'clock lecture given by American artist James McNeill Whistler (1834–1903), Wilde stated that: "there are not many arts, but one art merely: poem, picture, and Parthenon, sonnet and statue—all are in their essence the same, and he who knows one, knows all." (21 Feb. 1885; CW vi, No. 10, lines 77–80.) See also Gilbert Burgess, "An Ideal Husband at the Haymarket Theatre," *The Sketch* (London, UK), 9 Jan. 1895, 495, p. 643 ("All modes of art are one").

2. Reprinted from the daily edition (8 Jan. 1882, 2; which is H & S, b12). Reprinted in H & S, 22–5. The reporter appears to have been accompanied by the authors of "The Theories of a Poet," *New York Tribune* (New York, NY), 8 Jan. 1882, 7, 52–6; and "The Art of Dining," *The Cincinnati Commercial* (Cincinnati, OH), 14 Jan. 1882, 4, pp. 60–2.

3. Saturday 7 January. Wilde's private address: see p. 53, note 1.

you cannot teach anybody what is really beautiful. The true spirit of a painting or a poem cannot by any method be taught—it must be gradually revealed. A schoolboy, for instance, can arrive at an understanding of a scientific truth under a competent teacher, but the only way in which anybody can come to a knowledge of the beautiful is by being thrown among beautiful surroundings. I think if you desire a cultured society you must put the youth of the land into beautiful homes and let them gradually come to feel a necessity for such surroundings. A young man reared among such surroundings has not got to make a distinct effort to appreciate the beautiful. He will, if reading, come at once into sympathy with his author in his description of the true and the beautiful."

A DISCIPLE OF RUSKIN.

"When did you go to Oxford, Mr. Wilde?"

"In 1873, and entered Magdalen College.[1] It was at this time that this theory of the effect of beautiful associations began to manifest itself to my mind. This town was by far the most beautiful one that I had ever been in and I experienced its effect on myself. Ruskin was there and I became a disciple of his, and his teachings gave impetus to this thought. Very many of my theories are, if I may say so, Ruskin's theories developed. He was at that time giving a course of lectures upon Florentine art and had all the youth of the colleges after him. After we had listened to a lecture we would go out with him on the road. They were the most charming rambles imaginable. In 1876 I visited Italy and went through all the churches there, drinking in everything of the beautiful in art, and its whole splendor was revealed to me by association as it never could have been from any mere description.[2] I came back to Oxford more confirmed than ever in the correctness of my theories, and it was then that I began to write my poetry and gradually gathered around me a group of young men; an aesthetic clique, if you will. I had a beautiful house by the river side, which I fitted up in consonance with my peculiar ideas. We were very enthusiastic young men, and insensibly, as it were, we became extravagant in our expressions as compared with the common manner of converse. Meanwhile rumors began to reach us that this movement of ours, for such it might now be called, had reached London, but we did not realize how far it had gone until one Sunday in the University Church the preacher—we used to have the most distinguished men of the day to preach to us in town—opened his sermon by saying in effect that when young men in the University, not in polished banter but in sober earnest, declared that they were striving to live up to the level of their blue china, it must become very apparent that a form of heathenism had crept into these cloistered shades which it was

1. Wilde was matriculated at Oxford in Michaelmas (autumn) term, 1874.
2. Wilde had visited Italy in 1875 and 1877.

their bounden duty to fight with all their power. Well, all this was great sport for us. We were not martyrs, nor were we disposed to be. Just on top of this came Du Maurier's first caricature, and we found very much to our astonishment that we were becoming famous."

DU MAURIER'S CARICATURES.

"Then you went to London?"

"Yes. In 1878. I had then fully developed in my own mind what I may call my social idea of art; that is that in past times the artist was isolated to a wonderful degree—was cut off from his fellow-workers in all branches and also cut off from immediate contact with the public, the only medium of communication with whom being their books, their paintings or their sculptures. My idea was to sweep away these barriers and bring them more in unison as far as possible, and to establish what may properly be called a correlation of art, so that the artists in different lines should receive distinct assistance from each other. They are all striving to express essentially the same thing, only in different ways. So in the case of society my idea was the same, to sweep away all barriers and bring the artist in direct communication with his patrons."

"How were you received at first in London?"

"I found on arrival there that I was already known, and I was well received, and I took every possible opportunity to preach the doctrines I have evolved and crystallized during my college career. Du Maurier had not seen me when he made his first caricature, but he continued them after he did meet me in society, and I took especial pains to greet him cordially, praising his pictures when they were clever and pointing out defects if I discovered them."

HOW MR. WILDE ENJOYED "PATIENCE."

"And you found converts to your theory in London, did you not?"

"Oh, yes. I found myself surrounded by a clique there, just as I had in Oxford. I was somewhat surprised at this at first. I had not thought it strange that this should have been the case at Oxford, but I did not expect it at London. The movement, if you choose to call it that, grew from week to week and began to affect the drama. 'The Colonel' was written by Burnand and 'Patience' by Gilbert & Sullivan.[1] We attended at the opening night and had all manner of fun. I was not to be laughed out of my theory. I had arrived at what I sincerely believed to

1. *The Colonel* was a farce by *Punch* editor F. C. Burnand (1836-1917) that premiered on 2 February 1881 at the Prince of Wales's Theatre, ran for 550 performances, and gave a command performance before Queen Victoria. The plot concerns an American colonel's efforts to prevent two aesthetes from gaining control over a family fortune by converting its members to aestheticism.

be the truth in these matters, and the praise or blame of the public was to me a matter of no consequence whatever. I regarded it only as a help or a hindrance to the development of what I regard as an important social theory."

"What was its effect on society?"

"Through all the upper circles its effect was very general and marked, and no English gentleman would now think of building or furnishing his house without taking into consideration the ideas that have been developed during the progress of this aesthetic movement."

TRUE ART IN DRESS.

"Does it add to the expense of furnishing?"

"Not at all. On the contrary it tends to lessen the cost and so far as dress was concerned this introduction of a true art in women's attire cost much less than the former productions of French milliners or dresses from Worth."[1]

"Has the dress of men been at all affected?"

"Not much, as yet, but I hope that as the women's dresses have been so much improved, after awhile men will bring themselves unconsciously into harmony with their surroundings."

"Are the dresses in 'Patience' exaggerated?"

"Not much. I have seen among the advocates of my theory in society some that nearly equalled them, allowing, of course, for the necessity of larger decorations for stage effect. As to myself," continued Mr. Wilde, "I have gone somewhat in the true direction, conceding, of course, something to custom."

Mr. Wilde expressed himself as delighted with his reception in this country. "Nothing could have been more cordial," he remarked. He said he thought he should have to stay the winter out. "I shall go from here to Philadelphia," he said, "and from there to Boston."

1. Charles Frederick Worth (1825–1895) was an English fashion designer who founded the House of Worth in Paris. He is considered to be the father of haute couture and, through his innovative designs and self-promotion, became the arbiter of French fashion during the late nineteenth-century.

"The Art of Dining," *The Cincinnati Commercial* (Cincinnati, OH), 14 Jan. 1882, 4[1]

FORMULAS OF AESTHETICISM.

SOCIAL TRIUMPHS OF MR. WILDE

HIS APPEARANCE, THEORIES AND TOILETS—"MOSTLY OSCAR."

Correspondence Cincinnati Commercial.

NEW YORK, January 10, 1882.

✂ *A report of social events in New York, a description of recent fashions in dining, and accounts of Wilde's social engagements and his lecture in New York.*

Your correspondent called on Mr. Wilde this afternoon. He entered the drawing-room in a *negligee* costume of dark green. The short loose coat was buttoned high, showing a cravat of subdued cardinal. The coat was embroidered with green and cardinal cord, and there were a wide lapel and deep cuffs of quilted cardinal silk upon it. The trousers were long and full, and a round cord ran down the outside of the seams. He wore cardinal stockings and patent-leather pumps.

"What did you think of your audience last evening?"

"I was really much interested. I felt so keenly that it was a privilege I had never had before of telling a sympathetic audience what some of us were trying to do in England. The people seemed so near me, and I saw so many interesting faces of young girls and young men in the gallery. In England one never has the opportunity to speak in public, only those in politics, and I think it a great educational exercise."

"What do you think of American women?"

"I have the opinion that all sensible men have of American women. No sensible man ever tells that opinion."

As to his peculiar theory and its rise Mr. Wilde said: "My theory is that you cannot teach anybody what is beautiful. The true spirit of beauty must be revealed.[2] In 1873 I went to Oxford and entered Magdalen College.[1] It was at this

1. This article is similar in content to "The Theories of a Poet," *New York Tribune* (New York, NY), 8 Jan. 1882, 7, 52–6; and "The Science of the Beautiful," *The New York World, Semi-Weekly Edition* (New York, NY), 10 Jan. 1882, 7, pp. 56–9. It therefore seems likely that the author accompanied the *Tribune* and *World* reporters on the 7th. His claim to have spoken to Wilde on the 10th (the morning after the lecture) may be false, or he may have paid Wilde a second visit.

2. "Spirit of Beauty" is a phrase from a poem by Percy Bysshe Shelley (1792–1822), *Hymn to Intellectual Beauty* (1817): "Spirit of Beauty, that dost consecrate | With thine own hues all thou dost shine upon | Of human thought or form, – where art thou gone?" Wilde used the phrase

time that the theory of the effect of beautiful associations began to manifest itself in my mind. This town is by far the most beautiful I have ever seen and it had its effect upon me. Ruskin was there and I became a disciple of his, and his teachings gave an impetus to this thought. In 1876 I visited Italy,[2] and went through all the churches, drinking in all of the beautiful in art. I came back to Oxford more confirmed than ever in my theories, and it was then I began to write my poetry and to gather around me a group of young men—an aesthetic clique. I had a beautiful house by the river-side, which I fitted up in consonance with my ideas. We were very enthusiastic young men, and insensibly we became extravagant in our expressions. Rumors began to reach us that this movement of ours had reached London, and one day we were startled by a minister saying in effect that when young men in the University, not in polished banter, but in sober earnest declared that they were striving to live up to their blue china, it was apparent that a form of heathenism had crept into these cloisters which they were bound to fight with all their power. On top of this came Du Maurier's first caricature in Punch,[3] and we found ourselves famous. In 1878 I went to London. My idea was to sweep away all barriers and bring the artist into direct communication with his patrons, and I was well received. The movement had its effect upon the drama, as you know, and through all the upper circles of English society. It tends to lessen cost in dress. The dresses of the aesthetics in 'Patience' are not much exaggerated."

"What will be the practical outcome of all this?"

"That depends more upon America than upon myself. The movement deals with two kinds of people; those who create art, handicraftsmen, and people who enjoy art but do not create it. To the handicraftsman it gives perfect joy in his work, and puts an end to all the discontent of the working classes; that is the great danger of Europe, and will give him his opportunity of expressing his life in the work. The spread of machinery has nearly made man a machine, quite as soulless as itself. Love of art and the power of design make every handicraftsman a man. People who do not work in art are influenced by the beautiful and simple things that are about them every day of their lives. It will not merely be a constant source of joy and delight, but they will find that art is not a mere luxury nor an object of trade, but one of the great elements in the creation of all nobility of life."

"Do you expect to stay long in this country?"

---

repeatedly in his poem *The Garden of Eros*, first published in *Poems*. For example, "Spirit of Beauty! tarry still a-while, | They are not dead, thine ancient votaries," (CW i, No. 75, lines 103–4).

1. Wilde began his studies at Magdalen in 1874.
2. Wilde had visited Italy in 1875 and 1877.
3. The name is given here as "Der Maurier".

"I never make plans. I hate plans. If it interests me so much as I expect and hope it will, I shall stay until the end of spring. I must go to Italy every year. I am eager to see your western country, the Indian Territory and Mexico. Our middle class wear frock coats and high hats. I want to see those people who live in open air, hunt, fish and shoot. I want to study their perfect freedom, and I wish to see your flowers. There are so many more flowers in this country than in ours. So many new forms and subjects for studies in color. This is the young, new country to which we look for the perfect development of our themes." Concerning the architecture of New York, Mr. Wilde said: "It is not worse than the cities in England, and not better. There is not much Greek art on Fifth avenue."

M. P. N.

"Oscar Wilde," *The Catholic Union and Times* (Buffalo, NY), 12 Jan. 1882, 4

Interviewed by Our New York Correspondent

Your reporter found Oscar Wilde at home on Sunday morning at his residence in 28th street.[1] Mr. Wilde is tall—probably over six feet—has a strong, intellectual face, and wears his brown hair long, and falling over his collar. His manner is frank and genial, his language well chosen but not pedantic or affected, and his enunciation clear and distinct. Partly in reply to enquiries, but chiefly of his own motion, he said in substance:—"The end proposed by themselves by the cultivators of the beautiful in Nature and Art is twofold; first, the pleasure afforded to the senses, and secondly, the moral and intellectual advance which beautiful associations and surroundings cannot fail to promote."

This, thought the reporter, is quite true. The man who derides religion in a noisy bar-room, thinks other thoughts within some old cathedral aisles, or beside the roaring waters of sublime Niagara.

"But an education in Art is necessary. Not until the divine harmonies of color and of sound are understood, can the eternal truths they represent be felt and acknowledged, and the higher life of thought and feeling dependent on those truths attained."

True again, said the reporter to himself. The untaught peasant will admire an utterly hideous and impossible daub, while he will be quite insensible to the elevating influences of the grandest works of art.

1. Sunday 8 January. Wilde's private address: see p. 53, note 1.

"Those habituated to beautiful surroundings will seek for the beautiful, of which the good and the true are component parts. Let us cultivate the beautiful, and the rest will follow."

"What was the subject of your Newdigate Prize Poem?"

"Ravenna. I had just returned, curiously enough, from that delightful spot, when the subject was announced. The gaining of the prize was not to me the chief pleasure—it consisted in having my name inscribed on a roll where so many great names had been written. Macaulay, Tennyson, Ruskin, Mallock, and others not less distinguished had gained the Newdigate prize, in their day, and it was no small pleasure to be numbered with these men."[1]

"What is Ruskin's position with regard to the Aesthetic movement?"

"Ruskin has largely influenced both art and the appreciation of art. Many of my theories are, I may say, Ruskin's theories developed. By the time I went to London, in 1878, I had clearly-defined ideas of what should be done. In every branch of art, the artists were too much isolated from the public and from each other, and my thought was to bring poets, painters, sculptors and musicians, all striving for the same goal by different paths, into closer communication, so that they should react upon one another to the advantage of their various forms of art. This isolation was injurious, also, to the sympathy which should exist between artists and the public—a sympathy which is a powerful aid to the appreciation of art."

"How has the aesthetic movement practically influenced society?"

"Its influence is to be seen in the increased beauty of home decoration and furnishing, in the improved taste in dress—women will not now disfigure themselves with contracted waists and deformed feet—and in the growing love for pure and classic forms in everyday things."

"There has not been time or leisure for much art-development here?"

"Oh, Whistler, one of our greatest Academicians, is an American—more American than the Americans themselves. I have not yet found anyone so intensely American as Whistler."

"Do you purpose visiting Buffalo?"[2]

"I cannot say. I wish more of your cities had such names as 'Buffalo.' Fancy calling a town 'Leadville'?[1] And the streets, too—in Paris it was a continual

1. Thomas Babington Macaulay (1880–1859) was an English historian and politician. He won the Chancellor's Gold Medal, Cambridge University's equivalent to Oxford's Newdigate, in 1819 for *Pompeii* and in 1821 for *Evening*. Alfred, Lord Tennyson (1809–1892) was an English poet who served as Poet Laureate of Great Britain and Ireland from 1850 until his death. His poem *Timbuctoo* won the Chancellor's Gold Medal in 1829. Ruskin won the Newdigate in 1839 for *Salsette and Elephanta*. William Hurrell Mallock (1849–1923) was an English novelist and sociologist. He won the Newdigate in 1871 for *The Isthmus of Suez*.

2. Wilde lectured on *The English Renaissance* at Buffalo's Academy of Music on 8 February.

pleasure to find such streets as the 'Rue Balzac' and the 'Boulevard Malesherbes,'[2] but this numerical arrangement destroys the individuality of the streets. Surely there are sufficient great and glorious American names wherewith all the streets in the city might be named, recalling mighty men and noble deeds."

After some further conversation, your reporter departed, very favorably impressed both by Mr. Wilde personally, and by the slight insight into his peculiar views which a short interview permitted.

Oscar Wilde's published poems mark him as a man of ability and originality. His popularity at Oxford, which is really the Modern Athens, proves him to be no shallow pretender, and his manner, language, and evident habit of thought, proclaim him essentially a gentleman. There is no doubt that the justice of his cause, and the ability with which it will be advocated, will ensure him a patient and courteous hearing at first, and an enthusiastic following afterwards. His first lecture will be delivered at Chickering Hall on Monday evening, and your reporter hopes to give you an account of the proceedings in your next issue.[3]

"Like Cold Gravy," *The Daily Inter Ocean* (Chicago, IL), 14 Jan. 1882, 13

That Is the Shade of Velvet that Oscar Wilde Seems the Most to Favor.

"Cress" Captures Him and Tells The Inter Ocean How He Talks and Acts and Looks.

All the Mrs. Leo Hunters Worshiping at His Big Feet[4]—The Other Professional Beauties.

---

1. Leadville was founded in 1877 by silver mine owners and was soon the second most populous city in Colorado. Wilde lectured on *The Decorative Arts* at the city's Tabor Opera House on 13 April.

2. Honoré de Balzac (1799–1850) was a French novelist and playwright. Wilde was travelling with the works of Balzac and lamented that they took up so much room in his trunks (CL, 175). He described Balzac as France's "one great genius" (*The Woman's World*, Jan. 1888; CW vii, No. 91. line 245), and his *Comédie Humaine* as "the greatest monument that literature has produced in our century" (*The Pall Mall Gazette*, 13 Sep. 1886; CW vi, No. 37, line 7). Boulevard Malesherbes was named for Guillaume-Chrétien de Lamoignon de Malesherbes (1721–1794), a politician and royalist who was guillotined during the French Revolution.

3. A positive report of Wilde's first lecture was printed in the next issue: "Oscar Wilde's Lecture," *The Catholic Union and Times* (Buffalo, NY), 19 Jan. 1882, 5.

4. Mrs Leo Hunter is a character in Dickens's *The Pickwick Papers*, whose name suggests her desire to lionise famous and interesting people. In this context, it is a reference to Mrs John Bigelow, Mrs Paran Stevens, and other society women who were hosting Wilde at various receptions and dinners.

Special Correspondence of The Inter Ocean.

NEW YORK, Jan. 11.—The other day, in walking down Broadway, my attention was attracted to a gentleman with a crowd of small boys at his heels, and a number of well-dressed women, who seemed to be exerting themselves to keep up with his long strides in order to gain another glimpse of his face. In spite of the uncomplimentary remarks of the street gamins, and the eager glances of his fair pursuers, the gentleman pursued his way, his eyes fixed upon the unfathomable blue of the sky, his nose, as Bulwer would put it, "well up in the air," and his very large feet avoiding, as if by instinct, the obstacles in the pavement.[1]

Over six feet in height and proportionately broad in figure, he looked almost immense in a heavy coat that hung down to his heels, being unbuttoned flapped loosely in the breeze, and was trimmed with huge lapels, cuffs, and pockets of undressed sealskin. Long, loose, brown locks flowing over his shoulders and curled at the ends, framed a large and somewhat peculiar face, which suggested an ugly likeness of Tilton in his younger days, and, notwithstanding his uncommon size, there could be detected that same touch of the effeminate.

SENSITIVENESS AND SENSUOUSNESS

rather than strength were conveyed in his expression, and the hair combed well over the temples left only a little triangle of forehead to be seen, increasing by contrast the apparent heaviness of the jaw and mouth.

Of course you have guessed I am talking of Oscar Wilde, for it would be quite as unfashionable to begin a letter as it would a conversation without some reference to the apostle of the aesthetes. The day was excessively chilly, but that did not prevent the poet from wearing a low-necked collar, which exposed a long V of his muscular throat, but had none of the charms of Byron's unlaundried linen, being stiffly starched, sharply turned down, and fastening under a knot of violet plush.

This was my first view of the youth who calmly announces himself as the founder and father of art in America, but never did a self-proposed parent and originator meet with

A MORE VARIED RECEPTION.

The men, on general principles, detest him, the women suffocate him with the sweet incense of adoration, and the great unwashed roar at him. Eleven receptions and dinners have been given him since his arrival, to a number of which your correspondent was bidden, and it pays to go if for nothing more than to observe the precious price paid for notoriety.

1. Edward Bulwer-Lytton (1803–1873) was an English politician, poet, playwright, and novelist.

On presentation one of three things is sure to be said to him by each guest. It is, "Oh, Mr. Wilde, how good of you to come among us barbarians in art!" or words to that effect, or, apologetically, "I fear you find us very crude; but we are so dreadfully young, you know."[1] Perhaps a sweet young thing begs the poet to "have patience with us; we are intensely anxious to learn." Occasionally an unlettered savage, totally

DEVOID OF ARTISTIC IDEAS,

asks the Irish bard if he was seasick coming over, or how he likes America.

Clad "in a cobwebby gray velvet, with a tender bloom like cold gravy,"[2] or in a rich and mystic brown that suggests sweet simmering chocolate, for these are Mr. Wilde's favorite hues, he appears sufficiently different from other men to attract all eyes, and, therefore, the object of his toilet is attained.

The other evening, at Mrs. A. A. Hayes',[3] he appeared in dove color, made like all his dress costumes, with tight knee-breeches, terminating in silk stockings, that displayed limbs long and lithe, but which a ballet-dancer's ideas of beauty would find deficient to the extent of two or three bales of cotton padding. I asked him at Mrs. Mack's if he had adopted his present mode of dressing merely to gratify his own individual taste or with the hope that his example would make it fashionable.[4]

"Both," he replied modestly, in his even monotone. "To do away with the stiff conventionalities of a dress so unbecoming and displeasing to the eye would be a long way toward the development of art in this country.

CLARET COLOR, I PREDICT,

will be most favored by men, being generally becoming and picturesque (think of this fiery headed and red-whiskered men)[5] and next, shades of fawn gray and brown. In England I rarely ever wear black."

✂ *A report of Wilde's lecture in New York and his other social engagements.*

"CRESS."

1. Lord Illingworth in *A Woman of No Importance*: "The youth of America is their oldest tradition. It has been going on now for three hundred years. To hear them talk one would imagine they were in their first childhood. As far as civilisation goes they are in their second." (*Woman*, 20.) It may also be worth noting that in *The Picture of Dorian Gray* Lord Henry Wotton tells Dorian that "youth is the one thing worth having." (CW iii, 24.23–4.)

2. In *Patience*, the aesthetic Lady Jane dislikes the soldiers' red and yellow uniforms ("Primary colours!") and suggests they wear "a cobwebby grey velvet, with a tender bloom like cold gravy".

3. 5 January.

4. Wilde attended a reception at the home of Mrs John Mack, a wealthy socialite, immediately after his debut lecture on 9 January (Friedman, 76–7).

5. Presumably this parenthetical remark is the interviewer's.

[Augustus R. Cazauran], "Is it Aesthetic Taffy?" *The New York Herald* (New York, NY), 13 Jan. 1882, 10[1]

OSCAR WILDE'S ESTIMATE OF CLARA MORRIS—THE AESTHETE APPROVES OF AMERICAN STAGE SETTING.

Mr. Oscar Wilde visited the Union Square Theatre yesterday afternoon to witness Miss Clara Morris' performance as Mercy Merrick in "The New Magdalen."[2] The audience, made up chiefly of ladies, was rustling in when he arrived, and his name having been uttered by some of the ladies who attended his lecture at Chickering Hall, the tall aesthete became in a moment the centre toward which every glance was directed. He stood the shock of these multiplied batteries bravely, and the ushers having finally decided that his coupon entitled him to the lower left box he followed them calmly down the side aisle to it, seemingly unconscious that there were a couple of hundred opera glasses levelled at him.

Once in his box, *il s'effaça*, as the French say, till the middle of the first act, when he leaned forward, to better follow the acting. He kept that attitude till the final fall of the curtain on the last act, except when the *entre-acte* curtain was down, when he would peer at the house full of ladies through the slits of the curtains that drape the box. The play over, he was led on the stage and expressed his desire to see Miss Morris. As he waited for her Mr. Wilde delivered the following opinions:—

1. Reprinted as "Aesthetic Taffy," *The Daily American* (Nashville, TN), 16 Jan. 1882, 2; and "Wilde on Clara Morris," *The Topeka Daily Capital* (Topeka, KS), 17 Jan. 1882, 5. Excerpted in "Musical and Dramatic Notes," *The Chicago Daily Tribune* (Chicago, IL), 17 Jan. 1882, 7. Quoted in Ellmann, 156/163; and Sturgis, 213/205. "Taffy" was slang for flattery. The article was attributed by *The New York Mirror* (28 Jan. 1882, 3) to Augustus R. Cazauran (1820–1889), the Union Square Theatre's resident script doctor: "Her [Morris's] success being so genuinely great, we should think that M. Cazauran could safely be prohibited from the manufacture of such press notices as that recently foisted upon Oscar Wilde in regard to the acting and pronunciation of Miss Morris. Had Manager [Albert Marshman] Palmer [(1838–1905), proprietor of the Union Square Theatre] been aware that this absurd report was due to the misplaced ingenuity of M. Cazauran he would not have allowed it to be published. Neither the Union Square Theatre nor Miss Clara Morris needs any false bolstering." The *Spirit of the Times* (New York, NY), 25 Feb. 1882, 101, described it as "a bogus, advertising interview, written as a guy [i.e. a jest]." Nevertheless, Wilde's comments have the ring of truth.

2. Clara Morris (1849–1925) was a Toronto-born American actress. She and Wilde met at a reception at the home of American author and journalist Jane Cunningham "Jennie June" Croly (1829–1901) on 8 January 1882. *The New Magdalen* by Wilkie Collins premiered in London in 1873; Morris's revival opened on 5 January 1882. An undated letter from Wilde to Mrs [Augustus M.] Hayes, not included in CL, may refer to the performance on 12 January:

> Will you give me the pleasure of coming to my box tomorrow afternoon to see Clara Morris—if your husband is not engaged I will hope to see him too. (Christie's, 28 May 1999, sale 8404, lot 26.)

"Miss Morris is the greatest actress I ever saw, if it be fair to form an opinion of her from her rendition of this one *rôle*, Mercy Merrick. We have no such powerfully intense actress in England. She is a great artist, in my sense of the word, because all she does, all she says, in the manner of the doing and of the saying constantly evokes the imagination to supplement it. That is what I mean by art. She would be a wonderful success in London.[1] I don't think, however, that a play as worn as "The New Magdalen" is there would be the proper work in which to present her. She is a veritable genius. We have no one like her. From what I have heard of it her Miss Multon would be a sure sensation in England.[2] By the by, is this scenery of the parlors of Lady Janet Ray exceptional with you here?" Being told "not at all," he replied, "I was astonished at its fitness and beauty, the harmony of color, the elegance of the furniture—really, our London stage is not up to this sort of thing." When asked what he thought of the cast of the play as a whole he replied:—"Really, you know, the leading part is so strong, and Miss Morris played it so greatly that I saw nobody else, yet they must have been good or the contrast would have offended me, don't you know. I really hope Miss Morris will visit us in London. I was very pleasantly disappointed in one respect. I had been told Miss Morris's magnificent acting was somewhat marred by a provincial or Western pronunciation. This defect, if it exists, may be noticeable to an American ear, to me her voice and method of reading are perfectly delightful, and would be to our people at home I am sure. I really think a company like this, and such stage setting, should be seen in London." Being told Miss Morris was ready to receive him, Mr. Wilde bowed, shook his long locks and disappeared.

1. Morris had visited the United Kingdom in 1872, 1874, and 1875, but only to holiday and research her roles. She received offers for London engagements but never took them up. (Grossman, B. W. (2009). *A Spectacle of Suffering: Clara Morris on the American Stage*. Southern Illinois University. 12, 125–6, 241, 244, 286.)

2. *Miss Multon* was Cazauran's adaptation of a French play by Eugène Nus (1816–1894) and Adolphe Belot (1829–1890). The original had failed in Paris twice, but the version adapted for Morris, which was staged in 1876 at the Union Square Theatre, was a hit. Wilde saw the revival at New York's Grand Opera House on 11 September 1882 and would later tell his lecture audiences in the United Kingdom that Morris's "Miss Multon is a performance which can only be ranked with the achievements of Mme. Sarah Bernhardt." ("Amusements," *The New York Herald* (New York, NY), 12 Sep. 1882, 10; "London Society," *The Sunday Herald* (Boston, MA), 5 Aug. 1883, 16.)

"Aesthete Wilde on Greek Plays," *The Evening Telegram* (New York, NY), 13 Jan. 1882, 4th ed., 1[1]

His Views as to the Production of "Oedipus Tyrannus."

Mr. Oscar Wilde, the poet and apostle of aestheticism, breakfasted this morning by appointment with Mr. R. D'Oyly Carte at the Hoffman House.[2] To a representative of the TELEGRAM, who met him shortly after the repast and requested an expression of his views in regard to the proposed performance, in this city in a few weeks, of the "Oedipus Tyrannus" of Sophocles,[3] he said—

"The first modern attempt to perform a Greek play was the introduction on the stage, a year and a half ago, at my suggestion, at Oxford, of the 'Agamemnon of Aeschylus.'[4] I did not take part in it myself, as I had then left Oxford, but it was performed by my undergraduate friends. The elocution of the young men in the delivery of this play was characterized by great sweetness and correct modulation of the voice, and one of the actors, who took the part of Clytemnestra, was so successful that he has since decided to adopt the profession of an actor.[5] The distribution of the parts, the selection of the dresses, and the arrangement of the scenery for this play were mine.[6] I believe this is the first instance of a Greek play

1. Reprinted, with an abbreviated first paragraph and omitting the final paragraph, as "Wilde on Greek Drama," *Philadelphia Inquirer* (Philadelphia, PA), 20 Jan. 1882, 8 (which is H & S, b18). Referenced in CW vi, 286, note 7. This article did not appear in earlier editions of *The Evening Telegram*. The 4th edition was issued at 17:00.

2. The Hoffman House was a luxurious hotel in New York's Madison Square. D'Oyly Carte had arrived in New York on 11 January ("D'Oyly Carte and His Plans," *New York Tribune* (New York, NY), 12 Jan. 1882, 8, p. 755).

3. The play was performed at New York's Booth's Theatre on 30 January. Wilde would see it on the 28th, at the end of a week's run at Boston's Globe Theatre. Whether his opinion of it changed once he had seen it is unknown.

4. The play was staged at Balliol College in June 1880 and, later in the year, transferred to London for three performances. Wilde was very familiar with the play: in his final year at Portora School he was examined on it and received a mark 25 percentage points above his nearest rival (Sturgis, 35/41, 164/160).

5. Francis Robert "Frank" Benson (1858–1939), who played Clytemnestra, did indeed embark upon a career as an actor. He founded his own company in 1883, managed the Stratford-Upon-Avon Shakespearean Festival for 30 years, and was knighted in 1916.

6. Wilde is exaggerating his involvement. Benson was the stage manager and would later claim that he, along with Balliol man William Napier Bruce (who played Agamemnon), "practically organized and ran the whole thing". They cast the play within a week, mostly from the ranks of the university sports clubs, and Benson rallied cast and crew "with a somewhat despotic stage-management". Volunteers sewed the costumes from fabric that Benson dyed in his own bathtub. Benson's brother drew up the plans for the scenery. ("The players of the 'Agamemnon'," *The Graphic* (London, UK), 13 Nov. 1880, 467; Benson, F. (1930). *My Memoirs*. Ernest Benn Limited. 117–25.)

being performed in England, although Latin plays are acted at Westminster School every Christmas.

"I regret much to learn that the 'Oedipus,' when performed here, is to have only one actor who will speak the lines in Greek, while the other actors will make use of English.[1] The effect of this will be to destroy the unity of the performance, and it will be rendered only curious, whereas it should be beautiful. The play is the best acting play of the Greek literature, and is mentioned by Aristotle as an absolute type of perfection in the dramatic art. I saw it performed in the Comedie Française in Paris last summer.[2] The manager presented us with a good French translation of the Oedipus—so good that it was really worth listening to—and it struck me that not only in its plot, but in the construction, dramatic conception and effect, the Oedipus gives one an excellent motive for a modern play."

After these remarks Mr. Wilde took his departure, buttoning closely about him his fur-lined ulster and placing upon his head a large sealskin cap. Altogether, the apostle of aestheticism today looked more like a Russian than a Britisher.

"A Talk with Wilde," *Philadelphia Press* (Philadelphia, PA), 17 Jan. 1882, 2[3]

THE APOSTLE OF THE AESTHETES ENUNCIATES HIS VIEWS.

While on His First Railway Ride in America the Poet of the Utter Talks Entertainingly of His Mission in America.

As a Pennsylvania ferry-boat swung into her slip at Jersey City at a few minutes before one o'clock yesterday afternoon, the crowd scattered about the

1. George Riddle, an instructor in elocution at Harvard, played the title role in Greek. The rest of the cast, including Lewis Morrison who would later play the Czarevich in the ill-fated 1883 production of *Vera; or, The Nihilists*, spoke English. It is not known how Wilde heard of the production, but it seems likely that he would have read the interview with Riddle in "In Greek and English," *The New York World, Semi-Weekly Edition* (New York, NY), 3 Jan. 1882, 5, which appeared in the same issue as his own interview for that paper. Riddle thought that the dual language performance would "prevent the audience being four or five pages ahead of the actors."

2. This adaptation of Sophocles's play by Jules Lacroix (1809–1887) starred the one-time lover of Sarah Bernhardt, Jean Mounet-Sully (1841–1916).

3. H & S, b14. Printed simultaneously as "Wilde on the Cars," *The Boston Herald* (Boston, MA), 17 Jan. 1882, 4, which was reprinted as "Wilde on the Cars," *Cincinnati Daily Gazette* (Cincinnati, OH), 7 Feb. 1882, 3. Reprinted in Mikhail, 42–6; and H & S, 25–31. Excerpted with slight variations in "The Aesthete on His Travels," *Truth* (London, UK), 2 Feb. 1882, 175–7, p. 707. Reprinted, in slightly abbreviated form, in OWDA, 62–6. Quoted in OWDA, 41; Hyde, 52–3, 56–7; and Ellmann, 159–60/167. Referenced in Sturgis, 214/206, 214/208. The article is included in an album held at the Robert Ross Memorial Collection at University College Oxford, which includes many articles about Oscar and Lady Wilde, c. 1870–1893 (Ross b.6, 69).

dock exclaimed in subdued tones: "There he is; see him, that's Oscar Wilde." The tall figure of the apostle of Aestheticism, clad in his olive-green overcoat with its otter trimmings, and with his large face brightened by a smile and framed in long brown locks, blown about by the wind, was a conspicuous figure, as he stood in the very front of the crowd of passengers pressing against the gunwales of the boat. He had evidently been enjoying a breezy trip across the tawny Hudson, for his eyes sparkled and his face was flushed with pleasure as, with a long stride which kept him far in advance even of the eager rush with which a New York crowd escapes from a ferry, and which left his valet struggling hopelessly in the rear with a burden of baggage, he entered the Pennsylvania station, and passed to the waiting Philadelphia express. His sole companions were W. F. Morse, business manager for D'Oyly Carte, and a PRESS reporter. The party took seats in the smoking compartment of the Pullman car "Jupiter," and shrinking from curious eyes into a corner, Mr. Wilde alternately read "Fors Clavigera" and "The Poetry of Architecture," until the train had fairly started.[1] Then, as he saw through the window the dismal marshes which skirt Jersey City, his eye became melancholy and he contemplatively puffed a cigarette. As the train sped on its way through New Jersey, he scanned the flitting landscape closely, sometimes smiling like a child at a glistening stream or a stretch of yet green meadow, and again seeming to find the sorrow of old age in the frequent expanses of brown country and dripping black undergrowth, made more dreary by the overcast sky. The truth is, the poet had not had his breakfast; and thus unfortified against the horrors of a New Jersey landscape on a rainy day, it was no wonder that he finally relapsed into a state of hopeless dejection. Incredible as it may seem, the most non-aesthetic object on earth, a way-station sandwich, restored his spirits enough for him to enter into an animated conversation with the PRESS reporter.

"I am very tired," he said. "I have been so kindly received in New York, and so cordially welcomed by so many lovely people, that of course I wanted to see many of them before I went away. Was up late last night dining at Mrs. Paran Stevens' and afterward going to reception at Mr. S. L. M. Barlow's, and I was so late today that I had no time to breakfast.[2] Then I have been kept so busy an-

1. *Fors Clavigera: Letters to the Workmen and Labourers of Great Britain* (1871–1884) and *The Poetry of Architecture* (serialised in *The Architectural Magazine* 1837–1838) are works by Ruskin. Wilde's lecture on *The English Renaissance* borrowed heavily from works by Ruskin, including *The Two Paths* (1859) and *The Stones of Venice* (1851–1853), from *Hopes and Fears for* Art (1882) by William Morris (1834–1896), and *Studies in the History of the Renaissance* (1873) by Walter Pater.

2. Marietta Stevens née Reed (1827–1895) was a wealthy and influential socialite. Wilde also attended an evening party at her Fifth Avenue apartment on 8 January 1882. Samuel Latham Mitchill Barlow I (1826–1889) was a lawyer, art collector, and Democratic Party power broker.

swering letters. Why, it is strange how people seem to think I have nothing to do but answer letters."

HIS FIRST RAILWAY RIDE.

"This is your first railway ride in America, is it not?"

"Yes, this is the first time I have ever been in an American railway car. We go so swift—much faster than in England. There are but a few fast trains there—the Edinburgh and Liverpool trains. And then there isn't any such comfort as this. There are but two or three cars like this," indicating the sumptuous Pullman with a sweep of the arm, "in the country. I hate to fly through a country at this rate. The only true way, you know, to see a country is to ride on horseback.[1] I long to ride through New Mexico and Colorado and California. There are such beautiful flowers there, such quantities of lilies and, I am told, whole fields of sunflowers. Your climate is so much finer than that of England, so bright, so sunny, that your flowers are luxuriant," said Mr. Wilde, with a polite disregard of the clouds, and with a delightful ignorance of how hothouses are robbed of their treasures to let him breathe an atmosphere of fragrance.

"You have reason to be pleased with your reception in the United States?"

"O, yes, indeed. Do you know, the night before I landed I was wondering how it would be—thinking of the cloud of misrepresentation that must have preceded me, and wondering whether the people would wait to know me for what I am. But a poet must be indifferent to blame, as he must be to praise. He deserves neither till long after he is dead. Not till then can he be judged. While one is living, one can only work for what is to be. Do you know,"—his face lighting up with a sudden smile while his eyes roamed reflectively,—"our people in England took the greatest interest in my coming to America—No,"—in reply to a suggestion by the reporter,—"no, they did not regard it at all as an aesthetic mission to a barbarous clime; but our artists wish very much to have their ideas planted and growing in America."

"What are your plans for the development of aestheticism in America?"

"It is impossible to define them yet. In this, my first lecture, which I am now delivering, I endeavor to explain the *spirit* of our art theories. As for the particular form it may take I must wait to tell that in a second lecture after I have become acquainted with the country and have come to know something of its artistic materials and possibilities, and have learned to appreciate its national spirit. I must know something of your woods for ceilings, for example, and numberless things of that kind. Art must differ with place and people. What would be quite right in England might be quite wrong here. It is only the general principles that I can teach now; their definite application must come later."

1. Wilde rode through Greece on horseback in 1877.

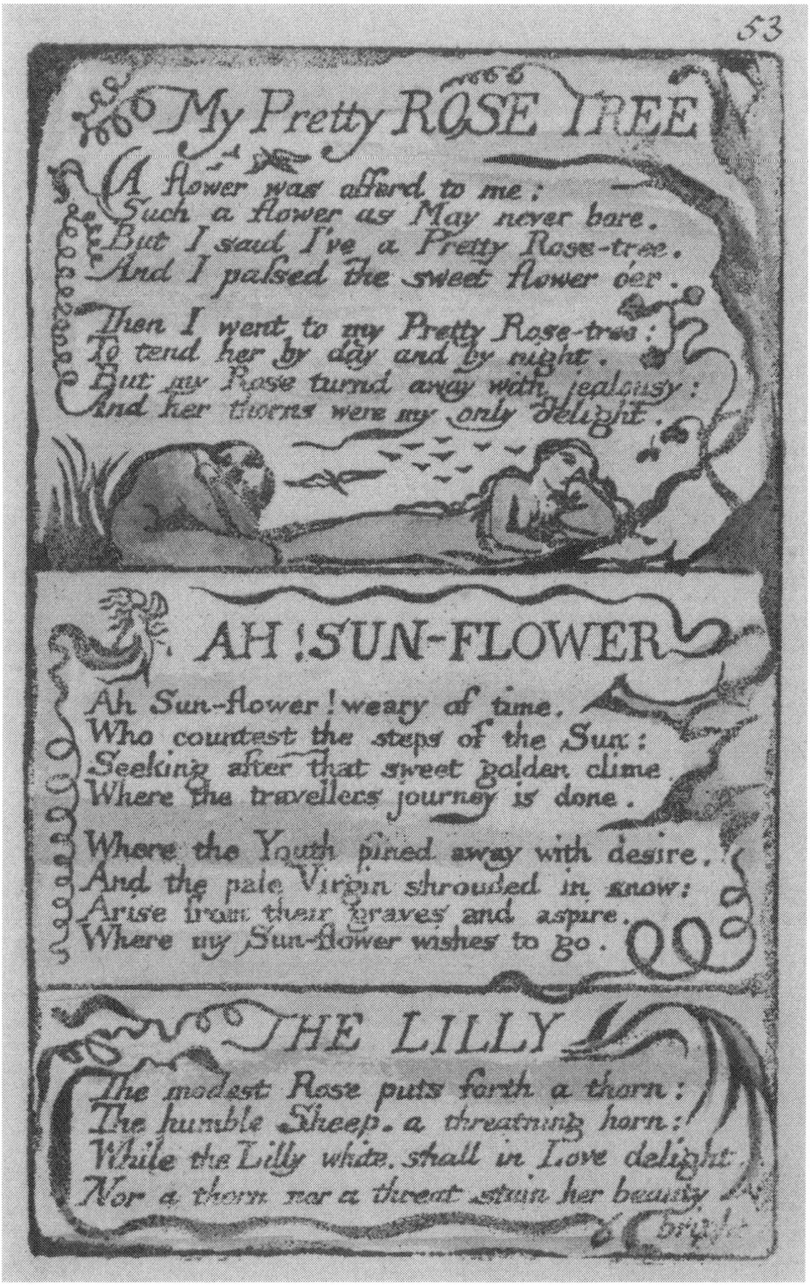

Figure 2. Songs of Innocence and of Experience, *Plate 53, by William Blake. "It is a page altogether exquisite." See p. 74, note 2.*

Here the poet gazed thoughtfully out of the window, and the reporter suggested that his impressions of American scenery must be as yet very limited. "Yes," was the reply, "but I enjoy very much what I have seen. But one cannot expect color in winter, when everything is so drear and brown. How dreadful those marshes are this side of New York. What a pity! and how unnecessary. They might plant them with something, so many beautiful things will grow in a marsh. Why, they might have great fields of callas growing there! Do you understand my line for lilies, and roses, and sunflowers? No? O, don't you know, there is no flower so purely decorative as the sunflower. In the house, it is perhaps too large and glaring. But how lovely a line of them are in a garden, against a wall, or massed in groups! Its form is perfect. See how it lends itself to design, how suggestive it is. So many beautiful, very beautiful wall papers have been designed from the sunflower. It is purely decorative," and the sunflower worshipper became lost in reverie.[1] Then, opening his eyes wide, his whole face radiant, he resumed: "And the lily. There's no flower I love so much as the lily. That, too, is perfect in form, and purely decorative. How graceful, how pure, how altogether lovely its shape, its tender poise upon the stem. And you have such beautiful lilies in America. I've seen a new one that we do not have in England, that star-shaped lily. I always loved lilies. At Oxford I kept my room filled with them, and I had a garden of them, where I used to work very often. As for roses, they are so full of color, so rich, so passionate. They suggest the feeling where the others suggest the form. They richly fill what the others outline. Why do not people grow them everywhere? I was pleased with the Raritan back there, with its brown current and brown banks; but still, those banks ought not to be bare and bleak—cover them with hardy lilies. Did you ever see those wonderfully beautiful books William Blake published so magnificently illuminated? In one of those books, enclosed in a charmingly appropriate border, are three lively [*sic*] poems—one on the Sunflower, one on the Lily, and one on the Rose. It is a page altogether exquisite."[2]

"Do you hope to teach the 'common people,' even the abjectly poor, to find these beauties, and by them to elevate their lives?"

1. Aaron Eames notes that in Wilde's *Poems* the references to lilies far outnumber those to sunflowers, and that in taking up the sunflower Wilde was playing to an audience familiar with dramatic works such as *The Colonel* (Eames, A. (2020). The herald of the helianthus: Oscar Wilde and sunflower symbolism. *The Wildean, 57*, 56–75).

2. The poems are *My Pretty Rose Tree, Ah! Sun-Flower*, and *The Lilly*. They were published as part of Blake's illuminated collections *Songs of Experience* (1789) and *Songs of Innocence and of Experience* (1794). There are multiple versions of the page on which the poems appear.

"The two classes we must directly work upon are the handicraftsmen and the artists. As for the class between, the idle people, rich or poor, it is useless to go to them, and tell them 'you must do this, and you ought to do that.' There must be a great mass of handicraft produced, before you can hope to affect the masses. And the handicraftsmen must be directed by the artists, and the artists must be inspired with true designs. It is only through those classes we can work."

"Do you not hope to bring back picturesque dressing, as one of the forms in which the spirit of your art will work itself out?"

"All that must take time. We have to move very carefully, you know. Prejudice cannot be carried by storm. And, by the way, one of the most delightful things I had in America is meeting a people without prejudice—everywhere open to the truth. We have nothing like it in England. But to return—we must get the women to dress beautifully first; the men will follow. Velvet is such a beautiful material,—why do not men wear it? Gray, or brown, or black velvet is always beautiful."

"You have been quoted as saying that the women's dresses in 'Patience' are not exaggerated."[1]

"Oh, the embroidery and paintings on the dresses are made for stage effect, and are larger than are worn in what is called good society. But in design they are correct. 'Patience,' by the way, has done our cause no harm. Ridicule may be a serious weapon, but there should be that in a true poet or a genuine cause which is indestructible; and there is indestructibility in our cause. Oh, no; people understand that 'Patience' is merely a burlesque. I enjoyed it very much. The music is delightful, and that is certainly on our side, even if the words are not."

"Speaking of dresses—how do you like the beauty of their American wearers?"

"I am charmed with American beauty. They possess a certain delicacy of outline surpassing English women. And there is a charm about this curve here," said Wilde, drawing his finger from cheek to chin, "that is peculiarly fascinating. But the color of English women is richer and warmer, I think. I saw Clara Morris on the stage in New York one evening,[2] and I was as delighted with her as with Sara Bernhardt, who had told me very much about her charm; and I have met many surpassingly beautiful young ladies since my arrival. Mrs. Langtry, I may tell you, is quite with me in all this movement.[3] She has an artistic house, de-

1. See "The Theories of a Poet," *New York Tribune* (New York, NY), 8 Jan. 1882, 7, p. 55; "The Science of the Beautiful," *The New York World, Semi-Weekly Edition* (New York, NY), 10 Jan. 1882, 7, p. 59; "The Art of Dining," *The Cincinnati Commercial* (Cincinnati, OH), 14 Jan. 1882, 4, 61.

2. See [Augustus R. Cazauran], "Is it Aesthetic Taffy?" *The New York Herald* (New York, NY), 13 Jan. 1882, 10, pp. 67–8.

3. Emilie Charlotte "Lillie" Langtry née Le Breton (1853–1929) was a British socialite, "professional beauty", and a friend of Wilde.

serves all her reputation for beauty, and sympathizes thoroughly with the aesthetic school."

MR. WILDE'S POLITICS.

"What are your politics, Liberal or Conservative, Mr. Wilde?"

"O, do you know, those matters are of no interest to me. I know only two terms—civilization and barbarism: and I am on the side of civilization. It is very strange, that in the House of Commons you never hear the word 'civilization.' They spend night after night squabbling over petty things, when they ought to be working against barbarism. Then, in our country there is seldom a piece of legislation that does not benefit one class more than another; and that perhaps makes the wretched party spirit more bitter. But Gladstone is the greatest Prime Minister England ever had.[1] A short time before I came to America, he said to me that from the United States would come at once the greatest danger and the greatest good to civilization. The greatest danger in the vast accumulation of capital, and the greatest good in the perfect simplicity of American politics, and in the fact that the only reason for the passage of a great law over here is that it is for the good of the whole people. The personal control of capital, with the power it gives over labor and life, has only appeared in modern American life. We have as yet nothing like it in England. We call a man rich over there when he owns a share of Scotland, or a county or so. But he doesn't have such a control of ready money as does an American capitalist. He is often pressed even for a matter of fifty or sixty thousand pounds," said Mr. Wilde, carelessly.

"What poet do you most admire in American literature?"

"I think that Walt Whitman and Emerson have given the world more than anyone else.[2] I do so hope to meet Mr. Whitman. Perhaps he is not widely read in England, but England never appreciates a poet until he is dead," said Mr. Wilde with a trace of bitterness. "I admire him intensely—Dante Rossetti, Swinburne,

1. William Ewart Gladstone (1809–1898) was a Liberal politician who served as Prime Minister of the United Kingdom for 12 years, spread between four terms, beginning in 1868 and ending in 1894. Wilde revered him as "the Greek ideal of the statesman" and sent to him a *Sonnet on the Massacre of the Christians in Bulgaria* (CW i, No. 33; Gladstone had written pamphlets on the subject) as well as copies of *Poems* and *The Happy Prince and Other Tales* (CL, 46–7, 113, 350).

2. Walt Whitman (1819–1892) was an American poet, a pioneer of free verse and author of the frequently revised *Leaves of Grass*. Wilde met him on 18 January 1882 (see "Wilde and Whitman," *The Philadelphia Press* (Philadelphia, PA), 19 Jan. 1882, 8, pp. 757–9). Wilde reviewed Whitman's "fascinating" *November Boughs* for *The Pall Mall Gazette* (25 Jan. 1889; CW vii, No. 114). Wilde told his tour manager that he wished to meet American poet and essayist Ralph Waldo Emerson (1803–1882); Emerson died shortly after Wilde's arrival in America and before any meeting could be arranged. In prison Wilde requested his *Essays* (Wright, 320). Josephine Guy (CW iv, 363) notes that Wilde alludes to Emerson's writings in *The Soul of Man Under Socialism* and *De Profundis*.

William Morris and I often discuss him.[1] There is something so Greek and sane about his poetry; it is so universal, so comprehensive. It has all the pantheism of Goethe and Schiller.[2] Poets, you know, are always ahead of science; all the great discoveries of science have been stated before in poetry. So far as science comes in contact with our school, we love its practical side; but we think it absurd to seek to make the material include the spiritual, to make the body mean the soul, to say that one emotion is only a secretion of sugar, and another nothing but a contraction of the spine. Why does not science, instead of troubling itself about sunspots, which nobody ever saw, or, if they did, ought not to speak about? Why does not science busy itself with drainage and sanitary engineering? Why does it not clean the streets and free the rivers from pollution? Why, in England there is scarcely a river which at some point is not polluted; and the flowers are all withering on the banks!" And Mr. Wilde again lapsed into melancholy.

ABOUT NOVEL WRITERS

"Do you think Mallock's 'Romance of the Nineteenth Century' a correct picture of a section of English society?"[3]

"No novel can include England," was the quick reply. "I enjoyed reading that book, though it has its many faults. But I have repeatedly upheld it against attack, because it is the first attempt by an English novel-writer to grapple with English society as it actually is. I mean by that, it is the first attempt to picture lives that are themselves interesting. George Eliot has made perfect pictures of lives in the provinces, and so have others; but Dickens and Thackeray are our only novel-writers who have touched London life realistically.[4] We have nobody in English

1. Dante Gabriel Rossetti (1828–1882) was an English painter and poet. William Morris (1834–1896) was a designer and poet. Wilde is exaggerating his intimacy with the men whose names he drops here: Swinburne, who disliked Wilde and his poetry, he only met once; Rossetti snubbed him; Morris came to enjoy Wilde's company, perhaps after a recommendation from his friend, Burne-Jones, with whom Wilde socialised regularly (Sturgis, 179–81/173–5).

2. Friedrich Schiller (1759–1805) was a German writer. Both he and Goethe were proponents of the Sturm und Drang movement, a precursor to the Romantic movement that Wilde identified as the root of the English renaissance.

3. *Romance of the Nineteenth Century* is an 1881 novel by W. H. Mallock. An earlier work by the same author, *The New Republic*, had included a thinly veiled cipher of Walter Pater, depicting him as an effete lover of young men.

4. George Eliot (1819–1880), William Makepeace Thackeray (1811–1863), and Charles Dickens (1812–1870) were English novelists, known for their realism and social criticism. Wilde described Eliot's style as "far too cumbrous" (*The Woman's World*, Jan. 1889; CW vii, No. 112, line 9) and, in *The Decay of Lying*, he had Vivian quote Ruskin's description of Eliot's characters as "being like the sweepings of a Pentonville omnibus" (CW iv, 79.11). Wilde thought that "Thackeray's delightful superficial philosophy, superb narrative power, and clever social satire have found no echoes", but that "Dickens has only influenced journalism" (*The Woman's World*, Jan. 1888; CW vii, No. 91, lines 250–2).

literature, for example, like Balzac, who has lived through so many changes of government and upheavals of society, and who mirrors all so exactly. A novel-writer must himself first live what he portrays."

At this point, the train reached Trenton, where Robert E. Winner joined the party, and the conversation became general. During the approach to Philadelphia, Mr. Wilde showed an eager interest in the many novel things he saw. He listened with wide-open eyes to an explanation of a long train of oil cars, but did not say whether he found any beauty in them. A glimpse of Fairmount Park brought back his happy smile, and he was greatly pleased with the ride over the elevated tracks and with the Broad street station. As his conspicuous figure walked through the waiting room, many a whispered comment flew about; but the aesthete dived into a cab, and was whirled quickly away to his quarters at the Aldine Hotel.

"The Aesthetic Bard," *The Philadelphia Inquirer* (Philadelphia, PA), 17 Jan. 1882, 2[1]

HOW HE LOOKS AND WHAT HE SAYS

A Lion That Will Roar You Gently—"Bunthorne" in Private and in Society—The New Gospel of the Aesthetes

Mr. Oscar Wilde, the English aesthetic poet, arrived at the Aldine Hotel yesterday afternoon, about four o'clock, and proceeded at once to his rooms, where he passed the afternoon in seclusion. He had been very busy during the morning in New York, and, with that and his journey to this city, and the trying two hours of lionization before him in the evening, felt the need of rest.

Toward six o'clock, however, he consented to receive a representative of THE INQUIRER, to whom he extended a welcome with the graceful courtesy which is always characteristic of good breeding. Whatever may be said of Mr. Wilde's costume and manner in society, in the privacy of his own apartment he was distressingly like any other gentleman.

The only peculiarity in his appearance was his very long brown hair, fine and glossy as silk, parted in the middle, and hanging below his collar and round a face essentially English—or Irish—but thoroughly refined, and endowed with a liberal share of the beauty of expression. His head has something of the Gothic arched poetical outline; the forehead is rather low, but broad and fair, though seemingly narrowed by the flowing locks; the nose is aquiline, the eyes bright

1. H & S, b15. Reprinted in H & S, 31–3. Excerpted in O'Brien, 33–4.

blue, and clear, as if you could see down into the lowest depths of thought within, and the mouth and chin are Hibernian, but of the highest Celtic type, and there is an air of refinement and gentle breeding pervading not only the face but the entire man, and idealized in the full, flexible, delicately finished lips. He has the low cultured voice of refined society, and his personal magnetism sufficiently accounts for the extent to which society both in London and New York has taken him up.

Any man in the same independent position, with the same charm of manner, and the same pleasant genial face and nature, would be a general favorite, had he never written a line of poetry or anything else but letters, or put forth to the world any even quasi-original ideas.

In reply to his visitor, who plunged at once into business, and asked for some concise information on his views Mr. Wilde replied:

"There is more in the movement, as you say, than appears upon the surface. Our aim is to unite all artists in a brotherhood of art, and to draw closer together those who cultivate the beautiful."

"Let me give you," he continued, "an illustration. Take, for example, Keats. When Keats was alive, how lonely he was. He had the fellowship of no brother artists. This movement is designed in part to remove that isolation, to bring all artists, whether in painting, sculpture, music or poetry, together, that they may aid each other in every way, and that each art may profit by the advance of its sister arts."

"And especially," he went on with increasing animation, "especially does the movement aim to reach the handicraftsman, and to raise him by familiarity with the truly artistic and by the sympathy of his brothers."

"The movement, then, is democratic in its tendency?"

"It is the most democratic impulse in the history of the world," said Mr. Wilde, earnestly. "I don't know, of course, how it is in this country; but we in England believe that the people, the artisan class, have toiled long enough at unloved labor and amid the unlovely, hard, repulsive surroundings. A man's work should be a joy to him. Make him an artist, make him a designer, and you render it so. What a man designs he delights in bringing to completion."

"Hence," said he, "you see the politico-economical importance of aestheticism. The toiling thousands of Great Britain are growing more and more dissatisfied every year with their dreary lives, filled only with incessant, unattractive toil. The time when they could be kept down with the strong hand has departed, and," with an evident allusion to Kingsley's "Yeast,"[1] "the problem of controlling them

1. *Yeast: A Problem* (1848) was the first novel by Christian Socialist, Charles Kingsley (1819–1875). It attacked the English social system insofar as it kept the labouring class in poverty. In his 1891 essay *The Soul of Man Under Socialism* Wilde declared that "Kingsley's prose was not of a very fine quality" (CW iv, 252.8–9).

is only to be solved by making them happy in their labor, and brightening their lives with such material surroundings as it is in the power of art to bestow."

As this seemed feasible only for such artisans as were also designers—though obviously of value to them—Mr. Wilde was asked by his visitor whether he deemed it possible to extend the benefits of aestheticism to the people most in need of his own theory of their blessings, and, on his replying in the affirmative, it was suggested, after a word of explanation, to the effect that the questioner was not arguing, but only seeking a clear conception of the inner light; that while designers and artists were no doubt in demand to a certain extent, yet that there was also a demand for operatives to carry out their ideas and designs, and that, however happy it might make the loomhand to go into the fields and study the flowers for his patterns, or the stonecutter to imagine his group of statuary, the tyranny of trade would prefer that the one should be in the stoneyard chipping at the marble for somebody else's designs, and the other hard at work in the factory keeping his loom in good running order.

To this Mr. Wilde replied that it was the tendency of aestheticism to raise all to a higher level, and to bring about among artisans a greater independence and a condition of things approaching in some respects to the better features of life among handicraftsmen in India.

In reply to the inquiry whether Tennyson sympathized with the movement, Mr. Wilde replied that within certain limits there could be no question of the laureate's sympathy with it, but added that ever since the severe criticism which had assailed his earlier poems, "an ordeal which," said he with a good natured smile, "every English poet has had to go through," the laureate had held himself in a great measure isolated from the world of art.[1] That his poems had endured was due to their intrinsic beauty, "for," said the aesthetic bard, "what is really beautiful has within itself an inextinguishable principle of life."

He would not say, however, he added, that Tennyson had absolutely held aloof from the movement; but, as one of its chiefest apostles, he might mention William Morris, whose rooms were a perfect museum of beautiful things, on every one of which he had bestowed somewhat of his own thought or handiwork in its organization.

Mr. Wilde, at a later hour in the evening, attended the reception at the residence of Mr. Stewart Davis,[2] Eighteenth and Spruce streets. The entertainment was a gentlemen's party from eight to ten P.M., on the principle of a conversazi-

1. Tennyson's early poetry was a major influence on the Pre-Raphaelite Brotherhood but met with such criticism that he chose not to publish for a decade. Wilde's poetry had also been harshly criticised (see Sturgis, 185–9/179–82).

2. Robert Stewart Davis (1838–1911) was an American newspaper publisher.

one with an elegant collation continuously served, and was attended by many of the most prominent judges, lawyers, merchants, bankers, physicians, clergymen and journalists.

✂ *A list of guests at the reception.*

The reception, though elegant in the highest degree, was purely informal, and the parlors were beautiful with floral decorations, the object in the disposition of the flowers being evidently rather their tasteful and artistic grouping than a mere profusion of display.

"Honors to an Aesthete," *The Times* (Philadelphia, PA), 17 Jan. 1882, 1[1]

MR. DAVIS ENTERTAINS MR. WILDE

A Representative Company of Philadelphians Gathered to Meet the Young London Poet. Mr. Wilde's Arrival and his Explanation of His Mission.

When Oscar Wilde, the aesthetic poet arrived at the Aldine Hotel yesterday evening one of the first things he did was to ring for wax candles. As he threw aside his cloak of sable with silver clasps he cast a glance of disgust at the plain wall paper on [*sic*] the room and heaved a sigh that expressed far more plainly than words his disappointment at not having dados of Japanese figures with borders of peacocks' tails.[2] The candles were brought and the gas turned out, and, throwing his cloak over the sofa and putting on his short embroidered jacket, with ruby silk cuffs and facing, the poet lit a cigarette, adjusted his nether limbs, encased in black cloth knickerbockers and silk stockings, and, with his enthusiastic Irish blue eyes directed away from the horrid wall paper towards the fireplace, he looked contented and happy and seemed for the moment quite at his ease.

In appearance this young member of the London coterie so humorously satirized by Du Maurier in *Punch* is not unlike the fictitious personage in the opera of "Patience," through which Gilbert and Sullivan have so cleverly burlesqued the advanced ideas of the aesthetic school. Although the irreverent New York reporters who described him as "a thin Beecher" went a little beyond absolute impartiality, it is nevertheless a fact that he bears a juvenile and embryonic re-

1. Excerpted in "Wilde Oscar," *The National Republican* (Washington D. C.), 20 Jan. 1882, 1; and "The Aesthete on His Travels," *Truth* (London, UK), 2 Feb. 1882, 175–7, p. 707.
2. Aesthetes were caricatured as being obsessed with dados and peacock feathers.

semblance to the great Plymouth apostle.[1] His face is smooth and he has what Mr. Beecher himself has described as "a whirlwind in the lower part of his face and a hurricane above." His lower jaws are strongly developed, but he has a fine, broad brow. The eyes are blue and, like all his features, are large. His long brown hair is carelessly parted in the centre of the forehead and allowed to fall in disorder over his leonine neck and Byronic shirt-collar. This collar is cut low and brought together by a wide white satin tie. At the reception given by Mr. Davis last night he wore an ordinary dress-coat, but in the hotel he lounged about in a magnificent short dressing robe. On both occasions he wore knee-breeches and black silk stockings, with low-cut patent leather shoes tied by wide silk ribbons. He is over six feet high and well proportioned. An observer, judging by his appearance, would take him to be about thirty years of age. His manner is quiet and he has the habit of leaning his head upon his arm and of placing one arm akimbo with his hand at the side, which is one of the favourite "Patience" positions. He also, in a seemingly natural manner, crooks his right knee when standing, which is one of the difficult poses that Calverley and Murgatroyd and Dunstable in the opera try so unsuccessfully to imitate.[2]

A LITTLE AESTHETICISM.

"The philosophy of aestheticism," said Mr. Wilde, in conversation, "is that the secret of enjoyment in life is to be able to understand and appreciate the beautiful. People cross continents to see a lake or a mountain or a waterfall, while the simple creatures who live about these scenes are able to discern only earth and water. The four great poets of the early part of this century—Wordsworth, Shelley, Keats and Byron—were grossly misunderstood in their lifetime by the British public, so much so that one was driven to the Cumberland wilds and the others to foreign graves.[3] Even today the masses of the people, owing to their groveling and unbeautiful surroundings, are not able to appreciate the poets. I would like to see everyone able to appreciate the artistic quality of the simplest things around them and thus learn of higher things than money-

1. Henry Ward Beecher (1813–1887) was an American clergyman, social reformer, and abolitionist.

2. Calverley, Murgatroyd, and Dunstable are officers of the Dragoon Guards in *Patience*. They attempt to regain the affections of the ladies by emulating aesthetic dress and behaviour. Aesthetes were caricatured as adopting crooked postures, sometimes referred to as "stained-glass attitudes".

3. William Wordsworth (1770–1850) was Poet Laureate of the United Kingdom from 1843 until his death. He was born in Cumberland but lived in Westmorland (both now part of Cumbria) from 1813 because he held the post of Distributor of Stamps for Westmorland. Shelley drowned while sailing in the Gulf of La Spezia; Keats died of tuberculosis in Rome; Lord Byron (1788–1824) died in Missolonghi from a fever contracted while fighting in the Greek War of Independence. Wilde had made pilgrimages to the graves of Keats and Shelley in 1877.

getting. My greatest object in visiting this country is to see what effect these ideas will have upon an unprejudiced people who are not wedded to the old conventionalism. I desire particularly to urge the importance of leading children to estimate the beautiful and teaching them to use their eyes and ears and hands. I would have Americans make for themselves the beautiful objects they bring from the older world. The key-note of this age is discontent. People are not satisfied because they do not enjoy life, and to enjoy life they must be able to understand the beautiful in the simplest things. The ladies are taking the right step in the decoration of their homes and in the draperies of their persons, but the men will be slow in receiving impressions. I do not believe in making society a fancy ball, but I see no reason why men should not wear brown or black velvet instead of cloth, nor do I see why knee-breeches are not more becoming and dignified than the ridiculous trousers which men adhere to."

✂ *A report of the Davis reception.*

[Florence Duncan], "A Chat with Oscar Wilde," *Quiz* (Philadelphia, PA), 25 Jan. 1882, 4[1]

Mr. Wilde's book of poems, published by Roberts Brothers, of Boston, was criticised at considerable length some weeks ago, in the columns of QUIZ.[2] The readers will not, certainly, accuse QUIZ of an overweening and unhealthy predilection in favor of the much be-paragraphed stranger within our gates.

I have learned since, that Mr. Wilde has written other poems, other things than he has given to the world in the book mentioned above—a book, notwithstanding that it exhibits a perfect familiarity with verse-making, a great deal of knowledge, reading, Greek and Latin, French and floriculture and the—antique, makes one say inwardly:—

"But all this has been said so much before—and why don't this poet read Keats? *He* was the real founder of all this. *This* man is a follower."

I must own that the courtesy with which I greeted Mr. Wilde, as he entered the *sanctum sanctorum* of QUIZ, was simply to honor the letter of introduction from the friend who gave it him, rather than the more paragraphed "Aesthete,"—so called—himself. I knew, of course, he was a gentleman in the conventional

1. Quoted in Sturgis, 217/209. There is no byline but Sturgis identifies the author as Florence Duncan, the editor of *Quiz*.

2. The review appeared in the issue of 15 Sep. 1881, 214–16, under the title, "Poetry as a Handicraft." The author, "Hamish", was not impressed: "Somewhat prejudiced in his favor before reading his book, we were thoroughly disenchanted on laying it down."

sense, and that he could read and write, but I was not prepared for one of the most delightful conversations of two hours and a half duration that I ever enjoyed, and almost at once I honored the man on his own account. Mr. Wilde can talk beautifully, and I am of the opinion that it is because he says the things that many of us think, but have not the courage to say *out*, that he has got himself into the rather peculiar scrape of being at cross-purposes with the editors of the precocious journals of our country. To be sure, what Mr. Wilde says on the lecture platform is familiar to those of us who had read the elders of his school, but that the majority of journalists are not familiar with the Ruskin–Morris–Rossetti thought is proved by their crass ignorance in their criticisms of Mr. Wilde.

Mr. Wilde's long hair may be fair game for the paragraphers in the funny column (no one need mind *that*)—but since when did it become honorable journalism for the *editor* of a respectable newspaper to abuse a man because of personal appearance or cut of his clothes?

It was good to hear him describe his visit to Walt Whitman. It was so respectful, reverential and truly sincere. "That grand, rugged, old man," he called him. "He was very kind to me, which made me glad at once, for I did not know that he would receive me."[1]

Mr. Wilde has the Ruskin-like descriptive power; he more than describes—he shows; a picture on Rossetti's easel, at which the artist was at work when Mr. Wilde was leaving home, he put before me as vividly as is possible, I think, to picture in words; he told of the back ground of country road and verdure; the cart laden with fresh green cabbage and garden vegetables of rich color coming over the brow of the hill; the farmer boy and market maiden—the simple beauty all around.[2] But he was at his best in talking of Keats. A man who can talk about "The Ode to a Grecian Urn" as Mr. Wilde can, is a considerable distance from being "a fool."[3]

Mr. Wilde expressed himself as greatly pleased with Philadelphia women. Like Arthur Sullivan, he thinks them the "most beautiful,"—though Mr. Wilde has not seen America as Mr. Sullivan had. He said the New York journalists had been very kind to him, kind and temperate, and I think he sincerely felt this.

1. See also later interviews and "Wilde and Whitman," *The Philadelphia Press* (Philadelphia, PA), 19 Jan. 1882, 8, pp. 757–9.

2. Wilde's description does not match any known picture by Rossetti.

3. In *The English Renaissance* Wilde praised Keats for poetry that possessed "that sense of calm and perfect repose which should be the effect of all fine, imaginative work [....] in Keats it seemed to have been incarnate, and in his lovely *Ode on a Grecian Urn* it found its most secure and faultless expression" (*Miscellanies*, 257).

"The most charming time I had was at Mr. Hurlburt's—of the *World*, you know—and *dear* 'Uncle Sam' Ward's, and Mrs. Bigelow's—but at Mrs. Paran Stevens' I met such beautiful women—so very lovely."[1]

"New York is very cosmopolitan, don't you think so?" he asked, very earnestly. I smiled, and so did he. We were both thinking of the Mrs. Leo Hunters, but we did not gossip—life is not long enough, especially when there is so much bric-a-brac to look at,[2] and so much work to do.

I liked his splendid defence of Mrs. Langtry, from the wicked and stupid talk about her.

"I saw her one night—we were at Ferdinand de Rothschild's[3]—the centre of the room, surrounded by the Prince of Wales and three Kings, all hanging on her words—and Duchesses waiting! It is not in human nature that people should not be jealous of her."

Mr. Wilde is singularly free from affectation in conversation, his expression is bright and sincere, and his manner courteous to a degree.

[Florence Duncan], "Some More," *Quiz* (Philadelphia, PA), 1 Feb. 1882, 4[4]

The mantle of Oliver Twist has descended!—This time, it is not for pudding, but for Wilde! Our subscribing correspondents, are converted into critics.

"But after all, you did not tell us much in last QUIZ what Oscar Wilde chatted about. Didn't he say anything more?"

Our attentive readers, and critical correspondents ignore that editors have to "condense." To be sure Mr. Wilde *did* talk about *more* than beauty and fashion—the aesthetic school and its priestess—America and Western Ozone. He talked of some people that he loved, "dearly" he said, and these people are little children.

(A man can't go permanently astray who loves little children.)

We were talking of flowers, and their healthy influence everyday in the home, above all, in the sick-room. Mr. Wilde has spent a great deal of his leisure time in visiting children's hospitals, he loved to take the little sufferers flowers,

1. Wilde was hosted by Samuel "Uncle Sam" Cutler Ward (1814–1884), political lobbyist and gourmet, at his apartments at 84 Clinton Place on 11 January (Friedman, 77–8). Mrs Paran Stevens invited Wilde to dinner for the second time. Jane Tunis Bigelow née Poultney (1829–1889), was the wife of John Bigelow Sr. (1817–1911), a Democratic politician and ambassador.

2. Aesthetes were represented as obsessing over ornaments and other small objects of aesthetic value, such as vases and teacups.

3. Ferdinand de Rothschild (1839–1898) was a British banker and art collector.

4. Reprinted as "Some More," *Canadian Illustrated News* (Montreal, QC) 11 Feb. 1882, 83.

and he bore earnest testimony to the power that flowers have to cheer the tired spirit and rest the weary eyes—and give respite from the plain square white—one could almost say too white—look of the hospital-ward.

All the members of the flower-missions have the same experience, and if our correspondents will turn to the pages of QUIZ, of some months ago, they will read the heart of the matter, very sweetly and nobly expressed by one of our contributors, a lady, who has as much practical knowledge of the flower-missions, and their true power, as any woman in the country. This article was widely copied, and I mention the fact because the parts of it most commented upon, were sentiments so perfectly in accord with Mr. Wilde's expressions.[1]

"One hears," said Mr. Wilde, "the sweetest things in the world said by children. One day, I was taking a lady friend a large bunch of great red lilies, (we have beautiful, rich, red lilies in England; they would never do for a lady to wear, but they are splendid in decoration), and a pretty little girl stopped me, one of the dirty, little street children, very pretty tho', saying:

"'Lor, Mister, *how rich you are!*'

"I thought it was such a beautiful thing to have said, and a thought so true, that there is so much that we have, so much real wealth in flowers."[2]

Some of the critical correspondents are desirous to know what I meant by saying Mr. Wilde "said *out*" that which others have not the courage to say.

Briefly, a great deal: few of us have the courage to run the risk of ridicule, by being, well—eccentric enough for a strong stand for what we know is right and proper—but is not usual or customary.

> The mission of genius on earth—to uplift.
> Purify and redeem by its own gracious gift,
> The world, in spite of the world's dull endeavor
> To drag down and degrade, and oppose it forever,
> The mission of genius—to watch and to wait,
> To renew, to redeem, and regenerate.[3]

1. Flower missions distributed fresh flowers and fruit to poor urban areas, hospital wards, and prisons. They became popular on both sides of the Atlantic in the 1870s. Katherine S. Hart ("The Philadelphia Flower and Fruit Missions," *Quiz* (Philadelphia, PA), 1 June 1881, 92–3) claimed that a gift of flowers could have a positive effect on a recipient's morals as well as their mood.

2. Wilde also told this story to his friend Charles Ricketts (Ricketts, 29). See also "Oscar Wilde on Children and Flowers," *New York Tribune* (New York, NY), 11 Sep. 1882, 8, pp. 461–462. The story inspired an exchange in *Vera* between the heroine and a child: "NICHOLAS. [...] Oh! Vera are those your flowers? | VERA. Yes you little rogue. | NICHOLAS. Your own flowers? | VERA. Yes. | NICHOLAS. How rich you are." (CW xi, 111.105–10.)

3. The lines quoted are from part ii, canto vi, verse xxxix of *Lucile* (1860), a verse novel written by Edward Robert Bulwer-Lytton (1831–1891) under the pen name Owen Meredith. The fourth line should read: "To degrade, and drag down, and oppose it forever."

Figure 3. Wilde photographed by Sarony in his usual interviewing posture: reclining on a sofa spread with a fur rug. He holds a copy of his Poems *(1881).*

But my corresponding critics are saying: "Now you are quoting Owen Meredith—and is Mr. Wilde, the first man in whom this thought has blossomed?"

Certainly not; not by a century; he is simply a popularizer of beauty. Suppose we look about and see if we are all such perfect joys forever—that we need no preachers in our streets, our homes, to our men and our women—and, oh, Plutarch! our business lives—here in this very country where politics is a trade, statesmanship gambling—and the greed of money-got-any-how—a leprosy.

This very day men blush if they are found doing a sweet, pure kindness to a fellow creature. From modesty? Not a bit of it, but because they think it feminine. (So it is, thank God.) A man who has his conception of beauty fully developed, will never degenerate into a mere house-tyrant. He need not be "too, too" "utter," or "intense" as we love chaff, now-a-days; he need not roll up his eyes, in ecstasy at the sight of a yellow crewel flower on a square of linen crash—but he may feel warmed to the very cockles of his heart, when he sees a youth showing promise of genius—let that promise be ever so crude or bizarre.

Beauty means something more than crewel-work and chromos. If Mr. Wilde only sets a few of the people thinking, will he not have done something?

"What Oscar Has to Say," *Baltimore American and Commercial Advertiser* (Baltimore, MD), 20 Jan. 1882, 4[1]

He Denies that He Had Any Falling Out with Mr. Forbes.
(Special to The American.)

WASHINGTON, January 19.—It having been rumored that the reason why Mr. Oscar Wilde passed through Baltimore today en route to Washington, without stopping in that city, was owing to some disagreement with Mr. Archibald Forbes, the English war correspondent, who is at present in Baltimore, the correspondent of *The American* called upon Mr. Wilde at the Arlington Hotel this evening.[2] He at first refused to be seen, and had denied admittance to several newspaper men, but a note from your correspondent proved effective. Before reaching the door a number of young ladies were seen hurrying in the direction of the room, anxious to catch a glimpse of its inmate. As the door was opened to admit *The American* man, Mr. Wilde was found reclining upon a sofa immediately opposite, attired in a tight-fitting dressing gown, trimmed with red, his long hair brushed carelessly back from his forehead. The waiter, in order to afford the ladies an opportunity to behold Mr. Wilde, held the door open until sternly told to shut it. Mr. Wilde advanced cordially and shook hands with your correspondent.

"I beg pardon for the intrusion, Mr. Wilde, but your passing through Baltimore without stopping has given rise to the unpleasant rumor that you and Mr. Forbes are not on amiable terms."

1. H & S, b17. Reprinted in H & S, 34–5; and, with a burlesque introduction and other additions, as "He is Here," *The Evening Critic* (Washington, DC), 20 Jan. 1882, 3. Referenced in Sturgis, 220/211. Preceded by an article titled "No Oscar For Us", which quotes Archibald Forbes (1838–1900), a war correspondent and lecturer managed by D'Oyly Carte. Forbes's lecture was *The Inner Life of a War Correspondent.* Although forgotten now, Forbes was a big draw at the time: in Hartford, Connecticut, he was introduced on stage by Mark Twain (Friedman, 116). The *American* has Forbes claim that Wilde had a "miff" on the train from Philadelphia: "The man of war was exceedingly cool on the question, and remarked 'that he did not take any stock in Mr Wilde: in fact, he was glad he did not get off at the depot [in Baltimore].'" Forbes later denied having said this (see "Wilde and Forbes," *The New York Herald* (New York, NY), 21 Jan. 1882, 3, pp. 102–4; and "Not a Battle, a Boom," *The New York World, Semi-Weekly Edition* (New York, NY), 24 Jan. 1882, 2, pp. 104–5). The *American* also suggested that "the Wednesday Club extended him [Wilde] an invitation to be present at their next entertainment, which takes place next Thursday night [26 January, the night of Wilde's lecture in Baltimore]. The super aesthetic poet cooly informed them that he charged $300 for his appearances at receptions other than at private houses. The Wednesday Club, it is needless to say, will not entertain him." The Wednesday Club met between 1858 and 1886. Its members played music, staged plays, and discussed literature and art. Wilde attended a meeting when he returned to Baltimore (see "Oscar Wilde," *The Sunday Herald* (Boston, MA), 29 Jan. 1882, 7, p. 124). The article in the *American* was a source of extreme distress for Wilde and he repeatedly spoke about it in subsequent interviews.

2. In the company of a *Washington Post* reporter: "Oscar Wilde Arrives," *The Washington Post* (Washington, DC), 20 Jan. 1882, 4, pp. 90–1.

"Well, really, this is most extraordinary. Mr. Forbes and myself are on terms of the greatest intimacy, and I cannot imagine the cause for any such rumor. Besides, why should I stop in Baltimore, as my engagement to lecture in Washington is prior to my Baltimore engagement? Lecturing here on Monday evening next, I shall go to Baltimore on the following Tuesday morning. So I left Philadelphia at noon today and came through to Washington, arriving here at 5 o'clock, and came right to my room, where I purpose spending a quiet, uninterrupted evening, which will be the first since my visit to your wonderful country."

"I regret having disturbed your quiet," remarked the correspondent.

"Not at all. I am only too happy to have had an opportunity to positively deny that any unfriendliness exists between Mr. Forbes and myself, which you will do me the kindness to state emphatically."

"You will no doubt see much to interest you in Washington."

"Yes, I have many letters of introduction to distinguished people in this city, and I have a great desire to see the politicians of your wonderful country, whom I shall no doubt find assembled here now: and I regret that my limited stay will prevent my making that earnest, careful study of your leading men that I earnestly desire."

"Yes," suggested the correspondent: "you will find at this season, during the assembling of our National Congress, a great many of the politicians of both the great parties."

"I expect so: and, by the way, tell me what city do you consider the most purely American city? I do not fancy that either New York or Philadelphia are true types of that American idea which we are impressed with on the other side."

"Well, I think you will find Baltimore about as near an approach to an American city as any we have."

"Yes, I have been told so; and as I propose visiting there, I shall, no doubt, satisfy myself."[1]

Mr. Wilde, in addition, stated that he had passed a charming time in Philadelphia, and one of his most delightful evenings was the one spent last night at the residence of Mr. George W. Childs, in that city;[2] that he desired very much to travel over this country, and store up knowledge which he purposed using in his books and poetry. He asked a great many questions regarding America, and dwelt in ecstasy over Walt Whitman, two pictures of whom were lying amid a mass of papers on the table in the room, and one of which he was to mail to

1. *The Washington Post* claimed that Wilde was responding to the suggestion that Washington DC was the most characteristic American city (pp. 90–1).

2. George William Childs (1829–1894) was a newspaper proprietor and philanthropist.

Swinburne.[1] He expressed himself as worn-out and tired, and stated that it was a positive luxury to have one night to himself. Your correspondent bade Mr. Wilde goodnight. "And pray contradict that report with reference to myself and Mr. Forbes," were his last utterances as the door closed.

"Oscar Wilde Arrives," *The Washington Post* (Washington, DC), 20 Jan. 1882, 4[2]

He Wants to See Our Politicians and Prominent Men.

Oscar Wilde, the apostle of aestheticism, arrived in the city at 5 o'clock yesterday afternoon and secured apartments at the Arlington Hotel. The first order he issued, after registering, was that he did not wish to be disturbed by anybody, as he was tired and desired to have one evening, at least, to himself. Persuasion and diplomacy, however, enabled a POST reporter to interview Mr. Wilde.[3] The passage leading to the room was thronged with females, anxious to get a look at the much-talked-of gentleman. When the reporter was ushered into the room, he held the door open that these ladies might have their curiosity gratified, but Mr. Wilde, noticing this, said sharply, "shut the door." He then rose from the sofa on which he was reclining, and advanced toward the reporter, extending a cordial greeting. He was attired in a tight fitting dressing gown, his long hair being brushed back behind his ears. He stated that he left Philadelphia at noon and came direct to Washington. Just here the reporter said:

"It was understood, I believe, that you were to have stopped over in Baltimore tonight and appeared in conjunction with Mr. Archibald Forbes, at the latter's lecture. It has been rumored since your arrival here, that you did not stop in Baltimore because you and Mr. Forbes had quarrelled."

"There is no foundation for such a rumor," replied Mr. Wilde. "Mr. Forbes and I are on the best of terms. I have no engagement to lecture in Baltimore until next Tuesday. I have been very anxious," he added, "to come to Washington, to see the politicians and prominent men, to many of whom I have letters of introduction. By the way, can you tell me which is considered the most characteristic American city? None which I have visited come up to the impressions we have on the other side."

1. Wilde's letter to Swinburne has not survived, but Swinburne replied to thank Wilde for the photograph (CL, 144). See also p. 415, note 1.

2. Reprinted as "Oscar Wilde's Eccentricities," *The Atlanta Constitution* (Atlanta, GA), 24 Jan. 1882, 4.

3. In the company of a *Baltimore American* reporter: "What Oscar Has to Say," *Baltimore American and Commercial Advertiser* (Baltimore, MD), 20 Jan. 1882, 4, pp. 88–90.

THE POST, with its usual delicacy, answered that Washington was.

"I have been told so," Mr. Wilde said, "and I shall no doubt have opportunity to satisfy myself."[1]

He then intimated that this was the first chance he had had to pass a quiet evening entirely to himself, whereupon the reporter took the hint and withdrew.

"Oscar and Our Man," *The National Republican* (Washington, DC), 21 Jan. 1882, 1

TAKE A TOUR AROUND THE CITY.

They Drop In to See Our National Sunflowers at the Capitol, Sip Tea, Smoke Cigarettes, and Talk Aesthetics Together—How Oscar Looks and Dresses.

A REPUBLICAN reporter had to see a lady friend off on one of the early trains yesterday morning, and consequently found himself up at an abnormally early hour. After having shed a silent tear at the Baltimore and Ohio depot he walked up the Avenue, and when near Fourteenth street he descried a tall figure in a gray ulster wending his way down Fifteenth street. Ranging alongside of the stranger the reporter discovered that he was standing in the presence of the great expounder of the English renaissance—Oscar Wilde.[2] The long-limbed aesthete was attired in a tight-fitting gray ulster, which blew open occasionally and disclosed underneath a pair of velvet knee pants. The upper garment could not be seen. A pair of black silk stockings and patent-leather low shoes, with large black silk bows, were seen beneath the skirts of the ulster. Round his neck was a wide Byronic collar and blue bow of the most delicate and ethereal shade, with long, streaming ends "borne on the soft zephyrs of the morning breeze."

A VERY HANDSOME DIAMOND PIN

was worn in the centre of the bow. On the poet's noddle reposed a "harmony" in the shape of a polo cap of a peculiar blackish-brownish hue, bound with pink.[3] A pair of semi-gauntleted, flesh-colored kid gloves and a light, fancy cane completed the garb. "How do you do, Mr. Wilde?" said the reporter. In a languid, slightly drawling voice, like a sick calf, he acknowledged the salutation, and said

1. The *Baltimore American* claimed that Wilde was responding to the suggestion that Baltimore was the most purely American city (p. 89).

2. It seems unlikely that this is how Wilde and the reporter met. Wilde was not an early riser and would not have worn his lecturing outfit at this time of day.

3. An allusion to Whistler, who saw a parallel between music and painting and titled many of his pictures "harmonies", "arrangements", and "nocturnes".

he was glawd [*sic*] to meet journalists, especially since his arrival in this country. "The newspapers," said Mr. Wilde, "have been passing some rather hard criticisms about me, ye knaw, but they won't do it when they know me better," this with a silly laugh. "Yes," replied the reporter, "the press rather likes to have something to 'guy,'[1] but they don't mean any harm by it." The time was passed in light converse until the Arlington was reached, where Mr. Wilde entered and told the reporter he would be "glawd" to meet him at breakfast at half-pawst ten. Shortly after noon Mr. Wilde went to the Capitol and wanted to see Speaker Keifer.[2] He called at the north door and asked if he could be admitted to the floor. The polite messenger told him he must first send in his card. "Card," said the aesthetic Oscar, "I never send a card to Parliament when I want to go in."[3]

"Can't help that, you will have to send one here," replied the Buckeye doorkeeper."[4]

"Ah, ha!" ejaculated the believer in sunflowers.

"WHERE CAN I GET A CARD?"

"Indeed, I don't know," was the answer. Oscar approached Mr. J. F. Bristow, who keeps a stand for writing cards, and told him that he wanted some cards. The facile knight of the pen took up his tools and asked what name. "Oscar Wilde, of England."

"You astonish me! Is your name really Oscar Wilde, the aesthete?" said Bristow. "Yes, that's my name." The Capitol card-writer flourished his name over a card and handed it to the aesthetic gentleman, who transferred it to the north door, and soon the card was in the hands of the Speaker, who read it, and said in reply: "Will see the gentleman at the hotel tonight." Mr. Wilde then passed the time in critically examining the Capitol and the pictures and statues that are contained in that noble pile. In the evening Mr. Wilde was again called upon at the Arlington, and found at room 151 on the ground floor. In answer to the knock the door was opened from the inside, and the lion of the hour was discovered half lounging, half reclining on a sofa covered with a large rug, facing the door. On seeing the visitor Mr. Wilde rose to his feet, and extending a large, soft hand, whispered a few words of welcome and then

1. To "guy" is to make an object of ridicule or derisive wit (OED).

2. J. Warren Keifer (1836–1932) served in the House of Representatives as a Republican from Ohio from 1877 to 1885 and 1905 to 1911. He was Speaker of the House from 1881 to 1883.

3. *The Evening Critic* (Washington DC, 20 Jan. 1882, 1) reported that Wilde was expected at the Capitol, by whom was not stated, "but at 2:30 he had not arrived."

4. A buckeye is a person from Ohio; in the late nineteenth-century the word also described a person or thing that was showy but inferior (OED).

SANK BACK ON THE SOFA.

A colored man advanced and took the guest's umbrella and hat and noiselessly retired. The room was in rather classic disorder, the table being littered with paper, letters, and material for writing. The room was heavily ladened with the odor of Turkish tobacco smoke, and the poet was puffing a cigarette through an amber mouthpiece. On a chair near the sofa was a large cup containing tea, from which the aesthete drank at intervals. Mr. Wilde wore a short, close-fitting dressing jacket of blue cashmere, with collar and deep cuffs of cardinal satin. The knee-breeches and silk stockings were the same as worn in the morning, with a low-cut vest, displaying a magnificent expanse of shirt-front. In the centre of the shirt was an immense stud of clustered diamonds. In place of the morning's blue bow Mr. Wilde wore a white silk tie. In appearance he is about five feet eleven inches tall, broad shoulders, slightly rounded, with long brown hair falling to the shoulders, parted in the centre. His features are heavy and prominent, his forehead broad, and a pair of blue eyes complete the *toute ensemble*. The conversation at first drifted into English channels. Then Mr. Wilde was asked his impressions on this country, and said he was charmed by the men and women he had met. The cities he did not care so much about. He is a delightfully colloquial talker, and it is a pleasure to listen to him. Talking in slow and measured accents, with a slight drawl and all the English accent of a high-bred gentleman, he speaks in a musical monotone, and his voice rises and falls in almost rhythmical cadence. When asked about what he thought the influence of his visit would have on the artistic world in this country

MR. WILDE BECAME ENTHUSIASTIC,

and, with considerable warmth, said he thought that single individuals could work great things if only they had the right ambition. "Ambition; yes, ambition; if a young, healthy man only has that he can do anything and be anything," said the poet.[1] Then the conversation wandered on through the realms of art, painting, and architecture. Mr. Wilde suddenly rose to his feet and said: "I would like to say something personal before you leave. You saw that stupid thing in the Baltimore papers about Mr. Forbes and myself? Well, now, I have just received a letter from him, in which he gives a denial to the assertions made by the Baltimore papers about certain remarks supposed to have been made by him relative to me.[2] He expressed great regret that any such stories should have been started, and is as sorry about the matter as I am. Now, there is another matter. You saw

1. In his *Phrases and Philosophies for the Use of the Young*, first published in *The Chameleon* in December 1894, Wilde would declare that: "Ambition is the last refuge of the failure." (*Miscellanies*, 177.)

2. See also "Wilde and Forbes," *The New York Herald* (New York, NY), 21 Jan. 1882, 3, p. 100.

that equally silly thing about the Wednesday Club in Baltimore, and my only attending their reception on receiving $300.[1] I don't think any *gentleman* (emphasized) would make such a proposition, and I certainly did not do anything so foolish. In fact, I have not received any invitation from the club."

Mr. Wilde then shook hands with the reporter, who retired.

"Mr. Oscar Wilde," *The Evening Star* (Washington, DC), 21 Jan. 1882, 1[2]

WHAT HE HAS TO SAY—ESTHETIC TAFFY FOR THE AMERICANS—THEY LOVE THE TRUE AND THE BEAUTIFUL—MR. WILDE ON THE TOO TOO BURLESQUES—HE THINKS "THE COLONEL" VULGAR—HE IS NOT LOOKING AFTER THE ESTATE OF HIS UNCLE.

A STAR reporter called upon Mr. Oscar Wilde, at the Arlington, yesterday, and was pleasantly greeted by the distinguished esthete. His looks and dress have been so minutely described that these points can be passed. In response to an inquiry from the reporter, Mr. Wilde said that he found a great deal more interest taken in this country in matters esthetic than he expected. "There is," he said, "much more true art here than I supposed; and true art, you know, is estheticism. I have had a great many inquiries from people who want to learn in art, and have seen a great many who have our ideas almost perfectly. I am doing all I can to encourage the spread of true taste. What I would like to see is a permanent standard of taste among the people in their lives and in all they do."

AMERICANS SHOULD NOT COPY.

"Would the standard be the same for all countries?"

"By no means. I think no greater mistake can be made than for one country to copy after another. There is an individuality of art for every people. The Americans should not copy the decorations of England. Their flowers, atmosphere and all external forms of art are different. American decoration should be entirely different from that of England or any other country. There is plenty of the beautiful in nature in this country for art's purposes without borrowing. And where there is borrowing there is a lack of individuality which makes the whole unsatisfactory."

1. See p. 88, note 1.

2. Reprinted, with a derogatory introduction that was possibly added by someone other than the interviewer, in "The Aesthetic Craze," *The Courier-Journal* (Louisville, KY), 22 Jan. 1882, 9. Quoted in OWDA, 88.

"What is your particular object in visiting America?"

"I want to see the country; and then I want to see how far the people here can love art and how far they can be led to love art. I would like to spread the truth of art and aid humanity to form the right idea of the true relations of art to life and of life to art."

NEW YORK AND PHILADELPHIA AUDIENCES.

"Did you notice any difference in the audiences to whom you have lectured?"

"I have only lectured in New York and in Philadelphia. I did notice a very marked difference. New York audiences are electric, and Philadelphia people are thoughtful. The latter make but very little demonstration, but there is an air over the whole assemblage which causes one to know that he is being listened to. I could see their faces listening."

O. W. AND W. W.

There was a picture of Walt Whitman on the table. The reporter asked Mr. Wilde what he thought of America's rugged poet.

"The most delightful day I have spent," he answered, "was in Mr. Whitman's little bare room in Camden. I think Mr. Whitman is in every way one of the greatest and strongest men who have ever lived. He is the simplest and strongest man I ever met. Eccentric? He is not; you cannot gauge great men by a foot-rule. The people in England, for whose opinion he would care, read him and read him, and wonder at him."

HE OBJECTS TO "THE COLONEL."

"Don't you find that many people here formed their opinions of you and your fellow-workers upon the basis of *Punch* and the criticisms of the newspapers?"

"A great many. In fact, the majority of them. I don't mind," with a little laugh, "'Patience' or the pictures of *Punch* so much. I can laugh at them both and enjoy them. I do object, however, to 'The Colonel.' It is vulgar. It is very vulgar. I don't see how anyone can enjoy such a vulgar picture as the play called 'The Colonel' presents. But the fun has not been wholly on the side of our caricaturists. I assure you we have pretty fully made ridicule of the Philistines. What is called the esthetic craze is not confined to a small circle in England. The whole artistic world of London is interested in the work of educating art tastes."

THE ESTHETE'S PROGRAM.

In answer to a question as to his future movements Mr. Wilde said: "I go from here next Tuesday to Baltimore—where, by the way, I was not engaged to appear Thursday night at Mr. Forbes' lecture, nor to go to any reception there. I lecture in Baltimore next Wednesday. I intend to visit New Orleans.[1] I think there is so much of deep interest to be found there in the remnants of old French life. I will stay in the United States until after spring."

YEARNS TO SEE AN AMERICAN SPRING.

"I want to see a spring in this country, and its flowers and growth of plants. Especially do I want to see a spring in California. I did intend to remain here as long as it was interesting to me, but that would be an unreasonable time. I was very anxious to see Washington and meet the intellectual people of the city."

NOT LOOKING AFTER PROPERTY.

"It is stated," said the reporter, "that you will attempt to recover a large estate owned by your uncle in Louisiana."[2]

"My uncle did, I believe, own a good deal of property in Louisiana, but beyond that I know nothing. I am not going to attempt the recovery of any property." This was said with a laugh.

During the interview Mr. Wilde reclined upon the sofa, over which was spread a buffalo robe. One leg was stretched at length upon the robe. His right arm was thrown over the back of the sofa. Upon his left hand he rested his head, when the hand was not making slight gestures.

"Oscar and Archibald," *The Washington Post* (Washington, DC), 21 Jan. 1882, 1[3]

THE TROUBLES AND ALLEGED MISUNDERSTANDING OF THE GENTLEMEN.

Why Mr. Wilde Failed to Appear in Baltimore—The "American's" Report of Mr. Forbes's Lecture Repudiated—Good Friends Both.

1. Wilde lectured in New Orleans on 16 and 26 June 1882.

2. John Kingsbury Elgee (1812–1864). The elder brother of Wilde's mother, as a young man he immigrated to Louisiana, where he made his fortune and purchased a sugar cane plantation. Mendelssohn, 203, records that by the 1860s he owned over 3000 hectares of land and over 500 slaves.

3. Printed simultaneously, excluding the first three paragraphs and with other minor differences, as "Oscar's Side of It," *Baltimore American and Commercial Advertiser* (Baltimore, MD), 21 Jan. 1882, 4 (which is H & S, b20). Quoted in Ellmann, 167/175. This is presumably the interview that Wilde referred to in his letter to Archibald Forbes of 23 January 1882: "Miss Meigs whom I had the honour of meeting last night tells me that some garbled interview appeared in the *Post* which contained certain foolish things supposed to have proceeded from me. I have not seen the paper at all, or I would have written to you at once about it." (CL, 130.)

It was mentioned in yesterday morning's POST that there was likely to be some trouble on account of the impression in Baltimore that Oscar Wilde was to appear in that city at Mr. Forbes's lecture last Thursday night, whereas he came to Washington instead.[1] The Baltimore papers yesterday mentioned the disappointment of the audience at not seeing Mr. Wilde and Mr. Forbes took occasion, according to the *American*,[2] when detailing his introduction to the late Czar of Russia by Gen. Ignatieff,[3] to refer to the apostle of aestheticism as follows:

"When I heard Ignatieff's invitation for me to come into the presence of the Czar," said the lecturer, "I glanced down at my clothing, which I had not changed for a fortnight, and in which I had ridden one hundred and fifty miles. Now, I want it understood that I am a follower—a very humble follower—of the aesthetic ecstasy (loud laughter and applause), but I did not look much like an art object then. I did not have my dogskin knee-breeches with me (laughter and applause), nor my velvet coat (laughter), and my black silk stockings (laughter) were full of holes. Neither was the wild, barren waste of Russia calculated to produce sunflowers and lilies." (Renewed laughter and applause.)

A POST reporter waited yesterday upon Mr. Wilde to hear what he had to say in reply.

"I am heartily pleased to see you," said Mr. Wilde. "I have read the article in the *American* today with reference to myself and I cannot really understand how any such an absurd and shameful jest regarding me could have been published. Now, in the first place, I had never expressed a desire to attend Mr. Forbes's lecture.[4] His subject does not interest me and practically I was not aware until this morning on reading the *American*, that I had been announced to appear at his lecture. Had Mr. Forbes made a personal request, I should, even at the risk of sacrificing personal convenience, been only too happy to have been present. However, as I have read a portion of his lecture in Baltimore, I am extremely pleased that I was not present."

1. "Oscar Wilde Arrives," *The Washington Post* (Washington, DC), 20 Jan. 1882, 4, p. 90.

2. "No Oscar For Us," *Baltimore American and Commercial Advertiser* (Baltimore, MD), 20 Jan. 1882, 4 (quoted p. 88, note 1).

3. Alexander II (1818–1881; reigned from 1855). Forbes was presented to the tsar by Count Nikolay Pavlovich Ignatyev (1832–1908), a Russian statesman, on 23 August 1877, bringing news from the Battle of Shipka Pass, where Russians and Bulgarians had repulsed an attack by Ottoman forces.

4. The *American* reports that on 16 January Colonel Morse sent a telegram to Forbes's Baltimore agent "authorizing the announcement that Mr. Wilde would *positively* appear at Forbes's lecture. [...] This announcement was greeted with great pleasure, and the seats for the lecture were in unexpected demand."

"It appears, however, Mr. Wilde, that your agent had arranged for you to be present, and that you had even gone so far as to accept an invitation to a reception at Mrs. Carroll's."[1]

"As to any arrangements of Col. Morse, I have only to say that I was to have met him at the depot at Philadelphia, instead of which, on my arrival at the depot, I found a telegram from Col. Morse, instructing me to proceed through to Washington. On my arrival in this city, or shortly after, I received another dispatch from him asking me if I could return to Baltimore and attend Mr. Forbes's lecture. I replied that it would be impossible; that I was worn out and tired, and desired and needed rest, and it would be utterly impossible for me to turn around and go back. I also sent a telegram of regrets to Mrs. Carroll."[2]

"Then it appears that the whole affair is the fault of your agent."

"It so appears. Certainly the citizens of Baltimore cannot possibly think for one instant that I would go so far forget myself as to disappoint them [*sic*], and I am greatly distressed that any such construction has been put upon the unfortunate affair. As I stated last night I shall go to Baltimore on Tuesday next, as originally intended."[3]

The reporter here called Mr. Wilde's attention to the statement that he had been invited to a reception by the Wednesday club, but had refused to appear for less than $300.[4]

"That is the most extraordinary thing of the whole affair," he replied. "I have never received an invitation from them, and how can anyone believe the absurd statement that I desired pay. I am only too delighted to visit the club, especially an artistic club, such as the Wednesday Club is said to be. It is quite too absurd to think of such an idea as pay."

"Then you cannot account for these statements?"

"Not at all. I do not care to associate with Mr. Forbes. I have never met him but twice. Our views are wide apart. I have no interest in him, and if it amuses him to caricature me in the manner which he did last night, well and good. It may serve a purpose, and judging from the fact, as stated, that his audience came to see me, it is answering one very good purpose. It is advertising Mr. Forbes at my expense."

1. The Carrolls were a prominent Maryland family. The *American* identifies the would-be hostess as "Mrs. Charles Carroll", presumably Caroline V. Carroll née Thompson (1830–?), the wife of Charles Carroll VI (1828–1895).

2. The *American*: "Mr. Wilde, on his arrival in Washington, telegraphed Mr. and Mrs. Carroll, through his New York agent, that he was ill, and regretted exceedingly having to absent himself from the reception last night. He added that he would write and explain himself later."

3. Wilde did travel to Baltimore on Tuesday 24 January.

4. See, p. 88, note 1.

Mr. Wilde will accept the hospitalities of Miss Sherwood during his stay in Baltimore.[1] He called yesterday afternoon upon Miss Robinson, and later on Senator Bayard, of Delaware, to which he had letters of introduction.[2]

Last evening he received a letter from Mr. Forbes, in which the latter pronounces as false the statement which appeared in yesterday's Baltimore *American* that there had been any "miff" between him and Mr. Wilde, and adds further that the relations between them are most cordial, and the affair is manufactured out of whole cloth.

"Wilde and Forbes," *The New York Herald* (New York, NY), 21 Jan. 1882, 3[3]

Grievous Charges of Discourtesy Against the Poet.

ABSURD REPORT OF A BALTIMORE PERSON.

An Indignant Protest and Denial from the Aesthete.

PLEASANT READING FOR AMERICANS.

What the War Correspondent Had to Do with It and What He Said.

(FROM OUR REGULAR CORRESPONDENT)

WASHINGTON, Jan. 20, 1882.

Some of the Baltimore papers today charge Mr. Oscar Wilde with having broken faith with the Baltimore public in not appearing according to advertisement on the stage when Mr. Archibald Forbes lectured in that city last evening. A graver charge is that he had snubbed Baltimore society by rudely neglecting to

1. Miss Sherwood may be related to the Mrs Robert H. Sherwood who entertained Wilde at her home at 107 Charles Street Avenue on the evening of 24 January ("Oscar Wilde in Baltimore," *The Sun* (Baltimore, MD), 25 Jan. 1882, 4, pp. 111–12). Another report claims that Miss Sherwood entertained Wilde at her Oak Street residence on the evening of 24 January ("Local Miscellany," *Baltimore American and Commercial Advertiser* (Baltimore, MD), 25 Jan. 1882, 4, p. 110). Mrs Sherwood appears to have been a wealthy widow, active in Baltimore society until the early 1900s.

2. Thomas F. Bayard (1828–1898) served as Democratic senator of Delaware from 1869 to 1885. Wilde told another interviewer that Bayard was "charming" ("Oscar Wilde in Baltimore," *The Sun* (Baltimore, MD), 25 Jan. 1882, 4, p. 111).

3. H & S, b19. Reprinted in H & S, 35–8. Excerpted in "Wilde and Forbes," *The Gazette* (Montreal, QC), 24 Jan. 1882, 7. Quoted in "Utterly Gross," *Cincinnati Enquirer* (Cincinnati, OH), 21 Jan. 1882, 1; OWDA, 79–80, 82; and Sturgis, 227/218, 233/224. Referenced in Sturgis, 220/211.

appear at a reception arranged for his entertainment last evening at the residence of Mrs. Charles Carroll, of that city, a disappointment which it is asserted caused the hostess much embarrassment. Another count in the Baltimore indictment against Mr. Wilde is that the Wednesday Club, of Baltimore, invited him to an entertainment and were politely informed that he charged $300 for his appearance at receptions not held in private houses.[1] It was represented that Mr. Wilde came from Philadelphia to Baltimore with Mr. Forbes and had a miff with Forbes on the train, so instead of stopping he came on to Washington. Mr. Wilde and Mr. Forbes are both lecturing under the management of Mr. D'Oyly Carte. A HERALD reporter found Mr. Oscar Wilde in all the glory of dressing gown, knee breeches and slippers in his parlor at the Arlington this evening. He was just sitting down to a repast of oysters, to what is known as "half a dozen raw" in this unaesthetic capital. Three colored waiters stood about his little table to hand him his wine and attend to his other wants.

"Pray be seated," he said, rising from his seat when the HERALD reporter was ushered in. Mr. Wilde then resumed his own chair and proceeded to the disposition of the oysters before him, pausing occasionally to press a dainty napkin to his lips. The reporter called his attention to the publication in a Baltimore paper charging him with having broken faith with the Baltimore public.

"This is an invention," he said, "an invention of someone in that city. It is shameful, disgraceful. I heard much about the character of American journalism in England. If you expect English gentlemen to come to your country, especially gentlemen of letters and art, you must improve the character of your journalism. I do not intend to come to this country again until this thing is changed. I received a letter from Mr. Forbes," said Mr. Wilde, rising and getting a letter from his writing table. He ran over the contents of the letter hastily and continued:—"It is a private letter and, of course, it would not be proper for me to give it for publication. You can say that I have received a letter from Mr. Forbes saying that he regrets that such insinuations have been made against me, and he assures me that he was not the author of them. I have only a slight acquaintance with Mr. Forbes."

"Was it true," asked the reporter, "that you were to attend the lecture at Baltimore?"

"The other day Mr. Carte asked me if I would not like to hear Mr. Forbes lecture. I told him that I had read some of his books; I was not particularly interested in the subject but I would go. It was arranged then that Mr. Carte or Mr. Morse would meet me in Philadelphia. Neither of these gentlemen could come with me, however, and Mr. Carte sent his clerk to the depot to tell me to go right on to Washington, as I am to lecture here Monday. Mr. Forbes took the train at

1. See p. 88, note 1.

Philadelphia too and we rode in the same car. He introduced me to two ladies whom he had with him. There was no difference between us at all. I came right on to Washington. Of course I could not think of stopping in Baltimore alone. I am a perfect stranger and could not go to any place like that unless someone was with mc."

BALTIMORE STORIES DENIED.

"It is said," pursued the reporter, "that the Baltimoreans are particularly incensed against you on account of your not attending a social entertainment to which you were invited."

"After I arrived here," replied Mr. Wilde, "I received a despatch from Mr. Morse asking me if I could not return to Baltimore and attend this reception. I replied that it was impossible. I had travelled all day, was worn out and it was utterly absurd to think of returning to Baltimore then. I presume Mr. Morse received some urgent telegrams and thought that he would telegraph me. I knew of this reception, but was told by Mr. Carte to come right through to Washington. Another thing in that publication is that some artistic club had tendered me a reception, and that I replied that I did not appear at evening entertainments unless I was paid for it. I never heard of this club before. As to the rest it is too gross to think of. When there are so many interesting truths why is it that these untruths should be published?"

CHARMED WITH NEW YORK.

"I am glad this thing did not come from New York. I was quite charmed with New York and with its men and beautiful women. The city had a cosmopolitan air, quite like Paris or Vienna. In England the papers would never publish such things. Since the publication of my poems few personalities appear against me. When a man has achieved a work they attack his work. There may be some satire, some announcement that Mr. Oscar Wilde wore a blue necktie or a red necktie or something else that will revolutionize the world, but that is all. I have heard before I came here," continued Mr. Wilde, "how journals here ridiculed the art movement in England."

QUITE TOO DISGRACEFUL.

"I did not expect such vile things. It is quite too disgraceful. If you expect to have art in this country you must first have good morals to back it. There are so many things worth thinking of and worth talking of that one hasn't time for such things. If I could live 10,000 years—and my poems may get me something like immortality—if I could live 10,000 years I might find time to write a letter to this editor and correct this thing.[1] I will go to Baltimore to lecture next Tuesday and I will tell them about art if they choose to listen to me, but I will say nothing about this."[2]

WHAT MR. FORBES SAID.

Mr. Archibald Forbes lectured here tonight. A HERALD reporter interviewed him at the Ebbitt House while he was enjoying his after dinner cigar.[3] Mr. Forbes was very pleasant in his discourse, but appeared to be blissfully ignorant of any delinquency on Mr. Wilde's part or any misunderstanding that had occurred between them. The reporter introduced the topic by calling attention to a publication intimating that Mr. Wilde and Mr. Forbes had had a "miff" on the train, which led to their parting company instead of remaining together in Baltimore.

"Miff! Miff!" said Mr. Forbes, in a quizzical manner, "I do not know the meaning of the word. It is a transatlantic word."[4]

The reporter translated the expression into terms more intelligible to Mr. Forbes, whereupon that gentleman replied:—

"Nothing of the kind occurred. I am friendly with Mr. Wilde, though my acquaintance with him is slight. I met him at the depot in Philadelphia when we were coming here. As I was a more experienced traveller than he I asked him if I could do anything for him. In that way we happened to get in the same car and sat together part of the time. I talked with him occasionally. I had two ladies under my care, and before arriving at Baltimore I introduced them to him. He took my seat between the two ladies and talked with them until they got out at Baltimore with me. At the depot in Baltimore a young gentleman, who, I understand, was a reporter, asked me where Mr. Wilde was, and I told him he was on the

1. A letter from Wilde was published in *The Sun* (Baltimore, MD), 24 Jan. 1882, 6. The letter is not included in CL.

> *Messrs. A. S. Abell & Co.*—Dear Sirs: America should be a country without prejudice, so I will pray you to permit me to say that my failing to visit your city was due entirely and absolutely to some misunderstanding on the part of a messenger from my manager's office, who met me in Philadelphia with instructions to proceed direct to Washington, and not stop at Baltimore, as I had hoped to do. Since my arrival in America I have received in each city that courtesy for which your country is famous, and I would not wish it to be thought that I could be willingly capable of any such unpardonable rudeness as your papers would seem seriously to charge me with. I remain, your obedient servant, OSCAR WILDE.
>
> Washington, D. C., Jan. 23. 1882.

2. Wilde arrived in Baltimore on Tuesday 24 January and lectured there on 26 January. While there he referred to the affair in an interview: "Oscar Wilde in Baltimore," *The Sun* (Baltimore, MD), 25 Jan. 1882, 4, p. 111.

3. Ebbitt House was a prestigious hotel in Washington DC, at this time known informally as "Army and Navy Headquarters" because of the number of military officers who stayed there.

4. "Miff" had been used to describe a petty quarrel since the seventeenth-century; in the nineteenth the word was in use on both sides of the Atlantic (OED).

train and gone on. He asked me where he had gone, and that I could not answer, as I did not know. I understand he came to this city."

AN ACCIDENTAL MEETING.

"Then," said the reporter, "you did not make your journey here together by any previous arrangement?"

"No, our meeting at the depot was entirely casual."

"What was the arrangement by which Mr. Wilde was to appear at your lecture and sit on the platform?"

"No one sat on the stage with me except Mayor Latrobe, the mayor of Baltimore.[1] I knew of no other arrangement. Mr. Carte is my agent as well as Mr. Wilde's. What arrangement he may have made I do not know. I have not seen Mr. Carte for a week."

NOT SEEKING A BOOM.

The reporter called the attention of Mr. Forbes to a published statement that the cause of the alleged "miff" between them was a difference of opinion as to which of the two was to be the real attraction at the Baltimore lecture. Mr. Forbes denied this with a laugh. "I got the fee for the lecture," he said. "What do I care for attraction in America? This lecture tonight will be almost my last lecture. I do not care to get up a boom now. I shall leave the country soon for Australia."

WHAT HE SAID OF AESTHETICS.

"There was a portion of your lecture as delivered in Baltimore last evening," said the reporter, "which was construed as arising from some ill feeling on your part toward Mr. Wilde."

"I know what you mean," said Mr. Forbes. "I have the words by memory and will repeat them. It is in my description of my visit to the Czar. I said, 'I glanced down at my clothing, which I had not changed for a fortnight, and in which I had ridden 150 miles. Now I wish it understood that I am a follower, an humble follower, of the aesthetic ecstasy, but I did not look much like an art object then. I did not have my dogskin knee breeches with me, nor my velvet coat, and my black silk stockings were full of holes. Neither was the wild, barren waste of Bulgaria congenial to the growth of sunflowers and lilies.' That was all there was to it. I would have said it if Mr. Wilde had been there. I have been saying it in my lectures for the last week, and you will hear me say it tonight if you come to my lecture. It is only intended to get a laugh. A man will do anything to get a laugh in a lecture. I told Mr. Wilde, after he lectured in New York, that I was going to men-

1. Ferdinand Claiborne Latrobe (1833–1911) served as Mayor of Baltimore seven times. His most recent term had ended on 7 November 1881; he would be re-elected on 24 October 1883.

tion his knee breeches. There was no ill feeling about it. I did not say it to injure him. If I should drop that part of my lecture now it might look as though I inserted it purposely as an attack on him. I would not wound any man that way, especially a countryman of mine. You must remember what I say. I am friendly with Mr. Wilde. I have a slight acquaintance with him—enough, I thought, to justify me in presenting to him two ladies who desired his acquaintance. We met casually and travelled together without any rupture in our friendly relations, and any arrangement by which he was to stop at Baltimore and appear at my lecture I knew nothing about. I thank you," he said as the HERALD reporter was taking leave of him, "for calling upon me, as I desire no misconstruction to be placed on my words and acts."

"Not a Battle, a Boom," *The New York World, Semi-Weekly Edition* (New York, NY), 24 Jan. 1882, 2

How Oscar Wilde Fleeing from a Lecture Lost a Reception

BALTIMORE, January, 20.—It is all an [?'oax] and an 'umbug about the deadly duel of the military with the aesthetic lion of the hour. They parted at the depot here (we say depot because they say station in Philadelphia) on the best of terms, each no doubt glad to have a city to himself. Mr. Wilde was expected to attend a supper at Mrs. Carroll's, after Mr. Forbes's lecture, but late in the evening came a telegram from Washington that he had been carried through and was really too unwell to return. He is expected here on Tuesday next.

WHAT MR. FORBES SAYS.

WASHINGTON, January 20.—Both Mr. Oscar Wilde and Mr. Archibald Forbes, who are here, say that they cannot imagine how the story could have started that they had quarrelled yesterday on the train from Philadelphia to Baltimore. When Mr. Forbes was found this evening at the Ebbitt House he was just parting from a reporter who, he said, had given him the first intimation that any canard as to trouble between Mr. Wilde and himself was afloat.[1] He said that there was absolutely no foundation for it. He has but a slight acquaintance with Mr. Wilde, having met him in England and again in New York. At Philadelphia, in the Union Depot, they had some casual conversation, and later, as Mr. Wilde is a new traveller in this country, Mr. Forbes went to him and offered to be of any service as to tickets. They travelled in the same drawing-room car, sitting near each other, and

1. Presumably the author of "Wilde and Forbes," *The New York Herald* (New York, NY), 21 Jan. 1882, 3, pp. 99–104.

occasionally conversing. Some little distance from Baltimore Mr. Forbes introduced Mr. Wilde to two ladies of his acquaintance, who were in the same car, and the party continued in conversation until Baltimore was reached. As the train ran into the depot Mr. Wilde mentioned that he was not going to stop at Baltimore, but going on, and Mr. Forbes and he shook hands, the latter wishing the former success. Outside the Baltimore depot a reporter, addressing Mr. Forbes, asked whether Mr. Wilde was in the train. That gentleman replied in the affirmative. The reporter asked whether Mr. Wilde was alighting at Baltimore. Mr. Forbes said no, that Mr. Wilde had told him he was going on. The reporter proceeded to say that Mr. Wilde was expected at Baltimore, and said something about a reception having been arranged for him, a matter which did not concern Mr. Forbes in the least, so he simply replied that he knew nothing about anything of the sort, but that Mr. Wilde was in the train and was continuing his journey. So far from being on bad terms with Mr. Wilde, Mr. Forbes said this evening that he had called upon Mr. Wilde this afternoon at the Arlington.

MR. WILDE'S STATEMENT.

Mr. Wilde's account of the alleged blood-curdling railroad encounter was quite as disillusioning as had been Mr. Forbes's. "The enterprise of American newspapers," he said, laughing lightly, "is astonishing in this case. It passes my comprehension. I have no idea how such a story could have started. Here is a letter that Mr. Forbes has sent over, assuring me that the origin of the story can be no more enigmatical to me than it is to him. I was certain of that without his assurance. He says that the newspaper statement that he alluded unpleasantly to me last night in his lecture is of the same character as that of the quarrel, and that whatever he may have said was in a pleasant vein, incapable of a harsh construction, being that the wardrobe of the Sultan was not so extensive as mine, or some pleasantry of that kind. Now, as to the story about myself. I had no idea of attending Mr. Forbes's lecture. I have read his book and never supposed I should get any new information by hearing him lecture. The matter of the reception by the Wednesday Club is utterly without foundation. The idea of my receiving money to accept their hospitality is too gross to talk about. Not a word have I heard from the Wednesday Club about a reception. Had they offered me one, I should have considered it an honor, and it would have given me pleasure to accept it if I was at liberty to do so. The private reception at Mrs. Carroll's I had expected to attend. I supposed Mr. Carte or Mr. Morse would accompany me from Philadelphia to Baltimore for that purpose, but at Philadelphia, just before taking the train, I received word from Mr. Carte that I had better go right on to Washington. That was after I had made all my arrangements to stop at Baltimore, and I was put to the trouble of changing my tickets, and after all had to leave a servant at Baltimore to look after my trunks and bring them on here. After reaching here a telegram came for me from Mr. Morse, at about [?6].30,[1] asking if I could not go over to the reception at Baltimore. I had been travelling all the afternoon and receiving callers after my arrival, and I was not only very weary but unwell, so I replied to Mr. Morse that I was too tired and that it would be impossible for me to go to Baltimore."

Mr. Wilde spent most of the day at his hotel, but this afternoon he drove out and saw the Department buildings and the Capitol besides making a few calls. He expressed his admiration of the Capitol, which suited agreeably his ideas of art. The smooth, wide streets of Washington and the general appearance of cleanliness also struck him favorably. His only grievance against this country, and that is one that he seems to bear lightly, is that he has had no time for rest since his arrival. Cards have poured in upon him almost continuously since his arrival here. His lecture here will be given on Monday night.

The Remorse of Morse.

Mr. Morse, who is associated with Mr. D'Oyly Carte in the management of the latter's enterprise and who has made nearly all the arrangements and dates for Mr. Oscar Wilde's lectures said yesterday that he left Mr. Wilde in Philadelphia last Tuesday morning. He was to have accompanied Mr. Wilde throughout his tour, but owing to a call for Mr. Carte to leave this city he was obliged to send out a representative to accompany Mr. Wilde. The despatches in the papers yesterday regarding a difficulty between Mr. Forbes and Mr. Wilde were in his opinion without foundation. "Mr. Forbes and Mr. Wilde, from what I know, are the best of friends," said Mr. Morse, "and I am informed by my agent that Mr. Wilde did not go to Baltimore to hear Mr. Forbes lecture, because he was physically unable to do so. Since his arrival in this country Mr. Wilde has had but little rest and was obliged to disappoint himself and the ladies and gentlemen of Baltimore who had arranged to receive him. I have no doubt he was most anxious to hear Mr. Forbes lecture." (It will be seen from Mr. Wilde's statement that nobody but Mr. Morse is really responsible for Mr. Wilde's failure to attend the reception prepared for him at Baltimore. Also, that Mr. Wilde conscientiously admits that he wouldn't have cared to attend his friend Mr. Forbes's lecture had he alighted at Baltimore.—WORLD.)

1. The number is unclear in the copy text and may be an 8.

"Our Aesthetic Visitor," *The Washington Post* (Washington, DC), 22 Jan. 1882, 1

His Evening Costume—How He Passed His Time Yesterday.

At the reception given by Dr. Loring, Superintendent of the Agricultural Department, and Mrs. Loring, on Friday evening,[1] Mr. Wilde was elaborately attired in a black frock coat, knee breeches, black silk stockings, Oxford ties, elaborately embroidered white vest and ruffled shirt, on which sparkled a solitaire diamond of great magnitude; quality unknown. The ladies craved an introduction, and the aesthetic hero of the evening was of a most accommodating nature. Among the other guests present were Assistant Secretary of State Davis, Senators Hill, of Colorado; Sherman and Hale, with their wives, and Representative Robeson and wife. The aesthete was introduced to the New Jersey Stalwart.[2]

Yesterday Mr. Wilde was busily engaged in doing the lions of Washington. At an early hour he secured a coupe and spent the entire day in inspecting the various points of interest about the city. From his personal comments made to a representative of THE POST, it can be authoritatively asserted that the angelican aesthete was much impressed with Washington and its surroundings. It is related at the Arlington that Mr. Wilde is what may be termed a healthy feeder. His orders for meals embrace such substantials as porter-house steak, mutton chops, etc, and in the bibulous line he sticks close to *Pommery sec* and Bass's ale.[3] Last night Mr. Wilde called on ex-Secretary Blaine with a letter of introduction from Mr. Archibald Forbes, and according to his own statement spent a most enjoyable evening.[4] Today it is expected he will attend St. John's church in the forenoon, and utilize the remainder of the day in a pedestrian tour through the West

1. George Bailey Loring (1817–1891) served as Commissioner of Agriculture from 1881 to 1885. He is not to be confused with Judge Edward Greely Loring (1802–1890), who, along with his wife, hosted a reception for Wilde on 22 January. Friday was 20 January.

2. Nathanial Peter Hill (1832–1900) served as a Republican Senator from Colorado from 1879 to 1885. "Sherman" is presumably John Sherman (1823–1900), Republican Senator from Ohio from 1881 to 1897; "Hale" is presumably Eugene Hale (1836–1918), Republican Senator from Maine from 1881 to 1911. George Maxwell Robeson (1829–1897) served as a Republican member of the House of Representatives from New Jersey's 1st district from 1879 to 1883. The Stalwarts, with which Robeson was affiliated, were a faction of the Republican Party during the 1870s and 1880s. They opposed the so-called Half-Breeds, who advocated for civil service reform.

3. Descriptions of Wilde's meals are a common feature of his 1882 interviews. See "Utterly Utter," *St. Louis Post-Dispatch* (St. Louis, MO), 25 Feb. 1882, 4, p. 208, note 1.

4. James Gillespie Blaine (1830–1893) was a Republican politician and leader of the Half-Breed faction. He served as Secretary of State twice: in 1881 and again from 1889 to 1892. Wilde told another interviewer that Blaine was "brilliant" ("Oscar Wilde in Baltimore," *The Sun* (Baltimore, MD), 25 Jan. 1882, 4, p. 111).

End, the Elizabethan architecture of that section of the city having attracted his curiosity. He will possibly end up the day with a visit to the Soldiers' Home.

"The Aesthete at Washington," *Springfield Daily Republican* (Springfield, MA), 30 Jan. 1882, 4–5[1]

A RECEPTION AT MRS BURNETT'S.

At Which Oscar Wilde Appeared in Character—How the Apostle of the Beautiful Conducts Himself in Society.

Correspondence of The Republican.

WASHINGTON, D. C., January 21, 1882.

✂ *A report of the 21 January meeting of the Literary Club in the home of Frances Hodgson Burnett, at which Wilde was present.*[2]

This afternoon a newspaper reporter for the "Critic" determined to interview Mr Wilde. He was refused, but planting himself on his rights, persevered until he succeeded. He found the aesthete sitting behind a high table dressed in a crimson silk dressing-gown turned back from his bosom, and up from his hands and his long locks displayed in such low folds that the boy, thinking this a woman, looked round for the man he had come to see. On the table was a fragrant bunch of hot-house flowers and a basket of fruit carefully arranged, the boy thought, to bring out the sage greens and old-golds of nature herself.[3] As he went on to talk, Mr Wilde threw himself down on the sofa, in his favorite attitude, with his arms over his head. At last a thought seemed to strike him. "How old are you?" said he to the lad. "Not 16," was the reply. "H'm, h'm. In England you would be getting flogged for not knowing your Latin, and here you are starting out in the world for yourself." Instead of interviewing the poet, the reporter soon found himself interviewed, until he put an end to it by asking some summary questions, to which

1. Excerpted in "Scraps," *The Indianapolis News* (Indianapolis, IN), 2 Feb. 1882, 2. Although the interview is attributed to a reporter for the "Critic", it was not printed in *The Evening Critic* (Washington, DC). This argues against its authenticity. However, it is corroborated by Wilde's account of a similar meeting with a sixteen year old reporter before he attended a dinner party in Washington: "Oscar Wilde," *The Sunday Herald* (Boston, MA), 29 Jan. 1882, 7, p. 120; "Utterly Utter," *St. Louis Post-Dispatch* (St. Louis, MO), 25 Feb. 1882, 4, pp. 205–6.

2. Frances Hodgson Burnett (1849–1924) was an English-American author whose best-known works are *Little Lord Fauntleroy* (1885–1886) and *The Secret Garden* (1911). Her first novel, *That Lass o' Lowrie's*, was published in 1877. See also "The Aesthete Entertained," *The Washington Post* (Washington, DC), 23 Jan. 1882, 4, p. 703.

3. Sage green and old gold were hues favoured by, or believed to be favoured by, aesthetes.

the stranger replied by the following heresies: Washington is not a handsome city. It has only one beautiful thing—the view from the base of the capitol. The government had made a mess of it by building in Greek fashion and omitting Greek decoration.[1] No! the streets were not fine, they were too broad and too straight! Streets should be winding and narrow, full of surprises, and the windows on the opposite sides should confront each other. Philadelphia was better than Washington!

✂ *A paragraph about the actor Lawrence Barrett's visit to Washington.*

"Local Miscellany," *Baltimore American and Commercial Advertiser* (Baltimore, MD), 25 Jan. 1882, 4[2]

✂ *Several paragraphs that are unrelated to Wilde.*

Mr. Wilde Finally Stops in Baltimore.—Oscar Wilde arrived at the Mount Vernon Hotel yesterday afternoon, where he was called upon by a representative of *The American*. Mr. Wilde is not as handsome a man as his photograph represents him to be. His hair is fully as long as in the photograph, and he holds his head a little to one side, inclining towards his left shoulder. He was attired in a long bottle-green cloth sack overcoat, with an enormous fur collar, which came down to his shoulder-blades. He wore a pair of brown trousers and a stiff felt hat, the counterpart of those worn by the Baltimore police force. His feet are large, and his gait not particularly elegant.[3] Referring to the unpleasant feeling which had been created by his failure to remain over in Baltimore on his way to Washington, Mr. Wilde said he regretted that, through misinformation, the press had been led to place a wrong construction upon his action, and it was his earnest desire that no further reference be made to the matter which, he thought, had been already as fully explained as it was possible it could be. Mr. Wilde speaks with a very slight brogue, and his intonation is that of an English gentleman. His face is clean-shaven, and his long hair and his habit of carrying his head at an angle toward his left shoulder gives him a simpering appearance. When he speaks, a faint, aesthetic smile covers his face, adding to this effect. His language indicates an extraordinary degree of intelligence—much more so that his facial expression. To sum up, Mr. Wilde is in appearance one of those men whom a lackadaisical school girl would call "too sweet to live." Last evening Mr. Wilde

1. See also "Oscar Wilde," *The Sunday Herald* (Boston, MA), 29 Jan. 1882, 7, p. 123.
2. I am grateful to John Cooper for identifying this article.
3. Wilde's friend Robert Baldwin Ross (1869–1918), a Canadian journalist and art critic, wrote of Wilde's "odd elephantine gait which I have never seen in anyone else" (CL, 842).

was entertained by Miss Sherwood and a literary circle at her residence on oak street. About nine o'clock he went to Holliday Street Theatre, and witnessed Lawrence Barrett's performance of Yorick's Love.[1] He sat in a proscenium box.

✂ *Several paragraphs that are unrelated to Wilde.*

"Oscar Wilde in Baltimore," *The Sun* (Baltimore, MD), 25 Jan. 1882, 4

Oscar Wilde in Baltimore—He Attends a Reception and the Theatre.—

Mr. Oscar Wilde, the esthete, arrived in Baltimore yesterday afternoon from Washington, registered at the Mount Vernon Hotel, attended a tea party at 5 o'clock at the residence of Mrs. Robert H. Sherwood, on Charles street avenue, Baltimore county, and at night went to the Holliday Street Theatre to see Mr. Lawrence Barrett play "Yorick's Love." Mr. Wilde occupied a box at the theatre, and attracted a great deal of curious attention. He is of medium height, stoops in the shoulders, has a slender figure and is graceful in movement. His head is rather large, of good shape and is covered with a luxuriant growth of straight brown hair, which is parted in the middle and drops with trained negligence on his shoulders. His face is effeminate. His forehead is high and narrow, his eyes pale blue, his nose prominent, his lips thick and his teeth large and uneven. He was dressed yesterday in a brown velvet, square-cut coat, brown velvet waistcoat and dark, tight-fitting pantaloons. Around his neck he wore a high white collar, around which was a dark, greenish-looking neck-cloth, tied artistically and drooping on his waistcoat gracefully. From his coat-pocket protruded a handkerchief of pretty much the same color as the necktie. His feet are shapely, and his shoes have sharp points. In manner Mr. Wilde is agreeable and polished, and when he becomes animated his words roll smoothly off his tongue, and his whole appearance changes, his face ridding itself of an uninteresting look and becoming genial and pleasant. He is not handsome by any means.

All modern cities, he said, referring to his travels in this country, are ugly, and New York is no exception to the rule. There are, he says, so many advertise-

1. Lawrence Barrett (1838–1891) was an American actor. In 1877 he created the eponymous role in *Yorick's Love,* a play adapted by William Dean Howells (1837–1920), the American novelist, from the 1867 Spanish original, *Un drama Nuevo,* by Manuel Tamayo y Baus. *The New York Times* declared the play "a constant strain upon the sympathies" of the audience, though Mark Twain wrote to Howells that the "magnificence of it is beyond praise". Wilde later spoke positively of Barrett's performance (see "Oscar Wilde," *The Sunday Herald* (Boston, MA), 29 Jan. 1882, 7, p. 126). In 1891 Barrett played the title role in *Guido Ferranti* (Wilde's *The Duchess of Padua*).

ments about the streets and houses that all traces of beauty, if there be any, are invisible. Besides, the continual bustle and confusion made by the railroads so upsets repose that it is almost impossible to appreciate anything that is seen. Philadelphia, he says, has a Puritanical look given to it by long rows of red brick buildings and white shutters, and is more pleasing to a stranger of his tastes than New York. Washington, he says, can make some pretension to architectural beauty in a few of its dwellings. Among the public men he met in Washington were Hon. Jas. G. Blaine, Senator Bayard and Gen. McClellan.[1] The first mentioned he thought brilliant, the second charming, and the third modest and exceedingly pleasant.

Of the ladies of America Mr. Wilde says that most of them are pretty, but that he has not see more than four or five who were truly beautiful. The Baltimore ladies, he says, are prettier than any others that he has yet seen. Speaking of American journalism, he said that if an American man of letters had gone to England and been written up there as he has been described by the newspapers in this country, the people of England would have become thoroughly aroused and expressed their indignation. English journalism is far ahead of American journalism in respectability, if not in news gathering. He repeated the explanation, heretofore published in THE SUN, relative to his non-appearance in Baltimore last week. He had not been invited to the reception, he said, except through his agent, but that he fully intended to come anyhow until instructed not to stop in Baltimore, but to go on to Washington. The instructions were owing to a misapprehension on the part of the messenger who delivered them. While speaking Mr. Wilde allows his animation to gradually slip away from him, and when he reaches a period he appears to be exhausted, and assumes postures that bring vividly to mind Gilbert's Bunthorne. Indeed, it is impossible to appreciate the depth and truth of Mr. Gilbert's satire without seeing the object of it.

The ladies whom Mr. Wilde met at Mrs. Sherwood's tea party express themselves as having been charmed with his manners but disappointed with his attire, as they had expected to see him in dress coat, knee-breeches and silk stockings, whereas he wore the clothes described above. Several gentlemen who were present at the party say that they had looked forward to meeting a brilliant conversationalist, but that in their opinion Mr. Wilde is a very commonplace young man indeed, with an outwarded show as picturesque as Bunthorne's and just about as easily seen through.[2] The tea party was quite a success, the dressing of many of

1. George Brinton McClellan (1826–1885) led the Union army in the Peninsula Campaign in southeastern Virginia and served as the Democratic Governor of New Jersey from 1878 to 1881.

2. "Commonplace": an allusion to *Patience.* See p. 32, note 1.

the ladies being rich and artistic.[1] Mrs. Sherwood was assisted at the reception by her daughters and the Misses Woods and Miss Goodwin, of Maine.

✂ *A list of guests at the reception.*

Today Mr. Wilde will visit the Johns Hopkins University, the Peabody Institute,[2] and other places of interest in the city.

"Local Miscellany," *Baltimore American and Commercial Advertiser* (Baltimore, MD), 26 Jan. 1882, 4[3]

✂ *Several paragraphs that are unrelated to Wilde.*

Mr. Wilde's Stay in Baltimore—He Goes to the Wednesday Club.—Mr. Oscar Wilde, the aesthete, who is now pretty well known to the American public, spent yesterday in making the acquaintance of Baltimoreans and taking a look at the city. His headquarters are at the Mount Vernon Hotel. About 2 o'clock he visited the Johns Hopkins University, where he met Professor Cayley, the English mathematician now lecturing at the university and an old acquaintance,[4] Professors Martin and Murray, and others connected with the institution, who extended to him every courtesy in their power. From the University Mr. Wilde returned to the Mount Vernon, and there remained until 6 o'clock, when, by invitation of Mr. Benjamin F. Horwitz, he dined with that gentleman at his residence on Cathedral street.[5] Mr. Horwitz had also invited Judge Gilmor, ex Mayor Latrobe, Mr. James Hodges, Mr. Richard J. Gittings, Mr. Robert V. McKim of New York, Dr. Herman Groesbeck, Dr. Delano Fitzgerald and Mr. Wm. Reed to meet Mr. Wilde, all of whom were present.

Mr. Wilde, who was called upon by an *American* reporter at his hotel yesterday afternoon, expressed his extreme regret that an impression had gotten

1. "Artistic" in the sense of being of aesthetic rather than conventional fashion. The differences between the two styles were recorded for posterity by William Powell Frith (1819–1909) in his painting *A Private View at the Royal Academy, 1881* (1883).

2. The Peabody Institute is a music and dance conservatory affiliated with the Johns Hopkins University. Its library, with its five stacked tiers fronted by Corinthian columns and overlooking a central hall, was built in 1877–1878.

3. H & S, b23.

4. Arthur Cayley (1821–1895) was an English mathematician. His name is given here as "Cayler". He spent six months in Baltimore in 1882, visiting his friend and fellow mathematician James Joseph Sylvester. It is unclear how Wilde would have been acquainted with Cayley, who since 1863 had held a chair at Cambridge University.

5. Benjamin F. Horwitz (c. 1831–1899) was a lawyer. He resided at 18 Cathedral Street, presumably with the wife and three children listed in the 1880 census.

abroad concerning himself and the Wednesday Club of this city, and expressed his desire that such impression might be removed. He said there was no word of truth in the statement that he had intimated he could not attend receptions at other than private houses without pay.[1] Mr. Benjamin F. Horwitz, whom the re-reporter saw after leaving Mr. Wilde, also said there must be some mistake in the matter, and showed the reporter an invitation from the Wednesday Club to Mr. Wilde, issued yesterday at Mr. Horwitz' solicitation, to attend the soiree at the club last night. This, Mr. Horwitz said, was cheerfully granted. "I do not know," said Mr. Horwitz, "whether Mr. Wilde will accept or not, as he has not yet received the invitation." Mr. Wilde did accept the invitation, and visited the club, where he was very kindly received. Mr. Wilde, during a conversation at the hotel, said he had not had much opportunity for observation since his arrival in Baltimore, but, from what he had seen, was of the opinion that there was very little that was beautiful in the architecture. The modern structures compared favorably with those of other cities he had visited in America. He said that he had been long enough in Baltimore to notice that its ladies were among the most beautiful he had seen. Everything points to a large audience at the Academy tonight to listen to Mr. Wilde's lecture. To avoid confusion, it is announced that tickets for the lecture, which will be given in the main auditorium, will be sold at McCaffrey's today, as well as at the box office at the Academy in the evening.

✂ *Several paragraphs that are unrelated to Wilde.*

"Oscar Wilde," *The Argus* (Albany, NY), 28 Jan. 1882, 8[2]

The Disciple of Aestheticism at Music Hall Last Night—His Appearance and Manner—The Lecture—A Brief Interview with Him.

✂ *An account and transcript of Wilde's lecture in Albany.*

AN INTERVIEW WITH THE POET.

An Argus reporter met Mr. Wilde after the lecture and found him to be a bright and sprightly young man, showing no signs of the languid demeanor so

1. Wilde may have been referring to this interview when he later told a reporter that, while in Baltimore, he had sent for the author of the article that was printed in the *American* on the 20th and asked him what he was paid for it ("Utterly Utter," *St. Louis Post-Dispatch* (St. Louis, MO), 25 Feb. 1882, 4, p. 206).
2. H & S, b24. Reprinted in H & S, 38. Quoted in OWDA, 103; and Hyde, 61.

noticeable upon the stage. He was seated at a desk writing autographs for a number of young ladies.

"I hope," said he, "that I am obliging beautiful young ladies, for I make it a point to grant my autograph to no others."

In answer to an inquiry as to how he liked America, the poet said: "I really have seen almost nothing of your country. As I came up from New York this afternoon, I caught occasional glimpses of the river and I was charmed with its beauties. The blue hills in the distance, the forests still green in places, and the strange, regular outlines of the Palisades formed a most pleasing picture. I am always delighted to study human nature, and I feel much richer by my contact with so many new phases of character. I think that the theories I have propounded in my lecture will be adopted to some extent in America, for your countrymen are not opposed to revolutionary ideas, and I believe truth will force its way to conviction."

Mr. Wilde complained that he could obtain no cigarettes to suit him in this country. "I smoke only Turkish tobacco, and that you do not have here. I have used up all I brought with me, and am now quite lost for a further supply."

A small and select reception was given to the poet at the conclusion of his lecture, at the Windsor. Mr. Wilde reached here from Baltimore at 4:30 yesterday afternoon and stopped at the Delavan until two o'clock this morning when he left for Boston.[1]

"Oscar Wilde in Boston," *Daily Evening Traveller* (Boston, MA), 28 Jan. 1882[2]

A Chat with the Apostle of Aestheticism.

His Dissatisfaction with the American Press.

The Object of Art and the Artistic Temperament.

An Injunction on the Duty of Reverence.

Mr. Wilde was found by a representative of the *Traveller* soon after his arrival this morning at Hotel Vendome, who accepted the cordial invitation of the young poet to enjoy a little chat in his private parlor. The talk drifted naturally to topics of art and the peculiarities of the movement known as aestheticism in

1. The Delavan House, a large hotel opposite the main railway station.

2. The copy text is a clipping that I am grateful to Elizabeth Adams for identifying in the Robert Ross Memorial Collection album (Ross b.6, 82). Excerpted in Lilian Whiting, "They Will Show Him," *The Daily Inter Ocean* (Chicago, IL), 10 Feb. 1882, 2, pp. 708–11 (which is H & S, b29).

England. Mr. Wilde is an intelligent and highly-educated young man and an exponent of the best thought in artistic life. His views have long been quite widely misrepresented, he feels, by the American press, much of whose outpourings about him he characterises as mere foolishness. Referring to the misrepresentation he had suffered, the question was asked in what manner, to which Mr. Wilde replied that misrepresentation requires no definition. These

PERSONAL DISCOURTESIES

are, he confesses, largely matters of indifference to him, many journals having been notoriously unfair to him, and he regards the difference between the American and the English press to be that the former relies too much on imagination, while the latter is controlled by existing fact.

"My object in coming to America," said Mr. Wilde, "is to tell the American people what is the latest and most important movement of thought in England, wishing that all should exactly understand what in England we artists intend to do. Our object is to produce more concentration, more definite artistic movements of value than ever before."

"Do you limit this movement to what are, distinctively, termed the 'Fine Arts,' or do you also include the decorative, Mr. Wilde?" was questioned.

THE UNIVERSALITY OF ART.

"No one art is finer than any other," he replied. "All true art is decorative art. The two finest paintings in Italy are those on ceilings in the palace of Pope Sextus [*sic*], from Michael Angelo.[1] There are in Venice decorations from Tintoretto,[2] and so I repeat that all pure art is decorative in its nature.

"The object of English aesthetes," resumed Mr. Wilde, "is to introduce beautiful designs in handicraft. It is not our primary object to procure more beautiful things for the rich to enjoy, but to teach the poor, the working people, to create beauty by educating them in designs and endow them with fine and permanent taste in handicrafts. To this end schools of design must be multiplied, and we have them in every city in England. The present movement is the most wonderful of anything that has taken place in the history of England within the last century. It is not to be called an imperceptible growth. All modern movements must have

1. The Sistine Chapel takes its name from Pope Sixtus IV, who restored it between 1473 and 1481. Michelangelo (1475–1564) painted *The Last Judgement* and the ceiling between 1508 and 1512 under the patronage of Pope Julius II.

2. Tintoretto (1518–1594) was an Italian painter who worked in Venice. His works include many paintings for the walls and ceiling of the Scuola di San Rocco and the massive canvas *Il Paradiso* for the main hall of the Doge's Palace. Wilde visited the Doge's Palace in 1875 and thought it "beyond praise" (CL, 10).

a definite form. We must know exactly what a movement means and what it intends.

THE AESTHETIC DEPARTURE

began with the pre-Raphaelites. Ruskin has aided it enormously. It is, indeed, an inspiration introduced in life. You remember Goethe said, 'Everything that is great promotes cultivation as soon as we are aware of it.'"[1]

"Practically, has the movement made a visible difference in England, Mr. Wilde?"

"It is widely noticeable," he replied; "yes," smiling in answer to a half-spoken question,—"yes, it is noticeable in ladies' dress, particularly in color. All beautiful color should be a gradation. The draperies, too, evince the education of the eye in form.

"Literature is, of course, a part of the movement. With the beautiful designs of Morris has gone the passionate and fervent eloquence of Ruskin; Rossetti, too, is not merely a painter but a poet also; Morris is not merely a designer, but the sweetest singer since Chaucer. As for a

DEFINITION OF AESTHETICISM,

the wider the definition, the more empty it is. Modern aestheticism is distinguished by its peculiar methods of approach. Philosophy used formerly to try to give a formula for beauty. We try rather to approach it always in its special manifestations. Every poem, every picture has a certain quality, certain virtues in it, and to disengage that particular quality, to discover that virtue, is the aim of the modern aesthetic critic. The truths of art cannot be taught. They are only revealed to natures that are receptive of beautiful impressions, and so we, in our aesthetic movement, want to create the artistic temperament which alone can discern the quality of aesthetic creation, and this is the reason of the immense importance we attach to what people call decorative art.

"The desire for beauty," resumed Mr. Wilde, "is the desire for life. It is the essential part of all great civilizations. Without it, civilization has, indeed, no meaning, because industry without beauty becomes barbarism.[1]

1. The reference is to *Gespräche mit Goethe in den letzten Jahren seines Lebens* (*Conversations with Goethe in the Last Years of His Life*; 1836 and 1848) by Johann Peter Eckermann (1792–1854). Eckermann records Goethe as saying that: "Byrons Kühnheit, Keckheit und Grandiosität, ist das nicht alles bildend? – Wir müssen uns hüten, es stets im entschieden Reinen und Sittlichen suchen zu wollen. – Alles *Große* bildet, sobald wir es gewahr werden." Wilde appears to be recalling the translation by John Oxenford (1812–1877), who renders this passage as: "the audacity and grandeur of Byron must certainly tend towards culture. We should take care not to be always looking for it in the decidedly pure and moral. Everything that is great promotes cultivation, as soon as we are aware of it."

"I hope," he continued, "that the newspapers of America will not mock what they should reverence, nor scorn what they should love. I can only hope that the American people will treat newspaper attacks on this movement with the indifference with which I treat them." Of

BURNE JONES,

the English poet said: "I consider that Burne Jones possesses the loftiest spiritual imagination, of the most fervid type, a splendid range of vision, a beautiful and joyous power of color and a wonderful fertility of design."

"The supreme object of life," said Mr. Wilde later, "is to live. Few people live.[2] It is true life only to realize one's own perfection, to make one's every dream a reality. Even this is possible."

The above is merely a hasty resume, compelled by the exigencies of an evening paper, of a long and most interesting conversation with Mr. Wilde. In manner the young poet well illustrates his own theories of the beautiful. With great refinement and courtesy he unites the perfect *savoir faire* of well-bred life and his running comments on current topics are full of insight. It is, indeed, the cheap wit that finds absurdity in all it does not understand and doubtless much of the misrepresentation of Mr. Wilde is owing to this cause. His lecture on Tuesday evening will be awaited with genuine interest.

"Oscar Wilde," *The Sunday Herald* (Boston, MA), 29 Jan. 1882, 7[3]

The Arrival of the Poet in Boston Yesterday.

A Conversation in Mr. Boucicault's Parlors.

His Thoughts About Art and a Poet's Life.

Mr. Wilde arrived in Boston Saturday morning, after an all-night railroad journey from Albany, and went straightway to the Hotel Vendome, and was assigned to pleasant rooms, which, however, had not been specially decorated in

---

1. Ruskin's *Lectures on Art* (1870): "Life without industry is guilt, and industry without art is brutality." The idea was a favourite of Wilde's: he had used it in *The English Renaissance* ("[...] if our days are barren without industry, industry without art is barren." *Miscellanies*, 296) and would use it again in *The House Beautiful* ("[...] when a child grows up he learns that industrious we must be, but industry without art is simply barbarism." O'Brien, 180). He also gave voice to it in a number of later interviews.

2. *The Soul of Man Under Socialism*: "To live is the rarest thing in the world. Most people exist, that is all." (CW iv, 239.1–2.)

3. H & S, b25. Reprinted in H & S, 39–47. Excerpted in Sturgis, 228/218–9. Quoted in Ellmann, 162/170, 176/185; and Sturgis, 216–7/208, 221/212, 228/219.

his honor, as announced by some imaginative writer. In fact, good friends of Mr. Wilde assert that at least three-quarters of what has been written about him since his arrival in this country is purely imaginative. Mr. Wilde's arrival in Boston was made particularly pleasant by the fact that his old friend, Mr. Boucicault, is here in the midst of his engagement at the Museum, and is also stopping at the Vendome.[1] Mr. Wilde's visit in Boston promises to be an enjoyable feature of his American journey, for, while he is not to be ostentatiously lionized, he will quietly meet with many of the most congenial people here, and be received with cordial hospitality. At 2 o'clock yesterday afternoon he lunched with the Literary Club, as the guest of Dr. Oliver Wendell Holmes; in the evening he dined with his friend, Mr. J. Boyle O'Reilly, who afterward presented him at the St. Botolph Club, where he met many of the leading literary and artistic men of the city.[2]

At noon Mr. Wilde received a caller from the HERALD in Mr. Boucicault's parlor, where he had been breakfasting with Mr. Boucicault and Mr. Charles H. Thayer, the manager for Mr. Boucicault's coming American tour, and also the business representative of Mr. Wilde for his Boston lecture engagement. It was seen at once that the eccentricities of Mr. Wilde have been much exaggerated, for his dress was not more of a departure from the ordinary than that of a dozen musicians and painters in Boston who might be mentioned. He wore a breakfast jacket of black velvet, and the rest of his costume was of the usual cut. Indeed, if his personal peculiarities had not been repeatedly heralded from England, it is hardly likely that they would have attracted unusual remark in this country. Mr. Wilde received his visitor with amiable courtesy, as he was presented by Mr. Boucicault, and the hope was expressed that his journey to Boston had been a pleasant one.

1. Dionysius "Dion" Lardner Boucicault (1820–1890) was an Irish actor and playwright. He made his stage debut in 1838 and three years later had his first success as a playwright with the comedy *London Assurance*. He debuted in America in 1854 and became a citizen in 1873. An interview with him appeared in the same edition: "Boucicault at Home," *The Sunday Herald* (Boston, MA), 29 Jan. 1882, 2, pp. 764–5. The Boston Museum, despite its name, was a theatre. Boucicault was appearing to packed houses in his old standards *The Colleen Bawn* (1860), *Arrah na Pogue* (1864), and *The Shaughraun* (1874), as well as a "new" play, *Suil a Mor*, that was a reworking of his *The O'Dowd* aka *Daddy O'Dowd; or, The Turn About is Fair Play* (1873).

2. The "Literary Club" was the Saturday Club, established in 1855. Oliver Wendell Holmes Sr. (1809–1894), an American physician and poet, was a prominent member. Wilde did not think much of his poetry (see "Oscar Wilde," *San Jose Daily Herald* (San Jose, CA), 4 Apr. 1882, 3, p. 315). Holmes visited the United Kingdom in 1886, and in London met Wilde again at a luncheon given by the American philanthropist Clara Bloomfield-Moore (Hoyt, E. P. (1979). *The Improper Bostonian: Dr. Oliver Wendell Holmes*. William Morrow. 263). He signed the autograph book of Wilde's wife, Constance Mary, née Lloyd (1859–1898), on 3 June 1886. John Boyle O'Reilly (1844–1890), an Irish-American poet, edited *The Pilot*, in which several of Wilde's poems had appeared. The St. Botolph Club was founded in 1880.

Figure 4. Dion Boucicault, with whom Wilde was interviewed in Boston.

"I came in a late train from Albany last night," said Mr. Wilde; "I lectured in Albany last night, you know."

"I suppose you have had all sorts of experiences with newspaper men?" remarked the caller, feeling that he might be apprehensive regarding the results of the present visit.

"Yes, some of them have been very tedious, while some others have succeeded in being very amusing. I was dressing one night, when I received the card of a person; on the card was printed his name, and also that he was a correspondent for a lot of western papers. 'This must be an immense newspaper man,' I said; 'I cannot dream of keeping him waiting.' So I put on my dressing gown and he was shown right up. A very young gentleman, or rather a boy, came into the room, and as I saw him I judged that he was nearly 16. I asked him if he had been to school? He said he had left school some time since. He asked my advice as to his course in journalism. I asked him if he knew French. He said, no. I advised him to learn French, and counselled him a little as to what books to read, and, in fact, I interviewed him. At last I gave him an orange and sent him away. That experience was really amusing to me, and the meekness with which he took it all was very charming."[1]

"It is a pity that you could not see America in a more pleasant season."

"I have been able to see nothing but newspapers so far. I have a great desire to see the beauties of America. Yesterday was the first day I have really seen anything of your beautiful country. Going up the Hudson to Albany—the beautiful, clear, bright day, the dark hills encircled with blue, I imagine in summer time it must be extremely beautiful."

"It is a pity you cannot be here in the summer, especially in Boston, where the suburbs are the most beautiful in America."

"Boston has the most beautiful surroundings?"

"It is more like England—exquisitely cultivated, but very natural," remarked Mr. Boucicault.

"I am hoping to see in New England many fine old houses like the 'Seven Gables,'" said Mr. Wilde.[2]

"Oh, yes, we have some old houses left; the Seven Gables is still standing in Salem, but, unfortunately, the most of the old-time houses are destroyed. Being

1. Wilde also told this story to the author of "Utterly Utter," *St. Louis Post-Dispatch* (St. Louis, MO), 25 Feb. 1882, 4, pp. 205–6. See also "The Aesthete at Washington," *Springfield Daily Republican* (Springfield, MA), 30 Jan. 1882, 4–5, pp. 108–9.

2. The House of the Seven Gables, also known as the Turner House, is a 1668 colonial mansion in Salem, Massachusetts. It was made famous by the novel *The House of the Seven Gables* (1851) by Nathaniel Hawthorne (1804–1864).

of wood, they have not lasted as long as they would in England. But you should take a drive out through the country while in Boston."

"Oh, yes, that I certainly shall have to do."

"Shall you be here in the summer?"

"I never have any plans in seeing a country; when it pleases me I stay, and go away when it ceases to please me. I should like to be here in the time of flowers."

"They are very beautiful."

"What are your trees here?"

"The American elm, maple, beech; also the hornbeam and the birch. These are among the principal deciduous trees."

"I wonder if we have the hornbeam in England; perhaps we call it by a different name.[1] What is it like?"

"It is a very graceful tree. It rises up about 30 or 40 feet, and then droops over, something like drooping willows, or a fountain."

"I remember of [*sic*] reading in William Morris' poems of the hornbeam, when I was a boy, and I was much puzzled to know whether it was a tree or an animal."[2]

"You spoke of Hawthorne—then you have read Hawthorne's stories."

"Oh, yes, I admire Hawthorne greatly. I think his 'Scarlet Letter' has the grandest passion, and is the greatest work of fiction ever written in the English tongue."[3]

Mr. Wilde was asked if he took any interest in politics, and he replied that he took an interest in everything in which humanity was active in thought and deed. "In Washington," said he, "I saw much of your leaders in politics, and visited in their houses, among them Mr. Blaine. Your American politics are a little difficult for us to understand, on account of the names of the two parties, Republican and Democratic. In Europe we have a greater difference in names. There they are the Conservative and Liberal."

"The origin of America was in democracy and in Europe it was centralization," said Mr. Boucicault; "and the tendency in America is from democracy to centralization, while in Europe it is the other way, from centralization to democracy."

1. The European or common hornbeam (Carpinus betulus) is native to Europe, including Southern England; the American hornbeam (Carpinus Caroliniana) is native to eastern North America (OED).

2. Morris was fond of Epping Forest, "certainly the biggest hornbeam wood in these islands, and I suppose in the world," (Mackail, J. W. (1899). *The Life of William Morris*. Longmans. 7).

3. *The Scarlet Letter* is an 1850 novel set in seventeenth-century Massachusetts. Hester Prynne conceives a daughter after an affair and is subjected to public humiliation, compelled to wear a scarlet letter "A" to advertise her adultery.

"In England it is a class interest that subdivides a party," said Mr. Wilde. "In England no measure is brought forward that does not touch the right of some particular class. You have no such distinction here."

"They have one class here, the moneyed class," said Mr. Boucicault.

"They never have in England such enormous capitalists as you have," said Mr. Wilde. "We call a man rich who has got a large amount of land, but who probably has not so much money as your magnates; that is, so much cash."

"Like our Jay Gould, for instance, who buys half a dozen railroads or so about every day, or sells them."[1]

"The moneyed interests are more solid in England, because the wealth is in the land, which has a fixed value; and not in stocks, which are constantly fluctuating. If, as I understand, the speculation is so great here, the commercial community must be always in that condition. The stocks and other securities are constantly changing in value, whereas the great values in England are in land, which has a fixed value."

"And not in Ireland," remarked Mr. Boucicault; "that has a very unfixed value."[2]

Mr. Wilde was asked if he had

THOUGHTS ABOUT ART,

visited any of the art schools in this country [*sic*].

"I went to a school of design in Philadelphia," said he. "I saw a young lady occupied in painting a moonlight landscape on a large plaque. Now a landscape, and above all, a moonlight scene, should never be painted on a plaque, or any round surface, but on canvas or paper. The surroundings of a school of design ought to be very beautiful. It is quite impossible to expect the designer to create beautiful designs in a whitewashed room with bare windows."

"Have you ever noticed one peculiarity of the studios of different artists? While the portrait painter or figure painter will generally have his studio decorated most delightfully, the landscape painter will have his studio perfectly bare, as if he were not dependent upon his surroundings?"

"Yes, but I think the true way for all artists to work is with the most beautiful surroundings. But I think in America the great future of your art lies with sculpture. You see, your clear, transparent atmosphere is best adapted to the grandest sculpturesque effects. It is so in Greece and Italy, where the greatest

1. Jason "Jay" Gould (1836–1892) was a railroad magnate and one of the wealthiest men of the Gilded Age.

2. The Irish National Land League was seeking to transfer ownership of Irish agricultural land from landlords to tenant farmers. In 1881 they issued the No Rent Manifesto. Wilde's family owned land in Ireland and their tenants were among those who withheld rent.

schools of sculpture in the world have existed, and I believe it will be so in America. In England, in our damp, dripping atmosphere, sculpture has a dreary look. It is absurd to attempt to revive Greek architecture without sculpture. That is the life of it, and the architecture is the life of it. So many public buildings in Washington in the Greek style, with most of their pediments empty, are lifeless. Sculpture gives animation to Greek forms in building; pediments full of figures, and a grand frieze around the sides, with reliefs—that is the beauty of it all. Without sculpture it is expressionless and purposeless as an empty picture frame."[1]

"One of the foremost sculptors here, whom I was talking with the other day, spoke of our lack of feeling for form in this country as yet, except among the very few."

"I suppose you mean by the lack of form the want of proportion," said Mr. Boucicault. "You can take the purest Greek form, and, by elongating or shortening it, you can turn it into anything that is most repulsive."

"That is an immense difficulty in art," said Mr. Wilde. "It is so absolutely dependent upon delicate proportions. The Parthenon in Athens is most beautiful, and the Madeleine, which is a copy of the Parthenon, is most abominable."[2]

"One is aesthetic proportion and the other is not," said Mr. Boucicault.

"No people went into the question of proportion as fully as the Greeks. There was a time in England, and always has been in Greece, when everything was beautiful. There was a time like that in England, and whatever we find built or made in that time, even for the most ordinary purposes, is beautiful. Then came the Puritan movement and destroyed all the artistic impulse. We are just beginning to recover from Puritanism in England."

"And we are also beginning to recover from the same in New England."

PHYSICAL BEAUTY.

"I am also a great admirer of the Japanese, of eastern art especially, in which there is a most delicate sense of the beautiful, but I object to the predominance of the grotesque. A people which has such an exaggerated sense of the grotesque is generally found not to have a love for the wonderful beauty in the human face and form."[3]

1. Sculpture in Washington DC: see "The Aesthete at Washington," *Springfield Daily Republican* (Springfield, MA), 30 Jan. 1882, 4–5, p. 109.

2. L'église de la Madeleine is a Roman Catholic church in Paris. It is similar in appearance to the Parthenon, though larger, but was in fact inspired by the much smaller Maison Carrée, an ancient Roman temple in Nîmes.

3. Wilde repeatedly complimented Japanese art. In an editorial for *The Woman's World* he wrote: "It is true that Japanese art, which is essentially decorative, is pictorial also. But the Japanese have the most wonderful delicacy of touch, and with a science so subtle that it gives the effect of exquisite accident, they can by mere placing make an undecorated space decorative." (Jan. 1889; CW vii, No. 112, lines 451–4.)

"Does not Mr. Ruskin ignore too much to beauty of the human form? [*sic*] Mr. Poynter, one of your leading British painters, makes that charge against him."[1]

"Yes; I know all sorts of things are said against Mr. Ruskin, but it is better to read what men have to say for themselves rather than what is said against them. Mr. Ruskin has an exquisite sense of the physical beauty of man. In the opening part of "Modern Painters" there is a fine passage on this very subject.[2] In England there is now a passionate love of physical beauty, so that if a woman there is very beautiful she becomes, just on that account, as celebrated as a great poet or a great artist."

"Where, on the whole, do you think you have seen the most beautiful women?"

"In London, I think. You know all things naturally come to London, and thus the finest examples of beautiful women may be found in London. Here in America I find a vast amount of pretty women, and the greatest number I have ever seen together in my life thus far I have seen in Baltimore; it was at the Wednesday Club, where I was entertained last week."

"Irish!" laughed Mr. Boucicault; "there is a deal of fine Irish blood in the old Baltimore stock! That accounts for the mass of feminine beauty there!"

POETS AND THEIR WORK.

"Do you know," said Mr. Wilde, "that the greatest fault I have to find with you Americans is that you are not American enough. You are all too cosmopolitan. What I am wishing to meet is a true American. I mean a man of whom it can be said, He is entirely the product of American conditions."

"You will find that in Walt Whitman," was suggested; "have you met Walt Whitman?"

"Indeed I have," said Mr. Wilde, his face kindling with enthusiasm. "I spent the most charming day I have spent in America with him. He is the grandest man I have ever seen. The simplest, most natural, and strongest character I have ever met in my life. I regard him as one of those wonderful, large, entire men who might have lived in any age, and is not peculiar to any one people. Strong, true and perfectly sane; the closest approach to the Greek we have yet had in modern times. Probably he is dreadfully misunderstood. If people would only know that no artist lives for praise; he only wants one thing, to be understood. I hope that

1. Edward John Poynter (1836–1919). Poynter claimed that "of beauty of form Ruskin seems to have no conception whatever."

2. Ruskin wrote five volumes in his *Modern Painters* series (1843–1860), which primarily argued for more truthful landscape painting. Wilde may be thinking of the chapter in the second volume titled "Of Vital Beauty in Man".

America will not treat its great poets as England too often has. Now, in France, it is different; they are proud that they have poets and artists there, but in England they not only expect them to look to posterity for their fame, but also for their bread and butter."

"Have you visited any of the universities in America yet?"

"I have visited the Johns Hopkins University in Baltimore, and certainly will not leave Boston without visiting Harvard."[1]

Mr. Boucicault here spoke, with earnest feeling, of the efforts that had been made in New York to make Mr. Wilde an object of ridicule, no slanders and malicious lies being too atrocious for certain people to invent. He compared the abuse heaped upon Mr. Wilde to that poured upon Mr. Millais, Holman Hunt and other artists of the pre-Raphaelite school in London 25 years ago.[2] There is no one better entitled to a respectful hearing than Mr. Wilde, who comes to this country with a friendly interest for it, and, therefore, a desire to become acquainted with the American people.

"All America naturally takes a great interest in what is done in England, as is natural," said Mr. Wilde, "for England is the mother of this country. I come here with a desire to tell you what the artists of England have been trying to do, for, of late, they have been doing some things which, I think, are worthy of telling about. It is on this account that I have prepared my lecture."

"It is to be hoped that you will have no fault to find with Boston's reception of what you have to tell us. At any rate, an entire community cannot be held to account for the disagreeable conduct of certain of its individuals."

"That is very true," said Mr. Wilde, "and I have not yet met any American gentleman who has not discountenanced and deplored all this ridicule and abuse. Whom are they harming? Not me, not the artist—for the artist, if he is an artist, must know what he is going to say, what he is going to do. He goes his way and produces his work. Keats wrote his poems and nobody read them at the time, but now you would think that that youth must have been loved, when he lived, by every man in England. Now to decry an artist thus is harm done to the public more than to the artist. There was only one artist in England who took any notice of what was said of him. That was Byron. Byron began by being a great lyric poet, and should always have been one. But he read the newspapers and it soured his

1. Wilde visited Harvard on 31 January.

2. John Everett Millais (1829–1896) and William Holman Hunt (1827–1910) were English painters and among the founders of the Pre-Raphaelite Brotherhood. On 29 January Boucicault wrote to Mrs George Lewis, also a close friend of Wilde, that D'Oyly Carte had left Wilde "at the mercy of the Press, making a market of their caricatures to advertise him in connection with *Patience* and Bunthorne." (CL, 135.) See also "Boucicault at Home," *The Sunday Herald* (Boston, MA), 29 Jan. 1882, 2, pp. 764–5.

nature, and at last he became a satirist, which is a low order of a poet. People in England condemn 'Don Juan,' but thereby they condemn themselves, for England is responsible for everything in 'Don Juan.'[1] An artist should not listen to, nor heed, ridicule and abuse, but he wants to be understood. Shelley was abused, but he did not heed it, and it had not the least effect upon him."

THE DRAMA.

Mr. Wilde was asked if his play was to be produced in this country.

"I cannot tell yet. I brought it with me, and Miss Clara Morris has it. She is one of the greatest actresses I have ever seen anywhere, here or in Europe."[2]

"Have you seen any of our leading tragedians?"

"I saw Mr. Booth in London, and Mr. McCullough, and I went to see Mr. Lawrence Barrett in New York. I thought Mr. Barrett had a thorough knowledge of his art, remarkable facial expression, and a striking quickness in adapting himself to his situations."[3]

"Do you not intend to go to the Pacific coast?"

"Well, I should like very much to go through to California when the snow on the mountains is melting and the flowers come out. I am told it is wonderfully beautiful then. And I want to see Mexico particularly, and to examine the wonderful remains of its ancient art. But one never sees a country by passing through it by railway. By racing through the country as we all do no one sees anything of

1. Byron's poem (1819–1824) reverses the traditional role of Don Juan as a seducer to one whom is easily seduced. He published the first cantos anonymously; they were criticised for their immorality.

2. Wilde had sent Morris a copy of the script from England (CL, 97, dates the accompanying letter to c. September 1880). Perhaps he gave her another copy on or about 11 January, when they were both guests at a luncheon. Wilde had previously sent Boucicault the script. Boucicault had tempered his criticism with friendly advice, but his general impression was that the "action stops for dialogue—whereas dialogue should be the necessary outcome of action exerting an influence on the characters." (Small, 96–7.)

3. Edwin Booth (1833–1893) was generally credited as the greatest American tragedian of his generation. He had visited London for the time in 20 years in 1880, but the season did not go well; Wilde blamed "the fiasco" on the poor stage management and company (CW iv, 529). However, he later claimed to have seen Booth often, "and enjoyed his acting highly" ("Sizing Us Up," *The Sunday Herald* (Boston, MA), 20 Aug. 1882, 12, p. 453). John McCullough (1832–1885) was an Irish-born American actor who played supporting roles in Booth's Shakespearean productions. Wilde praised Booth and McCullough's acting in a later interview ("Oscar Back Again," *The Daily Inter Ocean* (Chicago, IL), 1 Mar. 1882, 8, p. 235; "Oscar Wilde," *The Chicago Daily Tribune* (Chicago, IL), 1 Mar. 1882, 7, p. 239). Wilde had seen Barrett in *Yorick's Love* in Baltimore and met him in Washington DC at a gathering at the home of novelist Frances Hodgson Burnett ("District of Columbia," *The New York Mirror* (New York, NY), 28 Jan. 1882, 5.) Wilde cannot have seen Barrett socially or on stage in New York—at the time that Wilde was in New York, Barrett was playing in New Orleans, Charlotte, and Norfolk—so Wilde is presumably sharing his opinion of Barrett's performance in Baltimore.

it. The true way to see a country is to ride through it. I should like to ride through Mexico. I rode through Greece once; rode through the Peloponnesus; saw every little hill and tree, and knew it all. I want very much to see some of your Indians, to see men who spend all their life in the open air. I want to see how they carry themselves."[1]

"Have you noticed particularly our domestic architecture?"

"I have not had a chance to see much of it yet, but I saw in Washington some very beautiful new houses of red brick, with a great deal of charming woodwork about them and balconies to sit out on in pleasant weather. They were altogether very beautiful, and were full of flowers. I consider the most abominable style what they call Greek in New York, like Fifth avenue in New York, so depressing and monotonous, and entirely unadapted to the building material and the climate. In Philadelphia their old, red brick houses, with white doors and window shutters, were quaint and charming; so simple and unpretending. You could see that they were well built, and they were warm and clean-looking."

"You will find many brick buildings here in Boston. It is the prevailing building material here."

"That is right. The cheerful red, especially in the sunshine, combines so finely with the clear blue sky."

Here a visitor was announced and the conversation ended.

"The Aesthetic Apostle," *The Boston Sunday Globe* (Boston, MA), 29 Jan. 1882, 5[2]

An Interview with Oscar Wilde at the Vendome.

The Way He Has Been Treated by the American Press.

Searching for the "True American"—His Plans for the Future, Etc.

"Will Mr. Oscar Wilde favor THE GLOBE representative with a few moments of his presence and attention, with a view to rectifying some of the numerous misrepresentations that have preceded him to this city?"

1. Wilde later wrote to the actress Mrs Bernard Beere (1851–1915) from an unknown location in the American West that he had "seen Indians", and compared their appearance to a succession of British writers and actors: "in fact [F. C.] Burnand in a blanket and *quite* covered with scarlet feathers is now trying through the window to force me to buy a pair of bead slippers and making signs to a ruffianly looking [W. S.] Gilbert who is with him to tomahawk me if I refuse." (CL, 152–3.)

2. H & S, b26. Reprinted in H & S, 47–51. Quoted in Sturgis, 202/196, 224/215. Referenced in Sturgis, 223/215.

Such was the card borne on a silver platter to the apostle of aestheticism, as he sat in his elegantly-furnished parlors at the Vendome last evening, shortly after his return from dining with Oliver Wendell Holmes, James Freeman Clarke, Phillips Brooks and others at the Saturday club.[1] A gracious affirmative being received in reply, ye newspaper man, with his heart full of indignation at America's lack of appreciation of the truly beautiful and languid, soon found himself seated in a pensive chair by Oscar's drooping fireside—the fire, by the way, had drooped so much that it had gone out altogether, but what is the heat of vulgar coals when one is burning with a passion for sunflowers, crockery, poetry and all that sort of thing? The leader of the great English renaissance of the beautiful did not appear immediately, but through the half open door to an adjoining apartment came a few impatient words in undertone, which might have been occasioned by the total depravity of a necktie in refusing to be adjusted according to the standard of high art. On the lounge was carelessly thrown the heavy fur-lined ulster of olive green, with which the country has become so familiar. On the centre-table was a litter of letters, invitations of all kinds, a fine caricature and "A Thing of Beauty," one of Ruskin's books.[2] There was not a sunflower nor even a lily about the room. They had evidently not been unpacked. Without doors a disagreeable drizzle made Commonwealth avenue look particularly unpicturesque; in fact, the conduct of the weather was disgraceful in its supreme disregard of aesthetics. But

The Entrance of Mr. Oscar Wilde

put an end to all such observations. As the poet posed for a moment on the threshold it was evident how atrociously he has been misrepresented. Only the fertile fancy of the veteran interviewer would have described his luxuriant hair as falling upon his shoulders and flowing down his back. It seemed instead to be brushed forward over the ears and corners of the eyes, and indeed might have been tied under the chin and done excellent service as a muffler. To such extremes went the heated imaginations of the New York reporters that they impressed the public with the idea that his nether garments extended only to the knees; the writer can aver from careful observation they modestly reached an inch and a half below. The innumerable implications of this nature that have been spread before the public cast an indelible stigma upon American journalism.

Oscar has large, mobile and passably good-looking features, with full eyes that appear to languish, but are really very shrewd and all-observing. He wears no beard, and has only slight hirsute indications on the superior lip.

1. Phillips Brooks (1835–1893) was an American clergyman.
2. Presumably the 1880 reissue of Ruskin's "A Joy For Ever", the text of two lectures he gave in Manchester in 1857 "on the political economy of art".

"Ah yes," said he, lolling on the mantel and crossing his shapely calves; "interviews are a product of American civilization, whose acquaintance I am making with tolerable speed. You gentlemen have fairly monopolized me ever since I saw Sandy Hook. In New York there were about a hundred a day. I had to leave my house and go to a private house, when I wanted to push along my work, don't you know? But then, I am always glad to see you," with a benignant smile, "when you don't misrepresent the movement, you know."

"It is understood, Mr. Wilde, that you are very much dissatisfied with the manner in which you have been

Treated by the Press."

"Well, I don't care much. I don't read the papers a great deal. But if they were rather better strangers to fiction, and on somewhat more intimate terms with facts, there would be nothing lost."

"Will you kindly explain the true state of that Baltimore affair, Mr. Wilde, about which so many contradictory things have been said and written?"

"That was scandalous treatment," said the pioneer of the era of beauty, a trifle bitterly. "Those lies were invented by a Baltimore sheet, a rag of a newspaper, and every other paper in the country copied them like so many sheep. It was through a pure misunderstanding that I did not attend the lady's reception. I saw her when I returned from Washington, and we are now on charming terms. She is one of the most gracious ladies I have ever met. The idea that I made any amount of dollars a condition of my favoring a company with my presence is another malicious canard, but too absurd to do me any harm. The clout of a sheet that started these lies has never had the moderate amount of decency to retract them. The American papers are often a screed of falsehoods. Now, in England, you know," and the innumerable shining writers of English luminaries were here contrasted with the unfathomable frivolity and depravity of the American press. But through all this harangue a mysterious twinkle in the great aesthete's orbs seemed to intimate that he very well understood the advantage of free advertising, and didn't so much care whether he was represented or misrepresented, as long as he was as far from a failure as at present. As a matter of fact, had the American papers ignored him as the English have done, his venture in this country would probably have fallen short of its present measure of success.

"What were your impressions of New York society?" was queried.

"Charming, very charming—quite cosmopolitan. In fact, you are all cosmopolitan here.

I Have Yet to Discover the True American.

I searched diligently for him in New York and he was not there. All in vain was I on the qui vive for him in Philadelphia, Baltimore and Washington. I am getting sceptical now, and begin to doubt his existence. But possibly, as some of your people have told me, I shall find him further West."

"You have met many of our literary men, I believe, Mr. Wilde?"

"Well, yes, and for a young country your literary class, though very small, is highly developed, and evinces an acute appreciation of the more exalted ideals of thought and art. Longfellow is very pleasant, Dr. Holmes is extremely clever, James Russell Lowell, Aldrich and others rank high.[1] But, of course in the childhood of your nation, so to speak, you could hardly expect to produce such a glorious trio as burst upon England with the advent of Keats, Shelley and Byron. Of all your authors, I consider Walt Whitman far the grandest and noblest. Many of his lines are like a blast fresh from Olympus. I have met him and enjoyed his society more than words can express."

"In regard to your own poetry, it has been stated that you are at work on a new volume."

"Yes; I have been engaged for a long time in that direction, and devote all my leisure to its preparation. I intend that it shall be a great advance upon my first venture, and entirely distinct in tone and style—

More Soulful, More Throbbing, More Exalting, I trust."[2]

"Do you propose to publish it during your sojourn in this country?"

"Well, I have thought of so doing. It was at one time announced that I should do so. But on mature consideration I have come to the opinion that the American atmosphere is not conducive to the best development of poetic thought. I shall defer publication until my return to England. After my travels here are consummated I shall continue my work at home. To write true verse is the primary ob-

1. Henry Wadsworth Longfellow (1807–1882) was an American poet. Wilde would visit him at at his home in Boston on 30 January (Friedman, 127–8). For Wilde's brief account of the meeting, see "With Mr. Oscar Wilde," *Cincinnati Daily Gazette* (Cincinnati, OH), 21 Feb. 1882, 10, pp. 190–2. Wilde would later refer negatively to Longfellow's poetry in other interviews and tell the journalist Chris Healy that he was "a great poet only for those who never read poetry" (Mikhail, 384). In an article for *The Pall Mall Gazette* he would write that Longfellow "had a most charming and gracious personality, and he wrote some pretty poems. But his poems are not of the kind that call for intellectual analysis or for elaborate description or, indeed, for any serious discussion at all" (28 Mar. 1887; CW vi, No. 56, lines 35–8), but he conceded that the poet "was one of the first true men of letters America produced, and as such deserves a high place in any history of American civilization." (ibid, lines 30–2.) James Russell Lowell (1819–1891) was an American poet and former editor of the *Atlantic Monthly*. He also served as United States Minister to Great Britain (as the role of Ambassador was then known) from 1880 to 1885. It was a letter of introduction written by Lowell to Oliver Wendell Holmes that gained Wilde entrance into Boston society (CL, 118, 131). Thomas Bailey Aldrich (1836–1907) was a poet, critic, and editor of the *Atlantic Monthly*.

2. Wilde never published a second volume of poetry. It is unlikely that Wilde phrased his answer using the aesthetic slang given here.

ject of my life. Thus shall I best promulgate the principles of this great modern movement in the direction of the beautiful."

At this point the apostle, in a somewhat singsong and parrot-like way, gave an account of the great eternal and inevitable underlying principles of the "movement," what had been done, what was doing at present, and what it was hoped to accomplish in the near future. This, however, is already familiar to THE GLOBE readers.

Mr. Wilde dined last evening with John Boyle O'Reilly, dropped in at the St. Botolph Club, and later attended the Greek play at the Globe Theatre.[1] There is little doubt about his being received in what is known as "our best society," in case he cares to enter it. He lectures at Music Hall Tuesday night, and is already assured a full house, with three score of Harvard students in the front seats. From Boston he will go to Hartford, New Haven, and thence to the West.

"Oscar Wilde," *Morning Journal and Courier* (New Haven, CT), 2 Feb. 1882, 2

The Apostle of Aesthetics—His New Haven Effort—The English Renaissance—The Beautiful in Nature and in Art—High Flights—The Big Sunflower.

Oscar Wilde, the poet and apostle of aesthetics, lectured last evening at Peck's Grand Opera House to an audience of four or five hundred. It included not a few distinguished citizens, most of whom were accompanied by ladies. The lecturer arrived at the hall a few minutes before 8 o'clock. Outside there were thirty or forty persons waiting to catch a glimpse of the lecturer. They were probably much disappointed at finding him attired in ordinary dress like any other gentleman—no knee breeches, nothing but a plain black suit. The lecturer was accompanied solely by his agent, Mr. Vale, and his colored waiting man.[2] While Mr. Wilde was adjusting his toilet with an aesthetic, languid, composed air before the glass in the dressing room, Mr. Vale spoke with enthusiasm of Mr. Wilde's Boston success the evening before—a $3,000 house. Mr. Wilde having adjusted his long and flowing locks, which were parted duly in the middle and

1. This is the production of *Oedipus Tyrannus* that Wilde commented on in "Aesthete Wilde on Greek Plays," *The Evening Telegram* (New York, NY), 13 Jan. 1882, 4th ed., 1, pp. 69–70.

2. J. Sydney Vale (1856–?) was Wilde's travelling manager (Sturgis, 234/225). He was sometimes referred to as Vail, including by Colonel Morse; that is how his name is spelt in this article. Some authors have given his name as J. H. Vale. The identity of Wilde's African American valet (or valets) remains a mystery. He was probably called Stephen, and his last name may have been Davenport (Mendelssohn, 269–71). See also "Speranza's Gifted Son," *St. Louis Daily Globe-Democrat* (St. Louis, MO), 26 Feb. 1882, 3, p. 208, note. 4.

fell about his neck and collar, he was interviewed by a representative of the COURIER. He bowed with the air of an Apollo and our reporter took mental cognizance of the six feet of aesthetic humanity before him, finding him very much like the photographs displayed in Peck's window yesterday, minus the fur lined overcoat. He was dressed in a conventional dress suit, the pantaloons cut without special attempt at shadowy legs, black vest cut low, displaying a vast expanse of highly polished shirt bosom, in the exact center of which reposed a single stud composed of a pair of beautiful pearls. His collar was a low turn over, his tie a white, flowing silk tie or handkerchief. A pair of massive watch seals dangled from a fob chain. The following conversation ensued:

Reporter—"How were you pleased with Boston?"[1]

"Oh, very much, very much indeed," said Mr. Wilde, his face assuming a happy, genial smile. "I expected to be. Boston has indeed a great deal of culture, art and refinement."

"Did you visit the prominent people and places?"

"Oh yes, and my experience was very delightful. I think it was one of my pleasantest stopping places. I was honoured with an interview with Longfellow and others of note there. I had a charming time after my lecture at a party at Mrs. Julia Ward Howe's. I also took a run over to Harvard College and visited that institution. Harvard reminded me much of our English universities,—of our own Oxford. I liked Boston so well that I shall return there before my departure for my home."

"How long do you remain in America?"

"Oh," said Mr. Wilde, with a heavenly expression rolling his eyes slightly upward, "that depends somewhat. I have no fixed plan as yet."

"Do you remain in New Haven tomorrow?"

"Yes, I shall remain awhile. Professor Whitney, whom I have had the pleasure of meeting, has kindly consented to show me Yale University, in which I shall take great pleasure.[2] I afterward go to Hartford, where I lecture in the evening."

"Your poetry I see finds many American readers, and the newspapers have given many samples to their readers. Are any of your works published under your own direction in America?"

"Ah, they read my poems but through piracy.[3] It is a pity that the author is not protected in his work, as to its reproduction in this country. Yes, it is pleas-

1. This article makes no use of quotation marks. They are added here for clarity.

2. Presumably William Dwight Whitney (1827–1894), an American linguist and lexicographer. He was Professor of Sanskrit at Yale.

3. The Seaside Library had published a pirated edition of *The English Renaissance* and *Poems* in January, even going so far as to copyright it in the publisher's name. It was priced at ten cents.

ant," and here the author looked the ineffable again, "it is pleasant to be read, to have your thoughts read, to touch humanity in that way."

"May I ask do you confine yourself strictly to your manuscript in lecturing?"

"Oh, no. I often diverge. If the spirit of the audience moves me aright I give expression to new thoughts that occur to me. The inspiration of the moment gives me new currents of thought."

"You do not dress tonight in your regalia?"

"Oh, no; that is a matter in which I allow myself to be guided by circumstances and the weather. Knee breeches are a little cool for this evening. Dress should be aesthetic, not conventional. Beautiful colors should be considered in dress. I would allow liberality in the choice. My movement is to utilize the beautiful. Whatever is beautiful is a pleasure. So the beautiful should improve and grace the mind and add to the higher forms of feeling and life."

Just here the audience began to stamp vigorously. "What is that noise?" said Mr. Wilde, with a dreamy, far away expression.

"That," replied the reporter, "is your audience, who are impatient for your appearance."

"Impatient," said Mr. Wilde, dreamily. The reporter, with a goodnight, withdrew, Mr. Wilde retiring to converse with his agent, after which he placed his manuscript under the gaslight and read over a page or two, after which he stepped out upon the platform and calmly arranging his manuscript waited for the burst of applause which greeted him to subside, when he began the lecture.

✂ *A report of Wilde's lecture in New Haven.*

"Mr. Wilde in Brooklyn," *New York Tribune* (New York, NY), 4 Feb. 1882, 5[1]

"He looks like a love-sick young girl," was the remark of a sensible woman who listened to Oscar Wilde in the Brooklyn Academy of Music last evening. Mr. Wilde delivered his lecture upon "The English Renaissance," prefacing it with a brief explanation of his desire to arouse interest in artistic creations. There was a large and attentive audience, numbering about 2,000 persons. The lecturer's costume included black silk stockings and knee-breeches. The stage was set in a parlor scene, and a folding screen, ornamented with storks and Japanese illustra-

1. The reporter was accompanied by the authors of "Oscar Wilde in Brooklyn," *The Sun* (New York, NY), 4 Feb. 1882, 1, pp. 134–5; "Oscar Wilde In Brooklyn," *The New York Times* (New York, NY), 4 Feb. 1882, 2, p. 135; and "The Esthete," *The Brooklyn Daily Eagle* (Brooklyn, NY), 4 Feb. 1882, 2, p. 136.

tions, and a vase containing lilies and a sunflower, were the decorations. Many persons purchased at the door a "Comic Life of Oscar Wilde," sold by shrill-voiced boys.[1] The only interruptions in the delivery of the lecture were caused by an undue prolongation of applause by one or two instances. It was apparent, however, that a majority of the audience desired to give the lecturer a considerable hearing.

In conversation after the lecture Mr. Wilde said that he was much pleased with Americans, but not with their newspapers, which he thought, with a few exceptions, had not treated him fairly. He expressed regret that Englishmen are not trained in public speaking. He found lecturing very delightful when his listeners were apparently interested. As to the way the Harvard students acted at his Boston lecture, he remarked that probably he would have been received in the same way by students at Oxford.[2]

"Oscar Wilde in Brooklyn," *The Sun* (New York, NY), 4 Feb. 1882, 1[3]

How the Stage was Set and What he had to Say of the Cambridge Freshmen.

✂ *A report of Wilde's lecture in Brooklyn.*

Mr. Wilde was found in the dressing room after his lecture, half sitting upon the marble-topped table drawing off his kid gloves. He said that it was very kind to speak well of his lecture, because he had had no experience in public speaking. As to his Boston experience, he said that he found his audience there delightful.

1. Presumably *Ye Soul Agonies in ye Life of Oscar Wilde*, illustrated by Charles Kendrick.
2. At Wilde's Boston lecture a large group of Harvard students booked out the front rows. After the rest of the audience had taken their seats, the students entered wearing knee-breeches, colourful ties, and long wigs. Each carried a sunflower. As they paraded down the aisle they paused to strike aesthetic poses. Wilde had been tipped off, however, and when he came on stage he was in conventional evening dress rather than the aesthetic costume he usually wore. He addressed the students directly: "my sentiments are most friendly to all species of art, though I am free to confess that circumstances have sometimes occasioned me to sigh 'May Providence deliver me from my disciples.'" Wilde was rewarded with uproarious laughter and applause, and the students were chastened. See "Oscar Wilde," *The Boston Herald* (Boston, MA), 1 Feb. 1882, 2; "Sixty Bunthornes Present," *The Sun* (New York, NY), 1 Feb. 1882, 3; and *The Brooklyn Daily Eagle* (Brooklyn, NY), 2 Feb. 1882, 2.
3. H & S, b28. Reprinted as "Oscar Wilde in Brooklyn" *The Cincinnati Enquirer* (Cincinnati, OH), 6 Feb. 1882, 8. Excerpted in Hyde, 63. Quoted in OWDA, 129; and Sturgis, 254–5/243. The reporter was accompanied by the authors of "Mr. Wilde in Brooklyn," *New York Tribune* (New York, NY), 4 Feb. 1882, 5, pp. 133–4; "Oscar Wilde In Brooklyn," *The New York Times* (New York, NY), 4 Feb. 1882, 2, p. 135; and "The Esthete," *The Brooklyn Daily Eagle* (Brooklyn, NY), 4 Feb. 1882, 2, p. 136.

They were so quick to catch a thing. He could tell that they were bright. Referring to the sixty Bunthornes, he said laughingly:

"Oh, I could sympathize with them, because I thought to myself that when I was in my first year in Oxford I would have been apt to do the same; but as they put their head in the lion's mouth, I thought they deserved a little bite."

"The men and the women of America are splendid," he said, "but there is a broad chasm between them and the newspapers. I think the newspapers are simply outrageous. All? No, let me discriminate. I really haven't a complaint to make against but one—a Baltimore paper. That was simply villainous in its fiction about me in reference to an invitation to a lady's house. If any young American should come to England and be so treated by one of our newspapers, I think we should feel it very much. I am surprised that the Americans stand it. I suppose I shall lecture in the West, if there is anything left of me. I like the excitement of lecturing, and when one gets an interested audience it is a pleasure; but I hate travelling. I hate punctuality and I hate time tables. The railroads are all alike to me. One is simply intolerable; another is simply unbearable."

"Oscar Wilde In Brooklyn," *The New York Times* (New York, NY), 4 Feb. 1882, 2[1]

HE REPEATS HIS LECTURE ON "THE ENGLISH RENAISSANCE."

✂ *A report of Wilde's lecture in Brooklyn.*

Talking with a party of gentlemen after the lecture, Mr. Wilde said he found a wide difference between the men and women and the newspapers in America. He did not like the treatment he received from most of the papers, and from one in Baltimore in particular which treated him shamefully. "Before I left England," he said, "no one thought I would lecture. I find that if one's soul is in his subject he can talk for an hour without fatigue. I hate the railroads. I have to be too punctual. The cars are better, though, here than in England. If I survive," he continued, with a smile, "I shall go West. I want to be in California when the flowers are in bloom. I shall take dinner with Joaquin Miller, the poet, tomorrow, but I shall not lecture in the evening."[2]

1. I am grateful to John Cooper for identifying this article. The reporter was accompanied by the authors of "Mr. Wilde in Brooklyn," *New York Tribune* (New York, NY), 4 Feb. 1882, 5, pp. 133–4; "Oscar Wilde in Brooklyn," *The Sun* (New York, NY), 4 Feb. 1882, 1, pp. 134–5; and "The Esthete," *The Brooklyn Daily Eagle* (Brooklyn, NY), 4 Feb. 1882, 2, p. 136.

2. Cincinnatus Heine "Joaquin" Miller (1837–1913) was an American poet. He had visited England in 1871 and published a volume of poems, *Songs of the Sierras*, well-received by British

"The Esthete," *The Brooklyn Daily Eagle* (Brooklyn, NY), 4 Feb. 1882, 2[1]

Oscar Wilde's Appearance in Brooklyn.

His Lecture on "The English Renaissance" at the Academy—A Crowded and Fashionable Audience—Few Interruptions and Abundant Applause—The Poet's Bearing and Address—His Impressions of the United States and Intentions for the Future—He Hopes to be in California "When the Flowers Come Up."

✂ *A report of Wilde's lecture in Brooklyn.*

MR. WILDE'S IMPRESSIONS.

Mr. Wilde sat, unattended, upon a small, marble table in the cold, cheerless green room of the Academy after the lecture, when an EAGLE reporter entered. He shook hands pleasantly and without affectation. He expressed satisfaction with the result of his lecture in Brooklyn and his experiences in this country. "The men and women of America," he said, "are splendid; but there is a broad chasm between them and the newspapers. The people are delightful—the newspapers simply intolerable. Not all, however. I have but one complaint to make, and that is against a Baltimore paper. It contained a villainous attack upon me. I expect to go West, if there is anything left of me after I finish lecturing in the East, and I hope to be in California when the flowers come up. I feel that lecturing is pleasant, although it requires deep study and careful application. In England, you know, we write instead of lecture. I can hardly endure railroad traveling. The railroads in this country are superior to those in England. Still, there is not much to choose between them. One is intolerable and the other unbearable." Mr. Wilde, as he finished speaking, languidly drew on his long, pea green, fur lined overcoat, and entered his coupe.

---

critics and members of the Pre-Raphaelite Brotherhood. Wilde met Miller in January at a "crush" (Sturgis, 209/202). On that occasion Miller was reported to have invited Wilde to dine with him at his home (*The Chicago Daily Tribune* (Chicago, IL), 17 Jan. 1882, 4).

1. H & S, b27. The reporter was accompanied by the authors of "Mr. Wilde in Brooklyn," *New York Tribune* (New York, NY), 4 Feb. 1882, 5, pp. 133–4; "Oscar Wilde in Brooklyn," *The Sun* (New York, NY), 4 Feb. 1882, 1, pp. 134–5; and "Oscar Wilde In Brooklyn," *The New York Times* (New York, NY), 4 Feb. 1882, 2, p. 135.

"Wilde in Utica," *Utica Daily Observer* (Utica, NY), 7 Feb. 1882, 2[1]

YE LAST SWEET THING IN OSCARS.

A Genuine Sensation at the City Opera House—Wilde Unfolding the Flawless Essences of His Kosmic soul Under the Auspices of the Household Art Rooms—Getting Down from His Pedestal of Daffodils and Coming in Contact with Oneida County Snow Banks and an Inquisitive "Observer" Reporter.

Oscar Wilde reached Utica at 5:15 yesterday afternoon and departed at 11:22 today. The young poet was expected earlier, but, as Conductor Ferrell remarked: "The glaukous-haired disciple of poesy is nothing if intelligible."[2] Oscar's coming was eagerly anticipated. Public opinion in regard to the young Oxford graduate is so divided that while some insist he is only "utter," many urge that there is a method underlying it all which stamps Wilde as a level-headed money getter. Candidly, he doesn't look like a fellow whose nerves are constantly thrilling like throbbing violins in exquisite pulsation. In his eyes there is nothing of the "lone delight of soft communion with sweet antiphonal souls."[3] Not a bit of it. Wilde came to Utica in a drawing-room car like any one else, and when he shook hands with Commissioner Earll and Architect Cooper, no one about the depot suspected that the young Irishman had a Kosmic soul or that he dealt in mystic symphonies.[4] He did not even flaunt the burnished disk of the sunflower,[5] and as for a lily—it would have been paralyzed by the surrounding snow banks in seventeen seconds. Wilde is a remarkable creation. If he is playing a part in his tour through this country, he is a finished actor. If he is "acting out" himself, he is simply unique. No picture that has yet appeared does him justice. It has been either an extravagant burlesque or a colorless reproduction of his pale, classical features and long hair. Wilde is 26 years of age and six feet two inches in height. He has an interesting face of feminine mould, and when he speaks shows a fine up-

1. Reprinted in Gifford, J. J. (2006). *Glances Backward*. Broadview Press. 71–5. Quoted in OWDA, 154–5.

2. Presumably a reference to the burlesque interview in *Punch* ("Oscar Interviewed," *Punch* (London, UK), Vol. 82, 14 Jan. 1882, 14, p. 883).

3. Ibid, p. 884.

4. "Kosmic soul" is a reference to Wilde's poem *Panthea*, first published in *Poems*: "[...] We shall be | Part of the mighty universal whole, | And through all aeons mix and mingle with the Kosmic Soul!" (CW i, No. 62, lines 172–4.) "[M]ystic symphonies" is a reference to *Humanitad*, also first published in *Poems*: "When soul and body seemed to blend in mystic symphonies" (CW i, No. 58, line 408).

5. Wilde used the word "burnished" in a number of poems. The reference here is to *In the Gold Room (A Harmony)*, first published in *Poems*: "Her gold hair fell on the wall of gold | Like the delicate gossamer tangles spun | On the burnished disk of the marigold, | Or the sun-flower turning to meet the sun" (CW i, No. 86, lines 7–10).

per row of teeth. His accent and manner is that of a refined cockney.[1] He speaks slowly, with just a suggestion of the Dundreary drawl.[2] His sentences are long but he carries an idea with or behind them. He is perfectly self-possessed and his individuality or egotism is constantly apparent. Speaking to the writer of his experience in this country, last evening, he said:

WILDE'S IMPRESSIONS OF AMERICA.

"Your country is vast. I suppose I have no conception of it as yet but your distances are very remarkable."

"You are simply on the borders of the Continent, Mr. Wilde."

"Y-a-a-s, so I am informed. In our own ugly little Island we cannot appreciate the vastness of America. You call it a country, but I call it a w-o-r-l-d."[3]

"You have spoken every night since you began lecturing, have you not?"

"Ya-a-s, but not always to an audience.[4] It is not my lecturing that tires me. The sensation is so novel I fairly enjoy it. The exactions of traveling are wearisome, and then there have been so many receptions and pleasant little entertainments. America is a constantly growing wonder to me. You are decidedly cosmopolitan. There is a suggestion of all countries about you, and I have yet to meet the Yankee as a distinctive character."

Wilde attracts much attention. He wears an olive-green overcoat, gaily trimmed, a low, wide collar and necktie of mammoth proportions and gradated colors. As he stepped from the train he placed the fingers of his right hand gracefully to the side of his face and whether this movement was natural or mere affectation will never be known. His dress throughout was "a symphony of color" down to the patent leather shoes with decorated uppers of cream-colored broadcloth. He has the stooping shoulders and the gait of *Bunthorne*, but this, together with his cockneyed accent, is as natural as running water. In full evening dress Wilde is a revelation. He looks younger, more esthetic and more ethereal. Last

1. Here, and in several other American interviews, "Cockney" is used to refer to an inhabitant of London and not in the more specific sense of a person, usually working-class, from the East End of that city.

2. Lord Dundreary is a character in *Our American Cousin* (1858), a play by Tom Taylor. Edward Askew Sothern (1826–1881) created the role of the simple-minded, capering English nobleman, delivering his lines with a lisp and de-rhotacism.

3. It is unlikely that Wilde referred to Great Britain as "our own ugly little Island". Compare his words here with a similar passage in "Utterly Utter," *St. Louis Post-Dispatch* (St. Louis, MO), 25 Feb. 1882, 4, p. 205: "Oh, your country is so large. It is a world. But it looks so barren and rugged in winter time. To one accustomed to a little place like England, which has been tilled for centuries, this change is remarkable."

4. This self-deprecating joke would be uncharacteristic, and is certainly fabricated. The attendance at Wilde's lectures varied widely. Wilde boasted about his larger audiences and kept silent when they were less impressive. Also, he had not lectured every night since he began: he lectured ten times between 9 January and 6 February.

night he wore the most pronounced fashionable evening costume ever seen in the Valley of the Mohawk.[1] We shall not attempt to describe it save to remark that Wilde wore it with a naturalness and grace that is inimitable.

THE LECTURE.

The lecture was given under the auspices of the Household Art Rooms. The audience that listened to it was a large and cultivated one. The stage was handsomely set and covering the desk in the centre was a rich drapery embroidered with lilies. The lecturer glided upon the stage with a movement that suggested a change in the dance known as "the German."[2] In slow, measured motions he un-unfolded the text of his discourse. In England, he said, the aim of the new artistic movement was "to search out, in our great, ugly manufacturing cities, those men and women who can work with their hands as well as their minds and hearts. Such as your life is, so is your art sure to be. The spirit of art is one and eternally the same. Byron was a rebel and Shelley a dreamer, but Keats was the forerunner of the pre-Raphaelite school."

Before the lecture began Wilde said to the writer: "There is just one criticism which the American press has passed on me that I do not like. I do not think I deserve it. Here in this account (the reporter handed him a slip from the Albany *Argus*) they say I am not practical.[3] I should like to meet that horrid Albany fellow and I believe I could convince him that I am practical. I want you to listen to what I say about the workmen." His allusion to the handicraftsmen was made in these words:

"Great movements must originate with the workmen. I believe in practical art. I believe the musical value of a word is greater than its intellectual value and nowhere is this better exemplified than in that supreme imaginative work of the young American who wrote 'The Raven.'[4] To educate and refine a country you must begin with the masses. There must be stately and simple architecture in your cities and bright and simple dress for men and women. You should have

1. Utica is situated in New York's Mohawk Valley.

2. The German, also known as the German cotillion, was a dance popular during the second half of the nineteenth-century. A large number of persons would waltz a series of figures, or sequences, with a frequent exchange of partners. Parties arranged for the purpose of undertaking such a dance were also known as Germans (Dodworth, A. (1885). *Dancing and its Relations to Education and Social Life*. Harper & Brothers. 145–6).

3. The section of the article to which Wilde refers is: "Whatever may be said for or against the truth of Mr. Wilde's theories, no one who listens to him as he gives them utterance, can for a moment question his earnestness or sincerity. He is not a practical man, but having formed his aims and aspirations, he has the courage to live up to them regardless of the witticisms, the derision, and the sarcasm he meets on every hand," ("Oscar Wilde," *The Argus* (Albany, NY), 28 Jan. 1882, 8).

4. Edgar Allan Poe.

among your people some permanent canon and standard of taste. Creeds and philosophies decay, but beauty is the only thing time cannot harm. We should have in our houses things that give pleasure to the men who made them.

THE GOOD IN ART.

"The good in art is not what we directly learn from it but what we indirectly become through it. All the arts are fine arts and all the arts are decorative arts. By separating the handicraftsman from the artist you ruin both. Labor without art is merely barbarism.[1] Decoration is the form of expression of the joy the handicraftsman has in his work. Design is the study and result of cumulative habit and observation. I believe in the elevation and education of the poorer classes. I want to see the homes of the humble beautiful. The rich in England have too many beautiful things—more than their share—they might very well be divided."

After the lecture Wilde received an informal reception at the residence of Ex Mayor Hutchinson. He is more entertaining when met socially than upon the rostrum. He is a young man of ideas, a wide reader and a close observer. He says the assertion that he is not practical is the only distasteful stricture that has been passed upon him in this country.

"But your reception in Music Hall, Boston, by the Harvard boys?"

Wilde smiled. He rarely laughs. It was a smile that displayed to the best advantage that fine row of teeth and flashed the merest suspicion of "the whites of his eyes."

"Ya-a-s, you know, but I enjoyed it—merely a bit of badinage from the college boys. I understood it, for I know how it is myself."

"When do you expect to return to England?"

"Late in April. I shall spend June in Paris and then go to Venice. No, this is not my last visit to America. I want to see your country in the summer and autumn."

A gentleman asked Mr. Wilde to explain the secret of the sunflower and lily craze. The lecturer said: "I regard those flowers as the most perfect models of design—the most naturally adapted for decorate [*sic*] art—the gaudy, leonine beauty of the one and the precious loveliness of the other giving to the artist his best ideas. Here in Utica you have art rooms. Cultivate them. You have young artists. Cheer them on in their race through the meadows."

A full report of Mr. Wilde's lecture would fill five columns of this paper. We present below a few sentences verbatim, in order to give those readers who did not hear him an idea of his style:

1. Art and barbarism: see p. 117, note 1.

And so with you, let there be no flower in your meadows that does not wreathe its tendrils around your pillows, no little leaf in your Titian [*sic*] forests that does not lend its form to design, no curving spray of wild rose or briar that does not live forever in carven arch or window of marble, no bird in your air that is not giving the iridescent wonder of its color, the exquisite curves of its wings in flight, to make more precious the preciousness of simple adornment; for the voices that have their dwelling in sea and mountain are not the chosen music of liberty only. Other messages are there in the wonder of windswept heights and the majesty of silent deep—messages that, if you will listen to them, will give you the wonder of all new imagination, the treasure of all new beauty. We spend our days, each one of us, in looking for the secret of life. Well, the secret of life is art.[1]

After the reception at Mr. Hutchinson's last evening, Mr. Wilde was entertained at the Utica Club.

This morning, at half-past ten, upon invitation of Messrs. Earll, Cooper and Latimore, Mr. Wilde visited the Household Art Rooms and met a large company of ladies and gentlemen. He wore a light velvet coat and other apparel perfectly harmonized and attuned to said velvet coat. After the members of the company had been introduced the poet inspected the features of the art rooms alternately praising and criticizing what he saw. The tapestry struck his fancy; the bust of Venus he did not like. The embroideries were pronounced superior, "but," turning to Mr. Cooper, "don't let your young ladies paint landscapes on placques."

After half an hour's chat with the ladies, in which decorative art was discussed in all its length, breadth and border, Mr. Wilde shook hands with some, bowed comprehensively to the rest, donned his olive green overcoat, muffled his throat in a silken scarf of gradated wine color, put on his gloves and was driven to the depot. There he wrote his autograph and assured a friend that he should always remember with pleasure his visit to Utica.

Wilde is a brainy boy. Peculiar, but he makes his peculiarities profitable.

1. The closing lines of *The English Renaissance*. "Titian" is given as "Titan" in the texts in *Miscellanies*, 276–7; the Seaside Library, 31; and "The English Renaissance," *New York Tribune* (New York, NY), 10 Jan. 1882, 2. *Miscellanies* has "window *or* marble" (emphasis added).

"A Man of Culture Rare," *Rochester Democrat and Chronicle* (Rochester, NY), 8 Feb. 1882, 4[1]

OSCAR WILDE AND HIS MISSION ON EARTH.

His Lecture at the Grand Opera House—Rowdies in the Gallery—A Small Audience—A Brief Interview With the Great Leader in Modern Aestheticism—"I am Indestructible."

Oscar Wilde, his knee breeches, his business manager and his colored body servant arrived in the city late yesterday afternoon and were at once driven to the Osburn house, where rooms had been assigned them. The great leader in modern aestheticism at once retired to his apartment and did not again make his appearance until half past 7 o'clock, when he rode to the Grand Opera house, where a blushing reporter of this paper was presented to him in the dressing room.[2] There was certainly nothing limp nor languid in the hearty English grip with which he clasped the proffered hand, and had it not been for the singularity of his attire there would have been nothing in particular to distinguish him from an ordinary English gentleman. In appearance he was the typical *Bunthorne* of "Patience." He was dressed in knee breeches, black silk stockings marvelously fitted, low patent leather pumps, regulation dress coat, low cut double-breasted white vest, shirt collar turned low with a voluminous white tie, and a broad expanse of shirt bosom, ornamented with a single stud, in which were set two pearls and a diamond. A fob with double seals jingled below his vest, and the only other article of jewelry visible was a large seal ring upon the third finger of his left hand. The effect was curious if not picturesque, and it was heightened by the remarkable face and head. Thick and heavy hair, parted in the middle, fell nearly to the shoulders on either side, enclosing a long, narrow and oddly marked face. The forehead is low, the cheek bones high, the eyes bright and full of expression, the mouth large and mobile, the lips full, and the chin giving the impression of unusual length. It is not a handsome face; it is not a strong face, but it is an exceedingly interesting face, made doubly so, perhaps, by a knowledge of the man's life and position. It is emphatically the face of a dreamer, intelligent and refined, but not the face that would inspire confidence in earnestness of purpose and vigor of execution. This is the first strong impression, but the judg-

1. H & S, b30. Reprinted in Mikhail, 50–3; and H & S, 53–6. Excerpted in "Oscar in Rochester," *The Syracuse Morning Standard* (Syracuse, NY), 9 Feb. 1882, 1; the *Brooklyn Daily Union-Argus* (Brooklyn, NY), 10 Feb. 1882, 1; the *Utica Weekly Herald* (Utica, NY), 14 Feb. 1882, 4. Quoted in OWDA, 155–6; and Ellmann, 176/184. Referenced in Sturgis, 227/218.

2. The author perhaps alludes here to the maidens in *Patience*, who, before transferring their affections to Bunthorne, blush in the presence of the dragoons.

ment of the mind is wonderfully shaken by a brief experience with his conversational powers.

As the reporter perched gingerly upon the edge of a chair, Oscar Wilde inquired if art had gained any foothold in Rochester, which enabled the visitor with pardonable pride to refer to Powers' art gallery and the art exchange, never failing sources of inspiration. He admitted that the art exchange was good as far as it went, but that in reality nothing could be done until there was founded a school of design. "You must teach the people to do artistic work," he said, "and then the movement will begin to assume form. It is not to the rich who can afford to be patrons, but the workers in art to whom we must look for development."

"How about the treatment you have received from the newspapers in this country?"

"I have no complaints to make. They have certainly treated me outrageously, but I am not the one who is injured, it is the public. By such ridiculous attacks the people are taught to mock where they should reverence, to scoff at things to which they will not even listen. Had I been treated differently by the newspapers in England and in this country, had I been commended and endorsed, for the first time in my life I should have doubted myself and my mission. What possible difference can it make to me what the New York Herald says? You go and look at the statue of the Venus De Medici and you know that it is an exquisitely beautiful creation. Would it change your opinion in the least if all the newspapers in the land should pronounce it a wretched caricature? Not at all. I know that I am right, that I have a mission to perform. I am indestructible! Shelley was driven out of England, but he wrote equally well in Italy. It was not he who was injured, it was the people. I cannot expect,—I do not wish better treatment than Keats and Shelley received, and yet I must confess that I am surprised. You have sent many Americans to us in England, and at least we have received them courteously. You have sent us a good many actors, some of them good, some of them very bad; but I do not think they can justly complain of rudeness on our part. How would it have appeared had we accused Booth of blackmail, as I was accused in Baltimore?"

The listener gave expression to his vagueness and Mr. Wilde continued:

"We have many eminent men in our country, men eminent in art and letters, but they would not think for a moment of venturing here in a public capacity. They know well enough the treatment they would receive, the questionable courtesy I have experienced."

"How were you pleased with the demonstrations of the Harvard students?"

"There was nothing offensive in that. I understood well enough that it was meant as a good natured joke, and I entered into the spirit of it fully. It recalled to my mind many incidents of my life at Oxford."

"As you do not read what the newspapers say about you, I suppose you know nothing of the thousands of paragraphs that are flying about the country about you. Most of them, I presume originated in the newspaper offices. For instance I read the other day that you were presented to a prominent society lady in Washington, and she exclaimed, 'And so this is Oscar Wilde; but where is your lily? The quick reply was, 'At home, madame, where you left your good manners.' I suppose, of course, that had no foundation in fact?"

"On the contrary, it is absolutely true, with the exception that it happened in London and that the lady was a duchess."

"What did she do then?"

"She did what any duchess would do under the circumstances, I suppose—blushed and remained quiet."

"Well, then there is another story in which the boot is on the other foot. It is said that you complained that there were no quaint ruins in this country, no curiosities, and a lady replied, 'Time will remedy the one, and as for the curiosities, we import them.'"[1]

"Yes, that is an excellent story. It was first told of Charles Dickens when he visited this country. I find every community has its lady who is remarkably bright in her repartee and she is always credited with the latest *bon mot* going the rounds. Those two stories are following me all over the country, localised in almost every city."

"Pardon the digression, but I would like to know your opinion, from a thoroughly artistic standpoint, upon the prize fight which took place today?"[2]

Mr. Wilde laughed and said, "Even that has its artistic side. You know the ancient Greeks—"

At this point, Mr. Vale, the manager, made his appearance at the door and announced that it was 8 o'clock and time to go on. The lecturer at once sprang to his feet, excused himself, walked quickly to the back entrance, walked to the

1. Wilde used this story in *A Woman of No Importance*: "LADY CAROLINE. There are a great many things you haven't got in America, I am told, Miss Worsley. They say you have no ruins, and no curiosities. | MRS. ALLONBY. (*To* LADY STUTFIELD.) What nonsense! They have their mothers and their manners. | HESTER. The English aristocracy supply us with our curiosities, Lady Caroline. They are sent over to us every summer, regularly, in the steamers, and propose to us the day after they land. As for ruins, we are trying to build up something that will last longer than brick or stone." (*Woman*, 69.)

2. On 7 February 1882 the American heavyweight bare-knuckle boxing champion Patrick "Paddy" Ryan (1851–1900) lost his title to John Lawrence Sullivan (1858–1918) in a fight in Mississippi City. See "The Ring," *The Brooklyn Daily Eagle* (Brooklyn, NY), 7 Feb. 1882, 4. In his first Chicago lecture Wilde read from an editorial from the *Chicago Tribune* (12 Feb. 1882, 4) that humorously compared his school of aestheticism with that of Sullivan, telling his audience that he had no "wish to reproach that wicked and imaginative editor [...] because I know from experience that the conscience of an editor is merely decorative" ("Oscar Wilde," *The Daily Inter Ocean* (Chicago, IL), 14 Feb. 1882, 2).

front of the stage, and without preface, commenced at once to deliver his lecture on "The English Renaissance." There was a slight ripple of applause as he made his appearance. The lecture has been extensively printed, so that it is hardly necessary to reproduce even a sketch of it here. It was delivered in rather a tiresome monotone, but the small audience present was apparently interested and listened attentively until the close. At the beginning of the lecture, two or three young rowdies in the gallery attempted to make a disturbance by "Oh's" and "Ah's," and turning down the gas, but they were quickly suppressed by Ed. Moore, the officer in charge, and compelled to leave the house. It was said that the young men were students at the university, but it is sincerely to be hoped that none of the students are boorish enough to be guilty of such a stupid insult. Among those to arrive before the lecture commenced was Peter Craig, arrayed gorgeously in dress coat, white vest and knee breeches, a take off which some must have considered the essence of wit.[1]

"Oscar Wilde," *Buffalo Daily Courier* (Buffalo, NY), 9 Feb. 1882, 2[2]

The Apostle of Aestheticism in Buffalo.

A Large and Fashionable Audience at the Academy of Music.

The Poet's Appearance—How He Was Received—Full Text of His Lecture. A Talk With Mr. Wilde.

Mr. Oscar Wilde arrived in Buffalo yesterday morning from Rochester, and at once proceeded to the Tiffs House. He wore a long olive-green ulster trimmed with plucked beaver fur, was accompanied by a servant, and after registering quietly proceeded to his room, where he remained until it was necessary for him to proceed to the Academy of Music and give his lecture on "The English Renaissance."

✂ *A report of Wilde's lecture in Buffalo.*

A TALK WITH MR WILDE.

After the lecture, representatives of THE COURIER had a conversation with Mr. Wilde. He felt highly gratified by the reception which had been tendered him. "It

1. A local African American man, around 59 years of age. Rochester students had persuaded or compelled him to don aesthetic costume and parade into the theatre. They had also recently given him a mortarboard and stood him at a busy intersection to amuse passersby (Mendelssohn, 121–2).
2. Quoted in OWDA, 162.

was not long," he said, "after I began speaking before I found that I was addressing a refined and cultivated audience by whom I was understood. This is a very great comfort to me, for I need not tell you that I have not the gift of oratory. Indeed public speaking as an art is not cultivated in England. Unless a man is in political or parliamentary life, he has few opportunities of making himself heard, and thus you find many of our foremost men, who are consummate masters of language and thought upon paper, find it impossible to think upon their legs and express themselves engagingly. Besides I am not a good judge of the force of my own voice—very few men are—and I don't know whether I make myself heard to everyone or not.

"When I am on my way home," continued Mr. Wilde, "I will be in a better position to tell you something about my impressions of America. I have not as yet had any great opportunity of seeing men and things, but I am making the best of my advantages. I think I may say that I am noticing here a response to the mission which I consider my own. The work of decorative art is being more extensively carried on. People are beginning to see the sound wisdom of making their homes more beautiful, and some even think that there is joy to be had in stopping now and then to contemplate that which does not altogether partake of business. There is good, honest, practical work in art, and it should begin with the boys of your nation. Teach them to use their hands. Teach them trades that will employ hand and brain and make them love beautiful forms. The boy who loves the beautiful will not have much difficulty in learning to love the pure and the good for their own sake."

"I have been not a little surprised, in a country where wood is so generally used in building, that more wood carving is not employed, carving that is the product of the skill of your young people. In little Swiss villages you will find ragged urchins whose skill with the knife and chisel in carving wood ornaments is simply wonderful. I don't think it would be time thrown away were your boys taught to carve adornments for the plain wooden boxes which so many people consider perfect when they have a coat of white paint. Why not, also, paint these dwellings in bright and cheerful colors, instead of the uniform glaring white which one meets everywhere?[1]

1. Wilde made the same points in *The Decorative Arts*: "I wish to say little about your wooden houses, which are painted in the most oppressive colours I have ever seen, but it does seem to me that the adoption of the prevailing colour, white, with which you cover them, making the white walls appear as a sheet of white flame in the noonday sun, is a gross mistake when the barrenness of the houses is overcome so easily by wood carving [....] In Switzerland, the little barefooted shepherd boy that blows a horn all day on the hills after some stray goats will return home and there carve in wood over his father's door the figures of the birds and flowers he has seen, and beautifies the house with his art." (O'Brien, 160–1.) See also p. 318, note 2.

“As to architecture,” said Mr. Wilde, “in time you will doubtless have an architecture of your own with distinct characteristics. Anything would be better than the imitation of Greek architecture which loom up like nightmares in the leading streets of New York, Corinthian columns and Doric fronts and the most extraordinary admixtures of styles the world ever saw. Some people say such compounds are audacious: perhaps they are, but to me they seem little less than criminal. As to Decorative Art, those who are giving attention thereto should not be led into the mistake that the [?means] is the end. I see many excellent people who fancy they are busy with artistic decoration when they are really engaged in the perpetration of moonlight and landscape horrors on plates for the affliction of friends upon whom they may bestow them. I needn’t tell you that that sort of thing isn’t art at all; it is only the affectation of art by those who have not the earnestness to pursue the study of art with that thoroughness which is its due. But in time, as the minds of those who are to take our places become cultivated, all these evils will correct themselves. The trouble is that education usually begins in the wrong way, upon the assumption that children are started out already supplied with minds, when, as a matter of fact, they are only provided with capacities to receive what in time may become minds of greater or lesser force.

“As to the criticism I have encountered at the hands of the press I have rather enjoyed it. Had I been flattered and praised from the first I might have been misled; honestly criticised, I may have been shown my weaknesses. I may say that my lecture has been changed considerably since it was first delivered, and is likely to undergo further changes.”

Mr. Wilde left by the 6 10 o’clock train last evening, over the Central Railroad for Niagara Falls, where he will remain for a day or so, a guest at the Prospect House. On Monday night next he will lecture in Chicago.

“Utter Oscar,” *Buffalo Morning Express* (Buffalo, NY), 9 Feb. 1882, 4

AN APOSTLE OF AESTHETICISM.

The Knight of the Lilies and the Big Sun-flower—Mr. Wilde’s Visit to Buffalo—His Lecture on the English Renaissance.

✂ *A report of Wilde’s lecture in Buffalo.*

A CHAT WITH OSCAR.

After the lecture a representative of THE EXPRESS was introduced to Mr. Wilde, who was half-reclining in a large chair in one of the waiting-rooms just off the stage. On near inspection the disciple and expounder of aestheticism was found to be fully as masculine in his lineaments, sturdy in build, and genial in expression as he had seemed by the artificial lights. Sunlight pouring in a window illumined the long and heavy hair which has been particularly mentioned because of the outlandish, or rather aesthetical, way in which he wears it. It was not so dark as it had appeared viewed from the auditorium, but a genuine golden although dull hue—old gold, in fact. That just describes it. Old gold hair is just the thing for an aesthete, it may be presumed.

Mr. Wilde expressed much satisfaction with his reception here. He had felt that the audience were listening to him intently, and that many were interested in his subject.

"But I'm dreadfully tired," said Oscar, in a manner that was languid but a voice that sounded jovial rather than otherwise. "It isn't the lecturing, I delight in giving my lectures when I find there is interest in them, but it's the long distances. The traveling has nearly used me up. I haven't been used to it you know. At home I'd get up in the morning, have breakfast, do some writing, and then maybe start off for Egypt or some other distant part, but take my time about it all."

The reporter ventured to ask if he didn't find the American means of travel more comfortable than in Europe?

"The English railroads," replied Mr. Wilde, "are as bad as they can be. The American railroads are just as bad. There is no comfort on them anyway. One can't read or write comfortably, and if you look out of the window to see if an object is a house or a tree it's three miles behind you before you can determine."

Questioned as to what the extent of his tour of this country would be, he replied he hardly knew. He had wanted to visit California and Mexico. "They speak of your country," said he, "why, you have a world. I had no just idea of it." The scenery of the Hudson he referred to enthusiastically, and he was much interested in allusions made by the newspaper man to the mountain scenery on the Erie Railway and some of the Pennsylvania lines. Mr. Wilde had somehow conceived a great fancy for a Mexican visit. "I should like very much to ride through Mexico," said he. "I should like also to visit many parts of your country. Your cities have no architecture; they are too new. But you have grand rivers and mountains."

In the course of his conversation Mr. Wilde touched occasionally on the subject he holds nearest at heart, that of art improvement, and at such times he spoke enthusiastically, his big eyes full of light. "It is the subject to which your country must devote herself. She has had her war, she is prosperous, and now she must give her attention to art if she would obtain permanent good. The young women of the country must be expected to do the most.

"You have a decorative Art Society here, I believe. The mission is a noble one. It is not for the rich that we want art promoted, but for the poor."

Then somehow Mr. Wilde mentioned the newspapers. "You're a newspaper man," said he, "but I can't help saying that I am astonished at the ridicule, the mockery with which the American press treats lofty and serious matters."

Our representative could but admit that some American newspapers are a good deal given to levity.

"If in one of these papers an article were to be begun with a serious or noble expression of sentiment would the people take it for a joke?" asked Oscar.

The newspaper subject dropped, Mr. Wilde enumerated various things which had favorably impressed him.

"What is your opinion of American ladies, Mr. Wilde?"

"I have the same opinion of them that every sensible man must have," he said. But just what that opinion was he did not elucidate. He had, he said, seen many very beautiful women in this country—many in Baltimore, and a great many in New York.

Mr. Wilde's geographical and some other ideas concerning the United States are yet in an early stage of development. As he journeys further and investigates deeper, he will no doubt become still more firmly fixed in the opinion that here is a great field for the cultivation of the true and the beautiful in art, as well as any other fairly paying crop.

Mr. Wilde's first intention was to remain in Buffalo over night, and in that event was invited by Mr. H. L. Meech to attend the Theatre in the evening,[1] and subsequently the City Club. But on account of the little time at his command, Mr. Wilde late in the afternoon determined to pick up his grip-sack and start for Niagara Falls forthwith. He will do the Falls—aesthetically, as it is to be presumed, and will this evening start for Chicago, where he lectures next Monday.[2]

1. Henry L. Meech and John H. Meech were associated with the Meech Bros. theatrical company, headquartered at the Academy of Music. On the evening of 9 February the Academy was host to Haverley's New Mastodon Minstrels.

2. Wilde lectured on *The Decorative Arts* in Chicago's Central Music Hall on Monday 13 February.

"Wilde Sees the Falls," *Buffalo Morning Express* (Buffalo, NY), 10 Feb. 1882, 4[1]

And is at First Disappointed and Critical—But Grows Enthusiastic at Last.

Special Despatch.

NIAGARA FALLS, Ont., Feb 9—The day was all that could be desired for sight-seeing. Oscar Wilde, who made his headquarters at the Prospect House, breakfasted early, and wrapping himself in his long fur coat, stood out on the veranda of the hotel for nearly an hour steadily gazing at the scene before him. A carriage was ordered at nine o'clock, and in company with his agent, Mr. Vale, they started for the different points of interest. They returned at two o'clock. The change of scenery and fresh air seemed to please Mr. Wilde.

After dinner Wilde conversed on his morning's adventure. To use his own words, he said: "When I first saw Niagara Falls I was disappointed in the outline. The design, it seemed to me, was wanting in grandeur and variety of line, but the colors were beautiful. The dull gray waters flecked with green are lit with silver, being full of changing loveliness; for of all the most lovely colors are colors in motion. It was not till I stood underneath the Falls at Table Rock that I realized the majestic splendor and strength of the physical forces of nature here. The sight was far beyond what I had ever seen in Europe. It seems a sort of embodiment of pantheism. I thought of what Leonardo Da Vinci said once, that 'the two most beautiful things in the world are a woman's smile and the motion of mighty waters.'"[2]

Mr. Wilde wrote in the Prospect House private album:

"The roar of these waters is like the roar when the mighty wave democracy breaks on the shores where kings lie couched at ease.

"OSCAR WILDE."[3]

1. H & S, b31. Printed simultaneously, with minor variations, as "An Aesthetic View of Niagara," *The Boston Globe* (Boston, MA), 10 Feb. 1882, 4 (which is quoted in Ellmann, 185/195); "Oscar the Democrat," *Buffalo Evening News* (Buffalo, NY), 10 Feb. 1882, 1; and "Oscar Wilde on Niagara," *The New York Herald* (New York, NY), 10 Feb. 1882, 7 (which is quoted in Ellmann, 185/195). Reprinted as "Wilde Sees the Falls," *Wheeling Register* (Wheeling, WV), 27 Feb. 1882, 3 (which is reprinted in H & S, 57; and quoted in Sturgis, 235/226). An abbreviated despatch appeared as "Oscar Wilde at Niagara Falls," *Chicago Daily Tribune* (Chicago, IL), 10 Feb. 1882, 3. Quoted in "The Poet of Niagara," *New York Tribune* (New York, NY), 12 Feb. 1882, 6 (which is quoted in Ellmann, 185/195). OWDA, 163–4, quotes a version in the *Niagara Falls Gazette*.

2. *Personal Impressions of America*: "Every American bride is taken there, and the sight of the stupendous waterfall must be one of the earliest, if not the keenest, disappointments in American married life." (Dibb, 236.)

3. The author of the *Buffalo Evening News* version here notes that a "similar sentiment is found in one of Wilde's poems, where he says:— The roar of the democracies | Mirror my wildest passions like the sea." The quotation of *Sonnet to Liberty*, first published in *Poems*, should read: "But

This is the same album in which Sarah Bernhardt wrote: "How good is God to make such beautiful things."[1]

Wilde leaves tonight by the Great Western and Michigan Central railways for Chicago.

"The Apostle of Art," *The Daily Inter Ocean* (Chicago, IL), 11 Feb. 1882, 4[2]

St. Oscar de Wilde Arrives, Lilies and All, in Chicago.

Pen-pictured as, Upon His Couch Recumbent, He Accords Audience.

What Utterly Utter Replies He Vouchsafes on Non-fleshly Subjects.

Oscar Wilde, the apostle of aestheticism, the lover of all sweet, beautiful, and darling things in nature, the John the Baptist of the religion of art, the much-talked-of English lecturer, arrived in Chicago last night, and took rooms at the Grand Pacific. A reporter for THE INTER OCEAN called upon him and was kindly received. The aesthetic young man had been reclining in a very utter and languid attitude upon a sofa which was drawn up before the blazing grate, and the sofa was covered with a fine wolf-skin robe and a tiger skin, while where his head had lain was a silk shawl of the color of old gold and soft as the sigh of a maiden. He was found to be a tall and strongly-built young man, not too strong, not enough to be gross in flesh or muscle. His long hair, which curls up on the ends, was parted in the middle and fell to his shoulders. His face is smooth, oval, with no feature very strongly marked except the mouth. The lips are red, rather thicker than with most people, and have a little nervous trick [*sic*] of compression. The whole expression of the face is pleasant, especially when lighted up with a smile, which, when it happens,

---

that the roar of thy Democracies, | Thy reigns of Terror, thy great Anarchies, | Mirror my wildest passions like the sea" (CW i, No. 80, lines 4–6). Instead, Wilde was likely thinking of his poem *Louis Napoleon*, first published in *Poems*, which ends: "And that the giant wave Democracy | Breaks on the shores where Kings lay couched at ease" (CW i, No. 65, lines 15–16), and of a line from *Vera; or, The Nihilists*: "The star of freedom is risen already, and far off I hear the mighty wave democracy break on these cursed shores." (CW xi, 138.398–401.)

1. Bernhardt had visited Niagara Falls on 20 March 1881.

2. H & S, b32. Reprinted in H & S, 57–61. Excerpted in "Destroying the Beautiful in England," *St. Louis Post-Dispatch* (St. Louis, MO), 20 Feb. 1882, 2. Quoted in OWDA, 166–8; and Pearson, 66. The reporter was accompanied by the author of "Weary Wilde," *The Chicago Times* (Chicago, IL), 11 Feb. 1882, 6, pp. 155–8.

MAKES HIM VERY BEAUTIFUL.

The ears are entirely concealed by the thick locks, which he ever and anon brushes back carelessly, yet with a lingering and caressing motion. Mr. Wilde was dressed in a coat of black velvet, scarlet necktie, and handkerchief of the same color protruding from the pocket, light pantaloons, slippers, and red socks. He was smoking a cigar, and handled it with the grace which only comes from long practice. His greeting was kind, and the grasp of his hand cordial and soulful. The pressure was not intense, but the firm clasp of the white, nervous fingers was like the clinging of a vine.

"It has been a fine day for traveling, Mr. Wilde," said the reporter.

Mr. Wilde had thrown himself back upon the skins in a very picturesque attitude, and was gazing at the fire. He paused a moment, and then the sweet tones of his voice, full and round, and with a suggestion of a sea-shell held to the ear, made reply: "I have been traveling so long, you know. But," with a sigh, "it seems a bright and clear day." Then he relapsed into another utter attitude and

CARESSED HIS CIGAR THOUGHTFULLY.

"You have been often interviewed, I believe," said the reporter.

"Yes, but never with ordinary accuracy. All have relied upon their imaginations, and the result has been a libel upon that noble quality."

"Meaning—"

"The imagination."

"How do you like the West?"

"I should imagine it is far more free from prejudice. The East seems to catch too much of the little floating follies of Europe. For that kind of thing you in the West have no time. In the East I found many cities pervaded by some folly of misinterpretation which they are already tired of in England."

"What did you think of Niagara? I understand you paid the falls a visit?"

"When I saw the falls for the first time the thought came over me that they were not so noble in design and action as I had expected, perhaps; but the colors were beautiful. When in motion they were full of change."

"Did you change your mind?"

"Not till I had stood underneath the cataract did I realize how enormous was the physical force of nature in the midst of which I was standing."

"What are your general impressions of America?"

"That is a difficult question. I have only as yet seen your towns, not the country at all. I have not yet seen anything in the least that seemed definitely and absolutely American."

"How do you like the cities?"

"The best cities have a very high cosmopolitanism; in the lesser cities a curious provincialism. What strikes me most here in the West is really the type of civilization definitely American, created by yourselves and for yourselves."

"What is the nature of your mission?"

"THE WHOLE ESSENCE OF THIS ARTISTIC

movement in England is that we had a desire to discover in every city those men and women who have the power of artistic design; to give them the best models and expression possible to train them in the noblest surroundings to produce the noblest work."

"Is that its whole object?"

"In regard to people who are not handicraftsmen, who have not this power of design nor the capacity for artistic vocation, we wish to produce in them that artistic temperament without which there is no individuality in art, no real joy of life; in a word, no civilization."

"How can that be done?"

"There is only one way of producing this artistic temperament, and that is by accustoming them from childhood to the abiding presence in their own houses of beautiful and joyous color and noble and rational design. We want to make art not a luxury for the rich, but as it should be the most splendid of all the chords through which the spirit of any nation manifests its power, but to make it part of the daily atmosphere in which people live."

"What is art?"

This question seemed to arouse Mr. Wilde. He flashed a scornful glance at the reporter, but it was followed immediately by a sunny smile. He arose and stood with his back to the fire and his hands clasped under his coat-tails.

"AN ARTISTIC THING,"

he said, "is anything which, independent of its practical use, pleases one by the beauty and delicacy of its form, the wonder of its design, or the nobility of its color. A man who creates an artistic thing is a man who works not with his hands only, but with his heart and with his head."

"But what of industry?"

"Life without industry is barren, and industry without art is barbarism."[1]

"Do you think more of the works of Michael Angelo than of Edison?"[2]

1. Art and barbarism: see p. 117, note 1.

2. Thomas Edison (1847–1931) was an American inventor and businessman. Wilde and Edison shared a cordial meeting in the latter's New York offices in the summer of 1883 (Sturgis, 295–6/280–1).

"One production of Michael Angelo is worth an hundred of Edison. It is a sign of a nobler, fresher civilization among the people. Modern civilizations are not good or bad in themselves at all. They certainly increase one's wonder at the mysteries of nature and one's admiration for the genius of man. But their true use for civilization depends entirely upon the spirit in which they are used."

"Modern inventions are useful?"

"A tramway is an exceedingly useful and economical means of conveyance, but in Oxford today they are pulling down one of the most

BEAUTIFUL OLD BRIDGES

of England in order to substitute in its place what they call in England a light and elegant cast-iron structure."[1]

The last few words were spoken with undisguised contempt.

"This," he continued, "is in order to facilitate the running of a tramway. In this there is no gain to England at all, only the irreparable loss of stately and noble architecture."

"We are not troubled that way here," said the reporter, "for we have no old buildings or bridges to pull down."

"That is good fortune for you," he said. "There is hardly a beautiful thing left us. The history of a country should live not in books, but in its architecture. That is the most solemnly beautiful record of the past that man can create. There is hardly a single beautiful thing left in London," said Mr. Wilde with a sigh.

"But are not useful things more important to civilization that beautiful ones?"

"Useful is a dangerous word. Useful for what? I deny that between the noblest usefulness and the noblest beauty there is anything but the most complete accord and sympathy. Westminster Abbey is useful, and it's also beautiful—the most useful because it is the most beautiful."

"What is civilization?"

"That condition under which man most completely realizes the perfection of his own nature. Civilization without beauty or art is an impossibility. The best bookcase is the one which will best hold your books. Then add to it whatever you love best in the world as decoration."

"What do you think of our architecture?"

Mr. Wilde looked at his questioner pityingly.

"YOU HAVE NONE,"

he said. "You want in this country, to begin with, the primary element of beautiful cities, that is noble architecture. The old, red-brick houses your Puritan fathers

1. Tramway in Oxford: see p. 53, note 2.

built you are much more beautiful, much more simple, much more natural that the sham Greek porticos, the Doric chimneys, and Corinthian upper stories of Fifth avenue. In domestic architecture, there is nothing more suitable or beautiful than red brick."

"But it is not necessary for a building to be old to be beautiful?"

"Very true. A Gothic cathedral, with half the side chipped away by a storm, is not beautified by the operation. Age will add a certain charm, or what people call picturesqueness, to a building, but age will never make an ugly building beautiful."

"But is not modern civilization the greatest?"

"The greatest civilization of the world existed ages ago, and existed without steam engines. Of what use is it to a man to travel sixty miles an hour? He travels and then stops. Is he any better for it? A fool can buy a railway ticket and travel sixty miles an hour. Is he any the less a fool?"

"Weary Wilde," *The Chicago Times* (Chicago, IL), 11 Feb. 1882, 6[1]

ARRIVAL OF THE AESTHETIC PHILOSOPHER AND HIS RECEPTION BY "THE TIMES."

His Appearance, Actions, and Dress Not Materially Changed—Impressions of America Not Yet Fixed—Niagara Disappointing in Outline, but Beautiful in Color—A Discourse on the Artistic and the Useful—A Few Days To Be Spent in Looking About Chicago.

Oscar Wilde arrived in the city last evening, and was found at the Grand Pacific Hotel by a reporter of THE TIMES. The public has had so many descriptions of him that another one is hardly necessary. It is sufficient to say that he is tall, looks very much as he is represented in his photographs in the show-windows, wears his hair long, parted in the middle, and drooping down the sides of his face and over his neck, and was dressed last evening in a light suit of English goods, with sack coat and pantaloons, light red necktie, with a handkerchief to match just protruding from the breast pocket of his coat, and low shoes. He was reclining leisurely on a sofa smoking a cigar, and greeted THE TIMES representative cordially, speaking in a broad English accent. His face is long and extremely boyish,—in fact, he looks like a

1. H & S, b33. Excerpted in "Oscar Wilde," *Fort Wayne Daily Gazette*, 14 Feb. 1882, 5 (only the paragraph beginning "The whole essence of this artistic movement in England [...]"). The reporter was accompanied by the author of "The Apostle of Art," *The Daily Inter Ocean* (Chicago, IL), 11 Feb. 1882, 4, pp. 151–5.

VERY MUCH OVERGROWN BOY,—

and his features, while thoughtful, are somewhat effeminate. The conversation began with a casual reference to the pleasant weather, and he replied that he had been traveling so long that it hardly seemed pleasant to him. He was asked how he liked the west, and replied that it was freer from prejudices than the east, which catches too many of the floating follies of Europe, which the people in the west have no time for, and are too distant from it to contract.

"What are your general impressions of America?" was queried.

"That is a difficult question to answer. I have seen only the towns, not the country. I have not seen in the east anything that is distinctively American. In the best cities there is very high cosmopolitanism, but in the lesser cities a curious provincialism. What interests me most in coming to the west is that here I shall see that type of civilization which is definitely American, created by yourselves and for yourselves."

"What did you think of Niagara?"

"When I saw it, it was not so noble in outline and design as I had expected, perhaps, although the color was beautiful. All the most beautiful colors are those in motion; they are full of change. It was not till I stood under the cataract that I realized how enormous were the physical forces of nature amidst which I was standing."

COMING TO HIS FAVORITE THEME,

the reporter enquired: "What is the predominant idea of the philosophy which you teach?"

"The whole essence of this artistic movement in England is, on the one hand, a desire to discover in every city those men and women who have power of artistic design, to give them the best models and examples possible, to train them in the noblest surroundings, to produce the noblest work, and as regards the people who are not handicraftsmen, people who have not this power of design, nor the capacity for artistic creation, we want to produce in them that artistic temperament without which there is no understanding of art, no real joy of life; in a word, no civilization. There is only one way of producing this artistic temperament, and that is by accustoming them from their childhood to the abiding presence in their own houses of beautiful and joyous color and noble and natural design. We want to make art, not a luxury for the rich, but, as it should be, the most splendid of all the chords through which the spirit of any nation manifests its power. We want to make it part of the daily atmosphere in which people live."

"What do you mean by art and artistic?"

"AN ARTISTIC THING

is anything which, irrespective of its practical use, pleases one by the beauty and delicacy of its form, wonder of its design, or the nobility of its color. A man who creates an artistic thing is a man who works not with his hands only, but with his heart and with his head."

"Do you make art the chief end of life, then?"

"Life without industry is barren, and industry without art is barbarism."[1]

"You speak of civilization. Which, in your judgment, produces the greater civilization, an invention such as the telephone and the telegraph, or one of Michael Angelo's paintings?"

"If you mean which is the greater sign of civilization, the production of an Angelo or an Edison, I answer an Angelo. One Angelo is worth a hundred Edisons. These modern inventions are not good or bad in themselves at all. They certainly increase one's wonder at the mysteries of nature, and one's admiration of the genius of man, but their use for civilization depends entirely on the spirit in which they are used. To give you an instance: A tramway is an exceeding [*sic*] useful and economical means of conveyance, but in Oxford today they are pulling down one of the most beautiful old bridges of England in order to substitute in its place what they call in England a light and elegant cast-iron structure, to facilitate the running of a tramway. In this there is no gain to England at all—only

THE IRREPARABLE LOSS

of stately and noble architecture."[2]

"Which is the more important to civilization, beauty or usefulness?"

"Well, useful is a dangerous word. Useful for what? I deny that between the noblest usefulness and the noblest beauty there is anything but the completest accord and unity."

"What do you mean by civilization?"

"Civilization is those conditions under which man most completely realizes the perfection of his nature. And so civilization, without art, is a contradiction entirely, and civilization without beauty is an impossibility."

"What do you think of art in eastern cities as compared with art in England?"

"You want in this country to begin with the primary element of beautiful cities; that is, noble architecture. The old red brick houses that your Puritan fathers built are much more beautiful, much more simple and natural than the sham Greek porticoes, the Doric chimneys, and the Corinthian upper stories on Fifth avenue. For domestic architecture, there is nothing more suitable than red brick."

1. Art and barbarism: see p. 117, note 1.
2. Tramway in Oxford: see p. 53, note 2.

"Is age necessary to beautiful buildings?"

"Not at all. The beauty consists in the nobility of the architecture and the symmetry of design. Age often adds a charm, but it will never make an ugly building beautiful."

Mr. Wilde will spend the next few days in looking about the city.

"Oscar Wilde," *The Chicago Daily Tribune* (Chicago, IL), 11 Feb. 1882, 3[1]

His Arrival in the City.

Oscar Wilde, the poet, artist, and apostle of the esthetic movement, arrived in the city at 8 o'clock last evening, and was driven at once to the grand Pacific, where he was assigned the two parlors occupied by Mme. Patti on her recent trip.[2] He dined in his own room on a sirloin-steak and mushrooms, brook trout, boiled quail, and the usual amount of etceteras. He drank champagne, and "never thought such good wine could be obtained so far West." He expressed himself as perfectly happy, but expressed a desire for Turkish cigarettes, which could not be obtained in the hotel. After his dinner he was waited upon by a squadron of reporters, who were admitted in detachments to the rooms of the great esthete, occupying his time until midnight. THE TRIBUNE reporter went to scoff, but remained an hour, which was devoted to a delightful conversation.

On entering the room the reporter stood face to face with the great Oscar himself, the colored servant withdrawing after disposing the chairs properly. Before the reporter was fairly seated he became aware that the esthete was disposing himself in an artistic attitude which at once attracted attention. An ordinary lounge had been drawn out from the cheerful fire. It was covered with a magnificent robe of dark fur, while at the end dangled a delicate India shawl. The subject of the interview lounged in a carefully careless attitude with his arm thrown over the back of the sofa. Then it was that a good view could be had of his face and dress. He has a remarkable face, womanish, almost babyish in its innocence, clear olive complexion, dark eyes, full chin, entirely innocent of beard, rather heavy lips, large white teeth, and a contour which reminds one irresistibly of a Madonna. His dark hair hangs with a barely perceptible wave over his shoulders, and, as he talks, he brushes it back on one side or the other, making the part

1. Quoted in OWDA, 166–8; and Ellmann, 185/195. This article did not appear in all copies of the *Tribune*. The front pages of copies that included or did not include the article are identical and carry no edition numbers.
2. Adelina Patti (1843–1919) was an Italian soprano.

in the middle the more prominent. He wore a silver-gray jacket, buttoned only at the middle of the chest, and opened above to show a broad scarf of rose color tied in an indescribable manner. A handkerchief of the same shade dangled from his pocket. He wore light gray trousers, red stockings, and patent leather slippers, with large black bows. His appearance was irresistibly comic but when he talked he smiled, and the listener became so unconsciously absorbed in his conversation as to forget the ridiculous attire. His modulation is a trifle affected, but still it is essentially English. He talks slowly and evidently weighed his words. His careful manner of speech made it an easy task to obtain a verbatim report of the interview.

By way of breaking the ice, the reporter suggested that Mr. Wilde had possibly something to complain of about his reception here.

"Socially," he replied, "I was charmed with your people. I was received delightfully by some charming people. If you mean those Boston school-boys,[1] I assure you that it was not meant in earnest. It was only school-boy fun, and I appreciated it as such. As regards the newspapers it was different, and for one reason. In England one knows that if one tries to create a new movement, to produce any beautiful work in poetry or art, or to protest in any way against the commonplace life of the people—one knows that one loses all the ordinary rights of citizens, and that everything that folly or ridicule can do will be done. So, personally, I have long ago ceased to find any pleasure or to receive any pain from what anonymous newspaper-writers choose to say of me. The harm they have done in America is to the public and not to me. The newspapers seem to have raised again that mist of misrepresentation, that fog of folly which blinds people to all that is noble, and simple, and strong in a great movement. I feel, when I lecture, that the first half-hour at least I am merely struggling against the misrepresentation that has preceded me. Whether before I finish my lecture I am able to dispel that idea is not for me to say. I hope that I am."

Then, rising before the fire where his broad shoulders could be seen to advantage, he smiled winningly at the terrified reporter and continued:

"I do not think, however, that we in England would welcome any young American who had won himself any position in poetry or in art, who had something to say and could say it, in the way in which I have been received."

The reporter confessed to the same belief, and politely expressed regret.

"I am glad to hear you say that. You are the first newspaper man who has expressed the slightest concern as to my reception."

"What have been your impressions of the country?"

"I have only seen your cities, and you would not have me judge America by its cities, would you?"

1. Wilde refers to the Harvard incident: see p. 134, note 2.

The reporter intimated that even that might be permissible.

"No, no. Nature is what we must judge by. It is more to be admired than any work of man.[1] Thus far I have only seen two things which were wonderful in their beauty, the Hudson River and Niagara. I should imagine the beauty of the Hudson to be chiefly in the autumn, when the foliage takes on its grandest tints, but even as I saw it, with the trees all brown and leafless, it was wonderfully beautiful. As to Niagara, one knows nothing of it until one is underneath the falls. The outline is monotonous. It is not broken. There is nothing sublime about it. I do not think I ever realized so strongly the splendor and beauty of the mere physical forces of Nature as I did when I stood by Table-Rock. A wonderful thing is the calm directly underneath the falls, the rapids not showing themselves for a long distance down the river. There is a curious repetition of the same fall, of the same design almost, in the shape of the falling water, which gave me a sense of how completely what seems to us the wildest liberty of nature is restrained by governing laws."

"I have heard it stated that you were disappointed with the Atlantic."

"That old folly still clings, it seems. Why, I am passionately fond of the sea. But what is the sea in a calm? It is motionless. It is nothing. The grandest sight I ever saw in my life was a storm when coming from Athens to Naples, when a cyclone came up from the desert."[2]

"Ah," and the great esthete sank back in an ecstasy of blissful recollection.

Recovering his equilibrium he continued:

"I had an idea, when I came to America, that the people would listen simply to what I had to tell them about the most concentrated artistic movement we have ever had in England; that they would judge me by what I said, and that they would not rake up mere literally garbled folly against me. In Europe we are all so weighed down with prejudice, so trammeled by history, so old, that we always think of America as a country without prejudice. When we think of you in Europe, we think of you as a simple, practical, grand Nation."

"Could you, Mr. Wilde, give a brief definition of your aims in your trip to America?"

1. This contrasts with the position espoused by Vivian in *The Decay of Lying*: "If Nature had been comfortable, mankind would never have invented architecture, and I prefer houses to the open air." (CW iv, 74.1–2.) Also: "Sunsets are quite old-fashioned. They belong to the time when Turner was the last note in art. To admire them is a distinct sign of provincialism of temperament." (CW iv, 95.40–2.)

2. After his trip to Greece in 1877. Wilde's brother in law, Otho Holland Lloyd, later recalled a story that one of Wilde's travelling companions, probably George A. Macmillan, "during a frightful storm was sent crashing neck and crop to the keys of a piano in the small saloon." ([Otho Lloyd], "Stray Recollections," *The Soil*, Apr. 1917, 155–6.)

"I want to tell the American people what is the meaning of this movement in England to which England is giving so much of its genius and so much of its youth. You have heard the satire first. I think you should hear the truth now. We look to America for newer and more natural forms of art. We look for a school of sculpture particularly. 'Man does not live by bread alone.'[1] We feel that, with your wonderful climate, strong, healthy physique of your men and women, and the quick enthusiasm of life among you, you should be most noble artists.[2] Up to this time you have had much to contend with. You have had to conquer nature and to conquer your enemies. You have done both in a shorter time than any nation ever did before. There comes now a period of peace with you, a period for protection, for more wide-spread civilization. You have time yet to produce it. You have seen more than any other Nation the life without which industry is barren. You must remember that industry without art is barbarism.[3] All the wonderful material inventions which make life easier and wider for you, the steam engine, the telegraph, and the like, are noble or not entirely in the spirit in which you use them. The problem of modern life is how with all these wonderful inventions, far greater than ever Greek or Italian ever dreamed of, you can create a civilization greater or even as great as theirs."

"Then you think the Greeks were more civilized than we are?"

"Much more than the English are at any rate. They gave us speech, they gave us written characters. It is very valuable to be able to speak through a telephone to a man at the antipodes, but the value entirely depends on the worth of what he has to say. It is very valuable to travel sixty miles an hour, but the value entirely depends on how much the man who travels can gain from the places he sees or the things he visits. Most English people race over Italy in six weeks and bring back a memory of a bad dinner they got at Verona, or how their courier cheated them. That is all. To be content with merely the material substrata of evil, is as if man were to be content to know all the letters of the alphabet, and never care to combine them or to use them. There is a general idea that an artist has a supernatural horror of the steam-engine. Nothing of the kind is the case. One of Turner's most beautiful pictures, hanging in the National Gallery, in London, is the picture of an express train.[4] All that we feel about such inventions is that we

1. The reference is to Jesus's retort to the devil in Matthew 4:4: "Man shall not live by bread alone, but by every word that proceedeth out of the mouth of God."

2. *The Decorative Arts*: "You must have a strong and healthy physique among your men and women; sickly or idle or melancholy people don't do much in art, believe me." (O'Brien, 159.) Wilde presents an inverted version of this idea in *The Decay of Lying*: "Our splendid physique as a people [i.e. the English] is entirely due to our national stupidity." (CW iv, 74, lines 13–14.)

3. Art and barbarism: see p. 117, note 1.

4. Joseph Mallord William Turner (1775–1851) was an English painter. His painting *Rain, Steam and Speed – The Great Western Railway* was first exhibited at the Royal Academy in 1844.

want people to use them for the noblest purposes. Civilization has only one aim, to give every man the opportunity of realizing the perfection of our own nature. One must never mistake the means for the end."

The conversation turning on Irish subjects, Mr. Wilde said: "Ireland is the Niobe of nations. The noblest of materials for a great nation there were wrecked by the folly of England."

In conclusion, Mr. Wilde showed that he had other views outside of art, asking his former questioner sensible questions about pauperism, crime, and business statistics in this country, while he betrayed a lively interest in the story of the fire and the rebuilding of the city.[1] He leaves here after his lecture Monday evening, and delivers lectures week after next in St. Louis, Cincinnati, Detroit, and Fort Wayne. He will then return immediately to New York, to superintend the production of the play which he is shortly to bring out.

"Oscar Wilde Has Come," *Chicago Daily News* (Chicago, IL), 11 Feb. 1882, 3pm ed., 1

HIS IDEA OF HIS TREATMENT.

He Thinks America a Fine Country, But Believes the Press is Too Careless—The Ladies To Be the Developers of His Art Theories—An Interesting Talk.

"I am glad to see you," said Mr. Oscar Wilde, the famous Irish aesthete, extending his hand to the reporter, and placing a chair in parlor 3, Grand Pacific hotel. And the voice was full of music, the striking face bright and genial, and the extended hand warm with feeling not to be mistaken.

"What do you think of America as a country?" the reporter felt along.

"It is not a country. America is a vast world by itself, full of wonders to the visitor with eyes, and full of surprises. I liked New York very much for its cosmopolitan features; I liked Boston for its many literary reminiscences. In Baltimore I found pretty women, and in Philadelphia literary men."

"What is your theory on decorative art?"

"That it has been and will be done mostly by women. Men are so busy in the struggle for life and commercial supremacy that to the women must be relegated the task of sustaining and advancing decorative art; and this is proper and as it should be."

"And your reception in America?"

1. The Great Chicago Fire burned for three days in October 1871. It killed approximately 300 people; about 3.3 square miles / 9 km^2 of the city were razed.

"It has surprised me—that is, at first I could not understand it. But I very speedily became aware that this sort of thing resulted from gross misrepresentation by thoughtless and ignorant people and mismanagement of my business affairs. I feel it very bitterly and regret it to the utmost measure. When I begin my lecture I always feel that the first half of it is delivered in a mist of folly and misrepresentation; but if I can win over my audience by the time I finish, I am glad."

"What do you think of the eastern people as a class?"

"It is self-evident that they have caught much of the tinsel and flimsy nothings of Europe. Of course there is more art in the east than in the west, but I would much rather speak to a people devoid of art than to a people bad in art."

"You have an object in this new departure?"

"Well, yes; rather, perhaps, am I fully imbued with the Celtic love of rebellion. I am a rebel in art as many of my countrymen are rebels in politics. I am a rebel because I object to these crude forms and rules one dare not criticise. I imagine my mission to be that of a reformer, and I do not expect any more consideration from the general public than has been meted out to other reformers in the past—nothing more, but at the same time it shall not be less."

"And in the future—"

"I expect to be recognized properly in good time."

"What do you think of American newspapers?"

"They are particularly bright, but in many instances thoughtless. Why should a reporter—one of the calm, pleasant, polished fellows whom I delight to meet—call on me, receive my hospitality, and go out to his paper and causelessly and needlessly misrepresent me? Is that journalism? Is that the treatment a gentleman should receive from a gentleman? However, the time has long since passed when anything possible for a newspaper to print can make me glad or sad. One cannot pause to read and discuss and fret over everything about oneself in the prints—one might as well pause on the streets and dispute the right of thoroughfare with every urchin. Misrepresentation cannot have a lasting effect."

"You will doubtless meet a large and respectful audience in Chicago."

"I hope so. It will make me glad, and I am quite safe in thinking I shall leave friends here. I do not misrepresent myself, and hence the public will readily understand me and my work. Of all I have heard about Chicago, the good heart and intelligence of her people have been foremost."

"Will the decorative in art become popular?"

"Yes, as all things beautiful become popular.[1] The education of the eye pro-

1. This contrasts with a sentiment Wilde expressed in *Modern Art Training*: "Popularity is the crown of laurel which the world puts on bad art. Whatever popular is wrong." (Dibb, 226.) In *The Soul of Man Under Socialism* Wilde insists that: "Art should never try to be popular. The public should try to make itself artistic. There is a very wide difference." (CW iv, 248.27–9.)

duces precisely the same effect as the education of other organs or senses. Why should not a man or woman love that which adds charm to home and surroundings? Who will not turn about to gaze on a beautiful child, a beautiful picture or statue? Will not the people turn in love and admiration to that which is beautiful rather than cling to that which is uncouth and ill-shaped! 'Twould be strange indeed if the latter prevailed."

"Then you are an educator?"

"Something of that sort. Your Morse had a difficult time in teaching the people to believe in his telegraphy; Fulton met many trials and disappointments in applying his steam to shipping, and your William Lloyd Garrison and Wendell Phillips were maltreated in the public halls of Boston because they ventured the opinion that slaves should be free; because they were rebels against prevailing custom and popular opinion. However, the men triumphed, and in the city where they were most scorned are they now most loved and revered. Is not this poetic justice?"[1]

"On the whole, what is your impression of America?"

"Favorable, sir; favorable. Had I known as much of America ere I sailed as I have since learned, my reception in New York and my tour through this country might have been very different. However, that is a matter of the past which it is useless to discuss."

The reporter here withdrew and left Mr. Wilde to the consideration of a mammoth pile of mail. But the reporter left Mr. Wilde bearing away an impression far different from that with which he entered the aesthete's presence. To say that Mr. Wilde is a fascinating gentleman, polished and courteous in his manner and graceful in every movement, might not convey the desired idea of him. In form he is tall and well proportioned, and his face is one never to be forgotten—a long face, clear complexion, partially opened mouth displaying large, well-molded teeth, and, above all, a pair of wonderfully deep, clear, blue eyes, honest, generous and kindly in their expression. The only point about him differing materially from any other polished, elegant gentleman is the mass of brown hair partly shadowing the face. The hair is parted in the middle and hangs straight down to the neck, with never the suspicion of a kink or curl. So profuse is the hair

1. Samuel Finley Breese Morse (1791–1872) was an American inventor. He developed Morse Code, the single-wire electromagnetic telegraph, and, with the assistance of American chemist Leonard Gale (1800–1883), the technology that allowed telegraphic messages to be sent over long distances. Robert Fulton (1765–1815) was an American engineer and inventor. He is credited with building the first commercially successful steamboat (1807). William Lloyd Garrison (1805–1879) was an American abolitionist and publisher of the anti-slavery newspaper *The Liberator*. Wendell Phillips (1811–1884) was an American lawyer, orator, and abolitionist. Wilde lunched with him in Boston in January 1882 (Sturgis, 224/215).

that not a glimpse of the ears can be had. He was attired in a morning dress of modest brown, trimmed and faced on the coat lapels with dark crimson, a narrow cord of the same color running down the outside seams of ample pantaloons. Mr. Wilde's accent is decidedly English, but not of the cockney type. All in all, he is probably the most thoroughly misrepresented foreigner ever landed on American shores.

"Truly Aesthetic," *The Daily Inter Ocean* (Chicago, IL), 13 Feb. 1882, 2[1]

Of Course Oscar is Meant, with His Red-corded Seams,

And Calla-like Beauty of Answers to Supplementary Questions.

But He'll Pocket $1,000 Tonight, and Really Can Afford to Pose.

Oscar Wilde sat in his room in the Grand Pacific last night, a room made bright and artistic with beautiful things. A large center-table was heaped with choice old books, some of them rare old curios, with precious broken binding [*sic*] and soulful mediaeval dogs' ears. In the window's embrasure was a beautifully intense writing desk, all-inlaid with pearl, quite Japanese and early English,[2] heaped with letters answered and unanswered. The bright coal blazed in the grate. The sofa, with its covering of skins of wild beasts and its further curtain of the old-gold silk shawl, with netted fringe, was drawn up to a comfortable angle with the fire, and upon the couch thus made reclined the aesthetic young man, this time smoking a cigarette. He was dressed in a quilted black silk smoking jacket with scarlet collar, lapels, and waistbands. He wore the same scarlet necktie, handkerchief, and socks, or at the least they were of the same color as upon the previous visit of THE INTER OCEAN reporter. His pantaloons were black, with a

SCARLET CORD DOWN THE SEAMS

to match the trimming of the jacket. He greeted his visitor with languid grace.

1. H & S, b34. Reprinted in H & S, 61–4. Excerpted in "Wilde and Cheeky Reporter," *The Indianapolis News* (Indianapolis, IN), 15 Feb. 1882, 2. Quoted in Sturgis, 236/226, 238–9/229, 247/237. Referenced in Sturgis, 233/223–4.

2. An allusion to *Patience*. Lady Jane suggests that the soldiers improve their uniforms by surmounting them "with something Japanese – it matters not what – would at least be Early English!"

"As my former interview with you was necessarily brief," said the reporter, "there were a few questions I should like to ask you."[1]

Mr. Wilde made a gesture of assent, and the reporter asked him what he thought of Chicago.

"That is a difficult question to answer," he said. "I don't pretend to have seen the city yet. I have been here too short a time; but from what I have seen I like it much better than New York. The streets are wider, cleaner, and there are not all the railways overhead and in the middle of the street, and that dreadful noise is not here. It is wonderful to think how you have built such a large city in so short a time, especially after such a great calamity as your great fire. But of course it is a little sad to think of all the millions of money spent on buildings and so little architecture."

This he said with a sigh, and glance out of the window upon the twinkling lights of the city.

"But that will come in time, no doubt."

"Have you seen any art in Chicago?"

"I have seen one Chicago artist whose work is of the highest artistic quality, whose work is beautiful—more beautiful than the work of any sculptor I have seen yet, and of whom you should all be proud. I

REFER TO MR. DONOGHUE."[2]

"Is Donoghue a sculptor?" asked the reporter.

"Do you tell me you don't know him? He is a native of Chicago, studied in Paris, has come back to his own city, having done beautiful work already, and prepared to do beautiful work for you if any of you care for it," said Mr. Wilde, with ill-concealed sarcasm.

"Here is a plaque he designed for one of my poems—a figure of a girl—so simple, so powerful, so pretty. It is perfect."[3]

The reporter took his word for it.

"What do you think of the people of America?"

1. The reporter presumably refers to "The Apostle of Art," *The Daily Inter Ocean* (Chicago, IL), 11 Feb. 1882, 4, pp. 151–5, although that article is not brief.

2. John Talbott Donoghue (1853–1903) was born in Chicago. Wilde had visited Donoghue's atelier in the Reaper Block, two miles south of the Grand Pacific, that afternoon ("Art in Chicago," *The Chicago Daily Tribune* (Chicago, IL), 19 Feb. 1882, 16).

3. The clay plaque illustrated Wilde's poem *Requiescat*, first published in *Poems* (CW i, No. 4). An early manuscript version suggests that it was originally intended as a lament for a dead lover (Sturgis (2020), 29); Wilde rewrote it in memory of his sister Isola who had died in 1867 aged nine. A "gilt copper" version of Donoghue's plaque was later displayed above the drawing room fireplace at Wilde's Chelsea home (Sturgis, 317/299; Adele Marroc, "Oscar Wilde's Children," *The Philadelphia Inquirer* (Philadelphia, PA), 5 Nov. 1893, 23, p. 804).

"In the Eastern cities the people are very cosmopolitan. I think this is strongly characteristic as regards the men and women. It was in the West of America that I expected to find real American life—life made by yourselves and for yourselves."

"How have you liked your audiences?"

"At all important large cities I find the audiences intelligent, courteous, and sympathetic. In some of the small provincial towns which I have visited on my journey there have been attempts at disturbances. However, in all these cases the good sense and good feeling of the majority of the audiences entirely stopped any attempts of the kind."

"You refer more particularly to Rochester?"[1]

"Yes."

"How was it in Boston with the Harvard students?"[2]

"What the young men did there was a mere piece of

UNDERGRADUATE HIGH SPIRITS.

I received it in the same spirit, and my lecture at Boston passed off most brilliantly. It was not intended as an attempt to disturb my lecture, but merely a bit of school-boy fun. You don't suppose for a moment that a movement of any importance can be affected by sixty young men?"

"What do you think of athletic sports?"

"When I lectured in Boston I told these young men of Harvard that so far from their athletics being opposed to art, the best motives for the noblest sculptures would most probably be found on their running-ground, on the river, in the gymnasium. I reminded them that Greek sculpture never looked for any nobler motive than a young man starting for a race, tying his sandals before leaping, hurling the weight, and the like, and advised them to put up in their beautiful gymnasium a few casts of the best Greek statues of young athletes, so as to remind them that all their own physical perfection, and strength, and fleetness of foot and the like, might give to the artist beautiful subjects for his art."[3]

1. See "A Man of Culture Rare," *Rochester Democrat and Chronicle* (Rochester, NY), 8 Feb. 1882, 4, p. 145.

2. Harvard incident: see p. 134, note 2.

3. Reports of Wilde's first Boston lecture bear this out. "He had visited Harvard that day, and he begged to assure the students before him that there was more to the movement of aestheticism than knee breeches and sunflowers! [Laughter and applause.] He had been impressed there by things which promised well for the cause of art. He was charmed with the gymnasium. There was no antagonism between athletics and art, and he instanced the example of the Greeks. He suggested how finely the statue of a Greek athlete would look standing in the gymnasium, and what an ennobling influence it would have there. He would like to present them with one himself if they would accept it." ("Oscar Wilde," *The Boston Herald* (Boston, MA), 1 Feb. 1882, 2). See also "Oscar Wilde," *Boston Evening Transcript* (Boston, MA), 1 Feb. 1882, 2. A cartoon of

"Where does your lecture tour extend?"

"I lecture next week in Detroit, Fort Wayne, and Cleveland; after that in St. Louis, Cincinnati, and other cities."

"Will you go south?"

"I do not know yet whether I can go to Canada or your own Southern States."

"Will you go to the far West?"

"I don't think I shall have time to go to the far West. So many lectures to give, so much traveling to do. I am afraid I shall have to give up what I had looked forward to meeting in America—California in the spring, Colorado, and a ride in Mexico. I want to see Leadville immensely."

"Those mining towns are quite a curiosity."

"Yes; those new forms of life—new attempts at civilization that have sprung up in your mining cities—are objects of the keenest intellectual interest to us in Europe."

"IN SPEAKING OF ROCHESTER,"

said Mr. Wilde, rising and helping himself to a fresh cigarette, "I must say that I am trying to keep as good an opinion of your country as I can. Your great cities confirm me in my best opinion, while the pretty provincial villages are what such always are, entirely unimportant.[1] Let a young man go to England, and lecture on any subject he chooses, he will at least be treated with respect."

"Are you satisfied with the results of your tour financially?"

Mr. Wilde mildly stared with surprise at such an outrageous question, but evidently thinking that this was a type of civilization "created by ourselves and for ourselves," he confessed that he had done pretty well.

"I have had large audiences," he said. "By the way, how much easier it is to speak to a thousand people than a few dozen. Wendell Phillips told me that it was a test of a true orator for him to interest an audience of twenty."

"How much do you get a night?"

This was too much for Mr. Wilde. He pushed back his hair and threw his cigarette away. Finally he said:

"How much do your best lecturers get?"

"Some of them get $500 a night."

"Well, I got

Wilde distributing Greek statues to students from various Ivy League colleges was printed in *The Harvard Lampoon* (9 Feb. 1882, 94). There is no evidence that Harvard took Wilde up on his offer.

1. The context suggests that Wilde may have said "petty" rather than "pretty".

in Boston, and shall get the same here.[1] Of course, in little cities I don't expect so much. But it is merely filling in the time.

"I am extremely impressed by the entire disregard of Americans for money-making—"

Here the reporter was so surprised that he dropped his pencil.

"—as shown by the remarks made by many of the Western journals. They think it a strange and awful thing that I should want to make a few dollars by lecturing. Why, money-making is necessary for art. Money builds cities and makes them healthful. Money buys art and furnishes it an incentive. Is it strange that I should want to make money? And yet these newspapers cry out that I am making money!"

"Oscar Wilde," *The Chicago Daily Tribune* (Chicago, IL), 15 Feb. 1882, 3[2]

He Has Seen Quite Enough of Chicago—The Duty of Young American Journalists.

His Verdict on the Water Tower Unchangeable—A Dinner and Reception.

A representative of THE TRIBUNE called at the Grand Pacific Hotel yesterday afternoon and requested one of the gentlemanly clerks to transmit a bit of paste-board bearing his name to the parlor of Mr. Oscar Wilde, the celebrated esthete. A sable attaché of the hotel departed with the card, and returned in a few moments with the pleasing intelligence that "de gemman would see de gemman." The reporter started for the regions above, and on the way his guide asked:

"Is dat man an actor?"

Supposing that he referred to Mr. Wilde, the newspaper man informed him that he was the noted Oscar Wilde.

"What opery-house am he a playin' at?"

"Oh, he's a lecturer, not an actor. He's an esthete."

"Is he, dough? I thought he looked like one ob dem fellahs wat tumbles in a circus," said the wise-looking African, and the reporter saw that he had mistaken the great Oscar for an athlete.

The door of Parlor 3 was soon reached, and the scribe was solemnly ushered into the presence of the prophet of the beautiful. He arose from the sofa

1. Wilde was criticised for this boast. See p. 229, note 1.

2. H & S, b35. Reprinted as "Oscar in Chicago," *St. Louis Globe-Democrat* (St. Louis, MO), 17 Feb. 1882, 11. Quoted in OWDA, 31, 179; and Pearson, 67.

upon which he was reclining with a languid air, and allowed his hand to be pressed by the lead-stained hand of the journalist. Mr. Wilde is like unto the chameleon, as he has velvet coats of all hues. On this occasion he wore one of a drab tint, and this, together with a pair of baggy gray trousers, cloth-topped gaiters, a green necktie, and a handkerchief of the same shade, completed the outer toilet.

After greeting the reporter he sank back upon the sofa, which was covered with buffalo-skins, and dreamily sipped a cup of tea. The newspaper man ventured a question.

"HOW WERE YOU PLEASED

with your reception last evening," he asked.

There was a soulful gurgle of fragrant Young Hyson in Mr. Wilde's throat, followed by a painful silence which suggested that a tea-leaf had lodged in the region of his larynx,[1] and he said: "I was much pleased at the way my lecture was received by a Chicago audience. Don't you know it is wonderful to think that one man can stand before such a vast audience and sway people with your voice. It seemed grand to me last night that I was able to do this.

"By the way," he continued, "your newspapers seemed to think that I was to deliver the same lecture I delivered in New York City. The *Times'* report amused me very much, as I could easily see from reading it that they had no reporter there. All they gave me was a meagre half column."

"Mr. Wilde," said the reporter, "are you aware that you wounded the pride of our best citizens by referring slightingly to our water-tower?"[2]

"I can't help that. It's really too absurd. If you build a water-tower, why don't you build it for water and make a simple structure of it, instead of building it like a castle, where one expects to see mailed knights peering out of every part. It seems a shame to me that the citizens of Chicago have spent so much money on buildings with such an unsatisfactory result from an architectural point of view. Your city looks positively too dreary to me," and the esthete closed his eyes as if to shut out the view of a flat across the street.

"Have you seen much of Chicago since you have been here?"

1. Hyson is a tea blend; the young variety is considered better quality.

2. Wilde elicited laugher from his Chicago audience by describing the city's water-tower as "a castellated monstrosity with pepper-boxes stuck all over it." The *Chicago Tribune* reported that "[h]e felt amazed that any people could so abuse Gothic art and make the structure look not like a water-tower but like the tower of a medieval castle," ("Oscar Wilde," *The Chicago Daily Tribune* (Chicago, IL), 14 Feb. 1882, 7). In *Personal Impressions of America* he called it "a curious monstrosity in the shape of a Gothic Castle, seemingly built entirely of pepper boxes, and provided with all kinds of contrivances for emptying lead on the enemy." (Dibb, 235.)

Figure 5. The Chicago Water Tower. "A sort of castellated atrocity, with pepper-box turrets and absurd portcullises."

"OH YES, QUITE AS MUCH AS I CARE TO SEE.

I have driven through your parks, and viewed the principal objects of interest."

"Of course, then, you have been to the Stock-Yards and seen them kill pigs?"

"No, indeed," said Mr. Wilde, with a horrified look, "such sights have no interest for me," and he shrugged his broad shoulders so that the spoon in the tea-cup settled like a bean in a bladder.[1]

"How have you been impressed with our first social circles," asked the reporter, thinking to strike Oscar where he lived.

"I have been to one or two receptions," he said, "and I like your society people very much. They have all apologized to me for their newspapers, telling me that I mustn't mind what you reporters say."

"That is surprising. Chicago's people always swear by their newspapers, and declare them the best in the world."

"Oh, that's a bit of buncombe," said Mr. Wilde with a laugh. "Your newspapers are comic without being amusing. English papers are founded on facts, while American papers are founded on imagination. How long have you been a journalist?" he asked suddenly, turning the tables on the scribe.

"About three years."

"I should think you young men of the profession would have some ambition. Why don't you take your newspapers out of the hands of the old fogies, and make an effort to revolutionize the world?"

The reporter suggested that a man could not revolutionize the world to any great extent on $20 per week, and Mr. Wilde said with a laugh that he guessed that was a fact.

Here he reached for a box of Turkish cigarettes which reposed on the mantel, and the reporter posed himself for a bow of acknowledgement; but Mr. Wilde selected one cigarette, lit it, and replaced the box on the mantel, leaving the newspaper man to reach out longingly for an occasional whiff of the blue smoke. The reporter picked up a book which was lying upon a table and found it to be a volume of

MR. WILDE'S POEMS.

The edges were rough and uncut, and the poems were scattered through the volume without regard to order or neatness. It was unnecessary to look at the title-page to tell that the book came from an English press.

1. Wilde would inform later interviewers that "Sarah Bernhardt told me that there were only two things in America worth seeing, one was Clara Morris, and the other some dreadful way you have of killing hogs in the Chicago Stock Yards. I have seen Miss Morris; the other visit I have postponed indefinitely," (see e.g. "Oscar Back Again," *The Daily Inter Ocean* (Chicago, IL), 1 Mar. 1882, 8, p. 235).

"That," said Mr. Wilde, "is an English volume of my poems."

"Is it finished?" asked the reporter, gazing doubtfully at the rough edges.

"Certainly."

"I shouldn't think such a volume would appeal to the beautiful. It wouldn't do in America?"

"The American editions of my poems look frightful. That is the way a book should be gotten up. The contents and not the covers of a book are what we look for."[1]

Here a colored gentleman entered the room, deposited a few whispered words in the great esthete's left ear, and Oscar said, "Not this evening. I dine out, and I want a carriage at a quarter of 7," and the liveried lackey salaamed Mr. Wilde, went out, and slammed the door.

"I must say goodbye to you," said Mr. Wilde to the newspaper man. "I am glad to have met you, and hope that you will endeavor to infuse a new life into American journalism. You can tell people more interesting things than what sort of a necktie I wear. By the way, how it is that all American journalists aspire to be humorists?"

"Humorists are born in this country, not made," volunteered the reporter. "Men who are running country papers often attract attention by their witty sayings, their humorous remarks are copied, and they acquire a reputation as a humorist. Then they write a book, go on a lecturing tour, and give out."

"Well," laughed Mr. Wilde. "I hope you won't give out"; and he retired to dress for dinner.

✂ *A report of a dinner given for Wilde by Mrs H. O. Stone.*

"Oscar Wilde's 'Taffy'," *Chicago Morning News* (Chicago, IL), 16 Feb. 1882, 4

PLEASED WITH HIS RECEPTION.

He says Chicago Women are Beautiful—He is Delighted with his Audience's Personal Appearance—A Contrast with Baltimore and New York in Estheticism—But He "Cawn't" Consent to Marry Here.

"What do I think of Chicago?" repeated Mr. Oscar Wilde to a MORNING NEWS reporter yesterday. "I think it a charming city, full of intelligent, appreciative

1. In fact, Wilde had strong opinions about how his published works should appear; he involved himself in all aspects of their design, including cover decoration. See Frankel, N. (2000). *Oscar Wilde's Decorated Books*. The University of Michigan Press.

people; and your promise of a fine audience on Monday evening was more than fulfilled."

"You have also been granted a glimpse of Chicago social life, have you not?"

"More than a glimpse, sir, much more than a glimpse—a real experience, as it were, and one I shall remember very gratefully. Sorry you were not present. The assembled friends discussed the decorative in art very intelligently, and quite agreed with me on all essential points. Indeed, the home I had the pleasure of entering contains some elaborate specimens of advanced art."

"Do you think there is any hope for Chicago in the decorative in art line?"

"Oh, yes," and Mr. Wilde smiled. Continuing, he said: "I need scarcely repeat that I may be called a rebel in art, and, strange as it may seem, I find everywhere intelligent people who are also rebels on the same subject, and need only a little encouragement to give expression to their views. And this thing will grow, and those who today sneer at any departure from beaten paths and musty rules, will tomorrow be among the foremost to adopt and nurture advanced views on the subject."

"How will Chicago compare with New York and Boston in art matters from your standpoint?"

"More favorably than you could induce a New York or Boston man to believe, probably. Of course, these two cities have advantages over Chicago in such matters, but your people here are much more appreciative, and more ready to see and take up a good thing. The tinsel and shabby nothingness of Europe seem to have no place in Chicago, while in the Atlantic cities mediocre people accept them as facts—as solid realities. I have been shown works of art in Chicago, by local artists, fit to grace a grand salon in Paris, and what is better, your people know it."

"Is decorative art likely to be accepted by all classes?"

"Very likely, especially when classes come to realize the fact that it costs no more to have beautiful things than to have ugly substitutes. Why should it not be so? Surely it does not require stupendous inducements to make people [?take] old mine diamonds in place of French paste stones."

"How did your audience impress you?"

"Magnificently. I never remember having gazed upon an audience more handsomely and harmoniously dressed, and I am quite positive I never saw at one time so many elegant figures and handsome faces. The other morning when you called I said Baltimore impressed me as the city of beautiful women, but I am now convinced Chicago is quite equal to that place.[1] Ah, sir, why should not the

1. See "Oscar Wilde Has Come," *Chicago Daily News* (Chicago, IL), 3pm ed., 11 Feb. 1882, 1, p. 162.

beautiful in art flourish among so many beautiful people? Don't you find it quite a treat to reside in Chicago?"

"Well, yes. Why don't you come here yourself, get married, and settle down to the enjoyment of all these beautiful things?"

"Ah, my dear fellow, I can't, you know. I have my life work before me, and must devote my entire time and attention to it."

"One of these beautiful Chicago ladies might help you along, you know."

"It is useless for me to think of such a thing, much as I would like it. I may say it is far beyond the realm of possibilities. I leave Chicago today, very grateful to its good people for their friendly reception."

Mr. Wilde departed at 5 o'clock for Fort Wayne, where he will discuss the beautiful in decorative art this evening.

"Sunflowers and Lilies," *Fort Wayne Daily Gazette* (Fort Wayne, IN), 16 Feb. 1882, 6[1]

Reposeful, Soulful-Eyed Oscar is Here—The Gazette Aesthete has a Long and Pleasant Chat with Him on the Too Utterly Utter and the Too Intensely Beyond.

Oscar Wilde, the much-talked-of and heralded-on-every-breeze aesthetic young English poet, who lectures at the Academy tonight, arrived last evening on the Pittsburgh fast train from Chicago, and went at once to the Aveline house, where parlor No. 8 was assigned to him. As he did not arrive until 9:15, he complained both of hunger and weariness, and asked that he might not be disturbed. However, the young gentleman who looks after Mr. D'Oyly Carte's interest in the lecture tour acted as mediator with the great aesthetic, who, at 10:30, after Oscar had rested himself for an hour, ushered the GAZETTE apostle of the lily and the beautiful up to the room of his Gamaliel.[2] When the reporter and his escort entered Mr. Wilde was languidly reclining upon the sofa, which was artistically draped in a bear skin robe and mauve-colored traveling shawl, reading a crimson-bound volume of Joaquin Miller's poems, of which he is a great admirer and in whose writings he said he takes renewed interest since he met the wild poet of the Sierras, a short time ago. Oscar warmly grasped the hand of the GAZETTE aesthete and politely waved him to a seat, and then immediately but languidly returned to his recumbent position, daintily helping himself meanwhile to a fresh cigarette from his silver case upon the table. The first glance sufficed to show

1. Quoted in Bisch.
2. Gamaliel the Elder, or Rabban Gamaliel I, was a leading Jewish teacher in the first-century CE.

that he is all that fancy has painted him. He is a very tall and graceful youth. The much talked of golden locks were parted in the middle and hung in wavy masses down upon his shoulders, framing his large, expressive features. He wore the oft described gray traveling trousers, a mouse-colored velvet smoking jacket, a magenta neck scarf and slippers each embroidered with a golden sunflower surrounded by a spray of silver lilies, while from the side pocket of his jacket peeped a crimson pocket handkerchief, presenting a *tout ensemble* worthy of the gaze of gods and men.

As he puffed the fragrant cigarette, the reporter asked him how he liked America and his trip so far, he said:

"I like the Americans very much; when I first read what the newspapers said about me I was indignant, but now it amuses me. The audiences grow more respectful and I am delighted at the hearing Chicago gave me the other evening."

"What do you think of Chicago with all its vim and push?"

"Commercially it is a wonderful city, but knowing the millions of dollars that have been poured into the city to rebuild it, I was surprised at its poor architecture; there are no artistically beautiful buildings in the city."

"How do you like American railway traveling?"

"It is very tiresome, and if it was not for Howells' novels I could not endure it. He is your best novel writer."[1]

Being told that Genevieve Ward was at the Academy, and that the reporter has just come from there, Mr. Wilde said:

"I should have been glad to attend her performance. She is a very fine actress, thoroughly artistic. I knew her very well in England, and the author of her play, 'Forget-Me-Not,' which, by the way, is an old play to us English people, is an old friend of mine, Mr. Herman Merivale."[2]

"What do you think of American actresses?"

"Clara Morris is your only artiste. She is beyond criticism."

1. William Dean Howells (1837–1920) was an American novelist, critic, and playwright. His first novel *Their Wedding Journey* was published in 1872 and several others followed. An article about "The Novels of W. D. Howells" published on the same day as this interview in the *Boston Evening Transcript* stated that "[h]is novels are essentially love stories touched with as intense colors as the ameliorated conditions of modern life allow." Between December 1881 and October 1882 *The Century* magazine serialised his novel *A Modern Instance*, about the deterioration of a marriage.

2. Herman Merivale and Palgrave Simpson's play *Forget-Me-Not* was staged on 15 February 1882 in Fort Wayne. Genevieve Ward (1837–1922), an American actress and singer, played the Marquise de Mohrivart. *The Sentinel's* reviewer judged that "Miss Ward is a superb actress, and though suffering with a slight indisposition, nevertheless held enchained the attention of the audience." Ward was a friend of Wilde and his mother. In September 1880 Wilde had presented her with a copy of *Vera*, presumably in the hope that she would produce the play (British Library, Eccles 353).

"What do you think of Mary Anderson, our rising young American star?"

"Well, she may be a rising star, sir, but it will take her a long time to rise. I saw her as Juliet and I regret it very much, for I look upon Shakespeare as something sacred, and it was torturing to see his finest play so murdered."[1]

"How do you like American hotels as compared with English hotels?"

"In England we really have no hotels worthy of the name. They are so grand and gloomy that visitors once inside of them will submit to any extortion in order to get out of them."

From this point the conversation became general, and learning the writer has lived for several months in London, that great capital and its society was fully discussed, the poet being intimately acquainted with all its scholars and nobility, making a very fascinating running commentary on them. At this moment the colored valet who accompanies him, ushered in a waiter, bearing the great aesthete's dinner. It consisted of a huge steak smothered in mushrooms, a dozen raw oysters garnished with sliced lemon, some Saratoga chipped potatoes, all flanked by a bottle of Piper Heidsieck champagne, extra dry, all making a meal much more substantial that the odor of the lily or the bloom of the sunflower, the supposed aesthetical diet, and as the poet prepared to move on the tempting repast his confrere of the GAZETTE bowed himself out, mentioning as he did so an article that had been published in the morning about "east-thetics as compared with west-thetics," and which Mr. Wilde expressed a great desire to read, and at once sent out for a copy of the GAZETTE containing it.[2]

On the whole Mr. Oscar Wilde, Oxford graduate and poet is no ordinary man. He impresses one as being an exceedingly clever and intelligent Englishman with a knowledge of art and literature excelled by few men of the present day and whoever misses hearing him this evening will miss the event of the season and which the elite and intelligence of this country have crowded to hear. From Fort Wayne he goes to Detroit, thence to Cleveland, Cincinnati, Louisville and St. Louis. He will later in the season lecture in Dubuque, Indianapolis and several other western cities, having more engagements than he can fill. He is also busily at work on a new drama which will soon be produced in New York. It deals with Russian Nihilism.

1. See "In Honor of Oscar Wilde," *The New York Times* (New York, NY), 6 Jan. 1882, 8, p. 51.

2. The article referred to is a letter to the editor comparing the manners of Americans in eastern and western cities. It draws on reports of Wilde's reception in Boston, "where he was greeted by an exhibition of rowdyism that would have disgraced a mining camp on the frontier", and Chicago, where Wilde's audience was "very attentive, appreciative and at times decidedly enthusiastic." The correspondent concludes by expressing the hope that "no breach of true politeness may mar the visit of Oscar Wilde to our city" ("East-thetics and West-thetics," *Fort Wayne Daily Gazette* (Fort Wayne, IN), 15 Feb. 1882, 5.)

"Oscar Wilde," *The Daily Sentinel* (Fort Wayne, IN), 16 Feb. 1882, 3[1]

The Latest American Craze, Arrives in Our City—A Sentinel Reporter Accorded an Interview.

Last night, Oscar Wilde, the languishing young Englishman who is just now coining money from the insatiable desire of the American people to run after novelty of any sort, arrived in the city, accompanied by his business manager, J. S. Vale, and attended by his negro servant, an American addition to Mr. Wilde's service by the way. Wilde was met at the depot, as No. 6 came in, by a number of curious people, but with his face muffled and his head buried in the folds of his ample English ulster, faced with seal, he strode towering over the crowd from his drawing room car to a hack in waiting, and was driven to the Aveline house, where he was assigned parlor 8. Though Mr. Vale, the manager, said to a SENTINEL reporter that Mr. Wilde would be happy to accord an interview, the representative of this paper, in consideration for the aesthete's fatigue and hunger, postponed his visit until this morning.

The apostle of art does not rise at an early hour and when the reporter was ushered into his room at 11 o'clock, Oscar was found just about sitting down to his breakfast, a substantial one by the way, and which was prepared under the special direction of the African servant, who occupied a respectful position behind his master's chair. As THE SENTINEL man entered, Wilde put on his professional air and languidly looked up with a very slight and artistically controlled yawn.

This remarkable young person though not an exponent of the brawn and muscle of England is tall and compactly built and his frame shows signs of its fine physical development at a period before he set himself up as the St. Oscar, the patron of decorative art, and when he was stroke oar of St. John's crew, Oxford.[2] His brown hair is worn long and curls as it falls over the ample collar of his velvet coat. His face is square cut utterly without sign of beard and the expression of the face is sullen except when an occasional smile lights up his countenance and causes him to part a pair of very kissable lips, and display a range of white and even teeth. This morning, he was clad in a crimson silk dressing gown of Turkish pattern, hand painted with lilies and girded about the waist with a gold cord. His feet were covered with flesh colored silk hosiery and encased in slippers, of an

1. Quoted in Bisch.
2. Wilde enjoyed rowing recreationally with his friends and in his first semester at Oxford had tried out for the college boat at Magdalen (not St. Johns), but gave up after a few months, observing "I don't see the use of going down backwards to Iffley every evening," (CL, 70; Oliver St. John Gogarty, "A Picture of Oscar Wilde," *Esquire*, 1 Aug. 1945, 41).

Oriental pattern heavily ornamented with gold cord and into the decoration of which neither storks, lilies or sunflowers entered.[1] The reporter was cordially received and after some desultory conversation, the interviewer said:

"You must devote considerable of your time to the reception of representatives of the press, Mr. Wilde?"

"Yes sir, and I do not begrudge the time. You American newspaper men are wonderful fellows. I talk a moment to you and you go off and write two column interviews."

"Have you been fairly treated?"

"Yes, in the main I have. The American paragraphists have made something of a caricature out of me and my views on art, but I am amused by their fun at my expense."

"How do you like America?"

"I am coming to like it much as I travel more. I have so far seen little that is distinctly American. There are few things in your cities which differ from the ordinary hum drum of London life. A portion of State street in Chicago is quite like our Regent and Oxford streets in London."

"Did your Chicago experience please you?"

"Yes sir, I was treated handsomely there. Chicago is a very wonderful city and I have longed to see it. In my lecture I had occasion to say something about some of their architectural eye sores, and I presume my remarks were not appreciated. The social life of Chicago, I found during my brief experience of it to differ little from that of Park Lane in London. I found in Chicago more cultured and traveled people than any other point I have visited save New York."

"How about Boston? You do not certainly place the culture of the Chicagoan on a higher plane than that of the Bostonian?"

"I mean to say my dear fellow, that I found more cultured people in Chicago."

"May I ask, Mr. Wilde, the nature of your mission in America?"

"It is briefly to discover those men and women who are susceptible of artistic development and to give them best opportunities to expand. On the other hand we take those persons in whom there dwells no capacity for artistic vocation and produce in them that artistic temperament without which there can be no individuality in art; no actual joy of life; in a word, no civilization."

"How do you purpose to accomplish this?"

"By making art not a luxury for the rich, but by accustoming the people from childhood to color and design in their homes."

1. Wilde may have owned a second pair of slippers. Other interviewers noted that one pair was decorated with golden sunflowers or daisies ("Sunflowers and Lilies," *Fort Wayne Daily Gazette* (Fort Wayne, IN), 16 Feb. 1882, 6, p. 176; "An Aesthete in Undress," *The Sioux City Daily Journal* (Sioux City, IA), 21 Mar. 1882, 3, p. 266–7).

"What do you think of American architecture?"

"You have none. In this respect the American people need to improve. In the cities I have found few public buildings which pleased my eyes. Most of the buildings are *rococo* in construction."

Mr. Wilde here signified his desire to attack his matutinal meal and the reporter was about to take his leave of this very charming young man when he was motioned with a graceful wave of Oscar's white hand to keep his seat on the sofa draped with a pair of very fine skins. Mr. Wilde then showed his visitor a note from Miss Ward asking him to attend the performance of "Forget-Me-Not" last night.

"Please say that Miss Ward is a very particular friend of mine and I should have delighted to run in on the last act but fatigue prevented me. I was quite worn out."

The reporter then prepared to go, asking Mr. Wilde how he liked the flourishing metropolis of Fort Wayne.

"The day is bad and I shall be forced to remain within doors. I would have liked to look over your city but must I fear content myself by taking observations from my window."

Mr. Wilde is a charming conversationalist very little affected in his manners and in brief impresses us as an interesting, enthusiastic and eccentric young Englishman whose views however visionary, is thorough earnest about them.

A pleasant souvenir of the visit was a copy of Wilde's poems, the fly-leaf being traced in his own spidery handwriting: "Compliments of the author, Oscar Wilde."

"Wilde," *The Cleveland Leader* (Cleveland, OH), 20 Feb. 1882, 6[1]

The Advent of the Apostle of Aestheticism.

He Readily Consents to be Interviewed.

His Lecture on the English Renaissance.

What a Correspondent Thinks of the Illustrious Visitor.

1. H & S, b36. Reprinted in H & S, 64–7. Quoted in OWDA, 183; and Sturgis, 237/227. For another interview purporting to have taken place at the same time, see "Come and Gone," *The Cleveland Herald* (Cleveland, OH), 20 Feb. 1882, 8, pp. 183–7. The content of the two interviews is so different that they must have been given separately. That 5 o' clock is quoted as the starting time for both might be explained by the brevity of the interviews or that Wilde's promoter, the Mr Cotton mentioned here, had invited both reporters to attend at that time.

He came yesterday on the afternoon train over the Lake Shore road.[1] By 'He' is meant the great apostle of aestheticism; the man who proposes, so far as lies within the power of one person, to revolutionize modern English and American art, and bring us to a true conception of the beautiful, and a perfect understanding of the graceful. If he fail in this attempt, as fail he may, it is evident that Mr. Wilde has another object in view, and this latter purpose is more apt to result in full fruition than the former. He has an advance agent and a business manager, the same as any other attraction, and is fully prepared in other respects to increase the size of his bank roll. As his preparations for producing a regeneration in art are much less elaborate than his arrangements for swelling his own exchequer, and extend beyond nothing but suggestions without any practical place, it is fair to presume that Mr. Wilde's creed was adopted merely as a means to an end, and is not the moving cause in his present tour. To the energy and enterprise of Mr. Will J. Cotton the Cleveland public is indebted for a sight of the much advertised one. The terms, $500 per night, made the prospect look misty for a time, but Mr. Cotton perfected an arrangement, and brought the gentleman here.

THE ENCOUNTER.

Mr. Wilde was met at the N. Y., P. & O. depot by Mr. Cotton, and by him escorted to the Forest City House. At 5 o'clock, as per previous engagement, the aesthetic young man of the LEADER called at the hotel, and was presently shown into the presence of Mr. Oscar Wilde. The gentleman received his visitor with cordiality—not too cordial, but just the exact degree—and requested him to be seated. Having done so, the reporter took in the surroundings.

Mr. Wilde had caused his colored servant to cover the tete-a-tete with a silk shawl of an old gold tint, and over this a bear skin. A small table had been brought out into the center of the room, and on this rested a small teapot, one of the impossible blue kind, in which the ladies of two centuries agone [*sic*] delighted. A pair of cups and saucers to correspond and a box of cigarettes were the only other articles on the table.

A PENCIL PORTRAIT.

Mr. Wilde is a splendidly formed man of six feet or more in height. His head is large, almost ponderous, and well set on powerful shoulders. It is an undeniable fact that Mr. Wilde is most too fleshy. He wore a tightly fitting sack coat of brown velvet, vest of the same material, and loose trousers of a subdued tint but of very self-assertive cut. His throat was encircled by a pale green tie, and the corner of a handkerchief to match stood out in relief against the brown of the coat. A large seal ring made gesturing with the left hand somewhat wearisome.

1. Wilde arrived in Cleveland on 18 February.

Having satisfied his yearnings by a careful inventory of property and person, the reporter, by way of beginning, asked:

"What shall we do to be saved, with reference to art only?"

"What you need in America are good art schools, academies of design. They are the absolute essentials of aesthetic development and progression. The great popular mistake is that art should be of a national character. People forget that the great schools of art have been purely local. There never was a national Italian school of painting. Every city in Italy had a different school. From Venice to Naples they were unlike, but all beautiful. The same is also true of the styles of embroidery and metal working."

"Will you explain to me your conception of true poetry?"

"The essence of all art," said Mr. Wilde, "is a combination of perfect freedom with perfect beauty. If you ask me what attitude our school adopts toward poetry, I will tell you. A great deal of careless and bad work has been strutting about the world, sheltering itself under the name of inspiration. We don't care to discuss what inspiration may be, but we feel that it possibly belongs to a man's private life, and as a rule never appears in his work. We think that poetry is an art like the other arts, with rules and laws. A thing not to be kept as many young poets have for moments of deep depression, but an art dependent primarily on beautiful workmanship. A young poet, like a young painter, must study the great masters of style, and must be able to use language as a musical instrument. He should be a master of perfect technical excellence. Romantic sentiments and moral maxims are not the essence of poetry."

"May I ask why people generally associate you with sunflowers and lilies," asked the reporter.

"I will tell you why we have so loved and valued the flowers mentioned. It is because they are the two flowers of England which are the most perfect in design, and which lend themselves most materially to decorative art, giving the handicraftsman the most beautiful motives. But you must remember that there are no flowers in the valleys and gardens of England which we have not and will not use in the service of art. The flowers to be used in America are your own, not ours. You do not need to borrow our flowers any more than our money.[1] Then, as regards satire and caricature. Rebellions in politics are shot down; rebellions in art are slandered. It is the surest sign of the strength of any movement that it should be assailed by the impertinent insolence of ignorance and folly."

"Do the doctrines of your school extend any further than decorative art and poetry?"

1. Wilde appears to be unaware that sunflowers are native to North America and had been introduced to Europe in the sixteenth-century (Eames, A. (2020). The herald of the helianthus: Oscar Wilde and sunflower symbolism. *The Wildean, 57,* 56–75).

"We embrace all the arts, and in this the real strength of the movement lies. Art must no longer be the individualized expression, but must be democratic.[1] It must be an art that can appeal to the enormous masses of the people; an art that will not be a luxury for the rich, but the atmosphere in which men and women are to grow up."

"How do you like America as far as you have become acquainted?" asked the reporter preparing to leave.

"To begin with, America is not a country; it is a world. Every city has different types and there is no permanent type at all as regards her men and women. I think the society delightful. I find New York brilliant and cosmopolitan; Philadelphia, literary; Baltimore, pleasant; Washington, intellectual; Boston, more like Oxford than any city you have. The people in Chicago I found simple and strong, and without any foolish prejudices that have influenced East America. I found the audiences in Chicago very sympathetic, and it gives me a sense of power to sway such large multitudes. It is grand. In fact, the side of your American civilization those of us in Europe who are watching your young republics [*sic*] are most interested in is not the East but the West. We want to see what civilization you are making for yourselves and by yourselves."

During the conversation Mr. Wilde refreshed himself by frequent cups of the potent Oolong infusion, and blew out vast volumes of smoke inhaled from the fragrant "Old Judge" cigarette.

✂ *A report of Wilde's lecture in Cleveland.*

"Come and Gone," *The Cleveland Herald* (Cleveland, OH), 20 Feb. 1882, 8[2]

Wilde Sunflower Six Feet High

Blooms Only to Fade Away From the City.

Its Opinion of Art—Its Views on Newspapers—It Lectures—It Smokes Cigarettes—It is Dined and Wined.

"Oscar Wilde and servant, of England, Room 55."

1. When Wilde sent a copy of *Vera* to Edward F. Smyth Pigott (1824–1895), the Examiner of Plays for the Lord Chamberlain, c. September 1880 he wrote: "I am working at dramatic art because it's *the democratic* art" (CL, 97).

2. Quoted in OWDA, 183. For another interview purporting to have taken place at the same time, see "Wilde," *The Cleveland Leader* (Cleveland, OH), 20 Feb. 1882, 6, pp. 180–3.

That was the legend which a Herald reporter read upon the register of the Forest City House Saturday afternoon about 5 o'clock. A card asking the courtesy of an interview, and assuring the notorious stranger that the writer would be both brief and unaggressive, soon found its way up to the room of the aesthete; and by return porter an answer was sent granting the privilege asked, but craving ten minutes time in which to finish a midday repast. In precisely two minutes the reporter stood at the door of room 55, and rapped with gentle timidity.

Mr. Wilde did not answer the summons in person. His colored valet opened the door and ushered the caller into the presence of the far-famed apostle of the lily and the sunflower.

OSCAR WAS LOLLING

on an elegant sofa, and did not rise until his visitor had crossed the room. He then arose slowly, extended his hand reluctantly and pointed the reporter to a chair beside his own luxurious divan.

In the center of the room was a small, unaesthetic-looking table, at which the languid poet had just dined. The viands which remained unconsumed were just such as would be looked for in the menu of the aesthete—jellies, custards, pastry, etc., all served on decorated china. The sofa upon which the poet languished had offended his fastidious taste, and he had accordingly caused to be spread over it an afghan and a silk shawl of an old gold tint.

MR. WILDE HIMSELF

was attired in a velvet coat and vest of brown, and substantial looking pair of ordinary pantaloons. In personal appearance he is exactly what the prevailing photographs represent him to be, save that a pair of rather obtrusive front teeth are displayed in conversation, which have failed to appear in any of the representations of the poet. His face is even more smooth and girlish than would appear in the photographs, and caused to flit though the scribe's mind the horrible suspicion that Oscar has

NEVER YET HAD OCCASION TO SHAVE.

Between his thumb and fore finger he held a dainty cigarette, which, from time to time, he thrust between his rubicund lips, puffing the fragrant smoke above his head in circling clouds that delighted his yearning soul.

"Mr. Wilde," began the inquisitor, kindly but firmly, "may I inquire what first resolved you of your mission, and inspired you to champion this modern aesthetical movement?"

"Well, my passion for art was greatly encouraged, if not created, by a visit to Italy when I was a boy.[1] Then subsequently at Oxford I was greatly influenced by Ruskin. I was also much pained and saddened by seeing how unkindly

ALL OF ENGLAND'S GREAT MEN

were received, especially her literary men; how Byron, Shelley, Keats, Wordsworth, and all the rest were ridiculed! This, I now conceive to be the fate of all prominent men who depart from the common place in any degree, and I am no longer disturbed by it."

"Then you are able to take philosophically all the sarcasm and good-natured fun which has been directed at you since you came to America?"

"Philosophically? Why, I don't mind it in the least. At the very worst, it can only amount to a *personal inconvenience*, as though some one sought to throw mud at you while you were crossing the street. Why, all innovators must be indestructible. In crusading against

THE POPULAR STUPIDITY

and stagnation, I expect to hear ridicule; but I am absolutely impervious to it—it doesn't interfere with my serenity or my fixedness of purpose at all. It is not done from malice, and what is the use, then, in being troubled by it? It is done by a world which cannot understand; that has not been educated up to the aesthetical movement."

"How would you have the world changed?"

"I would create an artistic temperament. I would surround men with elevating environments that their lives might be beautiful. This is

THE SECRET OF ALL JOYOUSNESS

in life, and the keynote of all civilization—this artistic temperament; and it cannot be produced in any other way than by giving the people an opportunity to grow up in an atmosphere of noble and beautiful things. I think that every year in a great country, in America as much as in England, a certain amount of artistic intelligence and power is produced, and that the aim of any rational civilization is to seek out those men and women who have this power of design, this nobility of imagination, this love of the beautiful, and by means of a

SCHOOL OF DESIGN IN EACH CITY

to give men an opportunity of producing beautiful art. You in America don't want that we should look upon you as a mere collection of money-making merchants.

1. Wilde was 20 when he first visited Italy, and appears to have wished it thought that he had taken the trip earlier. See also p. 453, note 3.

You would like to influence the civilization of Europe. You are ambitious and should be so; but the only way you can influence us is by producing noble art and a noble civilization. Believe me, that we value your American poets much more than your American millionaires; and that we estimate you by the amount of great men you have produced, not by

YOUR HOARDED WEALTH."

"That's a rather severe implication, Mr. Wilde. Evidently you place a rather low estimate upon American art and civilization, when comparing them with English art and civilization?"

"Why, my dear young man," said Mr. Wilde, springing to his feet with a show of real enthusiasm, and addressing his visitor earnestly, "do you really think that American progress in these departments can be compared with that of England?"

The abashed reporter hung his head in mortification, and the poet went on:

"Can you seriously compare your art with ours? I have just been in Chicago, and while there I saw millions and millions of dollars sunk in public buildings, but I failed to find one single architectural triumph. Your poets are not to be compared with ours."

THE PRESS SAT DOWN UPON.

"Of course you have been misrepresented in the papers, Mr. Wilde. Would you care to disclaim, at this time, some of the things which have been identified with your aesthetical movement?"

"My dear sir," responded the aesthete, "when I read all this trash in the newspapers about some one whom the editors are wont to call Oscar Wilde, I really wonder what the young man is like after all, and wish that I might see him myself. If it really mattered in the least what the newspapers say, I might take pains to refute some things; but it won't pay."

"Then you don't have a very high idea of American journalism?"

"You know well enough how artificial and meaningless it is, if you have been in the business at all. The press is comic, without being amusing or fair. Nothing which I read by way of criticism gives me pain; nothing by way of commendation gives me pleasure. Who are the editors, anyway? Most frequently they are from the number of escaped convicts and other depraved characters."

The reporter only weighs 125 pounds, so he smothered his desire for revenge, and did not annihilate the six foot sunflower on the spot. Besides that, he did not care to mar the furniture or gore up the carpet. He left, and the aesthete still lives to roam through America.

✂ *A report of Wilde's lecture in Cleveland.*

A MIDNIGHT BANQUET.

After the completion of the lecture Mr. Wilde repaired to the Opera House, and occupied the north private box below during the last act of the Gladiator.[1] At the conclusion of the play Mr. Wilde adjourned to the Windsor club rooms, on Bank Street, where a substantial banquet had been prepared and a small party of friends were waiting to entertain him. The company that sat down to the sumptuous repast embraced besides the sunflower poet the following gentlemen: Messrs. James Carson, Thomas Walton, W. J. Cotton, R. J. Irwin, F. J. King, H. W. Begges, H. S. Stevens, and H. W. Gorton, the last named gentleman being from Buffalo. After the meal the party spent the time until 3:30 A. M. in story-telling, the recalling of reminiscences, and varied conversation.

SUBSEQUENT MOVEMENTS.

Mr. Wilde remained in his room at the hotel nearly all Sunday, receiving few calls and taking his meals at his room. At 7:30 P.M. he took the train for Cincinnati, pursuant to appointments to lecture as follows: At Louisville, Tuesday; Indianapolis, Wednesday; Cincinnati, Thursday, and St Louis Saturday.

"With Mr. Oscar Wilde," *Cincinnati Daily Gazette* (Cincinnati, OH), 21 Feb. 1882, 10[2]

THE GAZETTE ACTS AS CICERONE TO THE GREAT AESTHETE.

How He Looked Like and What He Wore—His Opinion of America and American Art—Doing the Aesthetics of Cincinnati—Oscar's Views on Men and Things in General.

Mr. Oscar Wilde arrived in this city yesterday morning from Cleveland, en route to Louisville, where he is to lecture this evening. He remained over a day, wishing to have a preliminary glance at certain objects of interest here before his

1. *The Gladiator* is a play by Robert Montgomery Bird (1806–1854). First staged in New York in 1831, it remained popular for decades. This production starred John McCullough. Wilde commented favourably on McCullough's performance in a later interview ("Oscar Back Again," *The Daily Inter Ocean* (Chicago, IL), 1 Mar. 1882, 8, p. 235; "Oscar Wilde," *The Chicago Daily Tribune* (Chicago, IL), 1 Mar. 1882, 7, p. 239).

2. H & S, b37. Reprinted in H & S, 67–71. Excerpted in "Oscar Wilde," *The Sunday Herald* (Boston, MA), 26 Feb. 1882, 9; "Studio and Gallery Gossip," *The Chicago Sunday Tribune* (Chicago, IL), 5 Mar. 1882, 16; "Oscar Wilde Discovers a Young Irish Sculptor Out West," *The Pilot* (Boston, MA), 11 Mar. 1882, 4; and "Personal," *The Irish-American* (New York, NY), 25 Mar. 1882, 4. Quoted in OWDA, 77, 116, 179–80; 189; Pearson, 67; Ellmann, 187/197; and Sturgis, 216/207–8, 224/215, 237/227. Referenced in Sturgis, 223/214.

return on Thursday for his lecture on "The English Renaissance" at the grand Opera House on the afternoon of that day.[1]

A Gazette representative having early information of the arrival of the great apostle of aestheticism, called upon him at the Burnet and was duly requested to follow his card to parlor No. 62, where Mr. Wilde was bestowed. The poet and aesthete was found rather languidly reclining upon a couch, over which was thrown, in careless grace, a rich fur lined railway traveling rug, smoking a cigarette in a thoughtful mood. There was a litter of letters upon the table, in the midst of which was a magnificent basket of roses, pink and red, which Mr. Wilde explained were a rest and comfort to his soul after the horrors of a railway journey. Against the side of the room stands a battered, but substantial English leather "box," which the Gazette representative gazed at reverently in the pauses of the conversation, knowing that it was the casket that contained the silken raiment which has excited the rage of the heathen in two continents.

Mr. Wilde was curiously like, but yet utterly unlike, the Maudle of the organ of the Philistines, Punch, and the fact reminds one of the proverb that a lie is never so dangerous as when it has in it a modicum of truth. The large, long face, framed in thick locks of brown hair, parted in the center and falling on either side of the cheeks almost to the shoulders, which gives to it a certain womanly air, is Du Maurier's, but in place of the vacant stare is a bright smile, and a perpetually changing expression, clear gray eyes, a tall and manly figure, a carriage the perfection of good form, and a bearing that bespeaks him a thorough man of the world. He wore a morning suit of light mastic colored tweed; the coat of velvet, a little pronounced in the matter of braid; a pale red silk handkerchief drooped from the breast pocket, and matched in color the ample neckerchief knotted in sailor fashion beneath his low turned shirt collar. He was faultlessly shod in patent leather, with gray gaiters, and wore no jewelry but a very large seal ring—a fine antique intaglio of Mercury cut in amethyst.[2] With this he seals his billet doux and those other "winged messengers" which have roused the dull British Philistine from his vulgar lethargy—or anyhow have showed him the true path out of the mire.

Mr. Wilde was most cordial. Would the GAZETTE act as cicerone, and show the stranger Rookwood, the School of Design, the Art Museum?[3]

Why, certainly; if the GAZETTE desires one good thing more than another, it is to stimulate the zeal and devotion of the people, and make room for what is

1. Wilde delivered his newer lecture on *The Decorative Arts* and not *The English Renaissance*. Promoters frequently made the same mistake in their advertisements of Wilde's lectures. See also "Oscar Interviewed," *The Rockford Daily Register* (Rockford, IL), 3 Mar. 1882, 3, pp. 245–6.

2. A facsimile of an impression in wax of Wilde's seal ring is reproduced in Mason, 181.

3. The Rookwood Pottery Company was founded in 1880, The McMicken School of Drawing and Design in 1869, and the Cincinnati Art Museum in 1881.

purely true and precious in art. Meanwhile, what does Mr. Wilde think of America?

"I am pleased with it. It has great possibilities; each city in the years to come will be the center of a school of art, as is Venice, Florence, Rome. It is folly to talk of a national art: there is no such thing. Each city has its center of inspiration. In Florence the inspiration was of a religious type, God and the angels; in Venice it was the noble men and women of the republic; in Rome, traditions and noble deeds.

"I am especially delighted with the West, it is so new and fresh, and the people are so generous and free from prejudice. The older cities in the East," Mr. Wilde said, musingly blowing little rings of smoke from his lips—"The people are enveloped in a perfect mist of prejudice, quite unlimited; they have imported so many old world ideas, absurdities, and affectations that they have lost all sincerity and naturalness." (The Boston Philistines made the aesthete have a thoroughly "bad time" evidently.) "You have no architecture, no scenery, but individuals are doing beautiful work, and you have great art possibilities."

"In what direction?"

"America is the country for a great school of sculpture, because it is dependent upon the sunlight which you have, and is an art which depends absolutely upon present and active conditions of life, and not upon remembrance or tradition. I met in Chicago," Mr. Wilde said reflectively, "a young sculptor whom we would love and be so proud of if he were in Europe—a Mr. Donoghue. He reminded me of the old Italian stories of the struggle of genius. Born of poor people, he felt a desire to create beauty. Seeing some workmen modeling a cornice one day, be begged some clay of them, and went home and began to model. A man who saw what was in him gave him money for a year in Paris. He went, and has come back. The way I found him was, he sent to me a little bas relief of a seated girl, illustrating a verse of my poem, 'Requiescat.' I went and saw him; found him in a bare little room at the top of a great building, and in the center was a statuette of the young Sophocles leading the dance and the song after the battle of Seramis, a piece of the highest artistic beauty and perfect workmanship, waiting there in the clay, to be cast into bronze. It was by far the best piece of sculpture I have seen in America.[1]

1. *The Young Sophocles Leading the Chorus of Victory after the Battle of Salamis.* Wilde reportedly promised "to advance Mr. Donoghue sufficient means to enable him to have his 'Sophocles' cast in bronze, with a view to exhibiting it in the Grosvenor Gallery in London." ("Art in Chicago', *The Chicago Daily Tribune* (Chicago, IL), 19 Feb. 1882, 16.) This did not transpire, but Wilde did send a photograph of the clay statuette of *The Young Sophocles* to Charles Eliot Norton, a professor of the history of art at Harvard whom he had met in Boston, encouraging him to commission a new statue from Donoghue (CL, 176-7). Donoghue executed a heroic-size version of *The Young Sophocles* in plaster in Rome in 1885 and exhibited it in Paris in 1886 and New York in 1887. It

"Meanwhile the artist starves upon a radish and a crust, the stoic's fare. Perhaps, but he will win in the end, and trouble is light if one is an artist. A man is not successful," said Mr. Wilde, sententiously, but truly, "because the world praises him, but because his work is good."

"What have you seen commendable in a decorative way in your visit?"

"Many good houses in Philadelphia, Boston, and Washington, and I have seen a Daisy Miller. I cannot tell you where (this in response to eager questionings),[1] because I am to go back there, and I should never be forgiven, but the sight of her has increased my admiration for Henry James a thousand fold.[2]

"Col. John Hay, of Cleveland, with whom I lunched yesterday, had a charming house.[3] But the room which has most impressed me was a little bare whitewashed room in Camden Town, where I met Walt Whitman, whom I admire intensely. There was a big chair for him and a little stool for me, a pine table on which was a copy of Shakespeare, a translation of Dante,[4] and a cruse of water. Sunlight filled the room, and over the roofs of the houses opposite were the masts of the ships that lay in the river. But then the poet needs no rose to blossom on his walls for him, because he carries nature always in his heart. This room contains all the simple conditions for art—sunlight, good air, pure water, a sight of ships, and the poet's works.

"I saw another of your great poets in his beautiful home." Mr. Wilde looked out of the window into the smoke and mist and sighed. It was a day to make the children of light to sigh and the heathen to mock and rage.

"This kind of weather," he continued, consoling himself with a fresh cigarette, "always gives me a sense of failure. I am always on the side of extremes—in winter I would always be sleighing, in summer always in a summer garden of flowers. I went to see Longfellow in a snow storm and returned in a hurricane,

---

was not cast in bronze until 1911, eight years after Donoghue's death (Tolles, T. (Ed.). (1999). *American Sculpture in the Metropolitan Museum of Art*. The Metropolitan Museum of Art, New York. 342–4).

1. In the source, this editorial remark is enclosed in square brackets.

2. Daisy Miller is the eponymous character in an 1879 story by Henry James (1843–1916). She is a young American woman whose flirtatiousness is frowned upon when she visits Europe. She is thought to have been inspired by Marian "Clover" Hooper Adams (1843–1885). As Wilde uses the indefinite article to refer to his Daisy Miller, it is probable he did not mean Adams but another woman representative of the type. Adams, who lived in Washington, wrote to Henry James in January 1882 to ask him not to bring Wilde to her home: "I must keep out thieves and noodles," (Friedman, 119–20). James was also less than enthused with Wilde, declaring him "a fatuous fool and a tenth-rate cad," (Friedman, 123).

3. John Milton Hay (1838–1905) was an American politician. He had been a private secretary to Abraham Lincoln; he would serve as the United States Secretary of State from 1898 to his death.

4. Dante Alighieri (c. 1265–1321) was a Italian poet. His works include *Divina Commedia* (the *Divine Comedy)* and *La Vita Nuova* (*The New Life*).

Figure 6. The Young Sophocles Leading the Chorus of Victory after the Battle of Salamis *by John Donoghue, 1885, cast 1911. Wilde thought the clay model "by far the best piece of sculpture" he had seen in America.*

quite the right conditions for a visit to a poet. When I remember Boston, I think only of this lovely old man, who is himself a poem, and the bright party of men I met at Dr. Holmes's."

At 1 o'clock Mr. Wilde donned his green overcoat, trimmed with otter, adjusted a bon silene rosebud in his coat lapel, drew on a pair of pale tan colored gloves, and with an ivory stick in his hand and a brown stiff felt hat on his head, was driven first to Robert Clarke & Co.'s, where he selected various books, among them the works of Howells, James, Miss McLaughlin, and others, and thence to Rookwood, the School of Design, the Art Museum, whose doors were inhospitably closed, and a half hour was delightfully spent at the delightful home of Mrs. Col. Nichols, on the Grandin road.[1] By request of Mr. Wilde, his impressions of the art industries of the city are not made public. He will embody them in his lecture on Thursday afternoon.[2] Mr. Wilde has a keen and quiet wit that enlivens his conversation upon worldly subjects delightfully.

When shown the School of Design, with its forlorn corridors and dark rooms, his eye lighted on the legend "No Smoking," painted in the window. "Great heaven, they speak of smoking as if it were a crime. I wonder they do not caution the students not to murder each other on the landings. Such a place is enough to incite a man to the commission of any crime," and then, 'most unkindest cut of all,'[3] "I wonder no criminal has ever pleaded the ugliness of your city as an excuse for his crimes!"

The suburbs Mr. Wilde kindly approved. Seen through the rain and mist, the stately villas of Grandin road were quite English with their green sweep of turf and crowding chimneys.

Of all men Mr. Wilde least loves a critic. "Let the poet sing," he cries, "and let the artist paint, and let the people look and listen—and so they would, and learn,

1. "James" is Henry James. Mary Louise McLaughlin (1847–1939) was a potter and ceramic painter based in Cincinnati. By the time of Wilde's visit to the city she had published *China Painting: A Practical Manual for the Use of Amateurs in the Decoration of Hard Porcelain* (1880) and *Pottery Decoration Under the Glaze* (1880). Maria Longworth Nichols née Storer (1849–1932) was the founder of Rookwood Pottery.

2. Despite making this request, Wilde did make brief comments to another interviewer that day ("Oscar Wilde," *The Cincinnati Enquirer* (Cincinnati, OH), 21 Feb. 1882, 4, p. 195). In his first lecture in Cincinnati he criticised what he had seen at Rookwood, but managed to keep his audience on side: "At a certain school of design—where, he would not say, as he hoped to deliver a second lecture at the place (laughter)—his artistic sense had received a severe shock by seeing moonlights and sunsets on dinner plates." In other cities he would repeatedly say that "nobody wanted to take soup off of moonlight or eat terrapin off of sunsets". He objected to the poor quality of some of the workmanship: "I am afraid that I saw some designs on your pottery that I feel quite sure were done by some one who had exactly five minutes in which to catch the train, and who thought he could decorate two vases and a dish in that time! (Great laughter.)" He complimented the School of Design, and the work of Mary McLaughlin and H. J. Breuer.

3. The reporter quotes Antony in Shakespeare's *Julius Caesar* (III, 2).

too—but the critic, a kind of middleman, comes between them, and, like the bird in Shelley's song, shuts his eyes and declares it is night.[1] Sometimes the critic himself, lured on by a hope of fame, paints, or writes, or sings, and then a great and sacred joy fills the soul of all artists, and his fate overtakes him." The real critic should be a poet, Mr. Wilde thinks, and in proof cites Coleridge, Keats, Goethe, Matthew Arnold, the greatest of living English critics, all poets,[2] and quotes with glee Theophile Gautier's reproof of a critic who lectured him on the iniquity of his ways. "It is of great advantage to a man never to have done anything, but he must not abuse it."[3]

"I forgive everything, the critics' ignorance, even. I applaud Bunthorne languidly from my opera box. I greet Du Maurier blandly at the club; but the unpardonable sin is to say I am impractical. That is to stick a dagger in me. This aesthetic movement is the first of any practical value in art in England. It has changed the whole character of English decorative art. It has given to every handicraftsman in England beautiful designs, which are at the foundation of all good art. We have relieved the whole English people from the incubus of the upholsterer. He now exists only in the museums as a warning."

Mr. Wilde looked in at the opera last night to see the diva and the audience, and was in the manager's box for half an hour.[4] He leaves this morning for Louisville, and returns, as before stated, for a matinee on Thursday at the Grand.

1. Hofer and Scharnhorst suggest that Wilde is recalling Shelley's poem *Archy's Song*, in which a nightingale "Sings like a fool through darkness and light" (H & S, 71).

2. Samuel Taylor Coleridge (1772–1834) was an English poet, critic, and philosopher. Best known for his long poem *The Rime of the Ancient Mariner* (1798), Coleridge also lectured on various topics, including education, Shakespeare, and the English poets. Matthew Arnold (1822–1888) was an English poet, critic, and inspector of schools. Wilde listed him among the "very few masters" of English prose (*The Queen*, 8 Dec. 1888; CW vii, No. 108, 155–8), and in prison requested his *Poems* (Wright, 320).

3. Théophile Gautier (1811–1872) was a French poet and critic. In prison Wilde requested his poetry collection *Émaux et Camées* (*Enamels and Cameos*; 1852, later revised) (Wright, 321).

4. The diva referred to is Adelina Patti. She performed on 20 February at the Music Hall. For Wilde's opinion of the concert see "Newport Gossip," *The Sunday Herald* (Boston, MA), 23 July 1882, 9, p. 444.

"Oscar Wilde," *The Cincinnati Enquirer* (Cincinnati, OH), 21 Feb. 1882, 4[1]

The Great Aesthete in the City.

Oscar Wilde, the aesthete, arrived in the city yesterday, and took up his quarters in Burnet House, where a representative of the ENQUIRER met him late yesterday afternoon. The original of "Bunthorne" was reclining on a fauteuil when our ambassador entered his apartments. He arose rather more quickly than poetic grace demanded, and with a pleasant smile extended his right hand and gave him a cordial greeting. In person he is very tall, with broad shoulders and a plethora of arms and legs—that is, he has the usual complement of limbs, but they appear longer and more loosely jointed than perfect accord with manly beauty requires. His face is long and narrow, and appears narrower than it really is on account of the length of his hair, which is light brown in color, is parted in the middle, and touches the shoulders like a dark flaxen mane. His eyes are large and light blue in color. Their outside corners are lower than the inside like a Chinaman's, though they are far from being almond-shaped. His nose is long, large and aquiline, and his mouth betrays his Hibernian origin, his lips being thick and the upper one so shut that his speech partakes somewhat of the character of a lisp. His teeth, especially the upper ones, are long, large and irregular. His chin is protuberant, and he has very high cheek-bones. His sack-coat and natty vest were of cobwebby grey velvet hue, with a cold gravy bloom;[2] his trousers were light in color and loose and limp in make. His shoes were of patent leather, with buff gaiters, and his low-cut Byronic collar was encircled by a silk cravat that was tied in a sailor knot, and was between a Dunducketty grey and a dull pink in color.[3] In the left lapel of his coat was a beautiful rosebud, and he held another in his left hand, whose delicate exhalations he ever and anon inhaled with evident rapture. Within easy reach stood a marble-topped table, on which was a vase containing four splendid calla lilies, whose faint perfume almost drowned the senses with olfactory delight. As soon as the greetings were over and our guileless youth took the chair which was proffered him by Mr. Wilde, he began operations by remarking: "Mr. Wilde, I presume by this time you are sufficiently acquainted with the customs of this country to know that you are face to face with the ubiquitous interviewer?"

1. H & S, b38. Reprinted in H & S, 72–4. Excerpted in "The Theme of Art," *Puget Sound Argus* (Port Townsend, WA), 16 June 1882, 2; "Aesthetic Subjects," *The Rock Island Argus* (Rock Island, IL), 1 Mar. 1882, 5; and *West-Jersey Pioneer* (Bridgeton, NJ), 2 Mar. 1882, 1. Quoted in "Esthetic Hog-Killing," *Chicago Morning News* (Chicago, IL), 1 Mar. 1882, 2; and OWDA, 190–1.
2. A reference to *Patience*. See p. 66, note 2.
3. Dunducketty is a "mud colour" or "an indescribable colour, but rather dull" (OED).

"Oh, yes," smilingly replied the aesthetic apostle, "and I am glad of it, for some of the brightest hours I have passed in this country have been with the gentlemen of the press who have interviewed me, and I have found them among the most intelligent men I have met here."

"Taffy," mentally ejaculated our reporter, and then said: "How long will you remain in this city?"

"Only until morning. I am on my way to Louisville, where I will lecture tomorrow evening; then I go to Indianapolis, and on Thursday I return to this city and lecture here. Today I drove to the Rookwood pottery, with Mrs. George Ward Nichols, and inspected its work very closely."

"How did you like it?"

"Some of it was very good, and much of it indifferent. On the whole I was very much pleased, as it showed what can be done for art even by one person, as in the case of Mrs. Nichols. There is one young man named Bowen at Rookwood whom I am sure has true poetic art and fervor. His productions are wonderful, and he should be encouraged."[1]

"I am going to tell you something that I fear will shock you," said our scribe.

"Shock me?" interrupted Oscar.

"Yes," was the reply. "Several years ago one of our promising young artists was employed by a number of our merchants to make a series of pictures for the Vienna Exposition. He executed the commission, his pictures attracted great attention, and, I believe, received a medal. What do you think was their theme?"

"Indeed, I can't tell."

"Hog killing!"[2]

"Well I don't know but even that could be treated in an artistic manner. You see there is no such thing as a poetic subject no more than that there is a natural school of painting. You hear people speak of the Italian school of painting, when no such thing exists. The Venetian style differs from the Florentine as it differs from that of other Italian cities. Each locality has its own school as distinct and

1. "Bowen" is H. J. Breuer. The spelling of his name is confirmed in "Oscar Wilde and Mr. Breuer," *Cincinnati Daily Gazette* (Cincinnati, OH), 25 Feb. 1882, 5. It had been given in various reports of Wilde's Cincinnati lecture as "Bauer", "Baur", and "Bower" ("The Aesthete," *The Cincinnati Enquirer* (Cincinnati, OH), 24 Feb. 1882, 5; "Oscar Wilde," *The Cincinnati Commercial* (Cincinnati, OH), 24 Feb. 1882, 4; and "Oscar Wilde's Lecture," *Cincinnati Daily Gazette* (Cincinnati, OH), 24 Feb. 1882, 5), and is given incorrectly in other interviews.

2. The French-born American painter and illustrator, Henry François Farny (1847–1916), was commissioned by the Cincinnati Pork-Packing Association to draw a series of cartoons representing the process of hog-slaughtering and pork-packing. The cartoons was exhibited at the Cincinnati Chamber of Commerce before being taken to the 1873 Vienna World's Fair, where they were awarded a medal by the "Commerce of the World" jury ("Farny's Pork-Packing Cartoons," *The Cincinnati Inquirer* (Cincinnati, OH), 21 Aug. 1873, 1). Farny is best known for his paintings depicting the life of Native Americans.

separate as the towns themselves. The so-called Dutch school is remarkable for its warmth of color, and yet its subjects are mostly commonplace. All through Holland you will see pictures mostly of brawls and quarrels in drinking-rooms. Yet every once in awhile you will see in one of them a gleam of light streaming through a window and tinting the glasses on the table with all the glories of the prism. Another will display a bit of coloring as warm and as sweet as the kiss of love. The men who painted these pictures poetized the subjects until the ordinariness of their character is forgotten. This shows that they were earnest and sincere, and that their heart was in their work. I have little faith in a young man who chooses what are called heroic subjects for his early efforts. It looks as though he was depending on his subject, and not on his own powers, for success. The lowliest subject, treated with loving earnestness and sincerity, will, if the artist is competent, give the best results, just as the plainest words are the most effective in the mouth of an actor."

"I understand that you will give us a new lecture here," inquired our representative. "What will be its subject?"

"Decorative art," was the answer.

"Will it contain any local allusions?"

"Yes, I think it will. I think I will speak of what I have seen at Rookwood. Wherever I go I try to see what there is of decorative art in it, and I speak of what I see in my lectures. I think it will be judicious to do so here."

As Mr. Wilde's task in decorative art is unquestioned, it will be seen that his lecture bids fair to be very interesting to our citizens. In the evening Mr. Wilde attended the opera concert at Music Hall, and was the central figure in the Director's box. He was dressed in black knee breeches and black silk stockings, white vest and black dress coat, with white tie and gloves. His presence speedily became known to those on the O P side,[1] and many were the opera glasses that were leveled at him as he stood up in the box listening to Patti and her supports. During the performance he was taken behind the scenes and introduced to the diva.[2]

1. Opposite or Off Prompt, i.e. stage right (the prompter is traditionally located at stage left).

2. For Wilde's opinion of the concert see "Newport Gossip," *The Sunday Herald* (Boston, MA), 23 July 1882, 9, p. 444.

"Oscar Wilde," *The Cincinnati Commercial* (Cincinnati, OH), 21 Feb. 1882, 8

THE APOSTLE OF THE AESTHETIC VISITS CINCINNATI.

HOW HE LOOKS, WHAT HE HAS TO SAY, AND WHY HE IS HERE.

Those who visited the Burnet House yesterday noticed at once that something unusual had happened. Proprietors, clerks, bell-boys and boarders wore a semi-amused, semi-puzzled expression, and the question was general, "Have you seen him?" followed by "What do you think of him?" "Him" was the famous aesthetic apostle, Oscar Wilde. He arrived from Cleveland yesterday morning and his entrance into the Burnet was the signal for a sensation, from which the dwellers in that hostelry have not yet recovered.

He was shown to a handsome apartment on the second floor. Soon after his arrival he remarked to his attendant that he felt slightly unwell, and requested him to send for some flowers. A smart young key clerk of the hotel, who wanted to get a good view of the famous aesthete, went to his room and asked what kind of flowers he would like to have. He replied that he was not particular about that, but flowers revived and brightened him when he was feeling badly. The clerk immediately telephoned Critchell to let him know how big a stock of sunflowers he had on hand, intending to order them all. The florist replied that he was out of sunflowers, but that he was loaded to the guards with lilies and rosebuds. "Send us three dollars worth mixed," said the clerk.

The flowers arrived, and Oscar felt better.[1]

In the afternoon he visited the Rookwood Pottery, and paid his respects to Mrs. Maria Longworth Nichols, its proprietor, at her residence.

Toward evening a representative of the Commercial called at the Burnet, and the response to a card sent to Room 62 was, "Come up at once." The reporter had read a great deal about Oscar, and was familiar with the great variety of pictures and caricatures of the poet; but he was scarcely prepared for the reality.

In the southwest corner of the room was a sofa. Over it had been negligently thrown a fur robe, covering about one-half or more from the foot. Over the other half was a silken drapery cloth of old gold. On the sofa reclined Oscar in an exquisitely medieval attitude. Before him was a table on which were lilies and roses. He rose gracefully and politely offered his hand to the reporter, with a pleasant smile, and then resumed his position on the sofa.

Oscar looks precisely like his picture by Sarony, and not unlike many of the caricatures. He is tall and rather powerfully built, and would impress a sporting

1. Stories of Wilde being restored by flowers should be treated with scepticism. However, in this case there is reason to suspect that Wilde did order the flowers. See p. 200, note 1.

man with the idea that a thorough system of training might give him a chance for the middle-weight championship. His brown hair falls about his ears almost down to his shoulders, and he has a feminine way of occasionally flirting it back with his hand. His costume was a study. He wore a sack coat and vest of the material so graphically described by Lady Jane as "a cobwebby gray velvet, with a tender bloom like cold gravy."[1] From the left pocket of his coat was a profuse display of old gold silk handkerchief, and from under his low and rolling collar hung a large silk neck scarf of the same color. His trousers were of a somewhat similar tint made loose, and his feet were encased in neat fitting shoes made of patent leather and yellow morocco.

His conversation was almost entirely about art, in spite of the fact that the reporter endeavored to turn his attention to the river, the streets, Patti. Concerning Patti, he said that he had been invited to go and hear her, and would probably do so. The three great arts, he said, were music, architecture, and decorative art. Of the "ceramic craze" he remarked that people who cannot paint pictures in oil or water colors imagine that they can decorate pieces of china, he believed that only artists who had the ability to design could be successful in decorative art. The ability to design is a requisite of the true artist. Referring to his visit to the Rookwood Pottery, he said that he noticed several vases on which the decoration showed original design, and was sure the same hand had designed them all. He found that he was right. The artist was a Mr. Bauer.[2]

He paused in his artistic talk long enough to remark that the wretched weather reminded him of London, and to say that the streets of Cincinnati were horribly dirty. Instantly the reporter's opinion of the poet rose several degrees.[3]

During all his conversation there was the suggestion of a mischievous twinkle playing about his eyes, which seems to say:

"This air severe
Is but a mere
Veneer!
This cynic smile
is but a wile
Of guile!
This costume chaste

1. A reference to *Patience*. See p. 66, note 2.
2. "Bauer" is H. J. Breuer. See p. 195, note 1.
3. The awful state of Cincinnati's streets was well known. The city's newspapers often rebuked the local Street Commissioners for failing to address the problem, hence why the reporter was pleased by Wilde's seeming insult.

Is but good taste
Misplaced!"[1]

Oscar's views on art are probably valuable, and they are certainly expressed in rich and flowing English. Indeed, he appears to have a wonderful command of the intricacies of his mother tongue; but, unfortunately, the reporter was too busy studying his physical peculiarities and eccentricities of costume to stem the flood of artistic eloquence, and as he gazed at Oscar, he murmured to himself:

"If this young man expresses himself in terms too deep for me,
Why, what a very singularly deep young man this deep young man must be."[2]

The poet came here principally for the purpose of getting some idea of decorative art in Cincinnati. He intends to devote a portion of his lecture at the Grand next Thursday afternoon to this subject. He lectures in Louisville tonight.

As the reporter walked away from the poet's room, he turned to the colored boy who had been his attendant all afternoon, and said:

"Well, Charley, what do you think of Oscar?"

With a puzzled shake of the head he replied:

"Hardly know what to think, boss; he looks like an Injun."

"English Renaissance," *Louisville Commercial* (Louisville, KY), 22 Feb. 1882[3]

AND ITS APOSTLE, OSCAR WILDE

A Visit to the Distinguished Aesthete in His Rooms—His Opinion of America and Americans—Lecture to a Large and Attentive Audience

"I find nothing unique in America," said Mr. Oscar Wilde, the distinguished English poet and apostle of art-culture to a COMMERCIALIST, who spent a short time in parlor 101 at the Louisville Hotel yesterday. "To a stranger like myself it appears monotonous." Mr. Wilde was reclining easily upon a sofa, over which was spread a dark skin and a soft olive cloth of some kind. He leaned easily on his right arm and his left was thrown behind his head, except when he removed his cigarette and puffed little pale-blue circlets of smoke above the marble-topped table which stood directly in front of him, and upon which was a vase containing

1. Lyrics of a song sung by Bunthorne, which also includes the lines "Then let me own | I'm an aesthetic sham!"
2. Lyrics of a song sung by Bunthorne.
3. Reprinted, without the account of the lecture, as "English Renaissance," *Salt Lake Daily Herald* (Salt Lake City, UT), 1 Mar. 1882, 6.

some lilies and roses and a slowly settling glass of champagne that had apparently been just touched.[1] The room was darkened a little, and the shutters of the window just behind his head were partially closed, throwing him, as a picture, into a soft but not indistinct light. It was a fine and graceful figure upon the sofa. Six feet of manly outline were displayed. He wore a dark olive smoking doublet, lined with rose-colored stuff, and profusely ornamented with cord and lace. This was turned back from the throat, encircled by a low-cut Byron collar, at which a dark necktie was negligently knotted. His pantaloons were light and loose and limp, the patent leather shoes pointed and topped with lavender gaiters. In all these details there was only the suggestion of the tastes and appearance of other men of leisure in their smoking parlors. The head and face, however, were remarkable, and disappointing to one who had become familiar with his photographs which, to say the least, "flatter" him. The face is very long, sallow and oval, the cheek-bones high, the chin prominent, the nose long and aquiline. His eyes, almond-shaped, full and dark, are unusually fine and intelligent, imbedded in the face as if upon cream cushions. His mouth is a poor feature. The upper lip is heavy but short, the front teeth long and protruding, and there is a slight suggestion of lisp in his enunciation. The forehead is not remarkable, but, on the contrary, his head is small at the crown and on either side falls a long, straight and ungainly mass of dark flaxen hair, which is not parted and is totally devoid of any beauty. It gives him an uncertain "womanish" appearance.

"I find nothing unique in America," Mr. Wilde said in answer to a question whether the peculiar bustle and rush of so representative a western city as Chicago had nothing unique in it. "Chicago is not unique. It is bare looking and monotonous. The architecture is so poor that it amounts to none at all. That is true of all American cities. And yet you must depend on the individual cities for your architecture as for all art. There is no National school of art. In Europe each city has its own school. This is more noticeably true of architecture, because when architectural monuments are raised they stand there forever, impressing a character upon the locality which cannot be removed. The same is true of painting. When you see Italian pictures it is not enough to know they were painted in Italy. You must know whether they were executed in Venice, or Florence, or Naples. These cities form schools of their own, and do not all form a National school. It is not so with music to as great an extent. A piece of music, when composed, goes out to all the world, and its influence is felt universally. Still there is a local coloring in the composition, and there are local schools. Buildings and art galleries

1. Wilde may have ordered fresh flowers, but the fact that a reporter noticed that he had also displayed lilies and roses in his hotel room in Cincinnati a day earlier suggests the possibility that he brought them with him. See "Oscar Wilde," *The Cincinnati Commercial* (Cincinnati, OH), 21 Feb. 1882, 8, p. 197.

remain where they are erected and formed, and are exclusively the result of local development. American architecture is cold and bare. It amounts to nothing as art."

"What do you think of the American himself?"

"I am exceedingly pleased with their kindness to me and the intelligence and appreciation everywhere to be met."

"In this respect how does the West compare with the East?"

"Oh, I have only lectured once in the West—in Chicago.[1] The people there were very cultivated and intelligent, and received me with every indication of attention. On the whole, I believe I think better of the West than the East. In the East you know there is much folly flying. It comes from European association and influence. In the West you are working out your own civilization by yourselves, and there is more readiness to hear thoughtfully suggestions and opinions."[2]

"You have not been annoyed in the West by the impertinences you met with in the East?"

Mr. Wilde had spoken before with an easy earnestness. His face was serious and there was none of the drawl which has been attributed to him, more than any man would display under the irksomeness of newspaper interviewing long continued. At this question, however, a furtive and half amused smile crossed his face.

"Oh," said he, "I met with some annoyances in two provincial towns, but I do not think the less of the Eastern people, because of the impertinence and ill-behavior of a few school boys. I assure you my reception has been too cordial for such incidents to weigh against.[3]

"I notice," he continued after a moment, "that your river is swollen and high."

It was hoped by the interviewer that he who had been disappointed in the Atlantic Ocean, and stood unmoved by Niagara, would express himself upon the waste that engulfed Shippingsport and the coal yards as in a maelstrom. Vain hope. He added:

"The worst of this is that it gives you very bad water."

1. After lecturing in Chicago and before arriving in Louisville Wilde had backtracked east, appearing in Fort Wayne, Detroit, and Cleveland. He may not have thought these cities qualified as Western; more likely he wished to focus attention on his Chicago lecture, which had been well attended and well received.

2. The *Salt Lake Daily Herald* has "thoughtful" rather than "thoughtfully". The *Herald* editor no doubt assumed he was correcting a typo, but it is plausible that Wilde intended to compliment the thoughtfulness of his audience.

3. The reference is to the disruptions to Wilde's lectures in Boston, New Haven, and Rochester, caused by students of Harvard, Yale, and Rochester University, respectively.

"The people of the great rushing West," responded the reporter, "have not the time to object to a few ounces of mud more or less to the gallon of water."

"Haven't the time?" inquired the great aesthetic with mild surprise; "why pure water is as necessary as pure air. Every drop of the water for your city should be filtered until it is pure."

The reporter paused and contemplated the suggested millenium when the Water Company would furnish more water than mud, and President Long and Councilman Feely would lie down together. The idea was so overpowering that he needed fresh air to recover in. Mr. Wilde said he would leave this afternoon for Indianapolis, where he lectures tonight, and bidding the reporter farewell, bowed him with evident relief out of the room.

✂ *A report of Wilde's lecture in Louisville.*

"Oscar Wilde," *The Cincinnati Commercial* (Cincinnati, OH), 24 Feb. 1882, 4

HIS LECTURE AT THE GRAND OPERA-HOUSE.

A LARGE AND FASHIONABLE AUDIENCE GREETS THE FAMOUS AESTHETE.

✂ *A report of Wilde's lecture in Cincinnati.*

It was an effort when behind the scenes to get the lecturer to descend from his clouds of rhetoric on art to a statement of the plainest kind. When the question as to the reason of his lecturing here in the afternoon was put to him he said: "Oh! that was business, and I never make any inquiries about business; I go like a lamb and lecture whenever the time is set for me." But when he was asked if he would lecture at 6 in the morning he was a little staggered, and without considering the aesthetic aspect of lecturing at the time of Aurora's coming, he was practical enough to say that would be a little early.

"Utterly Utter," *St. Louis Post-Dispatch* (St. Louis, MO), 25 Feb. 1882, 4[1]

Oscar Wilde, Smoking His Cigarette, Descants on "The Beautiful."

Some of his Rencontres With Newspapers—A Chat with the Apostle of Aestheticism.

An unusual bustle was visible about the corridors of the Southern this morning, which puzzled the guests as they entered. Knots of young men generally known in society stood around the pillars in attempted attitudes and seemed to be waiting intently. The clerks were more chipper than usual, and appeared to be expecting something. Many of the ladies who were down town shopping extended their promenade to Walnut street, a thing very unusual, and as they passed the hotel, craned their pretty necks in an attempt to gaze inside. Each carriage that stopped was watched curiously, and the appearances all indicated that something was going to happen. Every time a tall, slender young man with hair longer than usual advanced towards the register, the aforesaid young men would form ranks and follow him. As he registered "Fritz Hoffszleuttle, Omaha," or something equally astounding, the followers would turn, somebody would say, "Pshaw, that's not he," and back they went to the waiting place. The cause of the commotion was

THE COMING OF OSCAR WILDE.

He was expected on the morning train and the loiterers were on hand to see what he looked like. At 10 o'clock he had not come, and the watch was nearly given up. A half hour later Oscar alighted from a hack at the ladies' entrance, accompanied by his agent, stepped into the elevator and went to his room. He was clad in a large, heavy all-fur overcoat, with a slouched hat, such as Texans affect. His arrival soon became noised about, and the great question was what did he look like. A POST-DISPATCH reporter sent his card to parlor 70, where

THE AESTHETIC APOSTLE

had been domiciled, and was immediately invited to walk up. The tap at the door was answered by a musical "Come in," and the entrance was followed by disappointment. Anybody who imagines Wilde to be long, lank and angular is badly deceived. At the side of the room a sofa was placed, over one corner of which had been thrown a large and heavy drapery of old gold with tassels. The back was

1. H & S, b39. Reprinted in H & S, 75–8. Quoted in OWDA, 82, 89; Pearson, 62, 64; Ellmann, 176/185; and Sturgis, 227/218.

covered with a robe of long fur which hung down from the seat to the floor. Carelessly seated in the middle of the robe, and leaning back in a graceful pose, sat

OSCAR, WITH A TINY CIGARETTE

between his fingers.

As he rose to greet the visitor he looked as unlike the usual description of him as could well be imagined. He is a stout, rather heavily-built young man, possibly 5 feet 10 inches in height. His hair, which is of dark brown, is his distinguishing feature. It reaches his shoulders, is thick and heavy, not parted at all, but combed straight back in front, and he has a feminine way of tossing back stray locks which occasionally attempt to hang over the sides of his face. He wore a sack coat and high-buttoned vest of gray velvet, trimmed with wide braid of a like shade. His pantaloons were of a rough gray material, cut loose, and he wore shoes of patent leather and yellow morocco. His smooth face is large and pronounced and suggests at once the features of Henry Ward Beecher. The eyes are big, brown and almond shaped, the nose slightly aquiline, the lips rather thick, and the chin pronounced and heavy. Oscar's worst features are his teeth, the upper ones being large, projecting and uneven. He wore a dark pea-green scarf, under a turn-down collar, which concealed the shirt front. A handkerchief of the same shade appeared from his side pocket. He wore no jewelry save

A LARGE SEAL RING ON HIS LEFT HAND,

a pair of wide flapped cuffs at his wrists being fastened with plain pearled buttons. He looks like a stout, well-fed, active young Englishman, and his long hair gives him a poetical aspect. The reporter gazed anxiously over the room, but Wilde understood the glances and with a smile seemed to say:

"No, there are

NO SUNFLOWERS AND LILIES,

no flowers of any kind. I suppose you thought I could not travel without them. Well, I can. You see I did."

"You must be fatigued after your journey?" ventured the reporter, not knowing how to begin an aesthetic interview, and, therefore, dropping to every-day subjects.

"Oh no," said Wilde with a smile, in which the English accent was very noticeable. "I do not think I would have been able to endure it, however, but for one of your delightful novelists, W. D. Howells. I have read all his books since I came here, and he is a most charming writer." A pause occurred here while Oscar hunted under his yellow dog-skin gloves on the table. A little box was found, out of which a small cigarette was fished out and lit, and the aesthete was himself again.

"I was much disappointed in this way," continued he. "We in England have no idea of the distances in your country. The impression seems to be that all the large cities are located in the suburbs of New York, then come the Rocky Mountains, next the Indians, and then San Francisco and the ocean. We do not half understand that large cities like Chicago and Cincinnati are located in the heart of the country."

"How are you pleased with your visit so far?"

"Oh, your country is so large. It is a world. But it looks so barren and rugged in winter time. To one accustomed to a little place like England, which has been tilled for centuries, this change is remarkable."

"What do you think of your treatment by the newspapers?"

"I do not mind that," said Wilde, with a smile. "It does not cause me any annoyance."

"Do you read what is said about you?"

"Oh, yes, every line. When I come in at night, tired and weary, the reading of a good

VIGOROUS ATTACK ACTS LIKE A DISH OF CAVIAR.

Of course, some of it is not what I have been used to, as the English papers still have a sort of old fashioned regard for truth. They are not so much given to imagination as the journals here. Then the attacks come from such curious sources. I remember I was dressing at Washington for a dinner party, when a card was brought to me. The name was a curious one, and the card detailed for how many Western papers the owner was correspondent. I think there were eleven in all. I was slightly flurried, you may suppose. I said, 'Now, here is the man who moulds the thoughts of the West; I must be in [*sic*] my best behavior.' I requested the gentleman to come up, when in walked a boy, positively not more than 16. 'Is this your card?' I asked. 'Oh, yes,' said he. The scene was too ridiculous.

"'Have you been to school much?' I asked.

"The juvenile interviewer said he had.

"'Have you learned French?'

"No, he had not. I told him that if he wished to be a journalist he ought to study French,

GAVE HIM A BIG ORANGE AND DISMISSED HIM.

What he did with the orange afterwards I don't know, but he seemed very much pleased to get it.[1] Now I have had this experience several times. Boys have been my critics. What do I care about the expressions of a man who does not know anything in regard to my writings. It does not affect me any more than if the writer should say I had written a good sonnet or a bad sonnet. He does not know and I do not care."

"But there have been more bitter attacks?"

"Oh yes. Before I came to Baltimore, the American there published a most uncalled for attack upon me. It stated that I had accepted an invitation to attend a club reception there, and at the last moment had sent word that my terms were $500 [*sic*] for such services, that the club had very properly declined the offer, and that I would therefore not be present.[2] I had never heard of the club at that time, had never received any invitation, and the fact is that when I came to Baltimore they tendered me a reception. But the story was printed and was believed. There is no use denying such things, and I did not do so.[3] When I went to Baltimore, however, I found out the man who wrote the article and sent for him. He came. He was a young man about my own age. I simply asked him what he was paid for writing the article. He said, 'Six dollars.' 'Well,' said I,

'THE RATE FOR LYING

is not very high in America. That is all I wanted to ascertain. Good day.'"[4]

"It must have annoyed you considerably?"

"No. I mind nothing about their attacks but the effect they have on the public. I am not injured at all, but the public [?is] deceived. After all, there is so much to do [?in] life that there is not time to be troubled [?about] such matters. Our duty is to admire and worship the beautiful and the good. Everything else, including the annoyances, is mere failures, simply shadows." [*sic*]

"What are your impressions of the people as you have met them?"

"Ah, there is a wide difference between your papers and your men and women. From the latter I have always met with the kindest treatment. You have a great country, and the things that are said about me I am willing to bear. Of course the treatment is not fair. Some of our best lecturers would not come here, Ruskin, for instance, on account of the newspapers. When I declared I was com-

1. Wilde also told this story to the author of "Oscar Wilde," *The Sunday Herald* (Boston, MA), 29 Jan. 1882, 7, p. 120. See also "The Aesthete at Washington," *Springfield Daily Republican* (Springfield, MA), 30 Jan. 1882, 4–5, pp. 108–9.

2. The *Baltimore American* (20 Jan. 1882) had reported that Wilde demanded $300 (see p. 88, note 1).

3. In fact, Wilde repeatedly denied the story.

4. The reporter may also have been the author of "Local Miscellany," *Baltimore American and Commercial Advertiser* (Baltimore, MD), 26 Jan. 1882, 4 (see p. 113, note 1).

ing they all wondered. 'Why,' said Mr. Ruskin, 'everything will be said about you. They will spare nothing.' But I said I would come, and I came. The feeling there is almost fear of your papers, but I do not mind it. The ludicrous things are said in good part, and as for the rest I let it pass me by."

Mr. Wilde will remain in the city till Monday morning. Tonight he lectures at Mercantile Library Hall. Immediately after the lecture he will attend a reception, given in his honor, at the Press Club, No. 720 Chestnut street. Later in the evening he will be the guest of the Elks Social Club at the rooms of the People's Theater Building.

"Speranza's Gifted Son," *St. Louis Daily Globe-Democrat* (St. Louis, MO), 26 Feb. 1882, 3[1]

Oscar Wilde Arrives in St. Louis, Drives Around, Delivers a Lecture and Attends a Reception.

His Appearance and the Manner in Which He Talked to an Aesthetic Globe-Democrat Reporter—A Large and Fashionable Audience Bored by His Talk on Art at the Mercantile Library Hall—The Press Club Receives Him in High Style—His Autograph.

When the Ohio and Mississippi Railroad train rolled into the Union Depot three hours late yesterday morning, there alighted from the rear coach a young man conspicuously clad in a heavy fur overcoat, with a brigandish hat of mighty brim slouched over his head, but failing to conceal an open, boyish countenance and light brown locks, somewhat disheveled, which fell to his shoulders. He was closely attended by two men, who hurried him to a carriage in waiting, and the party were rapidly driven to the Southern Hotel. Were the young man a trifle taller, and his locks less tawny, he would have been mistaken for our own, America's own aesthete, Berry Mitchell, tragedian, poet and lecturer.[2] There was the same stately tread, the same disposition to press the overcoat into duty as a Roman toga, the same lofty indifference to the presence of gaping bystanders; and

1. H & S, b40. Reprinted in Mikhail, 53–7; and H & S, 78–83. Quoted in OWDA, 202–3, 204–5 (where the source is incorrectly given as the *Post-Dispatch*). Referenced in Sturgis, 231/222, 234/225, 237/227.

2. Berry Mitchell (1839–1912) was an American actor who mostly performed in the Southern states. According to "A Crushed Tragedian," *Public Ledger* (Memphis, TN), 22 May 1876, 3, Berry was left a fortune and, "[a] rather showy young man, he devoted himself to society and the stage." He was not a good actor, but drew audiences: "big houses laugh till they weep at seeing the drama butchered, poor Berry being innocently guilty of the crime." Like Wilde, he wore his hair long and was described as affecting "a Byronic air".

when he ascended the grand staircase on his way to Parlor 70, it was with the same air of Hamlet on his way to keep his appointment with the Ghost which all have observed in our Berry. This stagey individual was the apostle of aestheticism, the demi-god of the sunflower worshipers of England; the youth who walked into a Regent street restaurant, and, after gazing rapturously at a lily for a half hour, remarked, "I have dined," and departed untroubled with fears of indigestion;[1] the poet who has written a really meritorious book;[2] the author of unquestioned literary ability who, to quote a recent magazine, "has lent himself to a double scheme of advertising (both of himself and of a dramatic caricature of himself) unprecedented in the annals of either literature or the stage, and has thereby counted himself out of the company of self-respecting men of letters;"[3] the lecturer who, for $250 per night, invariably in advance, has appeared in knee-pants and velvet jacket before large audiences in the leading American cities, and talked of art and beauty. In short,

IT WAS OSCAR WILDE.

The two men with him were Mr. W. M. Traquair and J. S. Vale, manager of the mighty exhibition that the $250 young man makes of himself. Both are professional showmen, and handle Mr. Wilde as they would Tom Thumb, the tattooed man or the two-headed wonder.[4] Recognizing that curiosity to see Oscar Wilde is greater than to hear him, every precaution is taken that he is properly secluded previous to his public appearance, and no time was lost in immuring him in the sumptuous comfort of a private parlor which he only left during the day to enter a close carriage and pay a brief visit to the Crow Museum of Art.[5]

1. The reference is to the Du Maurier cartoon of Postlethwaite that appeared in *Punch* on 17 July 1880, depicting the poet seated alone at a table in a restaurant, gazing fondly at a lily. A waiter asks "Shall I bring you anything else, Sir?" Postlethwaite replies, "Thanks, no! I have all I require, and shall soon be done." The cartoon may have been inspired by Wilde's claim that he had "lived upon daffodils for a fortnight," (Sturgis, 161–2/157–8). The idea that aesthetes lived off flowers also explains why so many interviewers were keen to describe—and possibly exaggerate the size of—the more conventional meals Wilde ate in his hotel rooms.

2. *Poems* (1881).

3. The reporter quotes "On a Recent Social Phenomenon," *The Century* (New York, NY), Mar. 1882, 779–80. The article is critical of Wilde but does not mention him by name, referring to him only as "a young writer".

4. Ellmann, 177/185, states that "Traquair" was Wilde's African American valet. As the author of this article makes clear (and Mendelssohn confirms, 269), he was instead a theatrical manager. The correct spelling of his name is "Traguier".

5. Founded in 1879 as the Saint Louis School and Museum of Fine Arts (now the Saint Louis Art Museum). As the author relates later in the article, its building was erected by Wayman Crow (1808–1885), a St. Louis businessman and politician, as a monument to his son, Wayman Crow Jr., who died in 1878.

Oscar was followed to his room within a few minutes by his personal servant and two large tin-clad trunks of the Saratoga pattern.[1] The long ride of the night before, through from Cincinnati by boat and rail, had prepared the poet for something more substantial than a lily, and the aesthetic chief cook, who anticipated an order for a reed bird and the white of an egg beaten to a froth, was more than surprised when told by the "Jeems" of the languid creature that his young master would be made supremely happy by a tenderloin of beef, broiled lamb chops, stewed potatoes, three boiled eggs (not too boiled, but just boiled enough), buttered toast, a pot of strong coffee, a bottle of claret, and, "waitah, you may give me a nice, juicy onion, for Mr. Wilde is very fond of them, ye knaw." A reporter for an evening paper sent up his card while Oscar was waiting for the gastronomic poem, to the construction of which the chief cook of the hotel was giving his personal supervision, and was surprised to receive the answer brought by "Front:" "Tell the gentleman I am washing my neck, but will see him in five minutes." Mr. Wilde was accessible to the reporter only, sending a polite desire to be excused to all others, with a very few exceptions. Of the favored few was Mr. H. L. Dousman,[2] whose invitation to visit his house and inspect his art treasures was gratefully accepted, and 3 o'clock this afternoon set as the hour for the pleasure.

A GLOBE-DEMOCRAT reporter awaited an hour when the Prince of Languor had presumably suspended the delights of deglutition, and then sent up a lily-white card, decorated with the legend by which he is known to his creditors. "He will see you in ten minutes," said "Front" on his return.

Mr. Wilde evidently desired time in which to run through the

AUTHORITIES OF AESTHETICS,

in order to meet the reporter on equal terms. It must be remembered that he had entered the city at the Union Depot; had obtained a rear view of the Jail and the Four Courts, and had been whirled through the delightful boulevards known as Clark avenue and Myrtle street, and, having seen so much of the utterly utter in that brief ride, he was prepared to find in a St. Louisan a poet, and in one who assists to mold the opinions of St. Louisans he naturally anticipated a poem. When at last the reportorial aesthete entered the apartment where the lord of the lah-de-dah sat enthroned upon a sofa, over which had been carelessly thrown a dressed bearskin rug, it was to meet a boyish-faced young man, long-haired, smooth-faced, long nosed, thick lipped, uncertain-mouthed, of the general appearance of an overtasked medical student. His hair brushed back from his

1. A large travelling trunk with internal compartments and, often, a rounded top.
2. Hercules Louis Dousman II (1848–1886) was a socialite and art collector. After his mother died in 1882 he sold his art collection and invested in horse breeding.

forehead and hanging about his shoulders, gave him the romantic appearance of the tenor-lover in an opera, as he rose from the cushion on which he half reclined in an attitude that somehow suggested the backline of a ballet, for studied as it palpably was, graceful it positively was not. He extended in a very languid manner a large, soft, rather fat hand, which half closed upon the aristocratic duke of the inquisitor, then relaxed, and fell slowly to position, where it dangled at the end of an angular arm. As if exhausted by the effort, he sank back on to the sofa, and assumed another position suggestive of cramp colic. Our Berry could have done this much better. In a few moments he summoned strength enough to light a cigarette, which he puffed contentedly for a while, and seemed to await the first twitch of the reportorial rack. He said nothing, and the reporter hesitated to begin, for it is not often that a genuine worshiper of the sunflower happens along. Oscar sat, continuing to look intently at the reporter in the dim light. Oscar always affects Rembrandt shadows; he looks better in the dark, perhaps. The reporter, feeling that he was the object of the poet's attention and evidently filled his thoughts, at length ventured:

"Talking about the beautiful, what do you think of St. Louis?"

"I have seen so little of your city, of which I have heard so much. Tell me, have you

OLD FAMILIES

here? Old French families, that speak the delightful tongue, as handed down to them from generation to generation? I have heard that your city is so blessed. Am I wrong?"[1]

"Not exactly. There are some old families here. Came here many years ago. Set up as cobblers, tailors, etc., and took land in payment for their work. Couldn't sell the land; left it to their children. The "boom" set in, prices went up, they held on to their property, and left it to their children. Prices still booming, they in turn left it to their children. Prices are still booming, and the children have still got the property. Some of them talk French a little. Most of them talk German. It is very useful in trade."

"But your city has schools of design and art academies?"

"That is where you are wrong. There are no schools of design or art academies."

"Have you no art, then?"

1. *Personal Impressions of America*: "There were remains [in New Orleans] of the old monarchical grandeur, and French was spoken not as it is now in Paris but as at the time of Rabelais." (Dibb, 243.) François Rabelais (c. 1494–1553) was a French physician and writer.

"Yes, some. Mr. Dousman, a rich man, buys a great many pictures; and then there is the Sketch Club, and every year we have a picture show in connection with the Cattle Fair, and there is the *Hornet*, an illustrated paper."[1]

"The Sketch Club; that must be artistic."

"It is; it is aesthetic."

"Pray tell me all about it."

"The Sketch Club is an organization of all our leading artists."

"Good."

"And once a month they meet and each artist brings a sketch, illustrating some subject selected at the previous meeting by one of their number."

"How truly Bohemian!"

"Yes, the man who picks out the subject sets up a lunch of beer and sandwiches, and things like that, and he gets all the pictures to keep for his own."

Oscar looked disappointed and braced up on another cigarette. Then he said, "But you have certainly some art institutions?"

"Yes, there is one art institution. It is called the Crow Art Museum, and was built by a very wealthy gentleman who had a son who longed to be an artist. The father disapproved of the son's ambition, and discouraged it. The son died, they say partially of grief because he could not become a great artist, and the repentant father, recognizing the error of his judgment when too late, built this beautiful museum as a monument to his memory."

"How utterly pathetic, poor boy. I must visit that place this afternoon. St. Louis cannot be utterly without a love for the beautiful?"

"It is not, for you will find in St. Louis more beautiful homes than in any other large city. The artistic taste crops out also in the architecture of

PUBLIC BUILDINGS,

The City Hall, the Grand Tower block, at Fourth and Market, the Lucas Market buildings, and the church at the corner of Eighth and Washington avenue, are specimens that you should view before you leave the city."

"I shall endeavor to do so; but I have so many engagements. I shall at least view the church you speak of."

"Do; and you will never forget it. You have not seen our streets at their best."

"There are no avenues like the boulevards of Paris."

"You will certainly agree with most travelers that there are no such streets as our own in the known world. If fortunately it should rain tonight, you will see them as we know them best tomorrow."

1. The Sketch Club was founded in 1877 by male art students of the Washington University School of Art. It was dissolved and replaced by the St. Louis Artists' Guild in 1886. The *Hornet* was published between 1880 and 1882.

"I shall await the morrow with supreme interest."

"I had forgotten to ask you—how do you like our country?"

"I am lost in wonder and amazement. It is not a country, but a world. Englishmen know little of its extent, and but half believe when told of the existence of such cities as St. Louis, Chicago and Cincinnati thousands of miles from the seaboard. I confess that I myself was greatly deceived in your magnificent distances. Looking at a map while at home, I planned for myself a trip through Colorado, California, Mexico, the Southern States, and Canada. I now realize how foolish were such dreams. I shall barely have time to fulfil my engagements and return to Paris, where I expect to be by May 1. The West I like best. The people are stronger, fresher, saner than the rest. They are ready to be taught. The surroundings of nature have instilled in them a love of the beautiful, which but needs development and direction. The East I found a feeble reflex of Europe; in fact, I may say that I was in America for a month before I saw an American. My audiences in New York and Boston were cold, critical; in Chicago and Cincinnati they were so warm, cheerful and enthusiastic. I shall return to both of those cities, and lecture, before I go East. On Monday I go to Springfield.[1] Is that near the center of the State?"

"Yes, most of our capital cities are. The hardy pioneers located them in the days when the members of the Legislature traveled by horseback and canoe, and the geographical center was chosen instead of

THE CENTER OF WEALTH,

population or art. You would find a visit to the capital of this State of interest. It is most picturesquely located on bluffs, and would be considered a poem were it not for the boarding houses and the Penitentiary."

"Penitentiaries are not artistic."

"How do you stand travel by rail?"

"The long trips are more than wearisome, and I hardly think that I would be able to survive them were it not for the charming companionship of Howells' novels. He is America's greatest author."

"You have visited Mr. Tennyson?"[2]

1. Wilde lectured once more in Chicago, debuting his lecture on *The House Beautiful* at the Central Music Hall on 11 March. He returned to Cincinnati later than he anticipated, delivering *The House Beautiful* at the Grand Opera House on 11 June. He lectured on *The Decorative Arts* at the Springfield, IL, Opera House on 27 February.

2. The typesetter presumably misread the reporter's notes. The reporter must have asked about Longfellow rather than the Poet Laureate of the United Kingdom. Wilde had visited Longfellow on 30 January and afterwards often described him as a poem.

"Grand old man. I spent a delightful afternoon with him. He is not only a poet, but a poem. And there is your Walt Whitman, dear old fellow, a poet that indeed writes poetry. America, match him if you can."

"Have you found time to read the newspapers?"

"I read all that is written about me."

"Do you like it all?"

"I expected ill-treatment at the hands of the American press. I was warned of it by my friends before I left for America. It is the certainty of this unfair treatment that keeps our great men at home."

"Dickens, Hughes, Forbes and others were received with open arms, and treated with distinguished consideration on the occasion of their visit here, and lectured to large and delighted audiences until the press everywhere gave vent to nothing but encomiums."[1]

Without noticing the interruption, Oscar continued: "At first I was greatly annoyed, and with difficulty restrained my feelings, but latterly I have schooled myself not to notice them. When made the object of absolute falsehood, as in the case of the Baltimore paper, which stated that I had refused to attend the reception of a social club in that city unless I was paid $300, I endeavor to set myself right as I did in that instance. My critics have for the most part been mere boys, who knew nothing of the subjects of which I treat, and why should I annoy myself by paying attention to their utterances? I must say that my

EXPERIENCES WITH THE PRESS

in the West have been very pleasant, and I have met gentlemen whose intelligent conversation I have enjoyed. They have talked with me of art and literature, and understood the subjects. Such persons I like to meet."

Returning thanks upon behalf of the Western press, the GLOBE-DEMOCRAT reporter ventured a little way into the field of literature. Mr. Wilde is under the impression that England has no great story-writer today. B. L. Farjeon may be looked down upon as the successor of Dickens in the field of Christmas Stories. William Black is a delightful novelist. He deals with the beauties of nature and is a true poet. Walter Besant and James Rice he considers great writers. The purely English performance of writing a novel to accomplish a reform while ably carried out by Charles Reade and Wilkie Collins, savors of the mechanical and is perforce not beautiful. Justin McCarthy is a writer of brilliancy, and in the History of Our Times has given a most enchanting resume of the dry and repellent mass of in-

1. Thomas Hughes (1822–1896) was a social reformer, children's author, and Liberal politician. He wrote *Tom Brown's Schooldays* (1857) and was a Member of Parliament between 1865 and 1874. In 1870 he lectured across North America on British attitudes to, and activities undertaken during, the American Civil War.

formation found in the files of the London *Times*, and McCarthy has a son of great promise who may excel his father in brilliancy."[1]

"What has he done?" asked the reporter.

"He has written a volume of poems and several very clever sketches," replied Oscar, with a smile. He resumed his essay on literature, and had just remarked that the greatest writer since Shakespeare was Balzac, when a card was brought in. Oscar twirled the pasteboard in his fingers for a minute, arose and held out his hand for a farewell shake, remarking, "Another gentleman desires to see me now," and the GLOBE-DEMOCRAT reporter left, as another newspaper reporter entered the room to subject the by-this-time justly languid aesthete to what an Arkansas aesthete would call "a course of sprouts."[2] Oscar wore a look of calm resignation when last seen.

✂ *A report of Wilde's lecture in St. Louis, his attendance at a reception at the rooms of the Press Club,[3] and a description of his signature on the register at the Southern Hotel.*

1. This paragraph ends with quotation marks, indicating that part of it directly quotes Wilde, but there is no sign to indicate where the quotation begins. Benjamin Leopold Farjeon (1838–1903) was an English novelist, playwright, and journalist. A self-confessed disciple of Dickens, his first book was *Shadows on the Snow: A Christmas Story* (1865). William Black (1841–1898) was a Scottish novelist who was hugely popular during his lifetime. Walter Besant (1836–1901) was an English novelist and historian. He wrote a number of novels in collaboration with James Rice (1843–1882). Charles Reade (1814–1884), an English dramatist and novelist, wrote works that dealt with political topics, such as trade unions, women doctors, and abuses in private lunatic asylums. Wilkie Collins (1824–1889) was an English novelist and playwright, best known for *The Woman in White* (1859) and *The Moonstone* (1868). Wilde alludes to his more didactic novels, such as *Man and Wife* (1870), in which Collins attacked marriage laws and what he saw as the public's obsession with athleticism, and *The New Magdalen* (1873), in which a "fallen woman" puts her past behind her and marries a clergyman. Justin McCarthy (1830–1912) was an Irish Nationalist and novelist. *History of Our Own Times* (vols. 1–4, 1879–1880; vol. 5, 1897) begins with the accession of Queen Victoria. McCarthy's son, Justin Huntly McCarthy (1859–1936) was, like his father, a Member of Parliament and author. By 1882 he had written comparatively little, but he went on to pen many novels, plays, and histories.

2. Presumably the author of "Oscar Wilde," *The Republican* (St. Louis, MO), 26 Feb. 1882, 13 pp. 215–22.

3. Wilde is quoted in the report of the Press Club reception, but it does not seem that he spoke with the reporter. He described the American writer and orator Robert "Bob" Ingersoll (1833–1899) as "the most intelligent man of this century", and Henry Du Pré Labouchère (1831–1912), the English politician and journalist, as "the best writer in Europe, [...] indeed a most remarkable gentleman." (Labouchère would later draft the Labouchère Amendment, which made "gross indecency" a crime in the United Kingdom. It was the law under which Wilde was convicted in 1895.) Wilde told the President of the Merchants' Exchange: "You are ruining our English farmers and making them work for a protection policy against American produce. There is a universal demand in England for protection against your grain." Commenting on a disturbance during his lecture in St. Louis, he said: "I had a very delightful class of people who was of superior culture. I could converse with them as they were charming, but the noise and stamping of feet I always find in large cities, where the people are of such a mixed class."

His Wanderings.

Oscar kept himself to his room all day yesterday, except for a short time in the afternoon, when he was driven to the Crow Art Museum. This he pronounced the finest museum of its kind in the world. The Southern Hotel parlors were thronged all day by ladies, who hoped to gain a glimpse of the apostle of the lily, only to be disappointed. It was given out that he would visit the jewelry store of Mermod, Jaccard & Co., to view the artistic decorations of the window. Fully 200 ladies assembled and patiently awaited his coming, but in vain, although he had in the early part of the day accepted the invitation. He partook of a substantial dinner at 6 o'clock in his own room. He was not in a good humor, and spoke bitterly of the portraits of himself published in the evening papers. When at 8 o'clock he left his room, and promenaded the length of the parlor hall in the glory of his black stockings and smalls, fully a hundred guests of the house were treated to a free exhibition of his superlative and consummate presence.

Today at the Southern the dinner menu will be ornamented with a miniature sunflower, and Oscar is expected to do the dinner act in public. At 3 o'clock he will be driven to the residence of Hercules L. Dousman, where he will inspect that gentleman's art treasures. Monday morning he leaves for Springfield. One of the results of his visit will be the bankruptcy of numerous small-boy peddlers observed upon the streets last evening with unsold and unsalable stocks of yellow and black paper sunflowers, thrown upon the market by some enterprising dealer.

"Oscar Wilde," *The Republican* (St. Louis, MO), 26 Feb. 1882, 13[1]

He Arrives, Is Interviewed and Lectures.

Not So "Greenery Yallery" As He Is Painted.[2]

He Talks on Swinburne, Joaquin Miller and Walt Whitman.

His Impressions of America and Americans.

His Views of Journalism and Journalists.

1. H & S, b41. Reprinted in H & S, 83–8. Quoted in OWDA, 205, 209; and Sturgis, 246/236. Referenced in Sturgis, 224/215.

2. In *Patience* Bunthorne aims to be "A greenery-yallery, Grosvenor Gallery | Foot-in-the-grave young man!" Aesthetic painters, who exhibited in London's Grosvenor Gallery, were thought to be fond of subdued tints and secondary colours. Many interviewers in 1882 noticed Wilde's silk throw of old gold (i.e. greenish yellow).

His Lecture at Mercantile Library Hall on Decorative Art,

Before an Audience which He Did Not Understand and which Did Not Understand Him.

Oscar Wilde came yesterday, and this morning St. Louis has seen him, heard him, weighed him in the balance and found him wanting—in what was expected of him. Between him and his audience there is a mutual disgust. Yet no one who has seen him and conversed with him off the stage, taking him altogether aside from what he has said or written, but is forced to recognize that he has genius which seems to be of the abiding type. Few who heard his lecture will dissent from the opinion that his lecturing at all is a great mistake. The imagery which appears beautiful when condensed into poetry, in a prose lecture goes to seed and becomes absurd. Off the stage and off his guard he shows for what he is—a young man of no small talent, natural and acquired, but a talent which is yet to be matured by experience. On the stage, appearing before an audience which has paid two dollars a seat to see him dressed in knee breeches, he must not think it hard if forgetting the man of genius they remember only the

MALE PANTALOON

And laugh at him accordingly. It is their right and they have paid for it. But off the stage and away from constraint, he is a thorough gentleman, and not the "greenery yallery Grosvenor gallery" young man that he has been painted. The air of the college still clings to him; and there never was a better-natured, better-mannered collegian came out of Oxford. He is what he calls Joaquin Miller—"a splendid fellow." He arrived from Cincinnati yesterday morning with his manager, D'Oyly Carte,[1] and his valet, registering at the Southern, where he remained until afternoon, when he visited the Wayman Crow museum. How good natured he is, is shown by his ready compliance with the request of the Southern hotel bellboy whose asked him for his autograph. He wrote the following lines, which the bell-boy showed with infinite pride:

"The sea is flecked with bars of gold;
The dull dead wind is out of tune,
And like a withered leaf, the moon
Is blown across the stormy sea;
And overhead the curlews cry,
Where through the dusky upland grass
The young brown-throated reapers pass,

1. The reporter mistakes Vale, Wilde's travelling manager, for D'Oyly Carte.

Like silhouettes against the sky."[1]

Oscar As He Is.

The pen pictures which have been drawn of Oscar Wilde universally by American newspapers are like the reflections of the convex mirror, faithful and yet distorted. No one seeing the true Oscar Wilde could fail to recognize just as clearly that the man is not what has been described. The pictures have at once been true and untrue, with the untruth predominating. A REPUBLICAN reporter who called on him at the Southern yesterday afternoon and was shown up to his room was forcibly impressed with this.

Mr. Wilde met him at the door with a pleasant "good afternoon" and an invitation to be seated, speaking with the broad English accent which still obtains in portions of America, especially in Virginia, an accent which is rhythmic always, and which appeared to be perfectly natural with him. His appearance was much as it has been described so repeatedly in the different newspapers of the country, barring the exaggerations. His dress, which would have seemed *outré* enough on the street, did not seem out of place as a chamber *negligee*. He wore a short drab jacket, hanging open and showing a waistcoat of the same material, loose pantaloons, and a collar turned negligently over a neckcloth tied in

THE LOOSE SAILOR FASHION,

And there was something suggestive of the sea in his whole "make-up." The writer, who went altogether undecided as to the light in which the apostle was to be considered, found, after only a few words had been spoken, that there was a serious side to him which was altogether undeveloped for newspaper purposes, and which could be utilized to advantage. Perhaps no one has seen him who has not been disappointed in some way. The disappointment here was that he was not the grotesque being that has been described, but a thoroughly well bred and well educated young gentleman, with a large share of good humor; disposed apparently to carry out the maxim from his own beloved Greek of "especially thinking well of himself above all things;" apparently too with much theoretical and little practical knowledge of men. This was the impression, but in his conversa-

1. *Impressions I. Les Silhouettes* was first published in *Pan* (23 Apr. 1881; CW i, No. 87). The versions in *Pan* and *Poems* have four further lines, which come after the fourth line as given here. Three manuscripts of the poem are known to survive. The manuscript in the Bibliotheca Bodmeriana, Geneva, contains a draft titled *Impression du Soir* in which lines 5–8 of the *Pan/Poems* versions are omitted. Evidently Wilde recalled the Bodmeriana version when inscribing the poem for the bell-boy. All authoritative textual witnesses have "grey" for "gold" and "bay" for "sea". Wilde's use of "bars of gold" in *Panthea* (CW i, No. 62, line 106), argues for the authenticity of the first variant given here, as opposed to its being a typo attributable to the reporter or typesetter.

tion there were keen flashes of wit which made it doubtful after all if he were not more the man of the world than he seemed.

Taking a seat and motioning the reporter to another, he lighted a cigarette and waited to be questioned, while his servant, who evidently from frequent experience knew that his master required something to sustain him through the ordeal, placed a small glass of what appeared to be

SHERRY PUNCH, VERY WEAK,

On the table before him. Leaning his head against the easy chair, with his long hair flowing over his shoulders, Oscar waited with an air which was at once resigned and quizzical, not without a suspicion of embarrassment.

"Shall I put the question which was put to your countryman, Mr. Chuzzlewit, and ask you 'What do you think of our kentry, sir?'" asked the reporter.[1]

"You may if you like," was the reply, "though I might find some difficulty in answering it. It has changed greatly since Dickens' day, no doubt.[2] Every city in America is different from every other city—quite different. The West interests me more than the East, because the people of the West have created a civilization by themselves and for themselves. The East is a reflex of Europe, and therefore Chicago was more interesting to me than Boston, even though there I met Oliver Wendell Holmes, with whom I dined, and Longfellow, with whom I spent the afternoon. Eastern cities are imitations; Chicago is entirely American."

"I have read an account of your meeting with Joaquin Miller," said the reporter.

"That was true—one of the few true things that have been written about me. Yes, Joaquin is a very fine fellow, full of color; one of the first American poets, who is really from and of the New World. There is in his writings a resonance and an odor of not seen flowers; a breath of the sea; he is quite

SWIFT AND STRONG

As the sea, full of new imagery."

"And Whitman?"

"By the way, what do you think of Whitman, yourself?" was the parry which met the thrust.

1. *Martin Chuzzlewit* (1842–1844) is a novel by Dickens that was originally serialised. When the instalments were not as popular with the public as anticipated, Dickens contrived to send the eponymous character to America. He could thereby introduce into the story some of his own impressions of that country. Chuzzlewit is asked by Mrs Hominy, an American: "And how do you like our country, sir?"

2. Dickens toured America in 1842 and 1867–1868.

"There are lines in his 'Blades of Grass' [*sic*];[1] which, insane as he is generally counted, remind me of Homer. But my opinion is valueless, and my question unanswered."

He smiled as he took a fresh cigarette from a little box on the table and lighted it with air of one who was weighing his words before answering. When he did answer he said:

"Whitman is a great writer. You are right, as it seems to me. There is more of the Greek feeling in him than in any modern poet. His poetry is Homeric in its large pure delight in men and women, and in the joy the writer feels and shows through it all in the sunshine and breeze of outdoor life."

"And since we speak of living poets, what of your own Swinburne?"

"We look on Swinburne as one of the great poets of the day in England. In America, you seem to judge him entirely by his first volume, his *'Laus Veneris,'* which has in it many of the extravagances natural and proper enough, too, in the first attempt of genius. You judge him solely by this and not by his later writings, such as the 'Songs of Democracy' and 'The Songs before Sunrise.'[2] Swinburne, Shelley and Milton are the three great poets of liberty in England,[3] and Swinburne is the greatest master of the English language living,

WONDERFUL IN HIS POWER

Of expression and his control of words. Language to him is what the beautiful musical instrument is to the musician—the violin from which he draws what tunes he wishes. No one of our times has written poems more full of the fervor for liberty and the strength of democracy, and no one singer has sung such delicate and dainty little songs. Where else can you find the refinement of feeling that there is in his poem:

> "'If you were what the rose is
> And I were like the leaf?'[4]

Where such poems as his 'Garden of Proserpine' and his 'Hymn to Proserpine?'"

"You have been accused of imitating him,"[5] suggested the reporter. "Do you think it is worth your while to make a defence?"

1. *Leaves of Grass.*

2. *Laus Veneris* and the other Swinburne poems quoted or mentioned in this interview appeared in *Poems and Ballads* (1866). *Songs before Sunrise* was published in 1871 and is a collection of poems relating to Italy, and particularly its unification.

3. John Milton (1608–1674) was an English poet, best known for his epic, *Paradise Lost* (1667).

4. The opening line of Swinburne's *A Match* is: "If love were what the rose is".

5. *Punch* published a negative review of Wilde's *Poems*: "This is a volume of echoes—it is SWINBURNE and water [...] The Swinburnian jargon appears on nearly every page" ("Swinburne and Water," *Punch* (London, UK), 23 July 1881, 26).

"That accusation of imitating someone has been brought against every English poet, and besides, people forget that the first thing a young artist in painting or poetry should do is to study the great masters. The only way to do really original work is to acquire a knowledge of the style of all great teachers and to use that knowledge to produce

AN ENTIRELY NEW EFFECT.

No man in our age has studied Milton and Shakespeare so deeply as Swinburne, and yet from that study of Shakespeare and Milton he has produced a work entirely different from theirs. Take for instance the poems which appear in the periodicals through the country. Many of them show that the writers possessed feelings which, for lack of this study, they could not express. Hence their poetry is bad, although the idea is back of it. We of the younger school in England love Swinburne better than we love Tennyson, and consider him a much greater master. There is a breadth, a depth to him which there never was to Tennyson."

"You have been questioned so much concerning your school that I had not intended referring to it, but since you yourself have spoken of it, tell me if you think that your designs are practicable?"

"Do you think that we, the young men of England, would give our youth, our energy and whatever of intellect we may possess to their fulfilment if we had the remotest intention of failing. If it were an experiment we should achieve success, but with us it is a matter of actual accomplishment. We have already changed the whole condition of

ENGLISH DECORATIVE ART.

Every handicraftsman in England is now working with the noblest designs and models before him, and as for the opposition that people sometimes make, particularly in America, you must remember that only one thing is opposed to beauty, and that is ugliness. Everything is always beautiful or ugly, and utility always goes with the beautiful—never with the ugly. Anything that is ugly is merely what a bad workman makes. The only way to get good work then in any trade is by means of good designs. If you have bad designs no good workman will work for you."

"Did you meet Emerson while in the East?"

"I did not have the opportunity to call on him, I am sorry to say, and I understand that he confines himself closely at home. It would give me much pleasure to meet him on my return. He is one of the most brilliant men of the nineteenth century—the only man of letters in America who has influenced the course of English thought."

"The American press has not given you fair treatment, Mr. Wilde," said the reporter, changing the subject suddenly.

"I think," he replied, "that the ordinary critic belongs to the criminal classes, and that in many cases the newspapers of America would employ people to write on art whom in England we would not consider qualified to report any

CASE OF PETIT LARCENY

Above the value of five shillings. I think that if American journalism continues to supply nothing to the public but slander that is shameful and jokes that are bad, they will cease to have the slightest influence and will merely increase the already too large number of comic papers which are not amusing.

"In New York," he continued, in answer to another question, "they wrote entirely fictitious interviews with me after having called on me. I think that they might at least have spared me the trouble of talking to them. In Chicago they put down what I said more exactly. We have no interviewing in England, but it is not so objectionable after all if it is genuine."

"Does it not then strike you as objectionable that the details of a man's private life should be dragged before the public even in such small matters as his eating onions for breakfast?"

"The best answer that I can give to that question is perhaps the one I gave to a reporter in Washington who called on me and asked me to give him some of the details of my private life. I told him that I wished I had one."[1]

The conversation ended here, being interrupted by the entrance of his manager. Mr. Wilde stated before the reporter took his leave that he would lecture in Springfield Monday, and that he expected to be in Paris in May. It will doubtless be observed that in the interview, which is as near verbatim as it is possible for an interview to be given, the use of "aesthetic" terms which characterized the first part of it gradually disappeared as the speaker grew earnest, as when referring to Swinburne. The writer was forcibly impressed with it, and when he did leave the room he left it with a feeling that there was something under the sunflower and lily strangely akin to that practical system of metaphysics so unaesthetically styled "horse sense." And perhaps the young gentleman with the Sapphic speech and the mane of Absalom will not be so much ashamed of it when he has grown older and abandoned the lecture platform.[2]

1. This exchange does not appear in any of Wilde's known interviews, in Washington or elsewhere. *Personal Impressions of America*: "I was asked by an interviewer at Chicago for some details of my private life, but I told him I had not got one – it was stopped at the Customs House in New York." (Dibb, 246.) Wilde made the same claim in a later interview: "A Chat With Oscar," *The Times* (Philadelphia, PA), 2 Sep. 1882, 5, p. 458.

2. Sappho (c. 630 – c. 570 BCE) was a Greek poet from the island of Lesbos. Absalom is a Biblical character, identified in 2 Samuel 14:25 as the most handsome man in Israel. He was especially proud of his long hair, which led to his downfall when it was caught in a tree during a battle.

✂ *A report of Wilde's lecture in St. Louis.*

His lecture was somewhat abbreviated by the noise made by the handful of young roughs in the rear. He said that he had never met such treatment in any American city. "It was villainous, and so were the pictures and the articles published in the *Post-Dispatch,* whose representative he had treated with the courtesy due from one gentleman to another."[1]

"A Home Ruler," *St. Louis Daily Globe-Democrat* (St. Louis, MO), 27 Feb. 1882, 6[2]

Oscar Wilde Has Some Well-Settled Opinions on the Irish Question.

He Believes the Government Should Purchase the Land and Sell it to the Peasantry.

"What are your feelings with regard to the Land League?" queried a GLOBE-DEMOCRAT reporter of Oscar Wilde last evening.

The "aesthete" was sipping a glass of Appolinaris and smoking a cigarette. He promptly replied:

"As regards the general principle, that the only basis of legislation should be the general welfare of the people—and that is the only test by which the right of any citizen to hold property or possess any privileges should be tested—I am entirely at one with the position held by the Land League," replied Mr. Wilde. He continued: "The land of Ireland, like the land of England, is perfectly unfairly divided, and the peasantry of Ireland have never had the proper conditions necessary for any real civilization at all. They have lived in the most impoverished way, in a certain state of life in which the only opening for any improvement was for them to leave their own country."

"In this connection," interrupted the reporter, "I will ask you, do you believe in the wholesale emigration of the Irish from their native land?"

1. A cartoon, titled *The Darwinian Theory Illustrated*, comparing Wilde to an "aesthetic monkey", first appeared in *The Washington Post* (22 Jan. 1882, 4), and was reprinted in the *St. Louis Post-Dispatch* (25 Feb. 1882, 1). The accompanying editorial was not flattering: Oscar Wilde's "ancestry goes directly back to the melancholy monkey and any one who will carefully examine the two pictures will see the family likeness between the founder of the race and its nineteenth century representative." See also "Oscar Wilde," *The Dubuque Herald* (Dubuque, IA), 3 Mar. 1882, 4, p. 244; and "Gotham Gossip," *The Tribune* (Minneapolis, MN), 5 Mar. 1882, 1, p. 768.

2. H & S, b42. Reprinted in "Oscar Wilde," *The Chicago Daily Tribune* (Chicago, IL), 2 Mar. 1882, 5; and "Oscar Wilde on the Irish Question," *The Pilot* (Boston, MA), 11 Mar. 1882, 2. Quoted in Sturgis, 239–40/230.

Figure 7. A cartoon printed on the front page of the St. Louis Post-Dispatch, *25 Feb. 1882. It had first appeared in the* Washington Post *on 22 January with different text (see OWDA, 101). Wilde thought the cartoon and the negative articles that accompanied it were "villainous".*

The question was scarcely asked when Mr. Wilde replied, "I shall always hope that there shall be some people left in Ireland." After thinking a while he said: "With regard to emigration from Ireland, it has a great deal of influence in one way—in the way of reaction from America, not merely in people returning from America, a people bringing with them money to an impoverished country, but in a reaction of American thought on Irish politics. This modern public spirit with Irish politics is an entirely new departure in the history of Ireland. It is due entirely to the reflex influence of American thought."

The aesthete here lit a cigarette, and continued:

"With regard to the land bill, the mistake which I think the English Government are making is in thinking that they can permanently benefit one class in a community by permanently impoverishing the other. Up to this the gentry of Ireland have been rich and the peasant poor. They have merely transferred the burden from the peasant to the educated classes. They have not really alleviated the poverty of Ireland. They have merely removed its position and in one single act of legislation have swept away a great deal of the best civilization in Ireland. What I should wish to see would be the Government purchasing the land of Ireland from the landlords at a fair rate, giving them compensation as they gave the members of the Irish Church, and distributing that land amongst the people, issuing State bonds on which the people would pay an interest. This was the method adopted in Prussia, and it has there been in the highest degree beneficial."

"What do you think of the 'no-rent manifesto?'" asked the reporter.

"It is the one foolish thing that the Land League have done," replied Mr. Wilde.

"Why so?"

"Because," replied he, "it strikes at the root of all civilization, of all fair dealing and of all common sense."

The "no-rent manifesto" having been explained to Mr. Wilde, the latter replied:

"You must remember that a manifesto of that kind, besides the mere words of it, there is always a latent spirit in it which is always understood to mean more than it expresses. In Ireland it was understood to be absolutely 'No rent,' which, however, I have no doubt that the most thoughtful amongst the Land League would not approve of."

"You know Parnell, Sullivan, McCarthy and other members of the Land League?"[1]

1. Charles Stewart Parnell (1846–1891) was elected president of the Land League upon its formation in 1879, and became leader of the Irish Parliamentary Party in May 1882. For his connections with Wilde, see McCormack, W. J. (1998). Wilde and Parnell. In J. McCormack (ed.), *Wilde the Irishman*. Yale University Press. 95–102. "Sullivan" may be Timothy Daniel Sullivan

"I do," he replied.

"Do you think that they would advocate anything unreasonable or nonsensical?"

"It is no compliment to generalize about a man," answered Mr. Wilde. "With regard to any agitation of this kind it is entirely a question of result. The means of every revolution are justified only by one thing—by the success of that revolution. A compulsory sale and a fair compensation clause seems to me to be the remedy for the present evil system of land tenure in Ireland.

"It is easy," he added, "for one to point out in revolutions great excesses, even great crimes. No measure probably in the world ever produced so much immediate suffering and immediate crime as the French revolution, and no measure was ever productive of such permanent good afterward. It is very easy to object to the means of a revolution, to lay one's finger on certain excesses; the only way to judge of an agitation is by the success. In a political party it is not a question of whether they were wise or fair; the only way we can tell whether they are wise is by their success."

"Their measures are unwise if they do not succeed?"

"Certainly. Politics is a practical science. An unsuccessful revolution is merely treason; a successful one is a great era in the history of a country."

"Are you in favour of the total separation of Ireland from the United Kingdom?"

"There is another folly," replied Mr. Wilde. "It is only a question of whether a country is able to assert its independence. At present, I think it would be unwise in Ireland to claim total separation, because I do not think she would be able to preserve it, and to attempt anything that one cannot do is the only crime in politics. The first step to do should be a local Parliament, which I sincerely hope they will get, and it is an issue which my father was one of the first men in Ireland to advocate."

"Then," said the reporter, as he took his leave, "I may put you down as a Home Ruler?"

"You may," he emphatically replied.[1]

(1827–1914), or his brother, Alexander Martin Sullivan (1829–1884), both of whom were affiliated with the Land League. "McCarthy" is Justin McCarthy.

1. The grandson of the painter Ford Madox Brown (1821–1893) would remember Wilde sitting before the fireplace talking quietly with his grandfather "about public matters: Home Rule for Ireland and the like." (Mikhail, 364.) The British poet Theodore Wratislaw (1871–1933) once "made some slighting remark [to Wilde] about Home Rule. [....] 'Ah!' said he. 'My own idea is that Ireland should rule England.'" (Wratislaw, T. (1979). *Oscar Wilde: A Memoir.* Eighteen Nineties Society. 13.) In 1887 Wilde was elected to the Eighty Club, whose members were sympathetic to Home Rule, and, although he rarely engaged directly with Irish politics in his journalism, he made no secret of his opinions (CW vi, xxvii; Sturgis, 358–9/334–5 [Sturgis's discussion of this subject is more extensive in the British edition]).

"Oscar Wilde," *Chicago Evening Journal* (Chicago, IL), 28 Feb. 1882, 1[1]

Return of the "Apostle" to Chicago—A Chat with Him Concerning America, Journalism and Personal Matters—How a Baltimorean Lie Has Followed the Esthete.

Oscar Wilde arrived in the city this morning, and took up his quarters, as before, at the Pacific Hotel. He was visited, in the course of the forenoon, by a representative of THE JOURNAL, with whom he entered into a friendly chat concerning his personal impressions of America and Americans. He had just come from St. Louis, and had lectured in Cincinnati, and now he was booked for eleven consecutive nights in some of the smaller towns in the Northwest. His visit to the United States, he said, would terminate in April, and he proposed to spend the Summer, where he generally does, in Paris.[2]

Being asked the customary leading question,

HOW HE LIKED AMERICA,

Mr. Wilde said the country looked more dark and barren than he had anticipated. That, however, was to be expected, since he had come here in the gloomiest season of the year, and, in one sense, he felt he had missed much in not having seen the land in her Summer glory. He was not particularly interested in any of the Eastern cities, nor in Eastern men and women. He found there merely a reflex of European modes of thought and manners. But in the West, and right here in Chicago, he had found a distinctive type of American character, or at any rate what promised to develop into such, and therefore he had been more interested in the West than at any point in his sojourn.

The conversation drifted into the subject of

JOURNALISM.

Mr. Wilde said that to him there was something almost tragic about it. Never, he said, in the history of civilization, did literature have the advantage of such an audience. "Imagine," said he, "such a soul as Jean Jacques Rousseau having an audience of millions every day listening to him.[3] Now here, a boy of 16, just entering what may be a grand career, finds easily an opportunity to speak his thought [*sic*] in the presence of multitudes. It is a rare opportunity for an am-

1. H & S, b43.

2. Wilde did not generally spend the summer in Paris. His first extended stay was in the spring of 1883. However, he had holidayed there with his mother and brother in the summer of 1874, and also appears to have visited in 1867 (see p. 290, note 2).

3. Jean-Jacques Rousseau (1712–1778) was a Genevan philosopher. He is best known for his works *Discourse on Inequality* (1755) and *The Social Contract* (1762).

bitious soul. But somehow they seem to have no ambition, and they drift away into the current of humorous drivel."

"But," it was suggested, "the American newspaper covers in some ways a new field, and has acquired another kind of an audience. The audience that would listen to the philosophy of Voltaire or Rousseau is probably as limited as ever.[1] Journalism gives many things besides the results of science; it furnishes gossip, news."

"American journalism does not seem to me," said Mr. Wilde, "to have a deep influence on public sentiment. Everything that is written seems to be accepted as a joke. It would be all well enough for the America that Charles Dickens saw, but it does seem to me unworthy of great cosmopolitan America. The journalism of Paris is the concentration of the intellect of the city. It is a power, and has overturned dynasties."

The visitor happened to mention, in this connection, a ridiculous story to the effect that he (Wilde) had been in the habit of

LEVYING CONTRIBUTIONS

on the homes of persons where he had been invited. Such a bit of gossip had even found private circulation in Chicago.

Mr. Wilde said that was one of the most unaccountable things he had met in his tour. A story to that effect had been published in the Baltimore *American*, in an article of the dull stamp that seemed to have the aspect of being true. It had followed him from one city to another, and while he paid no attention to the comic squibs that were showered upon him here and there, he had been obliged to nail this copper shilling to the counter.

"I found," said he, "the young man who actually invented the lie, and asked him to come and see me. He was quite a young man. I said I should not care to express my opinion of his performance, but he must know himself he was a liar. I only wanted to know how much he received for writing the article, and he told me he got $6. I only wished to ascertain just what the tariff that an American newspaper was willing to pay for a lie."

Some reference was made to

PROFESSOR SWING'S CAUSTIC CRITICISM

of the esthete, which Mr. Wilde said he had not read. On its being stated to him in substance, the young poet said he imagined his critic asked too much of him. A man must work in any department of labor or art within certain limitations. At

1. François-Marie Arouet (1694–1778), better known by his pseudonym, Voltaire, was a French writer of the Enlightenment. In a list of books not to read at all, Wilde included "all Voltaire's plays, without any exception" (CL, 276).

Figure 8. Reverend David Swing, the Chicago preacher who condemned Wilde in the press. Wilde retaliated by inviting interviewers to his hotel room and telling them that: "There is nothing more depressing than to be attacked by a fool, as one cannot answer and does not fight with the same weapons."

the same time he contested the charge that his theories had no reference to moral esthetics.[1]

The visitor, seeing that Mr. Wilde was exceedingly busy with his correspondence, here took leave of him, impressed with the idea that he had met a very courteous, urbane, intelligent, and well-bred gentleman.

"Oscar Back Again," *The Daily Inter Ocean* (Chicago, IL), 1 Mar. 1882, 8[2]

Mr. Wilde Returns to Chicago to Lecture and to Be Interviewed.

Favorable Impressions on Art Prospects in St. Louis and Cincinnati.

Eulogy of John Millais, the Painter—Views on Drama and Actor.

Oscar Wilde is in the city for a short rest from his lecturing tour, and has rooms at the Grand Pacific. A reporter for THE INTER OCEAN called yesterday afternoon about 2:30 o'clock and sent up his card. The bell-boy returned in due time and said:

"Mr. Wilde is asleep, sah."

"Did he tell you so himself?" asked the reporter.

"No, sah," said the bell boy with dignity. "His servant told me so, sah."

The question then resolved itself into two points: Should the reporter wait for Mr. Wilde to finish his nap, or should he "rattle him up," anyway, and remind him of his duty to society? After some mental debate the latter course was decided upon, and he climbed the stairs and stood in front of No. 11. All was still. A

1. David Swing (1830–1894) was a popular Chicago-based preacher. His critique of Wilde, published in the 21 February number of his magazine, *The Alliance*, was titled "Oscar the Small". In it Swing described Wilde as "an intellectual and emotional abyss," criticised his egotism ("a large man would omit to boast of getting $1,000 a night while other great men were receiving only $300"—an allusion to "Truly Aesthetic," *The Daily Inter Ocean* (Chicago, IL), 13 Feb. 1882, 2, pp. 168–9), and concluded that "a woman kissing a poodle comes nearer expressing the unmanli-ness of this peacockism. He is a peddler of childish jimcracks and his domain is not the world, but the showcase of some notion store," (OWDA, 213–14). The article was reprinted in "Oscar Wilde," *The Chicago Daily Tribune* (Chicago, IL), 23 Feb. 1882, 8; and "Dr. David Swing on 'The Enigma of the Day,'" *St. Louis Globe-Democrat* (St. Louis, MO), 26 Feb. 1882, 3. For Wilde's response to Swing, see"David and Oscar," *The Chicago Sunday Tribune* (Chicago, IL), 5 Mar. 1882, 5, pp. 249–51; "Pr ofessor Swing and Oscar," *The Daily Inter Ocean* (Chicago, IL), 6 Mar. 1882, 8, pp. 251–3; and "Wilde and Swing," *The Boston Herald* (Boston, MA), 6 Mar. 1882, 2, pp. 253–4.

2. H & S, b46. Quoted in OWDA, 180, 216–7; and Pearson, 67, 68. The reporter appears to have been accompanied by the author of "Oscar Wilde," *The Chicago Daily Tribune* (Chicago, IL), 1 Mar. 1882, 7, pp. 236–40.

good solid rap on the door had the effect of producing a smothered sound from within, but whether it was an invitation to come in or go to—somewhere else, the reporter was not sure. He gave Mr. Wilde the benefit of the doubt, and rapped again. This time there was no mistake about it. "Come in" was hurled at the door as if it was a boot-jack. The reporter entered. The room at first glance seemed empty, but it was pervaded by an unseen presence that seemed to fill it to the transom. But where was the aesthete? There was no couch in the room. The reporter even glanced under the sofa, although he well knew it was useless. Upon a chair were Mr. Wilde's sacred breeches: at a little distance a pair of exquisitely all-but gaiters, and near them a pair of ecstatic socks. Various other articles of *lingerie* were scattered around in graceful if somewhat careless forms, but the reporter had no time to take an inventory.

HE IS FOUND.

A voice came from the alcove which the reporter now saw for the first time, and which was concealed by a closely drawn lace curtain, saying:

"Where is my servant?"

"I don't know," said the reporter, wishing he was at home, but taking off his hat to the pantaloons, gaiters, et al.

"Well, what do you want?"

"I am a representative of the press—"

Just then the missing servant came in out of breath, and brushing some cracker crumbs off his coat collar. Plainly, he didn't drink lemonade.

"I have been traveling night and day, and wanted some rest," said the gentleman behind the curtains, while the servant looked as if he would like to receive an order to bounce the intruder. "Ah, couldn't you come up again in an hour?"

"Certainly, I can," said the reporter, thanking heaven for the escape: and he went down to the office and matched pennies with Sam Parker.[1]

When the appointed time had expired, the reporter rapped again at the door of No. 11, and upon entering was much relieved to see that the gaiters, etc., were no longer on the chairs, but were on the graceful form of Mr. Wilde. He was as cordial as ever, and seated the caller with great politeness. His dress was a black velvet smoking jacket, light brown pantaloons, or perhaps a wood color, socks of the same grade, and patent-leather shoes finished at the top with cloth off the same piece as the pantaloons. The room was arranged with an eye to picturesque effect. The chairs were draped with skins of beasts, and Mr. Wilde's

1. Match pennies is a game in which two players each secretly turn a penny to heads or tails. They then simultaneously reveal the pennies, with one player receiving both pennies if they match and the other player receiving them if they do not.

own chair was ornamented with a silk shawl. A bright fire blazed in the grate, and the table was heaped with books, letters, and papers of all kinds.

THE INTERVIEW BEGINS—ST. LOUIS.

"What were your impressions of St. Louis?" asked the reporter.

"In St. Louis," he said, "they have the best arranged museum of art that I have seen in America. The collections are not extensive, but all is most excellent and beautiful. It has the first quality of a good museum—nothing in it that could possibly lead a young art student astray. Of all things in it—oil paintings, plaster casts, or statuary—there is nothing but good."

"That is high praise from such a source, Mr. Wilde," said the reporter.

He swallowed the taffy without winking, and continued: "But I think in America you are a little too exclusive—a great deal too exclusive—in your admiration for the French school. The examples of English art that I have seen in America all belong to the period of Benjamin West and Haydon, but of the modern school of English painters I have seen no examples.[1] I have not, for instance, seen in any of your public museums or private galleries any of John Millais' work. He is one of the greatest painters that England has ever produced. He will be remembered with Gainsborough and Sir Joshua Reynolds as one of our greatest portrait painters,[2] and no man now living in England, or, indeed, in the whole history of English painting, has done such a splendid amount of artistic work in style [*sic*] so entirely different. When he was a young man he belonged to the pre-Raphaelite brotherhood, and was their greatest painter. His early pictures are full of the most beautiful imaginations [*sic*] and most wonderful technical power, and his picture of "Christ in the Carpenter Shop" is the only beautiful religious picture, with the exception of Rossetti's 'Annunciation,' that I have ever seen.[3]

1. Benjamin West (1738–1820) was a painter of historical and religious subjects who was born in Pennsylvania and settled in London. Benjamin Robert Haydon (1786–1846) was an English painter who also specialised in historical paintings.

2. Thomas Gainsborough (1727–1788) was an English portrait and landscape painter. Sir Joshua Reynolds (1723–1792) was an English portrait painter and the first president of the Royal Academy of Arts.

3. *Christ in the Carpenter Shop* is better known as *Christ in the House of His* Parents (1849–1850); Rossetti's *Annunciation* is better known as *Ecce Ancilla Domini* (1850). Wilde exaggerates when he says that these are the only beautiful religious pictures he has ever seen: he had previously praised several religious paintings, including Titian's *Assumption* ("certainly the best picture in Italy", CL, 11), the Scrovegni Chapel frescoes by Giotto ("He is the first of all painters", CL, 12), and Guido Reni's *St. Sebastian* ("[...] though pierced by arrows, [he is] raising his eyes with divine, impassioned gaze towards the Eternal Beauty of the opening heavens", *The Tomb of Keats*; CW vi, No. 2, lines 60–1). In his poem *Ave Maria Plena Gratia*, first published in *Kottabos* in Michaelmas Term 1879 (CW i, No. 41), Wilde complains that a painting of the Annunciation he saw in Italy failed to live up to his expectations; evidently he preferred Rossetti's version.

"From the earliest poetical sentiment of his pictures, when he chose his subjects from Florentine legend and sacred story, he passed with an increased realism of technical power to nature drawn from the life of our day. "The Highland Woman Delivering the Order of Release to the Jailer for Her Imprisoned Husband;" the 'Girl Bidding Good By to Her Sweetheart who is Going to the Wars,' are great witnesses of how much splendid imaginative work can be got out of modern life. Millais then passed to landscape, in which he is a really great master. His picture of 'Chill October' is one of the most pathetic and beautiful landscapes I have ever seen; and lately his fame rests upon his powers as a portrait painter, in which he will rank with Sir Joshua Reynolds and Gainsborough. No one has painted children with such delicacy and love of the beauty of childhood and perfection of treatment as he since Reynolds painted 'Penelope Boothby.' No one has painted great men with such dignity and strength. His picture of Mr. Gladstone is one of the great pictures of this century, and he was painting one of Lord Beaconsfield at the time when that wonderful genius died. Any museum or gallery is quite incomplete without a specimen of his work."[1]

"What do you think of the Mississippi River?" asked the reporter, getting ready to write "grand," "majestic," etc. he was surprised to hear Mr. Wilde say, quietly, and without a gleam of fun:

"I don't think a well-behaved river should run over that way, don't you know?"

The reporter thought it was rather reprehensible conduct.

"The want of pure water," he continued, "in each city, caused by the overflow, and the dreadful condition of the streets in nearly all the cities I have visited, seem to show a curious want of provision against what I suppose a not extraordinary test. It is quite impossible to have any art unless you have good air, good water, and clean cities."[2]

"You have visited a number of Western cities, have you not?"

"Yes; I have lectured at Cincinnati, St. Louis, Detroit, Cleveland, Indianapolis, Fort Wayne, Springfield, Ill., and some other cities."[3]

1. The picture Wilde refers to as *The Highland Woman Delivering the Order of Release* is better known as *The Order of Release, 1746* (1853). *Girl Bidding Good By* is *The Black Brunswicker* (1860). *Chill October* was painted in 1870. Reynolds painted *Penelope Boothby* in 1788. Millais's portraits of children include *Cherry Ripe* (1879); his best known is *A Child's World/Bubbles* (1886). Millais painted William Ewart Gladstone, Prime Minister of the United Kingdom, in 1879, and his rival, Benjamin Disraeli, Earl of Beaconsfield (1804–1881), in 1881.

2. Wilde made the same points in *The Decorative Arts*: "[T]he noblest art requires a clear, healthy atmosphere, not polluted as the air of our English cities is by the smoke and grime and horridness which comes from open furnace and from factory chimney." (O'Brien, 159.)

3. Wilde only omits Louisville from this list.

OPINION OF THE AMERICAN ATHENS.

"How did you like Cincinnati?"

"In Cincinnati I was particularly pleased. There is not merely a great love of art, but of fine collections. Of course, all schools of art which are young and inexperienced will commit many faults; but still their work is very good, a great deal of it, and they are going to work in the right way."

"You like the West better than the East, I believe?"

"The Western cities seem to be more distinctively American, and as such are objects of great interest to all Englishmen. In the West seems to be the civilization you have created by yourselves and for yourselves. So much in the East is a mere repetition of European thought, and so much that is a mere misunderstanding of it."

"What do you think of the London press?"

The two best written papers in London are the *World* and *Truth*. You have already heard Mr. Edmund Yates, the editor of the *World*, when on his lecture tour.[1] He is a very brilliant lecturer. I understand Mr. Labouchère, editor of *Truth*, is to make a lecturing tour in America. I am sure you will be interested to hear him."

"Are not the poor people of England all 'Radicals?'"

"There is no connection between poverty and radicalism, but there is between handicraft and republicanism. To work at any handicraft induces that sense of independence which is the key-note of all republicanism. In the great cities of England there is a constant spirit of discussion and certain clash of ideas which make men think for themselves, so that the political thought of England progresses always in the manufacturing towns, and never in the agricultural places. An agricultural laborer's view of politics is founded entirely on the weather."

ESTIMATE OF DRAMATISTS.

"Would you please talk a little about dramatic art?"

"Oh, yes: I love to do so. Henry Irving is our greatest tragedian.[2] He stands at the head of our Shakespearean actors. He is a man of most curious and wonderful personality, with an interesting realism in his acting which was for us in

1. Yates toured America in the early 1870s.

2. Henry Irving (1838–1905) was an English actor. In a review of Irving's 1885 production of *Hamlet* Wilde wrote: "I call him a great actor because he brings to the interpretation of a work of art the two qualities which we in this century so much desire, the qualities of personality and of perfection." (*Dramatic Review*, 9 May 1885; CW vi, No. 16, lines 28–30.)

London an entirely new departure from the new found school of Macready.[1] He is certainly as great an artist as Charles Kean.[2] If he comes to America he will bring with him our most beautiful and fascinating actress, Miss Ellen Terry."[3]

"Do you not have a dramatic censor in London?"

"Yes. He would not allow Sarah Bernhardt to play 'La Dame aux Camelias' for a long time, and has recently decided that the most moral system of British morality would be undermined if the Paris Royal Company played 'Divorçons.'[4] If there was a censor to prevent bad acting we would all support the office with all the means in our power, but, unfortunately, there is no law to prevent any man or woman from murdering any great part in public."

"That kind of a censor would be popular in Chicago," said the reporter. "Do you think Mrs. Langtry will come to America?"

"She will probably come. She is one of the most beautiful women in the world. Her figure is molded like a Greek statue. She is not petite, and I wouldn't say she is tall. She is a perfect artistic height. She has a most beautiful voice. On the stage she has a joyousness of manner which is the beauty of all good comedy acting, and when she has studied her art she will be able to act Shakespeare's Rosalind in a way in which most of us have never seen the part."[5]

"Better than Neilson?"[6]

1. William Charles Macready (1793–1873) was an English actor who performed in several Shakespearian tragedies and histories.

2. Charles Kean (1811–1868) was an Irish-born English actor and son of Edmund Kean. He revived several Shakespearean tragedies.

3. Irving's partnership with Terry lasted 24 years. They arrived in New York on 21 October 1883, Irving's Lyceum Company beginning a season at the Star Theatre on the 29th.

4. *La Dame aux Camélias* is a tragedy about a courtesan that was adapted for the stage in 1852 by Alexandre Dumas *fils* from his own 1848 novel. It was the play for which Sarah Bernhardt was most famous. She successfully toured North America with it in 1880–1881, and was permitted by the Lord Chamberlain to stage it in London in 1881 after the Prince of Wales intervened on her behalf. *Divorçons* (1880) was written by Victorien Sardou (1831–1908) and Émile de Najac (1828–1889). It deals with a young woman who decides to divorce her husband so she can marry an attractive scoundrel. Her husband's kindness leads her to change her mind.

5. Langtry made her London stage debut as Kate Hardcastle in *She Stoops to Conquer* at the Haymarket on 15 December 1881. It was a charity performance in aid of the Royal General Theatrical Fund. Wilde was present, as were the Prince and Princess of Wales. She had previously appeared with her mentor, Henrietta Labouchère (see p. 480, note 2), in *A Fair Encounter*, a one act "comedietta", as part of an entertainment given in aid of St. John's Hospital, Twickenham. Her visit to America was confirmed in July ("The Jersey Lily Coming," *The New York Times* (New York, NY), 24 July 1882, 1); she arrived in October. She appeared in several roles, including Rosalind in Shakespeare's *As You Like It*.

6. Lilian Adelaide Neilson (1848–1880) was a British actress who, like Langtry, was famed for her beauty. She successfully toured America several times during the 1870s, playing Rosalind and other roles. In the years after her death she was often invoked as the standard against which new actresses should be measured.

"You can't compare artists, but you can easily compare mediocrity. I have not the slightest doubt of her dramatic genius. She is one of the most remarkable women of this age in England."

How do you like Jefferson?"[1]

"I saw him in 'Rip Van Winkle.' He is one of the greatest artists I have ever seen. His acting in London was, for all of us who loved and studied acting, one of the greatest we had ever seen in that play."

"How do you like Booth?"

"Booth is a very, very great artist. He speaks English much better than almost any of our own actors. His perfect enunciation, perfect ideas of blank verse and knowledge of emphasis, and consciousness that when he is speaking Shakespeare he is speaking music is a source of the greatest delight to all of us in London. His acting of King Lear I consider to rank along with Salvini's Othello, Henry Irving's Shylock, or the greatest thing in acting I have ever seen."[2]

"Do you like McCullough?"

"I saw him the other night in Spartacus. He is very strong, exceedingly powerful, and is a master of stage effects."[3]

"You have seen Clara Morris?"

"Yes; she interested me wondrously. Sarah Bernhardt told me that there were only two things in America worth seeing, one was Clara Morris, and the other some dreadful way you have of killing hogs in the Chicago Stock Yards. I have seen Miss Morris; the other visit I have postponed indefinitely."

"You lecture here again, I believe, Mr. Wilde?"

"Yes, at Central Music Hall, on Saturday evening, March 11, on Interior and Exterior House Decoration."

"Would you mind giving me a few points on the lecture?"

"No. I can't do that," he said, good naturedly. "But I will begin with the doorknob and end with the attic. Beyond that there only remains heaven, which subject I leave to the church."

1. Joseph Jefferson (1829–1905) was an American actor, most famous for his portrayal of Rip Van Winkle. He played the character in America, the United Kingdom, and Australia for 40 years.

2. Booth played Lear in London from 14 February to mid-March 1881. Tommaso Salvini (1829–1915) was an Italian actor, most famous for playing Othello. He performed in London, where Wilde must have seen him, and first visited America in 1873. Wilde saw his Othello again in New York in November 1882.

3. Wilde saw McCullough as Spartacus in *The Gladiator* on 19 February ("Come and Gone," *The Cleveland Herald* (Cleveland, OH), 20 Feb. 1882, 8, p. 187).

"Oscar Wilde," *The Chicago Daily Tribune* (Chicago, IL), 1 Mar. 1882, 7[1]

The Apostle of the Dado, After His Visit to the Suburbs

Cincinnati Art Museum Caught Him, and St. Louis' Museum Was All but Too-Too.

America Too Exclusive in Art Matters—The Esthete's Enthusiasm over Millais.

Mrs. Langtry Moves Him to Raptures—His High Opinion of American Actors and Actresses.

Utter Ignorance on the Subject of Prairies—The Mississippi Beautiful, but Not Well Behaved.

Mr. Oscar Wilde, the celebrated esthete, arrived in the city yesterday morning from Springfield, Ill., where he lectured Monday evening. He registered at the Grand Pacific Hotel, and was assigned to Parlor 11. About 2 o'clock yesterday afternoon a TRIBUNE representative called at the hotel to see the apostle of the beautiful and to obtain his impressions of the Great West. The reportorial card was returned by a bell-boy, who also brought the information that Mr. Wilde was asleep, and could not be disturbed. A journey to his parlor was then made, but a stalwart African stood guard at the door and would allow no one to pass him. With the assurance that Mr. Wilde would arise in an hour or so, the reporter repaired to the rotunda and waited.

About 3 o'clock a second tour was made to the regions above, and it was discovered that the colored gentleman had abandoned his post. A rap at the door brought forth a timid "Come in," and the reporter cautiously turned the knob and entered. No one was visible, but

THE EFFEMINATE VOICE OF THE ESTHETE,

proceeding from behind a pair of lace bed-curtains, asked what he wanted.

"The TRIBUNE would like to see you, Mr. Wilde," said the reporter.

"Well, you can't see me now," he answered. "I am very tired after a long journey, having come clear from Springfield, Ill., and I want to take a nap. I'll see you in about an hour."

The colored gentleman entered at this point, and the reporter withdrew while Mr. Wilde was giving his servant an angry talking-to for having deserted his post.

1. H & S, b44. Reprinted in H & S, 88–93. Quoted in Sturgis, 237–8/228, 239/229. Referenced in Sturgis, 237/228. The reporter appears to have been accompanied by the author of "Oscar Back Again," *The Daily Inter Ocean* (Chicago, IL), 1 Mar. 1882, 8, pp. 229–35.

At 4 o'clock the newspaper-man approached Parlor 11 a third time, and the "Come in," in answer to his rap, was delivered in a firmer tone of voice. On entering the room, Mr. Wilde was discovered sitting in a tastefully-draped chair near one of the windows. He wore a black velvet jacket, a pair of brown breeches, a brick-red necktie and handkerchief, low shoes, and maroon socks. His long hair fell gracefully over his shoulders, and his taper fingers toyed delicately with a cigarette. He gave the reporter a cordial hand-shake and bade him be seated.

"When did you arrive in Chicago, Mr. Wilde?" asked the reporter.

"I reached here this morning from Springfield, Ill., where I lectured last evening."

"What cities have you visited since you left here?"

"I have lectured in Cincinnati, St. Louis, Detroit, Cleveland, Indianapolis, Fort Wayne, Springfield, and other places."

"Which one of the Western cities are you most favourably impressed with?"

EASILY PLEASED.

"In Cincinnati I was particularly pleased, not merely at the great love of art shown there, but the people are doing a great deal of beautiful work. Of course, old schools of art disagree, when adopted by a young people, but experience will correct many faults. Still, a great deal of their work is very good, and they are going to work in the right way."

"How do you think the West compares with the East?" asked the reporter.

"The West interests us in England more than the East. You are making civilization by yourselves and for yourselves. So much in the East is a mere reflection of European thought, and so much of that a mere misunderstanding of it."

"What do you think of St. Louis?"

"I think St. Louis has the best arranged museum of art I have seen yet. It does not contain very much, but all it does contain is excellently and brilliantly chosen. That is the first qualification of a good museum. Nothing in it could possibly lead a young student astray. Out of everything in it, oil-paintings or plates, cast or etching, there is nothing but good to be got.

"But I think," continued Mr. Wilde, "that in America you are a little too exclusive in art matters—in fact, a great deal too exclusive. In your admiration for the modern French school, examples of English art seen in America all belong to the most dreadful period of English painting—the period of Benjamin West and Haydon. The wonderful modern school of English painting has no examples here. I have not, for instance, seen in any of your galleries any of John Millais' works. He is one of the greatest painters that England has ever produced, and will be remembered along with Gainsborough and Sir Joshua Reynolds as one of the greatest portrait painters, and

NO MAN IN MY TIME IN ENGLAND,

or indeed in the whole history of English painting, has done such a splendid amount of artistic work in style so entirely different."

Here Mr. Wilde paused, drained a glass of lemonade, lit a fresh cigarette, and, having gained his second wind, continued:

"Millais, when a young man, belonged to the pre-Raphaelite brotherhood, and was their greatest painter. His early pictures were full of the most beautiful technical imagination and most wonderful technical power, and his picture of 'Christ in the Carpenter-Shop' is the only beautiful religious picture, with the exception of Rossetti's 'Annunciation,' that I have ever seen. From the pastoral sentiment of his pictures, when he chose his subjects from Florentine lyrics and sacred story, he passed with increased realism of technical power to motives drawn from the life of his own day. The Highland woman delivering the order of release to the jailer for her imprisoned husband, and the girl bidding goodbye to her lover going to the war, are great instances of how much splendid imaginative work may be got out of modern life. He then passed to landscapes, in which he is a really great master. His picture of 'Chill October' is one of the most pathetic and beautiful landscapes I have ever seen. And, lastly, his fame rests on his powers as a portrait painter, in which he will rank, as I said, with Gainsborough and Sir Joshua Reynolds. No one has painted children with such delicacy and love of

THE BEAUTY OF CHILDHOOD,

and perfection of treatment as he has since Sir Joshua Reynolds painted 'Penelope Boothby,' and no one has painted great men with such dignity and strength as he has. His portrait of Mr. Gladstone is one of the greatest pictures of the century, and he was painting one of Lord Beaconsfield at the time when that wonderful genius died. Any modern gallery is quite incomplete without a specimen of his work."

"You call Millais your greatest painter, Mr. Wilde," said the reporter. "Who do you consider your greatest actor?"

"I call Henry Irving our greatest tragedian, as he stands at the head of our Shakespearean actors. He has a curious and remarkable personality, with intensity and realism in his acting which was for us, in England, an entirely new departure from the more formal, declamatory style of Macready. He is, in the matter of scenery and costume, as great as Charles Kean."

"Is he thinking of visiting America?"

"I believe he is. If he comes here he will bring with him our most beautiful and fascinating actress—Miss Ellen Terry."

"Mrs. Langtry is expected to visit this country soon. Is she as beautiful, do you think, as she is said to be?"

"She is one of the most beautiful women in the world," said Mr. Wilde, enthusiastically. "She is possessed of

A FIGURE MOLDED LIKE THAT OF A GREEK STATUE,

and is of a perfect, artistic height. She has a beautiful stage voice, is joyous of manner, which is the element of all good comedy acting, and when she has studied her art more she will be able to act Shakespeare's *Rosalind* in a way in which most of us have never seen the part acted. There is not the slightest doubt of her dramatic genius, I truly believe that she is the most remarkable woman of this day in England."

"Have you seen any of our great actors?" asked the reporter.

"Oh, yes; I have seen those of your actors who have visited England, and others I have seen since my arrival here. I think Joseph Jefferson is one of the greatest actors I ever saw. I saw him play *Rip Van Winkle* in London, and was greatly impressed with his acting."

"Have you seen Edwin Booth?"

"I have, and I think him one of the greatest actors I ever saw. I saw him in all his great parts in England, and I think he speaks English much better than almost any of our own actors. His perfect enunciation, his perfect delivery of blank verse, his knowledge of emphasis, and his consciousness that when one is speaking Shakespeare he is speaking music, was a source of the greatest delight to all of us in England. His *King Lear* I consider to rank along with Salvini's *Othello* and Henry Irving's *Shylock*, as the greatest thing in acting I have ever seen."

"What do you think of John McCullough?"

"I saw him the other night as *Spartacus*, and I think he is very strong, exceedingly powerful, and a master of stage effect."

"Who of our actresses have you seen?"

CLARA MORRIS INTERESTED ME ENORMOUSLY.

Sarah Bernhardt told me that there were two things in America worth seeing—one was Clara Morris' acting, and the other was some dreadful method of killing pigs in Chicago. She advised me to go and see both. I went to see Miss Morris immediately upon my arrival in New York City,[1] but the other I have deferred quite indefinitely."

"You have what is called a Censor of Plays, I believe, in England?"

"Yes, we have. The Lord Chamberlain has control of that department, and the Censor of Plays reads all new works before they are produced. His decision is final. He has recently decided that the whole moral system of the British nation

1. See [Augustus R. Cazauran], "Is it Aesthetic Taffy?" *The New York Herald* (New York, NY), 13 Jan. 1882, 10, pp. 67–8.

would be undermined if the French Palais Royal company acted 'Divorçons,' which he considers an immoral play. If we had a censor to prevent bad acting we all would support the office with every means in our power; but, unfortunately, there is no law to prevent men or women from murdering great parts."

"Do you lecture in Chicago again, Mr. Wilde?" asked the reporter.

"Yes, I shall lecture at Central Music-Hall Saturday evening, March 11, on the subject of 'The Decoration of Houses.'"

"What are your ideas on that subject?"

"Well, it wouldn't be fair to tell you before I delivered my lecture. The subject covers an immense amount of ground, and I shall

BEGIN WITH THE DOOR-KNOCKER AND GO TO THE ATTIC.

Beyond that is Heaven, and I shall leave that to the Church."

"Will you remain in Chicago long?"

"No, sir. I lecture every night now until I reappear here."

"How do you fancy making these one-night stands?"

"Oh, I don't mind it much. In fact I rather like traveling in this country."[1]

"Have you seen any of our prairies in your travels?"

"What are they?"

"Why, vast stretches of rolling lands as far as the eye can see."

"No, I don't think I have seen anything like that. I have done most of my traveling in the night."[2]

"How did the Mississippi River strike you?"

"Well, I think no well-behaved river would overflow as it has done, though I am quite ready to admit its beauty. I noticed a want of pure water in each city along its banks, caused evidently by the overflow. The streets are also in a dreadful condition in nearly all these cities, and this fact seems to indicate to me a serious want of provision against these extraordinary catastrophes. It is quite impossible to have any art unless you have good air, good water, and clean cities."

At this point Mr. Wilde arose from his recumbent position and extended his hand to the reporter. The hint was taken, and a retreat was made in good order, while Mr. Wilde turned to the window and contemplated the sea of mud beneath him with a feeling, it is to be feared, that Chicago was not an art centre.

1. Wilde had previously told an interviewer: "I hate travelling." ("Oscar Wilde in Brooklyn," *The Sun* (New York, NY), 4 Feb. 1882, 1, p. 135).

2. For Wilde's comments on American prairies, see "Aesthetic," *Dayton Daily Democrat* (Dayton, OH), 3 May 1882, 4, p. 370.

"Philosophical Oscar," *The Chicago Times* (Chicago IL), 1 Mar. 1882, 7[1]

Second Visit of the Young Aesthete to Chicago—What He Thinks of This Country—Opinions of Men and Woman in England.

Oscar Wilde returned to the city yesterday from Springfield, where he lectured the night before, and is at the Grand Pacific hotel. During his western trip he has occupied platforms in St. Louis, Detroit, Cleveland, Indianapolis, Fort Wayne, and other cities. He says he was particularly pleased with Cincinnati. Its people have not only a great love of art, but they are doing much beautiful work. All schools of design, he says, which are young and inexperienced commit many faults, but in Cincinnati the work is good, and the workers are going at it in the right way. As to the west, he says it interests the English more than the east, because its civilization is made by the people for themselves. There is so much in the east that is a mere reflection of European thought, and so much a misunderstanding of it, which is not met in the west. The reporter called attention to the reports that Mrs. Langtry and Henry Labouchère were to come to America, and asked him concerning them. Of Mrs. Langtry he said:

"She is one of my greatest friends."

"What is she like?"

"BEAUTIFUL WOMEN

Are quite indescribable. The beauty of her face is in the extreme sweetness and loveliness of her expression and the wonderful delicacy and transparency of her complexion. The real wonder of her beauty to all of us who are artists is that whether one carved her in marble or painted her in color she is equally lovely, the lines of her face being as strongly worked and as definite in outline as a Greek bronze, and yet so perfect in proportion that the effect is one of the simplest loveliness. In acting, she has a wonderfully musical and well-modulated voice, a delightful joyousness of manner, and real capabilities for her art. The part that, when she has had more study and practice, she will make her greatest success in will, I think, be Rosalind, in 'As You Like It.'"

"Was her first appearance really good?"

"No art would be worth doing if it could be done easily the first time, but there has been no debutante on the stage in London for many years who showed such really remarkable power and such great promise. She is now going to study

1. H & S, b45. Reprinted in H & S, 93–5. Quoted in Ellmann, 195/206.

Frou Frou to make a tour of England.[1] She is very nervous about visiting America, but, like many of us, most ambitious to see your country and to make herself a position here."

"Are there many young actors of promise in England?"

"Yes; there are four or five now there on whom we all rest great hopes for the future of the English stage—Mr. Conway, who will probably accompany Mme. Modjeska on her return to America; Mr. Bellew, whose father was well known as a reader in our country, and the Messrs. Forbes Robertson, the elder of whom, besides being a most romantic and beautiful actor, is also a painter, who has done most excellent work; and the younger, Mr. Norman Forbes Robertson, who has made several brilliant successes with Mme. Modjeska, and who is anxious to act over here."[2]

"WHAT ABOUT LABOUCHÈRE?"

"He is one of the most brilliant conversationalists and the most brilliant journalist in England, one of the many democrats which the English aristocracy has produced. He is Bradlaugh's colleague in representing Northampton,[3] and is a man of great importance in the radical party, through his keen knowledge of all foreign affairs, having been attaché at all of the important courts. He is the only brilliant enemy I ever had in England. He has had more libel cases to defend than any man in England, and he always wins them."

"How old is he?"[4]

"Men are always as old as they feel and women as they look, and I am sure that Mr. Labouchère feels eternally young, because he is always successful. But if we were obliged to go down to relentless facts, I should say he was a man of 50."

"How do he and Bradlaugh work together?"

1. *Froufrou* (1869), a play by French dramatists Ludovic Halévy (1834–1908) and Henri Meilhac (1830–1897). Sarah Bernhardt had brought the play to New York in 1880 and revived it in 1883 in Paris.

2. Harry Blenkinsopp Coulson (1850–1909) was an English actor who performed under the name Harry B. Conway and was known for his good looks. Harold Kyrle Money Bellew (1850–1911), better known as Kyrle Bellow, was an English actor. Johnston Forbes-Robertson (1853–1937) was an English actor, theatre manager, and painter. Wilde reviewed his portrait of the Duchess of Westminster, exhibited at the Grosvenor Gallery's inaugural exhibition in 1877: "He has succeeded very well in reproducing the calm, beautiful profile and lustrous golden hair, but the shoulders are ungraceful, and very unlike the original." (CW vi, No. 1, lines 360–2.) Johnston's younger brother, Norman (1858–1932), was also an actor and a friend of Wilde. He toured America with Modjeska the following season as "Norman Forbes"; contrary to Wilde's prediction, Conway was not with Modjeska's company.

3. Charles Bradlaugh (1833–1891) was an English Liberal politician, activist, and prominent atheist. He served as a Member of Parliament for Northampton from 1880 and founded the National Secular Society.

4. Labouchère had turned 50 in November 1881.

"Politically, he has been Bradlaugh's staunchest defender, and has been most loyal to his brother member. The two best written papers in England are *The World* and *Truth*. You have already heard the editor of *The World*, Mr. Edmund Yates, lecture. A very brilliant lecturer he is. So I am sure Americans will be interested in hearing the editor of the other paper."

"How do you account for the radicalism of Northampton? The voters there are mostly poor and shoemakers, are they not?"

"I do not think there is any connection between poverty and radicalism, but there is between handicrafts and republicanism. I mean that to work at any handicraft produces that sense of individualism which is the key note of all republicanism. Then, in great cities there is a constant spirit of discussion and a certain clash of ideas which make men think for themselves, so that the political thought of England progresses always in the manufacturing towns and never in the agricultural places. An agricultural laborer's view of politics is founded entirely on the weather."

Mr. Wilde looks as if his western trip had agreed with him.

"Oscar Wilde," *The Dubuque Herald* (Dubuque, IA), 3 Mar. 1882, 4[1]

A Random Talk with the Apostle of the Dado—What He Thinks of Ingersoll, Etc

Mr. A. Kitson, the gentleman who induced Mr. Wilde to lecture in our city, is evidently a wiser man today than he was before the nomadic English specimen introduced himself to a Dubuque audience. The lecture was not rendered in full, neither did Mr. Wilde give his lecture in as glowing colors and in as luminous a manner as Mr. Kitson was led to believe he would, and it evidently was quite fortunate for Mr. Wilde that he got his money in advance, for the man who engaged him did not think he came up to his agreement, and would evidently have questioned the payment of the amount agreed upon in full. In conversation with some gentlemen after the lecture, Mr. Wilde expressed his opinion on the press of America and many other features concerning the American people. The press he thought had no comparison with the English journals. He considered American newspapers nothing but a lot of garbage; that they are the cullings of police courts and circulators of immodest literature, and he considers them so much beneath his notice that he will not attempt to answer any of their slanderous and unjust attempts to hurt his business in this country. He says he had been from London so long that he is beginning to believe himself a vagrant, and that he is

1. H & S, b47.

losing all self respect toward his own sex. He thinks, however, that if he is degrading himself, he is converting a large number of the American people to the appreciation of the beauties in scenery, and also cultivating their tastes in a manner that will be of great benefit in the future. He contradicts the statement made by Harvey Young, that the aesthetic movement started in France.[1] Mr. Wilde says that the aesthetic enthusiasm first started in England about a half dozen years ago. His most intimate associate in Europe is the English crank, Whistler, a man of considerable prominence in London for his many eccentric ideas.[2] He thinks that the scenery in the vicinity of Dubuque is too utterly utter.[3] He also was very much pleased with the ladies of Dubuque, thinking them quite refined. He remarked that his audience was small, but he considered it quite classic.[4] Robert Ingersoll is, in the mind of the aesthete, one of America's greatest men. Oscar says he shall positively have an interview with Robert, on his return to the east. In answer to the accuracy of his general manager, Mr. D'Oyly Carte of New York, paying some of the eastern newspapers to advertise Oscar as a Baboon, presenting himself before the American people with an apple in his hand, he said it was positively false.[5] Mr. Wilde says he heartily wishes he had some enemy in this country that he could consider worthy of his notice, that he would like to make a defense in his own behalf, but that the American newspapers are too low for him to associate with. Mr. Wilde left yesterday morning for Rock Island.[6] He lectures in Chicago on the 9th if nothing prevents.[7] He flatters himself on his appearance at the Opera House, because, he says, any man can make a speech or deliver a lecture before [?1,000] people, but it requires nerve to deliver a lecture to empty benches.

1. The reference is presumably to Harvey Otis Young (1840–1901), an American painter and prospector, known for his Western landscapes and depictions of frontier life. In February 1882 Young was working on several paintings in St Louis, MO, but was preparing to depart for Colorado to work in a mine ("Art Notes," *St. Louis Globe Democrat* (St. Louis, MO), 12 Feb. 1882, 15). His comments on aestheticism are untraced.

2. Whistler was born in Massachusetts. From the late 1850s he resided mostly in London.

3. Wilde may have praised the scenery, but not using aesthetic slang.

4. Wilde's audience in Dubuque numbered 200; the venue seated 900 (Cooper, Dubuque lecture, 1 March 1882).

5. See "Oscar Wilde," *The Republican* (St. Louis, MO), 26 Feb. 1882, 13, p. 222, note 1; and "Gotham Gossip," *The Tribune* (Minneapolis, MN), 5 Mar. 1882, 1, p. 768.

6. Either the interviewer or Wilde is in error. Wilde lectured in Rockford on 2 March, a day after appearing in Dubuque, and would not have travelled via Rock Island.

7. Wilde lectured in towns and small cities in Illinois and Wisconsin every day between 1 and 11 March, when he made his second appearance in Chicago.

"Oscar Interviewed," *The Rockford Daily Register* (Rockford, IL), 3 Mar. 1882, 3[1]

After the lecture last evening a REGISTER representative dropped behind the scenes and met Oscar face-to-face, in his dressing room where an extended interview was had. Mr. Wilde was semi-reclining, like a withered sunflower, upon a cushioned seat while he held a darling cigarette between his teeth from which saffron smoke, probably the effect of the reflection of his countenance, lazily lingered a moment and then disappeared in upper air. Near at hand the great aesthete is very large and towering but his form tapers down in the tight breeches and stockings almost to a point.

To an interrogation as to how he liked the Opera House he responded, "I am charmed, I assure you with its beauty and beautiful design. It is artistic in coloring and neat in detail. Your audience too, though not large as I have been accustomed to, displayed their culture and sympathy by their intent attention."[2] He then went into a sort of aftermath lecture, until the reporter fearing he was in for another hour's dissertation on art, broke in with the query as to where he found his best American audience. He replied, "In the west, you are more natural here and one finds a deeper appreciation than in the East. There they are too permeated with European ideas and follies, which throw a sort of London fog before anything new, and accept too readily all the ridiculous notions engendered in Europe. In the West, you are new and progressive, and ready to accept an innovation if it comes well founded. But of all audiences I have been most charmed with those in Chicago. They have been delightful, so warm, so receptive, I cannot express my full delight with my Chicago audiences."[3]

"I see you were advertised to speak on the 'Renaissance.' How did you come to change?"[4]

"Oh! that is a very stupid piece of blundering, and about equal to the unbusiness-like capacity of every business manager I have met in this country. I once delivered a lecture on the 'Renaissance' in New York, and never intended to deliver it again.[5] Yet these foolish managers persist in unaccountably advertising that as my lecture wherever I go. I have protested and begged, but to no purpose,

1. A negative review of Wilde's lecture in Rockford appeared on the same page under the headline "The Only Oscar".

2. Wilde's audience in Rockford was about two hundred, a quarter house (*The Rockford Journal* (Rockford, IL), 4 Mar. 1882, 4).

3. Wilde refers to his Chicago audiences in the plural, but at this time he had only lectured in Chicago once, on 13 February. He would return for a second and final lecture in the city on 11 March.

4. Wilde had been delivering *The Decorative Arts* exclusively since 13 February.

5. Whether he intended to or not, Wilde delivered *The English Renaissance* eleven times between 9 January and 8 February.

until finally I allow them to do as they choose and when I come to lecture I do as I choose."[1]

Reporter—"Would you have any objection to my taking your manuscript for a short time to give extracts of your choicest ideas?"

Oscar—"The childlike simplicity of you gentlemen of the press throughout this entire country is something startling. In my early innocence when I first arrived, I once loaned my manuscript to a reporter; I did not get it back for four days, and it caused me an infinite amount of annoyance before I obtained my property again. Since then I have guarded it myself most rigorously, and have made it my rule never to allow any one to touch it."

At this juncture Oscar himself turned interviewer and suddenly said: "Who is the most interesting person you ever interviewed?" This was rather a sudden jump at an inoffending Bohemian, and for an instant his cheek deserted him and he murmured something about that being "a leading question." After his blushes had subsided the reporter stated that after this noted interview had been filed away in the archives of his memory it would always be a mooted question, whether P. T. Barnum, Forepaugh's $10,000 girl, George Francis Train, Susan B. Anthony, Dr. Mary Walker or his Royal "Nibs," were the most remarkable individuals who had dawned upon the reportorial horizon.[2]

The carriage was then announced and Apostle Oscar drew on an intensely all but overcoat extending to his knees, with a too-too sincere soulful binding of mink fur the entire length, and placing his pickerel-like hand in the reportorial digits, withdrew, and where the sunflower had bloomed was darkness and fleshliness again.

1. Wilde took this up with his manager, Colonel Morse, writing to him in early March: "Kindly see that I am not advertised to lecture on 'The English Renaissance.' I have not delivered that lecture since February 11 [no lecture is known for the 11th; Wilde delivered *The English Renaissance* on the 8th in Buffalo], and yet I am always advertised for it. It is very annoying [...]" (CL, 147).

2. P. T. Barnum (1810–1891) was an American showman and circus owner. He sat in the front row of Wilde's 11 May lecture in New York (Sturgis, 254/242). Adam John Forepaugh (1831–1890) was also a circus owner, and Barnum's main rival. In 1881 he sponsored a $10,000 beauty contest. The winner was Louise Montague, a 21 year old actress from New York. She appeared under Forepaugh's management as the "Queen of Beauty." George Francis Train (1829–1904) was an American entrepreneur and candidate for US president. In 1870 he travelled around the world, a journey that may have inspired Jules Verne's novel *Around the World in Eighty Days*. In the 1870s he became increasingly eccentric and attempted to stand for the position of dictator of the United States, drawing large crowds to his rallies. Susan B. Anthony (1820–1906) was an American abolitionist and women's rights activist. Dr Mary Edwards Walker (1832–1919) was an American surgeon and abolitionist, awarded the Medal of Honor for her efforts to treat wounded civilians during the American Civil War.

"Oscar Interviewed," *The Rockford Daily Gazette* (Rockford, IL), 3 Mar. 1882, 4

The Gazette Reporter talks with Mr. Wilde in Bed,[1] and Ascertains that He Fails to Practice what he Preaches, viz: Aestheticism

A reporter of the GAZETTE called on Oscar Wilde, the aesthetic apostle, at his rooms in the Holland House, this morning. By looking over the house register it was ascertained that his room was No. 29. We rapped at the door of his room, and a voice came from within, "come in."

On entering we found everything in perfect chaos; knee breeches, gaiters, shirts, stockings and shoes scattered indiscriminately about the room, on the chairs and floor.

A something in bed covered with a blue checkered shirt called out, "Pray what do you want, I thought it was me sarvant."

We pulled out our pasteboard, and after looking it over, the object with the hair, for this was about all that could be discerned, except a huge and ungainly mouth, remarked with a broad grin, "Pray, wait until I have finished me breakfast, I have been traveling constantly for months, and would like a short respite. Ca-r-n't you come up in 'arf an 'our?"

We replied that we certainly could and would, and retired with the lasting impression that Oscar was not very aesthetic, nor as neat and tidy as has been reported of him, and that he failed to practice what he preached.

At the appointed time we returned to the room, rapped, and was admitted [*sic*]. Upon entering we were much relieved at the sight, for no longer were the articles scattered about the chairs and floor, everything was in as perfect order as could be under the circumstances, as the room was quite small. Mr. Wilde was dressed in a black velvet smoking jacket, light brown pantaloons, socks of the same color, and patent leather shoes with cloth tops to match the pantaloons. He was just getting ready to depart and had on a seal brown overcoat, lined with fur, with fur collar and cuffs to match.

We were greeted with "Awh! I see, young man, that you are on time, and pray what can I do for you, something aesthetic I suppose."

We asked for his autograph, which was given at once, after giving a volume of directions to his colored servant, and which scrawl is now on exhibition at this office.

In reply to a question whether or not he thought the audience was a small one last evening, replied: "Yes, but very select, and seemed to be composed of your best people, who gave me very close attention throughout. I do not care to

1. Wilde's name is spelt "Wild" throughout.

address idle people, but on the contrary to speak to manufacturers and merchants, of which your beautiful city seems to be well supplied."

He referred to the action of the Harvard students in Boston and said they put their heads in the lion's mouth, and with the same result as might be expected. Their parading was indeed grotesque and was simply a school boy's affair. At Brooklyn the audience in the gallery were ill behaved people and applauded at the wrong points in my speech,[1] but I paid no attention to them and finished my talk without interruption.

The very worst place I have lectured thus far was at Rochester, N. Y., where the audience bellowed, clapped, and acted like a pack of blarsted fools.

At this point we were interrupted by the announcement that the hack was ready, and after a good morning, and cordial shake we left. He took the train for Aurora where he lectures this evening.

"Oscar Wilde in the West," *The New York Herald* (New York, NY), 6 Mar. 1882, 4[2]

(BY TELEGRAPH TO THE HERALD.)

Racine, Wis., March 5 1882.

Oscar Wilde made his first appearance before a Wisconsin audience last night. There were not more than seventy persons in the hall. The Racine College lads had arranged to give him a "sunflower reception," but were deterred by the professors. The lecture was only marked by occasional snickerings of an unappreciative audience. The HERALD correspondent subsequently interviewed Mr. Wilde as to any impression he might have formed of the West. He said:—"I like Chicago even better than Boston, but then I have been to so many incipient little places of late and I am almost worn out with hunger. I love my cigarettes and do not know what I should have done without them. I have not been able to obtain a morsel of food that I liked and have lived on cigarettes." The correspondent then asked him if he had given up his lily and he replied that the lily story was a newspaper joke. He broke down in the midst of his lecture here, saying he was exhausted and could not read his manuscript. He goes to Milwaukee tomorrow.

1. There are no quotation marks in this paragraph to indicate where Wilde's speech begins.
2. H & S, b49. Quoted in OWDA, 215.

"David and Oscar," *The Chicago Sunday Tribune* (Chicago, IL), 5 Mar. 1882, 5[1]

Mr. Wilde Replied to Prof. Swing's Recent Criticism of Him.

Mr. Oscar Wilde was in the city yesterday afternoon, and, understanding that he had something to say in answer to Prof. David Swing's criticism of him, published in a recent number of the *Alliance*,[2] a representative of THE TRIBUNE called on him at the Grand Pacific Hotel. He lectured Friday evening in Aurora, appeared in Racine last evening, and discourses on the beautiful in art to the Philistines of Milwaukee this evening. As Milwaukee has been represented to him as a good town for Sunday shows, he thought he would try his Sunday experiment there first. He greeted the reporter in his usual cordial manner yesterday, and, in answer to a question regarding Prof. Swing's article, he said:

"While in Rockford, Ill., recently, I was informed that an important attack on me had been published by Prof. David Swing, of your city, in a paper called the *Alliance*.[3] I was told that this article has so

INFLUENCED THE PROPRIETRESS OF A LADIES' SCHOOL

there, who had purchased two tickets for my lecture—one for herself and the other for the best behaved pupil—that she returned the tickets to the box office in consequence of Prof. Swing's attack. Of course I felt that any attack which would have such a marked influence on a whole city must be most remarkable and intellectual, and I quite looked forward to the pleasure of reading it this morning, for, next to a staunch friend, the best thing that a man can have is a brilliant enemy. There is nothing more depressing than to be attacked by a fool, as one cannot answer and does not fight with the same weapons.

"I confess, however," he continued with a smile, "to have been greatly disappointed at what I read this morning, because if a man attacks one for the clothes that one likes to wear he should go for his answer to one's tailor, and if a man assails one for the flowers that one admires he should discuss the matter with one's gardener; and, as regards the learned Professor's sneer at me for receiving a fee for lecturing, he is not the first clergyman that has visited me with such a bitter reproach, which derives all its sting from the fact that it comes from a body of men most of whom receives large salaries for preaching

1. H & S, b48. Reprinted in H & S, 95–8. The reporter was accompanied by the authors of "Professor Swing and Oscar," *The Daily Inter Ocean* (Chicago, IL), 6 Mar. 1882, 8, pp. 251–3; and "Wilde and Swing," *The Boston Herald* (Boston, MA), 6 Mar. 1882, 2, pp. 253–4.
2. "Swing's article": See p. 229, note 1.
3. Wilde was told about Swing's article four days before he lectured in Rockford by the author of "Oscar Wilde," *Chicago Evening Journal* (Chicago, IL), 28 Feb. 1882, 1, pp. 227–9.

"As regards his remarks on me, omitting the esthetics of mind and heart," said Mr. Wilde, "as I feel sure that he is too honest an antagonist to wilfully misrepresent one, I can only conclude that he did not attend my lecture. Had he done so he would have seen that I divided my lecture into two portions, in the first of which I dwelt on the necessity of teaching the handicraftsmen to work not only with his hands, as though, indeed, he were a mere machine, but with his head and heart always, for unless a man does so his work will always be commonplace and poor and have no beauty at all in it. I dwelt on the moral education that working in every art would give a man—for all good art is founded on two things—truth and honesty. In the world of business, indeed, the liar and the cheat may escape detection all their lives, but in art it is not so. A workman who is dishonest in his labor or who tells a lie in his art, such as painting wood to represent marble, or staining paper to represent stone, or pretending that the thing is solid when it is probably merely a hollow sham, that man knows that in consequence of it his work is worthless and will not last for any time. So much for those who work in art.

"In the second part of my lecture," said Mr. Wilde, languidly knocking the ashes off his cigarette and throwing away all but the butt, "I treated of those who only look at art, and do not create, or the ordinary man and woman of life, and I showed of what value the refining influence of noble and beautiful art would be to them from their childhood to their manhood, and I spoke of what influence the arts would have in producing between all countries a common intellectual spirit, for no truth of history is clearer than this, that national hatreds are always strongest where civilization is lowest.

"And I acknowledge that I am surprised," continued Mr. Wilde, "to find that

ANYONE WITH THE NAME OF DAVID

should be fighting for the Philistines. He should be taking a pebble from the river brook and hurling it at that monstrous Goliath of Chicago architecture, the water-tower, instead of praising it as being, as he calls it, calm and rational—two most unfortunate epithets.

"But perhaps I am wrong in taking the Professor seriously, for, from what I have seen of American literature, I have found that the sermon of the divine is always humorous and the writings of the humorous always depressing. In my next lecture I hope to dwell at length on the relations between art and morality, which have been so much misunderstood. I lecture at Central Music-Hall in your city next Saturday evening on 'Interior and Exterior House-Decoration.'"

"How have you been pleased with your reception in the smaller towns, Mr. Wilde?" asked the reporter.

"Very well, indeed. In Aurora, where I lectured last evening, they have recently started a decorative art school, and are very enthusiastic."

"In any of the cities which you have visited have art schools been established as a result of your lecture?"

"Oh, yes. In Philadelphia and in some other cities."

"When do you leave this country?"

"I leave about the 1st of May, and go to Paris to visit the salons and see the artists. I shall return to New England and lecture in Boston and some of the New England cities before I sail, however. On leaving Paris I shall travel through England and deliver lectures before the various art schools there."

"Have you ever lectured in England?"

"No, sir. I made my début as a lecturer in New York City."

"Have you ever delivered your Saturday evening's lecture before?"

"No, I have not. In fact, I have not completed it yet. I shall probably deliver it in Boston, but it is not a lecture to give a city at first—I think it best to start by giving the principles of art, and then enter into the details."

"Professor Swing and Oscar," *The Daily Inter Ocean* (Chicago, IL), 6 Mar. 1882, 8[1]

The Apostle is Rather Disappointed Over the Professor's Alliance Article, and Gives Forth No Uncertain Sound.

Professor David Swing's criticism of Oscar Wilde, published in the *Alliance* recently, seems to have been read by the latter and to cause him some annoyance. Mr. Wilde was interviewed by a representative of THE INTER OCEAN on Saturday at the Grand Pacific Hotel in response to a written request from the apostle of the lily and kneebreech.[2] He said: "I lectured in Rockford, Ill., lately, and there learned that Mr. Swing's article had induced the lady principal of a seminary who had purchased a couple of tickets to my lecture to return them to the box office. The audience was small. I felt that an attack that could so influence a whole city must be at least remarkable, and I looked forward to reading it with pleasurable emotions. I usually pay no attention to newspaper ridicule or criticism, and have long ago learned to entirely disregard it. But next to having a stanch [*sic*] friend is

1. Quoted in OWDA, 214–15. The reporter was accompanied by the authors of "David and Oscar," *The Chicago Sunday Tribune* (Chicago, IL), 5 Mar. 1882, 5, pp. 249–51; and "Wilde and Swing," *The Boston Herald* (Boston, MA), 6 Mar. 1882, 2, pp. 253–4.

2. Wilde presumably wrote to all the Chicago papers. He reported in a letter to Colonel Morse dated by Mason to 21 March that the *Chicago Herald* "signified that they would not have any more interviews, that I was seeking notoriety" (CL, 155).

the pleasure of having a brilliant enemy. There is nothing so depressing as to be attacked by a fool, for you cannot answer or fight him with his own weapons."

"You have read the article, then?" said the reporter.

"Yes; but I confess to having been greatly disappointed at Professor Swing's article. If a man attacks one for the clothes that one likes to wear, he should go for his answer to the tailor who made them; and if he assails me for a preference in flowers, he should argue the matter with a gardener. As for his sneer at me for receiving a fee for lecturing, I can assure him that he is not the first clergyman who has thus condemned me. But this shaft loses its sting when I consider that it comes from a body of men, most of whom preach for a salary.

"I can only conclude," continued Mr. Wilde, "that Professor Swing did not attend my lecture. If he had done so he would have seen that I divided it into two parts, in the first of which I dwelt upon the necessity of teaching the handicraftsman to work not only with his hands, like a machine, but with his heart and with his head. If he does not do so his work will be nothing more than commonplace and have no beauty of art in it at all. I dwelt on the moral education that working in every art would give a man the two things upon which all good art is founded—truth and honesty. In the world of business it is possible for the liar and cheat to escape detection all their lives—not so in art. A workman who creates a sham or does dishonest work in his art, such as painting wood to represent marble, or staining paper to represent stone, or pretending that a thing is solid when it is merely a hollow sham, knows that in consequence of it his work is worthless and will not last. In the second part of my lecture I treated of those who only look at art and do not create, the ordinary man or woman of life, and showed of what nature the refining influence of noble and beautiful art would be to them from their childhood to their manhood. I spoke of what influence the arts would have in producing between all countries a common, intellectual spirit, for no truth of history is clearer than this, that national hatreds are always strongest when civilization is lowest. I acknowledge that I am surprised to find that any one with the name of David should be found fighting in the ranks of the Philistines. He ought to take a pebble from the banks of the Chicago River and hurl it at that monstrous Goliath of Chicago architecture, the water-tower, instead of praising it as being, as he calls it, calm and rational. Those two epithets are very unfortunate in this connection. Perhaps I am wrong in taking the Professor seriously, for, from what I have seen of American literature, I have found that the sermon of the divine is always humorous, and the writing of the humorous always depressing. I hope in my next lecture to dwell at length on the relations between art and morality, which have been so much misunderstood."

"When will you lecture here again?"

"Next Saturday evening, in Central Music Hall, on 'Interior and Exterior House Decorations.'"

"Did you ever lecture in England?"
"No; I made my debut as a lecturer in New York City."

"Wilde and Swing," *The Boston Herald* (Boston, MA), 6 Mar. 1882, 2[1]

The Poet's Reply to the Pastor's Criticisms.

(Special dispatch to the Herald.)

CHICAGO, Ill., March 5, 1882. Oscar Wilde was smoking a cigarette when your correspondent saw him this afternoon in a Grand Pacific Hotel parlor.[2] He wore a dove-colored sack coat of velvet, trimmed with drab silk braid, vest to match, pantaloons of light-colored Scotch tweed, shoes of patent leather and very pointed at the toe, neck dress of brilliant red and pocket handkerchief to match. "I am fond of sweet odors, I love perfumery passionately," he remarked as he paid a boy $4 who came into the room bearing six pint bottles of perfumery.[3] Dictating in a deliberate, distinct utterance, he spoke as follows regarding the recent attack upon him in the Alliance: "Knowing of Prof. Swing as a brilliant man, I had hoped that his attack upon me would at least be brilliant; for, next to having a loyal friend, there is for me no pleasure like that to be found in having an intelligent enemy; simply because one can answer him. I was very much disappointed when I read it; for if a man has anything to say against the clothes I wear he should write to my tailor; and if he cares to speak unfavorably of flowers, which I think beautiful, he should address himself to my gardener; and, as regards his solemn attack upon me for receiving fees for the trouble of lecturing, nothing could, of course, be more foolish, coming from a practical man of the world, such as Prof. Swing is said to be. Every man should be paid for the work he does. The bitter reproach which comes from the clergy to me has a grotesque side, when one considers that it comes from a body of men who receive large salaries for

1. The reporter was accompanied by the authors of "David and Oscar," *The Chicago Sunday Tribune* (Chicago, IL), 5 Mar. 1882, 5, pp. 249–51; and "Professor Swing and Oscar," *The Daily Inter Ocean* (Chicago, IL), 6 Mar. 1882, 8, pp. 251–3.

2. Although the report is dated 5 March, the interviewer must have met with Wilde on the 4th and not "this afternoon". Wilde departed for Milwaukee later that day, so was not available to interviewed in Chicago on the 5th.

3. Wilde's second son, Vyvyan, recalled that his father "lived in an aura of cigarette-smoke and eau-de-cologne." (Holland, V. (1954). *Son of Oscar Wilde.* Rupert Hart-Davis. 200.) After his release from prison Wilde described how Robert Ross "detected me at Dieppe in the market place of the sellers of perfumes, spending all my money on orris-root and the tears of the narcissus and the dust of red roses. He was very stern and led me away. I have already spent my entire income for two years." (CL, 855.)

preaching the beauty of voluntary poverty. As regards his statement that I omit to take account of the moral element in art, as I feel sure that he is too honest a man to try to misrepresent me, I can only conclude that he neither attended nor read my lecture. Had he done so, he would have seen that I divided it into two parts. In the first part I said that the moral elements were necessary for good workmanship; that the ordinary workman worked with his hands and his heart, if the work has any beauty at all, and that all good art rests on two things—truth and honesty; that work dishonestly done, or which pretended to be something else than what it really was, such as the painting of wood to represent marble, or the staining of paper to represent stone, was all dead, bad art, quite worthless and very ugly. There is no better school for anybody than is to be found in work in art, for, while in the world about us the cheat and the liar may often go unpunished for a long time, if a man does untruthful work in art, he knows that he is bringing upon himself his own punishment, that he will be found out and won't last. In the second part I dwelt on the effect that art would have on ordinary men and women who do not work in art, but merely enjoy it. I showed what its influence might be on children and that it might have on nations. Now, as regards children, it would teach them to love the beautiful and the good and hate the evil and the ugly quite naturally and simply, the lesson coming to them so unconsciously and in such a joyous way that they would never forget it. As regards the nation, I advance the thought that art, by producing a common intellectual atmosphere, might be laying a sure basis for some universal brotherhood of man and a humanity which would include all patriotism, and I reminded the audience how Goethe had felt this and how he had no surer lesson to show one than that national hatreds are always strongest where civilization is lowest. I am very much surprised that anyone bearing the name of David should be fighting on the side of the Philistines. Rather should he be the first to take the pebble from the river brook and hurl it at that monstrous Goliath of Chicago architecture, the water tower, instead of calling it a calm and rational building—two most unfortunate epithets. But perhaps I am wrong in taking the learned professor so seriously to task, for of what I have read in American literature the sermons of your divines always seem to be humorous, and the writings of your humorists most depressing.

"Oscar Wilde," *Milwaukee Sunday Sentinel* (Milwaukee, WI), 5 Mar. 1882, 6[1]

Arrival in Milwaukee of the Distinguished Apostle of the Beautiful.

How the Sunflower-and-Lily Young Man Looked and What He Had to Say.

A Lecture on Aestheticism This Evening—His Impressions of the Country.

Long on Hair and Short on Breeches the Only Striking Peculiarities.

Oscar Wilde, he of the sunflower and the lily, the distinguished apostle of aestheticism, arrived in Milwaukee on the 11:35 o'clock train last night, and was driven in a closed carriage to the Plankinton House. There a number of men who were anxious to catch a glimpse of the young aesthete were waiting for his arrival, and eyed him critically when he came tripping into the office. The poet presented a striking appearance. He is somewhat tall, but disguises his lanky proportions by rounding his shoulders. His hair, brown, waving and fluffy, was parted in the middle, and fell, like that in the pictures of Charles II., to his shoulders. His face looked forth as between a set of soft window curtains, white, beardless, smiling and mild. The features were of Irish, much toned down, prominent, but not strong. The brow—the little triangular area to be seen of it, that is—was wholly placid and unmarked, and the eyebrows were neat, delicate and arched, and of the sort coveted by women. He was dressed in a traveling suit of some dark material,

BREECHES CUT EN TRAINE,

so to speak, having discarded his short clothes and silk hose, no doubt, on account of the change in the weather.

Oscar Wilde was born in Dublin, Oct. 16, 1855. He is, therefore, 26 years old.[2] His father was Sir William Wilde, of Merrion Square, Dublin. Sir William was a remarkable man. He was a celebrated physician, and widely known through England and on the continent. Lady Wilde, the poet's mother, was fully as remarkable as his father. She was a woman of splendid beauty and conspicuous

1. Quoted in Bobby Tanzio, "Wilde Didn't Impress Milwaukee Much," *On Milwaukee*, 17 Oct. 2004. Much of the *Sentinel* article is taken from earlier interviews. It seems unlikely that Wilde would have agreed to a lengthy interview if, as the author states, he had arrived in Milwaukee at 23:35. The author may have spoken with Wilde briefly and then padded out the interview. As Wilde had claimed earlier, after he talked with American interviewers for a moment they would "go off and write two column interviews" (see "Oscar Wilde," *The Daily Sentinel* (Fort Wayne, IN), 16 Feb. 1882, 3, p. 179).

2. The author may have obtained this information from a previous report, or Wilde had again shaved a year off his age (see p. 25, note 2).

talent. Under the pseudonym of "Speranza," she published several volumes of poems, which demonstrated an undoubted poetic gift, and achieved an honorable place in English literature. He was mostly educated in the colleges of Ireland, entering Magdalen College, Oxford, at the age of 19, graduating with considerable honor in 1878.[1] His literary career at once commenced, and since that time he has been struggling as a disciple of "The Beautiful," and has been lecturing in America for several months past. He will lecture at the Opera House this evening.

HOW HE LOOKED.

After Mr. Wilde had been comfortably settled in one of the elegant parlors of the hotel, a Sunday Sentinel reporter called and paid him his respects. When ushered into the luxurious apartments, Mr. Wilde was found reclining on an easy chair, but arose immediately and crossing the room courteously bade his visitor to remove his wrapping and make himself at home. As he strode toward the reporter, to welcome him, Mr. Wilde's figure is represented in the accompanying cut.[2]

A TALK WITH HIM.

Mr. Wilde talks with ease and there seems to be nothing extraordinary about him, with the exception of his dreamy eyes, somewhat effeminate ways and looks and his long, wavy hair. He said that his stay in America had been made pleasant in many ways and that he was glad to visit Milwaukee, which he had heard spoken of as a beautiful city. The weather permitting he expected to see a good deal of it today.

"Have you seen very many picturesque landscapes in America?"

"Comparatively few. My expectations in this respect have not been realized."

"Mr. Wilde, would you kindly state the purpose of your visit to America, regardless of financial considerations?"

"My purpose in visiting America is to propagate the ideas of the aesthetes of England, of whom I am one.[3] Money is a secondary, if at all a consideration."

"What is the purpose of the aesthetes?"

"That I will state at length in my lecture. I will say, however, that the aesthetic movement has for its object the revolutionizing of English and modern

1. Wilde was awarded his Demyship at Magdalen when aged 19 and matriculated the day after his twentieth birthday (Page, 3–4).

2. The article is accompanied by a stock illustration of a long-haired and moustachioed aesthete, posed in a stained-glass attitude with a sunflower in his hand.

3. As D'Oyly Carte had noted ("D'Oyly Carte and His Plans," *New York Tribune* (New York, NY), 12 Jan. 1882, 8, p. 755), Wilde did not like to refer to himself as an aesthete. The author of this article had no scruples about plagiarising other interviews, and he likely fabricated or rephrased this response.

poetry and painting. The aesthetes are pre-Raphaelites, that is to say, they believe nature to be the most beautiful of all things, and hence adopt it in its most beautiful forms and conditions as a model for their poetry and paintings. The prevailing school in America and that which is fast disappearing in Europe, and in England especially, is opposed to our school and believes the works of man

TO BE MORE BEAUTIFUL

than those of God, who is our teacher."[1]

"By what direct means do you intend to create in American artists a belief in your theories and inculcate in the American people a love for the beautiful?"

"Presumably, by means of my lectures, but my entire plans I have not arranged as yet."

"Do you expect to awaken an interest in this matter among the poor, or even the middle classes, who have not had the advantages of a careful training?"

"Those who have not had the advantages of a careful training," replied Mr. Wilde, "are already displaying the fact and manifesting their interest in the aesthetic movement by displaying in their places of business, or about their uncouth persons, huge pieces of cardboard furnished by quack doctors, whose advertisements they bear, and formed and colored in the resemblance of a sunflower. These too utterly practical (Mr. Wilde smiled) people I have despaired of ever reaching by a direct appeal. The fact is, the mass of Americans seem to be skeptical of all new theories in art, and even seem to be prejudiced against the sentimentalism of their own artists. I must therefore address myself more particularly to those who have cultivated a love of art and the beautiful and who, if they accept my theories, may, in time, influence the masses to the same end."

LILY AND SUNFLOWER.

"Your fondness for the lily and the sunflower has caused some extravagant caricatures."

"Yes, but I assure you they do not disturb me in the least. On the contrary, they are rather amusing. Neither they nor the extravagant and exaggerated opera of 'Patience' can prejudice sensible people against me."

"You have been quoted as saying that the women's dresses in 'Patience' are not exaggerated."[2]

"Oh, the embroidery and paintings on the dresses are made for stage effect, and are larger than are worn in what is called good society; but in design they are correct. 'Patience' has done our cause no harm. Ridicule may be a serious

1. Wilde's invocation of God is uncharacteristic.

2. This and the following question, as well as Wilde's responses, are taken from "A Talk with Wilde," *Philadelphia Press* (Philadelphia, PA), 17 Jan. 1882, 2, p. 75.

weapon, but there should be that in a true poet of a genuine cause which is indestructible, and there is indestructibility in our cause. Oh, no. People understand that 'Patience' is merely a burlesque. I enjoyed it very much. The music is delightful, and that is certainly on our side, even if the words are not."

"Speaking of dresses, how do you like the beauty of their American wearers?"

"I am charmed with American beauty. The women possess a certain delicacy of outline surpassing English women; but the color of English women is richer and warmer, I think. I saw Clara Morris on the stage in New York one evening, and I was delighted with her, as was Sarah Bernhardt, who had told me very much about her charms, and I have met many surpassingly beautiful ladies since my arrival."

MILWAUKEE BELLES.

"By the way," he added, "have you any beautiful women here?"

"Oh, yes," replied the reporter, "we consider ourselves very fortunate in that respect."

"I have been informed that the society of Milwaukee is very good, and that you have many wealthy, fashionable and cultured people here."[1]

Mr. Wilde stated that he had just received a telegram from his American manager, D'Oyly Carte, announcing that the latter had completed arrangements for the presentation of his (Wilde's) drama in New York at an early date, and that Miss Clara Morris would assume the leading character.[2]

"How do you think the West compares with the East?" asked the reporter.

"The West interests us in England more than the East. You are making civilization by yourselves and for yourselves. So much in the East is a mere reflection of European thought, and so much of that a mere misunderstanding of it."[3]

✂ *The remainder of this article is copied verbatim from "Philosophical Oscar,"* The Chicago Times *(Chicago IL), 1 Mar. 1882, 7: read from "The reporter called attention to the reports that Mrs. Langtry and Henry Labouchère were to come to America, and asked him concerning them" (p. 241) to the end of the article.*

1. It does not seem likely that Wilde would have asked after "wealthy" people; he does not do so in any other known interview.

2. Neither D'Oyly Carte nor Morse had "completed arrangements" but there was correspondence at this time about Morris (CL, 150–2), and it is characteristic of Wilde to exaggerate.

3. This paragraph is taken from "Oscar Wilde," *The Chicago Daily Tribune* (Chicago, IL), 1 Mar. 1882, 7, p. 237.

"Oscar's Opinion," *Sedalia Weekly Bazoo* (Sedalia, MO), 14 Mar. 1882, 7[1]

Says the Chicago Herald of yesterday: Oscar Wilde returned to Chicago yesterday. The lecturer has been very successful, pecuniarily, since leaving here, especially at St. Louis and Cincinnati, at both of which places he met crowded houses. At neither, however, did the receipts come up to those of the night when he lectured in this city, although they were satisfactorily large and the management has no cause to be dissatisfied. The reason why the proceeds of the lectures at these places is said to have been less than here is because those who flocked to see the apostle of culture were for the most part not willing to pay for the highest priced seats.

"I am glad to see you back in Chicago," said the reporter, as he entered his presence. "I think that the readers of the Herald would be glad to read another interview with you. Have you returned here to lecture?"

"I shall lecture a second time in Chicago on next Saturday week."[2]

"You have been to St. Louis and Cincinnati?"

"Yes."

"Did you like those places?"

"Yes; especially Cincinnati."

"Oscar Wilde," *The Jacksonville Daily Journal* (Jacksonville, IL), 8 Mar. 1882

The Lecture at the Opera House Last Night by the English Aesthetic.

Decorative Art Treated of by the Poet and Philosopher.

✂ *A report of Wilde's lecture in Jacksonville.*

Oscar Wilde's Movements

Mr. Oscar Wilde arrived in the city yesterday morning, coming here direct from Chicago. From here he goes to Decatur, to lecture there. In Chicago, as he informs us, he had a pleasant meeting with Rev. Henry Ward Beecher, and accepted an invitation to visit him in his Hudson river home in May.[3]

1. The *Bazoo's* source in the *Chicago Herald* is untraced.

2. Wilde lectured for the second time in Chicago on Saturday 11 March, when he gave his new lecture, *The House Beautiful*.

3. Wilde lectured almost every day in May and will have had to make his apologies to Beecher. Beecher invited Wilde again in July (CL, 177–8).

"Our Aesthetic Visitor," *The Daily Republican* (Decatur, IL), 8 Mar. 1882, 3

✂ *A paragraph puffing Wilde, seemingly drawn from advertising materials provided by his management.*

A REPUBLICAN interviewer found Mr. Wilde in room 72 at the New Deming Hotel this afternoon. He is a young man of fine physique, tall, large head, high forehead, long brown hair parted in the middle, and languid eyes. He wore a Seymour velvet coat with a purple handkerchief peeping out of the left hand upper pocket, and a tie of the same colour appeared at his neck. The young Englishman, who is a graduate of Oxford, is one of the finest conversationalists the writer has ever met. He talks fluently, has a fine command of language, and loves to converse principally about art and her devotees. He wanted to know at parting if there were any lovers of the beautiful in nature and the decorative art in Decatur, and fortunately the scribe was able to answer that there were "quite a number, and that no doubt a few of them would avail themselves of the opportunity to hear your lecture this evening." While in Chicago, the other day, Mr. Wilde met Henry Ward Beecher, whom Oscar thinks a capital good fellow – a man with whom it is indeed a pleasure to associate and converse. After closing his lecture engagements in America, he will return to England and spend the month of May in Paris.

"Gush and Greed," *The Daily Republican* (Decatur, IL), 9 Mar. 1882, 3[1]

Oscar Wilde, the Traveling Aesthete, in Decatur—His Personal Appearance, and the Talk.

Mr. Oscar Wilde, the aesthetic bundle of egotism from England, who has an unmistakeable and vulgar greed for American dollars, filled his appointment to "lecture" at the opera house in this city last evening. It was not expected that Oscar would be greeted by a large or enthusiastic audience, because westerners are not given to running after long-haired novelties, no matter what ism they may represent. The residents of Decatur are distinctively a discriminating people, and pretenders and egotists generally look upon vacant chairs when the curtain rises in our temple of music and comedy. The audience which greeted Oscar last night numbered less than 125 people, and was made up principally of members

1. Excerpted in Cooper (Decatur lecture, 8 March 1882).

of the two art classes in this city and the curious, who went to the hall expecting to be dreadfully bored, and a few of them were not disappointed, though they lingered until the snob had made his farewell aesthetic bow.

✂ *A report of Wilde's lecture in Decatur.*

Oscar told a reporter that he thought the provincial cities in Illinois very commonplace towns, and asked his visitor if he didn't feel bored living in such a small place—a town where he said there was "no opportunity to mingle with men of art, of science and of letters." He said *he* couldn't exist in such a town. What an unfortunate lot of people we Decaturites must be as seen through Wilde's telescope.

On the rostrum Wilde poses and talks gushingly, and has nothing to say that will particularly offend his hearers, but taken aside and alone, he is the queerest piece of humanity that ever struck Decatur. In private he assumes the manner of the pampered English swell and will talk about little else except the nobility and his art. Everything else is commonplace and vulgar to him, except perhaps American dollars.

The polished fraud departed for Peoria early this morning. He will lecture in Chicago on Saturday night on "Interior and Exterior House Decorations."

"Oscar Wilde," *The Daily Leader* (Bloomington, IL), 10 Mar. 1882, 4[1]

The Leader Interviews the Famous Exponent of Aestheticism.

Oscar Wilde, the latest and greatest furore in the modern lecture field, arrived from Peoria at 11:30 this forenoon and was installed in No. 9 at the Ashley. This afternoon a LEADER representative called on the gentleman in the interest of the reading public and for personal satisfaction. In response to a cordial "come in," the writer opened the door and stepped into the presence of a handsome specimen of physical development, tall with broad shoulders, full chest and well rounded neck—a smooth face, effeminate, perhaps, in some of its outlines, but beaming with intelligence, strongly marked by a tolerably prominent nose, and large, expressive eyes and lighted by an almost perpetual smile, revealing large but even and not ungainly teeth. His hair is long and flowing, parted hardly in the middle, and completes a picture resembling the engraving of prominent characters of past ages. He wore a brown velvet sack coat, black pants cut in the prevailing fashion, and patent leather shoes, while a light blue tie caught in a sailor

1. Quoted in *Decatur Daily Republican* (Decatur, IL), 14 Mar. 1882, 3.

knot and a handkerchief of a corresponding hue protruding from a side pocket were the utter features of his wardrobe. He was reclining on a sofa in the center of the room confronting a small table covered with writing material. Other articles of the room were a mammoth fur coat, a satchel and a handsome morocco case, containing sundry bottles, which, perhaps in turn contained diverse spiritous concoctions. There was an air of delicious languor in the appearance of the room which was in keeping with the character of the occupant. Mr. Wilde received THE LEADER man kindly and gracefully entered into an easy flowing conversation developing a number of interesting facts without a very severe application of the press pump. His experience in traveling to the small cities of the West through the monotonous prairie country had been anything but pleasurable. He considered the inevitable jostle against the rabble, and the draughts from the constantly opening doors at way stations as "dreadfully dreadful." He is considering an extremely flattering offer to visit California, but the dread of the long and wearisome ride is weighing in the balance against an acceptance. He goes from here to Chicago, by request, to deliver a new lecture which he has prepared while traveling, and thence projects a tour of the Canadas. He inquired the writer's opinion of Anna Dickinson's "Hamlet," and thought that it must necessarily be shockingly defective.[1] He spoke very kindly of Booth, whom he had seen frequently on the stage in London, and whom he pronounced a "charming fellow, with such a handsome face."

Mr. Wilde is a personal friend of Irving, the pet English actor, and said that the latter had assured him that he would make an American tour, but feared that the people would not like his voice and certain mannerisms peculiar to the London stage.

The reporter innocently mentioned the name of Mrs. Langtry, the English beauty, whose prominence in the London papers for a few years past has rivaled the Queen, and whose advent on the stage is the absorbing topic, and evidently awakened a responsive chord in the bosom of Mr. Wilde, who by the way is quite intimate with the charming lady. He said that he had remained in London a month longer than he had originally intended in order to witness her debut. He considered her the most promising debutante on the modern English stage and was quite rapturous in describing her qualities. He says she will visit America

1. Anna Elizabeth Dickinson (1842–1932) was an American orator and lecturer, famous as the first woman to deliver a political address before the United States Congress. Although not known as an actor, she appeared as *Hamlet* for one night only on 8 March 1882 at the Opera House in Bloomington. Wilde was lecturing in Decatur that evening and so was unable to attend. The *Leader* of 9 March declared that Dickinson's performance was "excellent and pleasing in many respects [...] but as an interpretation of Hamlet it is entirely inadequate and effeminate," and lamented that she had not stuck to the lecture platform "instead of descending to stage mediocrity".

professionally. The genial Oscar seemed to disparage American scenery and by way of a "corker," the writer mentioned Niagara Falls, and paused for the effect. Mr. Wilde laughed pleasantly, and said that from above the view was too unbroken, and was sadly defective as an ideal of grandeur, but from below, the view was both captivating and imposing.

Mr. Wilde spoke in the highest terms of the American women and their efforts to cultivate true art, but had little to say of the men, and laughed heartily at the newspapers.

The writer left the presence of the aesthetic young poet with the opinion that he is nobody's fool, being a young gentleman of superior education and culture, but with an eye to the main chance and his making a fortune out of the credulity of his fellow creatures.

"Oscar Wilde," *The Minneapolis Tribune* (Minneapolis, MN), 16 Mar. 1882, 6[1]

Oscar Wilde, "the apostle of beauty," and the most talked about young man of the day, arrived in Minneapolis from Chicago yesterday afternoon and registered at the Nicollet. Seeing his name in the hotel register a TRIBUNE reporter concluded to pay this "ultra-poetical, super-aesthetical, out-of-the-way young man,"[2] a visit and sent in his card. He was at once informed that Mr. Wilde was "at home" and almost before he knew it was ushered into the parlor where the celebrity was sitting. The sight that met the reporter's eyes when he entered the room was "quite too utterly utter," and nearly took his breath away. Mr. Wilde was reclining upon a handsome fur robe carelessly thrown upon a lounge. He was dressed in a black velvet "cutaway" coat and vest, tightly fitting pantaloons of a light brown color, patent leather shoes and brown stockings. His vest was cut very low and displayed a good deal of a shirt front, which the bell-boy who escorted the reporter to the room swore positively was "frescoed." A low turn down collar and a light blue cravat completed his by no means unbecoming attire. His "bonnie locks," which were parted in the middle, fell to his shoulders, but the fact that he was slightly pigeon toed detracted somewhat from his lion like appearance. He arose in a languid manner to greet the reporter, extending a "lily white hand," speaking with a slight drawl with a strong English accent. Seeing that it was too late to back out the reporter assumed as aesthetic a position as he knew how and entered into conversation with Mr. Wilde.

1. H & S, b52. Referenced in OWDA, 223.
2. How Bunthorne describes himself in *Patience*.

WILDE STATEMENTS.

In the course of his remarks Mr. Wilde said that hitherto England had not expected much of this country from an aesthetic standpoint. In fact she could not, logically. Now, however, the great questions were settled; the war was over; and Europe generally felt interested in the question as to whether or not this country would become civilized. According to Mr. Wilde if this country wants to be civilized she must give herself up to art. Industry without art is barbarism.[1] When asked what the object of his visit to this country was he stated that it was to create and foster a love for the beautiful, which he thought was greatly needed. The West, he said, was the place which attracted the eyes of Europe as the East was a copy of England. He could not understand Americans, nor the gap that existed between the literature of the country and the people. Americans lived seriously, but never wrote of life seriously. Though simple and crude they had some elements of greatness about them and he felt hopeful concerning their future.

✂ *A report of Wilde's lecture in Minneapolis.*

A CLOSING VENTURE.

It is understood that the gentleman under whose auspices Mr. Wilde came here is decidedly out of pocket by this speculation. Mr. Wilde charges $250 a night expenses for inculcating a love for the beautiful among our "peasantry,"[2] and it is doubtful if the receipts amounted to $200. This will, therefore, probably be the only time that Mr. Wilde will favor Minneapolis with his presence. He lectures in St. Paul this evening, after which he goes to Omaha, and thence to the Pacific coast to weep on the bosom of Joaquin Miller.[3]

1. Art and barbarism: see p. 117, note 1.

2. During the lecture Wilde was reported to have "dilated upon the necessity of teaching our 'handicraftsmen' and 'peasantry' the beautiful in art". Wilde's parents repeatedly refer to "peasants" in their books about Ireland. See also "Chats With Celebrities," *Hearth and Home* (London, UK), 30 June 1892, 219–20, p. 799.

3. Wilde never returned to Minneapolis. He lectured on *The Decorative Arts* at the Opera House, St. Paul, on 16 March 1882, and at Boyd's Opera House, Omaha, on 21 March 1882.

"The Apostle of Aestheticism," *St. Paul Pioneer Press* (St. Paul, MN), 16 Mar. 1882, 6[1]

He was Greeted by an Audience of Only Fair Proportions Last Evening, and Delivered His Lecture on the English Renaissance in a Monotonous Tone to a Curious Audience.

Oscar Wilde, the aesthete arrived from Chicago yesterday afternoon, and was assigned to room No. 113 at the Nicollet, where an interviewer was cordially greeted by him. Mr. Wilde, in the course of conversation, gave expression to remarks not particularly differing from those contained in interviews in other cities, and heretofore printed in the PIONEER PRESS. Mr. Wilde, as he stepped from the train, was dressed in the dark green coat with a fur collar so frequently described in the newspapers, and was the object of much curious interest.

✂ *A report of Wilde's lecture in Minneapolis.*

"An Aesthete in Undress," *The Sioux City Daily Journal* (Sioux City, IA), 21 Mar. 1882, 3[2]

Oscar Wilde as He Is When Off the Lecture Platform—Views and Raiment of the Apostle of the Beautiful.

The aesthetic-minded reporter called around yesterday forenoon to pay his respects to Oscar Wilde. On applying to the clerk at the Hubbard house he was told that Mr. Wilde's servant would take up his card. The servant indicated sat by the office stove, and was a likely-looking young man with just a tinge of the warm color of the tropics on his intelligent face. So this point is settled that the aesthetic thing in body-servants is the light mixed liver. Ere long the servant returned. Mr. Wilde would see the gentleman, he said, and the reporter followed to the floor above, and was ushered into the presence.

Mr. Wilde greeted the man of the pencil kindly, in fact much as a forgiving maiden aunt might have done. His demeanor throughout was ladylike, and his talk garnished with modest old English confidences. He expressed his surprise at finding a daily paper in so small a town, and his subsequent talk betrayed no hint that he had read THE JOURNAL'S railroad news. He had been riding in a carriage through the country back of the town the day before, he said, and found the brown prairies so somber and lonely. They are so different from England, where

1. H & S, b51.
2. H & S, b53. Quoted in OWDA, 226–7.

the grass is green, even in winter. But he preferred the west to the east. New England is much like old England, and being a copy is of course uninteresting, as copies must be. But if he were to live in this country away from civilization, from London, he would live in the mountains. He anticipated much pleasure in his trip to Colorado, where he was going, and was enthusiastic in the distant view of San Francisco, that city looking toward the east, toward Asia.

Of his mission Oscar Wilde spoke briefly, kindly reserving that for a paid lecture. The people of this country understood making money, but do not know how to spend it. The rich man builds a hideous square house of marble, at an immense expense, and there settles down for the rest of his life. This was because his knowledge of the beautiful was limited. In England the science of the beautiful is cultivated. The museum at South Kensington is supported by the government at great expense, and to it come artisans—carpenters, furniture makers, and every kind of workmen, to take notes and improve their taste.[1]

In no country did the artisan—and Mr. Wilde divided the word to show that the mechanic has to do with art—occupy so low a place as in America. It is the ambition of parents that their sons be physicians, or clergymen, or professional men of some kind, but not artisans. This was because due importance was not attached to art in everyday life. A lamp-post made 200 years ago was an object of beauty because the artisan who formed it had good designs to work from. Mr. Wilde complimented the Cincinnati School of Design and the Cooper Institute at New York.[2] He wondered that a great city like Chicago had nothing of that sort. He had suggested, in his second lecture in Chicago, a museum where artisans could be instructed, and thought that something of that kind would be opened.[3]

While inducting this aestheticism into the newspaper man, Oscar Wilde occasionally moistened his wrists in a preoccupied way with perfume from a tiny flat vial. His large, liquid eyes rolled upward at times as he became interested, something as a school girl's when she speaks to an intimate friend of her latest love affair. The full, ripe cheeks and long chin of the apostle of the beautiful seemed alike guiltless of razor or beard. The heavy black hair that was pushed back and fell almost to the shoulders, was not parted exactly in the middle, but careless like, a little to one side. Soft leather slippers, void of heel backs, and

1. The South Kensington Museum, now the Victoria and Albert Museum, was opened in 1857. It is a museum of applied and decorative arts and design.

2. The Cooper Union for the Advancement of Science and Art was founded in 1859 by industrialist Peter Cooper (1791–1883).

3. Wilde was reported to have said in his second lecture in Chicago: "[...] there should be established in all the great American cities museums where artisans and handicraftsmen might study the styles and patterns of the noble designers and artisans who had worked before them. [...] From such a museum workmen could learn more in a year or two than in a lifetime at books." ("Oscar Wilde," *The Chicago Daily Tribune* (Chicago, IL), 12 Mar. 1882, 5.)

navy-blue hose-silk, apparently, and embroidered with simple golden daisies—ornamented his ample feet. The knee breeches were not visible, nor in fact much of any garment excepting a dressing gown of some dark woollen stuff, with facings of flame-colored silk. A flowing silk tie, of color to match, completed the costume. Neither the tie nor dressing gown were unaesthetically new or tidy, but rather in old English disorder, as it were.

But seriously, Mr. Wilde is a most entertaining talker. His words come mellow and rippling like a meadow brook in his own England. Judging from his conversation—and one cannot hear him without believing that he is honest and in earnest—he has read nothing, knows nothing, cares nothing for the ridicule that crowds the press and convulses the street. Only once did he allude to it slightly, and then only to say that the art movement was not understood. What strikes one most forcibly is utter absence of anything masculine in the appearance of the man. Not only his voice and countenance, but his unconscious enthusiasm, his gentleness, his way of arriving at a conclusion, all seem to belong to the sex of which he is the admirer, and by which he is admired. Oscar Wilde is very different from other men.

"Oscar Wilde," *The Omaha Daily Herald* (Omaha, NE), 22 Mar. 1882, 8[1]

The Famous Aesthetic Poet and His Visit to Omaha

His Earnest and Instructive Lecture on "Decorative Art"—A "Herald" Interview With the Leader of "the Artistic Movement"—A Pleasant Greeting Given Him.

Oscar Wilde, the aesthetic poet and leader of what is termed "The Artistic Movement," delivered his lecture on "Decorative Art" at Boyd's opera house last evening, under the auspices of the Social Art club.[2] There was a large audience composed of our best people, with numbers from Lincoln and from Council Bluffs.

✂ *A report of Wilde's lecture in Omaha.*

OSCAR WILDE INTERVIEWED.

Mr. Wilde and his servant and Mr Vale, his business manager, arrived in Omaha yesterday from Sioux City and ensconced themselves at the Withnell

1. H & S, b54. Reprinted with omissions in "Oscar's Arrival," *The Daily Nebraska State Journal* (Lincoln, NE), 23 Mar. 1882, 4; and in Mikhail, 58–9. The version that appeared in the *Weekly Herald* on 24 March is reprinted in H & S, 98–100; and quoted in Ellmann, 182/191.

2. Omaha's Social Art Club was founded in 1881 and staged its first exhibition in May 1882.

house. The day without the four walls of the hotel was blustering and the wind swept occasional eddies of dust along the streets, rendering it very disagreeable for any one not habituated to the climate who should venture out.

Consequently when THE HERALD ambassador was admitted to Mr. Wilde's presence toward evening after sending up his card, he found that gentleman not prepared to speak advisedly upon the architecture of or other salient points of Omaha and the conversation was rather general in its scope. *En passant*, it may be remarked for the edification of those who desire to know how Mr. Wilde exemplifies his ideas of dress in private life, that his negligee consists of a black velvet jacket, dark trousers, leather gaiters faced with yellow cloth, and that a maroon silk scarf is tied at his throat and a handkerchief of like color and material peeps from the breast pocket of his jacket.

IMPRESSIONS OF THE WEST.

One of the first questions put by the HERALD representative was:

"How do you find our western cities?"

"You have not the lower orders of the eastern cities," replied Mr. Wilde. "I find less prejudice and more simple and sane people." He added, however, "The west part of America is really the part of the country that interests us in England less, because it seems to us that it has a civilization that you are making for yourselves and by yourselves—not the complementary echo of British thought."[1]

AMERICAN ARCHITECTURE.

"You have pronounced ideas upon our architecture."

"I find in all the eastern cities these general characteristics: the fault in American architecture is in an entire want of any definite conception of what style is suitable for your cities. The architecture should be as universal as the country and as easily understood. Most of the buildings are mere constructions of incongruous anachronisms."

A LIFE'S AMBITIONS.

"You have plans for future work, I presume?"

"For my life, do you mean?" and Mr. Wilde laughed merrily and lighted a cigarette as he threw himself back in his chair. "Well, I'm a very ambitious young man. I want to do everything in the world. I cannot conceive of anything that I do not want to do. I want to write a great deal more poetry. I want to study painting more than I've been able to. I want to write a great many more plays, and I want to make this artistic movement the basis for a new civilization."

1. The reporter almost certainly misheard Wilde. Elsewhere Wilde consistently expressed the opposite opinion: that he was more interested in the west than the east of America.

"THE ARTISTIC MOVEMENT."

"That is the highest and greatest of all your ambitions, I take it," said the interviewer. "But do you consider that there is an organized aesthetic school?"

Mr. Wilde replied: "There is a definite school of criticism and of attitude toward art. Up to this in England we have always had great artists, great portrait painters—for instance, in the last century; and the great landscape painters at the beginning of this age. But there has been an entire want of any concentration of artistic power. The great men stood, as it were, in a sort of sublime isolation, and their work was not understood by the common people and so not loved by them; and so both sides suffered, the artists missing the sympathy to which all artists are so sensitive; and the people not understanding their work. We, on the other hand, are concentrating all the stylistic genius of England, so that each art will gain and learn so much from its brother arts that the people will understand and love art more; for the decorative arts will indeed become part of their daily life. It will make beautiful the common vessels of the house, and it will become so natural to beautify their surroundings that even if the people wish to escape from it they will not be able.

"We also are making our artisans artists by giving them beautiful designs and noble models,—for all the decorative arts of England have been gradually falling into disuse and nothing that was made for the ordinary service of the house was either honestly made or beautiful. We look to this as the real strength of our movement. It is indeed to become a part of the people's life. It must begin not in the scholar's study—not even in the studio of the great artist, but with the handicraftsmen always. And by handicraftsmen I mean a man who works with his hands; and not with his hands merely, but with his head and his heart. The evil that machinery is doing is not merely in the consequences of its work but in the fact that it makes men themselves machines also. Whereas, we wish them to be artists, that is to say men. Now you see what we want.

AUDIENCES IN THE WEST.

"How do your audiences in the west impress you?" asked the interviewer.

"I should never wish—and no man could—to have a better audience, more simple, more understanding, more quick in their appreciation than the audiences I had in Chicago, Cincinnati and many of the western cities."

CONCERNING PHYSICAL BEAUTY.

Mr. Wilde remarked that he had seen many men of marvelous physique and many beautiful women in the west and this elicited his opinion that "Physical beauty is really, absolutely the basis of all great and strong art."[1] He believes, too, that all true art work must be wrought by healthy and happy men and women.

"Oscar's Expectations," *The Omaha Daily Bee* (Omaha, NE), 23 Mar. 1882, 5[2]

He Pines For a Sight of the Wild Jack Rabbit and Army Mule.

Oscar Wilde left on the noon train yesterday for San Francisco, accompanied by his manager Mr. Vale.

Speaking to THE BEE reporter, Mr. Wilde said he presumed he had a very tedious and monotonous ride before him. On being told that the rugged mountain scenery was very fine, he said, "Oh! How very, very beautiful that will be. Will we see any wild animals—from the cars I mean?"

"Oh yes!" was the answer, "you will see Jack rabbits between here and Cheyenne, and herds of antelope on the mountains, with here and there a drove of grizzly bears, buffalo and Rocky mountain lions."[3]

"How unutterably lovely," said the poet, "Is it really so. That will be too beautiful."

The disciple of aestheticism was not dressed in a very tasteful style and looked like "Big Nose George," the famous mountain bandit,[4] but his voice was mild and pleasant and his smile childlike and bland. He is anything but good looking and in his fur collared overcoat, slouched white hat, gray velvet coat and light gray pants and a faded red ribbon at his throat, he looked like a travel stained tourist. He will stop at various places in his return from the coast, having an immense number of engagements on the books already.

1. For Wilde on the relationship between physical beauty and art, see p. 161, note 2.

2. Quoted in OWDA, 231.

3. *Appleton's General Guide to the United States of America* (1879) reports that, in Nebraska, rail passengers could see antelope and prairie-dogs; the hills adjacent to the route in Wyoming abounded in mountain-sheep, antelopes, and bears (355–6).

4. George Parrot, aka Big Nose George (1837–1881), was a cattle rustler and highwayman of the American west.

[Ed. Berne], "Words with Wilde," *Ogden Daily Herald* (Ogden, UT), 25 Mar. 1882, 3[1]

Opportune Observations of the Original Oscar.

Oscar Wilde arrived in Ogden on Friday evening on the eastern express train.[2] A large number of people were at the depot anxious to get a glimpse of him. They went because they were full of curiosity and desirous to see for themselves the man whom the American press has so ridiculed. Upon arrival he was immediately engaged in conversation with a fellow countryman (an Irishman) of Ogden, who held him the greater part of the time until supper.

Mr. Wilde is a young man, above the average height. He has long dark-brown hair, which is parted in the middle, and hangs down over the neck and shoulders. His eyes are large and full; they are of a mild, dreamy, poetic cast, yet bright and wonderfully alert. His face is clean-shaven; when he smiles he shows his upper teeth which, in connection with his long face, gives him the appearance of

A BASHFUL SIMPLETON.

He wore a green-colored overcoat lined around the neck and in front with fur. A red silk tie and a turndown collar adorned his neck. His pantaloons were gray as was also his broad slouch hat; his apparel would go well with a Wasatch cow-boy.[3] The boots he wore were nicely polished, were pointed in the toe, all of which gave an English aristocratic appearance to his dainty feet.

When the conversation began to lag, and when the crowd became too numerous around the stove of the waiting room, where he had been standing, he asked his Irish friend for some "Mormon" publications; he was then taken up to the news stand of Mr. AH. Low and shown the "Book of Mormon" and other works.

THE OGDEN HERALD

was also handed to him with which he expressed himself highly pleased, saying, "A very fine papah. Is it Mormon?" He was told it was, and was then handed other Territorial papers, all of which he carefully folded and put away for reference.

1. H & S, b55. The author identifies himself in his later account of the same interview: Ed. Berne, "'Ed. Berne' and Oscar Wilde," *The Logan Leader* (Logan, UT), 7 Apr. 1882, 4, p. 274. Berne wrote a regular letter to *The Logan Leader*.

2. Friday 24 March.

3. The Wasatch Range is a mountain range that runs from northern to central Utah, and is to the east of Ogden.

While in conversation here, he was handed a bunch of cigarettes one of which he took, lit, and smoked, with the remark to those who offered him, "You are very kind." When the curiosities of Mr. Low's shop has been shown him, he was taken to the dining room where it is probable he ate a lily and gazed upon a glass of water.

When he returned from supper he was tackled by a HERALD man. His eyes did not look calm when he saw he had been tracked, but he smiled an aesthetic smile, shook hands with the reporter, and

THE FOLLOWING CONVERSATION

took place:

Reporter:—You are on your way to Salt Lake, as I learn from the papers of that city?

Oscar Wilde:—That is a mistake, I go direct to San Francisco.

R.—How long will you remain?

O. W.—The tour will occupy about three weeks during which time it is expected I will visit many of the cities on the Western coast. I will lecture in all I visit, hence will be kept very busy, but am in hopes that time will be given to visit the Yosemite Valley and other places of beauty and interest before leaving for the East.[1]

R.—Will you visit Salt Lake on your return trip?

O. W.—Am not prepared to say, but should very much like to, as I should hate to leave America without having seen that city.[2]

Here Mr. Wilde again questioned the reporter. He asked if there were

ANY FLOWERS

in this country, what they were called, and whether they grew in abundance. Also if the woods abounded in fierce wild animals and game. When he was told that the bear, wild cat, deer, prairie chicken, &c., were quite numerous, he said with a fancy gesture and a poetic voice, "O, I should so very much like to hunt through the wild-woods and the mountains."[3]

This outburst of enthusiasm was not manifested, however, until after the reporter had said that if his arrival here had been about two months later the valley would have been much more beautiful. The meadows then bloomed. The willow branches hung in lines and vied with the bending grass to kiss the brooks

1. Wilde toured California for two weeks and not three. He lectured almost every day, and would not have had the time to visit Yosemite. See also "Rare Oscar Wilde," *The Stockton Daily Evening Mail* (Stockton, CA), 4 Apr. 1882, 3, p. 321.

2. Wilde lectured on *The Decorative Arts* in Salt Lake City's Salt Lake Theatre on 10 April 1882.

3. As a young man Wilde had enjoyed hunting (CL, 31).

which, tripping over their pebbled beds, decked leaves and flowers and grass with crystal pearls, that shone

LIKE GOLDEN DROPS

resplendent in the sun. Then each breeze that fanned the earth brought scents from wild-flowers that blossomed over meads of waving green, while sweet-songed birds resounded their morning lays tuning one's ears to the sounds of melody.

R.—How do you like the western country as far as you have gone?

O. W.—The country, this side of the Mississippi, for a long distance I did not like so well, but that which we have traveled over, today, is grand. I like the air; it is so fresh and free. I rode on the platform, all day. The sky is so clear; (enthusiastically).[1] I like the gray stones and the high hills. It must be a beautiful country when the vegetation is growing, considering the delight variations and beauties as it is today [*sic*].

R.—I see by the papers that you were to lecture in Denver, Colorado. How do you like that place?

O. W.—The papers say a great many things of me that are not true. I have lectured in no place west of Omaha.[2]

R.—When do you return to England?

O. W.—Very likely I will return in May, but will first visit the New England States and Canada.[3]

At this juncture the time was up, and it was necessary that Mr. Oscar Wilde should

GET READY

for the westbound train; he, therefore, grasped the hand of the reporter and bid goodbye, not, however, before the latter had expressed a desire to have him stay in Ogden and lecture on his return from the Coast, to which desire Mr. Wilde partially yielded, stating, "I shall be glad to do so, if it can be made possible on my return."[4]

1. *Personal Impressions of America*: "The atmosphere was so abnormally clear that they had no vistas at all, and everything looked like a gigantic foreground. So clear, in fact, was the atmosphere that, looking down the street, I could see to read the names on a brass door plate two and a half miles away." (Dibb, 236.)

2. Wilde lectured in Denver and other cities in Colorado on his return from California, between 10 and 15 April.

3. Wilde made his first tour of Canada between 15 and 31 May. He briefly visited New England a couple of times in the following months, toured there for a week in late September, and then spent early October in the Canadian Maritimes.

4. Wilde did not lecture in Ogden.

Ed. Berne, "'Ed. Berne' and Oscar Wilde," *The Logan Leader* (Logan, UT), 7 Apr. 1882, 4[1]

EDITOR LEADER:—Oscar Wilde the darling Aesthete passed through our city on Friday, the 24th, on his way to San Francisco. He is the son of Sir William Wilde who was an eminent oculist, and surgeon oculist to Queen Victoria. His mother was a poetess and novelist. Oscar had splendid school opportunities, but neither at school nor college did he manifest much ability.[2] During the last three years he has been the leader of a class of persons in London society who profess to find the secret of life in beauty, and who spend their time, or fancy they do, in the enjoyment of the beautiful where less gifted mortals fail to find it. Some months ago he published a volume of poems which contained some good verses, but was quite severely condemned by some critics. He has been in the United States since Jan 2, 1882.

✂ *Two paragraphs that are identical to those in [Ed. Berne], "Words with Wilde,"* Ogden Daily Herald *(Ogden, UT), 25 Mar. 1882, 3, from "Mr. Wilde is a young man" to "all of which gave an English aristocratic appearance to his dainty feet." (p. 271.)*

He was tackled by your reporter, after he had dined (after Mr. Wilde had dined. Reporters never dine, they eat when they get a chance.) A long interview was had during which the aesthete said he would be absent on the coast about three weeks; that he liked our western country very much; that the papers told many untruths about him; that he would not visit Salt Lake; that he had lectured in no place this side of Omaha; that when he returned in May he would visit Canada. He also asked numerous questions about flowers, horses, and wild animals in Utah. We gave him a vivid description of the country that we had learned from some book when we were young, which so fascinated him that he paced up and down exclaiming, enthusiastically, "O, I should so very much like to seek the lair of the fierce Wasatch bear, and over the lovely glade track the wild sage hen." Ed. and Oscar then clasped hands and parted friends forever.

✂ *Several paragraphs that are unrelated to Wilde.*

ED. BERNE.
OGDEN, March 27th, 1882.

1. Although this article partially repeats Berne's longer account in [Ed. Berne], "Words with Wilde," *Ogden Daily Herald* (Ogden, UT), 25 Mar. 1882, 3, pp. 271–3, it is included here because there is some unique material.

2. On the contrary, Wilde excelled at school and university (Sturgis, 27/33, 35–6/40–1, 129/126.

[J. A. Woodson], "Oscar Arrives," *The Daily Record-Union* (Sacramento, CA), 27 Mar. 1882, 3[1]

THE APOSTLE OF ESTHETICISM TALKS PLAINLY.

He Develops as the Poor Man's Friend—What He Believes—The Creed of His Religion.

As a fitting introduction to the apostle of modern estheticism, a RECORD UNION representative yesterday morning met Oscar Wilde at the depot with a bouquet of the choicest flowers that could be culled from Sacramento's floral wealth, and being received by that gentleman with cordiality, the twain sat down to breakfast and had a chat, which, being unconcluded when train time was up, the apostle and the news-gatherer, having found themselves upon pleasantly-debatable ground, continued the conversation in the cars as they went Bayward.[2] Mr. Wilde is one of the

BEST TALKED ABOUT MEN

Of the day. This cultured young English poet is, his friends claim, the most misrepresented of foreigners that ever visited the country. The Oxonian, who is a genial companion and an admirable conversationalist, showed no disinclination to unbosom himself, and the determination being announced to give him for once a perfectly "fair show" in a representative American newspaper, responded to the questions propounded to him with ready fluency and sincere earnestness. He is scarcely 26 years of age, very tall and quite slender. This "build" gives him the appearance of slightly stooping in the shoulders when he addresses men of ordinary stature. He dresses plainly, to severity, indulges in a broad turn-down collar, a simple knotted scarf without jewelry, and wears a broad-brimmed white sombrero decidedly Spanish in style. His clean-shaven face is long, broadest at the lower jaw, with a full, round and over-sized chin; a large and well-developed nose, a broad mouth, with full lips opening over large, prominent teeth, the upper lip a shade too short, and eyes very full, large and handsome and an apology between gray and blue, are arched by delicately lined eyebrows. His forehead is

1. H & S, b59. Reprinted in Mikhail, 67–75; and H & S, 115–23. Quoted in OWDA, 241–3. A Mr Woodson is identified as the person who presented Wilde with a bouquet at Sacramento in "Lo! The Esthete," *San Francisco Chronicle* (San Francisco, CA), 27 Mar. 1882, 3, p. 298. J. A. Woodson was the literary editor of the *Record-Union* (*Maxwell's Directory of Sacramento, 1880–1881*).

2. Trains heading west on the Overland Route between Omaha, Nebraska and Oakland, California passed through Sacramento. Since 1879 they had continued on to Benicia, where they were driven onto the ferry steamer *Solano* and taken across the mile-wide Carquinez Straits to Port Costa. They then proceeded to Oakland. From the lack of overlap between this article and those written by reporters who met Wilde at Port Costa, it seems likely that Woodson travelled with Wilde as far as Benicia.

high, narrows as it ascends, and on either side his straight brown hair, which from a middle parting falls to a level with his chin in unstudied negligence, and shades a neck rather long and with a tendency to crane forward.

THE EXPRESSION

Of his countenance is very amiable, and a constant smile of perfect content rests upon his over-full features, which are almost effeminate in apparent lack of vigor and force, but which in that respect belie the man, whose conversation proves him to be shrewd, perfectly self-possessed, and entirely able to take care of himself in this world. With a Chesterfieldian bow, he returned his thanks for a button-hole bouquet a Sacramento lady sent by the news-man for "the lover of the beautiful," and the esthete settled himself in the cushions of a palace car, and signified his readiness to be put upon the categorical rack.

WHAT HE BELIEVES.

The news-gleaner opened the ball: "Are we to correctly understand you, Mr. Wilde, that your belief is that a true love for art for its own sake, and in its highest development, marks the best forms and systems of civilization most easily attainable?"

The Esthete—Yes. Life without industry is barbarism; industry without art is barren.[1] We should first teach the people to use their hands in the work of art. All that is artistic must begin in handicraft.

DEVOTION TO BEAUTY.

"You have been quoted as pronouncing the devotion to beauty and the production of the beautiful as making a man's life immortal. Would you be understood as erecting that into a creed of a religion of culture?"

The Esthete—The best service of God is found in the worship of all that is beautiful. Such a worshiper can do no wrong wilfully. We should remember that all things worthy should be satisfying. The religions of the world too often tell us to love the Creator without keeping in view the created things. How starved is such a belief—it sees the Creator and is blind to His work; it teaches of Him, but makes no effort to teach of His work's beauty and grandeur.

PLEASURE.

"In one of your addresses, Mr. Wilde, you speak of the necessity of every household possessing the things that give pleasure to the user and were a pleasure to the maker. Do I understand from you by that, that if we surround our-

1. This echoes a phrase used by Wilde in *The English Renaissance* and elsewhere: see p. 117, note 1.

selves and children by beautiful things, and keep both within, as you put it, 'the atmosphere of fair things,' that we will soonest bring the race to the purest state, and to despise and utterly forsake the vulgar and coarse and wicked?"[1]

The Poet—Yes, indeed. The man who lives in such an atmosphere must be a better man, a better workman, a better citizen; and there will follow such a better civilization. The mistake in our educational systems has been that we have sought to teach truth abstractly. Great special truth must grow up in us. Truth comes to the child through the atmosphere of his surroundings. Purify that, and you purify him. Surround him by the beautiful, the useful and the good, and what must result? The theory of beautiful surroundings that finds expression in Europe is true of nations. The life of every nation is influenced by its surroundings. Taine, in the history of literature, is constantly turning to the hills and the valleys—to the scenery of England.[2] He could not resist it, nor dissociate them from his theme. Formerly the products of the man's mind were treated abstractly—the man was treated abstractly, and not as to his surroundings. The first thing to teach the boy is to use his eyes, his ears and his hands. But we are always trying to educate his mind before we give him a mind, for mind is creative. The child is endowed with intellectual faculties, but the mind is the result of growth; and I need not say to what extent we control that. To a child the teaching of abstract truth is folly.

THE SECRET OF LIFE.

"You conclude one of your lectures with the words: 'The secret of life is in art.'[3] Would you add a word, and tell us how the masses can best attain a knowledge and love of art?"

Mr. Wilde—I hope that the masses will come to be the creators in art. That is what I mean—that art will some time cease to be simply the accomplishment and luxury of the rich; but the possession, as it is the rightful heritage, of all, poor and rich alike. The difficulty I have felt and met in America is, not that there is a lack of interest in art; not that they do not love it; not that they are not receptive—no, they have a great love for the beautiful—but the difficulty is that they do not hold the handicrafts in greater honor and respect. I would dignify labor by stripping it of its degradation, and that by developing all that is beautiful in the

1. The reporter refers to *The English Renaissance*: "So, in years to come there will be nothing in any man's house which has not given delight to its maker and does not give delight to its user. The children, like the children of Plato's perfect city, will grow up 'in a simple atmosphere of all fair things'" (*Miscellanies*, 270).

2. Hyppolyte Adolphe Taine (1828–1893) was a French critic and historian. His *History of English Literature* was published in five volumes in 1863.

3. *The English Renaissance* ends: "We spend our days, each one of us, in looking for the secret of life. Well, the secret of life is in art." (*Miscellanies*, 277.)

laborer's surroundings and opening his eyes to it. Ah! I would speak to the hard-working people, whom I wish I could reach through the prejudice that shuts them and me away from each other. Why, it is to the mechanics and workers of your country that I look for

THE TRIUMPH

That must come. Why, back here in the West I met a railroad-repairer—a man working out on the line at a hard, laborious task. It was his daily business. He talked with me, wanted to know what we are trying to do. Why that man quoted Pope to me,[1] analyzed his method, discussed my positions with me, understood me, and where he doubted gave his reasons in homely phrases, but unmistakeably and clearly. He took an interest in the best of life; was keen, kindly, receptive and pugnacious in need, withal—altogether a charming fellow. Now, in England, in men of his class such a conversation would be simply impossible. Here I learn that a man is fairly representative of a myriad.[2]

THE DECORATIVE "CRAZE."

"Mr. Wilde, the decorative art rage, as it is called, is thought by many to be indulged in to the extreme. Do you think there is a danger to the true art culture in the rush and push in the former line, or is it one of the signs of our renaissance?"

The Poet—Oh, of course; for the people have not had the opportunity, in all respects, as yet to get on well, so they are constantly going wrong. Still the desire to go at all is something, and much has been and is being accomplished. But if this desire is to culminate in anything great, it must be by the affectionate study of art and beautiful things. The truth about decorative art, like all in art, is to be revealed to those who are receptive of the beautiful. The present revelation is the cause of the revival in decorative art.

THE DRAMA'S PLACE.

"There is one question I much desire to ask you, whether you think the drama most popular now, the spectacular and the class that appeals more to the fancy and the eye and the emotions than to the intellect and the reason—whether it is not a stumbling block in the path to higher art culture?"

Mr. Wilde—No, no. so far from that being the case, the fault I find with the modern stage is the departure from the true spirit that intended it for the pag-

1. Alexander Pope (1688–1744) was an English poet. He is best known for *Rape of the Lock* (1712, 1714), his *Dunciads* (1728–1743), and *An Essay on Man* (1734–5).

2. Wilde's account of this meeting is also given in "The Only Oscar," *The Daily Report* (San Francisco, CA), 27 Mar. 1882, 3, p. 306, where the man is described as a miner.

eant. In this modern life, where we have given up so much of color, so much of the beautiful, let us leave on the stage all we can in beauty of dress, in richness of scenery, in graceful groupings. The trouble is the controllers of the stage belittle these spectacular effects by sensational scenes of the most improbable kind, and work up all sorts of morbid situations, with flying trains and sinking steamers, and all that. The stage is art in action. See how much we have fallen away from that ideal. On the stage we should see all we can of rich color, beautiful drapery and grouping, and all things that will cultivate a taste among the people for beautiful and chaste things. When they thus see how beautiful things can be made by their surroundings, they will look to their own, and discover possibilities before unknown to them.

GOOD FOR AMERICA.

"In your first address in America you spoke of the hope of perfection in your movement that you felt there was in America, because we are 'young.' Do you mean by that that the absence of the influence of the architecture, the art schools and culture of Europe, etc., is no drawback to our people in art advancement?"[1]

Mr. Wilde—No art is better than bad art. I'd sooner the people studied no art than some of the bad art of Europe—they would be more receptive of the true when it does come to them. Why, sir, architecture in England is deteriorating. The handicrafts are falling into disrepute. Against this it is to be said that England has had great examples and eminent exemplars; but they have isolated ones, like Turner.[2] They were surrounded by masses that did not appreciate them. They had admirers, votaries, supporters, but not in the masses. Against this non-appreciative spirit we are fighting. So I say that a new people, not under the dead weight of crowded Europe, give hope for quicker appreciation of the true and the beautiful. As I have said, "the very absence of tradition with you is the source of your freedom and strength."[3]

1. *The English Renaissance*: "It is rather, perhaps, to you [America] that we [the English] should turn to complete and perfect this great movement of ours [....] For you, at least, are young; 'no hungry generations tread you down,' and the past does not weary you with the intolerable burden of its memories nor mock you with the ruins of a beauty, the secret of whose creation you have lost." (*Miscellanies*, 265.) Wilde quotes from Keats's *Ode to a Nightingale*: "Thou wast not born for death, immortal Bird! | No hungry generations tread thee down; | The voice I hear this passing night was heard | In ancient days by emperor and clown".

2. Ruskin had singled out Turner for extended praise in the first volume of his series on *Modern Painters*.

3. *The English Renaissance*: "That very absence of tradition, which Mr. Ruskin thought would rob your rivers of their laughter and your flowers of their light, may be rather the source of your freedom and your strength." (*Miscellanies*, 265.) Ruskin is repeatedly critical of America in *Fors Clavigera*: e.g. "I could not [...] live in a country so miserable as to possess no castles." (Letter X.)

MAKING FUN OF HIM.

"You have been much caricatured, and your theories much satirized. How has that affected your judgment of the American people?"

Mr. Wilde—I rarely think of it; when I do, I think nothing of it. It does not in the slightest degree represent to me the strength or the sanity of a great modern nation. One must always remember that wisdom does not brawl upon the street. The voice of folly is always shrill and very loud, but it passes away. Of one thing I am convinced, and that is, the fool has no influence; he may for the moment—that is all.

"Harper's Monthly criticises you in a little dash this month, and dislikes your extravagance and eccentricities."[1]

Mr. Wilde—Do you call that a little dash? I call it as cruel as it is unjust. Suppose it is true—admitting it for argument sake only—that people come to hear me out of curiosity? Well, I get a hearing, and still hope to do some good in my day. But it isn't true. I've found in America truly appreciative audiences. True, caricature and misrepresentation have excited curiosity. Why in Chicago I had an audience of 3,000 people, and spoke for an hour and twenty minutes. And only one man left the room before the close, and he came to apologize for the necessity requiring it. That speaks of appreciation, at least for respectful hearing. I think the West is very fair to those who address it.

"So you do not fear ridicule?"

Mr. Wilde—Indeed, no. I want what I have to advance to stand on its merit. I ask no quarter. I have not the remotest doubt as to which side will win. I think the school I am in will win, because it represents great principles, and they are working for us, no matter what I may do.

"BLISTERING THE PRESS."

"But has the press given you a fair show?"

Mr. Wilde—Oh, the papers! They run in grooves a good deal. They might just as well take the other side. The praise of the man who can't understand me is quite as injurious as the abuse of any enemy can be. There is no limit to the nonsense some men will write if it raises the circulation of the paper from one to two.

1. George William Curtis, "Editor's Easy Chair," *Harper's Monthly*, 64, Apr. 1882, 786–90 (the comments about Wilde are on page 790). The article argues that Wilde's audiences have gone to see him chiefly because of his "oddities of apparel," and that his complaints about America are unjustified as he would have been treated in much the same manner if he had toured in knee-breeches in England.

AN OPINION.

"What do you think of this country so far as you have had opportunity to observe? Does it come up to or fall below your preconceived ideas?"

Mr. Wilde (with a merry twinkle of the eye)—My dear sir, I was sensible enough (pardon me) not to have any preconceived ideas about it. I came to see and learn. Well, thus far I find far more independence of thought here than in Europe.

THE COMMERCIAL SPIRIT.

"You are reported as saying that the commercial spirit in England is killing nobility and purity.[1] Coupling this with your expression of hope for art culture in America, are we to infer that you think this nation of traders less sordid than your people?"

Mr. Wilde—I mean the spirit of commerce is misunderstood. Some of the most beautiful cities have been built by commercial men, as Genoa, Florence, Venice. But in England men have been made machines, quite as soulless and ignoble as the whirling wheels of machinery. I don't speak now of the flood of bad patterns and ugly designs as resulting; but I speak of the injury to the workmen themselves, so deep that they cannot realize the nobility of life. In America I don't think it goes to that extent. I don't think the American workman will submit to such a position.[2]

ART EXPRESSION.

"I have read in Emerson's essay on 'The Poet' these words: 'The beautiful rests on the foundations of the necessary.'[3] Do you agree with that sentiment, Mr. Wilde?

The Esthete—The moment art becomes a luxury it loses, for it must arise out of necessity. All art is the expression of the noble and joyous in life. Luxury gives us the gaudy, the vulgar, the transient. It may help but it never creates art. For instance, luxury gives great prices for French landscapes of the modern school. Now, while I admire French landscapes, the indulgence by luxury in them does not dignify American handicraft at all, or help home effort.

1. *The English Renaissance*: "For there can be no great sculpture without a beautiful national life, and the commercial spirit of England has killed that; no great drama without a noble national life, and the commercial spirit of England has killed that too." (*Miscellanies*, 263–4.)

2. Wilde appears to have broached this subject again later that day: see "The Only Oscar," *The Daily Report* (San Francisco, CA), 27 Mar. 1882, 3, p. 305.

3. Emerson's essay was published in his *Essays: Second Series* (1844).

AN ART QUESTION.

"But, Mr. Wilde, if surroundings have so great an influence, does not the architecture, the great models, the atmosphere of art in Europe, account for the preference?"

Mr. Wilde—Familiarity with the beautiful in architecture does not belittle it with him who appreciates it. It grows on you. Italy is the loveliest country of Europe, but Italy gives you no landscapes from her studios. You speak of the broad field for the study of the lofty and the beautiful and awe-inspiring in California. Well, it is not necessary to have great natural wonders at home to develop art. It is in the eye and the heart of the artist that we find the secret of success. The landscapes of Italy are all-satisfying, and so the Italian artist does not reproduce them. You must go to the cloudy, the misty lands, for great landscape painters—the blue and the golden light of Italy is unapproachable.

"An American woman, Mr. Wilde, has written of beauty in lines with which you will accord, I presume: Mrs. Sarah J. Hale.[1] Never heard the lines? They are:

Beauty was lent to nature as the type
Of Heaven's unspeakable and holy joy,
Where all perfection makes the sum of bliss.

Mr. Wilde—Yes, certainly.

COPYRIGHT.

"By the way, Mr. Wilde, what do you in England think of the international copyright question?"

The Poet—That a country gets small good from a literature it steals.

"But you are retaliating now?"

Mr. Wilde—Very little. It don't change the principle. Why, in all your cars I find newsmen selling my poems—stolen! I never can resist the impulse to read out a lesson on the heinousness of the offence.[2]

"But there is a genuine American edition?"

Mr. Wilde—Oh, yes! by a Boston house.

"I heard you were getting out a work in America."

1. Sarah Josepha Hale née Buell (1788–1879) was an American writer and editor.

2. In *Personal Impressions of America* Wilde would describe his encounter with newsboys who sold pirated copies of his *Poems*: "Calling these boys on one side I told them that though poets like to be popular they desire to be paid, and selling editions of my poems without giving me a profit is dealing a blow at literature which must have a disastrous effect on poetical aspirants. The invariable reply that they made was that they themselves made a profit out of the transaction and that was all they cared about." (Dibb, 237.) A version of the story appeared in several American newspapers in 1882 (see e.g. "The Poet and the Peanut Boy," *The Silver State* (Winnemucca, NV), 23 Apr. 1882, 1).

Mr. Wilde—That is a volume of poems by a friend, Rennell Rodd, an English officer. It will appear in Philadelphia.

"Why not issue it in your own country?"

Mr. Wilde—I desire to introduce the author to the American public. I think it will appreciate him. It will have an introduction that I have written. In that I point out the strong quality of this young man's work, and show how the artist can best use the life around him. Young workers in art are apt to go too blindly in. They perceive too often without rule or principle, and don't cultivate our sense of beauty. They are slow to perceive how all art is a desire for perfection.

CONCLUSION.

The conversation was continued at much length. What has been given exemplifies its tone and character.

Wilde has an apparently affected drawl in his speech, but it is evidently his normal style of delivery. Divest him of his flowing locks, add crispness to his enunciation and vigor to his tone, and there would be nothing about him to give ground for ridicule, except, perhaps, his expressive and languidly poetic eyes, the almost boyish fullness and effeminacy of his face, and the full lips that speak of the possible voluptuary. His friends on the train complained bitterly of the rudeness of the crowds at small stations on the road beyond the Sierras—especially of the attempt at Corinne, Utah, of a grotesquely-accoutered crowd, with a band, that sought to invade the car.

Some of the crowds will probably be chagrined to now learn that the Oscar Wilde many of them saw was not *the* Oscar Wilde, but was that inimitable comedian John Howson, of the Comley-Barton Opera Troupe, who, being on the train, several times put on his "Bunthorne" wig, contorted his features into an admirable resemblance of the ever-dwelling smile on Oscar's countenance, and showed himself at times to save his friend and to have a bit of fun on his own account.[1]

At Sacramento there was no embarrassing staring at Wilde, and no crowd gathered about him. He was not subjected either to any vulgar inquisitiveness by the great crowd on the Oakland ferry-boat. The people hunted him out, glanced at him and passed on without offensive staring.

Mr. Wilde expressed often his warm admiration for what he had seen of America and its people. In all his conversation many will be disappointed to learn he never used the words "superlatively beautiful," "ravishingly beautiful," "too utterly utter," "too too," or any phraseology to which ridicule and satire have given point as to esthetes.

1. John Jerome Howson (1842–1887) was an Australian comic actor. The Comley-Barton Opera Company's production of *Patience* was authorised by D'Oyly Carte.

Concerning the sunflower, which is in the popular mind so intimately associated with Wilde's name, it may be added that he has himself explained about it in a lecture, in these words:

You have heard, I think, a few of you of two flowers connected with the esthetic movement in England said (I assure you erroneously) to be the food of some esthetic young men. Well, let me tell you that the reason we love the lily and the sunflower, in spite of what Mr. Gilbert may tell you, is not for any vegetable fashion at all; it is because these two lovely flowers are in England the two most perfect models of design, the most naturally adapted for decorative art.[1]

The poet, esthete and romantic philosopher, will remain on the coast three weeks, and will put in one day at Sacramento, when all the curious can for themselves see the present lion of curiosity.[2]

These things impressed the press representative yesterday after a long conversation with Mr. Wilde, and after observing him in a great crowd of representative people and making note of their expressions. He is scholarly, studiedly polite, a gentleman, shrewd, fearless, observant, self-possessed and of poetic temperament. He has been considerably misrepresented and unduly ridiculed. He is apparently sincere and earnest. He is, however, ludicrously odd to the American eye in personal appearance; is eccentric (or affected) in this regard, and lacks the manifestations of manliness in his countenance, and frequently in his manner. If he was more an object of curiosity than respect to Californians yesterday it was due to the latter causes, to the ridicule showered on him at the East, and in part to the present public conception of the tendency of his teachings.

1. *The English Renaissance* (*Miscellanies*, 276).
2. Wilde lectured in Sacramento's Congregational Church on 31 March and 8 April.

"Oscar Wilde," *The Daily Examiner* (San Francisco, CA), 27 Mar. 1882, 2[1]

An Interview With the Apostle of Aestheticism.

THE SUNFLOWER POET DESCRIBED.

A Talk About Art—His Favorite Poem—The New School of Poetry and Design Explained.

Oscar Wilde arrived in this city at noon yesterday by the overland train. The news that he was on the train induced hundreds of curious persons to go over to the Oakland depot in order to catch a first glimpse of this new lion. To these persons a cursory inspection revealed a tall, well-built, clean-shaven, eccentrically-dressed young man with remarkable features, a somber, melancholy face, lighted up at intervals in the conversation going on around him and directed entirely at him, by a frank, pleased smile that came readily and passed away quickly, leaving the face in repose, as before. Wherever he moved the crowd, guided by a large, wide-brimmed, white slouch hat he wore, followed, not obtrusively, but quietly and respectfully. Mr. Wilde was dressed in a style that would attract general attention anywhere outside of an artist's studio or chambers, and there was no need for anyone to point in order to identify him. From beneath his large white hat fell long light-brown hair, reaching in somewhat straggling masses to the shoulders, half hiding a face inclined to sallowness. A close-fitting black velvet frock coat showed off strong, square shoulders, manly waist and hips. Pants dun brown, highly polished pointed shoes, a velvet waistcoat, low, wide collar, puce-colored tie folded wide, yellow gloves completed the appearance in dress of the outward man. A boutonniere, somewhat withered, made up of heliotropes, a brightly-foliated daisy and a tuberose, decorated his coat front. A dark olive-green Summer overcoat was carried carelessly over his left arm, and the right hand, when not resting lightly against the chin as if aiding the poet in thought, grasped a thick ivory cane. Thus the object of curiosity appeared to those who yesterday saw him crossing the bay to this city.

1. H & S, b56. Reprinted in Mikhail, 59–64; and H & S, 100–5. Excerpted in Mason, 326. Quoted in OWDA, 243–5; and Sturgis, 244/234. Referenced in Ellmann, 186/196. The reporter was accompanied from Port Costa by the authors of "Oscar Wilde's Views," *The Morning Call* (San Francisco, CA), 27 Mar. 1882, 4, pp. 291–6; "Lo! The Esthete," *San Francisco Chronicle* (San Francisco, CA), 27 Mar. 1882, 3, pp. 296–303; "The Only Oscar," *The Daily Report* (San Francisco, CA), 27 Mar. 1882, 3, 304–9; and, from Oakland, by the author of "The Ideal Esthete," *Oakland Daily Evening Tribune* (Oakland, CA), 28 Mar. 1882, 2, pp. 310–13.

A FIRST GLIMPSE OF THE BAY.

A quiet conversation with Oscar Wilde would have disclosed nobler material than dress anomalistic of the man. Unfortunately this converse could not be had yesterday in the rush of car and boat, each bend in their rapid onward flight cityward, revealing to the ardent lover of nature scenes of picturesque beauty, silencing ordinary speech and thought; a changing panorama of soft murky outlines and hazy tints of color, the center always the sea-green bay, spangled with grassy Yerba Buena, and the gold of Alcatraz, which sparkled like brilliant splotches against indistinct backgrounds of black and indigo, coloring the far-off, woody mountain summits and curving shore-lines; the Golden Gate lost in a sunlit mist beyond;[1] San Francisco's hills, roadways, houses, dimly seen; at its feet a mist from which rose the tall, straight masts of merchant ships, tapering above the mist that hung over the wharves. Not alone the poet, but everyone ending the weary journey here were impressed by what to nearly all was the first view of the "uttermost Occident." Mr. Wilde was met at Port Costa by several persons, who, for one reason or another laid a claim to his attention, among them an EXAMINER representative. All were met with the quiet, dignified courtesy of a gentlemen and a man of the world. In speaking Mr. Wilde preserves a cold but polite and attentive air, and it is only when some favorite subject is touched upon that the face lights up and the gray–green eyes seek those of the person who has aroused his deeper attention, and smiles encouragement or appreciation. The long, rather thin face, the pointed chin and well-shaped nose seem to feel the influence of the smile, and an otherwise homely face appears momentarily handsome. A second later, the spurt of enthusiasm or interest having passed, the face becomes again immobile, the eyelids lower, the eyes grow dull with a far-away glance, or seek the ground as the tall body bends slightly to come to a nearer level with its companion.

MR. WILDE'S TALK.

Talking, Mr. Wilde speaks in a low, melodious tone, the broad English pronunciation being harmonized almost to rhythm. He gesticulates very little, and from constant practice has a habit of brushing loose hairs back behind his ears.

After apologizing for the intrusion, the reporter asked Mr. Wilde if the trip overland was a pleasant one?

"Partly," he replied, "but excessively long and tedious."

"Does the mountain scenery meet your expectations?"

1. Yerba Buena, like Alcatraz, is an island in San Francisco Bay. The Golden Gate is the strait that connects the bay to the Pacific Ocean; the Golden Gate Bridge spanning the strait was built in 1937.

"Hardly; I saw it at an unfavorable time, I suppose. The view from the top of the Sierra Nevadas, however, was beautiful."

"Do you like our country, Mr. Wilde, or are you disappointed with America and Americans?"

"There is very much here to like and admire. The further West one comes the more there is to like. The Western people are much more genial than those of the East, and I fancy that I shall be greatly pleased with California." Mr. Wilde merely smiled when told that California audiences would never think of showing him disrespect, and the only thing that might appear annoying to him will be the curiosity of all classes to see the man who has lately been so much read and talked about. "I like your country and its people," he said, as though apologizing for the latter.

"There is something quickening in the young life of a powerful nation. There is a wonderful opportunity for the growth and expansion of art in a country where a national life is unfolding. But there are too many amateurs here. Amateur art is worse than no art."

A DISSERTATION ON POETRY.

Reporter—Mr. Wilde, do your admirers believe that you have created a new school of poetry?

Oscar Wilde—They certainly should not—that is if I have any admirers. The pre-Raphaelite school, to which I belong, owes its origin to Keats more than to anyone else. He was the forerunner of the school, as was Phidias of Grecian art,[1] Dante of the intensity, passion and color of Italian painting. Later, Burne-Jones in Painting and Morris, Rossetti and Swinburne in poetry, represent the fruit of which Keats was the blossom.

The turn which the conversation had taken had evidently aroused Mr. Wilde from apathy, for his face and manner showed that he was thoroughly interested in the theme. The reporter improved the occasion to remark: "Judging from the tenor of your own poems, I fancy that 'Charmides' (pronouncing the name with the soft accent) is your favourite poem, Mr. Wilde?"

"Char—Charmides," he replied correcting; "yes, that is my favourite poem. I think it my best. It is the most finished and perfect. The people of America have taken very kindly to my 'Ave Imperatrix,' however."[2]

"Perhaps a feeling of nationality prompts this choice."

1. Phidias (c. 180–430 BCE) was a Greek sculptor and architect. His works include the lost massive chryselephantine sculptures of Zeus for the Temple of Zeus at Olympia and of Athena for the Parthenon.

2. *Charmides* was first published in *Poems* (CW i, No. 55). *Ave Imperatrix! A Poem on England* was first published in *The World* on 25 August 1880 (CW i, No. 76).

Mr. Wilde—Probably so.

Reporter—Does the "Sonnet to Liberty" voice your political creed?

Oscar Wilde—You mean the sonnet beginning:

"Not that I love thy children, whose dull eyes
See nothing save their own unlovely woe,
Whose minds know nothing, nothing care to know"——

No, that is not my political creed. I wrote that when I was younger. (Mr. Wilde is 26 now.)[1] Perhaps something of the fire of youth prompted it."

Mr. Wilde's recital of the lines was surprisingly impressive and pleasing, a perfect modulation and an earnest, almost pathetic tone giving the recital deep interest.

"If you would like to know my political creed," he said, after a short pause, "read the 'Liberta Sacra Fames'—I think it is the seventh sonnet."

The sonnet referred to is as follows:

Albeit nurtured in democracy,
    And liking best that state republican
    Where every man is kinglike, and no man
Is crowned above his fellows, yet I see,
Spite of this modern fret for Liberty,
    Better the rule of One whom all obey
    Than to let clamorous demagogues betray
Our freedom with the kiss of anarchy.
Wherefore I love them not whose hands profane
    Plant the red flag upon the piled-up street
    For no right causes, beneath whose ignorant reign
Arts, Culture, Reverence, Honor—all things fade,
    Save Treason and the dagger of her trade,
    And Murder, with his silent, bloody feet.[2]

HIS VIEWS ON POETRY.

"Mr. Wilde, one of your critics has denounced your poetry as impure and immoral."[3]

1. Wilde was 27.

2. *Liberta Sacra Fames* was first published in the *World* in November 1880 and revised in *Poems* (CW 1, 148). This is the revised version. See also "The Only Oscar," *The Daily Report* (San Francisco, CA), 27 Mar. 1882, 3, p. 309.

3. This is presumably a reference to Thomas Wentworth Higginson (1823–1911), an American minister and author. His attack on Wilde appeared in *The Woman's Journal*, 4 Feb. 1882. He questioned the morality of Wilde's poems and of their author's masculinity: "is it manhood for her [Ireland's] gifted sons to stay at home and help work out the problem, or to cross the Atlan-

"A poem," replied Mr. Wilde, "is well written or badly written.[1] In art there should be no reference to a standard of good or evil. The presence of such a reference implies incompleteness of vision. The Greeks understood this principle, and with perfect serenity enjoyed works of art that, I suppose, some of my critics would never allow their families to look at. The enjoyment of poetry does not come from the subject, but from the language and rhythm. Art must be loved for its own sake, and not criticised by a standard of morality."

The conversation turning somewhat upon his life, Mr. Wilde said that he felt proud of his Irish birth and parentage. "I live in London for its artistic life and opportunities," he said. "There is no lack of culture in Ireland, but it is nearly all absorbed in politics. Had I remained there my career would have been a political one."

"When do you expect to return to London, Mr. Wilde?"

"If lecturing does not kill me, very soon."

"Then you do not like lecturing?"

"Yes, I do," he responded quickly. "I like lecturing because it brings me face to face with those I desire should hear me. In England this is impossible."

By this time the train had run into the new depot on Long Wharf, and the passengers filed into the waiting-room.[2] Here the conspicuous figure of the coming lecturer attracted general attention. Even the shaggy fur overcoat, made famous by Du Maurier's sketches in *Punch*, caused a crowd to gather where the porter laid it with a valise in the corner.

THE FERRYBOAT.

On the ferryboat Mr. Wilde placed himself so that his back was turned to the crowd. The sights on the bay interested him greatly, and he asked many questions about the city, whose streetways, appearing like huge bleached ribs of a gigantic skeleton with the head pointing oceanward, were distinctly visible.

He asked many questions about the Chinese, and had the Chinese quarters pointed out to him.[3] Speaking of Chinese art, he said that it possesses no element

---

tic and pose in ladies' boudoirs or write prurient poems which their hostesses must discreetly ignore?" (OWDA, 118–19.)

1. *The English Renaissance*: "[...] one should never talk of a moral or an immoral poem—poems are either well written or badly written, that is all." (*Miscellanies*, 267.) Wilde would later rephrase this aphorism for the preface of *The Picture of Dorian Gray*, replacing "poems" with "books" (CW iii, 167.14–15.) He was cross-examined on it by Edward Carson (1854–1935) during the Queensberry libel trial (Holland, 80–1). See also p. 295, note 4.

2. The new terminus at Oakland's Long Wharf had opened in January. Passengers travelling on to San Francisco were obliged to take the ferry from here; the San Francisco–Oakland Bay Bridge was opened in 1936.

3. In 1880 there were 104,468 persons resident in the United States who had been born in China; 73,548 resided in California.

of beauty, the horrible and grotesque appearing to be standards of perfection. "Their art and music," he said, "are extraordinary developments of national life. I have seen much that is admirable in Japanese art but nothing of excellence in Chinese art.[1] When I was a lad I heard a Chinese fiddle, or so it was called, at the Paris Exposition, but I could discern no music in it.[2] When the Shah of Persia was in London the only music he cared for was the violin."[3] In answer to a question as to whether the harbor is fortified, Alcatraz and Fort Point were pointed out.

Mr. Wilde impressed all those with whom he came in contact as being "a veray parfit gentil knight."[4] His manner is courteous, deferential and self-possessed, his language clear and forcible, without ever descending to those excesses commonly attributed to him as daily talk. Nothing in his manner would attract unusual attention, and certainly not ridicule.

The Market-street slip reached, Mr. Wilde and his agent, Mr. Vale, took a carriage for their hotel.

1. Colin Cavendish-Jones notes that Wilde's view of China as expressed here owes much to the writings of German philosopher Georg Wilhelm Friedrich Hegel (1770–1831) and that by elevating Japanese over Chinese art Wilde was "conforming to a popular Victorian prejudice." (Cavendish-Jones, C. (2014). Oscar Wilde's radically revised view of China. *Studies in English Literature, 1500-1900, 54*, 923–41, 924.) Wilde revised his opinion of Chinese art after visiting San Francisco's Chinatown: see "Oscar Wilde in Chinatown," *The Daily Examiner* (San Francisco, CA), 30 Mar. 1882, 3, pp. 313–314.

2. The International Exposition of 1867 (1 April – 3 November). Wilde would have been 12–13 years old at the time.

3. Naser al-Din Shah Qajar (1831–1896) was the Shah of Qajar Iran from 1848. He visited London in the summer of 1873. *The Morning Post* (5 July 1873, 6) noted that "the Shah has a rooted dislike to music *pur et simple*", and this is perhaps why he was entertained with mixed programmes. For example, when he attended the Theatre Royal, Drury Lane, an incidental ballet was given between the first acts of the operas *La Traviata* and *Mignon*. In his memoir of his visit the Shah describes in great detail London Zoo, the acrobatic display he saw at the Crystal Palace, and the waxworks at Madame Tussaud's (*The Diary of H. M. The Shah of Persia During His Tour Through Europe in A. D. 1873*, 158–60, 193–4, 204–6), dedicating less space to musical entertainments. However, he does praise the singing of Canadian soprano Emma Albani (1847–1930) and Adelina Patti (ibid, 158). While he dined bands played music by, among others, Mozart and Strauss ("Visit of the Shah of Persia," *The Times* (London, UK), 19 June 1873, 9–10; "The Shah of Persia," *The Times* (London, UK), 23 June 1873, 11–12).

4. The reference is to Geoffrey Chaucer's *The Canterbury Tales*.

"Oscar Wilde's Views," *The Morning Call* (San Francisco, CA), 27 Mar. 1882, 4[1]

He Expresses Some Characteristic Ones to a "Call" Reporter.

He Caustically Reviews His Reviewers, and Tells why he Loves the Sunflower and Lily—His Arrival Here Yesterday.

Oscar Wilde arrived here yesterday on the overland train. A CALL reporter who met him at Port Costa, was introduced to a tall, large-faced man, with pleasant light brown eyes, winning smile, muddy complexion, and a charming manner. The two things about the gentleman which have given Gilbert's pen and Du Maurier's pencil such an amount of material to work upon, are the use of extravagant and unusual adjectives in praise of art or anything artistically pleasing, and an unusual style of dress. Gilbert has outrageously but brilliantly burlesqued the first; Du Maurier has faithfully reproduced the other, together with a heavy sensuousness in Wilde's face when in repose. On the train yesterday he wore a wide brimmed white felt hat, a velvet jacket, concerning the fit of which he should have a word with his tailor, and ordinary trousers and shoes. The striking features of his costume were his cravat and handkerchief—so much of the latter was shown that it can be classed as part of his costume. They were both, apparently, from one piece of material, and were of a startlingly brilliant yellow. A bouquet of wild flowers pinned to the lapel of his jacket, and his long straight light brown hair completed the peculiarities of his appearance. Deprived of them he would be voted on sight by the average American "a strapping big clever fellow." The much advertised aesthete, in conversation, quickly showed himself to be a man of quick perceptions, deep insight and practical views. In the hour and a half's trip in Mr. Wilde's company the reporter conversed with him on subjects

1. H & S, b57. Reprinted in H & S, 105–9. The reporter was accompanied from Port Costa by the authors of "Oscar Wilde," *The Daily Examiner* (San Francisco, CA), 27 Mar. 1882, 2, pp. 285–90; "Lo! The Esthete," *San Francisco Chronicle* (San Francisco, CA), 27 Mar. 1882, 3, pp. 296–303; "The Only Oscar," *The Daily Report* (San Francisco, CA), 27 Mar. 1882, 3, 304–9; and, from Oakland, by the author of "The Ideal Esthete," *Oakland Daily Evening Tribune* (Oakland, CA), 28 Mar. 1882, 2, pp. 310–13. *The Daily Report*, p. 308, notes that one of Wilde's San Francisco interviewers had "evidently expended 10 cents on the 'Seaside' edition of Wilde's lecture on 'The English Renaissance' and made Mr. Wilde's conversation consist of extracts from it." The next day the *Record-Union* complained that: "Yesterday the San Francisco papers all published what pretended to be interviews with Oscar Wilde, but in nearly every instance it was perfectly clear that the imagination of the reporters had supplied the greater part of the matter. One of these reporters had the effrontery to fabricate an interview by taking a report of Wilde's lecture, and making answers to a number of questions out of it." Neither article names the offender, but both must have been referring to *The Morning Call*. Although the *Call* quotes extensively from the Seaside Library's pirated edition of *The English Renaissance*, much of the interview does appear to be genuine.

ranging from Chinese art to the cause of the muddiness of the Sacramento River. Any subject he was not already familiar with he displayed a vivid interest in being informed about.

IMPRESSIONS OF OUR PEOPLE.

In the course of the conversation the reporter asked: "Have you been in this country long enough to have formed any general impression about it and its people?"

"Well, this country is too large to admit of its being comprehended in one general impression. In fact, no one impression would answer for two regions of this country. I find not only different degrees, but different kinds of development in different cities. My various impressions of them may be stated in detail in the future."

"What!" asked the reporter aghast, "You propose to write a book about us?"

"Human nature may be hardened to almost any degree of endurance," Mr. Wilde responded, laughingly. "I may even dare to write a book that mine enemies may read—and criticize it."

"If you are not yet prepared to give impressions regarding the Eastern States, you, of course, are not regarding this State."

"Not regarding the State, certainly, but I must say that after the brown barrenness of the States and the endless snows of the mountains, it was very joyous to me to see the harmony of color Nature has painted upon the California hillsides and plains we have crossed today."

"Californians always expect that much praise—"

"Yes," interrupted Mr. Wilde, "and I have another pleasant impression about this State—the names of its towns. Now, in one of the States I stopped in a place called 'Greggsville.'"[1]

A SHOCKING NAME.

The aesthete shuddered. "Now, is not that the ultimate of vulgarity? Why not Greggtown, or Greggs? but Greggsville! Here you have beautiful names," and he ran over, with every evidence of delight, a score of the euphonious Spanish names of the coast county towns.

"But you have yet to visit the mountain counties, where they have Murderers' Gulch, Hangtown, etc."[1]

1. Griggsville, Illinois was named for its founder, Richard Griggs. Wilde was aware of the correct spelling (CL, 149). *Personal Impressions of America*: "The introduction of the French word *ville*, with the Anglo-Saxon *Griggs*, was enough to drive any professor of philology into the grave. Supposing I had founded a school of art there: fancy 'Early Griggsville.' Imagine a School of Art teaching 'Griggsville Renaissance.'" (Dibb, 244–5.) Schroeder, 79–80, notes that Wilde's indignation at unaesthetic place names echoes that of Matthew Arnold.

"What are they compared to Greggsville? Proper. They at least convey an idea, an association, an—"

The reporter interrupted, in order to restore, if possible, Mr. Wilde's tranquillity, and boldly asked:

"What, Mr. Wilde, is your own definition of the English renaissance of art, concerning which we have been chiefly misinstructed by the satirists?"

"Yes, satire has paid the usual homage which mediocrity pays to genius, blinding the public to what is noble and beautiful."[2]

"Then the satirists have not followed this subject sufficiently closely to outline it?"

"Not only those who have written of it, but all those who have not asserted it, are supremely ignorant of the work that Morris, Rossetti, Burne-Jones and Swinburne and Keats' admirers have undertaken. To know nothing about these great men is one of the necessary elements of English education,[3] and to disagree with three-fourths of England on all points is one of the first elements of sanity, which is a deep source of consolation in all moments of spiritual doubt."[4]

This savage sword thrust at his English burlesquers was delivered with a charming coolness.

The reporter, after a moment's admiration of the poet's vigorous prose, again returned to the attack, and said: "But your comprehension of the art renaissance, after all else that we have heard, will be doubly acceptable."

ENGLISH RENAISSANCE.

"Well," said Mr. Wilde earnestly, "the English renaissance has been described as a mere revival of the Greek modes of thought, and again as a mere revival of medieval feeling; rather, I would say, that to these forms of the human spirit it has added whatever artistic value the intricacy and complexity and ex-

---

1. These towns were located in the mountains to the north east of Sacramento; Hangtown was later renamed Placerville.

2. The Seaside Library text of *The English Renaissance*, 30, has: "Satire paid the usual homage which mediocrity yields to genius, blinding the British public to what is noble and beautiful", as does the report of the lecture in "The English Renaissance," *New York Tribune* (New York, NY), 10 Jan. 1882, 2. The text in *Miscellanies*, 250, has: "Satire, always as sterile as it is shameful and as impotent as it is insolent, paid them [the Pre-Raphaelite Brotherhood] that usual homage which mediocrity pays to genius".

3. *The English Renaissance*: "To know nothing about these great men is one of the necessary elements of English education." (*Miscellanies*, 250); The Seaside Library, 30, and the *Tribune* have "their" for "these".

4. The article quotes this sentence verbatim from the Seaside Library text of *The English Renaissance*, 30, which matches the *Tribune*. The *Tribune* records that the audience at Chickering Hall laughed at this line. *Miscellanies*, 250: "For to disagree with three-fourths of the British public on all points is one of the first elements of sanity, one of the deepest consolations in all moments of spiritual doubt."

perience of modern life can give. It is from the union of Hellenism to its breadth, its variety of purpose, its calm possession of beauty, with the adventive,[1] the intensified individualism, the passionate color of the romantic spirit that springs out of the nineteenth century in England, as from the marriage of Faust and Helen of Troy sprang the beautiful Lady Euphonia.[2] The modern love of landscape dates from Rousseau, and it is in Keats that one discerns the beginning of the artistic renaissance of England. He was the forerunner of the pre-Raphaelite school."[3]

"Speaking of the pre-Raphaelites, what are they?"

"If you ask nine-tenths of the British public what is the meaning of the word aesthetic, they will tell you that it is the French for affection or the German for a dado," said Mr. Wilde, switching off slightly to give another vigorous slap at his scoffers. "If you inquire about the pre-Raphaelites, you will hear something about an eccentric lot of young men to whom a sort of divine crookedness and holy awkwardness is drawing all the chief objects of art."[4]

"Yes; but the pre-Raphaelites?"

"Well," said the aesthete, smiling at the reporter's unaesthetic impatience, "in the year 1847 a number of young men in London, all admirers of Keats, were in the habit of meeting together and discussing art. They had determined to revolutionize poetry and painting. To do so was to lose, in England, all their rights as citizens. They had those things which the English public never forgives—youth, power and enthusiasm.[5] These young men called themselves pre-Raphaelites, because as opposed to the facile obstructions of Raphael they thought they had

1. Adventive: that which comes from outside or from some external source; extrinsically added; extraneous; foreign (OED).

2. In the third act of Goethe's *Faust, Part 2,* Faust and Helen of Troy have a son named Euphorion. The Seaside Library, 30, and *Tribune* texts of *The English Renaissance* have Wilde say: "the beautiful Lady Euphonia". *Miscellanies,* 244, has "the beautiful boy Euphorion".

3. These two sentences are taken verbatim from the Seaside Library text of *The English Renaissance,* 30, which matches the *Tribune.* The first sentence appears in *Miscellanies,* 249, but is followed by another paragraph on Byron, Shelley, and Keats that includes the words: "[...] Keats was the pure and serene artist, the forerunner of the pre-Raphaelite school [...]". Théodore Rousseau (1812–1867) was a French landscape painter of the Barbizon school, which arose in the context of the Romantic Movement.

4. The reporter's question and Wilde's answer are taken verbatim from the Seaside Library text of *The English Renaissance,* 30. The passage in *Miscellanies,* 249–50, begins: "And these pre-Raphaelites, what were they?" The *Tribune* has: "Speaking of the pre-Raphaelites, what are they?" *Miscellanies* and the *Tribune* have "affectation" for "affection". The *Tribune* and Seaside Library agree on the end of the passage, but *Miscellanies* has: "[...] holy awkwardness *in* drawing *were* the chief objects of art." (emphasis added.)

5. Wilde's answer is taken almost verbatim from the Seaside Library text of *The English Renaissance,* 30, which matches the *Tribune* version. The passage in *Miscellanies,* 250, is phrased somewhat differently.

found a stronger realism of imagination, a more careful realism of technique, and individuality more intense. But of all things, it was a return to nature."[1]

GILBERT'S SATIRE

"Your explanation is, indeed, radically different from that humorous portrait of Gilbert's," the reporter said, vaguely conscious that he had taken down much more than he had taken in.

"But you must not judge of aestheticism by the satire of Mr. Gilbert any more than you judge of the strength and splendor of sun or sea by the dust that dances in the beam or the bubble that breaks on the wave. Don't take your critic as any sure test of art, for artists, like the Greek gods, are only revealed to one another."[2]

"You have found some savage critics in this country, have you not?"

"Yes, like a rainy day, such things are inevitable, but like a rainy day, I accept them as unpleasant in themselves, but not of a character to make me unhappy, if I only do not notice them."

"What have you found the American reviewers most object to?"

The aesthete was thoughtfully silent for a moment, as though trying to determine in his own mind which of the many American objections to his works had been the nearest universal.

Then he said, slowly, "Well, I suspect some of my verses have come in for the greatest amount of attack, and on the ground of their immorality, as set forth by one Higginson.[3] They insist upon an increased moral sense, or moral supervision of literature. Indeed, one should never talk of a moral or an immoral poem. Poems are either well written or badly written; that is all."[4]

"Mr. Wilde, there is one point I know you could satisfy thousands of CALL readers upon; by telling me why it is that two certain flowers have become connected with the aesthetic movement in England, and said, I hope erroneously, to be the food of some aesthetic young men."

"Well, let me tell you that the reason we love the lily and the sunflower, in spite of what Mr. Gilbert may tell you, is not for any vegetable fashion at all; it is because these flowers are, in England, the two most perfect models of design, the

1. This passage follows the preceding sentence in the Seaside Library, 30, and *Tribune* texts. In *Miscellanies*, 251, the passage comes later, is phrased somewhat differently, and is longer. All three texts have "abstractions" for "obstructions".

2. Wilde's answer is taken verbatim from the Seaside Library text of *The English Renaissance*, 31, which matches the *Tribune*. The version in *Miscellanies*, 262–3, is phrased slightly differently. Wilde had quoted the same passage in his 28 February 1882 letter to Joaquin Miller (CL, 141–2).

3. Thomas Wentworth Higginson. See p. 288, note 3.

4. These two sentences are taken from *The English Renaissance* (the *Tribune*, Seaside Library, 31, and *Miscellanies*, 267, versions match). See also p. 289, note 1.

most naturally adapted for decorative art—the gaudy leonine beauty of the one, the precious loveliness of the other giving to the artist the most entire and perfect joy."[1]

Coming along the bay, Mr. Wilde frequently expressed his delight with its loveliness and the beauty of the surrounding hills.

On the train and boat he was the observed of curious hundreds, many of whom had apparently made the trip across the bay purposely to see him. He hurried from the boat upon its landing, and with Mr. Locke drove directly to the Palace Hotel.[2]

"Lo! The Esthete," *San Francisco Chronicle* (San Francisco, CA), 27 Mar. 1882, 3[3]

Arrival of Oscar Wilde in San Francisco.

SUNFLOWER AND LILY IN FULL BLOOM.

The Poet's Reception on the Cars—Shocked by a Yellow Handbill and Restored by a Violet.

The 8 o'clock ferry-boat to Oakland yesterday morning carried a Committee of Reception, self-appointed, to meet Oscar Wilde, the apostle of estheticism. The committee consisted of Manager Locke, several Bohemian Club men and the usual flock of reporters that gathers on the railroad approaches to the city when some hapless celebrity is to be waylaid and ruthlessly rifled of his ideas of Cali-

1. Wilde's answer is taken verbatim from *The English Renaissance* (the *Tribune*, Seaside Library, 31, and *Miscellanies*, 276, versions match).

2. Charles E. Locke was a promoter and the proprietor of San Francisco's Bush Street Theater and a bric-à-brac store. He had arranged for Wilde's tour of the West. Several months after Wilde's tour Locke was arrested for embezzling large sums from various associates and lost control of his businesses.

3. H & S, b58. Reprinted in H & S, 109–15. Excerpted in "Oscar Wilde in San Francisco," *Auckland Star* (Auckland, NZ), 6 May 1882, 4 (supp). The reporter was accompanied from Port Costa by the authors of "Oscar Wilde," *The Daily Examiner* (San Francisco, CA), 27 Mar. 1882, 2, pp. 285–90; "Oscar Wilde's Views," *The Morning Call* (San Francisco, CA), 27 Mar. 1882, 4, pp. 291–6; "The Only Oscar," *The Daily Report* (San Francisco, CA), 27 Mar. 1882, 3, 304–9; and, from Oakland, by the author of "The Ideal Esthete," *Oakland Daily Evening Tribune* (Oakland, CA), 28 Mar. 1882, 2, pp. 310–13. The section of the article that describes Wilde being shocked by a yellow handbill and revived by the whiff of a bunch of violets is clearly a burlesque. The subsequent sections, which accord with other accounts published the same day, appear to be genuine.

fornia.[1] The committee having evidently had little more than forty winks of sleep, showed on its countenance the esthetic pallor which bespeaks a true appreciation of utter beauty and too joyous sympathy with poetic sentiment. Manager Locke, as the uncommissioned Chairman of the committee, hastened to show that the estheticism of his party was not merely skin deep by dashing instinctively for the lunch counter, where the too exquisitely utter cooking range was imbuing a plate of fried sausage with the exalted spirit of culinary art. The lofty example of the managerial esthete, proudly poised on a stool as high and dangerous as a Norman charger and wielding half a yard of steel with the vigor of a thirteenth-century Crusader, was instantly followed by the committee, and the range glowed and flamed in the intensity of its industrial zeal until the sunkissed citizen in front of it looked like a spot on a harvest moon. Before the refreshed esthetes laid down their napkins and readjusted their sunflowers the ferry-boat had touched the Oakland side and been made fast. This is especially worthy of note, as it is the first instant on record where anything but a collector was made fast by touching at Oakland.

THE ESTHETIC COMMITTEE OF RECEPTION.

As the committee filed out to the train for Port Costa an opportunity was given to note the esthetic beauties of their attire. Manager Locke, who had evidently been studying a cut of a medieval saint, had donned a dark-blue coat and a bright yellow necktie, which contrasted so violently with the unsubdued hue of his mustache that he looked like Julian Rix's sensational picture of the "Redwoods on Fire."[2] Each of the Bohemian Club men sported a large breastpin, on which a one-legged silver stork gazed pensively on a bronze frog, as if deliberating whether to go hungry or risk the terrors of strangulation and dyspepsia. The reporter of a morning journal, which caters to the esthetic aspirations of Jess and Natoma streets, and keeps the Police Department and the aristocracy of Minna street mutually intimate, boasted that in humble recognition of the coming esthete he had shaved off his mustache. On careful examination this was found to be a fact. The other journalists who found themselves attached to the tail of the Committee of Reception had contented themselves with the most ordinary attempts at esthetic adornment, and by their sameness of color helped to distract public attention from the party and save it from the suspicion that it was the advance guard of a milliners' picnic or the Board of Trustees of the Oakland cockpit.

1. The Bohemian Club of San Francisco was founded in 1872 by and for journalists, although artists, musicians, and, later, wealthy businessmen, were permitted to join.

2. Julian Rix (1850–1903) was a landscape painter from Vermont who worked in California. The painting referred to is *Redwoods* (1873–1881).

MEETING THE ESTHETE.

The run to Port Costa was pleasant and rapid. Flying over broad fields, green as the imagination of an esthetic poet, and whirling along the pebbly shores of the bay, with its sparkling waters, blue as the theatrical managers who have not dug into the bonanza of estheticism, the Committee of Reception met the overland train and Oscar Wilde at 10 A. M. Marcus Meyer, formerly of the Democratic party of San Francisco and now the agent of the divine Patti, conveyed to the committee from the fore platform of the train the pleasant news that the poet had breakfasted.[1]

"He was presented with a magnificent bouquet of sunflowers and camellias by Mr. Woodson at Sacramento," said the cheerful agent, unconscious of the intimation which the remark conveyed.

The medieval splendor of Manager Locke's attire gained him an immediate audience with the poet, who was in the rear portion of the sleeping car, paying his morning devotions to a pansy presented by a Benician esthete. The moment the manager entered the floral sanctuary the door was closed by the poet's colored valet and the committee was left to its own envious thoughts. After minutes which seemed hours to the anxious esthetes the door of the sanctum was opened and the manager came out hurriedly, and looking as if he had been worshiping a thistle or paying a compliment to a nettle.

MANAGER LOCKE'S MISTAKE.

"I ought to have known it myself," said he, bitterly, to Mr. Vale, the poet's traveling agent, and he took a poster out of his coattail pocket and exposed the offensive advertisement.

"What," gasped the terrified agent; "is that the way you've billed him? A plain yellow poster, without sandhill cranes, or lilies, or sunflowers—not even a line in old English text."

The guilty manager looked utterly woebegone.

"Not even a marguerite or a frog on the border," continued the agent, with a withering glance at the offender.

The manager groaned and hung his head.

"You haven't shown it to him, I hope," gasped the agent.

The manager nodded despairingly.

1. Marcus R. Meyer was elected President of the Young Men's Central Democratic Club in San Francisco in 1877 ("Central Democratic Club," *The Daily Examiner* (San Francisco), 22 Aug. 1877, 3). Later in 1882 he was acting as an agent for the theatrical manager Henry E. Abbey (1846–1896), booking dates in the West for the Swedish operatic soprano Christina Nilsson (1843–1921) and Lillie Langtry ("Nilsson and Langtry," *Salt Lake Daily Herald* (Salt Lake, City, UT), 21 Nov. 1882, 1). In the source his name is given as "Mayer".

"Great Caesar," exclaimed the agent, and he bounded into the poetic retreat.

The alarmed spectators were about to follow, but the valet closed the door, and faced the crowd grimly. Presently the agent reappeared, looking very pale.

"Where's that camellia that was presented us at Reno?" he anxiously inquired.[1]

SAVED BY A VALET.

The valet fished the previous souvenir out of a silver ice-pitcher, and the agent, snatching it, dashed into the sanctuary once more.

"Bring them violets!" he yelled, a moment after to the valet.

While the colored servant was climbing over the baggage on the rear platform to reach the box of violets on the roof of the car, the audience heard a deep sigh of relief from the sanctuary.

"Ah, that is so beautiful, so joyous. Put it away, Vale. I feel much better already."

"Take another sniff," replied the sturdy voice of the agent, and immediately the painful suspense of the audience was relieved by hearing a long-drawn inspiration, followed by another exclamation of esthetic gratification.

"How delicious; how sweet; how surpassing and too utterly sweet is the incense of the wild flowers in the joyous spring time."

"I guess so," replied the soulless agent, as he handed the poet his cherished bunch of violets, and came out to announce that Mr. Wilde would immediately appear to the visitors.

THE RAPTUROUS ESTHETE.

In a few moments the eminent esthete stepped through the doorway of the sanctum, and, bowing to the group of admirers, advanced to the middle of the car. The poet was still pale from the effects of the severe shock to his sensibilities, but the sight of the distant hills purpling in the morning sun completely restored him.

"They looked nice," remarked a prosy admirer.

"Ah—y-e-s—how utterly lovely—how exquisitely beautiful—observe the softness of the outline so full of the grace and perfect harmony of Nature's handiwork."

Having delivered himself of the rapturous compliment to the wooded peaks of Marin, the poet clasped his hands and gazed out of the window for some mo-

1. Wilde's train passed through Reno, Nevada on the way to California. In commenting on this interview, a reporter for the *Reno Evening Gazette* (28 Mar. 1882, 3) noted that "Oscar kindly made no mention to the press representatives of his masterly retreat out of the back door of the Depot Hotel, in order to avoid the further howling reception which the mob here had in store for him."

ments, lost in the too utterly joyous abstraction of the esthetic. While the poet's eyes were fixed on the environments of the hoary Tamalpais the CHRONICLE'S representative was making a mental sketch of the midday dreamer,[1] and found, when the picture was completed, that it was an odd one for this outlying post of civilization. In an older community the esthete might have passed with slighter attention, but his figure was certainly one calculated to excite the most intense curiosity in California.

AN OFF-HAND SKETCH OF THE ESTHETIC.

He did not look more outlandish than a trapper from the wilds clad in the trophies of the clime, but the outlandishness was of a kind to which Western people have not been in the smallest degree accustomed. Mr. Wilde's hat was of the sombrero pattern, light brown, pliable and of itself would not astonish the Californian. The poet's face was almost boyish, and the closer we examined it the more juvenile it seemed. It was the face of a man of 21 years; a long face made up on a pair of eyes set rather deeply, a large aquiline nose, full lips and a decidedly heavy chin. The dress of the poet was not less remarkable than his face, and consisted of a short velvet coat, rose-colored necktie and dark-brown trousers. The lower garments were cut with utterly sublime disregard of the latest fashion, but the esthete had yielded sufficiently to his shoemaker to allow that worthy artisan to fit him with the newest production of his last. The poet wore the perennial sunflower in his buttonhole,[2] and allowed his brown locks to float over his shoulders and just show enough ambition to curl to prove that they shared the wearer's hatred of the rigidly straight. The amount of ink that has been expended in England and America to prove that Mr. Wilde in the dress of estheticism is a very remarkable person is the best proof that his figure is sensationally uncommon,

MATTER-OF-FACT AND RHAPSODY.

The CHRONICLE man had expected to meet an odd-looking person, and prepared himself against surprise, but, as the poet lounged into the railroad car and leaned out of the window to revel in the picture of blue sky and purple hills, the reporter forgot his resolution, and stared and stared again in mute astonishment. What was particularly mystifying was the fact that this strange being, who looked as if he had no part in the every-day affairs of our prosy life, could not

1. Mount Tamalpais is a peak in Marin County.

2. Wilde was not wearing a sunflower: the *Record-Union* interviewer claims to have given Wilde "a button-hole bouquet" (p. 276); *The Daily Report* interviewer noted that "some faded wild flowers adorned [Wilde's] lapel" (p. 304); *The Daily Examiner* interviewer that Wilde's "boutonniere, somewhat withered, [was] made up of heliotropes, a brightly-foliated daisy and a tuberose" (p. 285).

only talk of the matter-of-fact when he pleased like a man of education and refinement, but like a man who was capable of deep thought and vigorous conclusions.

As Marcus Meyer, who has carefully watched the esthete for days, elegantly remarked in forming his estimate of the poet: "Anyone who picks him up for a fool will get left, and don't you forget it."

Though occasionally willing to show his ability to discuss the affairs of the world of man, the esthete could with difficulty be kept from raving over the world of art. He appeared to be able to give points to Ruskin in artistic rhapsody, and to discount everyone but Charles Warren Stoddard,[1] whom he so greatly resembled in manner and sentiment that the Bohemian Club-men could scarcely believe that the poet of Hawaii had not come back in disguise to greet them with a poetic and tender embrace.

THE ESTHETE'S TALK.

"I like your names here so much," said the poet, after he had fed his soul to satiety on the purple of Tamalpais and the blue of the sky over San Rafael. "How delightful it is to hear such names as San Antonio, San Pablo and San Lorenzo, after one's ears have been horribly shocked by such terms as Gringsville [*sic*].[2]

"The fierce suggestiveness of your Western names, such as Bloody Gulch and Murderer's Bar,[3] have in them something of interest," he continued, "but in such a name as Gringsville there is nothing but utterly, unmitigated and offensive vulgarity, ugh," and again the esthete's coat shook with the violence of his emotions.

Coming to a stretch of green meadow, enriched by the wealth of wild flowers, the poet exclaimed with the enthusiasm of a woman, and not a very strong type of Western woman at that:

"How joyous it is to see a spot of green after one has grown so weary of the desolate stretches of brown and gray! The lack of color in your American landscapes has been to me a source of much regret. In the old countries neither the winters nor the summers make much difference, for the landscape is always green—always full of color. It is a garden throughout the year, and there one can at all seasons appreciate to the fullest the beauty and the perfection of Nature."

1. Charles Warren Stoddard (1843–1909) was an American author of travel books. By 1882 he had published *Summer Cruising in the South Seas* (1874); his *A Trip to Hawaii* would be published in 1885. He was also a foreign correspondent for the *Chronicle*.

2. Griggsville, Illinois. See p. 292, note 1.

3. Bloody Gulch was to the south east of Sacramento. Murderer's Bar is to the north west of the same city, a few miles from Murderer's Gulch.

HIS CRITICISM OF THE EAST.

When asked how he felt towards his critics of the East the esthete sighed for those sordid and shortsighted persons, who in the blindness of their ignorance of estheticism know not the rapture that they miss.

"It would be more profitable," said he, "to listen to the sighing of the wind, for that tells of the power of the infinite, but to listen to those who can only see in the well of truth the reflection of their own substantial ignorance would be time misspent."

The poet refrained from speaking the kind words of the American people and expressing the unstinted praise of California which distinguished visitors generally bestow before they have reached the Oakland wharf.

"I find the Eastern States," said he, "too much of a reflex of English manners and customs, and reflections of themselves are not admirable. What I like best is the civilization which the people of the West have formed for themselves."

At this stage of the esthete's recovery an English admirer thought it advisable to drag him into a controversy on the Land League, the poet having several times intimated that the St. Patrick's Day celebrations throughout the country had greatly interested him.

"I read of a great demonstration in San Francisco on the 17th of March," said he. "You had an oration and a magnificent parade, and a poem. Who, by the way, was the poet?"

"Don't mention it," said one of the paraders. "He is already dead."[1]

ESTHETIC VIEW OF THE LAND LEAGUE.

"The Land League," said the poet, "is the most remarkable agitation that has ever taken place in Ireland, for it has, through the influence of America, created a republican feeling in Ireland for the first time. The agitations that preceded it, would, if successful, have resulted in the establishment of a monarchy. Now, success would mean the foundation of a republic."

"Do you think so?" said the British esthete, with a glare.

"I don't think so; I know it," said the poet, with so much energy that a second after his nervous system utterly collapsed, and hastily apologizing he staggered back to his sanctum, and for half an hour had to be treated to fresh applica-

1. After the parade, "literary and musical exercises" were given for the benefit of the Irish National Land League at Haverley's California Theater. Henry Hogan (1860–?), a law student who had been born in California to Irish parents, was the elected "Poet of the Day". He delivered a poem of 80 lines calling for Ireland's liberation "from tyrants' thrall." ("The Parade," *The Daily Examiner* (San Francisco, CA), 18 Mar. 1882, 3; "Poem of Henry Hogan, Esq," *Napa County Reporter* (Napa, CA), 24 Mar. 1882, 1.) The date of Hogan's death is unclear, but he was certainly still alive at the time this article was printed. He is probably the Henry Hogan who in 1900 was practising law in Albany, New York.

tions of violets, with an occasional whiff of the Reno camellia and Mr. Woodson's floral offering.

ARRIVAL IN THIS CITY.

On arriving at the Oakland ferry and during the passage the poet was the observed of all; but though his strange appearance provoked many smiles, he was treated with the courtesy of silence by the curious crowd. The only question he deigned to ask about the city, which he viewed from the upper deck of the steamer, where he stood poised on one leg like the decorative fowl of estheticism, was: "Have you no old ruins in your city?"

When told that the Mission Dolores boasted of an old church and a number of adobe shanties the poet's face brightened, but the joy was short-lived. Presently, borne on the wings of the western wind, came the odoriferous offerings of the water front, churned into aggressive life by the ferry-boat, and the poet, with an appealing look at Mr. Locke, turned and fled to the cabin. On arriving at the San Francisco side the poet was adroitly whisked into a carriage and driven to the Palace Hotel.

He will remain some weeks on this coast, and meditates a visit to Japan.[1] His fellow-passengers, including John Howson, the actor, speak of him in the kindest manner, and tell sorrowfully of the reception which he got at Corinne, where forty bogus esthetes, with big sunflowers and a terrible brass band, serenaded him.

1. Wilde's desire to visit Japan, shared with many interviewers for the next several months, was never realised.

"The Only Oscar," *The Daily Report* (San Francisco, CA), 27 Mar. 1882, 3[1]

Arrival of the Poet and Pioneer of the New Esthetes.

A Pen Picture of the Patron of the Sunflower and Lover of the Lily—How He Appears in the Garish Light of a California Sunday—His Manners, His Words and His Ideas

Oscar Wilde, the disciple of the intense, the prophet of the utterly too-too, arrived in San Francisco yesterday morning by the overland train. He was met at Port Costa by Manager Locke, of the Bush Street Theatre, under whose pecuniary auspices the lily-worshipper comes to this Coast, and by a heavy delegation of journalistic interviewers, to whom he in due time submitted himself. First he and his manager and Manager Locke had a little business confab. in the alleged poet's private compartment of the sleeping-car, and then the a. p. emerged with languid step, drooping eye lids, and wide, loose smile to greet the waiting newspaper men. He was attired in a broad brimmed, light drab, soft felt hat, a velvet coat, brown trousers, a rose-colored silk neck tie, and varnished shoes with very pointed toes. His hair hung, or, rather, stuck out down to the collar of his coat, a handkerchief, or what might have been one, of the same color and material as his necktie, protruded in a rumpled bunch from the outside breast-pocket of the coat, and some faded wildflowers adorned the lapel.

IMPRESSION DU WILDE.

The newspaper men, on being presented to Mr. Wilde and invited to take a seat with him, removed their hats. Mr. Wilde did not remove his, seeing which the DAILY REPORT representative at once resumed his tile, and wore it as long as Mr. Wilde did his; in other words, to the end of the interview. As Wilde left the

1. Quoted in Rodecape, L. F. (1940). Gilding the sunflower: a study of Oscar Wilde's visit to San Francisco. *California Historical Society Quarterly, 19*, 97–112, 100. The reporter was accompanied from Port Costa by the authors of "Oscar Wilde," *The Daily Examiner* (San Francisco, CA), 27 Mar. 1882, 2, pp. 285–90; "Oscar Wilde's Views," *The Morning Call* (San Francisco, CA), 27 Mar. 1882, 4, pp. 291–6; "Lo! The Esthete," *San Francisco Chronicle* (San Francisco, CA), 27 Mar. 1882, 3, pp. 296–303; and, from Oakland, by the author of "The Ideal Esthete," *Oakland Daily Evening Tribune* (Oakland, CA), 28 Mar. 1882, 2, pp. 310–13. A number of paragraphs about Wilde were printed on the same page of the *Report*, separately from the interview but apparently written by the interviewer. One is: "'Are you an American?' asked Oscar yesterday of one of the reporters who interviewed him. 'Yes, sir,' answered the graceless scribe: 'I am a native of the United States of Ohio,' 'Ah, indeed!' replied the aesthete." Another is titled "Bold, Bad Men" and quotes Marcus Meyer: "Oscar Wilde was only insulted twice during his trip across the continent. At Corinne a delegation of knee-breeched, sunflower-bearing citizens received him on the platform and at Reno he was hooted at. Marcus R. Meyer says Oscar was 'hurt' by the manifestations."

Oakland ferry-boat and walked to the carriage to enter a hack that was waiting to convey him to the Palace Hotel, a lady in the crowd of bystanders was heard to remark: "That Oscar Wilde! Why, I thought he was a gentleman!" and she had not seen the hat episode at Port Costa either.[1] Mr. Wilde condescended to converse, in low tones, with the newspaper men. He considered himself somewhat disappointed with the continent of America, there being, in his opinion, a sad lack of color and variety about its great landscapes. He had been ineffably bored and distressed by the vast brown levels over which the Central and Union Pacific men had been inconsiderate enough to build their transcontinental railroad, not knowing Wilde was coming, and the snow had wearied him too. The change to the green grass and varied foliage of California had, therefore, been "very joyous."

OUR WORKING CLASSES.

He had also, it seemed, been partly saddened and partly inspired by the lack of appreciation of the truly beautiful and the really artistic which he had observed in this large and vulgar land. Inspiration and hope had, however, been aroused in his velvet bosom by the fact that the working classes of the United States were actually freemen and not merely nominally freemen and actually slaves, as were those of England.[2] They were therefore at liberty to go in for the intense and brace up to the transcendental, as it were, and his mission was to give them a leg-up in that direction at one dollar a leg. However, as the Mohammed of the new art movement Mr. Wilde is hardly as supremely satisfactory as he might be; he is "all but" the very reverse. As a Britisher, who has come across the ocean to tell Americans how to attain the beautiful and worship the truly lovely, Mr. Wilde is hardly a representative of his own profession or an exemplar of his own aims. He is

A RATHER UNTIDY PERSON,

And does not suggest even personal cleanliness. In the poet of the aesthetic and the herald of the latest renaissance, frayed and grimy shirt cuffs are disappointing, and a wretchedly ill-fitting coat, wrinkled all up in the back of the shoulders is a dreadful shock to all beholders, to say nothing of the trousers, which are evidently English. Besides, Mr. Wilde's teeth were not submitted to the professional eye and hand of a dentist in early life, a disadvantage which in later life has not attracted as much attention as it might have from the person principally concerned. The leader of the aesthetes is, in brief an untidy prophet and is not as

1. This is perhaps the same woman whose remarks are quoted in "The Ideal Esthete," *Oakland Daily Evening Tribune* (Oakland, CA), 28 Mar. 1882, 2, pp. 311–12.
2. Wilde had also broached this subject earlier that day: see [J. A. Woodson], "Oscar Arrives," *The Daily Record-Union* (Sacramento, CA), 27 Mar. 1882, 3, p. 281.

clean as the average English gentleman prides himself on being. Seen upon the streets of San Francisco by an ignorant and benighted American who had never heard of "Charmides" or read "Panthea," Mr. Wilde would be taken for a corn doctor in reduced circumstances, or

A DETHRONED "KING OF PAIN."

That Mr. Wilde believes himself to know a great deal is evidenced by his poems, that he believes American working men to know very little is evidenced by a remark he made about a miner with whom he conversed on his passage through Nevada. "Why" said Mr. Wilde, "he quoted four lines from Pope! He actually did, and I was so pleased to see that men of his class read such authors. I should dearly have liked to have seen that man's home."[1] This very complimentary allusion to a man who preferred to express himself in the words of an old poet instead of puzzling his listeners by becoming a new poet himself, was a pretty good clue to the knowledge Mr. Wilde has of the intellectual status of the Americans whom he comes to teach. Oscar Wilde is very vain. Vanity sticks out—to use an aesthetic term—in all he does, says, and looks. For example, he remarked to the DAILY REPORT representative that he had been particularly struck by the lack of personal beauty in the Chinese he had seen, and he considered that this lack of personal beauty had had its effect—was reflected—in the absence of beauty which their works of art showed, their decoration being involved and obscure and the effects simply grotesque.[2] Yet Mr. Wilde professes to be ready to lead the world into realms of newer and more perfect artistic beauty, and Mr. Wilde is not beautiful himself—quite the reverse. His face is homely, his figure is ungainly, and his manners are not very good. Talking about his manners,

THE NEW ARRIVAL'S DEMEANOR

is very peculiar. It is exceedingly effeminate, and would lead the listener and observer to the conclusion that Oscar was a "mother's boy"—that he had first been endowed with his mother's mentality, then instructed at her knee and through her lips, and altogether pretty thoroughly coddled and spoiled, as such boys generally are. Pre-eminently English himself, after a certain fashion, Mr. Wilde expressed regret that he should have found the American people so Anglicized. The DAILY REPORT representative informed him that we were certainly Anglicized a good deal just at present but not enough to hurt; that our adoption of English

1. Wilde's account of this meeting is also given in [J. A. Woodson], "Oscar Arrives," *The Daily Record-Union* (Sacramento, CA), 27 Mar. 1882, 3, p. 278, where the man is described as a railroad-repairer.

2. For Wilde on the relationship between physical beauty and art, see p. 161, note 2. For Wilde's opinion of Chinese art before he visited San Francisco's Chinatown, see p. 290, note 1.

modes and fashions was merely a craze of the hour, and that next year we might be as German or Russian, as before we were English we were French. The poet admired very much the names of California towns and stations. "San Pablo" he thought was just quite too lovely for anything and he rolled his eyes at "San Rafael." The reporters maintained

A DISCREET SILENCE

Regarding "Geyserville," "National City," "Petrolia," "Shingletown," "Yocumville," "You Bet," "Yankee Jim," "Red Dog," "Linkville," "Shingle Springs" and "Twenty-six Mile House,"[1] for Oscar looked absolutely ill when he spoke of a place called "Griggsville," somewhere in the East.[2] Mr. Wilde, who names his poems "Impression du Matin," "La Bella Donna Della Mia Mente," "Amor Intellectualis," "Impression du Voyage," etc.,[3] thought it was too awfully dreadfully vulgar to append to the name Griggs the word "ville," forgetting, perhaps, that old Griggs had as good a right to tack "ville" on to his shebang as Wilde had to affix a Latin or Greek title to an English poem.[4] Marcus R. Meyer, the distinguished dramatic agent and Democrat, who had had the privilege of traveling across the continent with Oscar confided to the reporters his opinion that "Wilde is no sardine, and anybody who picks him up for a d—d fool will get left." That was precisely the impression Mr. Wilde gave the DAILY REPORT representative. If Wilde had been born in the United States, and had by a kind Providence been

DENIED PEN AND INK

And preserved from the perusal of poetry, he would very likely have made a fortune as a traveling physician, and would have attracted the attention by carriages and four, academic robes, and the other favourite advertising methods of that class which he now attracts by peculiarity of dress and affectations of speech and manners. Mr. Wilde is quite a shrewd young man, and probably knows every time on which side his bread is buttered. He is quite careful to avoid expression of opinion upon topics which would have an effect upon the size of the audiences at his lectures and changes or stops the conversation adroitly when he can,

1. All are, or were, towns in California, except for Linkville, which is in Oregon and is now named Klamath Falls.

2. Griggsville, Illinois. See p. 292, note 1.

3. *Impression du Matin* was first published in the *World* on 2 Mar. 1881 with the title *Impression de Matin* and in *Poems* with the present title (CW 1, No. 85). *La Bella Donna della mia Mente* was first published in *Kottabos* in Trinity Term 1876 as part of the longer poem *The Rose of Love* and in *Poems* with the present title (CW i, No. 9). *Amor Intellectualis* was first published in *Poems* (CW i, No. 46). *Impression de Voyage* was first published in the Boston *Pilot* on 28 July 1877 as *Hellas! Hellas!* and in *Poems* as *Impression du Voyage* (CW i, No. 29).

4. "Shebang": North American slang for a hut, shed, one's dwelling; a vehicle; a low drinking establishment, a tavern (OED).

rudely when he must, as soon as dangerous ground seems to be have been reached.[1] His conversation is exceedingly wordy and delivered with an air of superiority and authority which might with some listeners cover up its vagueness and indistinctness. What ideas the boss aesthete may have, in conversation, are clouded by his words to such an extent as to lead to the belief that the speaker himself is not as certain about them as he might be. One could imagine a spiritualistic medium who had graduated at Oxford and read much poetry talking in very much the same strain at Charter Oak Hall on a warm Sunday afternoon.[2] As a proof of the vagueness spoken of it may be said that the

THREE VERY INTELLIGENT GENTLEMEN

Who yesterday interviewed Mr. Wilde for the morning papers, have had for their reports today to draw upon their own resources very largely in order to supply a tolerably connected and intelligible conversation, and one of the enterprising gentlemen has evidently expended 10 cents on the "Seaside" edition of Wilde's lecture on "The English Renaissance" and made Mr. Wilde's conversation consist of extracts from it.[3] As for the DAILY REPORT representative, he remembers that Mr. Wilde embroidered his sentences considerably, but he cannot recall anything original or striking that he said. Travellers have before rejoiced in the green of California, noted its Spanish nomenclature, admired the line of its [?coast] range, said its Chinese were not pretty, and professed a desire to remain in California longer than their money-making engagements elsewhere would permit, but they have not been able to do it in quite the same style as Oscar. For example, when he says merely "I should like to visit Japan," he says it with such a rolling eye, such a sweeping smile, such a languid accent and such a general "air," that the unaccustomed hearer is really at first almost forced to believe that Mr. Wilde has given him a new revelation of the beautiful, till he pulls himself together and remembers that he could have said the same thing himself and said it just as well—perhaps better—had he thought it worth while or that anybody cared to know his wants and wishes.

Mr. Wilde was driven to the Palace Hotel when he landed and will lecture tonight at Platt's Hall upon "The English Renaissance."[4]

1. This is perhaps a reference to the moment noted by the *Chronicle* interviewer when an Englishman attempted "to drag [Wilde] into a controversy on the Land League" (p. 302).

2. Charter Oak Hall was a venue in San Francisco. In 1882 a group of spiritualists regularly met there on Sundays.

3. A reference to "Oscar Wilde's Views," *The Morning Call* (San Francisco, CA), 27 Mar. 1882, 4, pp. 291–6.

4. Wilde resurrected *The English Renaissance* for his first San Francisco lecture, presumably because he had been contracted to lecture four times in that city (Cooper, San Francisco lecture, 27 March 1882).

Newspapers and Lecturers.

When Oscar Wilde remarked yesterday to a newspaper man that American newspapers seemed to be written to create a laugh rather than to impart instruction, his answer was that American newspaper men, like English lecturers, accommodated themselves to the popular taste, because they wanted to make money—if they thought any particular course of conduct would advertise them in a manner that would produce the needful coin, they would adopt it, regardless of who laughed at it or failed to be instructed by it.

The journalist thought it unnecessary to add that some newspaper men would dress in knee breeches and carry a sunflower if they could thereby gain even one more small [?ct.]

✂ *A paragraph about the Women's Christian Temperance Union.*

The Effect of Age.

"You are the author, I believe," said an alleged journalist yesterday to Mr. Oscar Wilde, "of the poem beginning:

'Albeit nurtured in democracy,
  And liking best that state republican
  Where every man is Kinglike and no man
Is crowned above his fellows,[1]

Etc." "Yes" said Mr. Wilde "but I was young then." The inference was that now he is older and has, in his own estimation, been crowned above his fellows, he does not like republicanism and democracy as well. Though it will be noted that Mr. Wilde rather mixes up the two ideas of republicanism and democracy. There are those who say that Oscar ceased to be "young" when the Prince of Wales honored him with his patronage.[2]

1. This is the beginning of *Liberta Sacra Fames*. The "alleged journalist" is the author of "Oscar Wilde," *The Daily Examiner* (San Francisco, CA), 27 Mar. 1882, 2, who instead quotes *Sonnet to Liberty*, with Wilde suggesting that *Liberta Sacra Fames* better represents his "political creed" (see p. 288).

2. The Prince of Wales (1841–1910; from 1901, Edward VII) had requested a dinner at which he could meet Wilde, reportedly stating: "I do not know Mr. Wilde, and not to know Mr. Wilde is not to be known." (Sturgis, 181/175.) *Ye Soul Agonies in ye Life of Oscar Wilde*, 11–13, the comic biography of Wilde sold in America in 1882, includes a drawing of Wilde dancing with the Prince and claims that "Wales and Wilde became pals. The Prince discovered a subject in this subject, and the poet a host who gave excellent dinners, and expected no entertainment in return." See also "An Interview with Oscar Wilde's Brother," *The New Zealand Herald* (Auckland, NZ), 8 Apr. 1882, Supp. 2, pp. 770–1.

"The Ideal Esthete," *Oakland Daily Evening Tribune* (Oakland, CA), 28 Mar. 1882, 2[1]

Arrival of Oscar Wilde at the Terminal Depot.

How he Crossed the Bay—His Receptions Along the Line—His Appearance, and how he Travelled across the Country—Observations and Incidents—His Lecture and Reception this Evening at the Cavalry Armory.

Under the regular head, the record of the overland train for Sunday morning would naturally be, "Arrived—Oscar Wilde and ninety-one emigrants." Somehow or other quite a crowd gathered at the Oakland pier, in which were noticed several county officers and a sprinkling of the legal fraternity. San Francisco sent over delegations, prominent among whom were two distinguished representatives of the Young Men's Hebrew Association,[2] the whole numbering about sixty esthetic souls, anxious to catch a first glimpse of the apostle of beauty. As the train rolled in, and the engine in its fury shivered the guard timbers at the end of the track, the crowd broke into two solid lines, and in a few minutes

OSCAR APPEARED

Walking patiently under the mosquito-like buzz of a San Francisco reporter, and closely followed by several others who had gone to San Pablo as a self-constituted committee of reception.[3] Oscar is a heavy man with very light extremities, and can hardly be considered evenly balanced. His style of dress was not unfamiliar to the average Oaklander, as it has been seen once before. He wore the Buffalo Bill hat with wide brim, but of a soft sand shade instead of black. His coat was a short velvet cut-away, with vest of the same material, and pair of tight pants cut regardless of the latest styles. He had a little delicate flower in his button hole, wore a pair of brown dog-skin gloves and twirled a light frivolous cane. His long hair of soft-hued color rolling raggedly down his back; his face was boyish and looked as if it had never felt a razor; his accent, for an Irishman, was, to say the least, a well-copied cockneyism,[4] and his style pleasantly nonchalant and imposing.

1. The reporter was accompanied by the authors of "Oscar Wilde," *The Daily Examiner* (San Francisco, CA), 27 Mar. 1882, 2, pp. 285–90; "Oscar Wilde's Views," *The Morning Call* (San Francisco, CA), 27 Mar. 1882, 4, pp. 291–6; "Lo! The Esthete," *San Francisco Chronicle* (San Francisco, CA), 27 Mar. 1882, 3, pp. 296–303; and "The Only Oscar," *The Daily Report* (San Francisco, CA), 27 Mar. 1882, 3, 304–9.

2. The Young Men's Hebrew Association was founded in New York in 1874, and associations were founded in a number of American cities in subsequent years.

3. San Pablo was the last station before the terminus. The San Francisco interviewers had gone all the way to Post Costa to meet Wilde.

4. "Cockney": see p. 138, note 1.

HIS RECEPTION

Must have been very flattering to his vanity, as he was closely followed into the waiting-room and intensely gazed upon by scores of interested spectators. As the crowd pressed upon him en route for the boat, one enthusiastic maiden, not over prepossessing, moved near and pressed her chin upon the soft velvet of his coat, after which she looked up with a perfectly self-satisfied smile. On the boat he was posed at the front and center of the utter deck, where he could take in the beauty and grandeur of the approach to the city of the sand hills.

HIS INTENSE ATTENTION

Was directed to Goat Island, and he was told that the classical and botanical name was Yerba Buena. He was charmed with the sweet Spanish accent of his reportorial informant, and asked if there was any legend connected with the island. His curiosity was immediately gratified by having his attention called to the light-keeper's house, where the informant located the old Beowawa story, with the addition of losing the emigrant's child over the bluff, and the erection of a lonely cross over the nameless grave, and Oscar thought it was truly touching.[1] As the steamer neared the wharf, the distinguished guest was wafted down the stairs, and allowed to stand, with his attendants, where the mail truck usually reposes, at the bow of the boat, in front of the checking rope, where he calmly reposed upon his cane, with his easy fourteens crossed over his dun-brown unmentionables, and easily and pleasantly

TOOK THE CITY.

It was a calm and serene scene. San Francisco resting in Sunday repose, unconscious of the approach of the wonder of the age, and that great and good person just crushing the metropolis of the Pacific with his sad, soft gaze. It was a picture for a painter, but the tin-foil artist was out at Shell Mound with the San Francisco Cadets. The charm was broken, however, when a large Irish woman, with a strong sand-lot accent, shouted, "That's the way the Ahrestochracy is favored in this country. Here is a long-haired foreigner, who pays no taxes and is a barnacle himself, parmitted to ride in the favored place on the boat, and we honest people, who pay full fare, are huddled here like sheep in a pen, with a rope

1. Beowawe is a town in northeastern Nevada, founded in 1868 and situated along the route of the railroad to California. The town is named for the shape of the hills outside the town, which have the appearance of a gateway, "Beowawe" being the Piute word for gate. A local landmark is the "maiden's grave," burial place of Lucinda Duncan. A myth took hold that she was an 18 year old girl who had either been killed by Native Americans or fallen to her death from a cliff. It was later discovered that Mrs Duncan was an elderly woman who died after a brief illness while on a wagon train headed west in the summer of 1863.

around us."[1] A laugh followed, but Oscar stood calm and unmoved, and when the boat touched the apron he was hurried into a carriage ahead of the *oi polloi* and driven to the Palace. An occupant of the same sleeping-car informed THE TRIBUNE representative concerning his trip from Ogden to Oakland. The first eventful circumstance was

A BRILLIANT OVATION

At Corinne, Utah, where he was received by forty improvised esthetes with sunflower accompaniment and a dingdong brass band. At the Humboldt Wells, Elko, Winnemucca and Reno,[2] crowds swarmed at the depots, and he was hailed with cheers. After passing the region of sage brush, where anything goes for excitement, the interest in the curiosity waned. At Truckee and Colfax but a few persons gathered,[3] and at Sacramento there was no reception at all, except by the *Record-Union* man, who came down on the train with the esthete.[4] Keen observers on the train kept an eye on the brilliant youth, and by means of an acquaintance with the *valet de chambre*, it was discovered that he uses five hair brushes of different styles and patterns, from the steel scraper to the ordinary hog bristle and four combs of metal and bone. His suspenders are of light yellow, woven in flower and vine, and his soaps and perfumes are brilliant in variety. His valet is a gentleman of African descent, and was in constant attendance upon him while making his toilet. Mr. Wilde shaves himself regularly every morning. On the train his career was marked with a quiet though somewhat forced simplicity. He was averse to conversation, and devoted his attention principally to the members of the Comley-Barton troupe who were on the train. He has made a decided impression upon the coast, and his lecture in San Francisco, last evening, was well attended by a fashionable audience. Today

HE COMES TO OAKLAND,

And will lecture at the Armory of the Oakland Light Cavalry, corner of Twelfth and Washington streets, and will receive at the hands of the refined and cultivated as polite and gratifying a reception as he received last evening. It has been suggested by the members of the Light Cavalry having charge of the arrangements that, to prevent a blockade at the door, those wishing to avail themselves of the opportunity of attending the lecture this evening and on Thursday should procure tickets beforehand, and go early for good seats. Mr. Wilde will hold an

1. This is perhaps the same woman whose remarks are quoted in "The Only Oscar," *The Daily Report* (San Francisco, CA), 27 Mar. 1882, 3, p. 305.
2. Towns in Nevada.
3. Towns in California.
4. See [J. A. Woodson], "Oscar Arrives," *The Daily Record-Union* (Sacramento, CA), 27 Mar. 1882, 3, p. 275.

informal reception after each lecture in the company's parlor, giving Oaklanders the opportunity of personal interviews. Both lectures should be patronized, for they depend on each other for practicality and utility in application. Members of the company and Messrs. Kelsey & Flint will supply tickets on demand, and from the many applications already made for them indicate that there will be a large attendance.

"Oscar Wilde in Chinatown," *The Daily Examiner* (San Francisco, CA), 30 Mar. 1882, 3[1]

Last night, after the close of his lecture, Oscar Wilde, accompanied by Charles E. Locke, Mr. Vale, his business manager, Thomas Keogh and an EXAMINER reporter, and guided by special officers James Hamilton and Edward McLaughlin, made a thorough inspection of the Chinese quarter of the city. Mr. Wilde having expressed a wish to see all the finer secrets of Chinatown, no matter at what cost to his olfactory and optical nerves, the two experienced guides fulfilled his desire to the utmost extent of their ability. Joss-houses, Chinese hospitals in Ellick alley, theaters, lodging-houses, underground burrows, Murderers' Alley, the haunts of the high-binders, the holes of the rag-pickers, opium dens, gambling-houses, places of the most questionable character, restaurants, slaughter-houses, offal depositories, merchants' residences, pawnbrokers' stores, junk stores, fish and hog markets, and all the thousand and one queer haunts of the Celestial people were thoroughly explored.[2] "This is just like a chapter from the Arabian Nights," said Mr. Wilde, on leaving the principal Joss House, "and I feel exactly like Haroun al Raschid on an anonymous tour of the streets of Bagdad [*sic*]."[3]

1. Reprinted in *Bruno's Weekly*, *3*(25), 16 Dec. 1916, 1221. Quoted in Rodecape, L. F. (1940). Gilding the sunflower: a study of Oscar Wilde's visit to San Francisco. *California Historical Society Quarterly*, *19*, 97–112, 106.

2. In *Personal Impressions of America* Wilde would describe visiting a theatre and a teahouse in Chinatown (Dibb, 239–40), with one reviewer noting that the theatre "came in for more approval than did any other building referred to throughout the lecture." ("Mr Oscar Wilde on America," *The Dundee Courier and Argus* (Dundee, UK), 10 Oct. 1883, 4.) Chapter 16 of the book version of *The Picture of Dorian Gray* includes an account of Dorian's visit to an opium den: "Dorian winced and looked round at the grotesque things that lay in such fantastic postures on the ragged mattresses. The twisted limbs, the gaping mouths, the staring lustreless eyes, fascinated him." (CW iii, 327.18–20.) It was reported in *The Bookman* (*1*(3), Dec. 1891, 88) that the scene was "a purely imaginary description, as Mr. Wilde recently said that he had never set foot in an opium den in his life."

3. Harun al-Raschid (763–809 CE) was the fifth Abbasid Caliph. Parts of the fictional *One Thousand and One Nights* are set in al-Raschid's court and include the Caliph himself. The reporter spells the title of the book as "Arabian Knights".

"What a picture for Burne-Jones or Val Prinsep," he exclaimed, when a lamp was procured and light shed upon about a dozen heathens stowed away in a cellar.[1] Mr. Wilde was particularly pleased with the barbaric decorations of the large restaurant on Jackson street, and stopped there to feast his appetite on tea and preserves. It was nearly half-past 1 o'clock when the party separated, and Mr. Wilde thanked his guides for their attention.

"Oscar Wilde," *San Jose Daily Herald* (San Jose, CA), 4 Apr. 1882, 3[2]

A Conversation With a Herald Representative—The Lecture

The High Priest of the Esthetes lectured last night to an audience which filled the dress circle of the California Theater. All the most fashionable and cultured people of San Jose were there and the attention they paid to every word of the lecture showed how deeply they were interested in the lecturer and his subject. Mr. Wilde was dressed in the usual velvet coat, knee breeches and silk stockings, ruffled shirt front and lace ruffs. He is a tall, well proportioned man, with a very boyish face, smooth as a woman's, and made to look more effeminate by the hair, which is long and hangs down round the face. His eyes are beautiful, shaded with long lashes and full of expression which varies as the subject changes though their ordinary expression is that of gentle kindness. The face in repose is rather dull but the moment he opens his mouth to converse

THE WHOLE FACE LIGHTS UP

And is positively beautiful. His voice is mellifluous and his lecture was a beautiful word painting in the most perfect English. In a conversation with a representative of the HERALD Mr. Wilde said that when he first thought of coming to America he did not know that the people were so full of deep seated prejudice as he found them. He said that he had expected a certain amount of ridicule to be thrown on his school and himself, thinking that would be the natural result of their having read the ridiculous things which had been published on the other side of the water, but he did not think that when he had an opportunity of delivering his lectures and explaining the object he and his school had in view, that an apprecia-

1. In the source the names are given as "Burne, Jones, and Val Priuseh". Valentine Cameron "Val" Prinsep (1838–1904) was a British artist and writer associated with the Pre-Raphaelites. A number of his paintings were based on his Indian travels: *A Nautch Girl* was exhibited at the Royal Academy in 1878 and *The Roum-i-Sultana* in 1879. His 27-foot-long *The Imperial Assemblage Held at Delhi, 1 January 1877* was exhibited in 1880.
2. H & S, b60.

tive and practical people like the Americans would have understood him, but the great mass of them did not seem to, although there were many of the most cultured people here who fully appreciate the benefit which would accrue from raising the standard of men's morals by teaching them

TO LOVE THE BEAUTIFUL

And good and discard the evil and ugly. In speaking of the country itself he said he had never seen anything so grand and beautiful as the scenery on this coast, and, in fact, all over America. Nature had been most lavish in her gifts, but art had done nothing—art was dead. Speaking of poetry he said that there were really no great poets in America; that the only one who approached to greatness was Joaquin Miller and that he was not appreciated by his fellow-countrymen; that Longfellow was more a beautiful poem himself than a poet; that he was not original but more a copy after English poets; that Oliver Wendell Holmes did not deserve the name of poet; that the man who puts his tongue in his cheek, meaning those who descend to writing funny poetry, do not deserve the name of poets.[1] He considered Walt Whitman as the finest poet America has ever produced, and is surprised to see how little he is thought of among literary people in the United States. He thought that if

EDGAR ALLAN POE

Lived he would have been the greatest of all the American poets,[2] for what little he had done was much finer than anyone else has done since, in this country. He says that no country can produce poets, or artists of any kind until it discards the work of other countries and turns to its own mountains and rivers for inspiration, and build [*sic*] up a school of its own, peculiar to itself. That all American art should treat of American subjects, and copy from nature as seen in America. He said there never would be any art in the United States until the decorative art is better understood and people were surrounded by more beautiful things. Speaking of his dress which he said many had stigmatized as effeminate, he said that people forgot when they said that the fact that the men who won the independence of this country, won it in just such cloaks as he wore. That he thought it would be very inconsistent in him to preach art and beauty dressed in an ugly costume; that he wears the clothes to be consistent and that he believes ere long that it will be adopted by everyone. Only a bare synopsis of the lecture can be

1. Some of Holmes's poetry was comic. It is tempting to speculate that Wilde may have been particularly unimpressed by *A Familiar Letter*, in which Holmes's humorously encourages the reader to churn out their own poetry by imitating "the bards you so greatly admire" and using "words that run smoothly, whatever they mean", thereby winning such fame that "[a]t length your mere presence becomes a sensation".

2. Edgar Allan Poe died aged 40.

given, hardly enough, indeed, to give a fair idea of the subject. He spoke about as follows:

✂ *A report of Wilde's lecture in San Jose.*

"Rare Oscar Wilde," *The Stockton Daily Evening Mail* (Stockton, CA), 4 Apr. 1882, 3[1]

THE ARRIVAL OF THE NAUGHTY IRISH POET.

What He Thinks of California and Its People—His Compliment to American Elocution and Joaquin Miller.

Oscar Wilde has gazed upon the Stockton Court-house!

He rested his lily-white cheek upon his strong hand—the hand that penned "Charmides" and hefted $5,000 in twenty-dollar gold pieces for his six lectures on this coast. This statement is, however, a little bit of poetic license. He has not hefted it yet except in his mind's eye. It is now under Locke and key.[2] But this is an aesthetic digression.

The poet's eye swiftly took in the noble proportions of the massive pile before him. The poet groaned. "I have stood in the mighty Coliseum," he said; "my soul has drank in the harmony of St. Peter's Dome; I have leaned against the Pyramids; I have stumbled over the marble ruins of ancient Greece, and I have angled for catfish in the Hellespont, but this sight has been reserved for me until this day![3] Henceforth let no man say, 'See Naples and die.' I have smelled Naples and still live. But O! O! O!—" Here the poet broke down. He was aroused by a tap on the shoulder, and a rich, sweet voice, suggestive of the groves of Blarney, rang cheerily upon his ear: "Thiggin thu Gaelic?"[4]

"Ennoia poth emon egeneto," replied the poet quickly.[5]

"Hanaman Dhoul, vouz [*sic*] parlez tres bien comme un Irlandais,"[6] shouted his interrogator in joyful accents.

"Didn't I tell you, boys, he was Irish to the core?"

1. I am grateful to John Cooper for identifying this article. The opening is clearly fabricated, but the interview itself appears to be genuine.
2. A pun on the name of Wilde's promoter, Charles E. Locke.
3. Wilde had not visited, nor would ever visit, the pyramids of Egypt or the Hellespont (the Dardanelles).
4. An dtuigeann tú Gaeilge? Do you understand Irish?
5. ἔννοια ποθ' ἡμῖν ἐγένετο (ennoia poth' hemin egeneto). An idea once came to us/me. The opening words of the *Cyropaedia* (*Education of Cyrus*) by Xenophon (c. 430–355/354 BCE).
6. You speak very well, like an Irishman.

"Yes, and Orange Irish at that,"[1] replied a distrustful man. "What does he pack that yaller sunflower around wid him for?"

"Sure it's imblimatic av the sunburst. He's a Faynean."[2]

"Yes; an' his father an Irish lord."

"Hooray for Wild Oscar; hup! hup!"

The poet modestly received these expressions of popularity with a pleased smile. Turning his eyes towards the Court-house he repeated the following impromptu verses:

"My soul is filled with subtle joy
  When viewing thee, thou ancient mine
Of memories sweet without alloy
  Of those who toiled in '49.

And when their day of life is past,
  Upon their tombs inscribe this line:
'They died—their noblest deed the last
  Since drifting here in '49.'"

Then a window of the old building opened and spake:

"Jayzee Gamble; Jayzee Gamble; Jazee Gamble; come into Court!"

Waving his hand gracefully to the crowd the poet walked sorrowfully back to his conservatory in the Yo Semite Hotel.

A small crowd assembled at the railroad depot to catch a peep at the apostle of aestheticism, and when the good-looking six-footer stepped into John Finnan's hack a murmur of admiration was heard from some of the ladies who had gathered for a glimpse of the author of naughty but nice, artistically speaking, "Charmides." He wore a profusion of long brown hair, as fine as a woman's. Indeed, his countenance exhibits more of the female than of the male type, and this likewise is heightened by a pair of large blue eyes and full red lips. He wore a heavy cloak,[3] a grayish-brown velvet coat and a white soft felt hat. He cast a look of disgust at the big black heating stove in the office,[4] and surveyed the plain hat-rack

1. The colour orange is associated with Protestant supporters of William III (William of Orange), who defeated Catholic King James II at the Battle of the Boyne (1690).

2. The sunburst flag was associated with early Irish nationalism and the Irish Republican Brotherhood.

3. Wilde was photographed by Sarony wearing this cloak during a second session in 1882 (plates 24–7). The exact date of the session is unknown (Cooper, J. (2019). 'A picturesque subject indeed!' The Sarony photographs of Oscar Wilde. *The Wildean, 55,* 3–33). See also "Oscar Wilde on Cloaks," *The Atlanta Constitution* (Atlanta, GA), 6 July 1882, 7, p. 438.

4. Wilde railed against American cast-iron stoves in his lecture on *The Decorative Arts*: "I did not imagine, until I went into some of your [America's] simpler cities, that there was so much bad work done. [...] I came across the small iron stove which they always persist in decorating with machine-made ornaments, and which is as great a bore as a wet day or any other particu-

in the hall with a withering look.[1] He was escorted by J. S. Vale, his manager, and a colored servant. His lunch, which was served in his room, was more of a substantial than aesthetic character, and consisted of fried potatoes, cold roast beef, a bottle of English ale and bread and butter and coffee.

A MAIL representative was accorded an interview this afternoon with the poet. He was seated before a small marble topped table, in room 21, with a cup of coffee before him, the plates and potatoes, skins and all, having mysteriously disappeared, being out of keeping with the aesthetic nature of the surroundings. When asked for his impressions of California he said, "It is by far the most beautiful part of America I have seen yet. Eastern America is so colorless at this time, nothing but great brown plains and leafless woodlands, and when I arrived in California, and saw the green fields for the first time since I left England, it seemed to be one of the most beautiful things I ever saw in my life—such purple mountains and such a wealth of wild flowers. It delighted me far beyond anything I ever thought I should see in America."

Referring to the lack of decoration on the houses of America he said, "I have been disappointed that your wooden houses show no carving at all on them, because wood carving is one of the simplest of the decorative arts, and is so very easy to teach. Every shepherd's house in Switzerland is covered with beautiful carvings done by the lads of the family. What a Swiss boy can do well an American boy ought to do better.[2] Wood-carving should be taught in the schools here. It is not only a beautiful but a useful art. I have been told that you Western people have not the time to devote to art; that you are engrossed in the pursuit of

---

larly dreadful institution. When unusual extravagance was indulged in it was garnished with two funeral urns." ("Art Decoration," *New York Tribune* (New York, NY), 12 May 1882, 2.) He also returned to the theme in later interviews: see "The World Wonder Wilde," *Iowa Daily Register* (Des Moines, IA), 27 Apr. 1882, 2, p. 368; "Aesthetic," *Dayton Daily Democrat* (Dayton, OH), 3 May 1882, 4, pp. 371–2; and "Oscar Wilde Interviewed," *The Daily Sun* (Saint John, NB), 5 Oct. 1882, 3, p. 466. A cartoon by Thomas Nast (1840–1902) of Wilde jumping from a hot stove was printed in *Harper's Weekly* (9 Sep. 1882, 575).

1. Wilde criticised hat-racks in his lecture on *The House Beautiful*: "Hat racks are, I suppose, necessary. I have never seen a really nice hat rack; the ordinary one is more like some horrible instrument of torture than anything useful or graceful, and it is perhaps the ugliest thing in the house." (O'Brien, 168.) "The modern hat-rack he despised, preferring the light Japanese rack to any other design for the hall" ("Oscar Wilde's Last Lecture," *Sacramento Daily Record-Union* (Sacramento, CA), 10 Apr. 1882, 3). Daniel O'Connell (see p. 320, note 1) later remembered Wilde recommending Albanian hatracks to his San Francisco audiences, and saying "you are well aware, my friends, of the importance of a hatrack. It impresses the stranger who visits you, and indicates to him whether you are persons of refinement or otherwise" ("Bohemian Experiences of Oscar Wilde and Sir Samuel Baker," *San Francisco Chronicle* (San Francisco, CA), 24 Oct. 1897, 5).

2. Wilde made the same point in *The Decorative Arts*: "Why should not American boys do a great deal more and better than Swiss boys?" ("Art Decoration," *New York Tribune* (New York, NY), 12 May 1882, 2.) See also p. 146, note 1.

OSCAR WILDE ON OUR CAST-IRON STOVES.
Another American Institution sat down on.

Figure 9. A cartoon by Thomas Nast. Wilde often criticised the cast iron stoves that he found were ubiquitous in American hotel rooms.

wealth. I think that is a sad thing. A country that definitely devotes itself solely to the accumulation of wealth has a terrible fate in store for it."

Mr. Wilde said further in speaking of the climate and scenery of California, that it reminded him very much of Italy in Spring, with its orange trees in blossom and its vines in full leaf.

"The best American poet you have," he said, "comes from California."

"Who is that; Dan O'Connell?" inquired the reporter.[1]

"I am surprised," responded the poet, "that you can be ignorant of the one I mean. I regard Joaquin Miller as the successor to the laurels of Longfellow. Some short time ago, when Longfellow died, there were articles in all the American newspapers discussing as to which of the American poets would be most likely to take his place. They mentioned every writer of poetry in America that ever scribbled a volume of poems, but the real man—the California man—they never mentioned at all. Joaquin Miller possesses the true warmth of imagination and that refinement which constitute the poet."

The San Francisco newspapers had been very appreciative and courteous toward him, he said. This lecturing tour was his first essay in public life since he graduated with the highest honors of his class in Oxford, two and half years ago.[2] The first time he ever addressed a public audience was in New York on the 14th January last.[3] "I am very sorry," he added, "that it is my first experience, because public speaking is an art, and I, who lay such stress on the technical side of art—I know that I am offending myself, that I am dealing in the art of eloquence without ever having been taught to speak. In England we are never taught how to speak in public. The eloquence of American speakers has been a matter of constant wonder to me. At the Bohemian Club in San Francisco last Saturday night, General Barnes—a well-known lawyer—proposed my health in a speech which, for beauty of sentiment and for wealth of metaphor I have never heard excelled in England.[4] A literary man in England writes what he wishes to say and prints it,

1. Daniel O'Connell (1849–1899) was an Irish poet and journalist. He immigrated to California in 1868, taught Greek for a time at St. Ignatius College, and wrote for and edited a number of periodicals in the San Francisco Bay Area. In 1881 he published *Lyrics*, a book of poems. The fact that one of these poems rhymes "paragraph" with "phonograph" is perhaps all that needs be said of their quality (coincidentally, another is titled *The Rose and the Nightingale*; Wilde would later write a short story titled *The Nightingale and the Rose*).

2. Wilde had graduated three and a half years earlier, in November 1878 (Sturgis, 132/129).

3. Wilde gave his first lecture in New York on 9 January 1882. He had previously read *Ravenna* to a large audience at Oxford's Sheldonian Theatre (Sturgis, 128/125).

4. Major-General William Henry Linow Barnes (1836–1902) was an attorney and Civil War general famed for his eloquence: "Few men in the United States could equal General Barnes as a raconteur or in making timely speeches, set or impromptu, whatever the occasion." ("Death Forever Stills Voice of Noted Orator," *The San Francisco Call* (San Francisco, CA), 22 July 1902, 3.) He became President of the Bohemian Club in April 1883. The dinner that Wilde mentions was given on 1 April. Daniel O'Connell was present and remembered that beforehand "the feel-

but it is an uncommon thing for him to lecture. When I go back to England I shall certainly write about the necessity of teaching our young men the art of elocution."

Mr. Wilde regretted that he would be unable to visit Yo Semite and the Big Trees, as his lecture engagements made his stay in this State a brief one. Tomorrow evening he will lecture on the "Irish Poets" in San Francisco, after which he will leave for Salt Lake City and Denver to fill his engagements there. The following short poems are given as examples of Mr. Wilde's style:

✂ *Wilde's poems* Ave Imperatrix *(first four and final four stanzas),* Magdalen Walks, *and* In the Gold Room.[1]

"Wilde on Poetry," *The Stockton Daily Evening Mail* (Stockton, CA), 5 Apr. 1882, 3[2]

Some Sensible Advice for Stockton Spring Poets.

In reply to a question as to what he considered the coming style of poetry, Oscar Wilde in an interview yesterday said: "The imagination, upon which poetry depends, is something so untrammelled that you can never attempt to limit it to any school at all. I should be very sorry if you wanted to clip the imagination, like the wings of an eagle, and confine it within a cage. All over the world in ordinary magazines and provincial newspapers a constant amount of poetry is published, of which the sentiments are irreproachable and the writers of which express the proper admiration for its right things. Against these sentiments and against the sincerity of the people who write them nothing can be said. As much sincerity is wasted in filling the poet's corner in some small provincial paper as ought to inspire a play of Shakespeare or a poem of Dante, and this amount of poetry is utterly worthless. That is very sad, indeed, when we consider the deep feelings under which it is produced. The reason is this: the young men and women who contribute such poetry forget that poetry is an art, the highest and the most difficult of all the arts, dependent no doubt on nobility of imagination and on a nature

---

ing in the club [towards Wilde] was one of mingled curiosity and antagonism." A plot was hatched for General Barnes and Judge Hoffman to "attack and demolish" Wilde in a discussion of the classics and English literature; Wilde apparently vanquished his opponents with ease, Barnes taking the defeat better than Hoffman, who went away "feebly babbling about the unfairness of his defeat" ("Bohemian Experiences of Oscar Wilde and Sir Samuel Baker," *San Francisco Chronicle* (San Francisco, CA), 24 Oct. 1897, 5).

1. *Magdalen Walks* was first published in *The Irish Monthly* (6 Apr. 1878; CW i, No. 49) and revised for *Poems*. The revised version was reprinted here.

2. Reprinted in Cooper (Stockton lecture, 4 April 1882).

sensitive to beauty, but dependent also on its technical side, its rhythm, its music, its melody, and all the technical part of the art of poetry, which is quite as necessary as the theory of harmony is to the musician or a scheme of color to the painter. Most provincial poets never learn their art; they trust entirely to their own feelings; whereas, if any one wishes to write poetry, he or she should study the great masters of style to begin with, just as we set students of painting to study a great picture, or student-sculptors some masterpiece of the artist's chisel. In this modern school of poetry of ours, we should first study style and the music of words, we should absorb all the work of the great masters that have gone before us, and we should not forget the technical side of art. The charm of poetry comes principally to us through its wonderful music. Every word in the English language has a certain definite musical value, quite as definite as a note on the piano or a chord on the strings of a violin. It is approaching poetry on its artistic side where it is really an art. That is what we insist on in England, so that at any rate the poetry that is now published in England has all the qualities of beautiful style about it."

Mary Watson, "Oscar Wilde at Home," *The Daily Examiner* (San Francisco, CA), 9 Apr. 1882, 1[1]

How the Apostle of the Beautiful Looks and Acts in His Room.

INTERVIEWED BY A LADY REPORTER.

The Young Aesthete's Conversation—His Poetry and His Views—The New Book Dedicated to Himself.

The English language is popularly supposed to be a vehicle of expression that was perfected long ago. It is intended not to conceal but to express thought, and only persons who labor after originality, like Robert Browning,[2] for instance, give themselves the trouble to twist its words into new meanings. Yet, strange to say, there are two words in the English language which of late are employed as

1. H & S, b61. Reprinted in H & S, 123–8. Quoted in Sturgis, 243/233. See also Mary Watson's reminiscences of her meeting with Wilde: Watson, M. (1890) *People I Have Met: Short Sketches of Many Prominent Persons.* Francis, Valentine & Co. 48–52 (reprinted in Mikhail, 64–6). This article is included in the Robert Ross Memorial Collection album (Ross b.6, 66).

2. Robert Browning (1812–1889) was an English poet and playwright. Wilde's dialogue *The Critic as Artist* (1890, revised 1891) includes a lengthy assessment of Browning: "[...] he was great: and though he turned language into ignoble clay, he made from it men and women that live. He is the most Shakespearian creature since Shakespeare. If Shakespeare could sing with myriad lips, Browning could stammer through a thousand mouths." (CW iv, 130.6–10.)

frequently as any other two that could be named, if we make due exception of "charming" and "awful," and they are "aesthetic" and "utter," about the signification of which there seem to be no general agreement; yet all concede that they apply to an unknown quantity in artistic niceness, and at once the more complex form of intensified aestheticism in the shape of "utter" presents itself. The most agreeable and perhaps the most effective solution of the much-used word outside of dictionarial definition would be to get the meaning from the fountain head, that is, from the apostoletic source of Aestheticism, Oscar Wilde himself. I saw the lion in his lair, saw him stirred up, poetically speaking, and an interesting process it was. It took place at the Palace Hotel, where the young poet resided during his stay here. Without further preliminaries I will endeavor to picture Oscar Wilde's at-home manner and how he exists in so unaesthetic a caravansary as the palace Hotel. Fortunately, there was plenty of time to get a good look at the room and peer about without transgressing any social rules, for when I arrived, as per appointment, there was no one but his servant at home, and the opportunity was afforded to get an uninterrupted few moments and jot down whatever there was remarkable. Between the fear of not seeing everything and of his sudden arrival, I could only get cursory glimpses of all the peculiarities the room offered, and had little time to think of what I was to ask him when he did make his appearance. At any rate, all the questions that I had in my mind in reference to Mr. Wilde flew from me when he entered a few moments after I did.

HIS LAZY MANNER

And my hard effort to explain in a depressed sort of way, occasioned by my feeling of strangeness, soon made matters rather one-sided. He talked, and talked well, and soon I regained my ordinary frame of mind, but with still a misgiving as to how to broach my subject; but his action in throwing off his circular cloak, the quick and well-rehearsed movement of the servant, who reached the center of the room just at the right moment to catch the outside wraps of the poet, and his subsequent position on the sofa, partaking rather of an easy posture, half reclining, half sitting, set me quite at ease; and the poet, whom I had expected to lead me in the empyrean ways of poetic fancy, for which I was half prepared, made me believe so utterly in the mere commonplace that I felt a sense of disappointment, for it is so awful to believe in a man's superiority and then find him out. The rooms were of the usual hotel order, with the walls as innocent of cheerfulness as the sunless light which filtered in from the window. It suggested a question and I haphazarded it.

"How do you manage to live in these rooms without any surrounding signs of the beautiful?"

Quoth he, with an accompaniment of a rather comfortable shudder, "Don't mention it."

Since the request of not mentioning it was so vigorously put to me, I dropped the question of the beautiful in art, or whatever else was in my mind pertaining to the subject, and naturally did what ninety-nine people out of every hundred, when a lack of material for conversation occurred, would do. I spoke of myself.

"Is not this something new for you, Mr. Wilde. You have never met a lady reporter?"

"No," replied he, smilingly; "I have not. We do not have them in our country."

I looked toward the bay-window, wherein was placed a table, and on it a vase with a large bouquet of white flowers, beautifully arranged, and, to give it effect, a silk handkerchief had been thrown carelessly across the two lower branches, and the air coming from the window swayed the ends in graceful movements. Glancing from the top of the table to the floor, the pile of newspapers met my gaze, and naturally suggested the next question:

"Are you pleased at the newspaper reports of yourself and the reporters' interviews?"

Evidently this had struck a rich vein, for he looked up with a peculiar and hearty smile; but, evidently remembering that his questioner was of the same genus as the subject spoken about, he seemed to restrain himself; but replied, with a laugh:

"Frankly, then, I read them all, and not only here but all over America I have been quite amused at the struggle each of the gentlemen have had to write what I did not say; but I have the most sympathy with the writers of the articles which strive to be what is called here in the United States 'funny.' Their hard work has been so apparent."

From this on the conversation was quite easy, and Mr. Wilde displayed a fund of

SHREWD COMMON SENSE

Hardly to be expected from an art enthusiast and a poet. The conversation on his part which followed gave me full opportunity to memorize the disposition of every article in the room, and that a certain eccentric individuality of the man was displayed in every phase of the furniture could not be gainsaid. There were three tables in the room, the one mentioned in the embrasure of the bay-window, one inside the room and one about the center, and all in a row. The sofa on which the poet was reclining was on the left hand and the mantel on the right. On the table where the striking posy of white flowers was placed were also strewn in confusion scraps of paper, letters, books, etc., and at the foot the newspapers, which fortunately suggested the opening of a conversation which by this time was flowing along smoothly enough. On the table in the center of the room were also a lot of papers and cards from various business houses, evidently intended to convey to the much advertised aesthete the pleasure every merchant would have in showing him his wares, to be used in the future as an advertisement no doubt. On the table near the window and about four feet from the other was a large silver fruit-dish, filled with oranges, two plates and a knife, and placed there innocently enough as a living example of an effective and suggestive picture of still life. On the sofa was carelessly thrown a dark brown rug with a pillow, over which was thrown a crepe shawl of the same color, with long fringe to match. During our conversation several cards were handed in, and among other things the servant brought in an autographic album with some one's compliments and a request for Mr. Wilde's little contribution to the general collection. He arose, seated himself at the table with the open book before him, and in a posture which excellently expressed "thought," he tried to evolve something for the inevitable autograph-hunter and great American nuisance. The inspirational mood was not on him them. He arose, gracefully spread his arm over an almost impossible distance, and, with an admirable breadth of reach, got hold of a copy of his own poems, sat down again and said to me:

"One sometimes forgets one's own lines."

The struggle was short and had to be given up, so he bade the servant—

"Tell the messenger to leave the album, as I am too much engaged just now." This with a glance at me.

A few moments later, another autograph album was sent in and the message repeated—without the glance, however. He then wheeled the sofa in front of me and threw himself upon it—not, of course, lying down, but in a careless posture, with his arm thrown careless over the pillow. I got a good glance at his necktie, and I noticed that the handkerchief in his coat pocket and the scarf were of exactly the same tint of satin—a peculiar shade of olive bronze.

HIS INSPIRATION.

Among the other questions, and they were a legion, I asked him:

"At what hour of the day do you find it most convenient to write?"

"At no particular hour. In writing a verse I sometimes wait for the exact mood, and it takes weeks at times before I get the right word to express my thought in the completion of a sentence or a line. Sometimes a subject is presented to me when I least expect it, perhaps in a company of friends, perhaps traveling, or in a crowded street."

In an animated conversation, and especially about himself, Mr. Wilde, in a youthful sort of way, becomes quite enthusiastic. From the conversation which followed I gathered that he was born at No. 1 Merrion Square, Dublin,[1] and that his mother, of whom he seems very proud, inspired him with a desire to become a poet. He showed me her picture, and, from her portrait, she seems to be a handsome woman of about 47,[2] with a clear sunny expression of face, and not at all like a woman who is given to writing poetry. Mr. Wilde does not resemble his mother a particle, although there seems to be a deep bond of sympathy between them. He assured me that until the age of 18 he never thought of writing a line; and in proof that others have the same enthusiasm, and entertain the same views of poetry, art and literature as himself, he pointed out the fact that a young classmate of his has written a volume on the same subject and dedicated it to Mr. Wilde himself. Mr. Wilde is now having it published and it will be out shortly.[3] He showed me a bit of manuscript which he declared he appreciated, and valued above anything which had ever been given him. It was the original manuscript of "An Ode to Blue," written by Keats in a handwriting peculiarly dainty and small. The manuscript, old and yellow, was presented to Mr. Wilde on his recent visit to Louisville. While there, he received a note from a young lady asking him to call, signed simply Miss. Keats. It was from this lady, to whom the poet was a relative, that the young disciple received his treasured ode.[4] That Mr. Wilde is not sure of his ground, nor has he a fixed idea, is best illustrated by his reply to a question relative to

1. The source gives the address as Marian Square. Wilde was born at 21 Westland Row; the family moved the short distance to 1 Merrion Square when Oscar was aged one (Sturgis, 3/11, 12/19–20).

2. There is no telling if Wilde carried a recent or older picture of his mother, but Lady Wilde would have been gratified by this assessment. She had recently turned 60, and was known for her attempts to obscure her age by keeping the curtains drawn and using rose-tinted lamp shades (Melville, 159).

3. Rennell Rodd's *Rose Leaf and Apple Leaf*.

4. Emma Speed née Keats (1823–1883) was the daughter of George Keats, the poet's younger brother. She wrote to Wilde on 12 March, enclosing the manuscript of an untitled poem on blue (Harry Ransom Center, The University of Texas at Austin, MSS_WildeO_3_1_011). Wilde replied to thank her on 21 March: "What you have given me is more golden than gold, more precious than any treasure this great country could yield me" (CL, 157). In an article for the *Century Guild Hobby Horse* Wilde published the manuscript and expanded upon his encounter with Speed: "When my lecture was concluded there came round to see me a lady of middle age, with a sweet gentle manner and a most musical voice. She introduced herself to me as Mrs. Speed, the daughter of George Keats, and invited me to come and examine the Keats manuscripts in her possession. I spent most of the next day [22 February] with her, reading the letters of Keats to her father, some of which were at that time unpublished, poring over torn yellow leaves and faded scraps of paper [....] Some months afterwards, when I was in California, I received a letter from Mrs. Speed asking my acceptance of the original manuscript of the sonnet which I had quoted in my lecture." (July 1886; CW vi, No. 35, lines 6–16.) Wilde hung the manuscript on the wall of his study in Tite Street (William Theodore Peters, "Oscar Wilde at Home," *The Sunday Inter Ocean* (Chicago, IL), 16 Dec. 1894, 31, p. 617). It was sold in the auction of the Wildes' household effects on 24 April 1895 (Munby, 383).

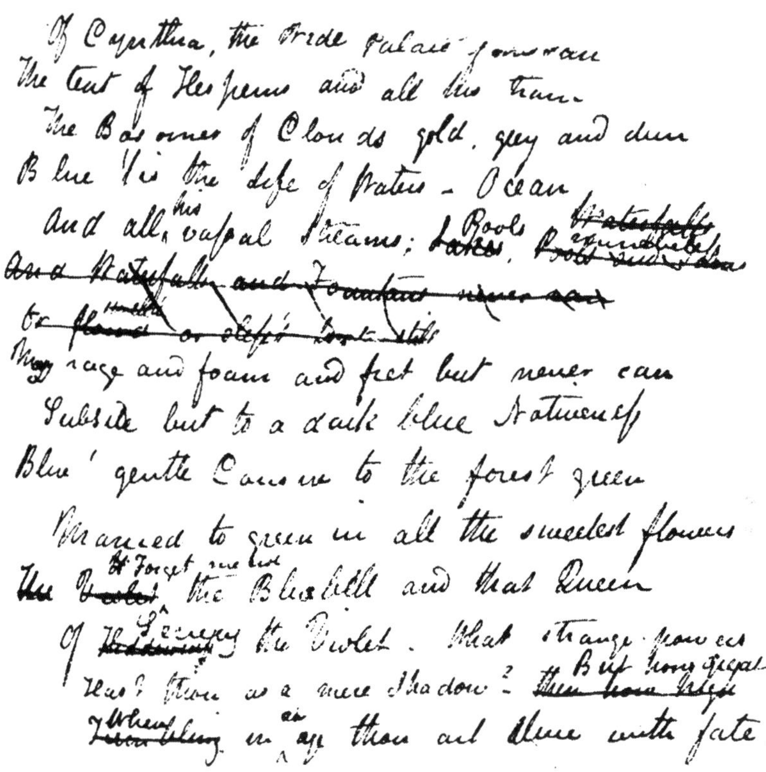

Figure 10. The manuscript of John Keats's untitled poem on blue, given to Wilde in America by a niece of the poet.

HIS NEW BOOK.

He said: "My other book may be a perfect contradiction of the first;"[1] and, on being asked about his return to England, he said: "I don't know. I never make plans, but go whither my feelings prompt. I wish, however, to be back in time for the salons."

Mr. Wilde regrets exceedingly that he entered into a contract with Sarony, the New York photographer, not to have any one else take his pictures while in this country. He admires the pictures produced by some of our local photographers, and, in an art sense, apparently believes in the superiority of San Fran-

1. Wilde's attitude here is echoed in his essay *The Truth of Masks* (1891; revised from earlier articles): "A Truth in art is that whose contradictory is also true." (CW iv, 228.24–5.)

cisco workmanship to that of New York. He had some fine specimens from the principal photographers of the city. On being asked as to the age expressed in the last words of his poem, which interests all women—

"I have made my choice, have lived my poems,
 and though youth is gone in wasted days,
I have found the lover's crown of myrtle better
 than the poet's crown of bays!"[1]

He replied: "Sometimes one feels older at 20 than he will at 40."

During his conversation about his poems he certainly evidenced a belief in them and gave way to his enthusiasm by frequent gestures. His voice, in ordinary conversation, does not partake of the same tone as that used on the rostrum, nor are the same unpleasant monotones employed with all their faulty intonations. Youthful fervor carries with it a sense of truth, and if the word "utter," as expressed by this aesthete, means ardor, coupled with a sense of art and what is beautiful in the world, it is a good word and ought to be a welcome one in our vocabulary, which, after all, is not replete with adjectives expressive of things that are beautiful, as a lady reporter can testify.

MARY WATSON.

"The Apostle Again," *Reno Evening Gazette* (Reno, NV), 10 Apr. 1882, 3

Mr. Wilde Goes East on Easter.[2] He is a Lover of Joaquin Miller.

A GAZETTE reporter rode a ways on the train yesterday morning and, a good opportunity offering, applied the screws to Oscar Wilde, who was a passenger, and found that he was highly pleased with his visit to the coast. He said the people were in danger of deifying money instead of allowing the love of beauty and the enjoyment of art to share their affections. He says California audiences are delightful ones both to talk to and to look at. His greatest complaint, however, is that people here do not appreciate Joaquin Miller, whom he ranks as America's greatest poet and as the coming playwright. His poem on Walker is the finest of his works.[3] Mr. Wilde thinks the man's private life has nothing whatever to do

1. The closing lines of *ΓΛΥΚΥΠΙΚΡΟΣ ΕΡΩΣ*, first published in *Poems* (CW i, No. 74). Wilde ended the poem with a full stop rather than an exclamation mark.

2. 9 April was Easter Sunday.

3. *With Walker in Nicaragua* appeared in *Songs of the Sierras* (1871). It is a long poem about William Walker (1824–1860), an American physician, lawyer, and journalist who led private military expeditions into Mexico and Central America in the hope of establishing colonies under

with our estimate of his work. If it is strong, good and beautiful, as he claims it is, the poet should be honored and enriched. The estimation in which great men are held is the standard by which he judges a community, and in that respect the coast is behind the East and the East far behind the old country. Speaking of the Press of America, Mr. Wilde said it was full of rubbish. He saw the New York papers, and it seemed that if people read them and were satisfied with them that this must be a nation of lunatics, but he found that an enormous gap lay between the papers and the people, who were bright, intellectual and imaginative. He was even more unfavorably impressed with the papers of the Pacific Coast. He says the East is ugly, but California is very pretty and Nevada by no means uninteresting. He begged of the GAZETTE man to refrain from painting the rocks with advertisements, which he held to be a high crime against the beauty of any country.[1]

"Oscar Wilde," *Salt Lake Daily Herald* (Salt Lake City, UT), 12 Apr. 1882, 8[2]

A Pleasant Chat with the Aesthete

His Impression of America and Her People and Poets.

The Courtesy of His Audiences.

His Peculiar Dress the Coming Thing in the Fashionable World.

Our reporter called upon Mr. Oscar Wilde on Monday and was received by the distinguished aesthete with characteristic courtesy, Mr. Wilde, speaking of his American experiences with the utmost candor.[3]

No part of America it appeared has struck Mr. Wilde so favorably as California, but as he said, "I have still to see Colorado." Whatever may be the effect of Denver and Leadville, it is at present certain that San Francisco and the west coast have captivated the poet, for Mr. Wilde intends to return there next year with a party of friends, "in the capacity," as he described it, "of a private gentle-

---

his own control. Walker was the President of Nicaragua for a little under a year between 1856 and 1857 before he was deposed. In 1860 he was captured and executed by the government of Honduras.

1. In *Personal Impressions of America* Wilde would complain that "one of the great features of America is the advertiser who defaced even the most beautiful parts of the Rocky Mountains with their advertisements, generally for some horrible medicine" (Dibb, 241).

2. H & S, b62. Reprinted in H & S, 128–30. Quoted in OWDA, 240, 275–7; Pearson, 72; Hyde, 62; and Sturgis, 224/215.

3. Monday 10 April.

man traveling for his own amusement and not as a public lecturer condemned to go on the platform at every place he stops."

Of the results of his tour, financially, the apostle of art decoration spoke very contentedly, and proposes devoting a portion of the proceeds to a lengthened visit to Venice, and a leisurely study of Italy.

But it was when he came to speak of his reception by the American public that Mr. Wilde was most interesting. "I am," he said, "more and more astonished and pleased every time I lecture at the courtesy with which I am received by my audiences. Everybody, they say, laughs at me, and says I am a fraud, yet not only do they fill any place I choose to lecture in, but they sit out all I have to say with surprising good humor and patience. I am quite conscious that much of what I say may be annoying, but after all I came to America to say it and so long as audiences with such forbearance and good breeding allow me to strut my brief hour upon the stage, I should be singularly stupid not to take advantage of the opportunities given me of trotting out my hobbies. I have no doubt that tonight there will be many people present, perhaps even most of them, who, after they have seen me and satisfied their curiosity as to my costume and my long hair, would be glad to go away again without sitting through a lecture on a subject that does not interest them; but at the same time I have no doubt whatever that they will, out of pure courtesy, sit it out to the bitter end. Sometimes I am inclined to laugh at this kindness, knowing that my audiences often laugh at me, but I really consider my opportunity so splendid a one for saying what I wish to say, that I only wish my delivery and my language were better than they are. Yes, you are right; my delivery has often been criticized *very* severely, and I confess it is abominable. But I cannot help it. I have never studied elocution—but I shall when I return to England, probably under Vezin.[1] As for my costume, I have several reasons for it, but the more important are these: that the present evening dress of gentlemen is the most objectionable possible, and then I should be glad to do something towards introducing a better. As it is, the Prince of Wales and some of his friends have already pronounced in favor of the velvet coat, ruffles, knee-breeches and silk hose, and it is quite possible that in another year or so all young men in England may be dressed as I am. Indeed, in New York, one very charming lady has ordered knee-breeches as *de rigueur* at her receptions, and New York has cheerfully submitted to her delightful tyranny.[2] But another reason for my wearing

1. Hermann Vezin (1829–1910) was an American actor and writer as well as a teacher of elocution. He immigrated to the United Kingdom when still a young man. When Wilde returned to London and was planning a lecture tour of the United Kingdom, he asked for Vezin's help in developing "a natural style, with a touch of affectation". Vezin replied: "Well, and haven't you got that, Oscar?" (Sturgis, 290/275).

2. Presumably a reference to Kate Field: see "The Question of the Hour," *The New York Herald* (New York, NY), 4 Mar. 1882, 9, pp. 766–7.

this costume is based on a principle, for live poets have principles, and that is that one should do as one preaches. Now Morris, the author of that exquisite *Earthly Paradise*,[1] is prophetically proclaiming the doctrine of artistic dress as a preliminary to a revival of true art; but he goes about himself in the very shabbiest and ugliest of nineteenth century clothes. I do not agree with this, so that when you call upon me as you do now, you find me dressed in aesthetic colors. My coat is a pearl grey velvet, my necktie Venetian green, and you will see that I spread a fur robe over this hideous sofa before I sit down on it. Tonight, for the same reason, if you come to the theatre, you will find me in black velvet lined with purple, and wearing the ruffles and seals of the regency."

Mr. Wilde then went on to speak of the American poets, expressing that special preference for Joaquin Miller and Walter Whitman, which he has so often tried to vindicate in opposition to other opinions. For Longfellow, he did not entertain so much reverence for the poet as love for the man. "Longfellow," he said, "was himself a beautiful poem, more beautiful than anything he ever wrote." Emerson's prose he considered poetry; the poetry of certain others he considered prose. But as he said "We rhymesters are without number; the real poet has not come once in a century." Mr. Wilde then quoted favorite sketches from Aldrich, Holmes, Lowell and others, showing an intimate acquaintance with American literature that justified his undertaking to criticise it. Of our novelists he places Howells and James easily first; "indeed," he said, "They are your only two."

Much more that Mr. Wilde said might be of interest to our readers, but our space compels us to be brief. To run up [*sic*], he appears to be thoroughly satisfied with the financial results of his tour, and more than satisfied with the good taste and courtesy of the audiences that have listened to him, and among the personal friends he has made in America, there are many who have exacted the promise that he will return to the country next year. "And so I will," said Mr. Wilde, "when I have got more to say, and learnt a better style of saying it."

"Art Decoration," *The Salt Lake Daily Tribune* (Salt Lake City, UT), 11 Apr. 1882, 4

Oscar Wilde Enlightens a Large Audience on the Subject.

At noon yesterday there was a large crowd of curious people on the steps of the Walker House, waiting to see Oscar Wilde. Presently a hack drove up to the

1. *The Earthly Paradise* is an epic poem by William Morris, and was published in volumes between 1868 and 1870. It concerns a group of mediaeval Norsemen who discover a lost city where the Greek gods are still worshipped. The travellers and their hosts share stories.

door with a tall man swathed in a cloak followed by a small man and a colored servant. He crossed the walk in a couple of steps and disappeared by way of the ladies entrance. The enterprising hotel keeper was ready for his guest and the boy who showed the poet to his room had a sunflower in his button hole. The boy looked quite ill at ease and embarrassed. The bar keeper hoisted a sunflower behind the bar, and at the dinner table a few ladies put lilies in their hair. The poet, however took his meals in his room. A TRIBUNE reporter found him in late in the evening and he gave an interesting description of his trip over America, and his impressions of the country. His opinions were given quite freely and will appear in tomorrow's issue.[1]

✂ *A report of Wilde's lecture in Salt Lake City.*

"Oscar Wilde," *The Cheyenne Daily Leader* (Cheyenne, WY), 13 Apr. 1882, 1

He Passes Through Cheyenne Once Again.

Oscar Wilde, of whom we have all heard so much, passed through Cheyenne yesterday for Denver, where he is booked for a lecture. Our reporter had considerable difficulty in rounding him up but finally found him in the car.

We shall not undertake to give the interview as it took place verbatim, but only the substance thereof.

Mr. Wilde looks and appears like any other respectable gentleman who travels through the country either on business or for amusement. He puts on no style and would scarcely be noticed among the ordinary run of travelers that pass back and forth over the U. P.[2]

He said that he saw no reason why the papers should assail him as they had done for he had not in his life, that he knew of, undertaken to say anything unjust or uncomplimentary to anybody else, and he hoped that the time would come when people would be considerate toward him and not take it for granted that he was a crank or an idiot. He had his views and ideas and had never sought to intrude them upon others, except in a reasonable way, and then only as any other person seeking to make an honest living would have done.

1. No interview with Wilde was printed in the next day's issue. An article positively appraising Wilde's visit to Salt Lake City appeared the following day ("Oscar Wilde," *The Salt Lake Daily Tribune* (Salt Lake City, UT), 13 Apr. 1882, 1).
2. Union Pacific railroad, i.e. the Overland Route.

His reception and treatment on the Pacific coast, he said, was cordial and friendly, and all that he could expect. He was going to Denver to lecture, but was undetermined where he should go next.

When asked as to his opinion in regard to poetry he said that he believed the only true poetry ever written was based on some actual incident, or occurrence, and cited as an example Robert Burns' "Farewell, the Bonnie Banks of Ayr," written by him just before he expected to leave his own country and sail for the West Indies, probably never to return.[1]

Mr. Wilde is a far different man from what most people who have read of him would expect to see. In appearance he is just as practicable and sensible about the ordinary affairs of life as a Cheyenne banker would be, and as the train started to roll out on the D. P. for Denver our reporter jumped off with the full belief that Wilde has been maligned and abused by the press unjustly and without reason.[2]

"Oscar Wilde," *Rocky Mountain News* (Denver, CO), 13 Apr. 1882, 8[3]

The Able-Bodied Esthete Dawns Upon Denver.

He Falls a Prey to a Keen "News" Reporter,

And Discourses Glibly on Many and Various Topics.

His Views of Art, Architecture, Dress and America.

Art Decoration Discussed at the Opera House.

An Interesting Lecture and a Fine Audience.

What Oscar Has to Say for Himself.

The esthete has come. The man whose life and talents are devoted to the study and cultivation of the beautiful, and the business of making money, has

1. Robert Burns (1759–1796) was a Scottish poet. When he wrote *Farewell to the Banks of Ayr* (1786) he had accepted a position in Jamaica (he later abandoned his plans to emigrate). In prison Wilde requested his *Poems* (Wright, 320). Compare Wilde's opinion here with that expressed in a later interview: "whatever actually occurs gives the artist no suggestion." (Gilbert Burgess, "An Ideal Husband at the Haymarket Theatre," *The Sketch* (London, UK), 9 Jan. 1895, 495, p. 645.)

2. The D. P. was the Denver Pacific Railway.

3. H & S, b63. Reprinted in H & S, 130–4. Quoted in OWDA, 248–9, 283–4; and Sturgis, 245/234. Referenced in Sturgis, 236/226, 237/228.

arrived in this prosaic city, where dollars and cents rank high, and where beauty is valued only for its money value.

Last evening's train over the Cheyenne division was delayed about half an hour, and seated in the drawing room car of that train was the much talked of Oscar Wilde, who manifested some regret and annoyance at the unexpected delay. The esthete is not handsome, and yet he is remarkably fine-looking. About his person there is an air of refinement, culture and grace that makes a striking contrast to the typical American man.

OSCAR WILDE

is tall and elegantly proportioned. His head is not large, and yet it is good-sized. His hair, a dark brown, is parted nearly in the middle and is worn long, giving him a somewhat peculiar appearance. His face is long and oval in shape. He wears no beard or mustache, his mouth is rather large and the lips are full and as bright colored as a girl's. His teeth are large and not particularly handsome, his forehead is low. His eyes are extremely beautiful; they are blue and very large. His nose is long and thin, and if breeding and blood are indicated by the nose, Mr. Wilde can lay claim to a large quantity of the genuine "blue." His complexion is so clear and beautiful that the maidens may well grow green with envy, for no balm or powder can give to their cheeks the peculiar beauty of the esthete's complexion.

HIS HANDS ARE WELL-SHAPED,

his fingers long and tapering as if made to handle beautiful objects or wield the pen while the poetic mind dictates words of fire. His feet are large and well proportioned to his body. Taken all in all, Mr. Wilde can be truly called an elegant looking gentleman. His looks would indicate that he was the descendant of a well-bred, fine, old English family, and his conversation marks him as a man of sense, strength and sympathy. During repose his face might be called plain, but when conversing his eyes grow bright, the color rises to his cheeks, his gestures are free and easy, and he is the picture of animation.

On the train last evening he wore a pair of dark brown trousers, well cut and neat fitting, and a black velvet coat, rather after the fashion of a sacque. It was cut high in the neck, leaving visible only the necktie, which was a cream colored silk scarf tied in a large bow. His collar was of fine white linen, and was not noticeably large. He wore a long heavy overcoat of *gen d'arme* blue cloth, lined throughout with fur, a broad fur collar and deep cuffs finishing the outside, of

THIS HANDSOME GARMENT.

Around his neck, a gold-colored embroidered scarf hung untied. The ends were fringed. Upon leaving the car, the scarf was carelessly drawn close about the neck under the overcoat. Upon his head Mr. Wilde wore a large black, or deep blue, slouch hat. Upon the third finger of his right hand he wore a large handsomely carved intaglio ring which was his only ornament.

After shaking hands with THE NEWS representative Mr. Wilde at once entered into conversation with an ease that is not ordinary even among public speakers. His voice is pleasant to listen to and gives one the impression of much power, yet he always talks in a monotone which must grow tedious. He talks rapidly, uses beautiful language and pronounces his words in a way which Americans will be very apt to call affected. His gestures during conversation are graceful and yet very emphatic.

Sinking back into the seat and assuming a comfortable position, Mr. Wilde said:

"Yes I am very sorry about this delay. I fear I shall be obliged to keep the audience waiting."

Upon being asked how he was impressed with the country through which he had recently passed, he said:

"OH EVERYTHING LOOKS SO BROWN,

bare and disconsolate. You know I have just come from California, which is a garden of beauty. Oh, it is so lovely! The cities of the Atlantic coast look bare and dreary at this time of the year. You know, at home, in England, it is always green. We have only the little island and it is well-tilled, every inch of it. It is always beautiful. For five months I have been longing for that garden spot, and California was such a delight to me. The green was such a rest to my weary eyes. It is the most restful of all colors. The California people are delightful; I disliked to leave San Francisco and should love to visit it again.

Mr. Wilde then asked a question which is only natural, considering what the ride from Denver to Cheyenne is. He inquired:

"What is there beautiful in Colorado?"

Being desirous of obtaining the esthete's views of the cities he had visited, the reporter said:

"Mr. Wilde, if it is not impertinent to ask, which city of those you have visited have you found the most esthetic?"

MR. WILDE, SMILING A LITTLE SARCASTICALLY,

replied: "You cannot ask an impertinent question of me. But really I cannot specify any one city. New York being so near Europe has many of the characteristics of a foreign city. Boston and Philadelphia both are paying considerable attention to art. But what especially pleased and interested me were the cities further removed from the Atlantic coast. Cincinnati has an art school and a good one, a school of wood-carving. Chicago people are very enthusiastic over art. I had large audiences in that city. I talked to about 3,[?3]00 people, who listened with the closest attention to all I had to say. St. Louis, too, is full of people who are interested in art, and San Francisco—"

Here Mr. Wilde was interrupted, but it is safe to infer all he had to say was in hearty praise of the esthetic movement among the dwellers in the

CITY OF THE GOLDEN GATE.

"You would bring art into the humblest houses, would you not? You would have art among the multitude? Is that your doctrine?" queried the reporter.

"It is. Art, but not poor amateur art."

Here Mr. Wilde shook his head in a disgusted manner and said:

"We had better have no art than bad art. We can live without art but we cannot live with bad art. Let our architects build good, substantial houses and let them be beautiful if they can. Let our chairs and tables be made first for use and second for beauty. Estheticism should begin with the handicraftsmen and when it does we will have more beautiful homes than we have at present."

"What about estheticism in dress?"

"Women's dress at present is too sombre, more bright colors should be worn. In England these ideas are being adopted rapidly. The milliner is being done away with, and the draper is taking her place. What is prettier than drapery, stately folds for the matron and becoming curves for the maiden? The milliner does away with graceful folds and gives us awkward bows instead."

SPEAKING OF PLACES OF AMUSEMENT, HE SAID:

"There should only be two things consulted in building a theatre—first the audience, then the actor. The trouble with too many theatres is, we have blue skies, red seats, green hangings, a great display of gilding, and then what is the actor to do? His costumes fall flat. Instead of this the house, the scenery and the stage should be only a setting. Let the woods used be dark and rich-looking. Let the hangings be of oriental materials, for they are the best example of correct tone in coloring. I was delighted with the Chinese quarters in San Francisco. Their theatre was plain and the stage was devoid of ornamentation. Those Chinese quarters fascinated me. I wish those people had a quarter in London. I should take pleasure in visiting it often.

"Common things should be made beautiful. When I was in San Francisco, at the hotel I was obliged to drink my chocolate or coffee out of a cup an inch thick, and I enjoyed going down into the Chinese quarters and sitting in a pretty latticed balcony and drinking my tea out of a cup so dainty and delicate that

A LADY WOULD HANDLE IT WITH CARE.

Yet this was not an expensive place for wealthy people to go to. It was for the common people. The laborers on the railroad came here, with pick and shovel, and drank their refreshing beverage out of a pretty cup of the two beautiful colors blue and white, while I was thought unworthy of anything better than a cup so thick that it suggested the idea that it was intended as a weapon, to be hurled at the heads of those seated at the next table.[1] Beautiful things for everyday use are what we want. The child is not taught by books and lessons alone. We know how we used to throw our books aside and rush out into the air and sunshine. The child must be taught by constant association with beautiful things. Beauty should be as free as the air and water, and then it cannot fail to leave its impress on all minds."

Talking of beauty in men's dress, Mr. Wilde said:

"WE DRESS WITHOUT THE SLIGHTEST REGARD

to beauty or even comfort. When a man is going to walk, or row or perform feats which require a display of strength and muscle, the trousers are done away with and knee-breeches are worn. Then again black broadcloth is chosen for dress suits, and no material can be more devoid of beauty than broadcloth. Velvet should be chosen instead, for it is a material which is always becoming."

Mr. Wilde believes that there will be a complete revolution in gentlemen's wearing apparel within the next few years; but for the sake of those gentlemen who are not of stately build it is to be hoped that knee-breeches will not become fashionable.

Mr. Wilde, speaking of the press, said: "When I read the papers and see what they say about me, it gives me a peculiar sensation. I feel as it I was traveling about in a country of barbarians."

The esthete spoke enthusiastically of the cordial way in which he had been received. Being asked how long

1. *The Decorative Arts*: "When I was in San Francisco I used to visit the Chinese Quarter frequently. There I used to watch a great hulking Chinese workman at his task of digging, and used to see him every day drink his tea from a little cup as delicate in texture as the petal of a flower. Whereas in all the grand hotels of the land, where thousands of dollars have been lavished on great gilt mirrors and gaudy columns, I have been given my coffee or my chocolate in cups an inch and a quarter thick. I think I have deserved something nicer." ("Art Decoration," *New York Tribune* (New York, NY), 12 May 1882, 2.) The story also appeared in slightly different form in *Personal Impressions of America* and the British version of *The House Beautiful* (Dibb, 239–40, 249–50). See also "The World Wonder Wilde," *Iowa Daily Register* (Des Moines, IA), 27 Apr. 1882, 2, p. 368; "Aesthetic," *Dayton Daily Democrat* (Dayton, OH), 3 May 1882, 4, p. 371; and "Oscar Wilde," *Dayton Daily Journal* (Dayton, OH), 3 May 1882, 4, p. 379.

he shrugged his shoulders and said: "If I survive, I shall remain until June." So it is evident that Mr. Wilde has not fallen desperately in love with America.

Of American women he said: "In this country I see any quantity of beautiful young girls, girls whose faces are charming with the flush of youth, whose eyes are radiant and whose forms are full of beauty. But there are few handsome matrons in this country."

Speaking of his first appearance in this country, Mr. Wilde said: "With the exception of speaking at an occasional wine supper at Oxford, I had never spoken in public until I lectured in New York, I then found out what a difficult task I had undertaken.[1] Americans are natural orators. I never heard a spontaneous burst of oratory until I came to America and listened to an American."

✂ *A report of Wilde's lecture in Denver.*

"Art and Aesthetics," *Denver Tribune* (Denver, CO), 13 Apr. 1882, 8[2]

Arrival of Oscar Wilde—A Tribune Reporter Escorts Him to the Opera House.

His Lecture of Decorative Art—Description of His Appearance—An Agreeable Disappointment.

Interesting Interview With the Poet.

The train which brought Oscar Wilde over the Denver Pacific railroad last night was thirty minutes late, on account of a delayed connection at Cheyenne, and for this reason alone he was exactly thirty minutes behind the usual time for raising the curtain at Tabor Grand Opera house. He arrived in the midst of a spell of weather that is not specially palatable to aesthetic taste, and for that reason only there was not an overflowing audience, but the parquet and dress circle were filled.

The train arrived just five minutes ahead of the time announced by telegraph, and baffled the designs of

A LARGE CROWD

of unaesthetics whose curiosity caused them to gather about the platforms, or take refuge from the snow storm in the sitting rooms of the Union depot. Even

1. Public speaking: see p. 320, note 3.
2. H & S, b64. Reprinted in H & S, 134–9. Quoted in OWDA, 282, 304, 305–8.

the enterprising advance agent, Mr. Locke, was thrown off his guard by the premature movement of the train and was two minutes late, while Mr. J. S. Vale, the manager of the athletic looking aesthetic, was out prowling around in unknown places for the agent.

A reporter for THE TRIBUNE had taken precaution against the uncertainties of telegraphic reports or railroad time, and having waited beside the track for half an hour, boarded the train the instant it landed. While the passengers of the palace car were hurrying to and fro with their baggage in the usual unaccountable haste of the railroad passenger to be the first out of the narrow door, the reporter was elbowing his way through, eagerly scanning the face of every man for a recognition of Oscar Wilde. At the rear end of the little smoking room the distinguished poet was found all alone, standing and waiting for somebody to receive him. The reporter, feeling that this duty devolved upon him in behalf of the city, introduced himself to Mr. Wilde, welcomed him to Denver, and relieved his uneasiness by the information that his carriage was waiting at the front of the depot. Mr. Wilde was dressed for the evening's entertainment, but covered with a pair of loose trousers and a large, heavy overcoat with a broad fur collar. A muffler was wrapped about his neck and he wore a broad brimmed felt hat. He was conspicuous for his splendid physique, his long hair and singular cast of features, which in repose would be that half of man and half of woman. In every movement of the man it was easy to detect a something which gave an effeminate shade to his masculinity, bearing a striking resemblance to the *Scribner* portrait of George Eliot.[1] But behind and beyond all that was, unusual or eccentric, to a man of observation, the strength of manhood and the character of genius.

When the reporter introduced himself Mr. Wilde received him cordially and began to say a great

MANY PLEASANT THINGS,

which he ended by declaring that his trip had been very tiresome. Just then Mr. Vale and Mr. Locke entered the car and conducted the poet to the carriage which was waiting for the party. A large crowd had gathered on the platform, and there were many young men who have not the slightest conception of the poetry that lives in the sunflower or the beauties that grow in the lily, followed in the footsteps and almost trod upon the heels of the aesthetic apostle. In still greater numbers they blockaded his way and surrounded his carriage, till the pressure of the crowd became disagreeable and even an annoyance. Some of them said such things as:

"Hello, Oscar!"

1. Paul Adolphe Rajon's engraving after Sir Frederic William Burton's chalk portrait of George Eliot in *The Century Magazine, 23*(1), Nov. 1881 (the successor title to *Scribner's Monthly*).

Figure 11. Reporters thought Wilde resembled this engraving of George Eliot .

"Let us see you, Oscar, old boy!"

"Put your head out the window, Oscar, for we know you're in there!"

And this they continued till the carriage drove away. One fellow was so anxious to see

THE FAMOUS POET

that he pressed his nose against the glass window till he got the full benefit of a peep into the carriage.

"I suppose this scene is familiar to you, Mr. Wilde," remarked THE TRIBUNE reporter, as the horses were turned and started off in a brisk toward the opera house.

"Yes; it is so everywhere," answered the poet artist, with a happy smile, which at once revealed a happy, philosophic disposition and a handsomely-formed and well-kept but somewhat irregular set of teeth. In such a smile there is less of the spiritual in the eye and a gentility of expression which makes the nose and the mouth a part of the index to a brain that is as practical as it is sentimental.

"Yes, such scenes *are* familiar," said Mr. Wilde. "This is simply curiosity, you know. It is the evidence of an unfinished civilization."

"But do you not find such curiosity universal?"

"Oh, yes, curiosity I find a universal characteristic; but in Europe the people are less curious about public characters, and they are not rude."

Mr. Wilde was evidently pained by the familiarity of the young men who called Oscar.

"Did you have many such experiences on your California trip?"

"Oh! my!" ejaculated the young man as he threw up his hands with a half languishing smile. "In daytime, at almost every station, they crowded the platforms, besieged the car windows and would become actually angry if I did not make an appearance. But," said Mr. Wilde, "this was only a manifestation of idle curiosity."

He mentioned a few exceptions among those he met enroute. One was that of an old gentleman who wrote him one of the most delightful letters he had ever read and then met him on the train. There were some evidences among the men he met, of deserved culture among the people of the west, but he had not had the time to cultivate them.

The carriage stopped at the stage entrance of the Opera house at 10 minutes after 8 o'clock. His audience had already gathered. He was ushered into the private dressing-room, where especial preparations had been made for his reception. While making his toilet he ordered a small bottle of Piper Heidsieck, which he touched quite temperately, leaving fully one-half till after the lecture.

✂ *A report of Wilde's lecture in Denver.*

SUPPER AND AN INTERVIEW.

At the close of his lecture Mr. Wilde, accompanied by THE TRIBUNE reporter, walked into his dressing room, remarking as he came off the stage, "Well, this is somewhat jolly; to travel in the close atmosphere of those coaches six hundred miles on a stretch and then give a lecture before resting."

"I suppose it must be very tiresome."

"O, no; not the lecture, but the miserable travel," and Mr. Wilde emptied the remaining half bottle of Piper Heidsieck into a goblet. After refreshing himself, he talked away to the reporter about art and poetry, art schools in Europe, and the lack of them in America, and said many pleasant things as chiruppy as though he had just awakened from a refreshing sleep upon a bed of posies.

Then the carriage was ready, and Mr. Wilde and his attendants were whirled off to the Windsor hotel, where all things were prepared for his quiet reception. Taking the elevator to the second floor, he was escorted straightway to his room, succeeding in escaping the crowd which had awaited [*sic*] all evening to see him. Only three gentlemen and three ladies who were promenading the hall caught a glance of the stalwart aesthete as he passed on to his room. There everything was prepared for his comfort and convenience. First of all was his supper, which was spread upon a small table. It was not by any means an extravagant bill of fare. There was a plate of fish, a dish of potatoes, an omelet, a pair of mutton chops, relishes, bread, butter and a cup of tea. Throwing off his overcoat Mr. Wilde sat down at once to the table.

"Take away this tea and bring me a bottle of this wine," said he, pointing to the wine list. "With two glasses," he added.

The servant quickly returned with a bottle of Grave Bordeaux. Mr. Wilde took one bite of the broiled fish and then ordered the plate removed. Just as he cut the first morsel from a mutton chop (after a glass of wine) and tested the bread and butter very sparingly, there commenced a series of raps on the door. Mr. Wilde abandoned his meal for the time, though he was almost famished, and gave himself to the duty of entertaining. Governor Tabor was among his visitors, and in the course of his interview, among other things, arranged to treat the poet to a visit to the Matchless mine at Leadville after his lecture tonight.[1]

Mr. Wilde expressed himself delighted, for he said of all things, that which he desired most was to see a mine.

When his visitors had ceased calling Mr. Wilde resumed his meal and THE TRIBUNE interviewer again unfolded his note book.

HIS NEW POEMS.

"When will your new book of poems appear?" asked the reporter.

1. Horace Austin Warner Tabor (1830–1899) was an American prospector, businessman, and politician. In 1878 a huge lode of silver was discovered at a mine in which he was a partner. He was elected as Lieutenant Governor of Colorado later that year. He bought the Matchless Mine, which Wilde visited on the evening of 13 April after his lecture in Leadville. Wilde vividly described his visit to the Matchless in letters to Fanny Bernard-Beere, Norman Forbes-Robertson, and Helena Sickert (CL, 162, 164, 166), in *Personal Impressions of America* (Dibb, 243), and in several subsequent interviews. See also "Wilde Under Ground," *Denver Tribune* (Denver, CO), 15 Apr. 1882, pp. 713–14.

"Not until after I return to Europe. I hardly think it practicable to write it here. There are so many things which I had intended which are impracticable, you know."

Mr. Wilde then related that in leaving Europe he left his preface to the work with a friend.[1] He said he could not write in America. His subjects would form a new departure, and he could not find either the time or the surroundings in America suitable to his themes. Besides, there were so many new experiences crowding upon him in his travels that he could only take notes. "When I return to Venice," said he, "I will begin to write, and whatever I have seen to impress me in America, whether of the beauties of nature or of men and women, I will write, and give America credit for it."

As to his drama, which has been prepared for two years past, he had little to say, except that it would soon be produced upon the stage.[2]

"How were you impressed by your trip to California?"

"How can I tell you? I could talk to you all night about it. California is a very Italy without its art.[3] There are subjects for the artist, but it is universally true that the only scenery which inspires utterance is that which man feels himself the master of. The mountains of California are so gigantic that they are not favorable to art or poetry. The scenery for definite utterance is that which man is lord of. There are good poets in England, but none in Switzerland. There the mountains are too high. Art cannot add to nature. There is no imitative art."

Mr. Wilde continued to illustrate by showing that the only landscape schools of art in the world were situated in countries where the scenery was less attractive and vice versa where the beauties and grandeurs of nature existed the schools were devoted to faces and figures.

"What class of people do you think are the most susceptible to the impressions that inspire poetry and art?"

"That depends upon the nationality. All classes of the Celtic race are the most susceptible to these finer touches of nature. With these people it matters little about their station in life. They are naturally sympathetic and their impressions are manifest in art and poetry."

1. No such preface survives and it is difficult to imagine why Wilde would have wanted to write it, unless he had temporarily entertained the idea of republishing *Poems* with a preface. It is also possible that the reporter failed to comprehend Wilde's reference to his preface for Rennell Rodd's *Rose Leaf and Apple Leaf*.

2. At this time Wilde was still hoping to convince Clara Morris to star in *Vera* (CL, 151). To state that the play would soon be staged was premature.

3. Ellmann, 185/194, quotes this phrase but does not provide a source. Wilde repeated the phrase in other interviews and in a letter to his friend, the actor Norman Forbes-Robertson (CL, 158).

Here Mr. Wilde finished one mutton chop and the omelet, pushed the dishes aside and took another glass of wine.

THE MORMONS.

The conversation was just beginning to assume a delightful form and Mr. Wilde, though weary, had become enthused with his favorite theme, and his words were pouring forth in a fluent stream of poetic beauties when he was abruptly arrested by a question as to the Mormons of Salt Lake and his impression of them.

"Oh, I could tell you a great many things. I was entertained by the president, Mr. Taylor. I found him a courteous, kindly and charming gentleman. The house had a good deal of feeling in it in the way of pleasing works of art and good furniture.[1] But the Tabernacle has the shape of a soup kettle and the decorations are suitable to a jail.[2] It was the most purely dreadful building I ever saw. There was not even the honesty to tell the truth, because they painted sham pillars. There are no pillars in the building. In the house of God, I think, no lies should be told. The city interested me because it was the first city that ever gave a chance to ugly women, and so with feelings of philanthropy he [*sic*] looked with kindly eye upon it; it is a city of execrable architecture, and yet I felt that it also robbed life of a great deal of its romance; for the romance of life is that one can love so many people and only marry one.[3] The people, as a body of humanity, have the most ignoble forms I ever saw, and the women are commonplace in every sense of the word."[4]

1. John Taylor (1808–1887) was born in England and immigrated to Canada in 1832. A few years later he was baptised into the Church of Latter Day Saints, and he rose to the presidency in 1880. In a letter to Fanny Bernard-Beere Wilde describes Taylor as "a nice old man" (CL, 161), and in *Personal Impressions of America* as "extremely charming, a highly educated gentleman" (Dibb, 240). The house Wilde refers to is Gardo House, then the official residence of the president. It was also mockingly referred to by "Gentiles" as "Amelia's Palace" (former president Brigham Young's favourite wife was called Amelia). Wilde visited the house on the afternoon of 10 April. In *Personal Impressions of America* Wilde would tell the story that, when Brigham Young died, Taylor "stood up in the Tabernacle and said that it had been revealed to him that he was to have the Amelia Palace, and that on this subject there were to be no more revelations of any kind!" (Dibb, 241.)

2. Wilde repeated this description of the Tabernacle in *Personal Impressions of America* (Dibb, 240).

3. Wilde reused this line in an impromptu speech about his American travels for Cincinnati's Musical Club: "He said that he had always thought it a very prosaic arrangement to marry so many women, because it is much more poetic to do as we are accustomed—marry one and love many." ("Oscar Wilde," *The Cincinnati Commercial Gazette* (Cincinnati, OH), 11 June 1882, 7.)

4. Wilde described the Mormons in his letter to Bernard-Beere as "very, very ugly." (CL, 161.) *Personal Impressions of America*: "The Mormons were very courteous and industrious, mainly very happy, the children beautiful, but the people themselves certainly not beautiful." (Dibb, 241.)

Mr. Wilde was asked what he thought of

THE AMERICAN PEOPLE

in comparison with the Europeans. He answered

"I came with only one idea about this country, and that was that it was free from prejudice. To us in Europe, America is looked upon as a nation simple and grand, and I thought that the moment they heard what I had to say they would understand me and realize what I meant by life and art. I find that I was wrong."

Mr. Wilde spoke further of the prejudices of those who criticised from ignorant views of the position he maintained, but he always felt that in every audience there were some intelligent listeners. He had found audiences in the West which listened with more simplicity, more real interest and desire to know what he had to say than in many audiences of the Eastern cities, showing that the West has kept itself free and independent, while the East has caught and spoiled itself with many of the flirting follies of Europe.

Mr. Wilde at the conclusion of the interview referred to the many foolish and unjust things which have been said of him by the newspapers, and then turned himself to a great pile of letters, which he glanced over, and many of them he threw away, saying, "If only I should read all of these I would not rest much tonight."

"And if you were to read all the letters you receive you would become pretty well acquainted with the people in America?"

"Well—," and Mr. Wilde significantly shrugged his shoulders for a reply, when the reporter extended his hand and bade the gifted young gentleman an affectionate adieu.

"Oscar Dear," *Leadville Daily Herald* (Leadville, CO), 14 Apr. 1882, 4[1]

Wilde Wrestles Wildly With the Art Decorative in this Mountain Wilderness.

He Falls an Unwilling Victim to Light Air upon His Arrival Here.

The Wonderful Aesthetic Demonstration Postponed on Account of the Weather.

The Much-Talked-of Disciple of Aestheticism Comes and Goes Without Any Fuss.

A Whole House Full of Curiosity Seekers at the Tabor Last Evening.

1. H & S, b66. Quoted in OWDA, 311–3.

Last evening's South park train brought Oscar Wilde to Leadville, and as soon as his arrival at the Clarendon became known the lobby filled up with a crowd of men anxious to have a look at the famous aesthete whose name has been heralded all over the country. All were doomed to disappointment, however, for Oscar left his carriage and was shown to his apartments by the ladies' entrance to the hotel. Immediately he sent for a physician, for his breath was short you know, and his weariness increased with every exertion to breathe. When the man of medicine heard the complaints he at once decided that it was a case of light air and prescribed accordingly. A HERALD representative then sent in his card and was soon ushered into the presence of the redoubtable Oscar.

As the quilldriver entered, Mr. Wilde arose from the bed on which he had thrown himself in utter exhaustion. After extending a cordial reception to the scribe, he excused himself and again sought repose on the couch. While giving him a chance to catch his breath the visitor took an inventory of the man who is setting the American people wild and what was seen in a glance or two was an individual some six feet tall, with long hair, reaching to the shoulders, a languid, far-away look in the eyes, and a mouth that vied with Soldene's for size.[1] His attire was that of any ordinary traveling man, and was by no means peculiar. He stated that he was extremely tired and had passed a most wearisome day. After a week in Kansas he goes to Canada, New England and New York, where he will lecture for the second time and return to the old world about the first of June.[2] His style of speaking is such that, not to see the speaker but simply hear the languishing words uttered one might suppose that they emanated from some "lah de dah" whose whole being depended upon seeing how much of his portion he could squander frivolously. This is not characteristic of the man, however, for he says he is ambitious and really when he is fired by his love of art he does exercise some symptoms of genuine manhood. This is his first visit to America and he remarks very evenly of the culture of some parts and the lack of civilization in other sections. Mr. Wilde is an Irishman by birth, but bears more the imprint of his foster country, England, than of his native Emerald isle. He still cherishes kindly feelings for the latter it would seem, for he said, "In coming up today I went out on the engine and found an Irishman was the engine driver and we had a good old talk. I saw blue birds, and oh, they were so beautiful, almost as beautiful as kingfishers." In speaking of his love for the beautiful he remarked, "I long to go back to sunny Italy, where to lie in my gondola, smoke cigarettes and write

1. Emily Soldene (1838–1912) was an English stage performer and writer. Her career as a gossip columnist did not begin until the 1890s, so the reference to the size of her mouth is probably literal.

2. Wilde's second lecture in New York, delivered at Wallack's Theatre on 11 May, was billed as his farewell to America, but he would go on to give around 70 more lectures before returning to Europe.

poems." When the subject of art was mentioned Mr. Wilde became almost rapturous, and said he loved to tell the people of the beautiful things in life and nature. "I love to travel and meet the best of men and look at the best and most beautiful of women so that when I die I will leave behind me a name that will be handed down to posterity as a lover of the beautiful." He recommended more beautiful art in America and sighed for the lack of it.

HIS RECEPTION.

Oscar Wilde must have appreciated most peculiarly the lack of art, as he calls it, in the Leadville people, for instead of receiving a grand ovation at the depot or hotel his agent quietly escorted him to a carriage and he was driven like any other arrival, to the Clarendon. The exercise of common sense may be what Mr. Wilde calls "a lack of art." The few who were curious, had to remain so, for they didn't catch a glimpse of the stranger, as he did not pass through the hotel.

✂ *A report of Wilde's lecture in Leadville.*

"Oscar's Oddities," *The Pueblo Daily Chieftain* (Pueblo, CO), 15 Apr. 1882, 3[1]

As Noticed by the Aesthetic Reporter of the "Chieftain."

A Man of Sense—A Brilliant Conversationalist, but Not of Tasteful Attire.

The noon train from Leadville yesterday carried through our city the far-famed aesthetic apostle, Mr. Oscar Wilde, who was returning from a lecturing visit to the great carbonate camp,[2] and en route to Colorado Springs, where he entertained the curious of that city with the delivery of one of his intellectual dissertations last evening. Mr. Wilde alighted from the train, and was met by the CHIEFTAIN apostle, who accompanied him to a room in the depot hotel. He expressed himself as being somewhat wearied by the tedium of travel, and was burdened with a hopeful feeling that a slight ablutionary indulgence would remove, to a telling degree, the provoking lassitude, and restore his temperament to its usual equipose [*sic*]. After the wash-act was neatly and tastily performed, Mr. Wilde freed himself of a deep sigh of relief, and the reporter knew that tranquility reigned supreme within his bosom.

1. Quoted in OWDA, 319–20.
2. A nickname of Leadville.

During the time occupied by Mr. Wilde in refreshing himself, the reporter noted the many peculiar and unique characteristics of the aesthete's dress and style, which have made him renowned in the two hemispheres. He is tall, and were it not for a preponderance of native grace, would incline to a slight awkwardness. He is extremely youthful in appearance, and his large intellectual face is as smooth and fair as a woman's; his hair does not know the touch of cold steel, and is profuse, and reaches below his collar. He wore a large black felt hat; brown velveteen coat, fastened before with embroidered clasps and silken cords; light pantaloons, gaiters of patent-leather and light colored cloth tops; thrown over his entire body, from his shoulders to his feet, he wore a black and richly trimmed mantle, that greatly added to his singular and attractive appearance. After noting his personal perfections and defections, the Faberonian fiend then applied the interviewing pump, and drew forth the following flow:

"Yes, I have been to Leadville and was favorably impressed with that wonderful city; just think of it! that great, large city, was built up within the lapse of time necessarily required for the erection of one house in England. I lectured to a splendid audience last night, who listened to me with rapt attention, and I have none but pleasant recollections of Leadville and its people. At the conclusion of my labor I visited the "Matchless" mine, as I had promised Mr. Tabor I would, while in Denver recently, and passed several hours under ground, being most deeply interested by the intricate and skillful work found there.[1] I am extremely sorry that a limitation of time compels me to hurry through the mountains and canyons of Colorado as I would, I know, be much profited both in beholding their grandeur and noting the comparisons with mountains abroad. From the few and hurried glimpses I have had of your rugged peaks and deep canyons, however, I am free to say that they are so sublimely grand that the brush of the artist cannot do them justice."

With these few kindly and well delivered remarks Mr. Wilde was spared by the reporter while a repast in the dining room was partaken of. The young foreigner was the cynosure of all eyes while he ate his dinner—to which was added a bottle of Piper Heidsieck.

After dinner Mr. Wilde returned to his seat in the coach and re-engaged in a pleasant conversation with the reporter. He seemed slightly perturbed by the staring of the crowd that had by this time gathered about the car, and mildly requested the porter to draw the curtains at the windows. Two ladies, more bold than the rest, entered the coach and begged the favor of an autograph from Mr. Wilde, who graciously and most happily complied.

About this time a be-hooded woman with her arms full of books and her face full of seductive smiles, elbowed her way through the aisle, and sidling up to

1. Wilde's visit to the Matchless Mine: see p. 342, note 1.

Mr. Wilde, exclaimed: "Why, don't you know me? I am the lady whom the state press says should be the one to take the nonsense out of you. I am Mrs. Churchill, editress of the *Antelope*." Mr. Wilde lost none of his complacency, but quietly replied: "You have, then, a prodigious task before you, madam; indeed, one that would take you until the end of the century to accomplish."[1]

The train beginning to move caused the reporter to withdraw, after bidding Mr. Wilde a hearty goodbye.

Mr. Wilde impressed the reporter as having more than the usual culture, and his conversation, carried on in a low monotone, showed that he is the possessor of a rich musical voice—not at all effeminate, as might be supposed from his face. The massive head and graceful contour of his features are partially hidden by his long hair, which, to a certain degree, conceals his forehead. His hands, from their appearance, receive much attention at the toilet, but are large, though as white as any lady's.

There is nothing aesthetic or beautiful about his autograph—indeed, as a chirographist, he is not a success. His name, in large scrawl, resembles a rail fence after an encounter with an enraged bull, more than anything else within the imagination of the reporter.

Altogether, Mr. Wilde is a pleasing gentleman to meet, and always commands respect from those with whom he converses. He is accompanied by Mr. Locke, his business manager, who is, without a doubt, reaping a harvest from the lectures given by his latest novelty. Mr. Wilde will not lecture in Pueblo, as has been reported on the streets.

1. Caroline Nichols Churchill (1833–1926) was a Canadian-born travel writer and newspaper editor, who wrote under the name Caroline (or C.) M. [*sic*] Churchill. In 1879 she settled in Colorado and founded a monthly newspaper, *The Colorado Antelope* ("A paper devoted to the interests of humanity, women's political equality and individuality"). In 1882 it was renamed *The Queen Bee*. Her meeting Wilde on the train was unlikely to have been a coincidence: the *Chieftain* had announced that morning that Wilde would be passing through Pueblo en route to Colorado Springs. Churchill had recently taken up the case of two of the "women of the town" of Denver, who had been arrested for adorning themselves with sunflowers and lilies ("Arrested for Aestheticism," *The Daily News* (Denver, CO), 6 Apr. 1882, 4).

"Quite Too Too," *The Evening Star* (Kansas City, MO), 17 Apr. 1882, 3pm ed., 1[1]

ARRIVAL OF THE APOSTLE OF THE UTTERLY BUT.

An Evening Star Aesthete Meets Him at the Depot, and Listens to His Sentimental Nonsense—The Long haired Divinity as He Looked and Acted—His Vague Ideas About Kansas City and His Endorsement of the Sun—A Very Transparent Humbug.

The alleged apostle of the beautiful just escaped the charge of stealing into the city like a thief in the night, as he arrived on the U. P. train at the hour of 5:30 this morning. An EVENING STAR reporter was at the Union depot earlier than that and not being certain as to what road he would honor with his precious person, Conductor Smith, of the Santa Fe, was accosted as soon as his train had pulled in and the all-important question put:

"Have you got Oscar Wilde on board?"

"No. At least if I have I don't know it, and it's a good thing for him too."

"Why?"

"Because if I had him and knew it, I would have drowned the d— fool in the Kaw river before he got here!"

This was not comforting, as the reporter had left his bed at an unearthly hour for the express purpose of seeing the Apollo who he supposed everyone worshipped as a god, and he hurried off down the track to meet the Union Pacific train, and boarding it at Hickory st, propounded the question of the hour to the colored porter of the sleeping coach. The colored man was in a different frame of mind from Conductor Smith, and replied with a smile that opened up his yellow face like

ONE OF OSCAR'S PET SUNFLOWERS,

"Yes, sah; we's got him. He's down dar in middle berth. See dat man wid de long harr and de big cloak and do piles o' little sacks and bags. Dat's him, suah!"

The EVENING STAR envoy passed down the car and found the famous Celtic poet contentedly reading a copy of the morning paper, his much talked of legs calmly resting across the cushion of the opposite seat. Beside him stood his secretary, a dapper little man with the snap and brusqueness of a professional show manager,[2] and a colored servant.

1. H & S, b67. Quoted in OWDA, 329–30.
2. J. S. Vale.

Wilde was dressed in the civilized costume of the 19th century with the exception of the large cloak which is made and worn in imitation of Tennyson. He had on a black slouch hat, a coat and vest of dark cloth, light trousers of Scotch goods, and a pair of shoes with extremely pointed toes, a la the regulation English snob. The Tennysonian cloak was thrown over one shoulder and under the opposite arm, and a large silk scarf of the shade of old gold was folded about his neck completely hiding the aesthetic collar, which probably occupied its proper place on his person.

Upon introducing himself the reporter was pleasantly met with the extremely aesthetic remark, "A-a-a-a-h, indeed!" drawled out with the soft, insinuating cadence upon which the distinguished scion of the house of Fitzgerald has made his reputation;[1] "have a seat. It is a beautiful morning, is it not? How lovely the sun looks as it rises in its grandeur through the azure blue of your lovely sky."

As he delivered this sample of the aesthetically poetical language upon which he is traveling the languid, effeminate,

TOO UTTERLY TOO SMILE

which the crazed damsels of New York and Boston went crazy over, made its appearance and gradually spread over his classic features until it rested in the lower corners of his triangular mouth. At this juncture the secretary, who by the way is much more of the all-firedly practical than he is of the utterly-too style, remarked:

"Have you a copy of THE EVENING STAR with you?"

The reporter replied that he hadn't, but one could be procured at the office or from the newsboys—price two cents.

It was plain that the secretary, as well as his master, had a decided weakness for the newspapers as a pile of them covered the seat adjoining and all had evidently been carefully perused and clipped for scrap-book purposes.

When the secretary had subsided, Wilde, who seemed impressed with the necessity of giving the reporter

ANOTHER SAMPLE OF AESTHETICISM

and poetry mixed in equal parts after his own formula, opened up with a description of Colorado and California, most of which is already familiar to the public through the medium of a myriad of reporters who have listened to the same thing under the same circumstances and have filled columns of valuable space with the repetition. He then began to question the reporter as to matters local, and was greatly surprised—or seemed to be—when told that Kansas City was in Missouri and not in Kansas and that its population numbered 80,000 souls exclu-

1. The Fitzgeralds were a family of high ranking Irish peers to which Wilde was not related.

sive of the festive Chinaman, whose color makes him aesthetic whether he will or no.

He desired to know the origin and significance of the word Kansas and was informed that it was Indian in origin but its significance was beyond the knowledge of the reporter.[1] The state capital, however, he was given some points upon. It was also an Indian name and signified small potatoes.[2] This seemed to please him and he went into

A DREAMY REVERIE,

in which some scene in his native land, where the potatoes are always large and the pigs fat, notwithstanding the eviction laws, was probably the central figure.

When the train pulled into the Union depot the secretary and servant bustled out to make preparations for the transit to the Coates house, and when all things were ready the poet stepped gently across the platform, still descanting upon the beauties of California to the reporter and passed into his carriage, which had been drawn up in the space between the depot and express offices, and when the valet had arrived with a truck full of traveling bags and robes, which were stowed away about the vehicle, the party was driven to its destination. Arrived at the Coates,

THE DISTINGUISHED CLOWN

passed directly to his room, leaving his secretary to make all arrangements, and as he closed his door a group of lady boarders and house maids, who had taken up a position in the hall, were heard to whisper, "isn't he too utterly beautiful!" "Too awfully too!"

"The Only Oscar," *The Kansas City Daily Times* (Kansas City, MO), 18 Apr. 1882, 5[3]

The Eminent Aesthete Arrives in the City from Colorado and Lectures at the Opera House.

He Drives Around in Quest of the Poet Warder and Praises the Bold Bard of the Kaw.

1. Named for the Kaw (or Kanza or Kansa) Native American tribe, known as the People of the South Wind.
2. The capital of Kansas is Topeka. The name is a Kansa-Osage sentence meaning "a good place to dig potatoes," or "the place where we dug potatoes".
3. H & S, b68. Quoted in OWDA, 332.

A Small Discussion on the Merits of the Renaissance—Why the People Failed to Turn Out.

What Mr. Wilde Wore on the Street and Before the Footlights—His Ability As a Lecturer.

The Lecture in Brief—The Necessities of Americans as Art Promoters—Our National Weaknesses.

Oscar Wilde arrived in the city yesterday morning and was at once driven to his rooms at the Coates house. The journey from Colorado was a tedious and wearisome one, and the eminent aesthete, poet and lecturer professed himself glad enough to arrive once more within the confines of a metropolis. He passed the greater part of the day quietly at the hotel, received a few of the callers who, partly as anxious pupils and partly as a means of gratifying curiosity, sent up their cards. Later in the afternoon he engaged the services of Peanut Joe and drove off on an errand of inquiry. Down town he was met and accosted by a representative of THE TIMES, who placed his knowledge of men and localities at the poet's disposal. "I am looking," said Mr. Wilde, "for Colonel Warder, your poet. I believe I read some verses welcoming me in your paper. Colonel Warder writes excellent poetry. The first and sixth stanzas showed deep thought." This tribute to the bard of Kansas City was delivered with heartiness, and demonstrated the fact that Colonel Warder's maiden effort in an aesthetic vein has secured the prompt approval of the master.[1] In his street attire Oscar Wilde appeared simply a robust, affable and ingenuous young man. He wears clothes of the English cut, speaks with a decided English accent and has not a little of the most pronounced English cordiality. He spoke pleasantly of his trip across the continent, and the various people with whom he had been thrown, all of which interesting facts have been duly detailed in exchanges and republished in THE TIMES.

1. George Woodward Warder (1848–1907) was a lawyer and poet. He had published collections of poetry in 1873 and 1878. Wilde refers to Warder's poem *A Greeting to Oscar Wilde* ("Poetry of the Period," *The Kansas City Sunday Times* (Kansas City, MO), 16 Apr. 1882, 11). The first of nine stanzas reads: "Like the purple tinted shadows of the never setting sun | Rising in effulgent glory as the ceaseless ages run. | Crowning with its golden vesture mountain tops and wooded plain | As a hollowed benediction resting over earth and main. | Is the spirit of all beauty—is the glad poetic thrill | Of the universe of nature that the ages can not still." The sixth stanza describes the sunflower "ever bending to the sun" and finds in it an example to be emulated: "So the soul should front its center, gazing up to truth and God: | Bowing ever to fair beauty as an angel on earth's sod." The eighth stanza addresses Wilde directly: "If thou gatherest truths like flowers, kind and gladsome as a child | True in heart and brave in spirit, then I greet you, Oscar Wilde". Warder's 1885 collection *Utopian Dreams and Lotus Leaves* begins with this poem, retitled as *Aestheticism* and with the eighth stanza rewritten to omit mention of Wilde. It also includes poems in praise of Lillie Langtry and Ellen Terry.

✂ *A description of an overheard conversation about aestheticism in a barber shop, and a report of Wilde's lecture in Kansas City.*

"Ah, Oscar," *The Topeka Daily Capital* (Topeka, KS), 21 Apr. 1882, 8[1]

BEAUTY'S GREAT EXPONENT.

A Short Talk With the Prince of Aesthetes—What He Says and How He Says It—His Lecture—His Looks—His Manner in General.

Oscar Wilde, who lectured at the opera house last night, arrived yesterday afternoon from Leavenworth and was the guest, while in the city, of the Windsor. The CAPITAL reporter called on him during the afternoon at his room at the hotel and had a pleasant conversation with him.

Mr. Wilde was reclining on a sofa drinking his tea from a blue-flowered china cup. His dinner, some strawberries and some cigars lay on the marble top table before him. He arose as the reporter entered and greeted him with a pleasant smile.

Mr. Wilde has a handsome soft womanish face, around which his long wavy hair fell in the finest decorative art. He is a very pleasant conversationalist, has a wonderful command of words, and expresses himself in a very clear lucid manner, much contrasted with the soulful utterances of his burlesquers. He said that when he landed in New York and read what the newspapers had to say about him, he thought that he was about to travel in an extensive lunatic asylum composed of the whole country, but that when he went out in society there, he found the most charming cosmopolitan people he ever had the pleasure of meeting. He thought the newspapers of this country were far from representing the true public opinion of the American people on art questions, he had met as intelligent, appreciative, sympathetic people in his travels in this country as in the highest art and social centers of England.

In England all society and all art is centered in one city—London—and in a very small part of that city, and to him the society of a large provincial city like Manchester was simply unbearable. In this country there is no similar center, but all over the country he found an element appreciative and intellectual. Rough was an unfortunate adjective for Americans to apply to themselves. The conflict which some shallow writers on art found between utility and beauty was a mis-

1. H & S, b70. Reprinted in Mikhail, 79–80. Quoted in OWDA, 336–7 (where Wilde's indirect speech is rendered as direct).

take. There cannot be anything useful which was not beautiful, and if ugly, it might be put down as of imperfect usefulness.

He thought that the present generation was a most impractical one. By impractical he explained to mean that they lived without making life worth living for—without any cultivation of the sense of pleasure, the beautiful. To him the life of the business man who ate his breakfast early in the morning, caught a train for the city, there stayed in the dingy, dusty atmosphere of the commercial world, and went back to his house in the evening, and after supper to sleep, was worse than that of the galley slave—his chains were golden instead of iron.

He said he had been annoyed less by the curiosity of unappreciative listeners than he expected. The rule was the most charming audiences quick to grasp and understand each point. At Rochester, N. Y., he had a very noisy audience who behaved very rudely. But these demonstrations interested him as all phases of nature, and especially human nature interested him. At Sioux City he had a large audience composed of common people, farmers, mechanics and others of a simple grade of life, and he said in all his lecture tour he had none more apparently interested and sympathetic.

He did not know how long he would remain in this country. He was without plans, and in fact hated plans. He thought of going to Japan, whom he regarded as the highest race of decorative artists in existence. While there was considerable aestheticism in his conversation, there was much less of that affected soulfulness about the talented young Englishman that one would suppose.

✂ *A report of Wilde's lecture in Topeka.*

[?Charles F. Howe], "A Stranger Within Our Gates," *The Atchison Globe* (Atchison, KS), 24 Apr. 1882, 1

Oscar Wilde lectured in Corinthian Hall Saturday night to an audience of forty-three people, including the door-tenders, ushers, janitor, etc., and the cash receipts did not exceed twenty-five dollars. This is an exact statement of fact, and Atchison had the honor of snubbing Mr. Wilde more effectually than any other city in the United States. The lecture was exceedingly short, and did not occupy to exceed thirty minutes. After it was over, W. G. Ellet, Archie Wells, Ed. Burke and Charley Howe, the last two connected with this office, asked the manager for an introduction to Mr. Wilde, which was granted.[1] They found him posing in a

1. Charley Howe is presumably the Charles F. Howe listed as a "traveling solicitor Daily Globe" in the 1882 Atchison Directory (also listed is one A. J. Howe, "with Daily Globe"). In 1880 Charley Howe (c. 1859-?) was a "merchant". *The Globe* was published by "Howe & Co." Burke is untraced.

dressing room, before his valet had relieved him of the absurd toggery which he wears on the stage, and on being introduced to the gentlemen, cordially shook hands with them, very much as a Kansas lecturer would have done, and talked with them quite freely. The first thing they noticed was his resemblance to an unsophisticated boy who had been encouraged in a hobby, and he seemed to feel that all the absurd things he said were quite new and startling. He is very tall, has a very large head with bushy hair, and long and thin legs, which were encased in velvet knee breeches, and black silk stockings, and when he talks he rests his elbow on a shelf or against the wall, in a very gawky manner.

After he had shaken each of his visitors by the hand, he said: "Ah! how kind of you to come! I did not expect any one; the night is so terribly dreadful. How did you like my lectuah?" The young men answered in a chorus that it was perfectly splendid, although they thought it was perfectly vile. "It is so difficult to lectuah to empty benches," Mr. Wilde continued. "When I was in New York, I had an audience of 5,000, and it was perfectly joyous. Chicago gave me an equally good audience. I was very much interested in that city in a young sculptor I met in an out-of-the-way place, who was really and truly an artist, and in my lecture I scolded the people for not encouraging him. I was afraid at first that they would not like it, but they took their scolding real well. I think it was so nice and good natured of them, and I have learned since that the young artist was greatly benefitted by what I said."[1] In speaking of his lecture, he further said: "We do not lectuah in England as you do here. We men of letters express our views by writing, and we have a great number of splendid magazines and reviews. You have more orators in America than we have in England, however, and a greater number of young men of capacity in responsible positions." Turning to one of the young men connected with this office, Mr. Wilde inquired: "In what business are you engaged?" Remembering that the poet had no occasion to feel friendly to the paper, he replied: "Me? Oh, ha; I am in the queensware trade."[2] This statement at once made Mr. Wilde enthusiastic, and he spoke of the splendid Cincinnati pottery, which was so artistic that he had visited the works, and lectured on the subject.[3] "Do the people in the West," Mr. Wilde inquired, "appreciate the beautiful in your line?"

1. The reference is to John Talbott Donoghue. Wilde repeatedly claimed to have spoken of Donoghue in his two lectures in Chicago, but this is not borne out by the reports of the lectures ("Oscar Wilde," *The Chicago Daily Tribune* (Chicago, IL), 14 Feb. 1882, 7; "Oscar Wilde," *The Daily Inter Ocean* (Chicago, IL), 14 Feb. 1882, 2; "Oscar Wilde," *The Chicago Daily Tribune* (Chicago, IL), 12 Mar. 1882, 5; "The Seraphic Oscar," *The Daily Inter Ocean* (Chicago, IL), 13 Mar. 1882, 2).

2. Queen's ware is a type of cream-coloured earthenware pottery, perfected by Josiah Wedgwood (1730–1795) and named for his patron Queen Charlotte, consort of George III (OED).

3. Rookwood Pottery Company.

"The fact is," the young man replied, "that I keep the books. I don't know much about the sales." Someone inquired if Mr. Wilde admired Wendell Phillips, and he answered that he admired every enthusiast, no matter what he did, or who he was. Mr. Wilde said he had thought seriously of going to Australia in June, but he didn't know whether he would or not, as an English colony was the most "barren" thing in the world, and decidedly "base," but he will certainly visit Canada and the South before his return to England.[1] Mr. Wilde said nothing about "too too," or "utterly utter," but his odd expressions are quoted exactly as they were used.

"Pike's Peak," *The Manchester Weekly Times* (Manchester, UK), 27 May 1882, Supp. 5[2]

(By a Correspondent of the Manchester Examiner.)

✂ *A lengthy account of the correspondent's ascent of Pike's Peak, the highest summit of the southern Front Range of the Rocky Mountains.*

Mountain climbing is not a subject of general interest, and some of my readers may be glad to turn from Pike's Peak to hear a word about Oscar Wilde the Great. I met Mr. Wilde a few days ago in Kansas,[3] and had a long conversation with him. I had previously had a strong impression that the apostle of the beautiful had not received justice at the hands of the newspapers, and my impression was confirmed by what he told me. It might be mere coincidence that all the newspapers in America have taken up a sneering attitude, but I do not think it is. Making all due allowances and exceptions, there is no doubt that Oscar Wilde has made a great sensation in America. He has received great social attention, and in many places he has had very large audiences. In Boston the Harvard students tried to turn his lecture into a burlesque, and this was duly telegraphed to England; but we were not informed—at least, not by wire—that Mr. Wilde completely turned the laugh against these young men, and emerged triumphantly

1. Between April and November 1882 Wilde repeatedly told interviewers that he planned to visit Australia; he never did.

2. H & S, b69. Reprinted in abbreviated form as "What Mr. Wilde Says About Himself," *New York Tribune* (New York, NY), 11 June 1882, 9 (which is the version reprinted in Mikhail, 87–8; and H & S, 139–40; and quoted in OWDA, 338–9). Also reprinted as "What Mr. Wilde Says About Himself," *The Macon Telegraph and Messenger* (Macon, GA), 15 June 1882, 1; "What Mr. Wilde Says About Himself," *The Chicago Daily Tribune* (Chicago, IL), 17 June 1882, 3; and "What Mr. Wilde Says About Himself," *Portland Daily Press* (Portland, ME), 19 June 1882, 2. Quoted in Sturgis, 260/249. Referenced in Sturgis, 256/245.

3. Wilde toured Kansas between 19 and 22 April.

from the ordeal. At a time when we were told that Boston society had turned its back upon the young poet, he was being entertained by Longfellow and Dr. Holmes. In the Eastern cities his photograph was most conspicuous (I saw it in a Washington shop window between those of Garfield and Arthur),[1] and Mr. Wilde told me that the demand for it far exceeded any possible supply.[2] He was enthusiastic about the kindness he had received in many of the western towns, particularly Cincinnati, Chicago, and San Francisco, and spoke most highly of the culture and intelligence of the leading people he had met in those cities. In New York he had a reception given to him such as in England is rarely given to a prince, and he has a promise that on his return an evening party shall be given in his honor, when all the gentlemen shall discard the odious trousers of dull respectability and assume the more becoming substitute of the aesthetic future. Mr. Wilde told me that in the West people had travelled long distances and waited weary hours at railway stations to see him pass. He was compelled, even when fatigued, to show himself on the platforms, and I presume the farmers went back to work cheered and refreshed by the phantom of delight on which they had feasted their hungering eyes. What the American press appears to resent is that Oscar Wilde should have achieved such a position in their country without his being generally looked up to at home. The idea that he is fooling their public seems to irritate them extremely, but in my opinion this is a most erroneous opinion. Oscar Wilde's message is one which is really wanted in the United States, and without some grotesqueness and exaggeration he would not have secured a hearing. He gave me a remarkable illustration of the Californians' detestation of the unforgiveable crime of horse stealing. Where murder is looked on rather as a fine art, a horse thief is regarded with universal loathing, and Mr. Wilde had dined with a gentleman in California who owned to having fired eleven shots at a predatory poet, and who could not be convinced that he had been guilty of want of respect for literature in so doing. When Mr. Wilde was lecturing in Chicago he received a present of a beautiful little bas-relief, quite precious in its delicacy, from a struggling sculptor.[3] Upon which the lecturer rebuked his Chicago audience for allowing such artistic merit to be unrecognized. "And instead of being offended," said Mr. Wilde, "they sent the young man more commissions than he could execute in two years." I only relate a very small part of what Mr. Wilde told

1. James A. Garfield (1831–1881) was the 20th President of the United States. His assassin, Charles J. Guiteau, was tried and executed during Wilde's tour of North America. Chester A. Arthur (1829–1886) was Garfield's successor.

2. Interviews with New York photograph dealers support Wilde's claim, although his popularity among their customers did not last: "The photographs of Oscar Wilde sold rapidly and extensively when he came to this country, but the demand has dropped off almost completely." ("Faces of Noted People," *The New York Times* (New York, NY), 25 Feb. 1883, 6.)

3. John Talbott Donoghue.

me, in order to show that his success in America has been much greater than has been reported. He said that he had no more attentive audience than the miners at Leadville. His intentions for the future are to lecture in Australia and New Zealand, and, above all, to visit Japan, and remain for two months at least in that wonderful country, contemplating its artistic treasures, while attired, if possible, in that grand old national Japanese costume which the natives themselves are so foolishly casting aside.

"Oscar's Return," *Omaha Daily Republican* (Omaha, NE), 25 Apr. 1882, 8[1]

Oscar Wilde spent an hour or two in Omaha, on Sunday.[2] He came up from Atchison, and went to Lincoln where he lectured last evening. For the last two weeks he has been lecturing in Colorado, Kansas and Missouri. He spoke of Denver in enthusiastic terms of admiration, saying it was a magnificent city, of marvelously rapid growth. While at Leadville he received quite an ovation, and inspected one of the leading mines.[3] He lectured once at Leadville and twice at Denver.

During his visit on the Pacific coast he lectured four times in San Francisco, twice in Oakland, once in Stockton, once in San Jose, and once in Sacramento.[4] He was delighted with San Francisco and California, and he thinks San Francisco the most picturesque city in America, affording the artist a fine field. He visited the Chinese quarters, which he found full of the most artistic effects which would have delighted the hearts of the old masters.

When informed that the legislature at Lincoln, at its last session, had passed a law ordering all sunflowers to be cut down, he exclaimed, "Is it possible! How unaesthetic the Nebraska legislators must be! Had I known this a little sooner I would never have gone to Lincoln."

Mr. Wilde goes east from Lincoln, and will make a tour of Canada. He will then return to the United States and deliver farewell lectures in Boston, Philadelphia and New York. He sails for England the last June [*sic*], and after a short rest he proposes to visit Japan to study Japanese art. He considers Japan the finest field in the world for artistic studies, and it has been the dream of his life to go there.

1. Reprinted in "Oscar Wilde," *The Sioux City Daily Journal* (Sioux City, IA), 26 Apr. 1882, 3.
2. Sunday 23 April.
3. Wilde's visit to the Matchless Mine: see p. 342, note 1.
4. This report of Wilde's Californian tour is correct except that he lectured twice in Sacramento: first on 31 March and again on 8 April.

[Champion Clement Chase], "The Poet in Lincoln," *The Omaha Daily Herald* (Omaha, NE), 26 Apr. 1882, 2[1]

Oscar Wilde Visits the University, the Penitentiary, and Insane Hospital.

His Address Before the Students—Comments Upon the Convicts—Sympathy With a Murderer—Dante in a Cell—The Lunatics Look at Him—His Remedy for Blues.

Staff Correspondence of THE HERALD,

LINCOLN, April 25, 1882.—On one of the front benches in the university chapel yesterday morning sat none other than Oscar Wilde, dressed as he usually dresses, and the students were so anxious to have him speak that he finally consented, though knowing that his manager would strongly object to any free lectures of that kind. For fifteen minutes he discoursed in a most entertaining manner on topics pertinent to the college and its work. He told the story, which those who have heard his lecture will remember, of Ruskin's humanitarian labors near Oxford, and how great is his influence there.[2] Mr. Wilde said that they in England looked to the universities of America to carry on and support the new art movement, and applying it practically here. He would wish that every one might learn some one of the decorative arts, so great a source of valuable pleasure are they.

Mr. Wilde did not hesitate to criticize the miserably poor architecture of the university building, and hoped that as the students grew up they would strive to improve [?that], as well as establish a gymnasium, where might be seen models of the old Greek athletes, such splendid examples of physical beauty.[3] He would have all strive to live up to the Greek ideal, "a sound mind in sound body." The whole spirit of Mr. Wilde's remarks was to show that it was quite as easy to build beautifully as badly.

Oscar was quite taken with some of the pretty faces on the right side of chapel and expressed surprise, as any Englishman would, at our co-educational system. "Why, if we fellows at Oxford had young ladies there we—well, we'd never study. Can you study under such attractions?" We assured him that we could, and that the young ladies were excellent students also. In conversation

1. Wilde spent much of 24 April in the company of George Edward Woodberry, Professor of Anglo-Saxon and Rhetoric at the University of Nebraska. Woodberry, in a letter written the following day to Charles Eliot Norton, his former tutor at Harvard, states that he, Harrington Emerson (1853–1931, Professor of Modern Languages), and "Clem Chase" (1860–1922; a correspondent for the *Omaha Herald* and *Chicago Times*) accompanied Wilde on visits to the Nebraska State Penitentiary and the Nebraska State Hospital for the Insane (Wimberley, L. W. (1947). Oscar Wilde meets Woodberry, *Prairie Schooner 21*, 108–16). See also Marland, R. (2021). Oscar Wilde at the Nebraska State Hospital for the Insane. *Notes and Queries, 68*, 328–31.

2. Ruskin's road: see p. 27, note 3.

3. Greek statues in college gymnasiums: see p. 167, note 3.

with some of the professors he expressed a regret that he had never studied elocution, and acknowledged that they made a rule *not* to learn extempore speaking. So he was told of our literary societies and how much they had done in this direction. "And do the ladies make speeches too? Well, well!"

In the afternoon some friends took Mr. Wilde out to see the penitentiary. He had never visited a prison and his horror at the bareness of the place and complete sympathy for the convicts was that of a child.[1] Going out those in the carriage were treated to a perfect flood of poetry; to a dissertation in which one British or American author was taken up after another and criticized in short, brief sentences, which showed perfect familiarity with their writings. "Longfellow," said Mr. Wilde, "was not a great poet; he was a great poem. Oh, a fine old man, a fine old man!" He was rapturous over Walt Whitman but said most stinging things of poor Joaquin Miller.[2] Emerson, he said, had been and was still a master for him; Carlyle had ceased to interest him.[3] He was surprised to learn that Emerson had lost his influence on our youth. Of his own countrymen he seems to be passionately devoted to Keats and quotes from him constantly. In fact, as to quotations Mr. Wilde has an abundant supply.

At the prison Warden Nobes showed the visitors the rogue's gallery, a large collection of convicts' photographs, and it was very amusing to hear Oscar's comments upon each.[4] "Oh, what a dreadful face, what a dreadful face; and what did he do?" Nobes did not hesitate to tell of the crimes in the most terrible way, calculated to shock sensitive poets. "Oh, here's a beast, an animal," exclaimed Wilde over one picture, "nothing of the man left." It was a negro's picture, but it had not done the man justice as we saw afterwards.

Mr. Wilde was very anxious to see all the prison had to show and while in the cell room conversed with Ayers of Grand Island, who is under sentence to be hung the 20th of June. "Do you read, my man?" asked the poet.

"Yes, sir."

1. Wilde had visited the Kansas State Penitentiary at Lansing (now the Lansing Correctional Facility) on 22 April ("Oscar Wilde in Prison," *The Leavenworth Times* (Leavenworth, KS), 27 Apr. 1882, 3; referenced in Cooper, "Gaul Post," 8 Dec. 2015).

2. Wilde had previously praised Miller (see "Oscar Wilde," *The Republican* (St. Louis, MO), 26 Feb. 1882, 13, p. 218; "The Apostle Again," *Reno Evening Gazette* (Reno, NV), 10 Apr. 1882, 3, p. 328). If it is true that he criticised Miller here, it may be that he thought his remarks would not be reported.

3. Thomas Carlyle (1795–1881) was a British author, biographer, and historian.

4. C. J. Nobes (c. 1850–1897) was deputy warden of the Nebraska State Penitentiary from 1874 to 1880, when the warden resigned and Nobes was promoted. In 1874, five years after the penitentiary was founded, there were 42 inmates; by the time of Wilde's visit there were 200. The inmates were put to work building their own prison (Andreas, A. T. (1882). *History of the State of Nebraska*. The Western Historical Company). Wilde saw prisoners making bricks in the sun. The next day he wrote to his friend Helena Sickert that the prisoners were "all mean-looking, which consoled me, for I should hate to see a criminal with a noble face" (CL, 166).

"And what?"

"Novels, part of the time. I am now reading the Heir of Redcliffe [*sic*]."[1]

Wilde said that his heart had been turned by the eyes of the doomed man, but if he read the Heir of Redcliffe it was perhaps just as well to let the law take its course. Further on they came to the dark cell where refractory prisoners are placed. At Nobes' invitation Mr. Wilde and one of the professors stepped in, whereupon Nobes slammed the solid door to with a terrible bang and gave them a very distinct impression of what black darkness is. Wilde went into another cell where he had caught sight of two neat rows of books which one of the convicts had arranged; quite a little library. He ran over the titles rapidly, until he struck Dante, when he came out, exclaiming, "Oh, dear, who would have thought of finding Dante here."[2]

After the penitentiary had been done, Mr. Wilde was asked if he would like to ride over to the insane asylum. He at first protested against additional horrors, but concluded that he would go as he was "in for it now." So over to the hospital they went.[3] The scenes just left were being forgotten in another literary discus-

1. *The Heir of Redclyffe* (1853), by the English novelist Charlotte Mary Yonge (1823–1901), was one of the most popular novels of the nineteenth-century. The plot reflects Yonge's religious outlook and centres on Guy Morville's clashes with a disreputable cousin, which he overcomes thanks to his Christian faith. In an 1889 editorial Wilde admitted he had still not read *The Heir of Redclyffe*: "I am not worthy of superhuman flights of virtue—in a novel. I want to see how people act and suffer who are as good-for-nothing as I am myself. Then I have the sinful pretension to be amused, whereas all our novelists want to reform us, and to show us what a hideous place this world is [...]" (*The Woman's World*, Jan. 1889; CW vii, No. 112, lines 205–8). It appears that Nobes encouraged prisoners to read. In 1882 he requested that his superiors allocate funds to provide the prison library with at least 500 new books: "The medium of a good library, well selected, is one of the most powerful means of reform advocated by prison authorities." (*Biennial Report of the Warden of the Nebraska State Penitentiary for the Years 1881 and 1882*, 10.) In his letter to Helena Sickert, Wilde wrote that reading novels was "a bad preparation for facing either God or Nothing," (CL, 166). During his own incarceration he found great solace in books (see Wright, 240–72), and, after his release, he would write to the editor of *The Daily Chronicle* that "[p]risoners should be encouraged to read, and should have whatever books they want," (CL, 1047).

2. Wilde's letter to Helena Sickert: "Strange and beautiful it seemed to me that the sorrow of a single Florentine in exile should, hundreds of years afterwards, lighten the sorrow of some common prisoner in a modern gaol." The prisoner also had a volume of Shelley (CL, 166). Wilde later told Chris Healy of his visit to the penitentiary: "I was shown a condemned cell where a prisoner, who had been sentenced to death, was calmly smoking a cigarette and reading 'The Divine Comedy' of Dante in the original." He also told Healy that, when he himself was imprisoned, and "[w]hen the greatest literary men of the world petitioned the English Government to treat me with less severity, the prison authorities allowed me, whilst I was lying in a hospital bed, to have one book to read. I chose the 'Divine Comedy,' and it saved my reason," (Mikhail, 384).

3. The hospital was, and is, approximately 2.5 miles north-west of the penitentiary. Its name was changed to the Lincoln State Hospital in 1921 and to the Lincoln Regional Center in 1969.

sion, in which Principal Shairp was rather roughly handled.[1] Dr. Mathewson showed Mr. Wilde around the asylum, the first he had ever visited.[2] The sad scenes here would move any heart, and it is no wonder that the aesthetic poet's was troubled to the extreme. He burst out in indignation against the white-washed walls and "sticky" floor, as he called it, saying that citizens would go insane with such surroundings, "with not even a bench to oneself, and one's neighbor's muttering. I would have the gayest colors possible in those wards, would furnish them with fantastic dresses, music boxes, means of enjoyment. Pooh! how dreary, how dreadful!"[3]

Mr. Wilde seemed glad to get away, and the visits to these two abodes of crime and insanity seemed to affect the rest of his afternoon. "I have greater respect than ever before for virtue and sanity," he said. He was thoughtful for a while and then remarked that whenever he had the blues or was disgusted with the world he took up Endymion and burying himself in that divine poem, forgot the world and its cares.[4] He said he had always been melancholy when a boy, though surrounded by every pleasure, until he went to Italy and learned the new life.

He expects to return to America some time, merely to lecture to universities of art, giving a fortnight's course at each college and refusing all public engagements. He will go again to California in July, with which place and whose people he is fascinated.[5] His lecture here was well attended, but Lincoln people do not like him and the criticisms upon him have been very severe. But Mr. Wilde is one thing above all, he is a perfect gentleman.

GARNET.

1. John Campbell Shairp (1819–1885) was elected Professor of Poetry at Oxford in 1877. His Oxford lectures were published in 1881 as *Aspects of Poetry*. When Wilde won the Newdigate Prize Shairp suggested amendments to *Ravenna*; Wilde did not adopt them (Sturgis, 127/124). In an article for *The Pall Mall Gazette* Wilde would write disparagingly of Shairp's critical faculties: "he was always confusing ethical with aesthetical questions, and never had the slightest idea of how to approach such poets as Shelley and Rossetti whom it was his mission to interpret to young Oxford in his later years; while, considered as a poet, he hardly deserves more than a passing reference." (24 Oct. 1887; CW vi, No. 80, lines 80–4.)

2. Harley P. Mathewson (1829–1901) had been appointed superintendent in 1877. In the source his name is given as "Matthewson".

3. Woodberry's letter to Norton: "I was much oppressed by the horrible things I saw, and thoroughly humiliated humanly. He [Wilde] bore it better—though he stopped at the last ward of lunacy and would not go on." (Wimberly, L. C. (1947). Oscar Wilde Meets Woodberry. *Prairie Schooner, 21*, 108–16.) The hospital had four floors, with the more difficult to manage patients on the fourth.

4. *Endymion* (1818) is a poem by John Keats. It begins "A thing of beauty is a joy for ever".

5. Wilde never returned to California.

"Argus and the Ass," *The Omaha Daily Bee* (Omaha, NE), 26 Apr. 1882, 1[1]

The Aesthetic Oscar Converting the Capitolines.

Lincoln Preparing for the Coming Session of the Legislature.

The Nucleus Raised for the State Home for the Friendless.

Temperance, Political and Other State Capital News.

Special Correspondence of THE BEE.

LINCOLN, April 25.—Oscar Wilde lectures here tonight under the auspices of the Presbyterian ladies of this city, and a full attendance of the "all but too-toos" is guaranteed. The languid disciple of Ruskin arrived on the afternoon train yesterday, and was domiciled at the Arlington. Your correspondent went around in the evening to make the gentleman's acquaintance, and, although he started out with the expectation of having a burlesque interview with the eccentric foreigner, he wholly abandoned the idea before he left. If your correspondent is entitled to an opinion on this subject, he considers Oscar Wilde as brilliant a man, intellectually, as he had lately met. The man's appearance as he greeted the reporter pleasantly by name was striking. He was stretched out lazily upon the bed, with a large bearskin robe drawn over his legs. His dress was neat and not especially outré. The long, dark hair, oval face and small mouth give him a decidedly effeminate appearance, though there was not the slightest visible trace of the sensuality so much alluded to by eastern correspondents. He talked rapidly and with excellent choice of language, proving himself a most excellent conversationalist and an entertaining host. During the interview he pulled away vigorously at a strong cigar in which he seemed to find much relish.

"I have come here from Atchison," he stated in response to a question, "having lectured at Topeka, Denver and several other points in Kansas and Colorado. My trip to the pacific coast has been one of supreme gratification to me. I should be contented to take up my residence there permanently. San Francisco I consider the most interesting and most beautiful of all American cities. Its location could not be surpassed. I lectured in that city four times, and at Oakland twice, having large and enthusiastic audiences. I also delivered lectures at San Jose, Stockton and Sacramento. I lectured twice at Denver and once at Leadville, at the latter place addressing an immense crowd of miners. The theme of my lecture there was "Handicraft" and I appealed to their sympathies and won their entire good will. In regard to my future plans, I expect to deliver a number of lectures between here and Chicago, reaching that city about next Sunday. Then I intend to

1. Quoted in Friedman, 212.

go to Canada for a season, after which I will lecture for the second time in Boston and Philadelphia, and about the end of June will give a final lecture at New York, sailing thence to England and after a little recreation I expect to go to Japan. There is a glorious feast of artistic treasures awaiting me there." Mr. Wilde then started off on a long and enthusiastic description of Japanese art.

In taking his departure, the reporter said, "Mr. Wilde, do you think that you could instil some of your artistic principles into the members of the Nebraska legislature? At the last session they passed a bill providing that all the sunflowers along our highways should be cut down."

"Is that a fact?" asked the aesthetic in astonishment. "If I had known that I think I should either have cancelled my engagement here or else engaged to lecture half a dozen times."

The impression which your correspondent took away with him after an hour's chat with the gentleman was that he was a man of great intellectual strength, in spite of numerous drawbacks in appearance and manner. However much opinions may differ on this point, he is certainly brainy enough to tell Nebraskans a great many things worth knowing in the special province to which he has so long applied himself.

ARGUS.

"The World Wonder Wilde," *Iowa Daily Register* (Des Moines, IA), 27 Apr. 1882, 2[1]

A Chat with the Irish Apostle of Aestheticism, and a Look at His Make-Up.

A Broadside at American Crockery—About the Practicality of Art in Nations.

HIS LECTURE LAST NIGHT.

The Irish apostle of aestheticism visited this aesthetic city yesterday, and lectured last evening at the Opera House. Further than this mere announcement, there should be no especial cause for wonder; but it is peculiarly the fact that this will not suffice, and believing that the aesthetic conception of this city needed food, THE REGISTER aesthetic visited the British peculiarity at his room at the Aborn House, and passed an hour with him in conversation on topics congenial to them both. As he entered Mr. Wilde was seated on a sofa smoking a very large cigar, with his idle hand lying across his lap. He arose at the chronicler's entrance and came forward, appearing a well developed man, perhaps five feet and a half

1. H & S, b71. Excerpted in "Oscar Wilde," *Iowa City Daily Republican* (Iowa City, IA), 28 Apr. 1882, 4.

high,[1] straight and full in bust. His hair, a dark brown, is combed back carelessly from his forehead, and is allowed to grow long and untrimmed. His complexion is not dark, nor exceptionally fair, but as soft and smooth as a lady's. His eyes are truly feminine, and in talking an expression of kindness plays in them, which gives the eyebrows the proverbial arch of good nature, and serves as an index to the true tenderness of his temperament. To begin where we should in telling of his clothes, let it be said that his trousers are long and cover a pair of patent leather shoes, cut low, and pointed in the toe. In sitting down the crook of the knee, in slightly elevating the pants, serves to display a rich red pair of silk stockings, clocked in the lighter shade of the same color, and fitting closely over the instep. When the chronicler took his seat, Mr. Wilde immediately asked as to the size

OF THE METROPOLIS,

and desired to know if it was not the busiest, and alike the largest city in the State. The question was of course answered in the affirmative, and in reply to his question as to the derivation of the name Des Moines, the chronicler said that it formerly served to designate the first inhabitants, the monks, from which the name was taken. Here he approaches the aesthetic subject, so near to his heart and pocket book, and desired to know if there were any ruins left here, of these first inhabitants, and if there were any ruins here of any kind. The answer was not acceptable, for every citizen of Des Moines knows there are no ruins here over thirty years of age, but the thought did come to the reporter's mind that if Mr. Wilde would visit almost any saloon in the city, he might find ruins, thirty, yes forty, sixty, eighty years of age. It would never have done to have told Mr. Wilde this, however.

"No," said he, "there are no ruins in this country, and it is a pity. For by the existing monument of other times, of an age when art was better, and existed in fact, the present would be the better educated."

The reporter spoke of art as it existed in England.

"Oh yes," he replied, "art attained to more perfect degree in England in the Seventeenth Century than it ever has in Italy. They build for beauty there, and a thing of beauty is not a joy forever but exists almost forever.[2] Ugly houses do not withstand the destroying power which man's conception impels him to; but a beautiful house, a house built with an eye to art appeals to the better nature of humanity, and it is permitted existence because the original conception of its erection and design was an artistic one. In that age of art in England, they builded artistically well, and that age is now displayed in England by practical results.

1. Wilde was over six feet tall, so this must either be a typo or an intentional slight.
2. "A thing of beauty": see p. 363, note 4.

is a practical one. In fact history shows this,"—but the reporter ventured to ask if Italy, with its history past and present, gave evidence to this statement, and he replied that it was a wide question. "No, I cannot say that, in this case, my statement holds good. Victor Emmanuel,[1] within the last fifty years, has, while destroying the first principles of republican government and instituting new ones, also destroyed Italy's national sense of art, and in the late wars what stood as art's monuments have been for the most part destroyed. Why, sir, Italian art is suffering today because America was discovered, and this is proved by the fact that your steam engines are introduced there. They are doing away with gondolas in Venice, which certainly furnished delightful means of conveyance, more rapid than a horse, more comfortable, and more delicious. In their place they are using the grimy, dirty steamers, which go puffing about, and are extremely horrid." This, allow us to add, is partial proof of the growth of practical ideas in Italy, which Mr. Wilde did not intend to assert, and which he unfortunately did do, but that it is testimony to the fact is somewhat doubted. However, it was not our purpose to interrupt him, and we will proceed with him to California, where he says nature has done what art has not, and in reality has made it an Italy without its art.

"I was deeply pleased with my sojourn on the slope; it is really the loveliest spot on earth. There are the peach blossoms, covering the orchards in their snow-white purity. The apple buds blossoming on the hills, resembling veritable red cheeks of nature, and the purple tipped mountains. All this comprising a picture with the blue Pacific as the back-ground. Oh! 'tis grand."

Of course the reporter was pleased if

MR. O. WILDE HAD SEEN

anything in this worry, hurry, work-a-day country that was satisfactory, and took the liberty to ask as to art out there.

"There is art in America but it is not common to any locality. I found that in San Francisco they have old established schools of design, and in all work, save that of handicraft, I find they are doing well. But the American people do not appreciate art as they should. The modern upholstery of today has destroyed the old beauty and true art displayed in that which took its style from the household furniture of the Puritans. In New England I was permitted to see some of the old furniture of the Puritan style, and I was deeply pleased with it. There are reasons

1. Victor Emmanuel II (1820–1878) was King of Sardinia from 1849 to 1861, when, after the Second Italian War of Independence, he assumed the title of King of Italy, the first king of a united Italy since the sixth-century.

for an immediate change in the style of your articles of use in this country. In the hotels of New York, Philadelphia, Chicago, San Francisco, in all of the hotels I have been so unfortunate to visit I have seen this demonstrated. In New York City the waiter brought me my chocolate at 10 o'clock in the morning, served in a cup of crockery ware at least three-quarters of an inch thick, and I thought as I lifted the unwieldy thing to my mouth, if the man who made it was born of a barbarous conception. Do you use these great, thick, ugly things for weapons, or are they used for drinking purposes in all times of peace? I was obliged to use them at my hotel in San Francisco, but while there I was permitted to visit the Chinese quarters, and to attend the Chinese theatre, and to sup at the Chinese restaurant. This is a nice, and cool resort. There is a cozy little latticed portico, lighted with Chinese lanterns, and there I was served with tea in dainty little cups, which were no thicker than the thin

TENDER PETAL OF A WHITE ROSE,

so dainty that a lady would exercise care in using them. Yet the Chinamen who use them every day are capable of doing, and do more coarse rough work in San Francisco than any other class of laborers, but they are that nice and proper in their mode of living as to use these dainty and beautiful articles of table furniture, and with a grace becoming the French Court."[1]

There is one thing which Mr. Wilde is pronounced in, and to speak of it would be to appeal to a very important issue of the people of the North. He does not like our stoves. Nearly every house he has entered, nearly every hotel room he has occupied in the West, is heated with a cast-iron stove, which, according to his aesthetic conception, is neither handsome nor shapely.

"Why," says he, "don't you do away with those horrid iron stoves? A porcelain stove is more elegant, and gives out more heat. I do not like the mechanical art displayed in their ornamentation, and the apparent custom with the designer of these stoves is to cap the climax of his crime on art, by surmounting them with a funereal urn, a cup of Jove, or with a poor suggestion of the Octagon of Thespis!"[2] This was a warm reminder, and the other newspaper man who was listening with THE REGISTER chronicler,[3] having the vision of a hotter futurity, changed the subject as to what time he would leave America.

"I wish to go to Japan, for I know there is art there, and I would like to remain there three long months, study their handicraft, improve upon the element of delicacy which pervades their artistic achievements, and teach my newly

1. Teacups in Chinatown: see p. 337, note 1.

2. Cast iron stoves: p. 317, note 4.

3. The other reporter's account is untraced. It may have appeared in the *Prairie City News*: see p. 683.

learned art axioms to the Americans, and the English." He stated that he longed to sail for Japan while in San Francisco, and probably it was only the anticipation of a visit to this city which contented him to remain.

After an hour's interesting presence with the peculiar aesthete, the chronicler took his leave, and with a full realization of a quotation from Horace Greeley,[1] who once said in effect that the fools are not all dead yet.

✂ *A report of Wilde's lecture in Des Moines.*

"Aesthetic," *Dayton Daily Democrat* (Dayton, OH), 3 May 1882, 4[2]

An Interesting Interview with Oscar Wilde

On Art, Decorative Art, American and European Art.

Sight Seeing About Dayton and the Soldiers' Home.

His Lecture on Decorative Art at Music Hall Last Night.

Our fair city was visited yesterday as most of our readers know by perhaps the greatest living art critic—one who at least is among the very highest and still on the ascendancy, while the luster of him, who has ruled supreme in the kingdom of art criticism hitherto, during the present generation, is rapidly waving and losing its power. The ignorant laugh at Oscar Wilde's eccentricities, but that matters naught in view of the fact that he is recognized by artists and connoisseurs of art as a man of almost unequaled taste and aesthetic judgement.

He arrived in this city last Monday night, and at once retired to his rooms at the Beckel House, where he remained during the morning.

A representative of the DEMOCRAT paid Mr. Wilde a visit, in his room at the Beckel House just after he had finished his dinner yesterday. A more opportune moment for an interview could not have been chosen for the old truth, well known, that a man's sociability and talkativeness are at their best when the inner man has been supplied with all that nature demands or culinary skill can supply, was here amply proven and promptly in answer to the reporter's card sent up from the office, came the invitation to walk in.

There sat the great Oscar Wilde half reclining on a sofa, a small table before him bearing writing materials in the use of which he had evidently been inter-

1. Horace Greeley (1811–1872) was the founder and editor of the *New York Tribune* and briefly served as a member of the United States House of Representatives from New York.

2. H & S, b73. Reprinted in H & S, 141–6. Quoted in OWDA, 342–3. Referenced in Ellmann, 187/197; and Sturgis, 230/220, 251/240.

rupted by the entrance of his visitor. Papers were strewn about his feet in profusion. The remains of his dinner stood on another table beside him, and the whole character of the room presented an air more of comfortable utility rather than orthodox neatness. Mr. Wilde himself was in perfect keeping with these surroundings as he sat there, whiffing a fine cigar. His face is well known to our readers through the thousands of pictures that have been scattered over the country since his arrival upon American soil. He looks exactly like these pictures with his long scraggy brown hair, wiry and oil-less, falling over his ears and neck, about his shoulders, his mild blue-gray eyes, his graceful nose but large lips, his soft effeminate flush, but withal his very large, massive head and graceful form. He is odd and eccentric in his dress and style, but it is an eccentricity which loses its conspicuousness in the charm of his conversation, the depth of thought and brilliancy of expression. Eccentric, it is true, but it is the eccentricity of a great man and not the eccentricity of affectation, or else he could not have won for himself the commendation of the greatest artists and literati of this continent and the old world as it [*sic*] undoubtedly has done ere he had reached the age of three decades.

His dress was peculiar although he did not wear his much talked of knee-breeches. He had on a mouse-colored, corduroy blouse with grey worsted pantaloons.

About his neck was tied an old silk tie of a warm green hue while from the left breast pocket of his coat protruded a silk handkerchief of the same color.

"How do American and American institutions impress you, Mr. Wilde?" asked the reporter by way of opening conversation after self introduction and cordial greeting had passed.

"Oh what is the use to generalize? This country is much like other countries, we do not find much difference. I think the West is grand; I was far more interested in that part of America than in the East. The East is much more like the countries of Europe. But in California I was perfectly delighted. Everything is so new and novel and interesting. I was charmed with California and the West. But what a dreadful barrier of desert separates you of the East from the West. It seems as though nature had exhausted her resources on the West and had nothing left for those prairies. Oh it is so dreary, so desolate with those miles and miles of level plain sweeping across the country with not a tree, not a flower, not even an animal."[1]

1. *Personal Impressions of America*: "One had to cross the alkali plains, which were so ridiculously vast that Nature, when it came to decorate them, seemed to have become alarmed and given up in despair. There were no trees or flowers – nothing of any colour – nothing of any shape. With the pitiless steel-grey sky overhead it was an expanse of monotony so vast that the train passing over it seemed immobile." (Dibb, 237.)

"I presume, however, that you do not find as much art in the West as in the East?"

"No; but still there are some good artists out there. We do not want to teach the people how to become great artists. We do not want to take a fine Italian masterpiece and put it in the workman's shanty. He would not appreciate it. He could not be made to appreciate it. It would give him no pleasure, what we want to do is to teach the people that they can have beauty in everything, teach them to open their eyes and look at nature, teach them to see the glorious panorama of color that is going on every day in the skies above their heads, and in all nature about them. We want to get them to quit using these horrid forms of furniture and household utensils, and make them understand that there can be beauty in the meanest vessel. We want to educate them to despise these dreadful combinations in color in their wall papers. Either they are so ignorant and insensible to these outrages to taste or else they are existing in utter misery. Now look at that chair. Can anything be more horrid in form, where it curves in it should curve out and where it curves out it ought to curve in. It will not last either; it is badly put up.

"All over the country, in all the hotels I stop at, they give me cups like this to drink my coffee or chocolate from. See how thick and clumsy it is. It is at least half an inch thick, and so barbaric in form that one would think it was made in a barbarous, savage age and intended to be used to hie at the head of an enemy as a weapon of defense. It disgusts me to drink from it. Such rude things make men rude who use them. We ought to have things of beauty in everything about our house. Let children when quite young be accustomed to see and handle delicate things and they will become refined. I was impressed, while out West, in going among the Chinese, to see these navvies who work hard all day on the railroad, shoveling dirt, go home at night and drink their tea out of cups of fine porcelain as thin and delicate as the petals of a white rose, so delicate, indeed, that our ladies even are afraid to handle them for fear of breaking them. That is what we should have for ourselves here.[1] I would place things of beauty, things of delicacy in the houses of all our mechanics as well as of the wealthy. This is the first hotel that I have been in for two or three weeks where my room did not have that horrid dreadful thing called a stove in it. I think the way people make stoves now is an outrage. If we must have them in our houses with their black iron bodies and ugly coiling pipe, let us have them plain and unornamented. But no, they insist on decorating them, and so they put a garland of roses around the bottom—black, grimy horrid machine made cast iron roses! What a desecration! And then on top they put a something that so much resembles a funeral urn that we think we are

1. Teacups in Chinatown: see p. 337, note 1.

living in a cemetery or sepulchre all the time. Why not make them plain? Then they can be accepted simply as a disagreeable necessity."[1]

"Mr. Wilde, do you think that this present so-called 'aesthetic craze'—?"

"O *do* not call it a craze. It is no craze. You Americans have such a way of treating serious things as a joke. And yet you are not a joyous people. In society there is all brilliancy and apparent joyousness, but on the railway trains I do not see happy men and women. Everybody has a troubled anxious look, and everybody is pushing forward in some business project. But the people do not appreciate art and so they call it a craze. But it will live, and spread its influences and be continuing in its good and it is no craze."

"You have answered just the question I was going to ask. I should rather have used the term, 'revival.' Do you think the present great revival of interest in art will pass away after a time or will its benefits be lasting?"

"Art and true beauty can never die. There may be a wave of barbarism sweep over Europe by an Asiatic invasion, but true art will not be lost."

"Pardon me for asking it, Mr. Wilde, but I have a great curiosity, as many other Americans have, to know why it is you have selected the lily and sunflower as the emblems of beauty. You know it has been only since your arrival in America that these flowers have really been discovered by Americans."

"I love the lily and the sunflower," answered the great aesthete, laughing, "because of their perfectness of form and adaptability for decorative purposes. What is more beautiful than the gracefully flowing outlines of the lily and the symmetry of the sunflower with its large round disk of rich reddish brown surrounded by its beautiful rays of yellow. Then with the lily there is such purity of color and it has so many beautiful legends associated with it. And the sunflower's fidelity to the great source of warmth, and light, and truth. It always looks to the sun, never drooping its head towards the cold shadows of earth. The lily is so beautiful for decorating rooms, but the sunflower is not gorgeous for indoor decoration, unless the room is full of richness and color. The rose is a beautiful piece of color, but it has no beauty of form and is not adapted for decoration."

"Do you think, Mr. Wilde, that you pre-Raphaelites of the present day, while tending to wean art away from the old heroic style of Michael Angelo, and introducing more of the realistic and more of nature as it is, and bringing it more within the power of appreciation of the masses than it has been hitherto?"

"Why, what could be more realistic than Michael Angelo? The truth is we are only beginning to appreciate the classic art. The infinite beauty of Greek art is only being discovered. But it is a mistake which the Americans so often make, to confuse me with the pre-Raphaelite [*sic*]. While I owe much to Mr. Ruskin and to

1. Cast iron stoves: p. 317, note 4.

pre-Raphaelite teaching, I do not class myself with that school, but I belong to a very different school entirely."[1]

"Whom do you consider the greatest living painter?"

"I think Mr. Whistler is by far the greatest artist living and I am glad to be able to say he is an American, although he lives in England."

"Have you found any artists in America whom you consider equal to your great painters of England?"

"It is hard to institute comparisons between artists and especially between men of genius, because to be a genius a man must possess certain qualities which are exclusively his own, and the value of these qualities cannot be compared with the value of qualities possessed by another. I think Mr. Duveneck of Boston is the greatest painter in America.[2] He and Mr. Whistler are leaders in this new school which I champion."

"Are there any other great artists who have become allied with this new school you speak of?"

"No, it is followed now only by the younger class of artists."

"What are the characteristics of the school?"

"Simplicity of treatment and the rendering of subjects taken from scenes of the present day in preference to the old subjects of history. The pre-Raphaelites estimate the worth of a picture by the story it tells. We do not consider that. It does not matter so much *what* you paint, as *how* you paint it. Our school lays greatest weight on the importance of color. A picture badly colored is no picture at all. Unless, as you approach a picture from a distance, the eye is pleased with the beautiful scheme of color, it is not a good picture no matter how good a story is told.

"I believe that art has a province of its own without invading the provinces of literature. If we want a poem, let us go to a poet; if we want a story, let us go to a story teller, but if we want a picture, a representation of the wonderful beauties around us, then let us go to the artist. Whistler has adopted this idea of the importance of harmony of color that he paints his pictures and names them, solely with this in view. He paints symphonies in color. You may laugh at the idea of a man painting a symphony, but he does it, and he names his pictures 'Symphony in Blue and White,' or 'Symphony in White.'

"Why, the most beautiful picture I ever saw is Whistler's 'Symphony in White.' It is so simple and yet so lovely. A grey sky lightly flecked with delicate white clouds, a grey sea dotted with white waves. And in the foreground is a

1. Wilde had previously been reported as saying: "The aesthetes are pre-Raphaelites" ("Oscar Wilde," *Milwaukee Sunday Sentinel* (Milwaukee, WI), 5 Mar. 1882, 6, p. 257).

2. Frank Duveneck (1848–1919) was an American portrait painter. He was born in Kentucky, found success in Boston, and worked for periods in Germany and Italy.

white balcony with all the varying shades of white, from the pearly white marble to the rich yellow-white of ivory. Upon the balcony are three little girls, oh! so beautiful, all dressed in white, and one is reaching over and tearing the petals of white blossoms from a tree, and they are borne away upon gentle zephyrs, like little white snowflakes. Could anything be more exquisitely lovely? What purity! What beauty! and then would you turn from this to some dreadful picture of "Mary, Queen of Scots, about to be beheaded," painted by some artist who ought to have been beheaded himself before he was ever allowed to paint such a picture? [1]

"This is the kind of art that is destined to win the day in the present age. We are tired of these bloody, ugly dreadful pictures we have had so long."

"What do you think of America, Mr. Wilde, viewed from an artistic standpoint?"

"It will never produce great landscape painters. It will be greater in figure painting than in landscape. But it will be greatest in sculpture. The country is new. People look upon the forests from a commercial point of view and do not appreciate them artistically. Men at hard labor in the mines or at agriculture form excellent subjects for figure painting while men who are confined in large cities become stooped and ungraceful. But no country which has the clear atmosphere and the cloudless skies, that America has or that Switzerland or Italy have, can be good for the landscapist. The great landscape painters of the world have been in Holland, France and England, where the hazy, damp atmosphere lend a charm to the view not see in clearer air."

"Well, I must express my thanks to you, Mr. Wilde, for this interview. I presume you have found us newspaper men a great annoyance since you have been in America."

"O no, not at all. I never allow anything to annoy me. If I don't want to see anybody I tell them so."

Soon after this, the carriage drove up which had been provided by Professor Isaac Broome,[2] through whose efforts Mr. Wilde was brought to Dayton, and

1. Whistler's *The White Symphony: Three Girls* and *Three Figures: Pink and Grey* both depict three women on a balcony tending a potted cherry tree, but several of the details Wilde describes are absent. In 1868 Whistler was commissioned to paint a frieze for F. R. Leyland, the shipping magnate. He prepared sketches for six scenes but finished only one, now lost, based on *The White Symphony: Three Girls*. Wilde may be describing this picture or one that has not survived, or he may be conflating *Three Figures* with another picture. A further possibility is that he is intentionally embellishing his description of Whistler's work. He wrote a letter to introduce an artist he met in Canada to Whistler: "She is already devoted to your pictures, or rather to my descriptions of them, which are just as good, I often think better." (CL, 172.) Wilde also spoke of *The White Symphony* in *The House Beautiful* (O'Brien, 170).

2. Isaac Broome (1835–1922) was a Canadian-born American ceramicist.

Figure 12. Montgomery County Jail, Dayton. Wilde thought it amusing that a building so ornamented should be a prison.

by the courtesy of Mr. Wilde and Professor Broome, representatives of the DEMOCRAT and *Journal* accompanied these two gentlemen on a trip of sightseeing.[1]

The new Presbyterian Church was first visited. Mr. Wilde admired its arrangement very much, and thought the granite pillars in the interior were beautiful, but would have been better if of different colors. He did not compliment the stained glass windows nor the frescoing, but said they were both barren and in bad taste.[2]

He was struck with the elaborately fine jail exterior and afterwards in expressing his admiration of the general beauty of the city said he did not wonder we have so fine a jail for with a city so beautiful people *could* not be very wicked.[3]

1. See also "Oscar Wilde," *Dayton Daily Journal* (Dayton, OH), 3 May 1882, 4, pp. 377–9.

2. The Westminster Presbyterian Church, or Third Street Presbyterian Church, was erected at Third and Ludlow Streets in 1881 at a cost of $65,000. It is not to be confused with the Summit Street United Brethren Church, dedicated 30 April 1882, or the Central Baptist Church at Clay and Van Buren Streets, dedicated 4 May 1882. (Crew, H. W. (1889). *History of Dayton, Ohio*. United Brethren Publishing House. 598, 605, 618.)

3. The Montgomery County Jail was built in 1874 on Third Street.

At the Art Pottery of the Ladies Decorative Art Society, he was not sparing in his praise of the works of Professor Broome and of the students.

He was particularly complimentary to the underglaze decoration of some pieces of pottery, the work of Miss May Broome, pronouncing them exquisite and in wonderful taste, and he was delighted when Miss Broome presented him a small piece of pottery which he had admired especially. Miss Broome has a right to feel proud of his praises of her work, for he is not accustomed to praise except when he means what he says.

At the Soldiers' Home a visit was paid to Governor Patrick who assisted by Chaplain Earnshaw, Colonel Thomas, Major Watson and Captain Giddinger, entertained their distinguished visitor to the very best of their ability. He was shown the principal attractions of the Home, although time was limited, and he freely praised the new theater and particularly the handsome drop curtain. Indeed although he has traveled so much and seen so many sights he still has a keen interest in all he sees.

✂ *A report of Wilde's lecture in Dayton.*

"Oscar Wilde," *Dayton Daily Journal* (Dayton, OH), 3 May 1882, 4[1]

Visit of the English Aesthete to Dayton.

He Inspects the Art School, the Soldiers' Home,

And Other Objects of Interest in the City.

What He Thought of It All—His Lecture.

Oscar Wilde and servant, Ireland, and J. S. Vale,[2] Manager, of New York, were among the names registered at the Beckel House yesterday morning. The JOURNAL man, having sent up his card, was duly ushered into the presence of the English poet and art reformer. He was seated on a sofa, with a table and writing materials before him, but rose to greet his visitor cordially, and requested him to be seated. The large athletic figure was attired in mouse colored velveteen coat, light pantaloons, low morocco shoes and dark blue embroidered stockings. There was little in the face to be called handsome. The smooth heavy boyish features were surmounted by a broad forehead and a profusion of long auburn hair, that was combed back without an attempt to part, and fell back of the ears without a

1. H & S, b72. Quoted in OWDA, 341–2. The reporter was accompanied by the author of "Aesthetic," *Dayton Daily Democrat* (Dayton, OH), 3 May 1882, 4, pp. 374–6.
2. Vale's name was frequently misspelt. In the source it is given as "T. A. Vaile."

wave, nearly reaching the shoulders. There was a suggestion of western picturesqueness in the long hair, but it was without the wavy ringlets of Buffalo Bill, and more vividly recalled the mannerisms of Joaquin Miller, the poet of the Sierra. The whole contour of the face was not unlike that of George Eliot, which appeared some months ago in *Scribner's Magazine*.[1] The lips are thick with a feminine expression about the mouth, the eyes are small and have a frank hearty expression, twinkling with amusement and brightening with enthusiasm, when he dwelt on subjects that pleased him. He proved an excellent conversationalist, with an easy manner that did not force itself on the listener but interested, by an apparent earnestness, and made him a confidant when the speaker threw back with a toss his heavy head of hair and indulged in a hearty laugh.

Professor Broome had arranged to conduct Mr. Wilde to such objects of interest as his time would permit during the afternoon, and directly after dinner a carriage was taken at the hotel by these gentlemen, accompanied by representatives from the *Democrat* and the JOURNAL. The first visit was to the Presbyterian Church, on Third street, which Mr. Broome desired to show to the guest as a specimen of the most advanced step taken in decoration. He appeared pleased and expressed admiration at the decoration of the interior.

"It is really quite excellent," said the poet. "I am surprised; its dimensions are perfect, and these polished granite columns are beautiful. They should not have been both alike, however; one of them of red Scotch granite would have afforded so charming a contrast. In America, you have such fine building stone. I do not like those windows though. Why were they made with so transparent a design and such flaring colors?"

Mr. Broome explained that the use of cathedral glass was in its infancy in this part of the country.

"Figures would have been much prettier and in better taste. The work in stained glass is a peculiar art, and so great an artist as Sir Joshua Reynolds has made in our country a flagrant error in it."

The drive from the city was through Dayton View,[2] and the conversation turned upon the objects of interest that encountered the eye. The comments these objects excited were not of affectation, but the expression of the school which he represented. The caricature of Oscar Wilde in "Patience" has no resemblance to the real. The criticisms which the aesthetic sense prompted were not ridiculous; they were always natural, and apparent truth suggesting errors or change in objects which have come to be regarded unchangeable as a matter of course. His eye quickly caught what was attractive or amusing, and his apprecia-

1. George Eliot in *Scribner's*: see p. 339, note 1.

2. An approximately 3 km^2 area of Dayton that was built in 1880. Wilde was presumably taken there to view the newest architecture in the city.

tion was always hearty. The jail, with its ornamented front, he found so amusing that he threw back his head and gave utterance to a hearty laugh, and for the instant thought it was only so called for a joke.

"What is the name of your river, here? Miami? Ah, how lovely are those Indian names; there are so many of them beautiful. But some of the eastern towns I have met have barbarous beastly names. There was one Greeksville [*sic*];[1] that is simply horrible. I would never lecture in such a town unless its name was changed. That is a beautiful scene!" he exclaimed, as the carriage passed over the river. "You should never let your manufacturers pollute the air with smoke. In many towns in England they have ordinances requiring all smoke to be consumed. Ruskin would not go to Manchester until they got rid of their smoke, and they finally did it.[2] When I called at the residence of Mr. Probasco in Cincinnati and looked down on the filthy cloud that hung upon the city, I was astounded—how long can beauty exist among so much that is vile?"[3]

"Your visit to San Francisco was pleasant?" asked Mr. Broome.

"Oh, I enjoyed it immensely. It is a wonderful country, a garden of the world. When I passed over that vast space from the mountains to the Mississippi, where everything seemed a monotonous brown, where even the animals and the Indians have fled from the rattle of the train, it seemed as if Nature had exhausted herself in forming the delightful country of California, and could do no more for these illimitable plains. There is a flavor of Bret Harte over this country.[4] He is a charming artist; his work is so finished and complete. And then there is Joaquin Miller. I love the West and its people. I like to visit your universities. There are so many of them distributed over the country. They make its life blood. Your universities reach into the people and effect a greater work than ours. They ought to cultivate more the physical as well as the mental man; a good gymnasium should be a part of every university. There is only one thing I utterly dislike in America; that is its cigarettes. At home I rarely smoked cigars, always cigarettes; they were African tobacco, rolled in Egypt; but I can't smoke those I find here; they are vile, and I have given them quite up. What a peculiar tint the brick has in so many of your houses? There should be more color in it. They have a sickly look."

1. Griggsville, Illinois. See p. 292, note 1.

2. Wilde had heard Ruskin lecture on the importance to artists' work of beautiful surroundings, "contrasting the sordid aspect of a great English city" and its "smoky chimneys, polluted streams, railways, and commerce" with the more picturesque surroundings enjoyed by artists of the Italian Renaissance (*Modern Art Training*; Dibb, 228).

3. Henry Probasco (1820–1902) was an American businessman with an interest in art. He commissioned public fountains and collected paintings and rare books.

4. Bret Harte (1836–1902) was an American writer of short stories and poetry. He is best known for his short fiction about the California Gold Rush of 1848–1855. Two of his novels were among the last Wilde purchased before his death (Sturgis (2020), 225).

Similar comments were called forth from time to time until the pottery was reached on Summit street. A number of carriages were drawn up before the building, and quite a number of ladies, including Miss Carrie Brown, the President of the Society, Mrs. Brainerd Thresher,[1] Miss Broome, and other members of the classes. Mr. Wilde was introduced to them, and he then passed a short time examining various articles of their work. Two vases by Miss Broome attracted his attention at once, and he complimented them highly for their simplicity. He was also particularly well pleased with the water colors made by members of the classes. In speaking of the work, he said that the amount was much smaller than what he saw in Cincinnati, but its quality was very much higher. Though the one young man there, a Mr. Brewer, he said showed the highest artistic talent.[2] He deprecated too great a freedom of style, and urged the cultivation of the senses before the mind. He referred to the use of glaring plain white dishes and the increase of decorated pottery of all kinds, and urged it in the articles of daily use. At the best hotels of New York and San Francisco he was daily served coffee in earthenware half an inch thick, that might serve as valuable weapons of defense. In San Francisco he saw Chinamen drinking from cups delicate as rose leaves, that ladies would have to handle tenderly.[3]

Proceeding to the Soldiers' Home a visit was made to the conservatory and the grotto, which were much admired. The party then proceeded to Governor Patrick's headquarters, where Colonel Thomas, Chaplain Earnshaw, Major Wilson, Captain Giddenger were introduced, and after a short stay there and a pleasant chat with the officers visited the Memorial Hall, the dining room and the library, and then returned to the city.

"Have you a poet in Dayton?" he asked on the return drive.

The newspaper man replied poets are numerous in the spring time, and there was the usual crop at present.

The aesthete sighed and, turning to the subject of actors, he said there were but two actors in the world, Bernhardt and Salvini. "Bernhardt told me," he continued musing, "there were two things worth seeing in this country, the acting of Clara Morris and the way they kill pigs in Chicago. I have seen Clara Morris, and I admire her. I have just come from Chicago, but I didn't care to see them kill pigs. What a beautiful flower this is (scenting a flower he held in his hand), single flowers are always the most beautiful. Double flowers always look to me like a woman with a pretty face but no figure," and he threw his head back laughing in his hearty manner.

1. Sarah Bliss Thresher (1841–1932) was a writer of hymn lyrics and the wife of Joseph Brainerd Thresher, an oil and varnish merchant.

2. "Brewer" is H. J. Breuer. See p. 195, note 1.

3. Teacups in Chinatown: see p. 337, note 1.

✂ *A report of Wilde's lecture in Dayton.*

"Oscar Wilde," *Harrisburg Telegraph* (Harrisburg, PA), 5 May 1882, 4[1]

His Impressions of Harrisburg—Other Topics Discussed.

A reporter of the TELEGRAPH wended his way last evening to the Lochiel Hotel, after Oscar Wilde's lecture,[2] to interview the "Apostle of the Sunflower and the Lily" in regard to his general treatment by the American public, and to hear some opinions from him in regard to his impression of this country.

Ascending the elevator to the third floor, and rapping at the door of the large, spacious room of the hotel fronting on Third street was but the work of a moment, after which the scribe was bade by a somewhat musical and rather feminine voice from within to enter the room. Accepting the proffered invitation, the man with the pencil found himself in the presence of the disciple of aestheticism. After glancing at Mr. Wilde's peculiar costume the reporter started the conversation with:

"Mr. Wilde, what is your opinion of Harrisburg from the little you have seen of it?"

"Well, one should not generalize about a place, having seen as little as I have of your city. I came here in the afternoon, and was engaged in writing a letter the remainder of the day, and consequently am unable to form any opinion of the "Capital City."[3]

"How were you pleased with your audience this evening?"

"I had a very charming audience, indeed, of perhaps 150 or 200 persons.[4] They were quite attentive and showed me the respect that the most sensitive lecturer would desire. Of course, I don't expect every one to agree with what I say—"

1. I am grateful to John Cooper for identifying this article.

2. Wilde lectured on *The Decorative Arts* in Harrisburg's Grand Opera House on Wednesday 3 May.

3. This letter appears to have been lost. At around this time Wilde was corresponding with J. M. Stoddart about the publication of Rennell Rodd's poems (CL, 167–8). Most of Wilde's long letters that survive from 1882 summarise his recent travels for friends in the United Kingdom. The Harrisburg letter may have been similar in content to the letter Wilde wrote to Helena Sickert on 25 April, in which he described his recent adventures in Colorado, Kansas, and Nebraska (CL, 165–6).

4. Wilde's audience was described as "very small" ("Oscar Wilde's Debut," *Harrisburg Daily Independent* (Harrisburg, PA), 5 May 1882, 4). The Grand Opera House's capacity was 1,324 (Cooper, Harrisburg lecture, 4 May 1882).

"What has been your treatment by the American press in general?" was the next question propounded by the scribe.

"It would be foolish for me to generalize on such a subject. When I came over to America, at first it seemed as if there was a want of sanative criticism on the part of the newspapers. The New York *World*, however, had quite a good article on my lecture, and deserves special mention in this connection, for the soundness and vigor with which it expressed itself with regard to my subject.[1] In almost every place I go, there is always one paper which writes in a becoming and serious manner on what I have to say, and the criticisms are, to say the least, quite good. In Denver, Col., the articles in some of the newspapers (the *Tribune* and one or two others) were excellent—in fact—nothing could have been better."[2]

"Speaking about the West, how were you received as regards your audiences?"

"I found not only the most charming audiences, but in every city I lectured I had always the people of the highest literary culture and intelligence."

The conversation was here interrupted by the servant who brought in an autograph album with the request that Mr. Wilde favour the owner with his signature, which he did, after which he returned the book to the owner. While writing, the reporter noticed a large black seal ring on the third finger of the aesthetic young man, which, however, was not graced by a sunflower or lily. Mr. Wilde's movements in writing are from the whole arm, giving him plenty of room to finish up with a sweeping curve line of beauty after having written his name.

"I see," resumed the reporter, "that Henry Ward Beecher has joined hands with you, as it were, in your endeavours for aesthetics. His last lecture on 'The modern uses of luxury and beauty in our homes.'"[3]

1. *The New York World* printed a glowing full-column review of Wilde's debut lecture: "He handled no prosaic subject nor was his handling prosaic. Long melodious sentences, seldom involved, always clear, unfolded his meaning as graceful curves reveal a beautiful figure. A vocabulary as wide as Swinburne's and well nigh as musical, modelled on that rich and flowing prose which is as marvellous as Swinburne's verse—how could such a style be dull?" ("Oscar Wilde's Lecture," *The New York World, Semi-Weekly Edition* (New York, NY), 10 Jan. 1882, 4). Extracts from the *World* article featured in puff pieces for Wilde's later American lectures. Wilde thought the account of the lecture in the *New York Tribune* was "badly reported" (CL, 170).

2. Wilde refers to "Art and Aesthetics," *Denver Tribune* (Denver, CO), 13 Apr. 1882, 8, pp. 338–45. The interview and accompanying account of Wilde's lecture ran to three columns.

3. Beecher was delivering a lecture titled *The Moral Uses of Beauty and Luxury*. He argued that piety and frugality did not necessarily go together, and that Christ only railed against those who amassed riches through immoral means. *The Atlanta Constitution* reported that the lecture contained "[g]reat beautiful thoughts linked to coarse jokes and ribald irreverence." Beecher saw no problem with Americans sending to Paris for their fashions but wished that Paris would not send "dresses six feet too long at the bottom and six inches too low at the top." He conceded that there was no use in his attacking fashion: "If it was the fashion to wear six monkeys tied to-

"Yes, so I see by the papers. Mr. Beecher is a man of great culture and intellect, and has that width of mind that enables him to comprehend people fairly. I have great admiration for him. He is one of those men whose broad humanity appears to understand everybody. When I was in Chicago he was kind enough to call on me. I hope to see more of him before I leave this country."

"Mr. Wilde, do you ever have any hesitation or apparent tremor in going before the public?" queried the reporter. "Mr. Beecher, Mr. Burdette, Mr. Tilton, Mr. Gough, and many illustrious lecturers, all testify to the fact that it is a terrible ordeal to pass through in coming before large audiences."[1]

"No, sir—not in the least—I am not at all timid," replied the aesthetic Oscar—"I know I have something to say, and I simply say it, that's all. I have confidence enough in American audiences from what I have seen of them, having lectured for a long time, to know that they will treat me in the most courteous and polite manner. I find this to be a rule. The only exception was at Rochester, where some roughs in the gallery of the hall when I was lecturing made themselves conspicuous for their want of sense by annoying me as much as possible. Of course, such things are unavoidable. These facts impress me every day with the sense of fair play among the American people."

"Then you don't concur in Charles Dickens' view of the people of the United States as set forth in his 'Chuzzlewit'?"[2]

"Oh, no—not in the least. I find them to be the most frank, ingenious and generous people I have ever met. Why, in Leadville, which has the reputation of being the roughest city of any in America, I could not have been treated nicer. I spoke to them about the ancient workers in metal, how they made the various kinds of coins from different metals, and told them of the many beautiful things in art that were wrought through the skill of the artisans of 'long ago.'[3] They

---

gether for a head dress all the women would wear them." He loved flowers, even though his old school chaplain had admonished him for trifling with them: "He [the chaplain] forgot that God had been trifling with them for thousands of years all summer long." ("Preacher Beecher," *The Atlanta Constitution* (Atlanta, GA), 2 Apr. 1882, 1.)

1. Robert Jones Burdette (1844–1914) was an American clergyman and humourist who wrote for the *Burlington Hawkeye*. His most popular lecture was *The Rise and Fall of the Mustache*. In 1882 he was lecturing on *Newspaper Humor*. John Bartholomew Gough (1817–1886) was a British-born American temperance orator.

2. *Martin Chuzzlewit*: see p. 218, note 1.

3. In a letter to Helena Sickert Wilde would claim to have "lectured the miners on the old workers in metal – Cellini and others. All I told them about Cellini and how he cast his Perseus interested them very much" (CL, 165). The Florentine goldsmith and sculptor Benvenuto Cellini (1500–1571) is best known for his bronze statue of *Perseus with the Head of Medusa* ("that green and gold god of Cellini's", as Wilde described it; CL, 589), and his *Autobiography*, one of Wilde's "books to read" (CW vi, No. 24, line 7). Wilde embroidered the story of his lecture to the miners on Cellini for *Personal Impressions of America*: "They [the miners] believed in the words of the poet that Cellini 'was a bully boy' and I was reproved by my hearers for not having

seemed to be interested in no ordinary degree in what I had to say, and the treatment I received at their hands could have been no better. This, too, after I had been warned by friends that I would receive some pretty rough usage. Why, I went down in the silver mines there and spent whole nights [*sic*] in them.[1] I cannot but remember the graceful motions of one of the workmen. His every movement would have been suitable for a bronze casting. There appeared to be a rhythmic pulsation in the beats of the hammer."

"Mr. Wilde, is it true that you really are *wild* over the sunflower and the lily?" continued the reporter.

"If you ask whether I admire those two flowers, I may say I love them for decoration—because they both have such perfect form. The flowers most essential to a young designer are those that are the most perfect. The rose has a most beautiful color, but the form of it is very loose. Of all flowers, the lily is the prettiest. It has the exquisite outline and perfect curve that adapts itself for decoration. It is the most constant flower in the paintings of Italy. In Florence not only is it seen everywhere in the flower gardens, but it is represented in marble, fresco and art. The sunflower, although not so constant, yet is especially adapted for decorative art, as its proportions are so symmetrical, and, with its great brown disk and golden rays, it forms no mean part in the designs in pottery, paintings, &c."

"Mr. Wilde, changing the subject, do you always deliver the same lecture?" asked the scribe.

"Oh, no. I have five or six different lectures.[2] I generally deliver the one that I think will suit the town. In a manufacturing place like Harrisburg, I think it best to lecture on the handicraft—on the calling of the man who works in wood and metal, &c. My *Renaissance* is a lecture given in New York on my arrival there. It referred more particularly to the theory of the art in its relation to life, and the history of the rise of this movement in England. I thought it best to show the people how it sprung up, what its conditions were, its birth—and, also, because I wish to mention with honor and reverence all those who had worked so nobly for the art in England."

---

brought him with me. I explained that he had been dead for some little time which elicited the enquiry 'Who shot him?'" (Dibb, 242).

1. Wilde to Helena Sickert: "I stayed all night there nearly, the men being most interesting to talk to, and was brought off down the mountain by a special train at 4.30 in the morning." (CL, 166). For Wilde's visit to the Matchless Mine see p. 342, note 1.

2. By this point Wilde was mostly delivering *The Decorative Arts*, a revision of *The English Renaissance*, with *The House Beautiful* serving if a second lecture in the same city was required. He had once delivered *Irish Poets and the Poetry of the Nineteenth Century* in San Francisco.

At this point Mr. Wilde entered upon a eulogy of Mr. Emerson, saying he was a man friendly to every movement for the amelioration of mankind; after which the reporter thanking the lecturer for his courtesy, withdrew.

"Oscar Wilde's Return," *The New York World, Semi-Weekly Edition* (New York, NY), 9 May 1882, 3[1]

Finding the True American in the Far West and Sublime Beauty at the Golden Gate.

Mr. Oscar Wilde arrived in New York early yesterday morning and went to the Grand Hotel, where, Friday afternoon, a WORLD reporter found him.

"After I left the East," said Mr. Wilde, "I found a people that struck me as more representatively American than those in the other States. It was west of Chicago that I found America. Here in the older country the people are very closely akin to the English. I arrived at last in San Francisco in the spring. The peach-trees were in bloom in the orchard, the apple-trees blossomed in the close, the beautiful sky was bright and the warm ocean, flooded with light, was pouring in through the Golden Gate. Oh! it was most beautiful, and for the first time I understood why nature had so clothed itself in green. It is because it is the most restful of all colors, and after yearning for it for three months I found it in San Francisco. Moreover, the place itself is most attractive; the people are warm and generous and are cultivated. I lectured four times there and twice in Oakland, a little place just across the bay."

AN ARTISTIC SIDE TO THE CHINESE QUESTION.

"Of course, I have no desire to enter into a political discussion, but I found the Chinese quarter in San Francisco most interesting, and, in my opinion, the Chinese have a decided artistic value, which I think Congress should consider in discussing the Chinese question.[2] Their quarter is full of artistic motives, and

1. Reprinted from the daily edition (6 May 1882, 1; which is H & S, b74). Reprinted as "Oscar Wilde's Return," *The Cincinnati Commercial* (Cincinnati, OH), 12 May 1882, 7; and in H & S, 146–7. Excerpted in *The Semi-Weekly Miner* (Butte, MT), 17 May 1882, 5. Quoted in Sturgis, 236/226, 244/234, 247/236. Referenced in Sturgis, 257/245.

2. Wilde refers to the debate that would culminate on 6 May in the signing by President Chester A. Arthur of the Chinese Exclusion Act, which prohibited the immigration into the United States of Chinese labourers. Wilde's reticence "to enter into a political discussion" was newfound: he had advised his San Francisco audience not to "borrow any Chinese art, for you have no need of it any more than you have need of Chinese labor," a remark that won applause from the "anti-coolie esthetes" in attendance ("American Barbarism," *San Francisco Chronicle* (San Francisco, CA), 30 Mar. 1882). It was immediately after this lecture that Wilde visited San Fran-

they have a constant eye to the value of color. We do not value color sufficiently—we do not recognize the element of joyousness that color brings into life. The Chinese have two theatres in San Francisco, and every actor is most nobly and beautifully attired, so that their plays are pageants, as every play ought to be, because the stage should be art in action. I learned many things from the Chinese."

THE RELATION OF PHYSIQUE TO INTELLIGENCE.

"How did the rough manners of the West impress you?"

"There, now; I object to that word 'rough' as applied to miners.[1] They are cordial and generous and not at all rough. One of my best and most interested audiences was composed of Leadville miners. One reason I liked them was because of their magnificent physiques. I spent a night in a silver mine, and it was one of my most delightful experiences.[2] The most unintellectual audience I had was in Salt Lake. The Mormons are the most unintellectual people I have met in America, because they have the worst physiques I have seen; and a people must have good physiques in order even to comprehend art.[3] I found President Taylor charming. I went to his house, and he and his three wives occupied a stage box at my lecture. The Mormons' Tabernacle is the shape of a tea-kettle and is decorated with the ornaments of a jail.

SEED BY THE WESTERN WAYSIDE.

"In Chicago I had delightful audiences. I was particularly struck with the courtesy of the Western audiences, which the tone of the press did not lead me to expect. In every city where I have been I have either found an art school—crude, to be sure—or, if they had not one, they started one on the occasion of my visit; so that I cannot doubt that my coming to America has had an effect. In the smaller cities most of the people have never seen any art whatever, and the idea of design is bad. The idea I had of America when I landed had been very strongly confirmed; it is that what this country needs principally is not the higher imaginative art, but the simple decorative art that can make beautiful for us the commonest vessel of the house. If an article is beautiful it must have been made by a good workman, because only a good workman can make a beautiful thing."

---

cisco's Chinatown (see "Oscar Wilde in Chinatown," *The Daily Examiner* (San Francisco, CA), 30 Mar. 1882, 3, pp. 313–14), which led to his revising his opinion of Chinese art (Cavendish-Jones, C. (2014). Oscar Wilde's radically revised view of China. *Studies in English Literature, 1500-1900, 54*, 923–41).

1. Wilde presumably misheard "manners" as "miners".
2. Wilde's visit to the Matchless Mine: see p. 342, note 1.
3. For Wilde on the relationship between physical beauty and art, see p. 161, note 2.

AN EXPERIMENT IN MEDIEVAL COSTUME.

Mr. Wilde said that his costumes described in THE WORLD of Thursday were an experiment.[1] They were very beautiful; so simple, yet so artistic. The age of Francis I, the era when the costumes such as he had ordered were worn, was an era of simplicity. He did not know whether he would wear them in public, but he would if he wore them at all. On Thursday afternoon next he will deliver a lecture at Wallack's Theatre on "the practical application of aesthetics to house decoration, dress and morals." He thinks it probable that he will go to Australia, as a strong pressure has been brought on him to do so. If he concludes to go he will sail from San Francisco on June 31 [*sic*], after having first visited Canada. He will remain in and about New York until he leaves for Canada.

"Oscar Wilde," *The Chicago Sunday Tribune* (Chicago, IL), 7 May 1882, 3[2]

HIS SURPRISE AND HIS VIEWS.

Special Dispatch to The Chicago Tribune.

NEW YORK, May 6.—Oscar Wilde was met tonight sauntering down Broadway with a friend.

"What! Thomas Burke assassinated! The friend of my father, and who has often dined at our house! And Lord Cavendish, too! I do not see why they wish to assassinate mediocrity, for he was just an easy-going, pleasant, mediocre gentleman whom no one could have a grudge against. Such, too, was Mr. Burke. He had filled many official positions, but none that brought him in contact with the Irish people. The assassinations were undoubtedly the result of intoxication at what the Irish thought a complete victory. They turned liberty into license; but

1. See "The New Costume," *The New York World, Semi-Weekly Edition* (New York, NY), 5 May 1882, 6, pp. 771–3.

2. H & S, b75. Reprinted as "Liberty Turned into License," *The Boston Herald* (Boston, MA), 8 May 1882, 2; and "The Assassination," *The Globe* (Toronto, ON), 9 May 1882, 2. Quoted in OWDA, 344; Hyde, 71; and Ellmann, 186/196. The version printed in "Bowied," *The Philadelphia Inquirer* (Philadelphia, PA), 8 May 1882, 1; and "The Dublin Assassinations," *Rochester Democrat and Chronicle* (Rochester, NY), 8 May 1882, 2, is identical to the *Tribune* except that the introductory paragraph reads: "A reporter met Oscar Wilde Saturday night sauntering down Broadway with a friend. Both wore long overcoats, flung open wide, and wide brimmed felt hats, nearly covering their long hair." The interview was preceded by lengthy coverage of the fatal stabbings of Lord Frederick Cavendish and Thomas Henry Burke in Dublin's Phoenix Park on 6 May 1882. Cavendish had recently been appointed Chief Secretary for Ireland; Burke was the most senior Irish civil servant.

MR. BURKE. LORD F. CAVENDISH.

THE DIABOLICAL MURDERS IN PHŒNIX PARK: SKETCHED BY A DUBLIN CORRESPONDENT.

Figure 13. The murders of Lord Frederick Cavendish and Thomas Henry Burke in Dublin's Phoenix Park. From The Penny Illustrated Paper and Illustrated Times.

when liberty comes with hands dabbled in blood it is hard to shake hands with her, eh?"[1]

"Hear! Hear!" said Mr. Wilde's friend.

"But, then, we forget

HOW MUCH ENGLAND IS TO BLAME,"

said Mr. Wilde. "She is merely reaping the fruit of seven centuries of injustice. There must be trouble ahead. I presume martial law will be proclaimed, and the Conservative party must come into power again, though I do not care to see it there.[2] Of course, we must not blame the whole Irish nation for the acts of a few men, but I am very sorry to hear the news, and hope it isn't true."

"Oscar Wilde," *The Montreal Daily Star* (Montreal, QC), 15 May 1882, 3[3]

THE ARCH-AESTHETE ON AESTHETICISM

How the Movement Progresses in England—The Use of Fashion.

Mr. Oscar Wilde arrived at the Windsor Hotel yesterday, where he very kindly received our reporter this morning. He was found amid the ruins of a substantial looking breakfast, and there was nothing in his appearance to indicate that he had been sitting up all night with a lily, unless, indeed, the fact of his breakfasting late might suggest something of the sort; but then again, the fact of his breakfasting at all refutes such a supposition. Some of Mr. Wilde's critics in

1. Charles Stewart Parnell had been imprisoned at Kilmainham gaol since October 1881 for his role in Land League demonstrations. Wilde refers to the release of Parnell on 2 May after Parnell and William Gladstone had reached an informal agreement (the so-called Kilmainham Treaty): Parnell would endeavour to quell the violence of his supporters, while Gladstone would allow Irish tenants to appeal for fair rent before the land courts.

2. The Liberal party, led by Gladstone, had been in power since 1880. In 1885 British-held Khartoum fell to Mahdist forces after Gladstone had been slow to send a relief expedition. He resigned soon after and the Conservative Marquess of Salisbury was appointed to lead a caretaker government. In a November general election the Liberals returned to form a minority government, but, after the party's Unionist wing split away to form the Liberal Unionists, another general election followed in the summer of 1886. Gladstone, who supported Irish Home Rule, lost over a hundred seats. With the support of the Liberal Unionists the Conservatives were able to form a government. The Liberal party had been the dominant force in British politics for much of the preceding 30 years, but would only be in power for three of the next 19. Wilde's prediction that the Conservatives would return to power, and that the Irish question would prove central to the Liberals' defeat, was therefore borne out, albeit after a delay.

3. H & S, b77. Reprinted in Mikhail, 84–6; and H & S, 151–3. Excerpted in O'Brien, 57–8. Quoted in OWDA, 348–9; and Hyde, 72.

addition to caricaturing his principles, have gone so far as to accuse him of affectation to an offensive degree, and as these statements have found their way into print, it is but the merest justice on the part of our representative to say that if affectation exists there, it is most artfully concealed and therefore can scarcely be offensive. To the tap of the Ethiopian lily who announced our representative, a remarkably musical voice replied, "Come in," and as the door opened a tall, well built gentleman with a very pleasing countenance arose from the breakfast table and advanced with extended hand and a smile of welcome to receive his early visitor. He was dressed in a delicate sage-green velvet coat and light cloth continuations of the Philistine order of architecture. A red necktie blended well with his dark complexion, which was thrown into striking relief by a profusion of long black hair surrounding it. The costume was decidedly indicative of good taste, and his movements, like his conversation, were easy and graceful.

"I am afraid, Mr. Wilde, that by this time you must look upon all newspaper men as a great nuisance," said our reporter, apologetically.

"Not at all," was the hearty response, "I am very pleased to see you."

"We have heard so much lately of aestheticism, have seen it so abundantly caricatured, and really understand so little about it that I am glad to have an opportunity of conversing with you on the subject."

"There is nothing I like talking about better."

"Do you think the aesthetic movement in England has arisen from a genuine appreciation of the principles you teach, or is the general adoption of aesthetic principles in decoration and dress a fashion in itself, one fashion being simply superseded by another?"

"It is not a fashion at all; it is a return to the right principles of art. This movement has entirely altered the whole character of ordinary English decorations. It would be impossible for anyone now to furnish a house without reference to our principles of design and decoration. Not merely are the ordinary houses of London so embellished, but when the Government wanted to decorate St. James' Palace last year, they at once gave the work to Mr. William Morris, one of the leaders of aestheticism."[1]

"You think, then, that this very general adoption of aesthetic principles has arisen entirely from a genuine appreciation?"

"I don't think anyone adopts beauty out of consideration for fashion. If a thing is beautiful, one cannot help liking it. People will adopt the *bizarre* for the

1. William Morris's company was commissioned to decorate the armoury and tapestry room at St. James's Palace in 1865 and completed the work by 1867. In 1879 he provided carpets for the same rooms. Wilde is probably referring to Morris's 1880 commission to redecorate the state apartments, grand staircase, and ambassadors' staircase.

sake of fashion, but not the beautiful. Even if they did, they would come to see it was beautiful after being with it for a time."

"May I ask, what is your conception of beauty?"

"In the last century, people were fond of finding an abstract definition of beauty. I am quite content to put that off for my old age, if lovers of art have an old age."

"Do they die young then?"

"No! But art is always youthful. I am quite content if I am able to surround myself and others with beautiful things. That is the difference between our aesthetics of this century, and those of the last century. The German philosophers of the last century were content to live in the midst of the most dreadful surroundings, provided they could call beauty long names. We want to produce beautiful things, which is very much more practical. It so happens that within the last two years fashion has been with us, and as you suggested just now, many people may have adopted our principles for fashion's sake, but those principles will never leave them. They educate the taste in color, for instance."

"Are English tastes improving?"

"In music, the taste of the English people has enormously improved. Ten years ago the fashion happened to be for German music and consequently for good music. Now all the works of Beethoven and the other great masters are loved and appreciated. When you can bend fashion to the service of anything good or beautiful, it is of immense importance."

"What do you consider the principal element of beauty in music, is it in association?"

"The charm of all art is founded entirely upon the senses. One of the uses of art is to cultivate the senses. The ears of people who do not often hear good music become very coarse. They have not cultivated the sense of hearing, a sense capable of infinite refinement. One of the great faults of all the education of children is the trying to educate the mind, when probably they haven't got one, instead of trying to educate the senses, which everybody has. We all have eyes, ears and hands, but most people never use either eyes, ears or hands. Any right theory of education, it seems to me (and by the way I want to write upon that subject) must be founded on a principle of educating the mind, not directly, but through the means of the senses. What Universities have you here, and what are they like? I take great interest in Universities everywhere."

Our representative having briefly explained a few of the characteristics of the Canadian Universities, and the educational system generally, evoked several expressions of approval from Mr. Wilde. "Yes," said he, "it is better for the country to have a good general standard of education than to have, as we have in England, a few desperately over-educated and the remainder ignorant. One of the things which delighted me most in America was that the Universities reached a class that we, in Oxford, have never been able to touch, the sons of the farmers and people of moderate means. These are the people to whose wants the University should adapt its curriculum and expenses so that it should be able to reach them."

"Is not Gower Street (i.e. London University) a move in that direction?"[1]

"Yes, Gower Street and Owens College, Manchester, are a move in that direction.[2] Really half of any good that comes from university life comes from the indirect influences from fitting the boy to live by himself; it teaches him independence of mind and common sense, too."

"But under our system it is possible for a young man to earn his living, while obtaining his education."

"I do not think any University which does not require residence on the part of the undergraduates is anything more than a good day school."

Mr. Wilde very much dislikes our bare walls, and called our reporter's attention to the white breakfast service, with the nearest approach to disgust he had yet exhibited.

"Do you recognize any primitive and intrinsic beauty in color?" asked our representative.

"Color! It is the greatest enjoyment of my life, from the rising of the sun till the setting."

And this was the first and last time in the interview that he became enthusiastic or "intense." His conversation was earnest, but practical and sensible. The arrival of a second visitor, many more being in the background, terminated a most agreeable interview.

"Oscar Wilde in Montreal," *Daily Witness* (Montreal, QC), 15 May 1882, 8[3]

THE APOSTLE OF ART IN OUR MIDST—HIS APPEARANCE—WHAT HE HAS DONE AND WHERE HE HAS BEEN.

Few men, at least of his age, have been so much talked about, and certainly none so much laughed at, as Oscar Wilde. Curiosity as to his personal appearance has

1. The institution that would later become University College London was founded in 1826 as a secular alternative to Oxford and Cambridge.

2. Owens College was founded in 1851 with funds bequeathed by John Owens, a textile merchant. In 1880 it joined the newly instituted Victoria University, a federal university for the North of England.

3. H & S, 76. Reprinted in Keller–Farmer, 122–9; *Bruno's Weekly*, 3(25), 16 Dec. 1916, 1220–1; Mikhail, 81–3; and H & S, 147–50. Excerpted in O'Brien, 58–61. Quoted in OWDA, 348–9.

been by no means abated by the many descriptions published, for readers at once recognize the fact that in some cases the most vivid language is useless to convey a correct impression, and Oscar Wilde has been considered a sufficiently unique personage to be one of those cases. Consequently, when a *Witness* reporter was ushered into the poet's room at the Windsor Hotel this morning, his personal as well as professional curiosity was somewhat disappointed to find no poet visible. He was there, however, and his apparent absence was only due to the tobacco smoke which hovered ethereally about his poetic form, and through which his countenance was presently revealed. Reclining in an armchair in the midst of anything but artistic, not to speak of aesthetic, surroundings was the apostle of art and aestheticism. Mr. Wilde as he rose and extended a large, gentle hand to the visitor, showed to full advantage. Tall, and well proportioned, his large figure was clad in graceful garments of soft homespun. The absence of knee breeches and hose was at first a painful shock, but the effect was partly removed by a glance at the massive throat; the broad turned down collar was decidedly "all but," while the aesthetic dull red necktie, baffling comprehension as to the manner of its putting on, can only be described as "quite consummately too." But attention could not remain long fixed on the attire. Mr. Wilde's face, surrounded and framed by a mass of long, untamed, tawny hair, is massive, almost colossal, and at the same time very pleasant in feature and expression, especially so far as the poetic eyes are concerned. But mere description, as was before hinted, is of necessity somewhat powerless.

Mr. Wilde, who speaks with the accent generally credited to the higher classes of London society, and by no means uncommon in the region of Pall Mall, showed no objection whatever to being interviewed, and kindly refrained from making any of those unpleasant remarks about journalists which his experience with them would seem to justify. When asked what opinion he had formed of the probable results of his campaign, he at once said that after all the nonsense written about him had been forgotten, good and lasting results would remain. In the cities where he had been, decorative art societies had been started, and old societies had been brought into more prominence. His immense correspondence was entirely on this subject. "Here," said Mr. Wilde, "is a letter only received this morning, referring to the effect of my visit to Philadelphia last week."[1] The letter was from Charles Leland, the famous "Hans Breitmann,"[2] and a member of "the school," thanking Mr. Wilde for the good he had done in connection with the teaching of art principles to the young. These results are being seen in the in-

1. Wilde lectured on *The Decorative Arts* at Philadelphia's Association Hall on 10 May.

2. Charles Godfrey Leland (1824–1903) was an American humourist and journalist. *Hans Breitmann's Ballads* (1871) was his collection of comic verses written in a mix of German and broken English.

crease of orders given to the art societies. Mr. Wilde mentioned an incident which showed the way in which he was able to help on native art. In Chicago he came across a young American sculptor of really extraordinary power and genius, but unknown.[1] He spoke about him, and told the people that they could not really appreciate art if they neglected the native talent in their own city. Now, that young sculptor has ever so many commissions.

The questioner asked how the British and American compared in their reception of his teachings. Mr. Wilde could hardly give a definite answer. "In America, you see, I have for the first time been face to face with people who have never seen any good art; as to their reception of what I say, while, no doubt, many come to hear me just from curiosity, yet afterward I am continually getting letters from these people saying how they have been pleased with this or that point in my lectures. The great thing is to get them to come, for when they come they always see what I mean. And," said Mr. Wilde, "what one really wants is not to be either blamed or praised, but to be understood."

"You have been all over the United States now, have you not, Mr. Wilde?"

"I have been all over the States except in the South and I suppose, though it is difficult to guess, that I have spoken to some two hundred thousand people. I have found the people very willing and ready to listen and appreciate."

Mr. Wilde has been in California, and is quite enthusiastic over it; "it is Italy without art," was his judgment of the Hoodlum city. Only he objected to its being called the Hoodlum city. He said, "No, it is the city of fine men and beautiful women! San Francisco has the most lovely surroundings of any city except Naples.[2] I lectured there six times, and had the most delightful and appreciative audiences.[3] People's imagination of beauty depends so much on what they are accustomed to see around them. It might be thought otherwise from those who live in beautiful places not speaking about beauty, but they have no need to talk about it. That is our object. We want to see the homes of the people beautiful, and when that is the case people will no longer talk of the beautiful at all. We are forced to do so now because there are so many ugly things in the world. In the ideal state of art there will be no art lecturer."

Mr. Wilde went on to speak of the knowledge of art in the different countries, England and America. "In England, now, we have the great advantage of models of art always with us, in the cathedrals, in the colleges of Oxford and Cambridge, and in many buildings of the finest architecture. In America the great

1. John Talbott Donoghue.

2. After his trip to Greece in the spring of 1877 Wilde sailed to Naples before proceeding to Rome (Page, 9).

3. Wilde lectured four times in San Francisco. Presumably he was also counting his two lectures in nearby Oakland.

want is of absolute models of art. The art which is learned from books is very worthless at best." Speaking of the aims of the movement with which he is identified, Mr. Wilde urged strongly that people should occupy a good deal more of their time with simple things. "It is all very well to devote time to little flower vases; they do for ladies' drawing rooms; but that is not touching the people. It is the people we want to touch, and this can only be done by beginning with simple things. The least things, every household article should be made beautiful, and I had far rather that, instead of designs for flower vases, a good design should be produced for a simple jug and basin, instead of the coarse pottery, inartistic in colour and outline, which is now common."

"What do you think is the present position of the movement in England, Mr. Wilde?"

"Well, you may best understand that from the fact that Mr. Morris has just received from Government the contract for the decoration of St. James's Palace.[1] The movement is one that must be recognized. We have already altered the condition of society in respect to art, and no one will now furnish a house without having regard to art principles."

Mr. Wilde said all this with a simplicity of language and manner, and a hearty sincerity which were quite refreshing after the caricatures which we have sometimes been led to imagine were imitations of the Arch-Aesthete. During the whole conversation "stained-glass" attitudes were conspicuously absent, and languid lackadaisicality was also entirely wanting. Once, indeed, the lithe-limbed poet sank into a position recalling in a faint degree certain creations of Du Maurier's imagination, and few could produce so aesthetic a yawn as once occurred in the intervals of puffing a cigarette. But these were evidently too natural to suggest even the ghost of a smile to the most risible. And when the visitor withdrew, leaving Oscar Wilde to plunge again into the wisdom of Mr. Shorthouse's sudden-famed "John Inglesant,"[2] and thinking as he went that behind the closed door there reclined neither a Postlethwaite, a Lambert Streyke nor a Reginald Bunthorne,[3] and that Messrs. Du Maurier, Burnand and Gilbert had all done him a grave injustice.

1. William Morris and St. James's Palace: see p. 389, note 1.

2. *John Inglesant* is an 1881 historical romance by English novelist Joseph Henry Shorthouse (1834–1903). The eponymous hero was, like Wilde, a Protestant who was tempted to convert to Roman Catholicism.

3. "Professor of Aesthetics" Lambert Streyke is a character in *The Colonel.*

[Arthur J. Graham], "A Chat with Oscar Wilde," *Canadian Illustrated News* (Montreal, QC), 20 May 1882, 306[1]

Mr. Oscar Wilde's lecture announced for tonight, will, unfortunately, leave us insufficient time to notice it in this number.[2] Mr. Wilde is, however, here, and may deserve himself that recognition which must for the present at least be denied his lecture. We have spoken before of Mr. Wilde's antecedents and his objects.[3] It remains to say a few words about his personality. With his appearance, probably most of our readers are acquainted. But what cannot be conveyed in a photograph is the manner of the man himself. Those who expect affectation and silliness of speech must be, to judge from our own experience, grievously disappointed in a man who acts and speaks simply as a gentleman of refined manners and accustomed to society—moreover, as a man to whom "the study of mankind is man." "The man who is bored by others," as Mr. Wilde remarked, "must be a bore himself," and the observation is a good gauge of his estimate of the interviewing, with which during his American trip he has been largely favored.

Our own visit was made not exactly in an interviewing spirit, but several hours spent in his company produced the impression recorded above, of a courteous, clever Englishman, with distinct views of his own, but little spoilt by the flattery which might have turned a wiser man's head, but which he has been shrewd enough to use for what it is worth, and to lay aside its effects in the presence of men of the world.

We talked but little of art, the subject in view of his lecture, perhaps, a little of "shop"—certainly no extravagant ideas obtruded themselves upon a somewhat matter-of-fact conversation. Mr. Wilde expressed his delight with the States, as a country in which young men were so highly esteemed—a very true criticism by the way, and especially noticeable to one who comes direct from the land *par excellence* of old fogeyism, where no man has a right, in the view of otherwise excellent people, to express any opinion at all before thirty.[4]

1. Excerpted in O'Brien, 70. There is no byline but O'Brien identifies the author as Arthur J. Graham, the editor of the *Canadian Illustrated News*. Graham (c. 1852–?) was born in England.

2. Wilde lectured in Montreal on 15 and 20 May 1882. This interview was presumably conducted before the first lecture. A negative review of the lectures appeared in the following week's edition. It ended: "Well, people went to *see* the man, not to listen to him, and thus no one can complain, if they saw much and heard little." ("Decorative Art a la Wilde," *Canadian Illustrated News* (Montreal, QC), 27 May 1882, 322.)

3. "Oscar Wilde," *Canadian Illustrated News* (Montreal, QC), 28 Jan. 1882, 51.

4. Wilde tended to value the perspectives of the young over those of the old. Lord Henry in *The Picture of Dorian Gray*: "It's absurd to talk of the ignorance of youth. The only people whose opinions I listen to now with any respect are people much younger than myself." (CW iii, 157.27–9.) Gwendolyn in *The Importance of Being Earnest*: "The old-fashioned respect for the young is fast dying out." (CW x, 787.89–90.)

About the courtesy of all his audiences Mr. Wilde is enthusiastic. He came to New York to speak and lecture for the first time in his life, and his audiences, with scarcely any exception, have treated him, he says, like an old friend.

But the pleasantest feature of his tour seems to have been his visit to California. The country, the people, the climate, are all, according to him, delightful, and certainly it is a fact not unworthy of record, that in a city like San Francisco, Mr. Wilde should have been enabled to lecture ten times, at short intervals, and always to fair houses.[1] A single lecture may attract many out of pure curiosity, but it says much for the San Franciscans, or for Mr. Wilde, or probably for both, that he should have been able to interest a people to whom Art of any description is somewhat of a novelty, and that they should have been ready to go again and again to hear the great truths and principles of Art, by whomsoever expounded.

Next week we trust to say something of the lecture itself, and the principles involved. For the present we can only wish Mr. Wilde a good audience, and his hearers a good lecture.

"From the Capital," *The Globe* (Toronto, ON), 17 May 1882, 2[2]

Disclosure of Affairs of Upper Canada Bank.

RE-GERRYMANDERING IN THE SENATE.

Mr. Plumb's Prospects of Getting a Portfolio.

OSCAR WILDE ON NEW WORLD ART.

Sir Leonard Tilley's Genealogical Tree in the Civil Service.

PROROGATION OF PARLIAMENT TODAY.

(From Our Own Correspondent.)

OTTAWA, May 16.

OSCAR WILDE.

Oscar Wilde arrived in the city this morning and put up at the Russell House. This evening he delivered a lecture in the Opera House, and afterwards paid a

1. Between 27 March and 8 April Wilde gave ten lectures in California, four of which were in San Francisco.

2. Excerpted in "Oscar Wilde," *Daily Witness* (Montreal, QC), 19 May 1882, 8; and "Oscar Wilde," *The Chicago Daily Tribune* (Chicago, IL), 20 May 1882, 2. Quoted in O'Brien, 78–9.

visit to the Parliament Buildings. Since arriving here he has been fairly besieged by autograph fiends and interviewers, but having become pretty well accustomed to this sort of thing, he treats it all in a businesslike manner. He is easily approached, and apparently cultivates a listless, "aesthetic" sort of air with a view to over-awing the visitor. His most prominent exemplification of the aesthetic consisted in his long flowing hair, drab velvet coat, tie of red silk with flowing ends, and red stockings. Being asked how long he expected to remain in America, he said he contemplated visiting in July next that home of art, Japan. He will leave here tomorrow for Quebec, and will afterwards visit Montreal and Toronto.[1] He thinks Montreal a glorious city, and was quite enthusiastic about it. Being asked his opinion of the frescoing in the French Cathedral he answered rather evasively, and said he did not admire the style. He apparently has not formed a very high idea of Canada from an artistic point of view, and wanted to know what we had been doing here all the time. He was somewhat surprised that the Princess Louise, who was such an admirer of art, had not accomplished greater results.[2] He had found a very nice art gallery in Montreal, and he had been particularly pleased with one painting, which he named. He is evidently not deeply versed in Canadian politics. He had heard that there was a good deal of talk here about free trade and protection, and said the same questions were exciting a good deal of attention in England. He asked who the leaders of the respective political parties were, and who were our best debaters, and felt rather disappointed at hearing that he had appeared rather too late on the scene to see Parliament to advantage.[3] He imagined that the Canadian North-West must be a fine country. He had been much pleased with what he had seen of the scenery about Ottawa, and fancied that it would be a nice place in summer time. Of all parts of the United States, Colorado and California had pleased him most. Being asked what he thought of art across the lines, he said he had not expected much, as America had contributed nothing to European art; but a younger school was coming up which was valued not so much for what it had accomplished as for what it promised. He had been pleased with the large audiences which greeted him in small towns in the United States, and with the attentive manner in which

1. Wilde lectured in Quebec City on 18 May 1882, Montreal on 20 May, and Toronto on 25 and 27 May. He delivered a total of 12 lectures in Quebec and Ontario in the final 16 days of May.

2. Princess Louise, Duchess of Argyll (1848–1939) was the sixth child of Queen Victoria and Prince Albert. Louise produced as well as admired art, and was a painter and sculptor. Her husband, the Duke of Argyll, was appointed Governor General of Canada in 1878, serving until 1884; Louise was viceregal consort. They founded the Royal Canadian Academy of Arts in 1880, and Louise was a patron of the Art Association of Montreal, the Montreal Society of Decorative Arts, and the Ontario Society of Artists. After she was injured in a sleighing accident in February 1880, Princess Louise spent longer periods in England.

3. The final session of the 4th Canadian Parliament ran from 9 February 1882 until 17 May 1882.

his lectures had been listened to. He found the masses on this continent better educated than in England, and attributes the fact to our university systems, which permitted farmers' sons and other classes, which English universities did not reach, receiving a higher education. He also thoroughly approved of the co-education of the sexes. What he most disapproved in connection with America was the ignoring of art by the Churches, and he regarded it as utterly impossible, for this reason, that they should succeed. They required something which would appeal to the emotions and imaginations of the people.

Oscar was introduced to a large number of persons in the speaker's rooms, and afterwards occupied a seat on the floor of the House near the Speaker's chair while the Senate amendments to the Redistribution Bill were being discussed.[1] He was attired as at the lecture, in a suit of black velvet, knickerbocker trousers, black silk stockings, and lace cuffs and tie, and was the subject of a good deal of attention.

✂ *Several paragraphs that are unrelated to Wilde.*

"Jottings from Ottawa," *The Montreal Daily Star* (Montreal, QC), 17 May 1882, 5[2]

Nearing the End—A Graceful Tribute—Niagara Falls—The North-West—Manitoba Better Terms—The Readjustment Bill—Oscar Wilde

[SPECIAL DESPATCH TO THE STAR.]

OTTAWA, May 17.—

✂ *Several paragraphs that are unrelated to Wilde.*

In a short interview which I had with Oscar Wilde, today, the great aesthete said he was going from America to Japan. "I shall go," said he, "by way of San Francisco, about the end of July. Japan is the most artistic country in the world,

1. The speaker was David Lewis Macpherson (1818–1896). The second reading of the Bill (158), "An Act to re-adjust the Representation in the House of Commons, and for other purposes" can be viewed in Hansard, Senate Debates, 4th Parliament, 4th Session, Vol. 1, 712–39. No reference was made to Wilde. However, two weeks earlier Wilde's father had been mentioned in a Senate debate on affairs in Ireland as one of the men who "met together to form the Home Rule party in Ireland, in 1870."

2. H & S, b79. Excerpted in O'Brien, 62–3. Referenced in "Oscar Wilde," *The Chicago Daily Tribune* (Chicago, IL), 20 May 1882, 2. Hofer and Scharnhorst cite "Jottings from Ottawa," *Montreal Daily Star* (Montreal, QC), 16 May 1882, 2; O'Brien cites "Jottings from Ottawa," *Montreal Daily Star* (Montreal, QC), 17 May 1882, 4. Neither citation is correct, and O'Brien and Hofer and Scharnhorst must have intended to cite the article transcribed here.

the home of art. I shall enjoy myself there so much," and he smiled a supremely happy smile in anticipation. "I like Montreal," he said, in answer to a question, and later he remarked quite gushingly, "Oh, indeed, it is a glorious city. It was glorious to stand on the mountain, and, looking down over the city, see that grand, broad river flowing along to the horizon.[1] I found much that was beautiful there."

"Did you find much art there?"

"Well, yes (with a shrug); I was in the Art Gallery. I saw one good picture, one very fine picture."

"Were you in any of the churches?"

"I was in the French Church," he answered, but he volunteered no opinion. Being pressed as to what he thought of it he said he thought its colors were healthy.

"Did you find as fine a class of art in the United States as you expected?"

"Well, I did not expect anything. I make it a point," he added, "never to expect anything."

"And you were not disappointed in this case?"

"Well, no, I don't know that I was. They are progressing rapidly, though. They seem to take a wonderful interest in the beautiful."

The poet then went on making numerous inquiries concerning the politics and political men of Canada. He came down from the subject of the beautiful for a minute and talked of Protection and Free Trade, and made the assertion that the feeling for "fair trade" was growing fast in England. He intended, he said, later on to visit Rideau Hall before he left Ottawa.[2]

✂ *Several paragraphs that are unrelated to Wilde.*

"Oscar Wilde on Decorative Art," *The Daily News* (Kingston, ON), 23 May 1882, 2[3]

A Thin Audience—Eloquent Discourse.

✂ *A report of Wilde's lecture in Kingston, Ontario.*

1. Lecturing in Montreal on 15 May, Wilde was reported to have "shocked not a few of his audience by calling a spade a spade. 'When I was on your beautiful *hill*,' said he, 'I noticed the clearness of your atmosphere so favorable to the development of art.' It was not nice to hear our cherished 'mountain' reduced to a hill." ("Oscar Wilde," *The Montreal Daily Star* (Montreal, QC), 16 May 1882, 2.) Mount Royal, a large hill or small mountain, has an elevation of 233 m / 764 ft.
2. Rideau Hall, or Government house, is the official residence of the governor general.
3. H & S, b81. Quoted in O'Brien, 90–1.

OSCAR WILDE INTERVIEWED

Oscar Wilde was visited at his room in the hotel this morning, and was found smoking a cigarette after having completed a breakfast which was not composed of poppies and lilies. In private conversation he displays an easy, good natured affability, and a rich poetical vein of discourse which is quite charming.

On being asked whether he had been much bored in America by Philistines in the semblance of newspaper men, he replied that he had never been bored in his life, and he thought that none but bores could be bored. He took an interest in everything that he saw or heard, and delighted to talk with all sorts of people upon topics concerning which they possessed any knowledge of which they appreciated. He thought it would be an immeasurable advantage if people would not attempt to carry on general conversation for which few had a gift.

Proceeding, he said he regretted that the wet weather had left him such a small house, although his audience had been appreciative. Wendell Phillips once told him that any man could speak well to a crowd, but it required a mighty effort to thrill empty benches, and he had found this true in his own experience. He could not say that he had been pleased in his American travels, but he did not come to be pleased. The eastern cities were immensely dreary and ugly in winter, but the delicious atmosphere, luxurious flowers, and lovely scenery of California had captivated him greatly. The St. Lawrence and Ottawa rivers struck him as glorious tides, and he meant all he said about their pollution.[1] The public, he thought, should compel manufacturers to consume their own smoke, make use of their sawdust, and discharge their effluvia somewhere else than into the beautiful rivers or the life giving atmosphere. Ruskin had induced Manchester to stop similar pollution. If the worst came to the worst, he would advise the people of any city to choose pure elements in preference to manufactures. On a verse of Keats being suggested as the creed of aestheticism, Mr Wilde said that he did not bother himself about metaphysics, but wished to interest people in the employment of honesty and beautiful ideas in handicrafts. He thought that such a town as Kingston should have a public library and night classes where drawing would be taught. One man in every four who attended would be found to possess considerable artistic talent. On being informed that there was a Mechanics' Institute here, he exhibited much interest and expressed a desire to visit the rooms. He gave some interesting opinions of newspapers, saying, among other things, that gossiping might be reduced to a fine art, as had been done by Madame de Recam-

1. *The Daily News* reported that Wilde had said in his Kingston lecture that "he had recently been in Ottawa, and had seen a noble river choked with sawdust. This he considered an outrage, as no one had a right to pollute the air or the water, which are the common inheritance of all."

ier,[1] and others, and that if newspapers were conducted in the proper way they would be the garner-houses from which future historians would draw their material.

John Hague, "Oscar Wilde," *Toronto Evening News* (Toronto, ON), 25 May 1882, 4[2]

SIR,—Coming up from the Capital yesterday, when seated at breakfast, in a far from aesthetic mood, who should be seated next to me but the renowned apostle of the beautiful, [?Mr.] Oscar Wilde. Trusting to the freemasonry of sympathetic ideas, I introduced myself as the friend of the late M—, one of the most gifted art critics of this generation, and the joint author with him of certain sketches of the Old Masters. We are at once *en rapport*, and I found that I had by this allusion, as the prophet in the wilderness by his rod made the waters to gush out, touched a copious spring of highly cultured intelligence, philosophical reflection, and acute criticism, both humorous and eloquent. Mr. Wilde is a brilliant conversationalist, a happy one in all senses, for he can listen as well as he can talk, and he can talk so that listening to his tongue, even to the garrulous, becomes more pleasant than to listen to their own. Well, although I am not garrulous I can prevent talk dropping into silence, and I listened yesterday morning to the only conversation worthy the name which I have had the privilege to share in since leaving England many years ago, for, unhappily here we cannot find anything to chat over save the virtues of our party and the wickedness of the opposite one, which is not a sufficiently varied theme to monopolize *all* one's lingual social capacity or mental sympathies. To my mind, one of the greatest disadvantages of life in Canada is the blank, the utter blank, of the charm of intellectual gossip, my talk with Mr. Wilde took me out of the dust and smoke and clatter of a noisy monotonous street into the heart of the country, rich in woodland beauty, redolent of floral sweetness, and soothing to the tired brain as a mother's lullaby to her child. We talked of art, of its present aspects here and at home, of art culture, of art schools, and their work and failures and needs. I told Mr. Wilde that years ago I had ventured to lay down as the glaring defect of all Canadian pictures that they showed an entire want of the power of drawing with exactitude

1. Juliette Récamier (1777–1849) was a French socialite, whose salons were popular with the leading literary and political figures of Paris.
2. Reprinted in Keller-Farmer, 85–90. Excerpted in *Bruno's Weekly*, *3*(26), 30 Dec. 1916, 1233; and O'Brien, 94–5. John Hague (1826–1906) was an English financial journalist and fellow of the Royal Statistical Society who had immigrated to Canada in 1871. Although formatted as a letter to the editor, in substance the article is an interview.

any living forms, trees or animals. This he earnestly and almost passionately approved. "Art," said he, "is not looked upon as an exact science, as it should be; there can be no art without truth of form, and no beauty can exist where is falsehood in drawing or colour." He then went on very suggestively, and with a delicacy of allusion to my own expressions which indicated the refinement of high breeding (for Mr. Wilde is a gentleman to the core), to insist that no true appreciation of form, or capacity to express it in any aspect, figure, drawing or architecture, can, unless there is in the draughtsman a keen, clear, pure conception and vivid sense of the charm and value of colour. A position which, though it will be "caviar to the general,"[1] and not acceptable to many artists and architects is, I believe, demonstrable. He heartily sympathised with and pushed to a humourous conclusion my ridicule of the ordinary methods of teaching in so-called Art Schools, their uselessness, their chilling and repressing effect upon the young. We then struck off at a tangent into a discussion as to the relative merits of Thackeray and Dickens, in which Mr. Wilde displayed, for so young a man, a remarkable familiarity with the whole field of fictional literature. He condemned freely the historical novels of Scott, as in the conversations of the characters, stilted and unnatural;[2] he placed Bulwer's historical romances on a lower level still, and, in doing so, used a phrase which is worth quoting. "Romance," said he, "what is it but humanity in its nobler, finer phases." To be truly romantic, therefore, is not to be unnatural, for that is to be false to nature, but it is to take human life into a higher expression and mood. Back again to art, we discussed the prevailing bad work done by artisans, the craze for cheap work and its results in degrading work and workers. His vehement condemnation of the preference given by young men for such occupations as clerks in stores or any similar work, over handicrafts, was to me most refreshing, as sweet, indeed, to hear as the red-hot gospel of a revivalist's thunder is to the religious fanatic.

Here he struck upon a vein of reflection which the so-called "working classes," that is handicraftsmen, will have to work before their social emancipation day dawns, their freedom from a ban which nowadays settles upon them, chiefly as the result of their own want of respect for their occupations. Mr. Wilde, with much fire and with graphic illustrations, touched upon the artistic aspect and claims to art treatment of the ordinary artisan's work. "To be done well," said he, "work must be done truly, and done with truth, it becomes artistic. This element of faithfulness is the only power able to raise labour into honour." The

1. A good thing that is not appreciated by the ignorant. The reference is to *Hamlet* (II, 2), in which the title character commends a play even though it "pleased not the million; 'twas caviar to the general".

2. Sir Walter Scott (1771–1832) was a Scottish novelist, poet, and historian. His novels include *Rob Roy* (1817) and *Ivanhoe* (1819).

thought is, of course, not original, but how few, how very few, see clearly wherein really consists the difference between work worthy of being respected, and which will bring respect to the worker, and work which is not respect, work of which the doer is made to feel that the very doing of it is in a sense a degradation. In a word I found Mr. Oscar Wilde a man of high useful capacity, wide reading and observation, clear headed, practical in his views as to the relation of worthy ends to fitting means to attain them, with deep, earnest sympathies with the socially depressed, and an almost passionate longing for the spread of refined tastes and habits among the humbler classes, an enthusiast doubtless, but enthusiasm has done every good work yet done in this world, and one in spite of some eccentricities, for all enthusiasts have been eccentric, is doing and will yet do, I believe and hope, a thoroughly good work in that sphere to which he deems himself called, the sphere of art reformer and teacher.

JOHN HAGUE

"Oscar Wilde," *The Globe* (Toronto, ON), 25 May 1882, 3[1]

Arrival of the Apostle of Aestheticism in Toronto.

WHAT HE THINKS OF LACROSSE.

His Opinion of Toronto and Toronto Ladies.

Mr. Oscar Wilde arrived in the city yesterday morning on the Grand Trunk express from the East. A deputation of gentlemen belonging to the city was at the station to receive him and escort him to the Queen's Hotel. By previous engagement he attended the lacrosse match between the Torontos and St. Regis Indians in the afternoon. He arrived on the grounds a few minutes before the game commenced, and when the grand stand and other available seats were densely packed.[2] As he passed through the gate someone shouted "Here's Oscar Wilde." The intelligence soon passed along the rows of seated spectators, and all eyes were at once strained to catch a glimpse of him. The juveniles were inclined to be boisterous at first, but they soon ceased their shouting, as Mr. Wilde appeared not even to notice their demonstrations. He was escorted to the space on the grand stand reserved for the Lieut.-Governor, where he was introduced to Miss

1. H & S, b82. Reprinted in H & S, 154–5. Excerpted in *Morning Chronicle* (Montreal, QC), 1 June 1882, 1; and O'Brien, 98–9. Quoted in OWDA, 352; and Sturgis, 254/243.
2. The first game commenced at 15:40 ("Lacrosse", *The Globe* (Toronto, ON), 25 May 1882, 8).

Robinson and a lady friend.[1] Without noticing the sensation his arrival had created he reclined his head gracefully on his hand, assuming the aesthetic attitude, and gazed earnestly into the field where the teams were preparing for the fight. He was dressed in a grey tweed pair of trousers and cobweb-coloured velveteen coat and vest;[2] his necktie was a dark green in colour, tied loosely around his neck, and covering his shirt front. He wore a handkerchief to match. He had a flowing coat, with a deep velvet collar, and secured to his form by a tasselated cord, which passed across his chest. He wore a black felt hat of unusual proportions. The earnest or intense expression of his almost feminine face, his long flowing hair, and his tall, handsome figure, and graceful movements gave him a striking appearance, producing immediately a favourable impression. When the game was started he evinced the most lively interest, and as it progressed his enthusiasm seemed to keep pace with the players, for he laughed heartily when any of them went unceremoniously to "grass," or clapped his hands when a good piece of play was done. He left the field shortly before the match was completed.[3] On being asked by a GLOBE representative how he enjoyed the match, Mr. Wilde said, "Oh, I was delighted with it. It is a charming game. That was the first opportunity I ever had of witnessing your national game, and I enjoyed it so much—but can you tell me who that tall, finely built man, that played defence for the Torontos, is?" broke off Mr. Wilde.

"That's Ross Mackenzie, one of the best lacrosse players in Canada."[4]

"I admired his playing so very much," said Mr. Wilde, "he appeared so thoroughly at home in the game. Lacrosse is so far ahead of cricket for physical development, and then everyone seems to get an equal share of the play, or hard work as I should term it. But don't you think," Mr. Wilde asked, "that the Indians, or at least the Indian umpire, should have been dressed in a manner to impress one with the position he occupied? I think he should have been dressed say in war costume, with his face painted, armed with a tomahawk, and wearing a

1. John Beverley Robinson (1821–1896) served as the fifth Lieutenant Governor of Ontario between 1880 and 1887. His daughter, Augusta Louise Robinson (1859–1935), was a singer and writer.

2. A reference to *Patience*. See p. 66, note 2.

3. The match consisted of five games, with each game ending after a goal had been scored. The Indians won the first game in seven minutes and the second in twenty-seven. The Torontos won the third game in seven minutes, the fourth in one, and the fifth in seven. Wilde left early, most likely after the second game (see "Oscar Wilde," *The Toronto Daily Mail* (Toronto, ON), 25 May 1882, 2, p. 407).

4. In the second game the Indians were on the verge of scoring, "but McKenzie was on hand and saved the goals, to the intense relief of the spectators."

head-dress of feathers.[1] I was greatly amused at the gesticulations of the Indians, and I wondered what language they were speaking."[2]

After asking some questions about the Indians and the origin of the game, Mr. Wilde said he was much pleased with the appearance and dress of many persons he had seen on the ground; "and," he continued, "I could not help admiring the dress of a little girl who sat in front of me. It was charming—such a beautiful blending of colour, that corresponded so nicely with her rosy cheeks."

"What is your opinion of Toronto and Toronto ladies, Mr. Wilde?"

"I have seen so little of the former that I have scarcely formed an opinion, but I judge from the appearance of your principal business street that it is a bright little town, and I have no doubt it is a commercial centre. But I cannot help wondering why your citizens build their houses with that horrid white brick when red brick is the same price. I think white brick such a shallow colour—in fact it spoils the effect of the architecture. I see the same fault here that I noticed in all Canadian cities.[3] The colour of the stone and other building material completely spoils the effect of the good architecture, which I could not help admiring in Canadian cities. As to the ladies, I think some of them are very nice and dress exceedingly well, but I will have a better opportunity of judging hereafter. I am gratified sometimes to see the monotony of an audience relieved by the presence of at least one well-dressed lady."

"Oscar Wilde," *The Toronto World* (Toronto, ON), 25 May 1882, 1[4]

Arrival in Town—Attends the Lacrosse Match—Besieged With Invitations.

Oscar Wilde arrived yesterday forenoon on the G. T. R. from the east.[5] He was dressed in the slate-colored suit of corded goods, blue silk tie with silk handkerchief to match. He wore an immense slouched hat. There were lots of people down to meet him, among them Mr. Patrick Boyle, the genial editor of the Irish Canadian.[6] Rushing up to his aesthetic countryman Mr. Boyle said: "Mr. Wilde I welcome you to Toronto on behalf of our Irish citizens." Mr. Wilde

1. The St. Regis Indians wore blue trunks with white shirts and red stockings.

2. From the report of the match: "The Indian team with proper discipline might be said to be invincible, but regardless of their captain's commands they rushed hither and thither, shouting and gesticulating wildly."

3. By this time Wilde had visited Montreal, Ottawa, Quebec City, Kingston, and Belleville.

4. Referenced in O'Brien, 71, 88–9.

5. Grand Trunk Railway.

6. Patrick Boyle (1832–1901) was an Irish printer and publisher. His family immigrated to Canada in 1844 and settled in Toronto. He launched the *Irish Canadian* in 1863.

thanked Mr. Boyle, and expressed a desire to see the Irish Canadian which contained his own portrait and that of his illustrious mother. Oscar put up at the Queen's, took a drive round the city, visited the lacrosse match, dined at the Toronto club, received a crowd of invitations, allowed himself to be interviewed, and generally put in a busy day.

AT THE LACROSSE GROUNDS

he was received with cheers and viewed the match in the company of the lieutenant governor's family. Speaking to a World reporter he said he enjoyed the lacrosse exhibition and considered it an interesting and exciting game. He thought, however the picturesqueness of the spectacle would be enhanced if the Indians wore more of their natural dress. Oscar admired the dress of the Toronto ladies, and was especially struck on the array of a little girl in print trimmed with embroidery.[1] Looking around Toronto, he said he was struck with its wide, regular streets. "But you should not build with white brick; it is not in good taste." But if your bricks won't burn any color but white what can you do? He did not like Montreal with its narrow streets—he was half a day in finding a book store. Quebec, he considered, looked like a small English town. The ladies of the ancient capital came in for high praise for their taste in dress.[2] Oscar will look around the city further today, and lecture in his knee breeches at the Grand tonight, where a big house is sure to greet him. Speaking of newspapers he said The World was the most artistic in its typographical arrangement of any he had yet seen in Canada.[3]

"Oscar Wilde," *The Toronto Daily Mail* (Toronto, ON), 25 May 1882, 2[4]

The "Apostle of Aestheticism" Arrives in Toronto.

AND IS FORTHWITH INTERVIEWED.

Mr. Wilde was enjoying with a friend what he termed an "afternoon tea," when he received a representative of THE MAIL. The reporter excused himself for

1. Wilde may well have commented on the material from which the girl's dress was made, although it also seems possible that the typesetter mistook "front" for "print".
2. Quebec City was the capital of the Province of Canada between 1852 and 1856, and again between 1859 and 1866.
3. The typography of *The Toronto World* was indistinguishable from that of any other North American newspaper of the period. The masthead was printed in a standard serif typeface with no decoration.
4. Quoted in O'Brien, 88, 99–100.

appearing at so inopportune a time, but Mr. Wilde hastened to assure him that he was quite at leisure.

"Afternoon teas are a custom with me," he said, "and the tea in Canada is very fine."

The reporter hoped that he had found other very fine things in Canada beside the tea.

"Oh, yes," was the reply, with a smile, "the cigarettes."

As both the articles mentioned were imported, the interviewer did not consider that any great compliment had been paid to Canada, and so he remarked.

"Well," continued Mr. Wilde, "your rivers are very beautiful, and your cities are so finely situated. Quebec especially has a noble situation, and I was sorry to see that there was so little life or spirit in it."

The reporter acknowledged that the Canadian rivers had all that was necessary in length, breadth, and depth, and referring to the [*illeg. wd.*] statement, said he did not think Toronto had any particular reason to boast of its site.

"The country is certainly rather flatter than what I have hitherto seen," admitted the young poet, "but with

THIS BEAUTIFUL LAKE

in front the city is not void of peculiar advantages."

After a few more words about the size and beauties of Lake Ontario, Mr. Wilde [?referred] to his disappointment in not yet having the opportunity of passing through the Thousand Islands, a trip he was anxious to make.[1] He next alluded to the lacrosse match in the afternoon, of which he had been a spectator. He thought it was [?full] of graceful movements, and hard knocks. He was pleased to learn that the Torontos had won the match, because not having waited for the conclusion of the match, he thought the Indians were going to win.

"How did you drift into the movement of which you are the leader?" asked the reporter.

"No man can drift into a movement," corrected Mr. Wilde. "He makes the movement. A man cannot drift into anything unless it [?might] be the Niagara. I will tell you how the movement originated."

He then went on to state that Oxford was the first really beautiful city he had ever visited, and he was as much impressed with the value of beauty to a city as to anything else. Ideas formed in connection with the subject led to the organization of a society of young men in the interests of Art.

1. The Thousand Islands are an archipelago of 1,894 islands in the Saint Lawrence River, where it emerges from the northeast corner of Lake Ontario. Wilde may have heard of the Thousand Islands while visiting Kingston, a city on the mouth of the Saint Lawrence River. He lectured there on 22 May.

that the ancient nations of Greece and [*illeg. wd.*] still lived.[1] Venice was still queen of the sea although there was no longer a galley in her port. But the works of the great painters [*illeg. wd.*] her galleries. Mr. Wilde then spoke of his plans for the immediate future. He intended after concluding his lecture season in this country, to sail from San Francisco for Japan, as he desired to study Japanese art, and [?consequently] the date of his return to England is not yet fixed. It is unnecessary to describe Mr. Wilde's personal appearance, as it is now well known to all readers of the daily press. It will suffice to say that in the generally accepted sense of the word he is about as unaesthetic looking a man as it is possible for a "six-footer" of his proportions to be. He is only twenty six years of age.

"Aestheticism's Apostle," *Toronto Evening News* (Toronto, ON), 25 May 1882, 4[2]

What Oscar is Doing—His Visits about the City and His Opinion of the Ladies.

Mr. Wilde kept pretty closely in his room at the Queen's Hotel today. He takes his meals in his room. Shortly after noon, on the invitation of the Society of Artists, the apostle visited the exhibition of paintings in the Society's rooms on King street.[3] The rooms were seldom so densely crowded since were opened [*sic*] as they were at the moment the aesthete stepped into the room. He is certainly a striking figure. But the fact that he wore a pair of light inexpressibles instead of the knee breeches, with which his name is so much associated, seemed to prove rather a disappointment. His hair is abundantly long; his manner is dignified; his voice is soft, and his speech that of the English aristocrat. He wore a garment over all which may be described as a toga, slung across his shoulders with a cord in the manner of the cloak of a French marshal. On arriving, he was introduced by his agent to Mr. Martin and the other artists who were present.[4]

1. The illegible word may be "Rome", although it is too indistinct in the copy text for this to be stated with any confidence.

2. H & S, b85. Reprinted in *Bruno's Weekly*, *3*(25), 16 Dec. 1916, 1221; and Mikhail, 86–7. For other accounts of Wilde's visit to the exhibition described in this article, see "Oscar at the Art Gallery," *Toronto Evening Telegram* (Toronto, ON), 25 May 1882, 4, p. 715; and "Oscar Wilde," *The Globe* (Toronto, ON), 26 May 1882, 6, p. 716.

3. The Ontario Society of Artists was founded in 1872. Wilde visited the 10th annual exhibition at the Society's Gallery at 14 King Street. There were 262 exhibits: mostly paintings in oil and water, and some sculpture and architectural design.

4. Thomas Mower Martin (1838–1934) was a London-born Canadian landscape painter and a founder of the Ontario Society of Artists. The 1882 exhibition included fifteen of his oil paintings

He has certainly a fine face of effeminate cast. His smile is sweetness and light itself. After the introductions, he addressed himself to inspecting the pictures. He was quite free in his criticisms, singling out both beauties and defects. Mr. Martin who acted as *cicerone* had to stand by and hear praise lavished on more than one of his own pictures. But Mr. H. R. Watson's paintings took Mr. Wilde's fancy most.[1] He expressed great surprise when he learned the artist's age and that he had never been to Paris. "He has the exact manner of the modern French artists."

Mr. Wilde afterwards went to the University in company with professor Pike, who is a college mate.[2] In conversation with the reporter, Oscar said that he approved of the outward designs of the Canadian architects, but in most instances the interior colouring was bad. In reply to a question as to whether he did not think the Toronto ladies the handsomest in the world, he said that the ladies of every town he had been in were the handsomest in the world. It may be mentioned incidentally that the sale of reserved seats warrants the belief that there will not be standing room at the Grand tonight.

"Oscar Wilde Again," *Rochester Democrat and Chronicle* (Rochester, NY), 1 June 1882, 4

An Interview with the Aesthete on a Car Platform.

Last night as the second Atlantic express rolled into the station in this city a representative of this journal espied the gentleman aesthete, Oscar Wilde, upon the platform of a palace coach. A bombardment of questions elicited the following facts in regard to his western tour:

"I have," said Mr. Wilde, "been warmly entertained at every place in which I have lectured, and all in all my trip through the western states of your country

---

and four of his watercolours (example titles: *A Seneca Chief*; *York Redoubt, Halifax Harbour, N. S.*; *Pair of Ducks*; and *Head of a Lion*).

1. Homer Ransford Watson (1855–1936) was a Canadian landscape painter. His seven oil paintings at the 1882 exhibition included *In the Gathering Gloom*, *A Cold Summer's Day*, and *Flitting Shadows*. Wilde's eye was caught by the latter picture and he exclaimed "the Canadian Constable! Where is the artist? I must know that man!" That evening Wilde praised Watson to his Toronto audience (O'Brien, 103). Neither *Flitting Shadows* nor any description of it has survived, although it must have been a major work as it was priced in the 1882 catalogue at $200. Wilde commissioned a landscape by Watson and showed it to William Hurlbert, editor of the *World*, in New York; Hurlbert at once commissioned a similar picture ([Arthur J. Graham], "The Week," *Canadian Illustrated News* (Montreal, QC), 2 Dec. 1882, 354; Floss, B. (2018). *Homer Watson: Life & Work*, 10; O'Brien, 102–4). When Watson visited London in 1888 Wilde invited him to Tite Street and advised him on where he could exhibit his pictures (CL, 340–2, 344).

2. William Herbert Pike was a professor of chemistry at Toronto who had graduated from Oxford in 1876.

has been a success and a pleasure to myself. I am now on my way to Boston, where I lecture on Friday night. From there I go to New Orleans, and thence again to California, where I sail for Japan. There I intend to study Japanese art. My western trip has given me the first idea I ever had of the greatness of the United States. California I love. I regard it as a perfect *facsimile* of Italy, though, of course, it hasn't the art of the latter. The Rocky Mountains and the snow-capped peaks of Colorado are among the most beautiful pieces of scenic grandeur I have beheld. They are most beautiful.

"The rivers of Canada are the finest of your country, and I consider the situation of Quebec finer than any city of America. My visit to Toronto was very pleasant. I delivered two lectures in that city, and enjoyed myself immensely."

During the interview the poet-scholar asked good-naturedly after the students of the university. He said he never allowed students' nonsense to trouble him, and after lighting a dainty cigarette, added: "Throughout my country and yours, until I was insulted in Rochester, I was always treated as a gentleman, but," smilingly he added, "I presume when I deliver my next lecture in your city, I will be treated as a gentleman, and not as the butt of a powerless joke."[1]

"Oh, then you contemplate visiting us again?" asked the interviewer.

"Yes, I shall return from Japan to America, and on my way through to San Francisco I am thinking of delivering lectures upon 'Japanese Art, and the Artistic Side of Japanese Life,' I shall then hope to visit you again.[2]

"In Japan," he said, "even the simplest utensil of the household is made beautiful," and he wished it might be so all over the world. After the reporter's questions, and the poet's answers as well, were well nigh run out, and there was danger of a disagreeable lull in the conversation, Mr. Wilde kindly interested himself in Rochester journalism and asked how many dailies the city afforded. When told that we gloried in eight he was indeed surprised and asked after a copy of one. He was supplied, and soon the locomotive gave its double toot and the gentleman was whirled on towards Boston, the city of his delight.

"Oscar Wilde," *The Boston Herald* (Boston, MA), 2 June 1882, Supp. 1

The Poet Revisits Boston After His Western Tour.

Art in Canada, and Some Young American Artists.

1. Wilde never lectured in Rochester again.
2. Presumably Wilde said, or intended to say, "on my way through *from* San Francisco".

Impressions of the West and the Western People.

Oscar Wilde arrived at the Vendome from Canada yesterday morning. When a HERALD representative called upon him later on in the forenoon Mr. Wilde was costumed in a pearl-gray velvet jacket, a flowing green tie, Canada-gray trousers, patent leather pumps and scarlet hose. He was both picturesque and charming. Mr. Wilde had just returned from a lecture tour in Canada, and it was but natural that the conversation should turn upon the Dominion and its people. "Canada," said the poet, "is distinctively a land of noble rivers. Away from the rivers the scenery is pastoral. Its cities are nobly situated. Quebec reminds me of Athens, with its high rock and purple hills. Ottawa, the capital city, is beautifully situated over a great rushing, yellow river. Montreal is on a sheet of water, and water and ships are always graceful. I never saw an ugly ship. I was particularly struck in Canada, as compared with the States, with the want of any real rush of life. The cities are wonderfully quiet. The streets of Quebec reminded me of a little village in Brittany."

"How did you like the Parliament buildings at Ottawa?"

"In proportion and in design they were extremely beautiful, and most delicately proportioned. Where they fail, and where all the public buildings in Canada fail, is in monotony of color. The only stone they have is a red granite. Now, a building should please one by its color, as do the old buildings at Venice, where lines of colored stone are used decoratively. The University of Toronto is one of the most beautiful buildings in Canada."

"Has Canada any distinctively national art?"

"I do not think that a country can have

A NATIONAL ART

until it feels two things—perfect independence and absolute unity. Canada, up to this time, has not yet realized itself. To begin with, there are two nations, the French and the English, in many cases absolutely distinct. Then, they have not developed the west of Canada, and, consequently, there has not come to them as there has to you the rush of fresh life. There has not been experienced that backward wave of newer, fresher life which you have had in America."

"But Canada must have individual artists of merit?'

"Oh, yes. In Toronto I found a young landscape painter, Mr. Watson, a most remarkable man. He has never been to Europe, but he has wonderful mastery over tone in color. His work in grays is exquisite. They have also a young sculptor, Mr. Dunbar, who has done one or two beautiful things.[1] At Ottawa they have a

1. Frederick A. T. Dunbar (c. 1849 – after 1919) was a Canadian sculptor who attended the Art School of Toronto and studied in Florence. He exhibited six works in the 10th annual exhibition

very good school of art—I call it a good school because they have the absolute essential of a school, which is a life class. Unless a school has that, it will never bring out anything good in a pupil. As long as the pupils draw from casts, there will be the coldness of death in their work. If the Princess Louise had stayed in Canada, she would have had a very remarkable influence on Canadian art; but her stay was too short.[1] But I must say that there is in Canada a great deal of growing feeling in art. I had there most interesting and intellectual audiences, in no city more than in Toronto, where I lectured twice."

Mr. Wilde then passed on to to pay a charming compliment to Mr. Howells. He said: "There is one perfect guide book to Canada. I know of nothing which can serve so well for Quebec as

MR. HOWELLS' 'CHANCE ACQUAINTANCE.'

The whole account of Quebec and Canada is most exquisite.[2] I thought on reading Mr. Howells' book how wrong it is to leave the writing of guide books to commonplace people; most guide books are dreadful."

"You have been to California since you last visited Boston?"

"Yes, I enjoyed myself greatly there. I think the future of America will lie in great measure with the West. Not merely is the country most noble, California being an Italy without its art, but the physique of the men and women is particularly splendid in California and in Colorado. They are the most courteous people. I lectured at a city which is supposed to be the roughest city in the United States, and that is Leadville, on the top of the Rocky Mountains. My audience was almost entirely composed of miners. I lectured to them on the workers in metal. I told them, as simply as I could, of all the wonderful things men had made out of gold and silver, brass and copper, and the like, and nothing could have been more delightful than their courtesy or more wonderful than their interest. They came around after my lecture and asked me to sup with them in one of their great silver mines, the mine called the Matchless mine. I spent my whole night in the silver mine with them, and I rank it as one of the golden memories of my life.[3] No one could have had more delightful companions. I saw that most of these miners

of the Ontario Society of Artists. Four were marble busts, or models for marble busts, of local politicians and clergy; the other two were bronze medallions (a head of a lady and a head of a boy). Aside from a pair of bronze medallions by his younger brother Ulric, these were the only sculptural works in the exhibition. None were for sale. Wilde praised Dunbar to his Toronto audience and afterwards sat for a bust that was completed by 30 May and immediately exhibited. It has since been lost (O'Brien, 103, 110). Dunbar later settled in Wilmington, Delaware.

1. Princess Louise, Duchess of Argyll: see p. 397, note 2.

2. Howells's *A Chance Acquaintance* (1873) is a novel. It is about the romance that springs up between a poor Western girl and a rich Bostonian man while they are travelling on the St. Lawrence River. It includes many descriptions of the scenery and places in Quebec.

3. Wilde's visit to the Matchless Mine: see p. 342, note 1.

were strong, simple, handsome fellows. In the whole West I had only one stupid audience, and that was at Salt Lake City, and I was not sorry that they were so, because so much depends upon our admiration of physical beauty in others; they had

THE MOST IGNOBLE PHYSIQUE.

They come, you know, from the ugliest peoples in Europe—the Welsh and the Swedes.[1] The president of the Mormons, Mr. Taylor, was very charming; a man of a great deal of refinement. He came to my lecture, and occupied a stage box with his five wives. But the faces of my audience were heavy, dull and common."

"You visited Denver?"

"Yes; Denver is a remarkable city. I went through Kansas to Missouri, where I had an opportunity of seeing a certain value placed on art. I was in the city of St. Joe when the effects of that picturesque brigand, Jesse James, were being sold at auction. A dustpan was knocked down to a millionaire, and the chromo-lithograph that he was in the act of nailing up when he was shot commanded a price which, in London or in Paris, only an authentic Titian could command."[2]

"And did you go to Chicago?"

"Yes; Chicago interested me very much because I found there a young sculptor who has an artistic power and a sense of beauty which are unequalled by any young sculptor of his age in France or England. His name is Mr. Donoghue. When I arrived at Chicago I found waiting for me at the hotel a package containing a little bas relief in clay of a seated girl, with a verse from my own poems graven on the side and a letter from the artist asking me to accept it. The delicacy of the work was so great, and the whole feeling for beauty so rare, that early next morning I went to find the artist, and, in a little garret in the top of one of the great business blocks of Chicago, I found a young man working away modelling—the artist of this bas relief. He had in his studio a little statuette of a boy dancing, which has

MORE OF THE REAL GREEK FEELING

in it than any work I have seen by any young man in Europe. I was so filled with wonder at finding in a great, new, commercial city, this young sculptor whose

1. In 1880 the foreign-born population of Utah stood at 43,994 persons, of whom 2,390 were born in Wales and 3,750 in Sweden. Other sizeable immigrant populations hailed from England (19,654), Scotland (3,201), Ireland (1,321), Norway (1,214), and Switzerland (1,040). Wilde had previously praised the beauty of the Swedish soprano Christina Nilsson (e.g. "Oscar Wilde," *The Chicago Daily Tribune* (Chicago, IL), 14 Feb. 1882, 7, p. 712).

2. Jesse James (1847–1882) was assassinated by Robert Ford in St. Joseph, Missouri, on 3 April. Wilde had previously described the auction in letters to Norman Forbes-Robertson and Helena Sickert (CL, 164, 166)

sense of beauty was so exquisite, as if he were the last of a long line of Italian artists, that I spoke about him in my lecture, and to everybody whom I met in Chicago society, and since that, they are, I am glad to say, taking much more notice of him, giving him commissions which he wanted very badly. On my return from California, he came to dine with me and brought with him a large bronze bas relief of two children which he had done for one of the rich Chicago merchants. Of his splendid future I feel quite assured. At Cincinnati I found in the art school a young designer with a real mastery over design, about whom I was able to speak in my lecture also.[1] At San Francisco there is a whole colony of excellent painters, among them a pupil of Mr. F. Duveneck. Indeed, there was hardly a city of any size that I visited in which there was not at least one young man working finely in art."

"How does provincial art in England compare with provincial art in the United States?"

"In England, you know, there is no such thing as England; there is London. We concentrate into one city all that is intellectual in men and all that is beautiful in women, and we have changed England into this great city. In America you have spread your artistic power over a whole continent: so, though it fails enormously in concentration, it gains in width."

Here the conversation turned upon the suppression of

WALT WHITMAN'S "LEAVES OF GRASS"

by the legal authorities of the state.[2] Mr. Wilde, a warm friend of the good, gray poet, chivalrously defended the persecuted bard. "I heard of that," he said, "through the Canadian papers. I think it will be a lasting stain on America if this thing continues. The man Walt Whitman is one of the noblest and purest men I ever met. I know no man in America who touched me more through the dignity and self-sacrifice of his life and through the simplicity and wisdom of his mind. I cannot believe that anyone who reads the prose preface of his 'Leaves of Grass' (Mr. Wilde must have had in mind an earlier edition than the one suppressed in Massachusetts, which had no preface, although earlier editions did have) can fail to reverence and to honor him. For creed of life there is nothing more noble. Besides, it should be remembered that the man is to be read as a whole. You must isolate no line from his context. No great book or no great poem could stand such

1. H. J. Breuer. See p. 195, note 1.

2. The seventh edition of *Leaves of Grass* was published in October 1881 by James R. Osgood and Company of Boston. Oliver Stevens, District Attorney of Suffolk County, Massachusetts, threatened to prosecute Osgood for selling obscene literature. Whitman was willing to make minor deletions but Stevens demanded that *A Woman Waits for Me* and *Ode to a Common Prostitute* be omitted in their entirety. Whitman refused, Osgood withdrew the book, and Whitman arranged for publication elsewhere (https://whitmanarchive.org).

a method of criticism. One must realize him as a whole and one must really give up the modern habit of trying to measure giants with a foot rule. The public don't see in general how that no artist neither desires praise nor will accept blame [*sic*]. He merely wishes one thing, and that is merely to be understood. If one understands Walt Whitman one will reverence him. If one does not understand him one should say nothing about him. But in no case should one dare to praise or blame him. In 50 years Walt Whitman will have taken his place as

ONE OF THE GREATEST WRITERS

that America has ever produced. In a letter which I had lately from Mr. Swinburne, he said, with reference to Walt Whitman, and I think it was a very just criticism: 'Whenever he writes on the noblest subjects he writes nobly.'"[1]

"Some of Whitman's finest and most modern lines have been inspired by machinery, his description of a locomotive in action, for instance—"[2]

"True. I have never seen any machinery that has not been graceful. The most beautiful machinery I ever saw was at Chicago. I never was so struck by the contrast between the ugliness of bad art and the beauty and utility of strength till I visited the water works at Chicago. They have built an imitation Gothic fortress, stuck over with ridiculous pepper boxes that they call turrets, the most foolish building that I ever saw, a mere architectural monstrosity—one of the many unpunished crimes of that great city. But inside was this noble and wonderful machinery—the stately orbit of the circling wheels, the rhythmic rise and fall of the long rods of polished steel, something to me as beautiful as anything undecorated I ever saw. The line of strength must be the line of beauty.[3] A man hauling a rope, hauls it straight if he does it gracefully; if he does it clumsily, he is hauling it crooked. There was nothing particularly graceful about the politicians at Ottawa, but the raftmen who were bringing wood down the river were some of them as noble as if they had stepped off a frieze on the Parthenon. There was a miner at

1. Wilde wrote to Swinburne of his first meeting with Whitman, passing on Whitman's compliments. Swinburne replied on 2 February, asking Wilde to convey to Whitman his "admiration of his noblest work—such parts, above all, of his writings, as treat of the noblest subjects, material and spiritual, with which poetry can deal." Wilde transcribed the letter and forwarded it to Whitman on 1 March (CL, 144–5).

2. *To a Locomotive in Winter*, first published in the *New York Tribune* (New York, NY), 19 Feb. 1876, 4, and included in the 1881 edition of *Leaves of Grass*.

3. *Personal Impressions of America*: "I have always wished to believe that the line of strength and the line of beauty are one. That wish was realised when I contemplated American machinery. It was not until I had seen the water-works at Chicago that I realised the wonders of machinery; the rise and fall of the steel rods, the symmetrical motion of the great wheels is the most beautifully rhythmic thing I have ever seen." (Dibb, 235.)

Leadville who was driving a new gallery, and at any moment this man could have become marble or bronze, and have been noble for eternity."[1]

After his lecture here this afternoon Mr. Wilde goes to New York, and thence to the South for a lecture tour, to extend through June. He is desirous of visiting New Orleans, where a deceased uncle formerly lived.[2] He anticipates much pleasure from meeting the warm-hearted southrons, and, in reply to the suggestion that, on leaving the United States, he would go home to old England, he said, with a laugh: "Oh, no; I shall first visit Japan, the most artistic country in the world."

[Lee Meriwether], "The Town Tattler," *The Free Trader and Journal of Progress* (Memphis, TN), 17 June 1882, 7–8[3]

When Oscar Wilde first landed in America he was one of the best advertised men on the continent. The New York *Herald* devoted several columns to the advertising of this new Messiah. The *Sun* and *World* took up the strain, and in the due course of the mails all papers followed. This is the secret of his wonderful

1. Wilde wrote to Helena Sickert of "the miners all at work, looking so picturesque in the dim light as they swung the hammers and cleft the stone, beautiful motives for etching everywhere" (CL, 166).

2. John Kingsbury Elgee.

3. Quoted in Friedman, 222–3, the source for which is Strode, H. (1964). *Jefferson Davis, Tragic Hero: The Last Twenty-Five Years, 1864–1889* (459). Strode dates the article correctly but states that it appeared in *Meriwether's Weekly* (the successor title to *The Free Trader and Journal of Progress*). Strode also states that "[m]aterial about Wilde's visit was given the author by Lee Meriwether" (1862–1966), whom he identifies as the interviewer. The material given by Meriwether to Strode evidently did not include a copy of the interview itself, as the accounts given in *The Free Trader* and *Tragic Hero* differ. Meriwether did not mention in his original account, but told Strode, that on the table in Wilde's room "were the two volumes of Jefferson Davis's *Rise and Fall*," and he was "amazed that the long-haired Britisher should have purchased such an expensive book or was even interested in the subject". Meriwether also quoted Wilde as saying that "Jefferson Davis is the man I would like most to see in the United States," and that he (Wilde) thought it remarkable that it took "Northern armies numbering three million soldiers four years to whip him". Upon being told where Davis lived (four hundred miles from Memphis), Wilde apparently said: "That's a long way to go to meet anyone, but not too far to go to see such a man as Jefferson Davis". Although Wilde's generally positive opinions of the Confederate President were recorded by other interviewers, it seems likely that Meriwether exaggerated them. The copy of *The Free Trader* in the Special Collections of The University of Memphis appears to be Meriwether's own: it includes the marginal note "My interview with → Oscar Wilde, June 17–1882". Some of the articles are marked by hand with the initials 'L', 'A', or 'EAM' to designate their authorship: 'L' is Lee Meriwether, 'A' is his brother Avery (c. 1858–?) with whom he "conducted" the paper, and 'EAM' is presumably their mother, Elizabeth Avery Meriwether (c. 1824–1916). The interview is marked 'L'.

monetary success as a lecturer. Not that he has no merit. Wilde is a shrewd man. Behind that simpering smile and affected manner of his, is concealed a profound knowledge of human nature.

Oscar Wilde's mannerisms on the stage are exaggerated for a purpose. He claims to be "so young," and proves that he is by his lack of training in lecturing. His delivery is wretched. He makes no pauses, but rushes on to the end of his discourse without a period, or even so much as a comma thrown between his sentences, to relieve the monotonous liquid flow of syllables. His gestures are limited to a wave of one hand. He fails to emphasize any word, and does not hesitate to elaborate an extensive parenthetical clause, thus breaking the thread of his discourse, and straining the attention of his hearers. The present reputation of Mr. Wilde, as a lecturer is, without doubt, ephemeral. But there is some body to the man's thoughts, and in time we trust he will gain a permanent reputation, akin to his master, Ruskin. But this will require hard work. He should put himself under an elocutionist, should strive to conquer his awkwardness on the stage, and drop that provincialism of speech which leads him to say "vah-ses" for vases, and to drawl out all his a's.

However much I was disappointed with Mr. Wilde, as a lecturer, as a conversationalist, I was delighted. In an interview at Gaston's hotel, I found him, just after his eleven o'clock breakfast, smoking long English cigarettes, such as Labouchère, of the London *Truth*, was so fond of. His room was in disorder. Photographs scattered all over the floor, flowers laying on the table, a lot of uncut French books and novels here and there, one laying open on the bed, and another at his feet, on the floor. Mr. Wilde was dressed in a very becoming gray velvet jacket, and a pair of fashionably-cut, light gray pants (not knee breeches), low-quartered shoes, very much pointed, and red-silk hose. He wore a large light-blue silk cravat, its folds drooping over his chest, hiding his shirt. He smoked cigarettes constantly—a half a dozen in the course of the interview.

"What feature of the South impressed you most favorably, Mr. Wilde?"

"Aw—I—aw—think the trees and the Negroes are the most striking points of the South. The forests are so grand and so beautiful. Nature seems to be unlimited here. In England the face of our land is molded into a series of beautiful gardens, which unfold a picture from whatever point we may observe it. I think the Negroes with their swarthy complexions, and crude countenances, lend a shade to the bright lines of the Southern picture. O, I so much wish I had a pretty little darkey, with his *red* lips and shining countenance, to sit in the corner of my room like one of those old curious Indian bronzes."[1]

"Would the word 'pretty' apply to a little darkey?"

"O, no! not in the sense you mean; but they are pretty in the sense that they are curious and quaint, and charm the eye, just as my antique block house from India. I wonder what the Negroes think of life! I have a mind to stop one on the street, and ask him his impressions. Are they religious?"[2]

"The negro, as far as I have observed, thinks more of cornbread and bacon than anything else. In summer time he is fond of cabbage and greens. Did you ever eat any greens, Mr. Wilde?"

"Aw! Aw! What are greens? Be so good as to explain."

"Greens," I sententiously replied, "are a national dish. They belong to the natural order *cruciferae*, and their cotyledons are conduplicate. They are generally boiled with hog meat and served up with vinegar."

"You are so kind. I thank you. I must taste some before I leave. But you have only answered part of my question. Have the negroes faith? For this is a most faith-bearing age. We have faith in everything. The philosophers are faithful to their creeds, Ruskin and I have faith in art, Frederic Harrison and Spencer have faith in humanity, Tennyson has faith in the beautiful. Even Voltaire had faith in God. When one speaks like Schopenhauer, of no faith, of perfect blankness, I cannot understand him, I know not what he means.[3] That old landmark of the ages,

1. Although Wilde described his valet and other African Americans using vocabulary that would today be condemned (see e.g. CL, 127), nowhere else is he reported to have used the word "darkey".

2. It seems likely that Wilde's question and the subsequent exchange are embellished if not entirely fabricated. This issue of the *Free Trader* also includes an obvious burlesque titled "Oscar Wilde and a Darkey", in which Wilde meets "an old colored man" in the streets of Memphis and asks him how his environment affects his thinking. Also in this issue is a brief article previewing the interview, marked in The University of Memphis's copy to indicate that it was authored by Avery Meriwether. It includes the following, which does not appear in the interview itself: "MR. WILDE expressed a great curiosity about the Negro character and dialect, and said he would read a little play called 'The Slave's Strategy,' with great pleasure, when it was suggested that it contained perfect specimens of the Negro dialect." The New York *Sun* (13 Jul. 1882, 2) reveals that the play was written by Mrs E. A. Meriwether under the pseudonym George Reeves, and describes the plot: "The scenes of 'The Slave's Strategy' are laid in and near Vicksburg during the days of fratricidal strife; and certain historical disadvantages under which the Southern characters labor during the three acts of the play are squared off in the last scene, wherein a Union Colonel is made to lead a negro woman to the altar. As to their subsequent bliss or woe the play offers no definite revelations." Elizabeth Avery Meriwether's other works include *Facts and Falsehoods Concerning the War on the South, 1861–1865* (1904), a book strongly critical of Abraham Lincoln and the motives and conduct of Northern politicians and generals during the Civil War.

3. Frederic Harrison (1831–1923) was a British Historian (in the source his name is given as "Frederick"). Herbert Spencer (1820–1903) was a British scientist and political theorist who was among the most famous intellectuals of the late Victorian era. He is best known today for

the Catholic church, is founded on faith, and grows today because of its wonderful faith. Are there many negro Catholics?"

"In New Orleans there are some. As a rule they are inclined to that church, which permits of a congregational worship. They are very emotional and prefer the Baptist and Methodist churches, where they can join in singing, shout and give their experience."

Here the conversation was interrupted by a procession of negroes, parading the streets, headed by a brass band.

"Ah, there is happiness for them," cried Mr. Wilde. "Fond of music, show and eating, it will take two centuries to bring them up to the realization of the truly beautiful in this world."

"Are the English masses in any better condition?"

"I can't say. But the English thinkers divided into two great classes, are rapidly changing the habits and thoughts of the masses. There is the school of scientists, who study the utilitarian and descry the soul. How foolish! The Scientist in describing the *Venus de Milos*, will say it is a block of marble, composed of so many grains of silica, lime, water, and so forth, and that this is cut into certain curves making up the statue. But this is not the Venus. This is not explaining the thing which speaks to the soul and elevates the thought. Only the philosophy of the beautiful can do this. I belong to the other class, small but growing, which teaches that the beautiful springs from the soul."

"In which class would you place Carlyle, Spencer, Huxley, Harrison, Ruskin and Buckle?"[1]

"Carlyle is a Titan to himself, an amorphous mass in literature, hurling his bolts at every person and everything. I have studied Spencer's philosophy and really do not think much of it.[2] It tells me nothing about the finer perceptions of man's nature, about his soul. Huxley is the same. Harrison's faith in humanity is optimistic. He deals in persons and ignores things. Ruskin is a truer interpreter of nature, he is a poet painter, and understands the finer harmonies of the soul. Buckle is a great teacher of our philosophy. Decorative art is nothing more than a section of the philosophy of the environment taught so eloquently by Buckle. This man with an unparalleled industry collected many facts for his "History of Civilization in England," and made it one of the seminal books of the century. I teach that wherever the eye lights, there should be an object of beauty to give

---

coining the phrase "the survival of the fittest". Arthur Schopenhauer (1788–1860) was a German philosopher.

1. Thomas Henry Huxley (1825–1895) was a British biologist and anthropologist. Henry Thomas Buckle (1821–1862) was a British historian who wrote *History of Civilization in England* (1857).

2. Elsewhere Wilde praises Spencer: "The Apostle of Beauty in Nova Scotia," *Halifax Morning Herald* (Halifax, NS), 10 Oct. 1882, 2, p. 469.

impulse and joy to the soul. Buckle teaches that our history as individuals, as a tribe and a nation is the result of the surroundings which impress themselves into the very innermost germs of our nature making the English and Germans phlegmatic as a race, the Italians and Spaniards frivolous and volatile."

Noticing an uncut copy of the criticisms of *Sainte-Beuve* lying on the table covered with flowers, perfumed notes and cigarette ashes, I asked Mr. Wilde if the English approached the French in critical ability.[1]

"Sainte-Beuve was the prince of critics. He was a poet. Only poets can criticise. They create, they build, and those who create are the only persons able to explain the manner of creation. A man cannot criticise a painting unless he understands the art. This is the secret of Ruskin's success. What a critic Shakespeare would have made. The only critics now living worthy of the title are Swinburne of England and Hugo of France.[2] While it is true that only a poet can be a critic, not all poets are critics. Your own Poe was a Messiah in a barren land. He came. He taught. America learned for the first time the essence of noble and lofty criticism.

"Can you give me the address of Mr. Jefferson Davis,"[3] said Mr. Wilde. "He is the one man I wish to see before I leave for Japan. How I wished his book was not so long.[4] Had he compressed an edition for England, it would have done him far more good. I read it with immense pleasure. I never could understand why John Stuart Mill sympathized with the North in the war.[5] Lord Beaconsfield favored the North because he always advocated Empire. But Mill was for the people, hence the strangeness of his conduct. I sympathized with the South, for I thought that if the Colonies had a right to secede, in 1776, the Southern States had a similar right in 1860. When Lincoln emancipated the negroes, the English who had

1. Charles Augustin Sainte-Beuve (1804–1869) was a French literary critic and poet.

2. Victor Marie Hugo (1802–1885) was a French poet, novelist, playwright, and critic. Wilde received a presentation volume from Hugo, which was sold in the auction of the Wildes' household effects (CL, 713).

3. Jefferson Davis (1808–1889) served as the president of the Confederate States from 1861 to 1865.

4. *The Rise and Fall of the Confederate Government* (1881) was published in a two volume edition and ran to more than 1,500 pages.

5. John Stuart Mill (1865–1868) was an English philosopher and politician. In the source his middle name is given as "Stewart". Mill supported the abolition of slavery, and thought that the breakup of the United States would damage democratic movements and encourage despotism in Europe, so his sympathy with the North is not difficult to fathom (Park, T. P. (1991). John Stuart Mill, Thomas Carlyle, and the U.S. Civil War. *The Historian*, *64*, 93–106).

spent many millions of pounds on freeing the slaves of a province, of course, lost sight of the great question of State rights, and poured forth their sympathies for the oppressed.[1]

As I arose to go, I asked Mr. Wilde if he believed in Free Trade.

"In my own country I was a protectionist in a measure. I believed at that time that tariff laws protected flesh and blood. What do we care so much for a market if we can create a set of artisans and workers in the handicrafts who will supply all our national needs? I thought that commerce should be as nothing in opposition to men. But I have changed since coming to America."

"What converted you so quickly?"

"The high prices."

"What, for instance?"

"Gloves. In New York the dealers charged me three and half to four dollars for a pair of gloves which cost me a dollar in London. You can get a good pair for fifty cents. Then there is velvet which I am very fond of wearing. I had a jacket made of that stuff in New York, which cost me fifty dollars.[2] In London the same cost me only twenty dollars. I find that tariffs do not protect flesh and blood. There is free trade in labor in this country while the products of labor are supposed to be protected. The result is that the manufacturers can import all the workmen they need to compete with Americans while they manufacture their goods at enormous profits."[3]

1. These words are unlikely to be Wilde's. Although in other interviews he expressed sympathy for the South in its defeat, he tended rapidly to turn the conversation towards the question of Irish independence (see e.g. "Oscar Wilde," *The Daily Picayune* (New Orleans, LA), 25 June 1882, 11, pp. 432–3; "Oscar Wilde," *The Atlanta Constitution* (Atlanta, GA), 5 July 1882, 8, pp. 435–6).

2. Wilde refers to the coats he requested Colonel Morse order for him in February (CL, 141). See "The New Costume," *The New York World, Semi-Weekly Edition* (New York, NY), 5 May 1882, 6, pp. 771–3.

3. Meriwether was critical of protectionism. The preface to the fifth edition of his *A Tramp Trip: How to See Europe on Fifty Cents a Day* (1886) is dedicated to an argument in favour of free trade versus protectionism. In his Appendix, Meriwether claims that a heavy overcoat he had purchased in London for $16 could not be had for less than $40 in America, because of the protection of American goods (271). Nevertheless, Wilde's comments are likely to be genuine, as they are repeated in a later interview: see "A Chat With Oscar," *The Times* (Philadelphia, PA), 2 Sep. 1882, 5, p. 460.

"Oscar Wilde," *The Daily Picayune* (New Orleans, LA), 16 June 1882, Friday's Afternoon Edition, 1[1]

A VISIT TO THE APOSTLE OF MODERN ART.

The Negro, the Indian and the Sunflower his Theme.

Mr. Oscar Wilde reached this city on Friday morning and took rooms at the St. Charles Hotel.

This gentleman is such a celebrity on account of the ingenious and peculiar manner in which he has been presented to the public everywhere, that many persons were desirous of visiting him at the hotel, and when a Picayune reporter called and was shown into his presence he found several gentlemen already there.

Mr. Wilde received his callers with much courtesy and sincerity,[2] and talked readily and pleasantly to all. He complimented his visitors by remarking that he had encountered more that was agreeable and courteous in the manners of the Southern people, than at the North.[3]

In Chicago he found people pushing their way with a brusque sort of energy, while in the South people were more quiet and polite. "It is always so in warm countries, and may be a result of climatic effects," said the apostle of modern art.[4]

Mr. Wilde said he had nothing to do with commerce and what was called progress. He was a student of art. He saw that in the rush and crush of business the native and characteristic picturesqueness of people was being rapidly destroyed, and he desired to do what he could to rescue from oblivion the truly artistic peculiarities that still survive.[5]

One must go to Asia and Africa for picturesqueness in human costume and habits. In America he had found it only in the Indians and in the negro, and he

1. H & S, b85. Reprinted in Mikhail, 89–90. This interview was not printed in the morning edition on 16 June, but was reprinted with more material and other minor variations the next day (page 3). The 17 June version is quoted in OWDA, 362; and Sturgis, 255–6/244. The reporter appears to have been accompanied by the author of "Arrival of Mr. Oscar Wilde," *The Times-Democrat* (New Orleans, LA), 17 June 1882, 3, pp. 424–6.

2. The 17 June version has "suavity" for "sincerity".

3. Wilde's experience of the South was, as yet, limited: he had lectured in Memphis on 12 June and in Vicksburg two days later.

4. At Oxford Wilde had been struck by the argument of French philosopher Victor Cousin (1792–1867) that the climate and physical geography of a country determined the character of its inhabitants (CW iv, 326).

5. Wilde took issue with this part of the article (see "Oscar Wilde," *The Daily Picayune* (New Orleans, LA), 18 June 1882, 11, pp. 426–7). Note that *The Times-Democrat* gives a similar though not identical quotation (p. 425), so this is less likely to be a case of misrepresentation than of Wilde failing to express himself as clearly as he would have liked.

was surprised that painters and poets had paid so little attention to these matters, and especially to the negro as an object of art.

He spoke of Mr. Cable in terms of great praise, and expressed admiration for some of his fine pictures of life and character in which the negro figures.[1] Father Ryan, the poet, also came in for favorable mention by Mr. Wilde.[2]

The poet expresses a desire to spend some time in New Orleans as it has many picturesque points which he wishes to examine.

As Mr. Wilde will present his peculiar views in his lecture, nothing further need be said of them.[3]

His personal appearance is perhaps the most striking thing about him. He is very tall, over six feet, with a large frame. His head is large, features all large and fat rather than strong in expression, but his face has an air of youthful, almost infantile sweetness, which perhaps is the real secret of Mr. Wilde's power over the people who admire him.[4]

His hair is long and straight, not curling, and hangs upon his shoulders in heavy masses. He was dressed in a black velvet jacket, gray tight fitting pantaloons, not knee breeches, red silk stockings and slippers. His shirt collar was loosely tied with a dark scarf.[5]

His entire appearance, if somewhat peculiar, is not unpleasing, and his manners are very agreeable and friendly.

Scattered around him, on the floor and on the sofa upon which he sat were a number of paper-bound, yellow-covered, novels in the French language, from the prolific press of Levy of Paris, while a bundle of cigarettes and a bottle of cologne water lay conveniently near.

1. George Washington Cable (1844–1925) was an American novelist. In 1880 he published his first novel, *The Grandissimes: A Story of Creole Life,* which follows the fortunes of a French Creole family in the early 1800s. In 1885 he relocated to Massachusetts after his articles calling for racial equality were met with hostility from Southern Whites.

2. Abram Joseph Ryan (1838–1886) was a Catholic priest and a poet whose work memorialised the Confederacy. The 17 June version has an additional paragraph here: "He spoke of his relatives in Louisiana, of whom Dr. J. K. Elgee, who once lived in Rapides parish, and was his mother's brother; and in reply to a remark that it had been reported that he had come to the State to look after some of the family possessions, said that however much he might desire to have a plantation in Louisiana, not the least of the attractions of which would be the proprietorship of groves of magnolia trees, he had no such object in view."

3. The 17 June version has "presented" for "will present", as Wilde had lectured the previous evening.

4. The 17 June version has an additional paragraph here: "He looks to be quite young, not much beyond 20, is beardless, with a florid complexion, brown locks and grayish eyes, and his face wears a somewhat over-fat or bloated look, but it does not at any time lose its attractiveness".

5. The 17 June version has "dark red scarf".

Mr. Wilde had but little to say about sunflowers, save to express the hope that the crop of this artistic and aesthetic plant had not been entirely destroyed in the great inundation to which Louisiana has been recently exposed.

Other visitors coming in the reporter took his departure with pleasing recollections of the apostle of modern art.[1]

"Arrival of Mr. Oscar Wilde," *The Times-Democrat* (New Orleans, LA), 17 June 1882, 3[2]

A Chat With the Disciple of the Aesthetic.

Yesterday Mr. Oscar Wilde, with his secretary, Mr. J. S. Vale,[3] and his valet, arrived in the city, and were at once driven to the St. Charles Hotel, where he was ushered to his apartments on the first floor.

In the forenoon a representative of THE TIMES-DEMOCRAT called upon him, and was at once requested to walk up. Entering his little parlor, the reporter found the poet enjoying the *dolce far niente* of a morning siesta, blowing clouds of cigarette smoke in the air as he lolled on the sofa. He arose, and advancing in somewhat of a constrained manner welcomed his visitor in a pleasant, cheery voice, and after shaking hands resumed his easy position.

Much taller than descriptions had led one to believe, he appeared at first sight to be a well framed and symmetrical large English boy, good-natured, frank, but fonder of playing with his sisters, than going into the ruder sports with the average boy at cricket or perhaps a village fight. He was dressed in a neat fitting velvet jacket, a pair of tight tweed pants, and above his low quarters were displayed scarlet half hose.

A large crimson cravat was the most pronounced article of his dress, and it caught the eye and held it perforce. His hair hung down to his shoulders in heavy masses, sometimes intruding on the face, but a languid movement of the hand would brush it aside.

His face is not masculine, although every feature is large. The feminine seems to overshadow the coarser ruggedness, and it leaves the impression that its owner could never have seen much of life's vicissitudes. Smooth and fair, it

1. The 17 June version has three additional paragraphs here, detailing Wilde's movements on the afternoon of the 16th and a brief tour schedule.

2. The reporter appears to have been accompanied by the author of "Oscar Wilde," *The Daily Picayune* (New Orleans, LA), 16 June 1882, Friday's Afternoon Edition, 1, pp. 422–4.

3. In the source, "J. J. Vale".

wanted force and decision. His eyes make one forget the face, for there is a dreaminess and liquidity about them seldom seen in men's.

His manner is open, frank and entirely free of affectation, and as a conversationalist he is always interesting. His sentences are well-rounded, clear, and his language chaste. There is little or no inflexion in his voice, and almost a total absence of vigor, and what Americans call vim.

During the conversation he pleasantly alluded to the fact that he had seen much more of the courtliness and grace of bearing in the South than in those places he had traveled North. It was natural with the climate. The manners here were better. Here is not so much of a battle for money as, for instance, say in Chicago.

Speaking of the weather, he said he was delighted to be where he could enjoy the almost Italian airs. This was the atmosphere of art. It was here that nature gave forth her most lively colors, most beautiful verdure and the forests were filled with the sweetest song birds. It was nearer Italy than the colder North.

He had felt an anxious desire to visit New Orleans from what he had read of it. Its beautiful creoles, gardens, magnolias, were all objects of beauty.

Mr. Wilde disclaimed having anything to do with commerce or progress. His mission was one purely of art. Trade and mechanics crushed out art genius, and what otherwise might be naturally developed into the great was dwarfed.

Speaking of dress he reiterated what had already been published—that the only well-dressed men he had seen in America were the miners of California and the Northwest. Their costumes were useful and at the same time picturesque. But in our cities the dressing was simply "dreadful." He could not understand why some painter had not taken up the negro as a study. There was a world of the artistic in his manners and curious habits, and little negro children amused him much. Their little black eyes shine like the lizard's, and their movements while basking in the sun were curious and wondrous to the artistic eye. He wanted to see our firemen in their ordinary fire dress, as he thought it would be much like the miners.

Among the things he most desired to see here was a voudou dance. He had read of them in Mr. Cable's novel, and wished he could be present at one.[1]

1. The passage in Cable's *The Grandissimes* to which Wilde is referring reads: "They gyrated in couples, a few at a time, throwing their bodies into the most startling attitudes and the wildest contortions, while the whole company of black lookers-on, incited by the tones of the weird music and the violent posturing of the dancers, swayed and writhed in passionate sympathy, beating their breasts, palms and thighs in time with the bones and drums [....] The amusement had reached its height. Many participants had been lugged out by the neck to avoid their being danced on, and the enthusiasm had risen to a frenzy, when there bounded into the ring the blackest of black men, an athlete of superb figure, in breeches of 'Indienne'—the stuff used for slave women's best dresses—jingling with bells, his feet in moccasins, his tight, crisp hair

The conversation drifted into other channels, and the reporter then withdrew.

During the day Mr. Wilde visited the rooms of the Southern Art Union, where he highly complimented some of the work exhibited.[1]

He leaves for Galveston on Sunday, and on his return will lecture at Spanish Fort. He has been invited by President Davis to spend a day or two with him at Beauvoir,[2] on his way from here to Mobile.

"Oscar Wilde," *The Daily Picayune* (New Orleans, LA), 18 June 1882, 11[3]

THE GUEST OF THE CLUBS AND PRIVATE CITIZENS.

HE RESTATES SOME OF HIS VIEWS AND ASKS TO HAVE SOME MISTAKES IN REGARD TO THEM CORRECTED.

On Saturday afternoon a reporter called on Mr. Oscar Wilde at his apartments in the St. Charles Hotel and was courteously received. The poet was in dressing gown and slippers. He wore a dark red or claret-colored necktie, tied in a loose knot, and there was nothing noticeable in his costume or general appearance different from what has been before described in these columns. He expressed himself much pleased with his reception in New Orleans. He had spent the morning with Mr. Geo. W. Cable, who had called on him and told him much of the interesting peculiarities of the traditional life and history of New Orleans. Later in the day he had called at the residence of "Xariffa,"—Mrs. Mary Ashley Townsend—of whose poems he spoke in praise, and whose charming hospitality the poet enjoyed.[4]

Mr. Wilde then accepted invitations from the Boston and Commercial Clubs, in which he had been elected to honorary membership, and where he had been treated to due hospitalities. He had likewise received a number of callers, and so his time was fully occupied.

"The Picayune has quoted me," said Mr. Wilde, "as taking no sort of interest in the advance of progress of civilization and commerce in contradistinction to

---

decked out with feathers, a necklace of alligator's teeth rattling on his breast and a living serpent twined about his neck."

1. The Southern Art Union was founded in 1880 and held its first exhibition in May 1881.
2. Jefferson Davis had been living at "Beauvoir", an estate in Biloxi, Mississippi, since 1879.
3. Quoted in OWDA, 363.
4. Mary Ashley Townsend (1836–1901) was an American poet and, under the pen name Xariffa, the author of humorous sketches.

art.[1] True, I am engaged in lecturing on art, while there are other persons who devote themselves to building railways and factories, but there is no conflict between these pursuits. On the contrary, there is entire harmony between art and commercial and industrial progress. The manufacturer strives to produce fabrics for human use in the various processes of life at such a rate that as many persons as possible shall have a cheap and good article. We say to the manufacturer, while you are making an article for the uses of men, make it beautiful. In doing so this need not add to the expense of the article. Why should not a man have the additional pleasure of drinking out of a beautiful cup, or of eating from a beautiful dish, or of sitting in a beautiful chair? The simplest articles of use can be as well made beautiful as ugly, but it is necessary that the taste of the artisan should be cultivated so as to enable him to work out beautiful forms.

"I am in full accord with the highest civilization. There is no need that civilization should make the world ugly, and true civilization does not. I spoke of a river in Canada which was defiled with sawdust from a mill.[2] If the proprietor of the mill had been a good manager he would have known enough to burn his sawdust for fuel instead of polluting a river with it. In the same way the manufacturers at Manchester, who formerly poured out the smoke from their thousands of chimneys, poisoning the atmosphere and darkening the sky, learned that they could save valuable fuel by burning their smoke, and thus a truer civilization has not only succeeded in adding to the profits of the manufacturer, or the cheapness of his fabrics, but also in purifying the atmosphere, and rescuing the beauties of nature from the abominations that have polluted and disfigured them. This is my position as to art and civilization, and I would be glad if the Picayune will set me right on the subject.

"In America your young men are a fine, intelligent, manly set of fellows, and they have a great opportunity to work for their country, and for civilization, and for art in a high class of handicraft and manufactures. This country affords the material for manufacturing everything the people consume. If you will attain excellence in the beauty of the products of your handwork you will work in a sphere far more honorable and useful than to sell haberdashery wares in a dry good shop. The Americans have too grand a destiny before them in manufacturing to neglect art, and they should have good schools of design everywhere, so that they may know how to make beautiful things, and to enjoy them after they are made."

1. See "Oscar Wilde," *The Daily Picayune* (New Orleans, LA), 16 June 1882, Friday's Afternoon Edition, 1, p. 422.

2. In Ottawa. See "Oscar Wilde on Decorative Art," *The Daily News* (Kingston, ON), 23 May 1882, 2, p. 400.

Mr. Wilde leaves for Texas this morning, and will lecture at Galveston, San Antonio and other places. He had heard that San Antonio is a place of much picturesqueness and pleasing peculiarities, and he expects to enjoy his visit to the Lone Star State.

The reporter, after promising to set him right as requested, bid the poet good evening and withdrew.

H. Ryder-Taylor, "Oscar Wilde," *The Evening Light* (San Antonio, TX), 21 June 1882, 1[1]

Oscar Wilde arrived in the city this morning by the 9 o'clock train, and the LIGHT was apprized of the distinguished arrival. We dispatched a local to the hotel to greet the aesthetic apostle. He found Mr. Wilde taking the world easy in his room at the Menger; he was dressed in drab velvet jacket, blue tie, white waistcoat, light drab trousers, scarlet stockings and slippers. A table covered with books, a lemonade—with a stick in it—and a huge bunch of mammoth cigarettes made up the array that confronted our aesthetic reporter, for Mr. H. Ryder-Taylor was the LIGHT representative who renewed an old acquaintance with Mr. Wilde. Mr. W. complained of a feeling of lassitude which he attributed to taking a bath at Galveston; he paid a high compliment to the Galvestonions, and generally complimented the people he had met with upon their advancement and civilization.

He spoke of his devotion to art and explained the objects of aesthetics being to give a high order of commendation to industry and would have workmen of intelligence working for the honor of their craft, as well as for his wife [*sic*].

Mr. Wilde branched out upon the general topic of his mission in a very interesting manner of the Mormons: he said he never saw such an unintelligent or ugly race in any part of the states; he was treated courteously by the Mormons—he found nothing about Salt Lake City worthy of mention, except the tabernacle, the theatre was well attended; children were innumerable, not pretty, but happy. He says the Mormons have no idea of art.

Mr. Wilde is an Irishman by birth, son of Sir. W. Wilde, and born on the 16th of October, 1856 [*sic*]; educated at Oxford, and since his graduation has taken a place in the literary circles of England.

1. H & S, b86. Reprinted in Mikhail, 90–1. Quoted in OWDA, 364–5. Henry Ryder-Taylor (1850–1908) was an English journalist who had settled in San Antonio, where he wrote books about local history.

H. Ryder-Taylor, "Oscar Wilde," *The Evening Light* (San Antonio, TX), 23 June 1882, 4[1]

Yesterday Mr. Oscar Wilde drove about the city and suburbs to inspect their art beauties. He was especially pleased with the St. Jose mission, its very fine door and window which he considered excelled anything of the kind in America, and he was charmed with the tout ensemble of the whole scene.[2] He met Mr. Grenet, our young painter, who was there sketching, and he spoke in very complimentary terms of his genius and knowledge of that art to which he is so devoted.[3] The Alamo interested Mr. Wilde very much, but he thought it is monstrous that such a noble and historic building should be used as it is now.[4]

Mr. Wilde expressed himself well satisfied with the excellence and accuracy of the LIGHT report of his lecture on "Decorative Art,"[5] which he described as the best published south of Boston, and presented our local with his portrait, autographed as follows, in recognition of his friendship: "H. Ryder-Taylor, from his friend Oscar Wilde, San Antonio, June '82." He also expressed a very strong opinion of the unprincipled conduct of the Times, in maliciously attributing to him words that he had not spoken nor even conceived, but he was not surprised at this when he found the same paper wilfully making a misrepresentation by saying that Mr. Ryder-Taylor walked (without invitation) with him to the hotel; whereas both persons, by pre-arrangement drove to the Menger Hotel, accompanied by Mr. J. S. Vale, his manager.[6]

1. Quoted in OWDA, 365.

2. The Mission San José y San Miguel de Aguayo was founded in 1720. The new church, which Wilde saw and which still stands, was built in 1768. The window referred to is the Rose Window. It was carved in 1775 in the baroque style by an unknown sculptor.

3. Louis Edward Grenet (1856–1922) was a native of San Antonio who studied in Paris and New York City before returning to his hometown to establish a studio in 1878.

4. The Alamo was built as a Spanish mission but, since the early 1800s, had been a military compound. In 1836 it was the site of a pivotal incident in the Texas War of Independence when 187 Texian soldiers and civilians defending the compound were overwhelmed and killed by a larger Mexican force. The United States Army later occupied the Alamo but abandoned it in 1876. The convent was sold to Augustine Honoré Grenet (father of Louis Edward), who erected an adjoining warehouse and used both buildings for his wholesale grocery business. When Wilde visited, Grenet had only recently died. His business was sold to mercantile firm Hugo & Schmeltzer and they continued to operate it during the 1880s. The Alamo was designated a UNESCO World Heritage Site in 2015. Wilde's remark on the use of the Alamo is echoed in his article on "The American Man" for *The Court and Society Review:* "He [the American man] is severe on the modern Romans for not covering the Colosseum with a glass roof, and utilising the building as a warehouse for dry goods (13 Apr. 1887; CW vi, No. 60, lines 51–3).

5. "Oscar Wilde's Lecture," *The Evening Light* (San Antonio, TX), 22 June 1882, 1.

6. *San Antonio Daily Times.* No library holds issues from the time of Wilde's visit (Library of Congress holdings information).

Figure 14. The Mission San José y San Miguel de Aguayo, San Antonio, Texas, photographed by Carol M. Highsmith.

Mr. Wilde was very grateful for the kindness and courtesy he has received in our city, and looks to its intelligence to bear in mind the lesson he had taught and as far as practical act upon them [*sic*].

According to his plan, Mr. Wilde left last night by the 6:30 p. m. train for Houston, where he lectures tonight, thence he goes to New Orleans, San Francisco and Japan. He gives return lectures in both the last two named places, lectures and studies art in Japan and from that place he returns to England.

"Louisiana Gleanings," *The Lake Charles Echo* (Lake Charles, LA), 24 June 1882, 1[1]

✂ *Several paragraphs that are unrelated to Wilde.*

To a reporter of the City Item, Oscar Wilde said, during the course of an interview: "I am ever so much desirous of seeing your Creole women; I understand they are very beautiful." We trust the aesthetic youth's curiosity was gratified.

✂ *Several paragraphs that are unrelated to Wilde.*

"Oscar Wilde," *The Daily Picayune* (New Orleans, LA), 25 June 1882, 11[2]

TALKS OF TEXAS, WHERE HE WAS DUBBED A "COLONEL" AND FELL IN LOVE WITH GALVESTON AND SAN ANTONIO.

His Views on the Southern Cause and that of the Irish People.

"There are in Texas two spots which gave me infinite pleasure. These are Galveston and San Antonio. Galveston, set like a jewel in a crystal sea, was beautiful. Its fine beach, its shady avenues of oleander, and its delightful sea breezes were something to be enjoyed. It was in San Antonio, however, that I found more to please me in the beautiful ruins of the old Spanish mission churches and convents, and in the relics of Spanish manners and customs impressed upon the people and the architecture of the city. America is so full of youthful vigor and

1. Based on an untraced interview in the *New Orleans City Item*. This is probably a genuine quote, as Wilde is reported to have said something similar in "Arrival of Mr. Oscar Wilde," *The Times-Democrat* (New Orleans, LA), 17 June 1882, 3, p. 425.

2. H & S, b87. Reprinted in Mikhail, 91–3; and H & S, 156–8. Excerpted in Hyde, 74. Quoted in OWDA, 366–7; and Sturgis, 255–6/243–4.

vitality that one sees those relics of a past age in the midst of so much that is new with a positive sensation of surprise and pleasure. Those old Spanish churches, with their picturesque remains of tower and dome, and their handsome carved stonework, standing amid the verdure and sunshine of a Texas prairie, gave me a thrill of strange pleasure."

These were the words of Oscar Wilde as he stood by the window of his parlor in the St. Charles Hotel on Saturday evening on his return from a brief pilgrimage to the Lone Star State. Mr. Wilde was looking fresh and bright, and he expressed the pleasure with which he had viewed the striking and picturesque scenery of the swamps in Louisiana and Texas. The giant cypress trees towering above the dense jungle of undergrowth and tangled vines, while long streamers of gray moss waved in the wind from the great branches which the trees thrust forth from the sky, attracted the poet's attention, while he had much to say of the alligators, which sprawled and yawned in the sunshine on the trunks of fallen trees and on the muddy banks of the bayous and the great morasses.

Nothing in the way of animal life, however, seemed to please the poet and art reformer so much as the young negroes.

"I saw them everywhere," he said, "happy and careless, basking in the sunshine or dancing in the shade, their half naked bodies gleaming like bronze and their lithe and active movements reminding one of the lizards that were seen flashing along the banks and trunks of the trees."

"You were in Texas long enough to acquire a military title. A week is quite sufficient, and I have no doubt I would be justified in addressing you as Col. Wilde," said the reporter.

"Oh, yes: I am a colonel by all the rules and regulations of a Texas brevet. I was dubbed 'Colonel' in Galveston and was fully invested with the title by the time I got to Houston. I shall write home to my friends of this new rank and promotion."[1]

After some further conversation the reporter spoke of Mr. Wilde's reported intention of visiting Hon. Jefferson Davis, on the way from New Orleans to Mobile. Mr. Wilde said he had an intense admiration for the chief of the Southern Confederacy. He had never seen him, but had followed his career with much attention. "His fall, after such an able and gallant pleading of his own cause, must necessarily arouse sympathy, no matter what might be the merits of his plea. The head may approve the success of the winners, but the heart is sure to be with the fallen.

1. *Personal Impressions of America*: "On approaching the borders of Texas I was called 'Captain'; when I got to the centre of Texas I was addressed as 'Colonel,' and, on arriving at the borders of Mexico, as 'General.'" (Dibb, 238.)

"The case of the South in the civil war was to my mind much like that of Ireland today. It was a struggle for autonomy, self-government for a people. I do not wish to see the empire dismembered, but only to see the Irish people free, and Ireland still as a willing and integral part of the British Empire. To dismember a great empire in this age of vast armies and overweening ambition on the part of other nations, is to consign the peoples of the broken country to weak and insignificant places in the panorama of nations; but people must have freedom and autonomy before they are capable of their greatest result in the cause of progress. This is my feeling about the Southern people, as it is about my own people, the Irish. I look forward to much pleasure in visiting Mr. Jefferson Davis."[1]

The poet had an engagement to go out for the evening, and he shortly took his departure with a party of gentlemen, as it was reported, to witness some mysterious and curious ceremonies of the devotees of voudou, which were to inaugurate the recurrence of St. John's night, June 24.

Mr. Wilde will lecture Monday night at Spanish Fort, on the internal decoration of the home, and on Tuesday will depart for Mobile, stopping at Beauvoir, the residence of Jefferson Davis, to spend a day with him.[2]

"Oscar Wilde," *The Daily Picayune* (New Orleans, LA), 27 June 1882, 3

LECTURE AT SPANISH FORT ON HOME DECORATIONS.

PRACTICAL TALK FROM AN APPARENTLY UNPRACTICAL MAN.

✂ *A report of Wilde's lecture in Spanish Fort.*

At the close of his lecture a reporter had a few minutes' conversation with the poet, in which he expressed his desire to return to New Orleans, where he had so much enjoyed his brief stay.[3] He goes this morning to Mobile, and at the close of his tour in America proposes a visit to Japan, the art land of the East.

1. The linking of the Southern cause with that of Ireland was a standard trope. For example, the Irish nationalist John Mitchel (1815–1875), who in 1845 was invited to take over "the chief editorial conduct" of the *Nation* (Melville, 21), the newspaper for which Wilde's mother wrote, and in the 1850s established a pro-slavery, pro-secession newspaper in Knoxville, Tennessee, asserted that "[t]he North is England; the South is Ireland" (Gleeson, D. T. (2016). *The Green and the Gray: The Irish in the Confederate States of America*. The University of North Carolina Press. 20–1).

2. Wilde visited Jefferson Davis at Beauvoir on 27 June as planned.

3. Wilde did not return to New Orleans.

"Oscar Wilde," *The Atlanta Constitution* (Atlanta, GA), 5 July 1882, 8[1]

ARRIVAL OF THE GREAT ESTHETE AND HIS LECTURE.

An Interview With Him at the Markham House Yesterday—How He Appears—What He Says of the South and of His American Tour—His Lecture at DeGive's Last Night.[2]

When Oscar Wilde reached Atlanta yesterday from Macon he disembarked from the train and stalked with measured tread to the Markham, flanked by his valet, when he entered the arcade of the Markham, he advanced to the radiator and came to a halt. There he posed, one hand sought the spot where his heart was supposed to be, and the other hung by his side. His head was thrown back, his long locks fell over his shoulder, and he gazed upon the frescoing in the ceiling apparently oblivious of the curious gazes that were directed toward him. His able secretary advanced, and put his autograph upon the register, and then Mr. Wilde was shown to a room on the second floor facing to the west, kept especially for esthetes. Mr. Wilde had scarcely had time to be dusted by his able valet before a CONSTITUTION reporter sent up his card. The response was an invitation to the young man to "come up at once," and accordingly after a very brief lapse of time THE CONSTITUTION was rapping at the door of the room of the great esthete. A deep voice from the inside called, "Come in," and the reporter turned the knob and entered. The room was rather narrow and one end opened by two windows upon Loyd street. Almost right under the window the colored people were yelling and shouting in true Fourth of July style. The spectacle that met the astonished gaze of the reporter was one long to be remembered. In the farther end of the room, seated in a large rocking chair, was the great esthete. His appearance was striking in the extreme, so odd he appeared. His hair was long and fell about his shoulders. It was parted near the middle and was rather stiff and in great abundance. His face was large, his lips exceedingly so, and his nose prominent. He would weigh evidently about 180 pounds. His dress was not the court costume which he wears while on the stage, but it deserves especial mention. His

1. H & S, b89. Reprinted in Mikhail, 93–6; and H & S, 158–61. Excerpted in Hyde, 74–5; "The Academy of Music Tonight," *The News and Courier* (Charleston, South Carolina), 7 July 1882, 4; "Oscar Wilde and Jefferson Davis," *The Daily American* (Nashville, TN), 8 July 1882, 1; "Oscar Wilde and Jefferson Davis," *The Daily Picayune* (New Orleans, LA), 11 July 1882, 1; "Oscar Wilde and Jefferson Davis," *The Pascagoula Democrat Star* (Pascagoula, MS), 14 July, 1882, 4; and "Oscar Wilde and the 'Lost Cause,'" *Northern Christian Advocate* (Syracuse, NY), 20 July 1882, 3. Quoted in OWDA, 372–3; Hyde, 7; Ellmann, 187/197; and Sturgis, 255/244. Referenced in Sturgis, 237/228, 256/245. This article is included in the Robert Ross Memorial Collection album (Ross b.6, 67).
2. The venue of the lecture was DeGive's Opera House.

coat was a black velvet jacket. He wore a white waistcoat with gray woolen pantaloons. A monster moonlight green tie surrounded his throat. His socks were exquisite silk and his shoes dainty gaiters. On a table near him lay a very fine cloth cloak with silk lining. On a bureau lay a large wide brimmed hat and near it an ivory cane. On a table lay a bouquet of sunflowers. Around the poet lecturer lay scattered several books, novels and books of poetry in French. THE CONSTITUTION was not long in making known its business. Mr. Wilde appeared to be irritated by the yelling outside, and rising said:

"Oh, the patriots, the patriots; let's shut down the window and shut out the noise."

"This is the first 4th of July you ever saw in America?"

"Yes."

"What do you think of it as you see it now?"

"I don't think that anything so fine as the declaration of independence should be celebrated at all if it cannot be celebrated in a very noble manner. Amongst the most artistic things that any city can do is to celebrate by pageant any great eras in its history. Why should not the 4th of July pageant in Atlanta be as fine as the mardi gras carnival in New Orleans?[1] Indeed a pageant is the most perfect school of art for a people. It shows them what otherwise they would not have a chance of seeing, noble costumes, beautiful colors and sculpturesque grouping. It would be quite impossible to over-estimate the influence on art that any celebration of the kind would have, for in an age like this, where there is such a growing feeling for what is merely grotesque and consequently ignoble, I think the people need to be reminded of the dignity of pure beauty. Amongst the many signs in Europe of a growing feeling for art, perhaps one of the foremost is the revival in so many cities of the beautiful pageants of the past. But I am afraid that the only pageants that most American cities have a hope of seeing are the glaring processions of their traveling circusses, and I feel that they deserve something very much better."[2]

"You have been to see Mr. Jefferson Davis lately. Tell me something about your visit to him."

"He lives in a very beautiful house by the sea, amid lovely trees. He impressed me very much as a man of the keenest intellect, and a man fairly to be a leader of men on account of a personality that is as simple as it is strong, and an

1. In 1882 the New Orleans Mardi Gras was celebrated between 16 and 22 February. Wilde did not witness the carnival as he was then touring the Midwest.

2. *Personal Impressions of America*: America "is a country that has no trappings, no pageants, and no gorgeous ceremonies. I saw only two processions during my whole visit, one was the Fire Brigade preceded by the Police and the other was the Police preceded by the Fire Brigade." (Dibb, 247.)

enthusiasm that is as fervent as it is faultless.[1] We in Ireland are fighting for the principle of autonomy against empire, for independence against centralization, for the principles for which the south fought.[2] So it was a matter of immense interest and pleasure to me to meet the leader of such a great cause. Because although there may be a failure in fact, in idea there is no failure possible. The principles for which Mr. Davis and the south went to war cannot suffer defeat. I had read Mr. Davis's book, which is a masterpiece, although to us in Europe the elaborate detail of military maneuver is at times a little burdensome. But there are passages in which he dwells on the principles of the southern confederacy that were read by us with the keenest interest and delight. It is impossible not to think nobly of a country that has produced Patrick Henry, Thomas Jefferson, George Washington and Jefferson Davis.[3] Besides its great men I admire in the south the wonderful beauty of its vegetation. I have seen no forests in Europe more wonderful, no flowers more exquisite in perfume or in color. It is worthwhile to come over here merely to see the magnolia in full blossom. It should be—the south—the home of art in America, because it possesses the most perfect surroundings: and now that it is recovering from the hideous ruin of the war I have no doubt that all these beautiful arts, in whose cause, I will spend my youth in pleading, will spring up among you. The south has produced the best poet of America—Edgar Allan Poe:[4] and with all its splendid traditions it would be impossible not to believe that she will continue to perfect what she has begun so nobly. The very physique of the people in the south is far finer than that in the north, and a temperament infinitely more susceptible to the influences of beauty."

"Tell me something about your sunflower ideas?"

"Oh, yes! I have some here that were sent up to me. The reason that we value the sunflower so much, is because it is so perfectly adapted for decorative art. Many flowers will merely be beautiful in color, without having a definite form, such as the magnolia for instance. But this flower is best suited for decoration, because its form is definite and perfect, and of all flowers, perhaps, the sunflower is the one which art has made noblest use of. It appears constantly in the medalic and tapestry of old Europe and is found all through Eastern art. Besides its beautiful form the imagination of the world has surrounded it with a halo of beautiful legions as golden as the halo of its own golden rays. I have been very

1. Davis's appraisal of Wilde was less favourable. The day after the visit he is supposed to have told his wife "I did not like that man," (Friedman, 234).

2. Linking of the Southern cause with that of Ireland: see p. 433, note 1.

3. Patrick Henry (1736–1799) was a Founding Father best known for his declaration in 1775: "Give me liberty, or give me death." Thomas Jefferson (1743–1826) and George Washington served as the third and first presidents of the United States, respectively.

4. Poe was born in Boston, but, orphaned as an infant, was taken in by a family in Richmond, Virginia.

pleased to find since I came to America, that the people have come to see and to appreciate its wonderful splendor far more than I think they did before, and indeed that is one of the noblest uses of art. It takes up some flower which people have thought common and shows them how beautiful it is."

"How do you find art in America?"

"The feeling of art and the admiration of beauty is, I think, more general than I expected. I found a greater appreciation of art in Boston, New York, Cincinnati, St. Louis and Chicago than anywhere else."

"What do you think after your American tour?"

"With regard to my American tour, I may say that nothing could be more interesting to any young man to have the opportunities that I have had of studying the civilizations in many cases very fine and in many cases very incomplete, of this new world. I have found a greater feeling for art than I expected, but far less knowledge of it, a great feeling for beauty and beautiful things, but a very vague idea about how a nation could acquire them. The real question that I have found in America standing in the way of its right artistic development is that the ordinary handicrafts are not held in their proper honor. So many young men whom I have met in railway cars and elsewhere, young men of a great deal of brightness of intellect being contented to select as a profession the occupation of clerks in stores, and the like, which in many cases means no little more than a form of salaried idleness, and on seeing how much finer it would be for them to select a profession in which they could use their hands and really do useful and good work."

"When will you return to Europe?"

"I shall not be in Europe for a year. After my tour through the south, I shall go to Canada, where I have to deliver ten more lectures.[1] I will then return to California, a part of America which I admire enormously—will go from there to Japan. In Japan I intend to study the method and the education of their ordinary artisans and to try and understand how it is that every ordinary Japanese workman has got this delicacy of hand, this feeling of beauty and this perfectly masterful power of design which are characteristics of their work. I am a wanderer by nature and I hardly know when I will be in Europe. I will sail for Japan about the 15th of August.

✂ *A report of Wilde's lecture in Atlanta.*

1. Wilde toured the Catskills and the New Jersey shore before giving nine lectures in the Canadian Maritimes.

"Oscar Wilde on Cloaks," *The Atlanta Constitution* (Atlanta, GA), 6 July 1882, 7[1]

Yesterday morning was as cool as September, and as Oscar Wilde boarded the Georgia railroad train, he was enveloped in his esthetic cloth cloak with its figured silk lining. He also wore his broad-brimmed white hat, and as he pulled it closer down over his ears, he remarked:

"One of the things I liked most in the west was the broad-brimmed hats, and cloaks too. The cloak is the most perfect form of drapery ever invented. It never can be ungraceful. I hope, in time, to see it far more generally worn that at present."[2]

Mr. Wilde lectured in Augusta last night.

"Oscar Dear, Oscar Dear!" *The News and Courier* (Charleston, SC), 8 July 1882, 4[3]

THE ORIGINAL OF "BUNTHORNE" APPEARS IN CHARLESTON.

Mr. Wilde's Advent at the Charleston Hotel—Waiting at the Ladies' Entrance—The Gathering Crowd—The Aesthetic Escapes by the Elevator—Barely has Time to take a Bath and brush his Long Hair and Mix his [?Tod] when a Reporter Calls—An Amusing Interview.

The arrival of the apostle of modern Aestheticism was an event which would have been marked by something of a demonstration, but for the fact that very few people knew at what hour the apostle would reach the city. A few moments after 1 o'clock yesterday an open carriage stopped in front of the ladies' entrance to the Charleston Hotel. From this emerged first a small but good looking American citizen, a little off color; then a dapper little red whiskered man, and finally two hundred pounds avoirdupois of aesthetic human flesh and bones done up in a mouse-colored velveteen shooting jacket and salt and pepper small clothes. The head was ornamented with long ambrosial locks of very dark hair, and capped with a broad brim, dim colored slouch hat, something after the style

1. H & S, b90.
2. This is presumably a reference to the dress of the miners Wilde encountered in Leadville (see "Wilde," *The Evening Telegram* (Providence, RI), 26 Sep. 1882, 1, p. 464). Wilde would also advocate cloaks in his lecture on *Dress*: "I would point out how graceful and comfortable the cloak worn in the time of Charles I was, how it could be thrown on one side when the weather was warm, and wrapped around the body when cold: how graceful the folds of such a garment were, compared with the hideous incongruity of modern garments." (Dibb, 273.)
3. H & S, b91. Reprinted in Mikhail, 96–100; and H & S, 162–5. Quoted in OWDA, 374.

of Buffalo Bill or Texas Jack.[1] "That's him," cried Ingliss, the barber, who had come out to see the sight, and there was a rush of the few persons who were loafing about the hotel in the direction of the show, while the store fronts in the immediate vicinity were speedily adorned with idle salesmen and drummers. The door of the ladies' entrance being locked, the 200 pounds of aestheticism posed about on the door steps, grim and dusty, and uncomfortable, but looking all the same like a magnified photograph of Geo. Denham in the role of "Bunthorne." There was no mistaking his identity. The face, form, figure, attitude and movement of the man brought "Bunthorne" forcibly to mind, and caused the spectators to look at once for the "Twenty love-sick maidens" who invariably accompany that aesthetical hero. The Reporter who had been sent to describe the event caught himself whistling the refrain which has of late become so popular:

Oscar dear, Oscar, dear,
How utterly, flutterly utter you are;
Oscar Dear, Oscar, Dear,
I think you are awfully wild, ta-ta.[2]

The door being at length opened Mr. Wilde was ushered in by an army of waiters, while his manager went around to the main entrance followed by the crowd and wrote upon the hotel register, "Oscar Wilde and servant of Ireland." The apostle was then hurried into the elevator and was anon comfortably put away in room 111.

THE INTERVIEW.

An hour or two afterward the Reporter sent up his card and was ushered into the awful presence of the founder of aestheticism, the apostle of decorative art, the only genuine Oscar Wilde. The off-colored *valet de chambre* "of Ireland" stood sentry at the outer door. To his knock came in sweet scents the answer to "come," and the Reporter entered the room now rendered famous.

The great aesthete was "lolling" upon a sofa, his ambrosial locks parted in the middle resting upon a pillow, and his feet, ornamented with red-striped socks and sharp-pointed shoes, occupying the other end of the sofa. Mr. Wilde wore the same mouse-coloured velveteen shooting jacket which he wore on entering the hotel, and the same pepper-and-salt small clothes, but his person showed evidences of a bath and the minor details of his costume were more attractively arranged. The ferocious "Buffalo Bill" slouch hat had been laid aside.

1. William Frederick "Buffalo Bill" Cody (1846–1917) was an American bison hunter and showman. John "Texas Jack" Baker Omohundro (1846–1880) was an American frontier scout, cowboy, and actor. Both were photographed in the 1870s wearing light-coloured slouch hats.

2. Lyrics from *Oscar Dear* by M. H. Rosenfeld, one of a number of comic songs about Wilde published in 1882. See Mason, S. *Oscar Wilde and the Aesthetic Movement*; and Sturgis, 230/221.

From his collar there hung the ends of a salmon colored silk neck handkerchief, while a pale violet-colored kerchief peeped out from the breast pocket of his coat. In front of the sofa upon which he lolled was a cane-bottom chair upon which stood a large tumbler filled with a liquid of some kind, and out of which protruded the end of two straws which ever and anon were conveyed to the lips of the apostle. Sundry pieces of lemon in the tumbler suggested lemonade, but the color of the fluid, a bright yellow, suggested "sunflower seed tea." A few moments later a gentle aroma of rum floated through the air, and at that moment the Reporter found himself in the hands of the great aesthete, who inquired very sweetly and solicitously after his reportorial health, at the same time requesting him to be seated. Then the business of the interview began. The apostle resumed his lolling attitude on the sofa and gave himself up languidly to the task of answering the questions that were put to him.

Mr. Wilde looks like an enlarged and magnified "lah-da-dah" young man and speaks with the "don't-you-know" yawp of the day.

"Ya'as," he said, "it was a very dusty journey don't you know, but the kentry is fine, a beautiful wooded kentry all the way from Augusta here."

ART IN THE SOUTH.

R. You've seen a good deal of the Southern people. What do you think of their capacity for aesthetic culture?

W. Well, you see, one can travel through a country, and see so very few of the people. It's awful when one realizes how *few* people one knows in the world; but upon the whole I'd rather travel through a country rapidly. I like the Southern people, although you have let the Northern people get ahead of you in art. I think you are more adapted to the cultivation of art. I mean decorative art. You are of a warmer temperament and of a more imaginative turn of mind, don't you know. I should think you would turn your attention more to art. You have magnificent forests, beautiful flowers. What you want is more diversity. I saw in your paper today that two carloads of furniture had been bought for an infirmary here and brought all the way from Chicago. Now, why shouldn't you make that furniture here in Charleston? The aim of our school is to educate the people into the love of the beautiful and to apply it to practical use in the manufacture of useful articles.

THE LILY AND THE SUNFLOWER.

R. Let me ask—if you won't think the question trifling—why is it that you are always pictured as posed with a sunflower of drooping over a lily?

W. Certainly I'll explain. (With a smile and a change of posture.) When the few of us young men got together to organize this movement we selected the lily and the sunflower for several reasons—as emblems of aestheticism. In the first place the outlines of these flowers are distinct and easily reproduced for wall papering and other proper uses. Now, there's your beautiful and fragrant Southern magnolia. Nothing could be more beautiful or more fragrant; ah, but you can't draw or paint the magnolia. Its outlines are not distinct, don't you see. And then the lily has always been associated with art in Italy and the sunflower with reverence and worship in the East. In Japan the worship of the lily is the foundation of religion; its emblem the pure white flower springing from a bed of dross. The sunflower, too, is the emblem of the sun worshippers.

R. The sunflower, as you know, grows wild in this land, and the people of Charleston, white and black, are affected with the craze. I saw a number of colored women on the Fourth of July parading the streets with huge sunflowers in their dresses and hats. Do you think this is owing to the love of the beautiful?

W. Who can say? To live one's life is to love the beautiful. I think the people are awakening to a sense of the beautiful. As you say, you have lived all your life among sunflowers, and never until now noticed anything beautiful in them. That is the mission of true art—to make us pause and look at a thing a second time. At Atlanta all the girls that passed the hotel wore sunflowers, and at Mobile an enterprising little boy made twenty-five dollars selling sunflowers to the people who came to my lecture. That boy will be a Congressman yet—who knows. It was a fortunate and harmless speculation for him. I wish all other speculations were as harmless and as innocent— (this *a propos* of nothing.)

R. It is printed in the newspapers that you are engaged to and will marry a young lady of Boston.[1] It would interest the ladies of Charleston and the South to hear whether this is true or not.

W. Ah! (with a smile). That you know is one of those things which must always remain a vast mystery. But if a man is engaged to be married he shouldn't come to the South, (this with an air which suggested "taffy.")

A gentleman who was in the room here suggested that the fair sex of Boston were hard to beat for beauty, to which the aesthetic apostle replied that that was true, but the women of the South were, upon the whole, much more beautiful than any that he had seen in this country. Their color and features, he said, were richer and more regular, and at this point the manager entered to bring an invitation to the apostle to visit the Charleston Club, and the Reporter seized the opportunity to take his leave and bow himself from the too awfully awful presence of the mighty aesthete.

✂ *A report of Wilde's lecture in Charleston.*

1. Reports were circulating that Wilde was engaged to Maud Howe (1854–1948), the daughter of poet and abolitionist Julia Ward Howe (1819–1910), whose Newport, Rhode Island, summer house he had stayed at in June (Fitzsimons, 112).

"Newport Gossip," *The Sunday Herald* (Boston, MA), 23 July 1882, 9

✂ *Several paragraphs that are unrelated to Wilde.*

Mr. Oscar Wilde left Newport for New York after giving a little dinner party at Hartmann's, the cuisine of which found much favor with him. He was introduced to its delightful mysteries by that well-informed *bon vivant*, his Uncle Sam Ward. I told you in the edition of Wednesday evening last of the entertainment given in his honor on Monday by Chaplain Hayward on board the United States war vessel Minnesota, but had not space to dilate upon the lightsome play of humor which marked the young aesthete in the catboat that bore him and his companions to the shore at the close of the dinner.[1] Oscar was in a frolicsome mood; a fog was falling, and the air was damp and chilly. Remarking that the texture of his white pongee silk coat was not suited to the atmosphere, I regret to say that the lecturer on 'The Decorative Arts' was forced to wrap himself up in one of the stuffed cushions covered with homely checked gingham! He did this laughingly at the suggestion of the skipper of the Zippo, who was disposed to be friendly. Mr. Wilde thought that, instead of eating down below decks, we should have dined up in the shrouds somewhere, stationed upon one of those convenient platforms, to which delicacies should have been hauled up by ropes! Guns should have been fired—bring me guns! A court-martial ought to have been held, and William, all in the Downs, should have parted from Susan, all in the dumps![2] Men who would not converse should be confined in the cockpit. In moments of ennui we would bombard the Casino; and, if perchance we sunk a boat full of journalists, *par hazard*, what reason for regret? Thus Oscar rattled on; custom cannot stale his infinite variety. From this [?frothy] badinage he passed as swiftly to the consideration of the relative merits of the

FAMOUS NOVELISTS,

Alphonse Daudet and Emile Zola.[3] Needless to say, he prefers the former, so superior in imaginative power to the gross writer who has aimed to substitute a

1. The correspondent's article, "Newport," *The Sunday Herald* (Boston, MA), 16 July 1882, 8, briefly mentions that Wilde is in the city and that there was an entertainment given on board the *Minnesota* "on Wednesday" (12 July). Another Newport correspondent reported that Wilde "visited the gunnery ship Minnesota today and dined with the chaplain on board" in a report filed on 17 July ("Newport Notes," *The New York Herald* (New York, NY), 18 July 1882, 4). Wilde lectured in Newport on the 15th.

2. The reference is to W. G. Wills's play *William and Susan* (1880), a nautical melodrama based on Douglas Jerrold's earlier play *Black-Eyed Susan* (1829).

3. Alphonse Daudet (1840–1897) and Émile Édouard Charles Antoine Zola (1840–1902) were French novelists. Later, in his dialogue *The Decay of Lying* (1889; revised 1891), Wilde would

purely scientific basis for the only true one in art: beauty. Mr. Wilde does not admire the nervous, sensual family whose mixed career pervades Zola's works, but he recognizes the power with which they are drawn;[1] he prefers 'Pot-Bouille,' one inexcusable chapter excepted, to 'Nana,' for which there is no excuse.[2] Daudet wins his undivided allegiance. He found 'Jack' stupid, but 'Numa Roumestan,' 'Le Nabab,' and, more particularly, 'Les Rois in Exil' delighted him.[3] He thought Henry James, Jr.'s critique on Alphonse Daudet, in a recent number of the Atlantic Monthly, rather weak and unsatisfying.[4] Returning to Zola, a little-known novel of his in the earlier days of his career pleased Mr. Wilde's sense of beauty. You may remember it—the story of the boy and girl who elope after an episode of a wall and well that divide, *à la* Cupid and Psyche, their respective homes. One incident—that of the boy becoming angry and throwing a stone into the well which has been accustomed to mirror the faces of the lovers who have never met save as reflected in its surface—particularly pleases the poet-aesthete. When the waters are thus troubled the boy has a sudden fear that he will never see his fair neighbour's face again. However, they elope, and the tragic ending shows the young girl killed by a stray shell from a battlefield, and dying "with the mute reproach of virginity in her eyes!"[5]

Oscar is now reading everything he can find about Japan; with our octavo standard ones he is scarcely satisfied, and Chaplain Hayward has recommended

---

declare through the character of Vivian that Zola's "work is entirely wrong from beginning to end, and wrong not on the ground of morals, but on the ground of art." (CW iv, 79.2–4.) Daudet "is better. He has wit, a light touch and an amusing style." (CW iv, 79.17.) In an article for *The Pall Mall Gazette* Wilde would compare Zola's "unimaginative realism" with Balzac's "imaginative reality" (13 Sep. 1886; CW vi, No. 37, lines 17–20). Chris Healy remembered Wilde describing Zola as "a third-rate Flaubert." (Mikhail, 385.) Lot 25 in the Tite Street auction was "M. Zola's Works, &c. 23 vols." (Munby, 376).

1. The Rougon-Macquart family featured in 20 novels by Zola. See also *The Pictorial World* (London, UK), 19 Dec. 1891, pp. 600–1. Wilde would disparagingly refer to the cycle in an article for *The Pall Mall Gazette*: "[...] the dreadful Rougon-Macquart family with whose misdeeds M. Zola is never weary of troubling us" (13 Mar. 1885; CW vi, No. 13, lines 42–3).

2. Zola's novel, *Pot-Bouille*, was serialised in *Le Gaulois* between January and April 1882. It is a satire of the manners of the bourgeois residents of a Parisian apartment block. *Nana* (1880) follows the eponymous character's rise from street-walker to high-class prostitute in late 1860s Paris. The novel was popular and drew praise from Gustave Flaubert and Edmond de Goncourt.

3. *Jack* (1876) is about a boy of seven who is sent to a boarding school; *Le Nabob* (1877) chronicles the rise and fall of a man who has made his fortune in Tunisia; *Les Rois en Exil* (1879) is about the deposed monarch of a Balkan state who lives in exile in Paris and dreams of returning to his throne; *Numa Roumestan* (1880) is a comedy that contrasts the character of the typical Provençal with the French of the north.

4. Henry James Jr is the author; Henry James Sr, his father, was an American theologian. James's article on Alphonse Daudet appeared in the *Atlantic Monthly, 49,* June 1882, 846–51.

5. *La Fortune des Rougon* (*The Fortune of the Rougons*; 1871), Zola's first novel in the Rougon-Macquart cycle.

to him a capital French volume, 'Le Japan de Nos Jours,'[1] and has told him he ought not to fail to see the Japanese returning home laden with camelias at a certain season of the year. Mr. Wilde thinks that Japanese young women will at least be 'decorative.' Among other subjects he spoke of music and painting. He is always sorry when Alma Tadema, who, too, is 'decorative,' attempts to paint any but purely lay figures, his men and women being mere accessories, and not human beings.[2] He regards Mme. Patti—to skip to lyric art—as a charming music box, and recalls with regret the spectacle of 4000 persons assembled at Cincinnati and listening to her singing of "Home, Sweet Home," a sweet ballad which ought to be reserved for the drawing room.[3] Mr. Wilde thinks that the lower classes in London care more for a higher order of music than the corresponding classes of Americans. In London they are not to be caught with cheap patriotic clap-trap. He prefers Nilsson to Patti, both as singer and actress, and instances her Margherita in 'Mefistofele' as a noble achievement.[4] You may not be surprised to learn that he apostrophizes her throat as "a marble pillar." On the whole, to return to Newport from the aesthetic clouds, Mr. Wilde was very well received. He won the respect of most of those who had been prejudiced against him, thanks to a lecture more practical than purely theoretical, and in 'society' he was a sufficient success to make his stay here agreeable. He is certainly, with all the affectations that have become second nature, a brilliant conversationalist and a most interesting individuality. As an example of his peculiarities, the following will serve: "What will you have to drink?" asked a friend in the Casino restaurant. "Oh, some of your American drinks, full of gorgeous coloring." "Do you mean gin-fizz?" queried a sprightly foreigner in his delightful *patois*. No, he did not mean gin-fizz, and no one could think what he did mean. At last the young lion tossed his mane impetuously and gave it a name. "Well, a sherry cobbler, then!" When it

1. *Le Japon de nos jours* (*The Japan of Today*; 1877), by Georges Bousquet (1845–1937). Bousquet was a French legal scholar who in the 1870s worked in Japan on the drafting of the country's civil code. His two volume book covers Japanese history, family life, religion, and politics, but the chapters on architecture, sculpture, painting, and dance will have been why the book was recommended to Wilde.

2. Lawrence Alma-Tadema (1836–1912) was a Dutch-British artist, best known for his depictions of classical antiquity.

3. Wilde attended Patti's concert in Cincinnati on 20 February. She sang the aria *Bel raggio* from Rossini's *Semiramide* (1823) and *Home, Sweet Home* by composer Henry Bishop with lyrics by John Howard Payne. She also appeared in the third act of Giuseppe Verdi's *Aida*.

4. Nilsson appeared in London as Margherita in Arrigo Boito's opera *Mefistofele* (1868) on a number of occasions. Wilde's most recent opportunity to witness her in the role would have been in July 1881, during her season at Her Majesty's Theatre. Wilde would attend Nilsson's concert at New York's Steinway Hall on 2 December 1882 ("Mme. Christine Nilsson," *The Chicago Daily Tribune* (Chicago, IL), 5 Dec. 1882, 5, p. 777). Despite his stated preference for Nilsson over Patti, Wilde would later have Lord Henry take Dorian Gray to a Patti concert (CW iii, 76.6, 81.20, 84.22).

was brought the comment was irresistible that there wasn't much "gorgeous coloring" in it. The poet regarded the amber brown fluid pensively, shook up the ice and said: "Oh, I don't know, I don't know;

A VERY GOOD TONE!"

✂ *Several paragraphs that are unrelated to Wilde.*

"Oscar Wilde," *Brooklyn Union* (Brooklyn, NY), 29 July 1882, 4

Oscar Wilde, who arrived in New York this morning from Long Branch, told a reporter that he dined with General Grant last evening,[1] and was going to Peekskill tonight to spend Sunday with Mr. Beecher.[2]

Utica Morning Herald and Daily Gazette (Utica, NY), 1 Aug. 1882, 2[3]

Oscar Wilde says he intends to visit Saratoga, August 10, and will lecture there. "Then I shall go to Richfield Springs and probably lecture there.[4] As to my movements after that I am unable now to speak. I intend to go to Japan."

"Pursuing a Venus," *The Chicago Daily Tribune* (Chicago, IL), 12 Aug. 1882, 6[5]

Oscar Wilde's Story of the Discovery of Mrs. Langtry.

Town.

"There are but two purely Greek things now in Europe," says Mr. Wilde, "one is the Venus of Milo, the other Mrs. Langtry!" The effect of Mrs. Langtry's

1. Ulysses S. Grant (1822–1885) served as the 18th president of the United States. He had led the Union Army to victory in the Civil War. Wilde and Grant conversed about Wilde's planned visit to Japan, with Grant advising Wilde to extend the trip to Siam ("Grant and Oscar," *The Times Democrat* (New Orleans, LA), 4 Aug. 1882, 6).

2. Beecher had a residence at Peekskill, New York, 50 miles / 80 km from New York City.

3. Quoted in Cooper (Catskills lectures, 9–19 August 1882).

4. Wilde lectured on *The Decorative Arts* in Saratoga Springs on August 10 and Richfield Springs on 14 August.

5. Reprinted as "Pursuing a Venus," *Portland Daily Press* (Portland, ME), 20 Sep. 1882, 2.

Figure 15. Lillie Langtry, whom Wilde befriended in London and greeted on her arrival in New York. "I would rather have discovered Mrs. Langtry than have discovered America."

beauty is, he estimates, that of extreme delicacy produced by really strong lines. The mouth is large; the jaw is heavily outlined; and yet, as the Pantheon, while in reality a large building, gives the impression of being a more delicate structure than it really is, so the "Jersey Lily's" face conveys an idea of softness and grace infinitely charming.[1] No photograph can do her justice, he holds, "for her complexion is like ivory stained with rose!" Even Millais has been comparatively unsuccessful with her portrait. He can paint children and men, but not a beautiful woman. Mr. Wilde considers Mrs. Langtry "the most charming of companions." There is no other woman in the world with whom he would rather go to look at a picture, or see a play or give a new book to. It is remarkable, however, that she herself is entirely untouched by the feeling she inspires. "She is beautiful and virgin as a fountain, and as cold!" It is a great treat to hear Mr. Wilde describe how he and a friend, an artist, presumably Mr. Frank Miles,[2] "discovered" Mrs. Langtry several years ago, when he was still at Oxford. One night at the Lyceum Theatre Oscar and his friend saw a beautiful unknown seated with a gentleman in a box. They asked every one in the house whom they knew and all the officials the name of this divinity, but no one could tell them. When the play was over they waited to see her get into the carriage and then rushed along the Strand in a state of enthusiasm only possible in young men and artists. They told everybody that they had discovered the Venus of Milos there in London, in the flesh, but no one could enlighten them concerning the incognita, and Mr. Wilde returned to Oxford, leaving his friend in town to prosecute the search. One day he received a telegram: "Come at once. I have found the Venus of Milos." He sought an audience with the university powers, whom he much distressed by a fable as to pressing family matters in London, and, gaining permission, took the first train to town and a hansom to Chelsea. Entering his friend's studio, he found Mrs. Langtry there, sitting for her portrait! At that time she knew so few people in London that they might have been counted on her fingers, but Mr. Wilde and his friend "told nations she was beautiful," and interested in particular the late Duchess of Westminster, and it was at Grosvenor House that the now celebrated beauty, "Jersey Lily," made what was virtually her social début. Mr. Wilde regrets almost that Mrs. Langtry should have decided to come to the United States to act before she is apt to be something more than merely a beautiful woman and an indifferent actress. He believes that she had the making of an accomplished artiste and in time will prove herself one, since she has that effectual substitute for genius—

1. Lillie Langtry hailed from the island of Jersey. Millais's portrait of her is titled *A Jersey Lily* (1878). "Pantheon" may be a slip for "Parthenon", a more common reference point for Wilde.

2. George Francis "Frank" Miles (1852–1891) was an English artist whom Wilde met at Oxford. The two lived together in London after university and before Wilde left for America. Miles introduced Wilde to Langtry after meeting (and sketching) her at a reception hosted by Lady Seabright (Sturgis, 110–11/109).

ambition. It was not singular that she should have made one of the best débuts on record, for her training as a "professional beauty" had been of great service to her. It was nothing new to her to know that a whole theatre full of people were fixing their lorgnets upon her face. People who are used to being stared at are obliged to cultivate the quality of unconsciousness of self, and Mrs. Langtry had taken a long course of lessons wherever she went. Among her fine qualities is, says Mr. Wilde, "a voice as musical as Sarah Bernhardt's." She possesses, moreover, rare powers of mimicry. He would like to see her play *Rosalind*, for she is the only woman of his acquaintance who would be apt to look like a boy in the doublet and hose, the contours of her uncorsetted figure giving her advantages in this respect. At all events he regrets that she does not create an entirely new part, in which she will run no danger of comparison with anyone else, since popular criticism consists so largely of comparison.

"Sizing Us Up," *The Sunday Herald* (Boston, MA), 20 Aug. 1882, 12[1]

Oscar Wilde's Opinions of America and Americans.

Some Harsh but Justifiable Criticism.

The Poet Five Times in Love Here.

(FROM OUR SPECIAL CORRESPONDENT.)

RICHFIELD SPRINGS, N. Y., Aug. 17, 1882. I have intercepted the laureate of art and unconventionality here, on his way to New York. He has grown more unconventional and conspicuous in his dress since I first met him, and the crude notions of America which then possessed him have been crystallized into positive opinions. He is some months older, too, and these have been eventful months to him. He says he has enjoyed every day of his lecture tour, and I have no doubt of it, for he has gained five pounds since he landed in January, and now turns the scale at 185. Yesterday it was so cool here that gentlemen wore overcoats and

1. Reprinted, minus the final paragraph, as "Sizing Us Up," *Daily Telegraph* (Saint John, NB), 23 Aug. 1882; and "Sizing Us Up," *The Daily Examiner* (San Francisco), 3 Sep. 1882, 1 (which is quoted in Rodecape, L. F. (1940). Gilding the sunflower: a study of Oscar Wilde's visit to San Francisco. *California Historical Society Quarterly*, 19, 97–112, 106–7). Excerpted in "Social and Personal," *Albany Evening Journal* (Albany, NY), 23 Aug. 1883, 2; and "Oscar Wilde Rebuking American Rudeness," *Utica Weekly Herald and Gazette and Courier* (Utica, NY), 29 Aug. 1882, 3. Quoted in "The Last of Oscar Wilde," *The Chicago Sunday Tribune* (Chicago, IL), 27 Aug. 1882, 4; and OWDA, 385. The author appears to have introduced fabricated or heightened elements into what is otherwise a genuine interview.

ladies shawls, but the Prophet of Beauty radiated on the piazza of the Spring House in a rather-too-short pair of white duck pantaloons; beside which, his costumes consisted of a gray Scotch cutaway, well worn, a broad, soft brown hat, a long, sailor-knotted, terra cotta necktie, over a broken-cornered collar, low shoes, black socks and white kid gloves. Nobody else in town wore any garments like unto one of these; so he was much besieged and bestared at.

"Yes," he said, responsive to my salutation and inquiries. "I am raking in the shekels—if that is what you call it in America. I have had large audiences, have made considerable money, have had tremendous experiences of various kinds, and now I am going home. To write a book about it? Yes, certainly. I do not now think of any other Englishman who has seen America so thoroughly as I have. I have seen the splendid South in its glory, and have eaten of its savory hoe cake, have partaken of New England's pie and pancakes, have witnessed the wonderful growth of the North-west, have seen the sun rise and set on your great midland ocean of grass and flowers, have camped with the miners of the Pacific slope and taken pot-luck with the Mormons, and now I am going home. About American women? Certainly. I have not found among them very much of the highest order of beauty. An astonishing amount of prettiness, daintiness, intelligence, vivacity, personal attractiveness—but of classic beauty not a great deal. In Europe there are only two Greek things—the Venus of Milo and Mrs. Langtry, and Mrs. Langtry has the advantage of having arms and movements. Do I think she is

THE MOST HANDSOME WOMAN

in the world? I hesitate to say so now. I said so once to Ruskin when I first saw her, and he answered, 'That utterance is a form of blasphemy. You might as well say of a particular flower that it is the finest flower in the world—and the world so full of flowers supremely beautiful.' The beauty of many of the prettiest American women seems to me so perishable. It is the beauty of youth, of life, fading tomorrow; but the highest form of beauty is perennial. I shall write sonnets to Mrs. Langtry when she is 95.

"That is a natural enough question of yours, 'How does Mr. Langtry take it?' He takes it philosophically. Perhaps he feels, somehow, that he is an intruder, because—No, little boy, I don't want to buy one of your sunflowers. Run away now and sell them to somebody else. Heavens! the idea of picking that gorgeous flower! The sunflower ought never to be picked. It is splendid on the stem, but preposterous in a vase or a girl's corsage. That is quite like marrying a beautiful woman. I have fallen into the habit of thinking that the husbands of beautiful women belong to the criminal classes.[1] They have committed sacrilege and rob-

1. Wilde would later commit this epigram to paper in a notebook he kept around 1890: "The husbands of beautiful women belong to the criminal classes: the husbands of plain women have

bery in attempting to monopolize what belongs to all mankind. They are fit candidates for the penitentiary. What if somebody should lock up the air and sunshine?"

When I had first spoken to Mr. Wilde, he sat alone on the porch reading Tennyson's poems, which he usually carries around under his arm. There was nobody near him, and few seemed to notice him. But now it was noised about that Oscar Wilde had come, that this flashing object on the piazza was he, and already 50 women, girls and children were gathered around as if he were a wild Choctaw or a polar bear, or a man from the moon, and groups of handsomely dressed ladies stood and gazed at him at a distance of six or eight feet, evidently catching all they could of the conversation that was conducted in a low tone.

"The most striking thing I have noticed," he repeated, dropping his voice another note or two and laughing, "is the curiosity of your people. They have reduced staring to a fine art. I have seen an exhibition of ill-breeding and impudence that amounts to positive barbarism. I do not let it trouble me, for I cultivate indifference to all such vulgarity.

THE PHILOSOPHY OF LIFE

is never to be annoyed. I am satisfied now that there is no affliction on earth that a man of serene temper cannot get used to in six weeks.

"Oh, yes; of course I have met thousands of refined and well-bred people who would be incapable of any discourtesy, but these are in a great and surprising minority. I cannot help thinking that good breeding is commoner in England. When Gladstone or any other well-known Englishman appears in public, he is kindly let alone—neither stared at nor followed. Even there, though, there was a furor over Mrs. Langtry, and, when I took her to the Grosvenor gallery once, she escaped from the mob with great difficulty. But the people who are thus intrusive and impudent are the lower class of our people, while here they seem to include the middle and nearly the upper class. For instance, in Saratoga, last week, I stopped at the States and Congress Hall—two of the best hotels, which one would suppose would be patronized by cultured people. While talking with Judge Brady there was a great crowd came around us, mostly women, and, finding it a bore to be thus stared at, I moved on into the office.[1] There they came flocking after us. I went to the billiard room, but found no refuge there. The women rushed there—ladies in silks, and crapes, and laces, with diamonds in their ears,

---

married into them" (Small, 145). He included a shorter version in the 1891 revised edition of his novel *The Picture of Dorian Gray*: "'The husbands of very beautiful women belong to the criminal classes,' said Lord Henry, sipping his wine." (CW iii, 317.20–1.) See Marland, R. (2021). Oscar Wilde on the husbands of beautiful women. *Notes and Queries*, *68*, 331–2.

1. Judge John Riker Brady (1822–1891) was a Justice of the New York Supreme Court.

bringing their daughters with them! To balk the pursuit utterly, I fled to the bar room. Will you believe me that they came there—in 10 minutes, 50 or 100 of them—filling up the place almost. It seemed to me a most painful and dreadful thing—the bold-faced staring and half-audible comment.[1] It seemed much worse than the conduct of abandoned women. Why didn't I say: 'What'll you have, ladies?' Oh, it wouldn't have done any good, and all the country would have said I had insulted the ladies at Saratoga.[2] There they came with a rush, and there, before and among them, were the horse racers and gamblers of Saratoga, smoking, drinking and talking loud. Was it not a horror? I was stupefied, and said to myself: 'What land is this I have come to?'

"Yes, as you say, I do not travel under normal conditions. I do not see the same average of people that others see. An atmosphere of

CURIOSITY AND IMPERTINENCE

seems to be created wherever I walk. Wretched me! I, who plead for gentleness and kindliness and gracious courtesy, am doomed to be the destroyer of courtesy every day and hour. I, who preach the importance of good manners, am the very Attila of good manners!"[3]

A group of children were looking up into his face, saying: "Here he is! That's Oscar Wilde!" etc. One of them stumbled over his patent leathers, and another, a boy of 8 or 10, came up boldly, put a hand on the white linen thigh of the guest

1. The Saratoga correspondent of the *Inter Ocean* reported that one woman stood before Wilde and exclaimed "Well! I'm glad I've seen a gorilla at last!" ("A Chicago Widow," *The Daily Inter Ocean* (Chicago, IL), 31 Aug. 1882, 9).

2. After this interview appeared some journalists attacked Wilde as he had predicted (see e.g. "Oscar Wilde's Insolence," *The Daily Inter Ocean* (Chicago, IL), 9 Sep. 1882, 12), although others took his side (see e.g. "Saratoga Springs," *The Courier-Journal* (Louisville, KY), 3 Sep. 1882, 8). The *Inter Ocean* paraphrased Wilde's remarks in an unflattering manner: "In a recent interview, he [Wilde] declares that the American people, particularly the women, are a set of rude and vulgar boors; that they have no taste in dress, no refinement of manner, no ability in conversation, and lack the attractions, moral, mental, and physical, which the ideal being should possess." The *Inter Ocean* article was reprinted elsewhere with the comments ascribed to Wilde placed inside quotation marks as if they had been taken down verbatim ("Kicked by an Ass," *The Cleveland Leader* (Cleveland, OH), 15 Sep. 1882, 4).

3. The following February, the New York correspondent of the *Chicago Tribune* remembered conducting this interview: "'I cannot understand this impudent curiosity,' he [Wilde] said to me in August at Richfield Springs. 'It is an astonishing spectacle. If they stare so at me, and run me down, and hedge me in, how must it be with Mr. Longfellow, and Herbert Spencer, and Darwin, and other such illustrious men?' 'They are let alone,' I said. 'When Gen. Grant travels people keep at a respectful distance.' 'Well, how do you account for the difference?' he persisted. 'Why is this?' I did not think it would be quite polite to tell him; and he went on: 'When I get back to England I shall write a book on Americans and their overmastering curiosity. Surely there was never anything like it on earth,'" ("New York Gossip," *The Chicago Sunday Tribune* (Chicago, IL), 18 Feb. 1883, 9).

and said in a high, rasping, nasal voice: "Gimme yer card, if yer please!" "Not now—I am busy," said Mr. Wilde; "by and by, perhaps."

"There's a specimen American child," he continued. "The children here are unrestrained savages. I never saw handsomer children than these little Americans, but they are left uncivilized, to grow up hoydens and blackguards. Such juvenile impudence exists nowhere else in the world. Only occasionally do I see your children pay any respect to their elders, even to their parents. It seems to me dreadful. Their audacity seems to me almost depravity. It cannot help harming the rising generation.[1] Yet I love children. They are living flowers. I think of adopting one or two.

"When I marry that Boston lady?[2] Don't speak of it! She is a charming lady, but no such thing as marriage was ever thought of by either of us. It was unspeakably cruel to set such a story afloat and cable it across the sea as they did. Your newspapers have been reasonably good to me, but I don't like them wholly. They are splendid and wonderful news gatherers, but they overdo it. They invade every home like the Goths, intrude on personal rights and make private reserve impossible. Reverence, I fear, is dead in America. I do not mean religious reverence—that I would care less about; I mean a true respect for personal liberty and dignity.

"Marry? Dear me, no! I never shall marry—till I find the one lady, beautiful in person and soul, who will let me go into raptures over all the other lovely women; who, when I come home and wildly say, 'My dear, I have seen the most beautiful and charming creature in the world!' would encourage me and sympathize with

MY PASSION,

and bring my slippers and tea and say, 'Now come and tell me all about this lovely creature, and you must go and see her again right away.'

"'Right away?' Oh, yes; I have learned nearly all of your Americanisms now, and have even adopted some of your most expressive slang, for slang is the reservoir and fountain of language. Well, as I was saying, I have been madly in love five times since I have been here—in San Francisco, in New Orleans, in Kalama-

1. Wilde expanded upon this idea in an article for *The Court and Society Review* titled "The American Invasion": "From its earliest years, every American child spends most of its time in correcting the faults of its father and mother. [...] In fact, it may be truly said that no American child is ever blind to the deficiencies of its parents, no matter how much it may love them." (23 Mar. 1887; CW vi, No. 55, lines 82–100.)

2. Maud Howe: see p. 441, note 1.

zoo and twice in New England—and I don't know what would have become of me if my agent hadn't dragged me along.[1]

"Much as I had heard of the progress and rapid growth of this country, it is quite startling to me, and somewhat alarming, too, for it is plain that the amenities of life, and the sweet graces which alone make existence worth having, are being forgotten and despised in the rush for riches. I wonder what this country, especially the West, will be in 20 or 30 years from now.

"Edwin Booth? Oh, yes, I have seen him often, and enjoyed his acting highly, of course. I gave a little breakfast party to him before leaving England.[2] The Prince of Wales was there, and I wondered what he would say to Mr. Booth, as I knew he had not been to see him play, and that, as he is so fond of the drama, the actor felt the seeming neglect. Shortly the prince said: 'I would like to know Mr. Booth.' So I brought Mr. Booth over and presented him. In the conversation the prince said: "I have not yet been to see you, Mr. Booth, for my friends said your support was very bad, and I felt it would be unfortunate to see you for the first time when you were poorly supported.' It seemed to me a most graceful speech.

"How came I to be such a devotee of beauty? I will shorten a long story. Coming into life, and finding myself born into a world where most of the things about me were ugly and uncouth, it seemed a tragedy, and I wept all through boyhood at my wretched lot. When I was 16 my father sent me to Florence.[3] On entering that lovely city my load of misery dropped off. Beauty surrounded me. I recognized in it the land from which I had long been in exile. Then I found that art was the panacea for all ills, and the love of art the secret of happiness. Recalled, I was sent to college at the beautiful city of Oxford, and there I met Ruskin, and in him saw the man I so long sought. He is possessed by the

TRUE SPIRIT OF ART.

A coterie of us there surrounded ourselves with beautiful things as far as practicable. A friend was admiring a set of blue china in my room one day, when I playfully remarked that I wished I could live up to the level of it. Next Sunday the dean preached to us on modern heathenism, and quoted my remark, in all seri-

1. Leaving aside whether Wilde really did list the cities where he had "been madly in love", it does seem that he had a brief romance in San Francisco. On 19 April [1882] he wrote a letter to "Darling Hattie", informing her that "I now realise that I am absolutely in love with you" (CL, 164–5). Sturgis, 246–7/236, suggests that the recipient may have been Hattie Crocker, the daughter of the director of the Southern Pacific Railroad, who resided in San Francisco.

2. Wilde may be referring to the séance that he and Frank Miles hosted in the spring of 1881. It was attended by Booth, the Prince of Wales, and other assorted luminaries (Friedman, 45).

3. Wilde first visited Florence in the summer of 1875 when he was 20 years old. He was not "sent" by his father. See also "Come and Gone," *The Cleveland Herald* (Cleveland, OH), 20 Feb. 1882, 8, p. 185, note 1.

ousness, as a very dreadful utterance. To be the subject of a sermon by the dean made me noted at once, and then Punch caricatured me, and Gilbert and Sullivan gave me the finishing touch in their grotesque and funny opera. My present 'mission,' as you call it, is to urge the introduction of beauty into the things of common life.

"No, I am not going home. I am now going to Japan, where I shall spend the autumn. That is a great and wonderful country—the home of art. The absurdity of our speaking of a people as heathen who can teach us in every form of beauty! I shall return here again on my way to England."

Mr. Wilde lectured here on Monday night to a large house. He wore his black velvet costume, ruffled shirt front and lace cuffs. Today he has gone to the Catskills—thence to Long Branch, and exit.

"Loveliness and Politeness," *The Sun* (New York, NY), 20 Aug. 1882, 5[1]

Many Cities in which Oscar Wilde has Seen the Handsomest American Girl.

The following extract from the New Orleans *Times* was shown to Oscar Wilde by a SUN reporter in a parlor car of the Long Beach railroad on Wednesday evening:

THE MOST BEAUTIFUL WOMAN IN AMERICA.

Oscar Wilde pronounced Miss Alsatia Allen of Montgomery, Ala., the most beautiful young lady he had seen in the United States.[2]

Mr. and Mrs. Steele Mackaye were in Mr. Wilde's party,[3] which was returning from Long Beach. Mr. Wilde was dressed in a light gray suit of Irish frieze, with a high-crowned slouch hat of light gray. He removed his hat as he read the

1. H & S, b92. Reprinted in H & S, 165–6. Quoted in OWDA, 388–9; Pearson, 75; and Sturgis, 256/245, 787 note 20/728 note 246 "Unfortunately, as Morse".

2. This paragraph was widely reprinted. The name is almost certainly incorrect: Wilde met and admired Miss Virginia Ball Allen (1861–1883). See also "Oscar Wilde," *The Montgomery Advertiser* (Montgomery, AL), 31 Jan. 1886, 3, pp. 580–1.

3. James Morrison Steele MacKaye (1842–1894) was an American playwright, theatrical producer, and inventor. Wilde was hoping to stage *The Duchess of Padua* in partnership with MacKaye, with Mary Anderson in the lead role. In a letter to Anderson, Wilde emphasised his confidence in MacKaye as the manager of the play, describing him as "a man of great practical knowledge, of exquisite taste, and sound experience. Except him there is no one can do it." (CL, 185.) In his review of Lillie Langtry's American stage debut for *The World* (New York), Wilde praised MacKaye—though without naming him—as "the master hand which designed the curtain at the Madison Square Theatre" (7 Nov. 1882; CW vi, No.7, 80–1).

paragraph, allowing his abundant long hair to descend about his face. Then he chuckled gently and said:

"That is a remark, my dear fellow, I suppose I have made of some lady in every city I have visited in this country. It could be appropriately made. American women are very beautiful, and some of the finest types of beauty I have ever seen I found in the South. But it is in the decay of manners that the thoughtful and well-bred American has serious cause for regret. I have repeatedly said this, but I am told in reply, 'We are still a young country. You must not be too severe upon us. Where we are raw and crude now these finer arts will come with time.' 'Ah, yes,' I answer, 'but when your country was still younger its manners were better. They have never been equal since to what they were in Washington's time—a man himself whose manners were irreproachable.' I believe a most serious problem for the American people to consider is the cultivation of better manners among its people. It is the most noticeable, the most painful defect in American civilization.

"I shall spend some weeks more in this country," Mr. Wilde continued. "I shall lecture at Long Branch, Cape May, and several other watering places.[1] I meet at these summer resorts people who are interested with me in these matters. Of course there are many disadvantages in lecturing in summer hotels. The lectures are apt to be badly managed, the rooms are often difficult to speak in, and there is an inevitable bustle and confusion, which nobody can help, and for which nobody is to blame. From America I shall go to Japan, the most highly civilized country on the globe. Nowhere else do good manners so universally prevail among all classes. The culture and attainments of these people are little understood in this country.

"Next to Japan is France, where in spite of frequent revolutions, good manners have reached a strange degree of perfection. If you visit France do not waste your time in Paris, among the ruined monuments of the empire, but go into the villages and the remote country hamlets, and note the instinctive politeness of the peasant, who will convince you that you have honored him and honored his country by coming into it.

"The Englishman abroad is in the main a man of good manners and an agreeable companion. I am a Celt, but I can tell the truth about him. At home the average Englishman is arrogant, ill-tempered, and tied down by prejudices which nothing will induce him to lay aside."

1. Wilde lectured at Long Branch on 22 August, Cape May on 26 August, and at a few other cities before taking most of September off from lecturing.

"A Chat With Oscar," *The Times* (Philadelphia, PA), 2 Sep. 1882, 5[1]

He is Going to Write a Book About the Country and the People.

HIS IMPRESSIONS OF AMERICA

Pleased With Newport and Disgusted With Long Branch and Fifth Avenue.

Special correspondence of THE TIMES.

CAPE MAY, August 30.

Oscar Wilde has been here with his sunflower and lily. He is going to write a book upon American life and manners. He said as much in a conversation the other night after his lecture at the Stockton. He is quietly collecting the material now. He will touch upon everything, from the beauty of true art to the price of potatoes. He says that he had had a better opportunity of acquainting himself with the subject than Charles Dickens had.[2] He had seen more of the country, met a greater number of representative people and made a closer study of our institutions and affairs. More than all, he flatters himself that he is entirely free from the prejudice which distorted the great novelist's vision, and can therefore draw a more truthful picture. He will not forget to speak his mind about the attentions, complimentary and otherwise, that have been paid to him. He will strike out from the shoulder at the Philistines who had been laughing at his legs, disturbing his lectures and burning him in effigy.

After all, Oscar is a very pleasant companion. Even the barbarians admit, after being ten minutes in his company, that he is observant and witty and a delightful talker. You don't mind his affectations after his tongue begins to go. He knows everything. He takes his morning paper with his coffee and roll, sitting in bed.[3] He is consequently at home on all the topics of the moment. He can make a rattling good argument for free trade from the English standpoint, as well as a touching plea from his own pedestal for Hogarth stovepipes; that is to say, pipes with a curve to them. He will chat with any decent-looking person. He had made it a point, he says, to meet and "draw out" the men of all classes. He particularly

1. Excerpted in "The Last of Oscar Wilde," *The Chicago Daily Tribune* (Chicago, IL), 5 Sep. 1882, 4; and the *Rochester Democrat and Chronicle* (Rochester, NY), 8 Sep. 1882, 2 (both cite their source as the *Philadelphia Press*). Also excerpted in *Decatur Weekly Republican* (Decatur, IL), 21 Sep. 1882, 3. Quoted in OWDA, 389–90, 396.

2. *American Notes for General Circulation* (1842) describes Dickens's travels in America from January to June 1842. The author ventured as far west as St. Louis and as far south as Richmond. Like Wilde, he visited Quebec.

3. Wilde told the audience of his first lecture in Chicago (13 February) that he was "in the habit of setting aside a pleasant half-hour for the perusal of the daily papers, a habit which had become a pleasant and delightful luxury in the morning." ("Oscar Wilde," *The Chicago Daily Tribune* (Chicago, IL), 14 Feb. 1882, 7.)

enjoys a study of those favorites of fortune who are commonly styled "self-made." They are "so rugged," he says, and so "truly racy of the soil."[1]

OSCAR AMONG THE LADIES.

United States Marshal Kerns took the apostle in charge here. The Marshal, you know, is completely up in art matters and is thoroughly en rapport with Wilde.[2] He introduced him to fifty ladies or more, who were delighted with the sensation. Then he got him into a private parlor with Ex-Mayor Stokley, Henry P. Brown, Assistant United States District Attorney, and two or three other gentlemen.[3] Oscar wore the extraordinary evening dress in which he had been lecturing. His legs, it was observed, are beginning to show the effect of constant work and travel. His black silk hose were not quite so well filled throughout as they might have been. Oscar said, in passing, that he did not see anything singular in his dress. It was the mode, he observed, "in Washington's time and is the only thing now permissible approaching a truly artistic conception." He could not understand how any gentleman could tolerate starched linen in summer, while as for himself, he prefers cambric for shirt bosoms, with a lace frill, so adjusted that it can be made to serve the office of the prevailing stiff and angular shirt collar. He wore no jewelry except a large ring on the index finger of his right hand. After he had got himself posed to his liking in a big arm chair a waiter was asked to be good enough to bring a bottle of wine and a box of cigars. That was a starter. The wine was old and the cigars were as black as ink; but they never phased Mr. Wilde. He smoked and drank and chatted until an unmentionable hour. Some one who got a glimpse of the merry company and a startling array of open-mouthed bottles in an atmosphere of smoke, started the rumor that a wicked attempt was being made to set Oscar drunk. But the wise did not interfere, for they knew that the Apostle of Beauty could put the whole crowd under the table and yet keep his own head as clear as a bell.

1. I.e. deeply connected to the land. In 1842, *The Nation* (the Irish nationalist newspaper of the "Young Ireland" movement) stated that its aim would be "to aid and organise the new movements going on among us; to make their growth deeper and more 'racy of the soil'; and above all, to direct the popular mind and the sympathies of educated men of all parties to the great end of Nationality."

2. James N. Kerns (c. 1829–1901) was made United States Marshal for the Eastern District of Pennsylvania in 1871 and held the post until 1887. The statement that he was "completely up in art matters" was presumably sarcastic. Marshal was best known for a scandal that had erupted in 1880 after it was shown that he had appointed hundreds of unqualified Republican sympathisers as Deputy Marshals with the intention of intimidating Democratic voters.

3. William Strumberg Stokley (1823–1902) served as the Mayor of Philadelphia from 1872 to 1881. Before entering politics he ran a confectionary business and worked for a volunteer fire company. Henry Billings Brown (1836–1913) was a judge of the United States District Court for the Eastern District of Michigan from 1875 to 1890. He was appointed to the Supreme Court in 1890.

A SHY YOUNG MAN.

Oscar said that he was pleased with his reception here, though he had to ride from the railroad station in a closed carriage and gain access to the hotel through a dining room window to avoid the eyes of a piazza full of women, who had gathered together in shining toilets to see the circus go by. It becomes annoying at times, he says, to be stared at wherever he goes, and he feels like retiring to a monastery for a rest. A newspaper writer called on him recently and said: "Mr. Wilde, I want to talk to you about your private life." "Private life," returned the aesthete; "private life? I have none, sir. I wish I had."[1] He was painfully treated by the ladies at Saratoga. He tells of his experience there with tears in his voice. "Mr. Secretary Blaine and two or three other gentlemen and myself," he said, "went out into the court yard of the Grand Union to sit under the trees and listen to the music. Not that I cared to hear that music, but I wished to while away the time. Would you believe it? In fifteen minutes, between three and four hundred women had gathered round and stood gaping at us. Old women and young girls, and mothers leading their daughters by the hand. We got up and went into the billiard room. They crowded in there. 'Let us go into the bar room,' some one suggested. 'It is the only place in which we can escape them!' Oh, how we had erred. In five minutes the bar room door was surrounded and the way to it packed by those unblushing women. A common bar-room! Oh, it was so pathetic! My heart ached for those women. They must either have been so secure as to be beyond the fear of scandal, or they must have been wholly without shame."

NEWPORT THE BEST PLACE.

Of all the places in the United States Newport pleased him best. "The life there," he said, "is true and beautiful. The wealth is not used in vulgar display. One finds a high refinement and culture. The people have a correct appreciation of art in personal adornment and household decoration as well as in that larger vocation to which men devote their lives." Long Branch, however, he did not like at all. He thinks it is new and crude and garish. The cottages "are a heavy mass of color, without picturesqueness or harmony of design. Mr. Hoey's Hollywood Park is simply horrid.[2] And, really, a police force for the protection of art ought to be established to prevent the residents of Long Branch from painting their fences in such awful reds and greens." Philadelphia pleased him best of all the cities in the country. "I loved its red brick houses, with their white stone trimmings," he said.

1. Wilde had made the same claim in an earlier interview. See p. 221, note 1.

2. John Hoey (1824–1892) was born in Drogheda and, as a boy, made his way to New York. He arrived penniless and without shoes, but eventually made his fortune in the freight business. In 1882 he opened Hollywood Park in Long Branch. The extensive grounds were decorated with sculptures and fountains.

New York he liked for its enterprising, bustling life. But it seemed to make his flesh creep to think of Fifth avenue. He detested the street, with its blocks of brown stone mansions, filled with artistic gewgaws that indicated only a vulgar and undisciplined taste. He could hardly think of Mrs. Stewart's residence and Vanderbilt's three-million-dollar palace without shivering.[1] The larger hotels, he said, are excellent all over the country. He does not know a restaurant anywhere that can equal Delmonico's or the Brunswick. Our smaller houses, however, he regards as the worst in the world. He could always obtain something good to drink even in them, but absolutely nothing fit to eat. "Why," said he, "at some wretched town in the West I subsisted wholly on cigarettes and spirits."[2]

He said that he was very favorably impressed with what he saw of the South. He observed the signs of progress and prosperity on every hand. The people and the social organization of Virginia reminded him strongly of England.[3] The people all over the South sang in his ears the old melancholy refrain: "You ought to have seen it before the war." "I was once sitting on the portico of a country house," he said, "with a young lady, admiring the beauty of a limpid stream under the rays of the moon, and I said to the young lady: 'How beautiful is the moonlight falling on the water.' 'It is beautiful, indeed,' she replied, 'but ah, Mr. Wilde, you ought to have seen it before the war.'" Oscar laughs when he tells that story, but there are people who say that they heard it years before Oscar came out.[4]

1. Cornelia Mitchell Stewart née Clinch (1802–1886) was the widow of Alexander Turney Stewart (1803–1876), an Irish-born American entrepreneur who made his fortune in dry goods. Stewart built a residence on the northwest corner of Fifth Avenue and 34th Street in 1870. The French Second Empire style building was faced with marble. It was demolished in 1901. The Vanderbilt Triple Palace was a mansion at 640 Fifth Avenue between 51st and 52nd Streets, commissioned by American businessman William Henry Vanderbilt (1821–1885). Construction began in 1880 and was completed in 1882. The mansion had separate residences for Vanderbilt and the families of two of his daughters. Its brownstone facade was designed in the Doric and Corinthian styles. It was demolished between 1947 and 1949. Wilde may have had Vanderbilt's mansion in mind when he criticised New York architecture in an earlier interview ("Oscar Wilde," *Buffalo Daily Courier* (Buffalo, NY), 9 Feb. 1882, 2, p. 147). He did not see the interior, but may have approved of the so-called Japanese room with its peacock decorations ("Mr. Vanderbilt's House and Pictures," *The New York World, Semi-Weekly Edition* (New York, NY), 24 Jan. 1882, 6).

2. The author of "The Last of Oscar Wilde," *The Chicago Daily Tribune* (Chicago, IL), 5 Sep. 1882, 4, commenting on this article, points out that: "He did not mention the place by name, but it is not difficult to guess that St. Louis was the 'wretched town' he meant, as his description accurately fits it."

3. *Personal Impressions of America*: "If I was going to settle in America I would choose Virginia, the pleasing country life of which was its chief characteristic, and in which it so resembled England." (Dibb, 244.)

4. *Personal Impressions of America*: "Among the more elderly inhabitants of the South I found a melancholy tendency to date every event of importance by the late war [....] In Galveston on the Gulf of Mexico I joined some gentlemen in their favourite pastime of bathing at night in the Gulf.

POOR CONKLING.

He was asked whether he had met other prominent men besides Ex-Secretary Blaine. "Yes," he replied, "many of them. But I shall count them as nothing until I see Roscoe Conkling.[1] Oh, how I long to meet Mr. Conkling! We have been maligned and persecuted together by the newspapers. I take up my daily journal, in bed in the morning, and I read with the liveliest interest something abusive of myself. And then, somewhere near that article, I am sure to find something infamous about Roscoe Conkling. I cannot leave the country content without meeting the man who has shared with me the venom of so many journalistic anonymuncles [*sic*]."[2]

He thinks that on the whole we are a money-getting people without as yet any great appreciation of or love for art. Our girls, he thinks, are not as modest as their English cousins. He ascribes that to our system of rearing them. They cannot, he believes, take part in great entertainments as they do and go about almost at will without becoming bold. He admires, however, the cleverness, the steadfastness and the warm hearts of our women and he feels sure that in time they will succeed in "teaching the men that there is something worth living for beyond dollars and cents." He believes that one who devotes himself to art does a good thing and elevates himself above the mere worker in material. He said, however, that it is not easy to do that in this country, because protection has made everything so high. "My gloves, for example, which I might have bought for a dollar in London, cost $2.50 here."

"So they ought," broke out Ex-Mayor Stokley gruffly. "They are luxuries."

"Luxuries, sir?" replied the aesthete, opening his big eyes wide in amazement. "Do you call gloves luxuries? How would you go on the street, how would you travel in the railroad cars without gloves?"

NO GLOVES FOR STOKLEY.

"Do you see those hands?" returned the ex-Mayor, warmly. "Before I became Mayor of Philadelphia I worked so hard at my shop making ice cream and candy that my hands became all covered with corns that you might have cut with

---

When the moon was gilding the bay with silvery streaks, I turned to a gentleman who was standing next to me and said: 'How beautiful the moon is tonight.' 'Yes,' was his reply, 'but you should have see it before the war.'" (Dibb, 244.)

1. Roscoe Conkling (1829–1888) was a Republican politician. After three terms in the Senate he resigned in 1881 over a conflict with President Garfield. In 1882 he was nominated to the Supreme Court by Garfield's successor, Chester A. Arthur, but declined to serve, instead returning to the practice of law in New York. Some journalists wrote disparagingly of his political acumen and gloated over his fall.

2. Wilde had used the word "anonymuncule" to describe Thomas Wentworth Higginson in a letter to Joaquin Miller that was printed in *The World* (New York, NY), 3 Mar. 1882 (CL, 141–3).

a knife, and those hands, sir, have never had a pair of gloves on them. And you talk about work! Why, it's good for you! I've worked nearly all my life, and I weigh two hundred and twenty pounds."

"I will take your word, Mr. Mayor; I will take your word for it," gasped the horrified aesthete.

Oscar afterwards made inquiries concerning Mr. Stokley's career and no doubt the energetic ex-Mayor will cut some sort of a figure in the apostle's book. Mr. Wilde, it was hinted, has gathered in already about $15,000 by his lectures here. He still keeps a hold on the people, too, socially. He receives fifty letters a day. They come from all parts of the world. He and his secretary spend half the night sometimes in answering them.

J. W. K.

"Oscar Wilde on Children and Flowers," *New York Tribune* (New York, NY), 11 Sep. 1882, 8[1]

In conversation with a TRIBUNE reporter recently, Oscar Wilde said that the most interesting reading that he had seen in the newspapers lately had been the letters in THE TRIBUNE describing the excursions of the Fresh Air Children.[2] He quoted from several of the letters the sayings of the children,[3] and said in that connection: "The best thing that has been said about flowers I believe since Christ talked about the lilies,[4] was said to me by a child in the streets of London. I was going along with a whole armful of flowers, when a street Arab playing in

1. Reprinted in the *Buffalo Morning Express* (Buffalo, NY), 13 Sep. 1882, 2; and Marland, R. (2021). Unnoted sources in Oscar Wilde's Vera. *Notes and Queries*, *68*, 446–8.

2. The Fresh Air Fund was founded in 1877 to allow poor children of New York City to take vacations in the countryside. In 1881 the *New York Tribune* began supporting the fund, reporting on the children's activities, and publishing letters from readers who had hosted children. One such letter describes a boy from a Brooklyn tenement who, on a visit to Northampton, MA, could not understand "why people have so much land about their houses. 'When is there going to be a house built between this one and the next?' he asks. 'Who owns all the robins?' was his inquiry on the first morning," ("Fresh Air in the Country," *New York Tribune* (New York, NY), 3 Aug. 1882, 2). When he redrafted the Prologue of *Vera; or, The Nihilists* to add a role for a boy, Wilde gave him the line: "Who owns all the robins?" (CW xi, 112.124).

3. See also Wilde's positive review in *The Court and Society Review* of Mark Twain's article "English as She is Taught", in which are quoted numerous amusing errors committed by American schoolchildren (20 Apr. 1887; CW vi, No. 64).

4. "And why take ye thought for raiment? Consider the lilies of the field, how they grow; they toil not, neither do they spin:" (Matthew 6:28). Wilde may have been thinking of this verse when, in *De Profundis*, he listed "the love of children and flowers" among the things for which Christ was responsible (CL, 747).

the gutter looked up and exclaimed in astonishment: 'Lord! how rich you must be.'"[1]

"Wilde," *The Evening Telegram* (Providence, RI), 26 Sep. 1882, 1

And His $2 Silver Shoe-Buckles,

His Diamonds and His Knee-Breeches.

What He Thinks of the Telegram's Aesthetic Tint.

✂ *A report of Wilde's lecture in Providence.*

An Interview with Mr. Wilde.

"Would you like to meet Oscar Wilde?" said my friend Moore,[2] his manager, last evening, just after the arrival of the New York team, as I stood in the lobby of the Narragansett Hotel.

"Why, certainly," said I.

"Well, come up with me," and we went up to Room 5, and, knocking, there was a cordial "Come in," and opening the door I was ushered into the presence of the most ridiculed and caricatured man of the nineteenth century. The general look of his features was the same that is so well known by the photographs of Sarony, and also the numerous pictures in the illustrated newspapers, but the aesthetic costume was lacking, he being clad in a drab linsey-woolsey suit, like ordinary mortals, with only some slight differences in style and cut, like any ordinary Briton.

"Won't you sit down, sir?" said he, "I am waiting for my trunks from the depot."

As he stood up beside me I could see that he was built in a powerful mould, being over six feet in height and broad-shouldered, and looking much taller and brawnier as he stood up in the room than when he affects the "stained-glass attitudes" in aesthetic togs upon the stage; but when he sat down upon the sofa he was limp and sort of spread out in the corner of it, due possibly to the fatigue of a long ride in the cars, or it was his usual manner.

1. Wilde repeatedly told this story. See [Florence Duncan], "Some More," *Quiz* (Philadelphia, PA), 1 Feb. 1882, 4, p. 86; and Ricketts, 29.

2. Moore was managing Wilde's tour of New England. Wilde complained about his management to Colonel Morse: "Mr Moore paid only 250 dollars, and *no expenses at all*. I did not like to stop lecturing as he entreated me to go on. [...] he brought me to wretched villages of 10,000 people where of course they did not come" (CL, 183). After Providence, these "villages" were Salem, Lynn, Pawtucket, and North Attleborough.

I suggested to him that the drizzly, foggy evening must remind him of some of the fogs and nights of his own city, London.

"Ah," said he, "we are too severe even ourselves on our climate. Of course the winters are beastly, but the summers are delightful in London. It is the smoke of the manufactories that adds to the disagreeableness of our atmosphere."

"How much longer do you remain in this country, Mr. Wilde?" (I could hardly bring myself to say "Mister," it seemed sort of inappropriate, and I almost found myself being overfamiliar by ejaculating Oscar whenever I spoke to him.)

"Well, I can hardly tell. Do you know I find it hard to make up my mind to leave. I have found so much that is interesting to me in your country. I expect, however, to make a tour of the provinces, then go to Australia and Japan."

"Does the country come up to your anticipations?"

"Oh, far ahead of what I ever realized. Do you know that we seem to think of this country over in England more from the standpoint of the West, of the limitless prairie and wildness of that region, than of the cities of the East, of which there is, comparatively speaking, little known. You see the average Englishman, especially among the nobility or rich commoners, land in New York and start right out West for the hunting, so that they see very little of your cities, which accounts, to a great extent, for the prevailing ignorance concerning your larger places. Now, I like New York so much; it is so cosmopolitan, bright, cheery and full of life; and Boston I was just charmed with, the delightful literary people one meets there; in fact, I think we know Boston better than any other city for the influence of its literary minds. Emerson is as well known and his works as great and known in England as in his own country. And then there are some fine buildings in Boston. There is Phillips Brooks' house and his church, both fine specimens of ornamental architecture.[1] Have you any fine buildings here?"

The question staggered me for a moment, and I thought to myself I only wished we had been coming up the river and I could have sprung the gasometer on him as the dome of some church, after descanting on the beauties of the Hospital.[2] However, our old First Baptist Church is always my stand-by, and I spoke of that with commendable pride as being the work of a countryman of his, Sir Christopher Wren, and the spire as one of the most graceful pieces of church ar-

1. Phillips Brooks (1835–1893) was an American clergyman. He became rector of Trinity Church, Boston in 1869. After the church was burned down in 1872, architect Henry Hobson Richardson built a new church under Brooks's direction. The church was completed in 1877 and lauded for its architectural innovations and decorations. Four stained glass windows designed by Edward Burne-Jones and executed by William Morris were installed in 1882. Richardson also built Trinity Rectory (1880). The name is given as "Philip Brooks" here.

2. The interviewer refers to the Gasometer at 82 Crary Street (built 1872), a domed structure with a diameter of 121 ft 6 in / 37 m used by the Providence Gas Company to hold gas, and the nearby Rhode Island Hospital (opened 1863).

chitecture in the country.[1] Then there was the City Hall, Narragansett Hotel, Court House—well, there were quite a number after all when I came to sum them up.

"In Newport," said he, "I found the most refined audiences I have lectured before, and the domestic architecture the finest I have ever seen.[2] I enjoyed Newport thoroughly. The cottage life is simply charming. More like my own country, where we care nothing for hotel life. Do not care for hotels [*sic*]."

"Your peculiar ideas of dress seem to be one of the principal things that have made you so well known and criticised."

"Not peculiar, exactly, it is common sense and comfort I aim at as well as the artistic look at the dress of men today. It is not comfortable, by any means—hats afford no protection from the elements, tight-fitting coats that are not warm. Just look at a crowd of men in the dress of the period; could anything be more unartistic, or ignoble? Why, the best dressed men I have seen were in Colorado; their outdoor life makes their dress consistent and comfortable, broad-brimmed hats that protect their faces from the rain and sun, and at the same time they are graceful.[3] I saw some fine specimens of manly beauty in the West. One great trouble with modern sculpture is that the artist has nothing to go by. The sculptors of earlier ages saw the lines of their models through the drapery and the resulting statuary is natural, easy and graceful. The artist must see something before him in order to reproduce it. It cannot emanate entirely from his own mind. There will be a change here in dress, and it is even now felt to a great ex-

1. The First Baptist Meetinghouse was built in 1774–1775. It was designed by Joseph Brown (1733–1785), an American industrialist, astronomer, and architect. Brown was inspired by illustrations of designs by Sir Christopher Wren (1632–1723), an English architect.

2. Wilde lectured in Newport, Rhode Island on 15 July. During the course of his lecture "[h]e complimented the Newport people upon the fact that they were painting their houses in colors, instead of adhering to the white which was so general throughout the country." ("Oscar Wilde in Newport," *The Sun* (New York, NY), 16 July 1882, 5.)

3. Wilde repeated his praise of the miners' dress in *Personal Impressions of America*: "I was received by a quiet, well-armed mob, altogether the best-dressed people I had seen in America amongst the men. They wore broad-brimmed hats which would protect them from sun and rain, cloaks which were picturesque and always graceful, and knickerbockers and high boots. I made them promise before I left that they would not change their dress even if they became millionaires." (Dibb, 242.) He made a related point in *Dress*: "I must acknowledge that all ugliness of dress had come entirely from those who were called the Upper Classes. [...] Among peasants and fisher folk generally – men and women – we never found ugly dress." (Dibb, 274.) See also "Mr. Oscar Wilde Interviewed in Glasgow," *Evening News and Star* (Glasgow, UK), 22 Dec. 1884, 4, p. 575; and Wilde's editorial for the November 1887 number of *The Woman's World*: "And yet how sensible is the dress of the London milkwoman, of the Irish or Scotch fishwife, of the North-country factory-girl! [....] Wherever physical labour of any kind is required, the costume used is, as a rule, absolutely right, for labour necessitates freedom, and without freedom there is no such thing as beauty in dress at all."(CW vii, No. 81, lines 413–19.)

tent in England, especially among the ladies, who are adopting these sensible ideas, and there are today in London the finest dressed ladies in the world."

"How do you think Mrs. Langtry will succeed over here?"

"Excellently. She is one of the most charming of women. She is very handsome, and the fact that she has had all England at her feet for three years and a half, is sufficient proof of her beauty, and you Americans like beautiful women, so that is half of the battle, and then she is really a fine actress, not anything great, of course, for it would not be art that could be acquired in six months, but she possesses one of the most musical of voices, and is thoroughly fascinating, and there is a magnetism about her that has made her, even the short time she has been upon the stage, unusually successful in her chosen profession. I know of no one upon the stage who has such a musical voice except Bernhardt."

"You see, Mr. Wilde, we are slightly aesthetic in the tint of the paper of the TELEGRAM."

"Ah, yes, like your namesake of New York. Well that gives the paper a cheerful look, and then again it is pleasant for the eye, not so tiresome as the glaring white. Very nice, I assure you."

Here the valet of the apostle of aestheticism arrived with the trunks, and as it was nearly time for the lecture, I took my departure and left him getting ready to don his aesthetic costume for the evening.

VALE.

"Oscar Wilde Interviewed," *The Daily Sun* (Saint John, NB), 5 Oct. 1882, 3[1]

His Lecture Last Evening—Court Items.

(Special to THE SUN.)

FREDERICTON, Oct. 4.—Oscar Wilde, the apostle of aestheticism, arrived here from Bangor by the 4:15 p.m. train today, and put up at the "Barker." THE SUN correspondent sought and obtained an interview with him. A colored valet waited at the door. On entering, the reporter was cordially received by the poet and invited to a chair. Mr. Wilde was reclining in elegant leisure on a sofa, amidst a profusion of furs, sipping a cup of tea and nibbling quite ordinarily at a bit of toast. He was attired in an ordinary travelling suit of dark stuff, and wore an orange tie of considerable dimensions. "Very glad to see you!" was his first exclamation, and then he plunged into general conversation on almost every conceivable subject, in all of which he seemed interested. He expressed delight with his

1. H & S, b93. Quoted in O'Brien, 119.

visit to Canada, and enthusiastically mentioned his admiration for the beautiful autumnal tints of our forests and the grandeur of our rivers and mountains. He evidently had made a study of Canadian politics and was warm in commendation of the ability and statesmanship of Sir John A. McDonald, whom he had met at a dinner in the Upper Provinces.[1] He spoke of the splendid possibilities of the North West and the wonderful interest in its future awakened in England; but his pet subject, Art, was recalled by his glancing at a modest appearing parlor stove that gave out its blazing heat in the room, upon which he made a most violent onslaught, characterizing it—aesthetically speaking—as an unparalleled monstrosity, a black-leaded horror, and an unpunished crime.[2] Turning to his travels, he said he intended visiting Australia after leaving Canada, and thence going to Japan, where, said he, art flourishes more grandly than in any country under the sun; but where it is being lowered in character by the advent of the English, who had produced a similar effect in India. He regretted being unable to sail down the river to St. John, and expressed his admiration for Fredericton, making minute enquiries as to its characteristics and trade. His manner of conversation is pleasant, winning, and simple, though impressing one as of an active and highly intelligent mind.

✂ *A report of Wilde's lecture in Fredericton.*

Mr. Wilde goes to St. John by the morning train.

✂ *A paragraph of news from the county court.*

"The Apostle of Beauty in Nova Scotia," *Halifax Morning Herald* (Halifax, NS), 10 Oct. 1882, 2[3]

OSCAR WILDE AT AMHERST.

The afternoon train from St. John on Friday, brought beauty's latest evangel to our province.[4] He came, not surrounded by a halo of blue and purple glory, not

1. Sir John Alexander Macdonald (1815–1891) was the Scottish-born first prime minister of Canada. He was returned to office in an election on 6 June. Wilde dined with Macdonald on 16 May, the day before parliament was prorogued (O'Brien, 44).

2. Cast iron stoves: p. 317, note 4.

3. H & S, b94. Reprinted in *Bruno's Weekly*, *3*, 30 Dec. 1916, 1232–3; Mikhail, 105–10; and H & S, 166–72. Excerpted in "Oscar Wilde on the American (and Canadian) Ladies," *Morning Chronicle* (Montreal, QC), 16 Oct. 1882, 4; and O'Brien, 41, 53. Quoted in Hamilton, 120–1; OWDA, 404; Pearson, 76; Hyde, 77; O'Brien, 80, 110, 128–9; and Ellmann, 195/206. Referenced in Ellmann, 188/197–8.

4. Friday 6 October.

in a carved car, nor in a Greek urn. He rode on an engine. He saw the little hills rejoicing merrily. He saw Moncton, and noticed the indecent wonder of the "Transcript" editor.[1] He took in the Pre-Raphaelism of Dorchester.[2] He rejoiced at the preciousness of Westcock, and was enraptured at the gaudy leonine beauty of the Tantramar.[3] Oscar praised the railroad and liked the appointment of the cars. He smoked the cigar of peace and he crossed the Missequash [*sic*] but he took no interest in Fort Cumberland, as the battles fought there were not fought for love of beauty but for love of territory.[4]

At Amherst he shook hands with the engine driver, gaily wished him a good day, gave him a stray cigar, and leaped lightly to the platform, declining the proffered help of a hand kindly outstretched to assist him. The station platform was crowded with citizens, trying to get a glimpse of "wild Oscar," as they called him, and these were anxiously watching the door of the car where the Evangelist might be supposed to be, while he was quietly getting into a carriage and getting under way for Lamy's. The first impression on looking at Oscar is that he looks like his pictures. You have seen that picture before and are ready to turn over a leaf.

A HERALD representative called upon Mr. Wilde in his room at Lamy's. He was received with a polite friendliness that was winning. The Apostle had no lily nor yet a sunflower. He wore a velvet jacket which seemed to be a good jacket. He had an ordinary neck-tie and wore a linen collar about number eighteen on a neck half a dozen sizes smaller. His legs were in trousers such as Greenfield might have made, and his boots were apparently the product of New York art, judging by their pointed toes. He wore a ring with a seal of great size. A consensus of the opinions of Amherst people decides that Oscar's hair is not good. It is the color of straw, slightly leonine, and straight as an Indian's. It is faded and bleached looking, and when not looked after goes climbing all over his features. Mr. Wilde was communicative and genial. He said that he found Canada pleasant. He liked the scenery of New Brunswick, as it lent itself readily to art. There were no towering mountains, and deep gulches such as he had seen in the West. There were no large rivers, but the scenery was always changing as one passed through.

1. *Daily Transcript*: a Moncton newspaper. Wilde's train passed through Moncton; he would lecture there on 12 October.

2. Dorchester is a town between Moncton and Amherst. Wilde probably only saw it from his train car.

3. Westcock is a town at the mouth of the Tantramar, a river in New Brunswick near the border with Nova Scotia. Wilde had referred to "[t]he gaudy leonine sunflower" in *Le Jardin* (CW i, No. 94, line 5).

4. Fort Beauséjour was built by French colonists between 1751 and 1753 to the west of the Missaguash River. After the Battle of Fort Beauséjour in 1755, the fort was surrendered to the British and renamed Fort Cumberland. In 1776 it was the site of the Battle of Fort Cumberland, when British forces repelled sympathisers of the American Revolution.

Every turn in the road brought a small surprise. The streams wound attractively through the land, and there were innumerable hills and valleys of all conceivable forms.

Had our autumn forests finer colors than those in England?

Well, he would not say that. Our timber was finer, but its beauty was of a different sort.

Mr. Wilde uses the word "timber" in a sense that he thinks American. He talks about the leaves on our timber, etc.[1]

The conversation turned on newspapers.

"The editor of a paper," said Oscar, "has an advantage over all other writers. He never waits for his audience, and he is sure that what he writes will be read."

(Oscar sighed here, doubtless thinking of his poems.)

"American journals are in many respects better than the English. I think the American newspaper is the journal of the future. It is filled with news. The reader of the large New York papers knows everything that goes on in the world that is worth knowing, and much more. Still there is a want of dignity, and an amount of scurrility in the American newspaper which ones gets in smaller towns that is terrible."

"Did they not discuss your appearance and your lectures in a somewhat unsatisfactory way?"

Oscar at this stage had brought in to him a cup of tea and having asked your representative to partake with him he laughed quietly and pushed his hair behind his ears, as he replied: "They talk in an incredible [*sic*] obtuse manner about my message and my work. I think nothing whatever about the criticisms now. It does not interest me as it did at first. I understand the people who say those things about me and I cannot bring myself to care what they say. I cannot possibly do it. At first it surprised me. I came out here, never having spoken in public, in earnest about my message, strongly feeling what I was saying, and I talked seriously to those people. They heard me and went away and talked about my necktie and the way I wore my hair. I could not understand how people could do such a thing. I thought it inexpressibly stupid."

This last with a sigh and a look of half wearied pity at the thought of these critics. He said "stupid" with a strong accentuation on the last syllable.

1. Wilde was probably not imitating what he believed to be American usage. Although "timber" commonly refers to wood trimmed into logs or otherwise prepared for use as a building material, it has also long been used to describe standing trees suitable for such use, including in the United Kingdom: English law classed certain species of tree as timber and prohibited their waste (OED). Sir William Wilde used the word to refer to standing trees (see e.g. Wilde, W. R. (1849). *The Beauties of the Boyne, and its Tributary, The Blackwater*. James McGlashan. 45, 128, 143, 152, 164, 169).

"The English Journals," he went on, "are much more serious and earnest in their tone than yours. But a man who has a name that is valuable will not be an English journalist. English newspaper articles are written anonymously. A good writer can get no credit for good work, and so will not write for an English paper. The proprietor is everything, the writer nothing there. In France, where the writers sign their names, better men become journalists."

"But as a matter of fact you can tell who writes many articles in England."

"Yes, in some cases you can. There is George Augustus Sala.[1] (This name was uttered with a weary look as if the physical effort of articulating it was nearly too much and the last syllable of Sala was clearly accented.) You can always tell what Sala writes. No other human being can write such intolerable English."

Oscar made enquiries about the institutions of Amherst.

"Do you tell me that it has only three thousand inhabitants? Why (lying back luxuriously on his bear skin rug and sipping his tea,) I never spoke in a town so small as that. Mr Townshend has driven me about the village and I consider it a beautiful little place."[2]

He spoke of our style of Government, of democracies generally, of sociology, of Herbert Spencer, whom he had read and admired greatly. He found nothing in his work or in any other work on evolution which differed from Plato and Aristotle.

"There is nothing in art or philosophy in which we are as wise as the Greeks. Spencer has prosecuted enquiries which have led him to verify the Greek philosopher. No, we should *not go back* to the Greek, we should try to get up to the Greek. All that remains for us anywhere is to corroborate the Greeks in everything. They reached a level, the summit of which we cannot yet see. True, they had simpler problems. Their common people were less stupid. It is a wonder we do not have twice the trouble we do have, with the elements that go to make up the countries we now live in. Our conceptions of beauty may reach the Greek conception some time. There is nothing higher to hope for.

"Yes, I have found America pleasant. Out in the West, delightful. At Denver I met the most interesting people I have ever seen."

"Rough and ready I suppose?"

"Ready, but not rough. They were polished and refined compared with the people I met in large cities farther East. Yes, I *did* see the common people. I spent

1. George Augustus Henry Fairfield Sala (1828–1895) was an author and journalist who signed his articles for the *Illustrated London News* as G. A. S. He is depicted in William Powell Frith's painting, *The Private View at the Royal Academy, 1881,* glaring at Wilde as the latter holds court before a coterie of female admirers.

2. C. J. Townshend was the son of a local clergyman; his wife produced *Patience* in Amherst (O'Brien, 127).

a night in a silver mine. I dined with the men down there. They were great, strong, well formed men, of graceful attitude and free motion. Poems every one of them. A complete democracy under ground.[1] I find people less rough and coarse in such places. There is no chance for roughness. The revolver is their book of etiquette. This teaches lessons that are not forgotten. I wish I could have gone to Winnipeg. I like free people without the resources of civilization. They are freer and more artistic in their surroundings because they follow nature."

"Speaking of ladies (he had spoken of them) do you consider American or European ladies the finest looking?"

"That I cannot answer here. I shall wait till I get in mid-ocean, out of sight of both countries. If I were to answer you I should find it to my advantage to be anything but candid."

Your reporter intimated that the last remark was a sufficient answer.

Oscar, smiling and drinking more tea, proceeded: "Your women are pretty. I never saw so many pretty women as I have seen here, especially in the South, but the prettiness is in color and freshness and bloom. A truly beautiful woman never grows old. The most of your pretty ladies will not be pretty in ten years."

"I believe you discovered Mrs. Langtry?"

A look of rapture came to Oscar's face. He flung his locks from where they clustered around his nose, and with a gesture, the first of the interview, he said:

"I would rather have discovered Mrs. Langtry than have discovered America. Her beauty is in outline perfectly moulded. She will be a beauty at eighty-five.

"Yes, it was for such ladies that Troy was destroyed, and well might Troy be destroyed for such a woman. Perhaps it may be true—they say it is—that the siege of Troy was brought about by a quarrel about a harbor, but they thought they fought for a woman; they had the conception that it was for beauty, and that is the same as if it was. It would be a fine thing if nations went to war with each other now over such questions as to which had the most beautiful women. How much better that than the senseless dispute about getting Egypt and possessing Arabi.[2] Now that we have caught Arabi we do not know what to do with him. When I was young I thought the wars of the roses were to decide whether a red or a white rose was the most beautiful. I learned afterward that it was a vulgar dispute. The right of one or two men to a crown or something of that kind."

1. Wilde's visit to the Matchless Mine: see p. 342, note 1.

2. Ahmed 'Urabi or Orabi Pasha (1841–1911) was an Egyptian nationalist, referred to in contemporary American and British newspapers as Arabi Pasha. In February 1882 he and his supporters launched what came to be known as the 'Urabi Revolt against foreign rule. On 13 September 1882 a British army defeated 'Urabi's army at the Battle of Tell El Kebir, and 'Urabi surrendered.

This last was spoken in a tone of injured susceptibility, as though York had thrown soup on Oscar's coat, or Lancaster had smoked a black pipe over Oscar's dinner.

"What do I think of your American Literature? I think you have had a great poet in Poe. He is your greatest poet. His sense of form and exquisitiveness of touch are intense. His gold is not to be gilt and his lilies are unpaintable. Joaquin Miller is also a beautiful poet. 'Arizonian' is a poem of great artistic excellence.[1] Fawcett, a new poet, whom we had not heard of when I left England, has written some of the most perfect poetry which I have seen.[2] Walt Whitman if not a poet is a man who sounds a strong note. He writes neither prose nor poetry but something of his own that is unique. He is one of your greatest men.[3]

"No I do not care for the Commemoration ode of Lowell.[4] It has no harmony in its conception. It is oratory of the strongest kind, and is eloquent but does not meet my idea of poetry. Lowell had written a poem on dedication which is delicate poetry. You must like it. You have poets with you. In New Brunswick a young man, Mr. Roberts, has published a little book.[5] You have heard of it."

The reporter had read Robert's published poems and was delighted to find that Mr. Wilde met and liked them.

"And Mulvany of Toronto, a countryman of my own, a man once well known at Trinity College.[6] He is a man of taste. Frechette, I believe is however your best poet.[7]

"Wordsworth was undoubtedly a poet. I do not read the poems he liked best of his. I do not care for his "Idiot Boy," "The Excursion," is nothing to me.

Your correspondent intimated that the poem was too long for what poetry it contained which reduced the average too low.

Said Mr. Wilde, "I do not like to hear poems spoken of as too long. 'The Excursion' is shorter than the Iliad. I would not have one line less in the Iliad. But I

1. *Arizonian* is the first poem in Miller's *Songs of the Sierras.*

2. Edgar Fawcett (1847–1904) was an American novelist and poet. His first published works appeared in 1871. In a letter dating to c. December 1888 Wilde describes Fawcett as "the best American poet there is – alive" (CL, 376).

3. Wilde's praise of Whitman is elsewhere unqualified.

4. James Russell Lowell recited his *Commemoration Ode* at Harvard University on 21 July 1865.

5. Charles George Douglas Roberts (1860–1943) was a Canadian poet who at the time of Wilde's visit was working as principal of Fredericton's York Street School. He began publishing poetry in 1878 and his first collection, *Orion and Other Poems*, appeared in 1880.

6. Charles Pelham Mulvany (1835–1885) was an Irish-born clergyman and poet. He immigrated to Canada about 1859. Like Wilde he studied classics at Trinity College, Dublin; like Wilde's mother he wrote poetry for the *Nation*.

7. Louis-Honoré Fréchette (1839–1908) was a Canadian poet, writer of short stories, and politician. He attended a reception for Wilde on 15 May and shortly afterwards gave Wilde an inscribed copy of his volume of poems *Les Fleurs boréales* (1881) (O'Brien, 65–6).

like Wordsworth's sonnets. That beginning: 'Milton thou should'st be living at this hour,'[1] is fine, as is that which commences:

'The world is too much with us.'"[2]

As your representative rose to go, having declined a cup of tea, which was again politely offered, he was asked about Halifax, the nature of the people and style of the town. Mr. Wilde had met Sir John MacDonald and his lady. "Sir John, (and Mr. Wilde sighed as he said it,) was a man of the world, but his lady was charming and so was he."

And your correspondent left. There was other talk about the classics, about the French idea of the Dramatic Unities,[3] about Shakespeare and Wordsworth and Keats and Rossetti, but this was of a nature too confidential to be communicated to everybody. It will be remembered that Mr. Wilde begins one of his sonnets with this line;

"I stood by the unvintageable sea."[4]

Your correspondent thought of this as he was leaving, and remembering that the Tantramar was very muddy as the aesthete passed over it, he asked, "Do you consider the Tantramar vintageable to any extent?" The apostle laughed gaily at this proof of the presence of a Philistine, but contented himself with praising other streams of less leonine beauty.

It may be said here that Mr. Bigelow deserves the greatest credit for his enterprise and daring in bringing so high priced a man to a small town like Amherst. Mr. Wilde had never spoken in so small a place before. He had a good house and a good hearing.

1. The sonnet quoted is *London, 1802.*

2. The sonnet quoted is *The World Is Too Much with Us.*

3. The dramatic unities refer to three principles requiring limitation of a drama to a set period of time, either the time taken to act the play or a single day (unity of time), to a single location (unity of place), and to the development of a single plot (unity of action). The principles, developed in the Renaissance from Aristotle's *Poetics*, were influential, particularly in France where they drew the support of, among others, the playwrights Jean Racine (1639–1699) and Voltaire.

4. The first line of *Vita Nuova*, first published in the *Irish Monthly* in December 1877 as *Πόντος Ἄτρύ γετος?* and retitled for *Poems* (CW i, No. 37).

"Oscar Admires the American Autumn," *The Boston Daily Globe* (Boston, MA), 13 Oct. 1882, 5[1]

(Bangor Commercial.)

Oscar Wilde is accompanied in his travels by an agent and a colored servant. He came direct from Boston to Bangor, and from this city he went Wednesday morning to Fredericton, N. B. From the latter city he went to St. John, N. B., today. The aesthetic gentleman expressed himself as well pleased with Bangor's beauties, the most prominent of which in his eyes, are the great river, and the stately elms which ornament the streets. The autumn coloring of the leaves was pleasing to the eminent lecturer, and he took occasion to remark, to the Commercial, that the American autumn has suffered at the hands of American artists abroad, who have libelled its gorgeous beauties with unfaithful brush and untruthful colors. Mr. Wilde thinks our autumn glorious, and a thing that must be seen to be appreciated.

"Oscar Wilde," *The Daily Sun* (Saint John, NB), 14 Oct. 1882, 4[2]

On Soldier's Dresses, Painting in Pottery and His Reception in the Maritime Provinces

JAPAN THE MOST ARTISTIC COUNTRY IN THE WORLD.

Oscar Wilde arrived in St. John by the noon train, yesterday, and during the afternoon was waited upon by a SUN reporter, who found him in his room at the Royal Hotel, enjoying the luxury of an after dinner cigar. He was received and welcomed very cordially by the poet and aesthete, who was dressed in a brownish gray suit, with knee breeches, and dark stockings. He had on a silk tie, of a shade which admirably harmonized with his dress, and from his pocket protruded the corner of a handkerchief of the same color as the tie. On the object of the visit being stated, Mr. Wilde, in reply to a question as to his impressions of his audiences in these provinces, said, "I have been charmed with the audiences I have had in Canada. The audience here was a charming one, quick to catch and understand every point, and very ready to give whatever appreciation the lecture may be worth. I had very nice audiences, both at Amherst and Charlottetown, and also at Halifax. At the latter place I had a very attractive looking audi-

1. Reprinted in Cooper (Fredericton lecture, 4 October 1882).
2. Excerpted in O'Brien, 124, 140.

ence, for all the military came with their red coats, which formed a great relief to the customary solemn black suits.

Mr. Wilde then branched off into a dissertation on the subject of military dress, saying that in the olden times the greatest arts seemed to be devoted to the glory of the soldier, but either he had deserted art or art had deserted him. For instance, the most splendid metal work for 400 years in Europe went to inlay breast plates and other accoutrements for the soldier, but that time has passed. He was particularly disgusted with the swords they use, which, so far as he knew, were got from the military tailors, who all keep a supply on hand. He thought they might have much more beautiful swords. As for their costumes, he said that although they were very pretty and of fine colors, still their shapes were very bad. The shell jacket, for instance, with its entire want of recognition of any of the principles of drapery, seems peculiarly monstrous. He did not see why soldiers should not go back a little to the splendid arts they once had. The guns and pistols of the olden time were so beautiful. And people take so much greater care of what is beautiful than what is not.

Speaking of his trip to Prince Edward Island, he expressed himself as very much pleased with the Island, though he had a very hard bit of travel to get there. He did not arrive in Charlottetown till 9 o'clock, and, as his audience had been waiting for an hour, he drove at once to the hall. He was very much pleased with the press notices. The reports of his previous lecture in St. John, which appeared in both the morning papers of this city, he considered excellent, and in their notices of him the papers wrote about him in a courteous way, just as a gentleman likes to be written about.

Rep.—There was rather a severe criticism on you in the Halifax *Chronicle.*

Mr. Wilde—In the same paper that contained a very appreciative account of my lecture, there was a scurrilous letter, the writer of which took refuge in vulgar personalities.[1] So far as I am concerned I have no time to listen to the shrill voice of folly. One is not made or marred by newspapers. One makes or mars himself. There is always hovering around newspapers a class of mosquitoes—pieces of dirt without a sting.

Rep.—You certainly had an attentive audience here.

Mr. W.—I was charmed with my audience here. People don't realize when they go to a play for example how much they contribute to the goodness or badness of the acting. If they are careless, and chatter and talk among themselves, they make the actors careless, whereas if they are attentive they make the actor

1. The letter was signed "Aesthete-Hater" and described Wilde as a "narrow-headed, spindle-shanked, shaky, ungraceful specimen of manhood". Wilde's lecture was declared "the dullest bosh, trash, commonplace talk and uninspired nonsense." (O'Brien, 131–3.)

better. I have heard people coming from a theatre complain that the play was dull. They probably made it so themselves.

Rep.—What are your movements after you leave St. John?

Mr. W.—I go from this place to Boston, where I will pass Sunday. I will lecture in Portland, Me.,[1] and two or three other places, and then I go back to New York. From that place to Australia, where I will lecture for three months, and I will pass next summer in Japan. Japan is the most artistic country in the world.

Rep.—Why so?

Mr. W.—Because in Japan the artisan is the artist. Everything in a Japanese home is in good taste. There is no separation between the man who makes a thing—and the one who decorates it. Every man is able to decorate what he makes and make what he decorates. Half the bad ornaments of this century come from people not having made what they decorate. This is particularly the case in the decoration of pottery. If the potter decorates the dish that he turns from his wheel he won't forget that it is a dish and will try and make of it a very beautiful dish to express by its ornamentation the use to which it is going to be put. If a person who had not made it undertakes to decorate it the chances are that he will treat it as a piece of canvas and paint a picture on it. He is merely painting a picture on wrong material. Hence comes the terrible habit of painting a landscape on china, a thing which never would be done by a potter. That I think is one of the great secrets of Japanese art.

Rep.—I suppose after you return you will give the world the benefit of your visit to Japan?

Mr. W.—Oh, yes, I expect I will have something to say about it.

Rep.—You spoke in your previous lecture in very complimentary terms of a cottage now being built here?

1. There is no known record of Wilde having lectured in Portland, Maine. According to Cooper's itinerary of Wilde's American lecture tour (accessed January 2022), Wilde lectured only twice after leaving Saint John for the last time: in Bridgeton, New Jersey, on 26 October, and in New York City on 27 November. In previous interviews Wilde had been fairly accurate about his immediate schedule, and it seems likely that there were at least plans for a Portland lecture. See also "Oscar Wilde Explains," *The Boston Herald* (Boston MA), 16 Oct. 1882, 2, p. 478, where Wilde states that his "next lectures would shortly be delivered in Maine and New Hampshire, but dates were not definitely arranged". Colonel Morse, who contributed a chapter about Wilde's American tour to a 1907 edition of his works, wrote that "a short lecture tour was arranged in October, 1882. Mr. Wilde, with Mr. Husted as his manager, left for New England, and after speaking at Portland and Bangor, Maine, arrived at St. John, N. B. October 4, speaking there October 6." (Keller–Farmer, 91–2.) As Morse was writing several decades after the tour, it is unsurprising that his account contains some errors (Wilde lectured in Bangor on 3 October, Fredericton on 4 October, Saint John on 5 October, and Amherst on 6 October), and he had probably forgotten that the plans for a lecture in Portland had not been realised.

Mr. W.—Yes, Mr. Allison's cottage.[1] If you have not seen it, it is worth a visit. Of course the outside is not finished yet, but I like the whole house. Inside there is a fine hall, excellent ceilings and beautiful staircase. The worst use you can make with wood is to varnish it. To be worth looking at wood should be nicely oiled. I also found at Moncton a house Mr. Cleveland built very much in the same style and very charming.

Mr. Wilde here begged to be excused, as he had promised Mr. J. C. Miles to visit his studio,[2] and after a few minutes' more conversation, in which he said he had had a very successful tour in America, the interview came to an end.

Mr. Wilde's visit to Mr. Miles' studio resulted in his purchasing a picture from that artist—a marine view.[3]

"Oscar Wilde Explains," *The Boston Herald* (Boston MA), 16 Oct. 1882, 2[4]

His Version of the So-Called Arrest at Moncton, N. B.[5]

Oscar Wilde has arrived in Boston from St. John, N. B., and, in an interview Sunday afternoon at the hotel Vendome, he gave an explanation of his recent "arrest" at Moncton, N. B., as stated in Saturday's HERALD. He regarded the affair as an ill-advised attempt to extort blackmail on the part of the Young Men's Christian Association of Moncton. "It seems," to use his own words, "that last week they telegraphed to my agent in Canada to ask whether I could lecture in

1. Allison was the architect of a house belonging to Mrs Zebedee Ring. It was in Queen Anne style (O'Brien, 121).

2. John Christopher Miles (1837–1911) was a Canadian painter of landscapes and figures. He was born in Saint John, trained and worked in Boston for a number of years, and returned to Saint John in 1877.

3. When Miles explained that he was compelled to offer his works cheaply because he was undercut by chromograph sellers, Wilde replied that painting "never will be duly appreciated until one of those dreadful chromographers is hanged." ("Oscar's Second Visit," *St. John Globe* (Saint John, NB), 14 Oct. 1882.)

4. Reprinted as "Oscar Wilde Explains," *The Morning Herald* (Halifax, NS), 19 Oct. 1882, 2; and (excluding the final paragraph) as "Oscar Wilde Explains," *Daily Transcript* (Moncton, NB), 18 Oct. 1882, 2 (which is H & S, b95; and is quoted in O'Brien, 138; and Sturgis, 260/249). Excerpted in "Oscar Wilde Explains," *The Montreal Daily Star* (Montreal, QC), 18 Oct. 1882, 2.

5. Inaccurate reports circulated widely in the days immediately after Wilde's visit to Moncton to the effect that he had been arrested and had settled the case by paying the YMCA $100 (e.g. "Oscar Wilde a Prisoner," *The New York Times* (New York, NY), 14 Oct. 1882, 5). A full account of the scandal is given in O'Brien, 137–9.

Moncton for them on Friday night. I replied that I was engaged to deliver my second lecture at St. John on Friday, and that Thursday was the only open night I had in the week. At the same time I stated my terms. No reply came for 36 hours, and then another gentleman of that town made application for me to lecture. My agent then telegraphed a second time to the Y. M. C. A. to ask them to reply immediately to the previous message. They took no notice of the telegram, and after 48 hours elapsed, he very properly closed with the gentleman who was not connected with the Christian association. These latter people having ascertained that I was engaged by the other party, telegraphed to my agent to say that they would accept his offer, but the agent replied that the date was already fixed for another lecture. On my arrival at Moncton on Thursday last I was waited upon by a representative of the Y. M. C. A. and a local attorney, who asked me whether, in consideration of the disappointment to the association, I would not contribute something to the funds. I replied that I did not consider that the association had any right to make such a claim, and that I was not sufficiently interested in it to subscribe to it. On my refusal they proceeded to the under sheriff, and presented him with a writ, which they had obtained that morning, and asked him to serve it on me as I was stepping on the platform to lecture. The sheriff, a gentleman of some knowledge of the world, naturally declined to do anything so uncalled for and so impertinent, but called on me at my hotel and explained to me the matter. Two gentlemen of Moncton accompanied him and entered into engagements with the sheriff to prevent my being given any further annoyance. The lecture went off very successfully. After the lecture this local attorney made a definite demand on me for $100, on receipt of which he declared he would withdraw his writ. My agent, by my orders, refused to accede to any such gross attempt at extortion, and the matter will proceed for trial before the local judge. Some gentlemen of the town have kindly promised to see to the matter on my behalf.[1] I am glad to say that great indignation was expressed at the behavior of the association and, before I left, most of the leading citizens had withdrawn their names as members of it. The whole thing shows the illegality of most law and the immorality of most moral institutions. Such associations are usually the refuge of the provincial Joseph Surfaces.[2] True, it afforded me an interesting insight into certainly not a very favorable side of Canadian ordinary life, and for experience one would go through a great deal, even to a sudden visit from a sheriff."

1. Wilde's manager offered to pay $20 of the $100 and, when this was refused, a judge set a bond of $35 which Wilde's local sponsors covered (O'Brien, 138). In Wilde's absence, the writ in the case was set aside by the Kent County Court, and the YMCA "repudiated the action of its committee" ("Oscar Wilde Comes Out Ahead," *New York Times* (New York, NY), 5 Nov. 1882, 8).

2. Joseph Surface is a character in *The School for Scandal*, a 1777 play by Richard Brinsley Sheridan. He is a hypocrite but nevertheless enjoys a reputation as a man of good morals.

Mr. Wilde further added that his next lectures would shortly be delivered in Maine and New Hampshire, but dates were not definitely arranged. He thought his departure from America would occur about December next and he proposed going to New Zealand and Australia before he went to Japan. He reluctantly admitted that the rumor that he was writing a book on the United States was not incorrect, but hinted that he was not going to publish it perhaps for some years. Speaking of Sala's latest work, "America Revisited," extracts from which have appeared in the Herald, he said no one ever believed Sala to be in earnest. He was one of those disciples of Dickens who indulged in "grotesque exaggerations."[1]

"Mrs. Langtry Arrives," *The News and Courier* (Charleston, SC), 26 Oct. 1882, 1[2]

HOW THE JERSEY LILY WAS STARED AT AND TALKED AT.

Not a Beauty but a Charming Woman—Oscar Wilde's Tribute and Aesthetic Antics—Mrs. Langtry's first American 'Interview.'

(FROM OUR OWN CORRESPONDENT.)

NEW YORK, October 23.—Last week Mr. Henry E. Abbey sent out invitations to all newspaper men of any importance in the city asking them to go down to the Bay to meet Mrs. Langtry. It was arranged that a boat should leave the foot of Twenty-second street, North River, at 5 o'clock this morning, and moreover it was provided that any invited guest who chose to do so could sleep on board, the boat being ready at 10 o'clock on Sunday evening.[3] Some guileless souls did so, and found that while Mr. Abbey kindly offered a bed he could not ensure sleep; several young gentlemen made night hideous and sleep a mockery. At five o'clock this morning, upon arriving at the dock, I found the *Laura M. Starin* with steam up and about one hundred and fifty persons—newspaper men, theatrical people and managers—ready for the trip, some of them very sleepy, having been awake on the boat. At 5 o'clock exactly we steamed out into the blackness of the North River with the lower cabin filled up with men who ranged themselves on each

1. Sala, Edmund Yates, and others, were known as Dickens's "young men," and acknowledged the older writer as their inspiration. Sala's *America Revisited: From the Bay of New York to the Gulf of Mexico, and from Lake Michigan to the Pacific* was published in two volumes in 1882.

2. Also present were the authors of "The Lily of Jersey Here," *The Times* (Philadelphia, PA), 24 Oct. 1882, 1, 484–7; and "The Jersey Lily," *The Boston Herald* (Boston, MA), 24 Oct. 1882, 4, pp. 721–5.

3. Wilde was among those who took up Abbey's invitation to sleep on board ("Mrs. Langtry's Arrival," *The Evening Post* (New York, NY), 23 Oct. 1882, 4th ed., 1).

side and watched the preparations for breakfast made by three French waiters, who prepared a breakfast worthy of Mr. Abbey's well known hospitality. It was yet dark when we passed the Battery,[1] and the morning promised to be foggy and chill. Within, however, matters were pretty bright, and the centre of attraction was Mr. Oscar Wilde, who, dressed in a bottle-green ulster many sizes too large for him, his long hair floating over his shoulders, and a flaming red cravat set with an intaglio pin, kept an eye on the head waiter and proved to be a better eater than a poet. It was understood on board that Mr. Wilde claimed a close intimacy with Mrs. Langtry as one of her earliest patrons and teachers. He, among the first, declared her to be the beauty which she was afterwards acknowledged to be, and it was no less than fitting that he should now shine by her reflected light. By the time that the breakfast was entirely ready and the hungry reporters, who had gone without sleep or breakfast, were sharpening their knives, there was a crash from the band above, and the strains of 'God Save the Queen' announced the proximity of the Jersey Lily. Breakfast was forgotten, and there was a rush to the upper deck, from which the *Arizona* was seen lying not two hundred feet off. It was now quite light, although the morning was foggy, and everyone on board the *Starin* eagerly scanned the throngs which lined the decks of the *Arizona* in search of a first glimpse of the famous beauty. The band played with a vengeance, but there was no response from the *Arizona*, except that the immigrants shouted at Mr. Wilde, taking him for an aboriginal not yet civilized. For half an hour we lay in waiting for some invitation from the *Arizona*, and watching for Mrs. Langtry. Suddenly a young and pretty woman appeared on the hurricane deck of the *Arizona* and the band struck up 'God Save the Queen' with renewed energy,[2] a British flag was thrown to the breeze, and the party on board the *Starin* were debating whether to cheer or not when it was discovered that the beauty was a member of Mr. Wyndham's company.[3] 'God Save the Queen' was cut short and the flag was rolled up again while ropes were thrown to the *Arizona* and we were made fast at the side of the gigantic vessel. It was now broad daylight and many were the shouted inquiries as to what had become of Mrs. Langtry. It was rumored that she had been dismayed at the sight of the hundred reporters, each with spectacles and notebooks, but a terrific rush was suddenly made to the rear of the boat, when Mr. Oscar Wilde was discovered bowling at the rate of twenty to a minute and leaning over the edge at the risk of his life in order to talk to a lady on the *Arizona* who stood with the captain on the promenade deck. It was feared that Mr. Wilde would go into the water with every bow,

1. A public park at the southern tip of Manhattan.
2. Hurricane deck: a light upper deck or platform in some steamers; the promenade (OED).
3. Charles Wyndham (1837–1919) was an English actor-manager. He would later contract with Wilde to produce *The Importance of Being Earnest.*

but his balance was good and he proceeded to recite a sonnet in honor of Mrs. Langtry which was no doubt very beautiful, but owing to the screech of a steam whistle was lost to the reporters and the world.[1] This, then, was the picture: The *Arizona* crowded with emigrants on its lower deck, and on the upper deck Mrs. Langtry, Mrs. Labouchère, her companion, and the captain of the *Arizona*.[2] On the *Starin*, not twenty feet away, a little group composed of Mr. Abbey, Mr. Wilde and a few particular friends, and as a background one hundred staring reporters gazing at Mrs. Langtry as critically as the most complete disregard of her feelings and the intervening distance would allow. Mrs. Langtry never flinched, but answered with pretty grace the customary questions which are shouted out upon such an occasion. Mr. Abbey asked her if she would like to come on board the *Starin*, and I cannot blame her for saying "No." A plank was let down from the *Arizona* and everyone climbed up to the bigger vessel, and crowded around while Mr. Abbey shook hands with his star. The way in which the reporters behaved was not calculated to raise one's opinion of the influence of interviewing upon newspaper men. She was examined from head to foot as a wild animal of some unknown species might be, and, after a good look, the note book came forth and down went Mrs. Langtry's points. If Mrs. Langtry's ears are sharp she may even have heard the expressions of disappointment which were whispered among the crowd. Her bearing under the ordeal was simply admirable. She never seemed to realize that she was being looked upon at all, and when three or four newspaper men, myself among the number, were introduced to her and apologized for this extraordinary reception, which could not have been more brutal if she had been the queen of the Cannibal Islands, she laughed pleasantly and said that she supposed it was a part of the business.

Everyone will naturally ask whether Mrs. Langtry is a beauty from our American standpoint, and the verdict of nine out of ten of the men who saw her this morning was that her reputation for beauty remained an inexplicable puzzle. To go into details, Mrs. Langtry is a trifle more than average height, solidly built, carrying herself with the grace of perfect health, and the high bred air of a woman of excellent society. Her head is large and so is her chin, which is unusu-

1. Wilde presumably recited *The New Helen* or another poem that may have been inspired by Langtry. *Madonna Mia* (CW i, No. 66), first published in *Poems*, with its references to a "lily-girl" with eyes "[l]ike bluest water", may have seemed an apposite choice. Langtry, 179, later recalled that, on hearing the band, she had "hurried on deck, and there found a tug alongside, with Henry E. Abbey, and his partner [John B.] Schoeffel, marshalling a perfect army of reporters, while Oscar Wilde, torn from his slumbers at an unearthly hour, still had the spirit to wave a bunch of lilies in welcome." Wilde's behaviour echoes his earlier dramatic welcome of Sarah Bernhardt to England, when he is supposed to have flung an armful of flowers at her feet (Sturgis, 146/143).

2. Henrietta Labouchère née Hodson (1841–1910) was an English actress best known for her comedic roles. She and Henry Labouchère had been in a relationship for a number of years, although they would not marry until 1887. She had introduced Langtry to the stage.

ally massive. Her mouth is also large, her teeth perfect, her nose small, her eyes gray and her hair brown, turning towards red. She was dressed in what appeared to be a tight-fitting, dark blue flannel dress, with gold braidings; around her neck she wore a handkerchief of olive brown, and her hat was of black straw trimmed with red and black striped ribbon. The whole effect was pretty and quiet, and I have Mr. Wilde's word for it that the costume was perfect. It was when Mrs. Langtry first opened her mouth that her real grounds for reputation became plain. Her expression in talking is one of the most fascinating imaginable. Her voice is full and musical, and even in an ugly woman the charm with which she greets men whom she would rather not see would make one forget all ugliness. When her face is in repose it is not at all the sculptor's idea. Most persons would call it cold, irregular, heavy and commonplace, the face simply of a healthy young woman who has the charm of health and some intelligence. Nineteen persons out of twenty meeting Mrs. Langtry in the street would never think of her as a peculiarly pretty woman, not to say beauty. It is probably for this reason that most of the pictures received in this country have disappointed the public. I never remember to have seen a face of which the charm lies so wholly outside the domain of photographic art.

It must be remembered, in saying all this, that Mrs. Langtry had just undergone a week's voyage, had been awakened by the strains of a brass band playing its loudest, had dressed in a hurry, had had no breakfast and was confronted by about as unpleasant a crowd of reporters as can be imagined. I have said nothing about Mrs. Langtry's famous complexion, because, to tell the truth, Mrs. Langtry had no complexion to speak of this morning, and it was scarcely to be expected that she would have in the circumstances. Mrs. Langtry on the stage enhanced by all the accessories of art, in a dress showing her very beautiful neck and shoulders is most probably an entirely different picture from the Mrs. Langtry I found this morning. There is an idea, however, that the Jersey Lily is a vision of classic grace, of red rose beauty, a sort of beatified [*sic*] wax-doll, who in the most unfavorable circumstances will always appear to step out of her bath and to have had ten hours of good country sleep. She is nothing of the kind. There is no suggestion of the wax-doll about her, and I venture to predict that if Mrs. Langtry makes a great success in this country it will be as an actress of intelligence and not as a woman of beauty.

After I had apologized again for the amount of staring with which she had been favored, I ventured to ask her what she thought of the country, or of as much of it as she had seen.

"I will tell you when the fog lifts and I get a good look at it; I can say at least that I think your water is beautiful and your fogs are almost as good as our own. If I am to be interviewed perhaps I can tell you all that I think I ought to tell you and then you can print as much of it as you like. In the first place, I act because I like it and not entirely because it means so much money in my pocket. If I had a fortune tomorrow left me I doubt whether I should leave the stage. The society life which I have led seems rather hollow now that I look back to it after my first year's hard real work. If I were to meet with rebuffs and failures it is possible that I might become discouraged, and one of my objects in accepting Mr. Abbey's offer was to come out here and play before a public to whom I am nothing more than any other actress whose name has been widely advertised. In England, it is said, and I fear it may be true, that my social position and my many friends among the aristocracy have been the real foundations for whatever measure of success I may have achieved. Some things have encouraged me to think this is not wholly so, for, although I might attract small audiences of society people, I could not fill the galleries, and, as you know, the public, in the larger sense of the word, have supported me very generously. If the same thing is repeated in this country I shall begin to feel that my hard work has really told, for all this talk about my beauty is the merest imagination, as you can see for yourself.

"Of course you know the history of my going on the stage. I needed money and some kind friends, Mrs. Labouchère among them, suggested that my success in some private theatricals pointed out the way for me to make an independence for myself if I wished it. I really had but very little training when I first appeared before the public, and I do not wonder that professional actors were inclined to criticise my pretensions rather sharply. I will say here that the profession upon the whole has behaved in the kindest manner towards me. As my power for making money grew and I began to feel that certain stage work produced certain effects upon the audience, I began to enjoy my work as I had never hoped to do. Here you see me actually coming across the Atlantic to show you how little I know about acting. That is about the whole story."

I stepped back to allow a timid young reporter to ask Mrs. Langtry whether *Lady Macbeth* was one of her parts—a question which filled her with merriment—and ran against Mr. Oscar Wilde, who having proved that he was actually on speaking terms with Mrs. Langtry and having discharged his sonnet at her, was composing another one, which he informed me he hoped to read upon the occasion of her first appearance.[1] He delays going to Australia on purpose to await this event, and will leave on the following day, stopping only in Chicago, to which city it seems he has taken a strong liking.[2] I asked Mr. Wilde how he explained Mrs. Langtry's great popularity, not alone with the aristocracy, but with the masses.

"Why," he said, "do not the masses realize the beauty and purity of the lily? Mrs. Langtry is like the lily, not only in beauty but in the certainty with which she

1. Wilde did not recite a poem on the occasion of Langtry's New York stage debut.
2. Wilde never returned to Chicago.

responds to everything that is beautiful in nature. The lily turns to the sun and reflects its warmth. Mrs. Langtry has a faculty for finding out beauty wherever it exists, and in some way translating it for the common herd. You might call her the medium which gives value to much that would otherwise seem valueless in our eyes. For instance take Rosalind's lovely words, and they acquire in Mrs. Langtry's mouth a new beauty. Even my own poor sonnets when recited by her make me quiver with delight.[1] It is a gift of heaven, and cannot be analyzed."

Mr. Wilde then went off after confiding to me that in case he could find a puddle between the gangplank and Mrs. Langtry's carriage he should put his precious fur-lined ulster into it in order to immortalize himself and save Mrs. Langtry's feet from getting wet. When I saw the last of him, as I left the dock, he was hunting for a puddle, and in case there was none to be found I suppose he hired someone to make an artificial one convenient for his purpose. To sum up the whole expedition we had a very pleasant excursion down the Bay, we began a very good breakfast at Mr. Abbey's expense, we heard 'God Save the Queen' played nineteen times by a wretched band, we had a little pleasant conversation with a famous young woman, who is not a beauty, but who is very charming, which is far better than beauty, and we satisfied a little curiosity of our own, and perhaps have satisfied, or partly done so, the similar curiosity of the readers of a great many newspapers. The curtain has now fallen upon the first act of Mrs. Langtry's début. She has been a success in one sense—the most important—and a failure in another; but this act has been merely a preliminary and the great one is yet to come.

Mr. Abbey is understood to pay Mrs. Langtry at the rate of $600 a night and all expenses. An auction sale will be held tomorrow night for choice of seats on the opening night, a week from today. It is expected that the average price of orchestra seats will not be less than $20 upon that occasion, and the critics of the daily newspapers have been asked to accept one seat instead of the customary two—a wholly unprecedented request.

H. H. H.

1. Ellmann, 195/206: "'Even my own poor sonnets when recited by her [Lillie Langtry] make me quiver with delight. I shall write them to her until she is ninety,' he [Wilde] commented to the same journal [*Andrew's American Queen*] on 18 November 1882.'" The relevant passage in *The American Queen* (New York, NY), 18 Nov. 1882, 322, reads: "'Even my own poor sonnets,' says Oscar Wilde, of London, of Mrs. Langtry, 'when recited by her make me quiver with delight. I shall write them to her until she is ninety.'" There follows a paragraph criticising Wilde as "utterly lacking in intelligence". It seems clear that the words in *The American Queen* were obtained not from Wilde but from *The News and Courier* or an unidentified reprint thereof and from "Sizing Us Up," *The Sunday Herald* (Boston, MA), 20 Aug. 1882, 12, p. 449, in which Wilde is reported to have said "I shall write sonnets to Mrs. Langtry when she is 95."

"The Lily of Jersey Here," *The Times* (Philadelphia, PA), 24 Oct. 1882, 1[1]

How the Reception Committee Met Mrs. Langtry on the Arizona—Her Personal Appearance and How She Dressed. She Has Left Society Forever.

Special Dispatch to THE TIMES.

NEW YORK, October 23,

Mrs. Langtry arrived today and created a furore. Long before daylight a steamboat containing Henry E. Abbey, Charles A. Mendum, Oscar Wilde and forty others moved down the North river to meet the steamship Arizona and the beauty.[2] On the trip down Oscar Wilde was the centre of attraction. He wore a sage green overcoat, lined with fur, a black velvet and braided coat, a salmon-colored neck-handkerchief and a two-story brown felt hat. Altogether he was made up for the occasion, but as his flowing hair was rumpled by the wind he became more an object of ridicule than of beauty. The members of the reception committee were "guyers" of notoriety, and Oscar had anything but a pleasant trip if he was at all sensitive. Just as day broke the Arizona was sighted at Quarantine and the band began playing "The Girl I Left Behind Me," an air, by the way, which Oscar applauded.[3] After the Health Officer had examined the passengers and crew of the incoming vessel Mrs. Langtry and her traveling companion, Mrs. Labouchère, appeared on the upper deck of the Arizona and the reception committee at once advanced on her.

THE JERSEY LILY.

She is a woman of middle height, with a well-developed figure, and at first sight she is not beautiful, as people have been led to expect by the flattering notices that have been published about her. Her hair, a rich red brown, was done up in two bunches, which were harpooned to her head by a silver skull. Her front hair, released from crimping pins, covered her forehead completely and gave foundation for the opinion that she was fixed for the occasion, although she has had neither powder nor paint on. Her features are regular and her eyes are large, gray-blue and expressive, particularly when she is talking. Her mouth would size

1. Reprinted in "The Lily of Jersey," *Daily Globe* (St. Paul, MN), 30 Oct. 1882, 3. Also present were the authors of "Mrs. Langtry Arrives," *The News and Courier* (Charleston, SC), 26 Oct. 1882, 1, pp. 478–83; and "The Jersey Lily," *The Boston Herald* (Boston, MA), 24 Oct. 1882, 4, pp. 721–5. Although Wilde does not speak directly with the reporter, he was aware that he was attending an interview with Langtry and that his remarks were on the record.

2. Charles Albert Mendum (1849–1945) was a theatrical manager.

3. The lyrics of *The Girl I Left Behind Me* can be traced to the eighteenth-century. It was played by the British Army on occasions of departure, and achieved popularity among American soldiers in the nineteenth-century.

up with Soldene's, and she has a set of fine, regular teeth, shown advantageously whenever she smiles. Much pains have been taken to spread the idea that Mrs. Langtry's complexion is as near perfect as complexions go, but when closely inspected her skin is not as remarkable as her friends would have the public believe. When animated by conversation her face is very captivating and her smile is extremely fascinating, so much so, indeed, that Oscar Wilde took occasion to remark to a companion that she was "delicious when her face lighted up with laughter." All in all, she is not as beautiful a woman as the public have been led to believe and after examining her critically Sarony, the photographer, remarked: "There are countless women in this country who are more beautiful than she."[1] It was generally admitted, however, that she will "make up" marvelously well for the stage and that her good looks, assisted by her bewitching smile, will make her a favorite, even if she is as poor an actress as those who have seen her say she is.

HOW THE BEAUTY DRESSED.

She wore a narrow-brimmed black straw hat, adorned with a soft-looking role of navy blue and red-striped silk. Her dress was of blue cloth, kilt pleated, with a tight-fitting waist and a bosom of old-gold braid, surrounded by dark buttons. Her kid gloves were brown and reached to her elbows. A plain gold pin was the only article of jewelry she wore, and around her fair throat was knotted a rich yellow handkerchief. Mrs. Labouchère, a stout person of middle age, with gray hair done up in cork-screws, wore a suit of blue flannel, and her head was covered by a flat blue and black hat almost the size and shape of a soup plate. She is past the age of beauty, but Oscar Wilde waited upon and chatted to her with great gallantry.

After Mrs. Langtry had shaken hands with every member of the reception committee she made herself solid with the Americans by requesting the musicians to play "Yankee Doodle," which was rendered with great vigor. During the rendition of that time-honored tune Mrs. Langtry appeared a trifle tired, but she stood it out and at its conclusion asked for an encore, which, fortunately for the ears of the people on deck, was not given. Mrs. Langtry looks a little worn, but while she chatted with a dozen or more of her visitors, she was perfectly ladylike, self-possessed and graceful. She talks fluently, but her conversation does not

1. Lewis and Smith report that Sarony paid $5,000 for the right to photograph Langtry (OWDA, 418); Sarony told an interviewer that he had paid her "$1,500, of which $1,000 were paid in cash and $500 in works of art." ("Popular Photographs," *The New York Herald* (New York, NY), 26 Oct. 1884, 14.) In another interview Sarony revealed that the deal was for the exclusive right to her photographs in America ("Theatrical Photography," *The New York Mirror* (New York, NY), 22 Mar. 1884, 10), a fact later corroborated by Langtry, 118. Upon seeing the photographs she is supposed to have remarked: "You have made me pretty. I am beautiful." (OWDA, 419.)

impress one as thoughtful, although perhaps that impression was attributable to the thinness of the subjects that were discussed. Mr. Wilde, as he buttoned his polar region overcoat over his manly bosom, declared that "she is very nice" and, of course, that settled it.

A CHAT WITH MRS. LANGTRY.

When the Arizona reached her pier on the North river Mrs. Langtry swung on to Mr. Abbey's arm and after running a gauntlet of several hundred people entered a carriage and was driven to the Albemarle hotel, where she occupies the three apartments which were last year fitted especially for Sarah Bernhardt. In the afternoon a representative of THE TIMES found her at home and had a pleasant chat with her. She wore the same dress that she landed in, but the absence of a hat added greatly to her appearance. Her voice is low, soft and pleasing, and her manners are extremely fascinating, although she talked about nothing but theatrical matters and much of her talk was sugar-coated.

"I have," she said, "left society forever. I have determined to live for dramatic art alone, and I feel confident that I shall succeed."

In referring to the difference between playing in England and America she said, with just a touch of simper:

"Oh, I will meet the people of America much differently from the manner in which I met the public at home. There I knew a great many people, and among them were critics, who treated me very kindly. Here I will have to play on merits."

At this moment Mr. Wilde, in most saccharine tones, added:

"Do you feel very ambitious?" and the beauty replied:

"Oh, Mr. Wilde, I am afraid I am very ambitious."

Oscar smiled and curried his tangled locks with his off hand as he murmured:

"Indeed, indeed."

During the pause which followed the lady thoughtfully contemplated her neatly-fitting little kid boots, and then went on:

"I will make my appearance as *Hester Grazebrook* in 'The Unequal Match,' after which I will appear in the 'Honeymoon' and 'As You Like It.'[1] Oh, no; I am too young an actress to say whether I will play the old comedies or not, but as I feel now I do not think I will. Of course I would like to, but I doubt whether I will be able to get up in them this season. Oh yes, people in the profession have treated me very kindly, much more so, indeed, than I had a right to expect, for you know," she added, in tones of thin compassion, "it does seem rather hard for me to go into the profession and take a leading place ahead of people who have

1. *The Unequal Match* (1857) by Tom Taylor (1817–1880). *The Honey Moon* (1805) by John Tobin (1770–1804). Langtry played Rosalind in Shakespeare's *As You Like It* (c. 1599).

been in training all their lives. Yes, whether I fail or not, I intend to make acting the study of my life, as I believe it to be the noblest of arts."

SHE DOES NOT PAINT.

"Do you paint?" asked a very utter young man, adorned with a pair of gold eye-glasses.

"Sir!" said the Lily, as her face crimsoned with a call-before-the-curtain blush.

"I mean," stammered he of the goggles, "do you paint pictures?"[1]

"No," replied Mrs. Langtry, "although I am very, very fond of them and when I have time I mean to devote it to that art. I saw Miss Davenport play in London and I think she is a charming actress, so charming that I am unable to understand why critics treated her so harshly."[2]

After some general chat she said: "I enjoyed the voyage to America very much, although we had such a dreadful storm last week that I feared we would be wrecked. Yes, I had an engagement in London for this fall, but I got out of it in order to play with Mr. Abbey," and she rolled her eyes at her manager in a way that made him blush to the roots of his hair. Then she slopped over a little on the United States, saying: "You cannot imagine how I have longed to come here, and now that my desire is gratified I am perfectly satisfied, for I do so love this beautiful country."

Considering that she had seen nothing of the country but a few North river piers and a row of dingy tenement houses on Twenty-second street this praise sounded a trifle extravagant, but no one ventured to say nay to her. She became quite demure when one of her callers asked her what she intended to do with all the money she will make in America. In reply she said, with a sigh: "I do not care for money. I fancy it makes one selfish, don't you?"

1. The embarrassment was due to the other meaning of "to paint", that is "to wear make up". Although at this time it was acknowledged that cosmetics were necessary on stage, there remained a social stigma attached to their use off the stage.

2. Fanny Davenport (1850–1898) was an English-American actress. Like Langtry, she was considered a great beauty. Langtry presumably saw Davenport at London's Toole Theatre, where she opened in *Diane de Lys* on 9 September 1882. Reviewers criticised Davenport's "remarkably strong" American accent, her "stage tricks", and the "want of *vraisemblance* [verisimilitude]" in her performance, while acknowledging that she had "gifts not to be ignored" and that she had been hampered by a poor choice of play ("Toole's Theatre," *The Standard* (London, UK), 11 Sep. 1882, 2; "At the Theatre," *The Pall Mall Gazette* (London, UK), 14 Sep. 1882, 4; "The London Theatres," *The Era* (London, UK), 16 Sep. 1882, 6;).

"The Sunflower Poet," *Camden Daily Courier* (Camden, NJ), 27 Oct. 1882, 1[1]

Oscar Wilde Delighted with His South Jersey Experience.

Oscar Wilde passed through Camden this morning on his way to New York. He lectured in Bridgeton last evening to an audience which filled Music Hall. A COURIER reporter found him this morning comfortably settled in one corner of the smoking car puffing contentedly at a cigar, and apparently oblivious of the noise and bustle occasioned by the arrival of the numerous military companies which take part in the parade today.[2] He expressed no interest in Philadelphia's celebration by either word or action, and was in turn observed by but few. When asked about his audience last evening he softly replied, and with evident satisfaction, "Ah! very nice! very nice!" He inquired after the "Good Gray Poet," and upon learning of his serious illness,[3] expressed his sincere sorrow, adding, "He is such a splendid man." In regard to his future movements he stated that he was bound for New York, from which point he should shortly depart for Australia.

"Mrs. Langtry on the Hudson," *The New York Herald* (New York, NY), 30 Oct. 1882, 5[4]

WHAT SHE THINKS OF THAT NOBLE STREAM, AND WHAT OSCAR WILDE THINKS OF NIAGARA FALLS.

Shortly after eight o'clock this evening a handsome woman attired in a housemaid's suit of buff, with white apron, and sleeves rolled up, displaying a white and pretty arm, will emerge from the wings and stand in the glare of a bright light at Abbey's Park Theatre.[5] At once she will become the focus of hundreds of opera glasses; hundreds of women "in silk attire" will exclaim "Oh!" and hundreds of men in correct broadcloth will say "Ah!" The tension will be re-

1. Reprinted in Cooper (Bridgeton lecture, 26 October 1882).

2. A parade was staged in Philadelphia on 27 October to commemorate the city's bicentennial. It was the culmination of festivities that began on 22 October.

3. Reports were circulating that Walt Whitman was seriously ill with Bright's disease (a kidney condition now known as glomerulonephritis) and was unlikely to recover. In fact, he lived another ten years.

4. H & S, b96. Reprinted as "Mrs. Langtry on the Hudson," *The Courier-Journal* (Louisville, KY), 5 Nov. 1882, 10. Excerpted in *The Pall Mall Gazette* (London, UK), Nov. 1882, 4. Quoted in "Wanted—A New Universe," *New York Tribune* (New York, NY), 31 Oct. 1882, 4; OWDA, 419–20; Pearson, 76; Hyde, 78; and Ellmann, 196/207.

5. Langtry was scheduled to debut as Hester Grazebrook in *An Unequal Match* at the Park Theatre on 30 October.

lieved; New York's citizens—or a representative number of them—will have decided for themselves what they have heretofore had a chance to decide but by proxy—whether the "Jersey Lily" is really as beautiful as enthusiastic admirers have represented. And the "Jersey Lily" herself? Well, it may safely be assumed that she will await with beating heart the judgment which the metropolitan audience may pronounce, not upon her beauty, perhaps, but upon her histrionic ability. She avows, with an earnestness of manner which cannot be mistaken, that the ordeal will be a trying one for her, but that if the verdict, which she will await with anxiety, is favorable to her it will be a welcome boon and make her a happy woman indeed.

All day yesterday the carpenters were busy arranging the scenic effects. No expense or labor has been spared in making the scenery for Mrs. Langtry's performances worthy of a distinguished debutante. After witnessing the performance at the Madison Square Garden on Saturday evening Mrs. Langtry was given an opportunity to observe the working of the double stage,[1] after which she went to the Park Theatre, where a scenic rehearsal was gone through with which lasted until half-past two in the morning. Several of those who are to take part in the play appeared upon the stage in full costume, and Mrs. Langtry, aided by Mrs. Labouchère, suggested changes here and made amendments there until she was compelled, from sheer exhaustion, to return to her hotel. About noontime yesterday, accompanied by one or two friends and Mrs. Labouchère, she went upon a steam yacht a short distance up the Hudson.

There were numerous callers during the day. Upon her return, about half-past five o'clock, she found Mr. Oscar Wilde, among others, patiently awaiting her arrival.

"What do I think of the Hudson?" she said, vivaciously, when the little party were again seated in her parlor, "why, I think it is simply lovely, grand, magnificent—or, rather, let me use that expressive American, somewhat paradoxical phrase, and say that I was 'agreeably disappointed.' I don't wonder that you call it the 'Rhine of America.' Do you know there is only one thing that would prevent me from settling down somewhere upon the banks of the Hudson and becoming Americanized?"

"And what is that?"

"Why, the horrid railroad that runs all the way along the bank. It destroys very much of the beauty. Why do they allow it here?"

1. The Madison Square Theatre was built in 1877. Its double stage was an innovation of Steele MacKaye: an elevator the size of the stage reduced the time necessary for scene changes. Langtry will have seen a performance of *Young Mrs. Winthrop,* a new play by Bronson Howard (1842–1908).

The reporter refrained from unfolding to Mrs. Langtry that peculiar phase of American government which gives to "soulless corporations" the right to levy upon all the choice lands of the continent regardless of the claims of beauty or the more substantial rights of citizens.

"I suppose now I must see Niagara Falls, that great American attraction," continued Mrs. Langtry.

"Oh, don't go to Niagara Falls," broke in Oscar Wilde.

"Why not?" asked Mrs. Langtry, laughing; "is there nothing of 'the beautiful' there? Oh, I remember now laughing heartily at your experience at Niagara Falls—pulling up the car window curtain, asking disappointedly, 'Is that Niagara Falls?' pulling the curtain down again and going to sleep."[1]

"They told me," said the London aesthete, "that so many millions of gallons of water tumbled over the falls in a minute. I could see no beauty in that. There was bulk there, but no beauty, except the beauty inherent in bulk itself. Niagara Falls seemed to me to be simply a vast, unnecessary amount of water going the wrong way and then falling over unnecessary rocks. You saw Jefferson the other evening," he continued, changing the subject. "What did you think of him? I admire him very much."[2]

"Oh, he was grand. I was, indeed, charmed—I might even say he was 'too preciously lovely,'" she added, laughing.[3]

"Do you know that I think of going to Australia?" said Mr. Wilde a moment later.

"To Australia! Why?"

"Well, I'll tell you. Do you know when I look at the map and see what an awfully ugly looking country it is I feel as if I wanted to go there to see if it cannot be changed into a more beautiful form," and he threw back his hair and laughed.[4]

1. Langtry, 90, would further embroider the story for her autobiography: "He [Wilde] was lecturing and I was playing at Buffalo at the same time that season, so we visited Niagara in a party, and in an interview he gave a reporter on his impressions of these mighty waters, he announced, 'that Mrs Langtry was photographed with Niagara Falls as an unpretentious background!'" Wilde told this joke in *Personal Impressions of America*, but about Sarah Bernhardt (Dibb, 236). Langtry played in Buffalo between 12 and 14 March 1883. Helena Modjeska filled out the rest of the week and the pair were reported to have visited Niagara together on the 18th. ("Amusements," *The Commercial Gazette* (Cincinnati, OH), 25 Mar. 1883, 3). Wilde could not have joined them as he was then in Paris.

2. Sheridan's comedy *The Rivals* (1775) was being staged at the Union Square Theatre with Joseph Jefferson starring as Bob Acres, a buffoonish country squire. Wilde saw the play c. 15 October and, in a letter that is not included in CL, invited Steele MacKaye to join him in his box (MacKaye, P. (1927). *Epoch: The Life of Steele MacKaye, Genius of the Theatre*. Boni & Liveright, Vol. 1, 447).

3. Langtry apes aesthetic slang.

4. The Duchess of Berwick in *Lady Windermere's Fan*: "Do you know, Mr Hopper, dear Agatha and I are so much interested in Australia. It must be so pretty with all the dear little kangaroos

"Will you rehearse at all tomorrow?" Mrs. Langtry was asked.

"No; I shall give tomorrow to rest," she responded; "I feel so very much worn out, and then, you know, I want to prepare myself to meet the ordeal which awaits me. And then I have such a mass of correspondence that ought to be attended to. I receive such queer letters, too. I received one the other day from a little girl, who said she was ill-treated at home and wanted me to send her money that she might run away and be an actress. Now isn't that very funny?"

After she had once more complacently acceded to the demand of the autograph hunter Mrs. Langtry's visitors rose and were smilingly bidden adieu by the "Jersey Lily."

"Mrs Langtry's Disappointment," *New York Tribune* (New York, NY), 31 Oct. 1882, 1[1]

The greater part of yesterday was spent by Mrs. Langtry in resting preparatory to her first appearance on the American stage in the evening. At about 1 p.m. she went to the Park Theatre to inspect the scenes which had been set. She was especially pleased with one for the second act. She returned to her hotel about 2:30 p.m. Mr. Abbey was one of the first to call on her after the fire was discovered. From her apartments at the Albemarle they had an excellent view of the flames. Oscar Wilde was one of those who were admitted to Mrs. Langtry's room. He said that Mrs. Langtry showed wonderful nerve, although she was greatly disappointed.[2]

While the fire was still burning Mr. Abbey went over to the Fifth Avenue Hotel, and after a few minutes' consultation with Mr. Florence,[3] came back and announced to Mrs. Langtry that he had engaged the Grand Opera House for next Monday. This cheered her considerably. Notes of sympathy were sent up in quick succession to her during the evening, but she denied herself to almost everyone who called. "I do not care so much for my own disappointment," said she, "as I do

---

flying about. Agatha has found Australia on the map. Quite an important size, I see. But what a curious shape! Just like a large packing case." (CW xi, 378.32–5.)

1. This interview is part of the extensive coverage of a fire that had destroyed the Park Theatre in the early evening of 30 October. The coverage occupied the first three columns of the first and third pages.

2. Wilde was also reported to have declared "It is a beautiful fire," although it seems unlikely that he did (see e.g. "An Unfortunate Fire," *The Boston Herald* (Boston, MA), 31 Oct. 1882, 1).

3. William Jermyn Florence (1831–1891) was an American actor who was playing at the Grand Opera House. An interview with Abbey on the same page of the *Tribune* indicates that Florence agreed to step aside so that *An Unequal Match* could be staged at the Grand. In the end, the play opened at Wallack's Theatre a week after the fire.

for Mr. Abbey's loss. He has been so generous. It is too bad. I am only sorry that I did not lose anything. It seems selfish." Mr. Abbey said she did not seem to mind her own loss at all. She was much grieved to hear that several of the men had been hurt, but she expressed gratitude that the catastrophe had not happened in the evening when the presence of a large assembly would have precipitated a panic and great loss of life.

Mrs. Langtry was just on the point of sending her costumes over to the theatre when she heard of the fire. A distressing feature of the evening was the arrival every little while of handsome floral tributes which had been prepared for presentation to her on the stage. Late in the evening Mrs. Langtry ordered that no cards should be sent up to her, as she was so upset by the excitement and the messages of sympathy had become too numerous for her to attend to. She ordered her carriage about 9 p.m., and Mr. Abbey took a drive with her about the city. Stopping in front of Wallack's Theatre for a minute she received expressions of sympathy from Lester Wallack and others.[1] Mr. Abbey was also the recipient of hearty hand-shakes and sympathetic words wherever he went.

[Harrison Grey Fiske], "The Usher," *The New York Mirror* (New York, NY), 18 Nov. 1882, 7[2]

✂ *Several paragraphs that are unrelated to Wilde.*

Oscar Wilde told me the other day at the Wyndham breakfast that his Langtry notice in the *World* was his first exploit in journalism.[3] He said it would be his last. He had only three-quarters of an hour in which to write three-quarters of a column. "If I transpose a comma from one part of a sentence to another, in one day," he exclaimed, "I consider that I have done a good day's work."[4] Neverthe-

1. John Johnstone "Lester" Wallack (1820–1888) was an American actor and theatre manager. His new theatre had opened in January 1882.

2. Harrison Grey Fiske (1861–1942) was an American journalist, playwright, and Broadway producer. After a stint as the dramatic critic of the *New York Star* he was appointed editor of *The New York Mirror* at the age of eighteen by his father, who had bought an interest in the paper.

3. The breakfast was given by A. M. Palmer on 9 November in honour of the actor Charles Wyndham. Wyndham's company was staging *Fourteen Days*, a play by the English dramatist Henry James Byron, at Palmer's Union Square Theatre. See also "New York," *Boston Evening Transcript* (Boston, MA), 18 Nov. 1882, 10–11, pp. 725–6. Wilde's review of Langtry's New York debut in *An Unequal Match* appeared in New York's *The World* (7 Nov. 1882, 5; CW vi, No. 7). It was not his "first exploit in journalism", although his earlier articles had been placed in magazines rather than daily newspapers.

4. Wilde would later tell Robert Sherard that, while staying at an American "country-house" (probably the Newport home of Julia Ward Howe), "he had told his host one evening that he had spent the day in hard literary work, and that, when asked what he had done, he had said, 'I was

less Wilde's article was a skillful specimen of non-critical eulogistic writing. The gentleman, by the way, is looking about for an agent to precede him to Australia who knows how to handle an attraction in the Colonies. Here's a chance for Tracy Titus.[1]

✂ *Several paragraphs that are unrelated to Wilde.*

"Persons and Things," *The New Haven Evening Register* (New Haven, CT), 24 Nov. 1882, 2[2]

✂ *Several paragraphs that are unrelated to Wilde.*

There is danger that in the near future, America will be deprived of the classic presence and the bewitching smiles of the original and unsurpassed Irish aesthete, Mr. Oscar Wilde. That gentleman has already spent a happy year in this country, but now that Lily [*sic*] Langtry has come to dispute his title to being regarded as the most beautiful among the children of men, he has become a prey to consuming depression, and has determined to make new conquests, and seek new laurels at the other end of the earth.

"Is it true that you are bent on taking an adieu of this country?" asked the N.Y. *Star* reporter of Mr. Wilde yesterday, as that gentleman was found admiring the bronze fountain in Union Square.

"Aye," replied the aesthete rather gruffly.

"Many persons will be interested in knowing your views of the American scenery and of Americans in general," suggested the reporter.

"America is a grand country. It is, in fact, too large; the distances are too great. When you say a country is big, you say something in its favor, and that is about all that can be said in favor of America. I mean the country, you will understand, and not the people."[3]

---

working on the proof of one of my poems all the morning and took out a comma.' 'And in the afternoon?' 'In the afternoon—well, I put it back again.'" (Sherard, 72.)

1. From the mid 1870s Tracy W. Titus (c. 1843–1887) toured various comic opera companies through America and Australia.

2. Excerpted in "Oscar is Off," *The Canton Daily Repository* (Canton, OH), 24 Nov. 1882, 1.

3. *Personal Impressions of America*: "one is impressed in America, but not favourably impressed, by the inordinate size of everything. The country seems to try to bully one into a belief in its power by its impressive bigness. It behaves like a big boy at a private school. Everything was twice as large and twice as far off as it should be." (Dibb, 235–6.) See also "The American Man": "It is only fair to admit that he can exaggerate; but even his exaggeration has a rational basis. It is not founded on wit or fancy; it does not spring from any poetic imagination; it is simply an earnest attempt on the part of language to keep pace with the enormous size of the country." (CW vi, No. 60, lines 128–31.)

"You do not, then, admire American scenery?"

"Pshaw! Niagara and that sort of thing? I am no admirer of horse scenery."

"And the people?"

"There are fine men and beautiful women in America."

"It has been stated, Mr. Wilde, that the two classes of persons in this country for whom you entertain real admiration are the tailors and the photographers."

"Ah!" said Oscar, with delight, "I have been up the avenue to my tailor's today. I have ordered some novel things for my trip to Australia—something they have not seen there before. New York tailors beat the world, Paris included."

"And the photographers?"

"Your clear skies favor the photographing art. My photographs, taken in all sizes and positions in this city, will astonish the antipodeans, if what I hear about that savage country be true."

Mr. Wilde is now completing his arrangements for his trip to New Zealand and Australia. Before he leaves America he will publish some poems, upon which he has been engaged during the summer.[1]

✂ *A paragraph unrelated to Wilde.*

"Oscar Wilde Prostrated," *The Cincinnati Commercial* (Cincinnati, OH), 26 Nov. 1882, 7[2]

THE APOSTLE OF THE GOOD AND BEAUTIFUL APPARENTLY IN A BAD WAY,

FOR WHICH HE HAD EVIDENTLY BETTER TAKE SOMETHING AT ONCE.

THE POET WAITING TO "GET RESTED" BEFORE MOVING—A SINGULAR MALADY.

Special to the Cincinnati Commercial.

NEW YORK, November 25.—Oscar Wilde is living in furnished rooms at present in West Eleventh street.[3] He has not delivered any lectures recently, and although he may occasionally appear upon the platform again in this country, he

1. If Wilde wrote any poems in the summer of 1882, they have not survived.

2. Reprinted as "Oscar Wilde Thoroughly Exhausted," *New York Tribune* (New York, NY), 27 Nov. 1882, 3 (which is H & S, b97; reprinted in H & S, 172–3; and quoted in OWDA, 431; and Sturgis, 260/249); "Oscar Wilde Prostrated," *The Daily American* (Nashville, TN), 28 Nov. 1882, 3; "Oscar Prostrated," *Pittsburgh Commercial Gazette* (Pittsburgh, PA), 1 Dec. 1882, 8; and "Oscar Wilde," *The Chicago Daily Tribune* (Chicago, IL), 2 Dec. 1882, 3.

3. Wilde was residing at 48 West 11th Street (CL, 189).

does not contemplate giving any further serious attention to the lecture business for the benefit and aesthetic enlightenment of Americans.[1] Since his return from the professional tour of the watering places in the summer, he has been living the life of a man about town. Through the kind offices of "Sam" Ward and other friends he obtained a visitor's card to the Manhattan Club, and has been for some time a frequent caller there. He still goes into society, although it is not exactly the same social crowd as that which took him upon his arrival here. He dines at well known restaurants about 7 o'clock every evening, and is a prominent figure at the theatres on first nights. He comes out into the lobby between the acts like a very commonplace young man,[2] lights a very small cigarette, and throwing himself into the attitude which a prominent photographer, on the payment of a satisfactory sum of money, was allowed to reproduce for the benefit of the people at large,[3] he furnishes a novel and altogether harmless diversion for the lobby loungers. After the play, and probably an incidental aesthetic agony over some "dreadful" combination of color in the scenery, he indulges in a little supper and an accompanying cogitation over a few critical paragraphs intended for publication[4]—In fact, it will be seen that Mr. Wilde has been leading a very seedy existence,[5] and he now declares that "he is thoroughly exhausted, you know, and—ah—suffering from severe nervous prostration."[6] In the meantime many persons have expressed a fear that Mr. Wilde intended staying here. An English paper printed a report that he intended marrying an American heiress.[7] There have

1. Wilde had lectured in Bridgeton, New Jersey, on 26 October and would give his final American lecture in New York's Parepa Hall on 27 November (see Cooper, "The Full List: Oscar Wilde's Lecture Tour of North America, 1882"; and Marland, R. & Cooper, J. (2013). Wilde's final farewell lecture in New York. *The Wildean*, 42, 57–61).

2. "Commonplace": an allusion to *Patience*. See p. 32, note 1.

3. The reporter here refers to Napoleon Sarony (Wilde was photographed by no one else in America).

4. A reference to Wilde's review of Langtry's New York debut: "The scenery was, of course, prepared in a hurry, still, much of it was very good indeed, the first scene especially with its graceful trees and open forge and cottage porch, though the roses were dreadfully out of tone, and besides their crudity of color were curiously badly grouped [.... T]he carpet is out of all color-relation with the rest of the room, and the table-cover is mauve." (CW vi, No. 7, lines 58–61.)

5. The *Tribune* has "speedy existence".

6. The *Tribune* adds here "He believes that he has four doctors." According to Ellmann, 195/206, Wilde told an interviewer for *Andrew's American Queen* that he was suffering from malaria. Ellmann's source is "En Passant," *The American Queen* (New York, NY), 23 Dec. 1882, 402, in which the passage relating to Wilde reads: "Poor Oscar Wilde, of London, has the malaria. The disease seems to sit upon him very gracefully, for it makes him appear more languid, drooping, and more aesthetic than ever. Malaria is an aesthetic disease, he says, with a shrug of his big shoulders, but it is a deuced nuisance. This last clause shows that he is a man, after all." It does not seem likely that Wilde's comment is genuine. See also "Lily Langtry's Friend," *Buffalo Evening News* (Buffalo, NY), 15 Dec. 1882, 3, p. 778.

7. Maud Howe: see p. 441 note 1.

been rumors of his starting a society journal in New York. The story has been circulated that his name had been posted for election at the Manhattan Club, and it has been wildly asserted that he intended producing his play, "Vera, the Nihilist," in a very short time. It seemed indeed that the life of the poet would for a long while be bound up with the life of the metropolis. A Tribune reporter, who called at the house, in West Eleventh street, was shown into Mr. Wilde's sitting-room. It is a commonplace room, with the paper portions of three Japanese parasols blown against one of the walls to denote a presence not in harmony with the remainder of the surroundings. Mr. Wilde presently sauntered in. There was a look of utter weariness on his long, smooth face. He threw back his hair in a manner that was both painful and poetic, and sank slowly, gracefully, but with an appearance of unutterable fatigue into an arm chair.

"Have you made any arrangements to produce your play?" was asked.

"Why do you ask?" said Mr. Wilde, opening his eyes.

"The public might like to know."

"Oh!" and Mr. Wilde closed his eyes and yielded himself up to thought.

"To persons of no reputation," he presently began, "small paragraphs are doubtless an advantage, but really I do not care for them."

"But the production of your play might be a matter of a big paragraph."

"Oh," and Mr. Wilde closed his eyes again. "Well, I have made no arrangements as yet," he added.[1]

"Are you going to Australia?"

"As soon as I get thoroughly rested. I am tired out. Really all is hollow, hollow."[2]

Mr. Wilde here passed his hand across his brow, and his eyes again denoted that life for him was full of fatigue and disappointment.

"I am waiting to go to Australia, because I cannot find anyone to go with. I shall probably stay here until January."

"And how about Japan?"

"Japan will keep. I shall doubtless go there before I am through."

1. Wilde had met with the American actress Marie Prescott (1853-1893) on 12 November to discuss *Vera* (Mason, 257–8.).

2. The *Tribune* has the reporter ask: "Are you going to stay in this country?" and Wilde reply: "No; I am going to Australia, as soon as I get thoroughly rested. I am tired out, now, really."

[Harrison Grey Fiske], "The Usher," *The New York Mirror* (New York, NY), 2 Dec. 1882, 7

I think Marie Prescott's information regarding the purchase of Oscar Wilde's play, printed a fortnight since in these columns, was premature.[1] Meeting Mr. Wilde on Fifth avenue the other day the subject came up, and he said the MS. had not left his hands. I suppose the matter is still in abeyance. The negotiations, if carried out, would be a good thing for both parties. Vera, I understand, is an exceptionally clever play, and Miss Prescott is an exceptionally clever player. Such a combination of cleverness, if brought about, ought to succeed.

✂ *Several paragraphs that are unrelated to Wilde.*

"Mr. Wilde Undisturbed by Rumors," *New York Tribune* (New York, NY), 25 Dec. 1882, 5[2]

A rumor which caused considerable consternation and excitement was abroad in the city last night to the effect that Oscar Wilde had been swindled by a "banco steerer" out of $1,100.[3] The report stated that Mr. Wilde had given the confidence man a check on the Madison Square Bank for the amount, and had afterward given notice to the bank not to pay the check. The report had the color of probability lent to it by the fact that Joseph Sellick, alias "Paper-Collar Joe," alias "Hungry Joe," etc., had been figuring on the police returns at the central office within two days.[4] A searching investigation by a TRIBUNE reporter revealed Mr. Wilde at midnight in Delmonico's cafe, seated at a table smoking, in company with two friends. Mr. Wilde was seemingly cool and imperturbable. He lit a fresh cigarette as the reporter spoke to him and blew a bold cloud of smoke into the

1. Prescott had written to the *Mirror* shortly after her 12 November meeting with Wilde to state that she was "very proud that he is willing to trust me with the creation of so grand a rôle as Vera" and that she intended to produce the play the following September ("Oscar Wilde's Play," *The New York Mirror* (New York, NY), 18 Nov. 1882, 7).

2. Printed simultaneously as "Bunko: Oscar Wilde Reported to Have Lost $1,100," *The Chicago Daily Tribune (Chicago, IL)*, 25 Dec. 1882, 2 (which is H & S, b98). Quoted in OWDA, 440; and Hyde, 81.

3. Banco or bunko is a dice game, but the name was also applied to card games or to any dishonest gambling game. A banco steerer was a member of a confidence trickster gang whose task was to entrap the victim. The first appearance of the rumour that Wilde had been so cheated was in *The Wall Street Daily News* (New York, NY), 22 Dec. 1882, 1.

4. The police inspector to whom Wilde reported the crime identified Joseph Bond as "Paper-Collar Joe" and Joseph Lewis as "Hungry Joe," but stated that other confidence men had also adopted the latter alias (Alexander S. Williams, "A Bunko Man's Work," *The Cincinnati Enquirer* (Cincinnati, OH), 5 May 1888, 12).

air, which enveloped a young man with an immaculate white tie just in front of him.

"Mr. Wilde, is it true that you have lost $1,100 in a banco game?" asked the reporter.

"I have heard the report," replied the poet. "I received a note while at dinner today asking me about it, and I sent the person a reply."

"Then I understand you to deny the story?"

"It does not concern me enough to either deny it or affirm it," said Mr. Wilde, in a soft, low voice. "Not," he added with a smile, after a moment's thought, "but that I should very much object, indeed, to losing $1,100, but I should not object to having it known if I had done so."[1]

The guileless smile of Mr. Wilde indicated that "Paper Collar Joe" would have met a foeman worthy of his steal.[2]

"Is Oscar a Gambler?" *St. Louis Post-Dispatch* (St. Louis, MO), 25 Dec. 1882, 1

A Story That Bunko Men Victimized Mr. Wilde,

Which he Explains Emphatically—How He Looks in Short Hair.

Special to the Post-Dispatch.

NEW YORK, December 25.—Mr. Oscar Wilde is still in the city. There is apparently no immediate prospect of his departure for England. Since he cut his hair Mr. Wilde does not present that complacent appearance so familiar to the public in his early portraits.[3] He seems ill and preoccupied, and during the intervals when his face is in repose he has a worried look. At least this was the impression he conveyed to a reporter when he saw the poet dining at Delmonico's with a few friends. The object of the reporter's call was to ascertain the truth of a story that Mr. Wilde had been made the victim of some "bunko steerers" who had swindled him out of $900 at cards in a gambling house on Twenty-eighth street near Sixth avenue. According to the ordinary accepted version of the supposed facts two fashionably dressed men made Mr. Wilde's acquaintance some two months ago at the Park Avenue Hotel. It is said that they ingratiated themselves into his confidence upon their supposed knowledge of his family, with whom

1. In a letter to John Boyle O'Reilly dated [c. 15 December] Wilde wrote: "I have fallen into a den of thieves, who are unscrupulous and lying: they owe me money which they won't pay me and I want to get back to England." (CL, 192.)

2. The *Chicago Tribune* has "steel" rather than "steal".

3. Wilde would not have his hair cut short until the following spring.

they claimed to be on the most friendly footing. They did not make any effort to entrap him for some weeks, until their intimacy had assumed a more permanent character. Having well established themselves in this respect, it is said that several small

GAMES OF CARDS

were proposed, chiefly ecarte, for trivial stakes, with alternate results to Mr. Wilde, sometimes losing and occasionally winning, but rarely beyond a few dollars in either case. Three days ago the grand strike for something higher was to be attempted, and the story runs that an appointment was made by one of the supposed friends to meet Oscar Wilde and the "steerer's" confederate at the latter's rooms in Twenty-eighth street. The meeting took place and the result was that, after several runs of "luck" Mr. Wilde's good fortune deserted him, and he found himself short by $960. Another version, differing in some respects from the foregoing, is to the effect that a well known bunko runner known in gambling circles as "Hungry Joe" (who is now under bonds for good behaviour) in company with an acquaintance saw Oscar Wilde walking along Broadway and proposed to him that they should fleece Wilde. The acquaintance replied that he didn't think it could be done and that no man in America could play that game on him. "At any rate, let's try," was the answer, and the attempt was made, as already stated, to the tune of $960. It is further reported that Mr. Oscar Wilde laid

COMPLAINT BEFORE CAPTAIN WILLIAMS

with the view to the arrest of the swindlers.[1] The police are, however, reticent upon the matter. As Mr. Wilde is the man who is most likely to know whether either rumor is true or false a reporter interviewed him upon the subject.

"This is the latest and most extraordinary fabrication that I have yet heard and I have been made the victim of several."

"Then this is not true?"

"True! there is not a shade of truth in it. It is totally untrue in every respect. I am not given to high play and certainly not with people I don't know. You can deny it in every particular; it is most absurd. A more ridiculous thing I never heard of; please oblige me by denying it altogether." From those who are in a position to know the reporter learned that Mr. Wilde is economically inclined; that he is by no means lavish in his expenditures, and lives in a retired and unostentatious style.[2]

1. Alexander S. Williams (1839–1917) was a Canadian-born American law enforcement officer. In 1894 an inquiry showed that he had collected protection money from gambling dens.

2. Wilde certainly was "lavish in his expenditures" (see Amor, A. C. (2014). Heading for disaster: Oscar's finances. *The Wildean, 44*, 37–56), but lacked a regular income at this time.

"Mr Wilde Closes his Bank Account," *The Sun* (New York, NY), 27 Dec. 1882, 1[1]

Mr. Oscar Wilde visited the Madison Square Bank yesterday and closed his account, preparatory for his departure for Europe today. He drew out some $2,900. A reporter of THE SUN who met him there asked what foundation there was for the story that he had been swindled out of $3,000 by bunko men. He replied: "It is one of the wonderful stories got up by you American reporters. You are really the most ingenious people in the world. I assure you there is nothing whatever in it, and I can't imagine how it started."

The paying teller of the bank was asked if Mr. Wilde had stopped any large check there. He replied: "I do not think it would be right for me to tell you. Mr. Wilde has done business here, and we are bound not to disclose his private affairs."

President Cryder said: "I don't think there is anything in the story. Certainly no such check has been presented here, and I have not heard that Mr. Wilde had any check stopped."[2]

"Oscar's Adieu," *St. Louis Post-Dispatch* (St. Louis, MO), 28 Dec. 1882, 1[3]

He Descants Upon American Topics Generally,

Including the Press, the Country, the People, Art, Mrs. Langtry and Mrs. Labouchère and Sails away on the Bothnia for Home.

Special to the Post-Dispatch.

NEW YORK, December 28.

1. Reprinted in "Oscar Wilde Draws His Money and Leaves the Country," *The Daily Picayune* (New Orleans, LA), 31 Dec. 1882, 7.

2. William Wetmore Cryder (1835–1918) was the president of the Madison Square Bank.

3. I am grateful to John Cooper for identifying this version of the article. Reprinted as "The Wide, Wide World," *The Evening Star* (Kansas City, MO), 29 Dec. 1882, 1; and, in a shorter version, as "Parting Words From Oscar," *The Chicago Herald* (Chicago, IL), 28 Dec. 1882; and "Parting Words From Oscar," *The Courier-Journal* (Louisville, KY), 29 Dec. 1882, 5. *The Courier-Journal* cites as its source the *Chicago Herald*. Also reprinted as "Oscar Going Home," *Irish Nation* (New York, NY), 30 Dec. 1882, 5; and "Exeunt Oscar Wilde," *The Memphis Daily Appeal* (Memphis, TN), 30 Dec. 1882, 2. Quoted in "Oscar Wants to Go Where He is Not Known," *The Boston Daily Globe* (Boston, MA), 28 Dec. 1882, 1; "Oscar's Parting Shot," *The Evening Critic* (Washington D.C.), 28 Dec. 1882, 1; and "Oscar Seeking an Undiscovered Country," *Buffalo Evening News* (Buffalo, NY), 28 Dec. 1882, 3rd ed., 1.

Oscar Wilde has sailed for Liverpool on the steamer Bothnia.[1] The fact of his going was not generally known, and he escaped the scrutiny of curious people who would have otherwise attended his departure. His friend Mr. Norman Forbes, of Mme. Modjeska's troupe, was the only person at the steamer with him.[2] The early morning was chilly, and Mr. Wilde wore his fur collar buttoned closely about his neck, and beneath was tied a heavy old gold silk scarf. It was bright moonlight when Mr. Forbes and a reporter greeted him.

"You see," he said, as he raised his hat and allowed his long hair to linger for a moment in the moonlight, "my going away

HAS BEEN KEPT QUIET.

Only a few of my personal friends know of it, and I persuaded them not to get up at so early an hour to see me away."

"Did you enjoy your visit to this country?" asked the reporter.

"Very much indeed," he replied. "I think America is a very progressive country, but it is somewhat behind in art, but that, of course, is to be expected. Nevertheless, I was much delighted with the progress that art has made here. There is much that is good, and, individually, I have met many talented gentlemen with whom I am delighted. Of course I had much to contend against, and had I not been a young man, I probably would have been forced to give up my object. I have been subjected to much ridicule and at the same time have made many friends. I have seen very much to be pleased with and believe that I have learned a great deal. I enjoyed my visit to the Western States and wanted to spend more time there."

"Were you pleased with your reception here, Mr. Wilde?"

"No, I was not," he replied smiling. "No man ever came to this country who had to contend with what I did. I am glad that I am on the bright side of thirty, for I do not think that a man past thirty could have accomplished what I have."

"What do you think of the Americans as a people?"

"Ah," he said, as he paused in his walk, "the Americans had a type fifty years ago but they have lost it. In fifty years hence, however, they may regain it. But I like the Americans." Mr. Wilde spoke with some hesitancy of Mrs. Langtry and Mrs. Labouchère, and said: "I am very friendly with both the ladies, and Mrs. Langtry is a particular friend of mind. I attach no importance to their quarrel.[3]

1. *The Courier-Journal* has "Oscar Wilde sailed for Liverpool on the steamer Bothnia, of the Cunard line, at 7 o'clock this morning."

2. Norman Forbes-Robertson.

3. There were reports that Langtry and Mrs Labouchère had fallen out over Langtry's relationship with Frederick Gebhard (1860–1910). Langtry had met the wealthy New Yorker shortly after arriving in America and Gebhard had accompanied her to Boston, the next leg of her tour. In an interview shortly thereafter Labouchère said, "I have not quarrelled with Mrs. Langtry. I

Mrs. Langtry has a perfect right to choose her friends, and I think I know that she would do nothing to injure her reputation. I think that Mrs. Langtry has been treated very unjustly here. She came to this country to act and to study. She has been misrepresented. Your people, who are so chivalrous, have not treated her with consideration.[1] The press has been too severe in its criticisms. She is young, and all this is very discouraging. A man, for instance, could contend with this, but you should be more chivalrous to the ladies."

"What's your opinion of the American press?"

Mr. Wilde did not answer directly. He placed his right foot on the rail, rested his chin on his hand, and gazed meditatively at the waning moon. Finally he said, with a smile:

"Of course the American press is very different from our English press. The English press is made up of facts, while the American press is imagination. But you have many brilliant writers and courteous journalists. But, as I said before, your dramatic critics have been rather hard on Mrs. Langtry. They should be a little more chivalrous."

"Will you ever return to this country, Mr. Wilde?"

"Oh, yes!" he replied, "I hope to return some time. I like the country very much, and when I return I hope to find a great improvement in decorative art. It is progressing, and I have great hopes of the future. At present I want rest and peace and would like to go to a country where I am not known—if there is such a country."

"Your lecture tour has been a financial success has it not, Mr. Wilde?"

"Oh, yes, quite a financial success," he replied.

It was now time for the steamer to leave, and Mr. Forbes and the reporter went on shore, and a few minutes later the Bothnia moved away from the wharf.

---

have no wish to quarrel with her, but I have had occasion to remonstrate with her in regard to a certain acquaintance formed by her in this city, which seemed to me likely to interfere with her success on the stage, and certain to interfere with my own comfort as her friend and companion. She did not take these remonstrances in good part, and insisted on keeping up this acquaintance at Boston," ("Mrs. Langtry's New Admirer," *The Cincinnati Commercial* (Cincinnati, OH), 5 Dec. 1882, 1).

1. *The Courier-Journal* has "with just consideration."

Printed in Great Britain
by Amazon

e8b71bda-4054-4c12-9ed8-66555fb4b24eR01